DIALECTICAL MATERIALISM

DIALECTICAL
MATERIALISM

*A Historical
and Systematic Survey
of Philosophy in the
Soviet Union*

by
GUSTAV A. WETTER

Translated from the German by
PETER HEATH

GREENWOOD PRESS, PUBLISHERS
WESTPORT, CONNECTICUT

Library of Congress Cataloging in Publication Data

Wetter, Gustav Andreas, 1911-
Dialectical materialism.

Translation of Il materialismo dialettico sovietico.
Reprint of the ed. published by Praeger, New York.
Bibliography: p.
1. Dialectical materialism. 2. Philosophy, Russian.
I. Title.
[B809.8.W433 1973]   335.4'11   72-12335
ISBN 0-8371-6727-2

Nihil obstat   ANDREAS MOORE, L.C.L.
                  Censor deputatus

Imprimatur   ✠ GEORGIUS L. CRAVEN
                  Epūs. Sebastopolis
                  Vic. Gen.

Wesimonasterii, die 30a Junii 1958

Cum licentia superiorum ordinis

© *1958 by Routledge & Kegan Paul Ltd.*

First published in the German language by Herder Verlag,
Vienna, as Der Dialektische Materialismus, 1952

Revised edition, translated with the author's additions

This edition originally published in 1958 by Frederick A. Praeger,
Publishers, New York

Reprinted with the permission of Praeger Publishers, Inc.

Reprinted by Greenwood Press, Inc.

First Greenwood reprinting 1973
Second Greenwood reprinting 1977

Library of Congress catalog card number 72-12335

ISBN 0-8371-6727-2

Printed in the United States of America

Contents

Preface

THE present work is the outcome of a course of lectures originally delivered by the author in the summer of 1945 at the Papal Oriental Institute in Rome, in which, as part of a more general survey of the history of Russian philosophy, he also had to deal with pre-revolutionary Russian Marxism, and with Soviet dialectical materialism. From these lectures there sprang the first version of this book, which was published in Italian late in 1947.[1] It was followed in 1952 by a very extensively revised German edition, which had to be reissued, in unaltered form, in 1953 and 1956.[2] The present English translation is based on the text of the fourth German edition, now in the press, which has again been very thoroughly revised and supplemented with new material.

The doctrinal edifice of Soviet philosophy is divided into two parts: dialectical and historical materialism. The author has here had to confine himself to the first of these, namely, dialectical materialism, including the philosophy of science; in effect to the properly philosophical portion, as the term 'philosophy' is understood in the West. Historical materialism, which in Soviet usage includes the theory of society, could not be dealt with as such. The problems of ethics, aesthetics and the philosophies of history and law are also assigned, under the Soviet scheme of things, to the field of historical materialism. There would certainly have been some justification for enlarging the scope of the account to some extent and bringing these subjects also within our purview, since in Western usage, at all events, they undoubtedly rank among the philosophical disciplines properly so called. The reason why this has not been done is that the author originally hoped later on to be able to follow up the volume on dialectical materialism with a second one on historical materialism, and because lack of both time and space have compelled him to this self-imposed restriction.

[1] Gustav A. Wetter, S. J.: *Il materialismo dialettico sovietico*, Turin 1948.
[2] Gustav A. Wetter: *Der dialektische Materialismus. Seine Geschichte und sein System in der Sowjetunion*, 1st edn., Vienna–Freiburg-i-B. 1952.

The present revised version of the book differs in the first place
from previous editions of the German version in that the historical
part has been carried up to the XXth Party Congress of the C.P.S.U.
(February 1956). In the systematic part, the chief need was to take
account of the changes wrought by the de-Stalinization campaign.
These have consisted chiefly in a reversion from the Stalinist account
of the theory of dialectic to that of Engels, and a corresponding
rehabilitation of the law of the negation of the negation, together
with the theory of categories and certain philosophical problems
raised by modern science. The chapter on 'Dialectical Materialism
and Modern Science' has therefore been completely rewritten and
very much enlarged. The section on the 'Unity of Theory and Practice' has also been rewritten almost in its entirety. In working over
the remaining chapters, however, the author has been compelled by
technical considerations of publishing to limit himself more severely,
and to depart less extensively from the earlier text. It has therefore
proved impossible to revise these portions as much as he himself
would have wished.

The author thinks it important to point out that he has had to
limit himself to the *Soviet* account of dialectical materialism as the
subject-matter of his inquiry. The first effect of this is to exclude the
philosophical writings of Western communists, which take their inspiration largely from Marx's early writings. The latter are quite
consciously and definitely set aside in Soviet philosophy. And—
short of embarking on an endless task—it has also meant omitting
the philosophical literature produced in the Russian zone of Germany, the satellite countries and Red China. Nor has it been feasible
to enter here into the complex problem of Titoism.

The treatment is divided into two sections: historical and systematic. But the main emphasis falls on the latter. The historical chapters are really designed only to provide the necessary background
for understanding of the systematic part, and make no sort of claim
to consideration as an original *historical* inquiry into the philosophical development of Russian Marxism—still less into the
origins of Marxist philosophy generally.

The main object, in fact, has been to provide an ordered selection
of documentary evidence sufficient for an intellectual show-down
with Soviet communism. But if such a show-down is not to degenerate into a futile babble of conflicting monologues, the first endeavour
of both parties must be to understand the other. This calls, from the
outset, for strict objectivity in presentation of the opposing viewpoint and readiness to acknowledge positive merits wherever they
are to be found. One could wish, at this point, that the Soviet
participants to the discussion had also adopted this attitude. There
has, indeed, been a great deal of talk there recently of the need for

more serious study of 'bourgeois' philosophy and science. But the object of this has been merely in order to 'refute' them more effectively; willingness to acknowledge their elements of truth and to learn from them can be found, at best, only in the scientific field, and this primarily on grounds of practical interest.

This aim accounts for the predominantly expository character of the book. It also explains its tendency to a certain diffuseness for which the author craves indulgence. The essential features of Soviet philosophy could certainly have been quite fully set out in a far more concise fashion, as has been done by Bochénski in his excellent book.[1] But owing to the Hegelian terminology of dialectical materialism, a compressed account of this sort can easily leave the reader with an impression of something 'deeper' lurking beneath the individual formulae of this philosophy. Only on a more thorough examination of the philosophical attitudes and arguments propounded in Soviet dialectical materialism does it become evident that this is not the case. More especially does the author believe that only a more detailed account can justify his opinion that in present-day Soviet philosophy there is very little left of real dialectics, and that it consists, rather, of a materialistic evolutionism, decked out in dialectical terminology.

So far as the author has adopted a critical attitude, in the systematic part, towards individual tenets of dialectical materialism, he has been guided in principle by the endeavour, not to set out from any preconceived philosophical position, but rather to criticize so far as possible from within. If, in spite of this, his criticism has often run in an almost compulsive fashion along Aristotelian and scholastic lines, he would again attribute this to the fact that owing to the above-mentioned disappearance of true dialectic from the conceptual scheme of Soviet dialectical materialism, the individual categories have again taken on the values they had in the pre-idealist scheme of things, which ultimately goes back to Aristotle, and hence that Soviet philosophy has come to share a common pattern of concepts with the Aristotelian and scholastic tradition—a situation to which we shall revert in more detail in the Conclusion.

The author regrets that only after completing the text of this new version did he come into possession of the communist rejoinder to the first German edition of this book, which appeared recently in East Berlin,[2] and that he has therefore been unable to deal with the counter-arguments it contains.

He would also wish to beg the kind indulgence of the English-

---

[1] I. M. Bochénski: *Der sowjetrussische dialektische Materialismus* (*Diamat*), Berne-Munich 1950.

[2] Georg Klaus: *Jesuiten, Gott, Materie. Des Jesuitenpaters Wetter Revolte wider Vernunft und Wissenschaft*, Berlin 1957.

speaking reader for having been virtually unable to take account of the exceptional wealth of English literature on the subject. But he hopes, by his treatment of original works in Russian, to have rendered a service even to the English-speaking student which may somewhat mitigate this defect.

Finally, he would like at this point to express his heart-felt thanks to all who have assisted him in the preparation of this English edition and more especially the translator, Mr. Peter Heath of Edinburgh, for his able and devoted collaboration, in a lengthy and troublesome task.

Rome, November 1957

Translator's Note

RUSSIAN SPELLINGS have been 'anglicized' throughout, with the usual anomalies and exceptions for well-known names, foreign authors, etc. I am grateful to Mr. Dennis Ward, of Edinburgh, for help in this matter, though he is not responsible for any remaining mistakes; also to Mr. V. G. Kiernan, for the loan of books; and to Mrs. F. Broadie, for her skill and endurance in typing the manuscript.

P. L. H.

PART ONE

Historical

CHAPTER I

The Philosophical Roots
of Marxism

MARXISM, according to Lenin, is derived from three main
sources: 'The doctrine of Marx . . . is the legitimate successor
of the best that was created by humanity in the nineteenth century
in the shape of German philosophy, English political economy and
French socialism.'[1]

The economic and political sources mentioned above cannot be
dealt with here. But in order to give a complete picture of the development of Soviet philosophy it will be worth while to enter at least
briefly into the philosophical background of Marxism; the more so,
since both Lenin and Stalin, as well as Marx and Engels, are continually referring to the 'materialistic inversion' of the Hegelian dialectic.

Marxism has prided itself from the beginning on its ancestry in
classical German philosophy. 'We German socialists', says Engels,
'are proud of the fact that we are derived, not only from St. Simon,
Fourier and Owen, but also from Kant, Fichte and Hegel.'[2] 'The
German working-class movement is the inheritor of German classical
philosophy.'[3]

[1] V. I. Lenin: *Tri istochnika i tri sostavnykh chasti marxizma* (Three
Sources and Three Component Parts of Marxism), in *Sochineniya* (Works),
issued by the Marx-Engels-Lenin Institute under the Central Committee of
the C.P.S.U (B), XIX⁴, pp. 3 f. (Translated in V. I. Lenin: *Selected Works*,
Moscow 1936-9, XI, p. 3; cited hereafter as *LSW*.)

[2] F. Engels: *Die Entwicklung des Sozialismus von der Utopie zur Wissen-
schaft* (Socialism: Utopian and Scientific), 4th edn., Berlin 1891, p. 5.
(Preface to 1st German edition 1882; translated in Karl Marx: *Selected
Works*, Moscow 1942, I, p. 137.)

[3] F. Engels: *Ludwig Feuerbach und der Ausgang der klassischen deutschen*

3

An inheritor too, not only in the sense that the founders of Marxist theory were to some extent influenced by this philosophy, but also because German socialism constitutes a direct continuation of the philosophy of the great German masters. The age of merely speculative theoretical philosophy is presumed to have ended, and a new era to have begun, in which its task is not merely to interpret the world, but also to change it.

Of all the great German philosophers, neither Kant, Fichte nor Schelling has had so great an influence on Marxism as Hegel.

1. HEGEL

The philosophy of Hegel is the most complete realization of the romantic urge to incorporate all departments of life and culture into a unitary scheme. Fichte and Schelling had already made the first moves towards deriving everything from a single ultimate principle. Fichte's first principle was the Ego, Schelling's the Absolute, conceived as a principle of absolute indifference, which is the source of all diversity and multiplicity.

But the Absolute as a principle of indifference cannot explain the diversity which is supposed to proceed from it. Hegel therefore endeavoured so to frame the concept of the Absolute that the basis of multiplicity should already be contained in it. In the nature of the Absolute itself a pattern would be thereby revealed, such that the multiplicity observable in Nature and history would become intelligible as a mere expression and development of this pattern itself.

Hegel therefore conceived the Absolute as a concrete Idea, as a concept unfolding by virtue of its own internal development. All concrete determinations are merely moments and phases undergone by the Absolute in its own process of self-development.

The means whereby the Absolute differentiates itself through its own internal activity is the celebrated Hegelian *dialectic*. In Hegel's sense of the term, dialectic is a process in which a starting-point is negated, thereby setting up a second position opposed to it. This second position is in turn negated, *i.e.*, by negation of the negation, so as to reach a third position representing a synthesis of the two preceding, in which both are 'transcended', *i.e.*, abolished and at the same time preserved on a higher lever of being. This third phase then figures in turn as the first step in a new dialectical process, leading to a new synthesis, and so on.

As against the interpretations of Hegelianism current in the

Philosophie (Ludwig Feuerbach and the End of Classical German Philosophy), Stuttgart 1888, p. 68. (Translated in Marx-Engels: *Selected Works*, Moscow 1951, II, p. 364; cited hereafter as *MESW*.)

Soviet Union and commonly met with in Marxist literature, it must be emphasized that this dialectical process is not considered by Hegel to be in any sense merely a method by which we think.[1] As can be seen from the presence of a dialectical pattern in the Absolute itself, it is definitely taken to be a genuine process in reality as well.

With these preliminaries we may now attempt a brief sketch of the Hegelian system.

In the first place, Hegel sets before us in his *Logic* the self-development of the Absolute, its self-determination by means of the predicates or 'categories', beginning with the most general and at the same time the emptiest, pure *Being*. From this primary category the self-determination of the Absolute proceeds by way of its negation (*Non-being*), to the first synthesis (*Becoming*) which represents the identity of Being and Non-Being. The Absolute thereby acquires a determination which then becomes the starting-point for a new dialectical step forward. In this way the Absolute gradually enriches itself through ever higher degrees of determinacy, until it finally reaches the highest phase of its dialectical development, in which it realizes itself as Absolute Idea. At this stage the Absolute embraces and includes the entire process whereby it realizes and determines itself under the lower categories. One must beware, however, of thinking of this process as a temporal one. It is merely an unfolding of what is simultaneously present in reality, an unveiling of the inner structure of the Absolute itself, as it exists 'prior to the creation of Nature and finite Spirit'.

The *Logic* therefore shows us the Absolute as it is in itself, prior to the creation of the world, Nature and finite Spirit, and independent of these. The second part of the Hegelian system consists of the *Philosophy of Nature* which depicts the Idea in its *self-external* aspect, as *otherness*. But the Idea thus outwardly embodied in Nature retains a tendency to revert to its own original unity. We therefore perceive in Nature an ascent towards an ever-higher unity, interconnection and inwardness. The mechanical, the physical and the organic represent stages whereby the Idea in Nature endeavours to regain this unity.

Eventually the Idea attains this goal, returning from its outer embodiment in Nature back into itself, and this returning-in-upon-itself constitutes Spirit. Hence the third part follows, the *Philosophy of Spirit*, which Hegel again sets forth in three stages.

The first consists of the doctrine of subjective (individual) Spirit, in which Hegel deals with psychology and anthropology. In the

---

[1] M. A. Leonov, for example, complains that 'In Hegel the laws of the dialectic are not derived from Nature and history, but rather imposed upon the latter as laws of thought'. *Ocherk dialekticheskogo materializma* (Outline of Dialectical Materialism), Moscow 1948, p. 94.

second phase of his philosophy of Spirit he develops his doctrine of the objective (universal) Spirit, which finds expression in law, morality and ultimately in their synthesis, ethical life. The highest realization of this ethical life is discerned by Hegel in the State, and more particularly in the Prussian monarchy of his own day. This doctrine of the objective Spirit is closely connected with his philosophy of history, which has exercised great influence on more recent philosophy. The culmination of Hegel's system is to be found in the doctrine of Absolute Spirit. The objective universal Spirit does not yet represent the highest stage attainable by the Idea in the course of its return to itself, since the universal Spirit is not conscious of itself. This occurs only in the synthesis of objective and subjective (individual) Spirit which gives rise to Absolute Spirit. At this level Spirit exists not merely 'in-itself', but also 'for-itself': it attains full self-possession. It arrives at this self-knowledge, moreover, in three different ways: in *Art* it contemplates its own nature intuitively; in *Religion* it represents this nature by means of imagery; and in *Philosophy* it finally achieves an adequate grasp of this nature by means of the concept. Hence there arise three complementary disciplines: aesthetics, the philosophy of religion and the history of philosophy.

Religion and philosophy, according to Hegel, have the same content; the difference lies merely in their mode of expressing it. In religion it takes the form of imagery and historical circumstance; in philosophy, of the concept. Philosophy is the highest stage in the development of Spirit since in it the Spirit gains access to itself in a manner adequate to itself, namely in the form of the concept.

Since Hegel considers philosophy and religion to have the same content, he makes it his business to offer a philosophical interpretation of Christian dogma; a rationalistic interpretation, naturally, directed against those who would separate knowledge and faith, whether in the name of clerical orthodoxy or rationalistic enlightenment.

The philosophy of Hegel is of great significance for Marxism, two of its features in particular exercising a powerful attraction on Marxist thinkers. The first of these is its revolutionary dialectical method, the advance beyond negation to the negation of the negation: it is this which constitutes the internal dynamic of the Hegelian system, whereby everything appears to be continually on the move, in process of becoming, and nowhere comes to a stop. But there is also its immense power of synthesis, whereby the whole range of human knowledge is apprehended in all its living unity. This is what Lenin had in mind in describing Hegel's scheme, for all its mysticism and empty pedantry, as a 'work of genius': 'the idea of a world-embracing, universal, living interconnection of all things one with another'.[1]

What Marxism could not tolerate, however, was Hegel's idealism, and the reactionary, anti-dialectical tendency of his system in presenting itself as the summit of philosophical development, and the Prussian monarchy as the final incarnation of the Spirit. This conservatism of outlook leads Stalin to interpret Hegelianism as a philosophy of aristocratic reaction against the French Revolution.[2]

For Soviet philosophy, the effect of Hegel's idealism upon his dialectic is to violate every single one of the 'principal features' of dialectic laid down by Stalin himself. The real connections in the world are supplanted by intellectual fabrications; an ascending order of development occurs, for Hegel, in the realm of Spirit only, and not in Nature; the transition from quantity to quality, in Hegel's sense, refers, not to the concrete historical development of the world, but only to the concept of quality as a logical category; and objective contradictions in reality are likewise transformed by him into merely logical contradictions between concepts.[3]

For these reasons, Marxism has set itself all along to preserve what is 'valuable' in Hegel, namely the dialectical method, while replacing idealism by materialism, and so transforming the 'idealist dialectic' into a 'materialist' one.

In thereby 'turning Hegel upside down', however, Marxism retains not only an immediate link with Hegel, but also an indirect one, by way of Feuerbach and the 'Hegelian Left'.

2. THE 'HEGELIAN LEFT'[4]

Soon after Hegel's death in 1831 his disciples split into two groups. The rift occurred chiefly in the field of philosophy of religion. The 'Right' remained more or less loyal to the traditional outlook expressed in the doctrines of the Churches; but there was also a 'Left' consisting of those who supported the liberal opposition to Prussian absolutism, and made use of Hegelianism as a weapon against it.

The 'Hegelian Left', led by David Strauss, Bruno Bauer, Ludwig

---

[1] V. I. Lenin: *Filosofskie tetradi* (Philosophical Notebooks), Moscow 1947, p. 121; German edition, W. I. Lenin: *Aus dem philosophischen Nachlass. Exzerpte und Randglossen*, Berlin 1949, p. 64. (Cited hereafter as *FT*, the German page numbers in brackets.)

[2] *Cf.* M. A. Leonov: *Op. cit.*, p. 89.   [3] *Ibid.*, pp. 94 ff.

[4] For this and the following sections, see Auguste Cornu: *Karl Marx. L'homme et l'œuvre. De l'hégélianisme au matérialisme historique (1818 bis 1845)*, Paris 1934; Karl Löwith: *Von Hegel bis Nietzsche*, Zürich-New York 1941; Wilhelm Windelband: *Die Geschichte der neueren Philosophie*, II, Leipzig 1922.

Feuerbach, Max Stirner and Karl Marx, pointed to the contradiction between Hegel's revolutionary method and the conservatism of his system. It arises from the fact that the dialectical method involves a continual progress, a ceaseless development, for which no specific state of affairs can be laid down in advance as an ultimate conclusion. The principle of dialectical progress implies that every reality is thereby already in process of losing the character of logical necessity it possesses at that moment. At any subsequent moment it is no longer rational and appears destined to give place to a new reality.[1] But this dialectical character of Hegel's method is at variance with his system, which differs entirely in recognizing a particular state of affairs as final (in politics, the Prussian State, in philosophy, Hegelianism itself).

The left-wing Hegelians simply took over the revolutionary method, and turned it into a philosophy of action. For Bruno Bauer this action consisted in philosophical criticism: its task is to ensure that the irrational element is eliminated from the historical unfolding of reality.

As Reinhard Lauth has recently shown, there were two Slavs in particular, in the ranks of the Young Hegelians, who played an altogether critical part in the intellectual development of the youthful Marx. Lauth regards this as one of the decisive reasons why Marx's doctrine should have proved so particularly influential in the Slavonic East.[2]

The first of these two, Count August von Cieszkowski, found the answer to the general perplexity which had overtaken the minds of Hegel's disciples after the master's death. If the Absolute Spirit has attained to self-awareness in Hegel's philosophy, what is there left for post-Hegelian philosophy still to do? In his book *Prolegomena to Historiosophy*, Cieszkowski bases history upon the triad of feeling (antiquity), thought (the period of internalization, inaugurated by Christ and terminated by Hegel), and will. In future reality is to be transformed by will, by action.

'Practical philosophy, or more properly speaking the *philosophy* of practice—the most concrete possible influence of the latter on life and social relationships, the emergency of *truth* in *concrete activity*—such is the future destiny of philosophy in general.'[3]

This watchword of concrete action now led the Young Hegelians

[1] *Cf.* F. Engels: *Ludwig Feuerbach, etc.*, pp. 6 f. (*MESW*, II, pp. 327 f.).

[2] R. Lauth: *Einflüsse slawischer Denker auf die Genese der Marxschen Weltanschauung*, in *Orientalia Christiana Periodica*, Vol. XXI, Nos. 3–4, Rome 1955, pp. 399–450.

[3] A. von Cieszkowski: *Prolegomena zur Historiosophie*, Berlin 1838, p. 129; quoted in A. Cornu: *Op. cit.*, p. 82, n. 19.

into the field of political and social activity, the Hegelian philosophy being transformed in the process into a political and social doctrine.

To begin with, however, the campaign against the 'Right' and political absolutism was opened, not in the political field, but in that of the philosophy of religion, with an attack on the churches and on Christian doctrine. Only later was the struggle against the churches, which were held to be the main pillars of absolutism, extended into a struggle against the Prussian monarchy as well.

In addition to Arnold Ruge, one of the leading figures in this struggle was the Russian, Mikhail Bakunin. He is the other Slav among the Young Hegelians whom Lauth regards as having exercised a decisive influence on Marx's mental development. In his well-known article *Reaction in Germany*, in the *Deutsche Jahrbücher*, he attempted to provide a theoretical foundation for the implacable hostility shown by the Hegelian Left, not only towards the churches, but increasingly also towards the Prussian State. Thesis and anti-thesis can only achieve reconciliation in synthesis in so far as the thesis remains capable of forming an organic synthetic whole with the antithesis. But as regards the opposition of freedom and unfreedom, this is at present no longer the case. Hence the thesis must now be simply destroyed by the antithesis. Bakunin then seeks to justify this primacy of the negative over the positive by way of a philosophical deduction, and ends his article with the fiery summons:

'Let us put our trust, therefore, in the eternal spirit, who shatters and destroys only because he is the unfathomable and eternally creative source of all life. The desire to destroy is itself a creative desire.' [1]

For Bakunin, therefore, the dialectic has a quite different ground-plan from the Hegelian one: the opposites are no longer reconciled in the synthesis—instead, the thesis is destroyed by the antithesis; the latter is thereby lifted at the same time to a higher qualitative level and becomes the general starting-point for the formation of an entirely new reality, which Bakunin took to be embodied in democracy:

'The victory of democracy will be not merely a quantitative change . . . , but a transformation of quality—a new, living and genuine apocalypse, a new heaven and a new earth, a young and splendid world, in which all present discords will be resolved in a harmonious unity.' [2]

---

[1] M. Bakunin: *Reaktion in Deutschland*, in *Deutsche Jahrbücher*, Vol. 17, 21st Oct. 1842, p. 1002; quoted in D. Chizhevsky: *Hegel bei den Slaven*, Reichenberg 1934, p. 203.

[2] M. Bakunin: *Op. cit.*, p. 986.

Cieszkowski's ideas are operative in the Marxian doctrine of 'practice'. Bakunin's antithetical dialectic may be traced wherever Marx envisages the proletariat in the rôle of a 'grave-digger', whose task it is to 'eliminate' the class-enemy and so bring about a 'new earth', a qualitatively different kind of reality, in which all anti-social tendencies will have been erased from the 'new man', where selfishness and crime exist no longer and where work has become the first necessity of human life.[1]

3. LUDWIG FEUERBACH

Of all the Left-Hegelians, it was certainly Feuerbach who exercised the greatest influence on the intellectual development of Karl Marx. Originally a follower of Hegel, he finally severed his connection in 1839, though without ever being able to free himself entirely from the influence of his master.

His objection to Hegel's system is based on a weakness in its philosophy of Nature. Here, Hegel's attempt at a general deduction of the infinite variety of individual objects in Nature had encountered a barrier which it could not get over. Hegelianism, as Feuerbach saw it, had certainly been able to provide an account of Nature in general, as outward embodiment of the Idea, and to derive from it forms and laws of a highly general kind; but it had not succeeded in deducing *a priori* the infinite multiplicity and diversity of individual concrete instances. Hegel had seen in this a lack of congruence between reality and the concept, which he entitled the contingency of Nature; ascribing it, not indeed to a weakness of the concept, or of philo-sophy, but to the weakness of Nature, which thereby betrays its subserviency in relation to Spirit.[2]

[1] On all this, *cf.* Reinhard Lauth: *Die 'verwirtschaftete' Humanität. Grundvoraussetzungen der philosophischen Weltanschauung von Karl Marx,* in *Neue Deutsche Hefte,* No. 17, Aug. 1955, pp. 334–46.

[2] Here, however, we have no wish to prejudge the issue as to whether the nature of the dialectical process in Hegel consists in an *a priori* type of deduction, or whether, as more recent authorities have maintained, it is really a sort of scrutiny of essences (*cf.* Nicolai Hartmann: *Die Philosophie des deutschen Idealismus,* II, *Hegel,* Berlin–Leipzig 1929, pp. 166 ff.). It is admitted, even by those who take this latter view, that it is in the field of Nature-philosophy that Hegel's system breaks down. Hartmann sees in the inability of Hegel's philosophy of Nature to lay hold of the entire multi-plicity of concrete instances 'only one among many indications that the plan and outline of Hegel's philosophy of Nature is not free from objection even from the standpoint of his own method' (*Op. cit.,* p. 287); the explana-tion being that Hegel was 'from the very start a philosopher of the Spirit', for whom the philosophy of Nature always remained a step-child (*Op. cit.,* pp. 282 f.).

Feuerbach reverses this relationship, taking it, not that reality is inadequate to the concept, but rather that the concept is inadequate to reality. In his *Critique of the Hegelian Philosophy* (1839) he sees it as a major flaw in the dialectic that it allows for succession but not co-ordination, time but not space. Hence it can justify history, but not Nature. Hegelianism, with its historical approach, is incapable of accounting for Nature, cannot understand it, and therefore regards it as 'contingent'. But in actual fact this 'contingency' is the true reality, since all the laws of Nature deduced by Hegel *a priori* can only have meaning in application to concrete cases; the individual, on the other hand, can never be deduced at all. The essence of Nature therefore resides in these individuals with which Hegel's doctrine is incapable of dealing. But if a philosophy cannot comprehend the individual, it ought to be rejected. In this way Feuerbach, having first supported Hegel, later turned against him.

But he also took a further step. True reality, he holds, is the individual, the singular, Nature; the universal, the Idea, Spirit, are correlative to these. In his *Outlines for a Philosophy of the Future* (1843) he argues that only the sensory individual is real, and the universal merely an illusion on the part of the individual. Here again he inverts the Hegelian thesis. Hegel considered Spirit, the Idea, to be the true reality, and Nature merely the external guise, a necessary self-division on the part of Spirit, which apprehends itself by means of this sundering and separation from itself. According to Feuerbach, however, the opposite happens: Spirit is merely a duplication and disuniting of the individual within itself, not a real entity, but only a pale reflection of Nature.

German idealism thereby terminates in a crude materialism; and there its tragedy lies. The basic flaw in idealism, its inability to derive Nature and the individual from the Idea and the universal, led, in Feuerbach's teaching, to its own self-destruction through the disavowal of its one creative principle, Spirit. And yet this materialism and naturalism still bears traces of its idealistic origin; the influence of the dialectic remains, as can be seen in the conception of Spirit as the 'negation' of matter, as a sundering of Nature over against itself. 'This materialism is the twin brother of dialectical Idealism. Feuerbach's teaching is merely inverted Hegelianism.' [1]

Starting from this point of view, Feuerbach carried Strauss's criticism of Christianity to its logical conclusion. Strauss's historico-philological methods had already shaken the foundations of religion; Feuerbach attempts to uproot them psychologically, by seeking to lay bare the origins of the idea of God, and so to liberate humanity from this idea.

---

[1] W. Windelband: *Op. cit.*, p. 393.

Religion, in his view, is an illusion arising from the fact that man ascribes reality to his own nature, of which he forms a concept for himself, and sets this up over against himself as something alien to him. 'Religion, at least the Christian, is the relation of man to himself, or more correctly to his own nature (*i.e.*, his subjective nature); but a relation to it, viewed as a nature apart from his own. The divine being is nothing else than the human being, or, rather, the human nature purified, freed from the limits of the individual man, made objective—*i.e.*, contemplated and revered as another, a distinct being.' [1]

Man sets up his own nature as God to himself by magnifying it to infinity. Hence this nature appears to him as something alien to himself. God is that which man would wish to be. Religion thereby becomes a product of human needs and wishes. 'Religion is the disuniting of man from himself; he sets God before him as the antithesis of himself. God is not what man is—man is not what God is. God is the infinite, man the finite being; God is perfect, man imperfect; God eternal, man temporal; God almighty, man weak; God holy, man sinful. God and man are extremes: God is the absolutely positive, the sum of all realities; man the absolutely negative, comprehending all negations.' [2]

The urgent need at present, however, is to transform this God back into man. God being in reality nothing other than man, he must be remade into the true, rational, philosophical man. Theology is to be transformed into anthropology, but anthropology of a philosophical kind.

In this way Feuerbach seeks to liberate man from the illusion of God, to restore him his full freedom, and to make a true man of him. 'The aim of my writings and lectures is this: to turn men from theologians into anthropologists, from lovers of God into lovers of humanity, from candidates for the hereafter into students of the here-and-now, from lackeys of a heavenly and earthly monarchy and aristocracy into free, self-respecting citizens of the world.' [3] And at the end of the final lecture Feuerbach expresses the hope that he has not failed in his task 'the task, that is, of turning you from friends of God into friends of man, from believers into thinkers, from praying men into working men . . . from Christians, by their own admission and belief *half-animals and half-angels*, into *men*, into *complete men*'. [4]

[1] Ludwig Feuerbach: *Das Wesen des Christentums. Sämtliche Werke*, VI, Stuttgart 1903, p. 17. (Translated as *The Essence of Christianity* (by Marian Evans), 2nd edn., London 1881, p. 14.)

[2] *Ibid.*, p. 41; (English, p. 33).

[3] L. Feuerbach: *Vorlesungen über das Wesen der Religion. Sämtliche Werke*, VIII, Stuttgart 1908, pp. 28 f.

[4] *Ibid.*, p. 360.

Feuerbach's atheistic humanism here takes on a religious note. 'Our relation to religion is therefore not a merely negative, but a critical one; we only separate the true from the false . . . But that which in religion holds the first place—namely, God—is, as we have shown, in itself and according to truth, the second, for it is only the nature of man regarded objectively; and that which to religion is the second—namely, man—must therefore be constituted and declared the first. Love to man must be no derivative love; it must be original. [Only so can love become a true, holy and positive force.] If human nature is the highest nature to man, then practically also the highest and first law must be the love of man to man. *Homo homini Deus est* —this is the great practical principle: this is the axis on which revolves the history of the world. The relations of child and parent, of husband and wife, of brother and friend—in general, of man to man—in short all the moral relations are *per se* religious.' [1] And when Feuerbach says of himself, in his *Philosophical Fragments*: 'God was my first thought, Reason my second, and man my third and last', [2] the implication is that his humanism has never quite renounced its religious origins. 'Man is man's God' and other such sayings confirm the irony of Stirner, who described Feuerbach as a 'pious atheist'. [3] The remark is more than a mere witticism, for the religious problem is the central issue in all Feuerbach's thinking. Bulgakov applies to him a saying of the hero in one of Dostoyevsky's novels, 'God has been tormenting me all my life'. [4] Feuerbach says of himself indeed, in the *Lectures on the Nature of Religion* delivered towards the end of his life: 'Apart from this difference among my writings they all, in the strict sense, have one and the same object, one and the same thought and endeavour, one and the same theme. That theme is religion and theology, and everything connected therewith.' [5]

This is all of considerable interest to our inquiry; this religious aspect of anthropologism, the cult of 'God-man', to borrow an expression from Bulgakov, is also evident, as a legacy from Feuerbach, in Marxism and Bolshevism; though it is not in fact acknowledged, Feuerbach himself being disapproved of precisely because of his religiosity.

But when Feuerbach asserts that man is man's God, he is thinking

[1] L. Feuerbach: *Das Wesen des Christentums*, p. 326 (English, pp. 270 f.; words in brackets omitted).

[2] L. Feuerbach: *Fragmente zur Charakteristik meines philosophischen Entwicklungsganges, 1843/44. Sämtliche Werke*, II, Stuttgart 1904, p. 388.

[3] *Cf.* S. Bulgakov: *Religiya chelovekobozhestva u L. Feuerbacha* (The Religion of God-man in L. Feuerbach), Moscow 1906, p. 7.

[4] *Ibid.*, p. 7.

[5] L. Feuerbach: *Vorlesungen über das Wesen der Religion*, p. 6.

of man as a social being, in community with other men: 'Man by himself is human (in the ordinary sense); man and man together—the unity of *I* and *Thou*—is divine.' [1]
So much for Feuerbach. We have dealt with him in some detail, since his doctrine had a great influence on that of Marx, and hence on the whole of Marxism. Feuerbach's influence on Marx is expressly underlined by Masaryk, who ends his exhaustive account by remarking: 'Anyone who has mastered these few pages on Feuerbach knows more of Marxism than he would from an undigested reading of the first volume of *Capital*.' [2] Bulgakov goes further still: 'I should like to endorse this judgement [of Masaryk's, above] with redoubled emphasis: even a well-digested reading of all three volumes of *Capital* will give no such idea of the basic standpoint, the ruling spirit of Marxism, as familiarity with Feuerbach.' [3]

Marx's chief debt to Feuerbach is the idea of humanism. This humanism, the struggle to free humanity from oppression, led Marx to socialism. Feuerbach is also the source of the notion of anthropomorphism, which Marx, as we shall see, was to apply not only to philosophy and religion, but also in the social field. The influence of Feuerbach, and that of all the 'Hegelian Left', especially the fact that they began their campaign against the 'Hegelian Right' and the whole social order dominant at the time, with an attack on traditional Christianity, also helps to explain how Marxism could take on such a violently anti-Christian and anti-religious character.

From the standpoint of contemporary Soviet philosophy, however, Marx's significance is not to be seen merely in the fact that he combined the Hegelian dialectic with Feuerbach's materialism. Such a view (of which Plekhanov and Deborin are accused) would mean looking at Marx's philosophical work too much from the logical angle, as a purely ideal development, whereas in reality his philosophical career must be viewed in the closest possible connection with the proletarian struggle for liberation.

In detail, the following objections are more particularly raised by the Soviet philosophers against Feuerbach's philosophy:

(*a*) In his revolt against German idealism Feuerbach paid insufficient attention to the importance of the dialectic; hence he confined himself to dissenting from Hegelianism without overcoming it. (Engels already makes this criticism in his tract on Feuerbach);

---

[1] L. Feuerbach: *Grundsätze der Philosophie der Zukunft*, No. 60; *Sämtliche Werke*, II, Stuttgart 1904, p. 318.
[2] T. G. Masaryk: *Die philosophischen und soziologischen Grundlagen des Marxismus*, Vienna 1899, p. 28.
[3] S. Bulgakov: *Op. cit.*, p. 11, n.

(*b*) Owing to his neglect of the objective significance of the dialectic in everyday life, his materialism has an excessively abstract, contemplative, 'metaphysical' character (as it has been called since Engels), in conceiving of man as an absolute, unalterable entity, given once and for all, regardless of his historical development and concrete situation;

(*c*) His humanism is too religious; Feuerbach does no more than replace the religious link between man and God by an equally religious relationship of men to one another.

4. MARXISM AND POSITIVISM

In addition to Hegel and Feuerbach, Masaryk also mentions positivism as a further source of Marxist philosophy. Apart from the latent positivistic elements in some of the German philosophical systems (in Schopenhauer and Stirner, for instance, and even in Hegel himself), Marx was especially influenced, in Masaryk's opinion, by French positivism, with which he came into contact particularly during his stay in France from 1843 onwards.

Communist reviewers of earlier (German) editions of this book have taken violent exception to this suggestion.[1] A Soviet reviewer in *Voprosy filosofii* (who lacked even the courage to reveal his own identity and signed his article 'Materialist'; this being the only instance known to us where an article in this periodical has appeared under a pseudonym) describes it as a 'scoundrelly fabrication' to identify the dialectical materialist rejection of metaphysics with that of positivism, since the latter also regards materialism as 'metaphysics' and rejects all philosophy whatsoever. A further major argument put forward is the hostile attitude which Marx and Engels adopted towards Comte.[2]

That the Soviet elaboration of Marxism does indeed concede the right of philosophy to exist, and differs from positivism in this respect, is something we have always been at pains to acknowledge, even in earlier editions of this book (in the very passage, indeed, which our Soviet reviewer singles out for attack, so that the charge of 'scoundrelly fabrication' recoils on his own head). But it still does not follow from this that in earlier days also Marxism was always similarly anti-positivistic in its attitude, nor yet that—even in Soviet Marxism—some other positivistic elements may not be discernible.

---

[1] So, for example, Giuseppe Berti in *Societa*, Vol. 3, No 5 (Nov.–Dec. 1947), pp. 705 ff.; 'Materialist': *Otets iezuit v roli kritika dialekticheskogo materializma* (A Jesuit Father as Critic of Dialectical Materialism), in *VF*, 1952, 6, pp. 125–37.

[2] *VF*, 1952, 6, p. 129.

And if Marx and Engels took issue on occasion against A. Comte, this too is no guarantee of their entire immunity from positivistic habits of thought, for positivism had already come into being earlier than this; indeed, Feuerbach himself, who exercised so decisive an influence on the two founders of Marxism, is commonly referred to as one of the main representatives of German positivism.

As for the concrete evidence of Marxism having absorbed a measure of positivism, it is clearly traceable from the first at many points in Engels. Thus many passages in his writings evince a tendency to dissolve philosophy into the special sciences, as when he says, for example, in *Anti-Dühring*:

'It is in fact no longer a philosophy, but a simple world-outlook which has to establish its validity and be applied not in a science of sciences standing apart, but within the positive sciences.' [1]

We shall have to return to this matter in more detail in Part Two.[2]

A second similarity between Marxist philosophy (this time including Soviet philosophy) and positivism consists in their common aversion for unchanging 'metaphysical' entities and restriction of attention to the perpetually changing flux of facts or appearances. In spite of this, dialectical materialism endeavours to validate the category of 'essence' as well as that of appearance. But we shall see more explicitly in Part Two how impotent it is to give a concrete account of this category,[3] based on the denial of any unalterable essentiality in things, such as would guarantee a certain stability throughout all change. But dialectical materialism, again like positivism, is concerned only with the dynamic aspect and pays insufficient regard to the static element, that which persists in all change and development. The result, despite all the renunciations of positivism, is a constant oscillation between anti-positivism and certain positivistic positions, an indeterminacy which will often emerge in the course of our survey.

---

[1] F. Engels: *Herrn Eugen Dühring's Umwälzung der Wissenschaft*, 3rd edn., Stuttgart 1894 (English translation (by Emile Burns): *Anti-Dühring*, London 1934, p. 155; page references throughout are to this version).

[2] *Cf.* Part Two, Ch. I.   [3] *Cf.* Part Two, Ch. IV.

CHAPTER II

Karl Marx and Friedrich Engels

1. KARL MARX

KARL MARX[1] was born in Trier on the 5th May 1818. His father, an advocate, was a Jew who became converted to Protestantism in 1816, in which faith his son was also brought up, after having received baptism in 1824.

The latter attended the *Gymnasium* in Trier and later studied at the Universities of Bonn and Berlin. At his father's wish he matriculated in the Faculty of Law, but was far more strongly attracted to philosophy and history, and devoted himself almost exclusively to these subjects after the death of his father in 1838.

The focus of his intellectual activities was provided, however, not by the teaching in the university, but by the meetings of a philosophical society in the Berlin suburb of Stralau, where both he and his respected teacher Gans were then living. The members of this circle consisted of young lecturers, zealous adherents of the Hegelian philosophy, and included Bruno Bauer, who had been a *Privatdozent* in the Berlin theological faculty since 1834. Under the influence of the discussions in this 'Stralau Graduates Club' Marx seceded from the philosophies of Kant and Fichte to that of Hegelianism.

Soon afterwards he was already in the camp of the Hegelian Left. In company with Bauer he cultivated 'Criticism' which held that reality could be transformed through the development of the Idea and the elimination of the irrational. But Marx soon became

[1] In the following chapter particular acknowledgement is due to the works of Auguste Cornu and Karl Löwith already mentioned (*cf.* p. 7, n. 4).

17

convinced that philosophy alone was not in a position to alter the real world and that for this purpose it had to be supplemented by practical action.

Frederick William III died in 1840 and was succeeded by Frederick William IV, who attempted to revitalize the régime on a basis of absolute monarchy and protestant pietism. This development brought about a simultaneous change in the position of the Hegelian Left. Till then the Hegelian philosophy had enjoyed the favour of the government, and even the Hegelian opponents of the régime, who confined themselves to the sphere of ideas, had been tolerated on that account. All this was now at an end. The veteran Schelling was recalled to the University of Berlin, the government hoping that he would counterbalance the influence of Hegelian radicalism. Cheated in their hope of winning over the authorities to their own ideas, the Hegelian Left was forced into opposition and transferred its campaign from the religious to the political field. Already in 1838 Ruge and Echtermaier had founded the periodical *Hallesche Jahrbücher* (Halle Annals), which furthered the application of 'Criticism' to the political sphere.

In spite of their opposition views the Hegelian Left remained loyal at first to the cult of the Idea of the State, and of its concrete embodiment, the Prussian State, which they had taken over from their master. Basing themselves on the Hegelian philosophy of Right they still saw the State as the embodiment of Reason and Morality. Their criticism was therefore chiefly directed against religion, which they held responsible for the faults of the régime. But very soon their opposition also turned against the monarchical principle and finally against the Idea of the State itself, so that only their faith in humanity was left to them (*cf.* Feuerbach's religious humanism).

This change did not take place without leaving a profound impression on the mind of the youthful Marx. He became increasingly estranged from Bauer and allied himself at first with Ruge. At this juncture he wrote his doctoral dissertation on *The Distinction between the Democritean and Epicurean Philosophies of Nature*[1] (1841). There he argues that Criticism, by secluding itself from reality, becomes incapable of having any effect on the world, and goes on, already clearly under the influence of Cieszkowski's ideas,[2] to call for a supplementation of critical theory by means of practical activity.

This thirst for activity soon brought Marx into politics. He began

[1] K. Marx and F. Engels: *Historisch-kritische Gesamtausgabe* (Collected Works), issued by the Marx-Engels-Lenin Institute, Moscow and Frankfurt-a-M., later Berlin and Moscow, 1927 ff. (cited hereafter as *MEGA*). Part I, l, i, pp. 5–81.

[2] *Cf.* R. Lauth: *Einflüsse slawischer Denker . . .*, pp. 427 ff.

contributing to Ruge's *Jahrbücher*, though somewhat dissatisfied with its policy, which seemed to him too remote from politics and life. In 1842 the *Rheinische Zeitung* (Rhineland Gazette) was founded in Cologne. Marx and Bauer were invited to become contributors. After obtaining his doctorate, Marx had originally returned to Trier; from thence he moved first to Bonn and later to Cologne. It was not long before he was in virtual control of the paper. He was lucky to be able to seize this opportunity, for this journal enabled him to apply the doctrines of criticism direct to political questions.

Marx's work on the *Rheinische Zeitung* had a great influence on his development, leading him to busy himself not only with political questions but also with economic ones. When he began he was still imbued with Hegel's ideas, believing that the progress of the Idea would necessarily bring about progress in reality, and that philosophical criticism must necessarily result in changes in the actual situation.

Traces of a Hegelian outlook are clearly visible in his first article, in which he criticizes the debates of the Rhenish Diet on Press freedom. He came out as a determined champion of the liberty of the Press. In order to support his claims he brings the Hegelian concept of the State into action:

'Present-day philosophy regards the State as a great organism, dedicated to the realization of legal, ethical and political freedom, in which the individual citizen, when he obeys its laws, is merely obeying the natural laws of his own, and indeed human, reason.'

In Marx's view this concept .of the State requires freedom of the Press, for the Press is the

'Seeing eye of the spirit of the people. . . . It is the intellectual mirror in which a people contemplates itself. . . . It is the ideal world, forever springing from the real and pouring new life back into it, from the ever-increasing riches of the spirit.' [1]

In October 1842 Marx became chief editor. In further articles dealing, *inter alia*, with the debates in the Diet on the law against theft of timber,[2] and the state of the peasant wine-growers on the Moselle,[3] he became increasing concerned with social and economic problems. Since the *Rheinische Zeitung* was also conducting a

---

[1] *Die Verhandlungen des 6 ten rheinischen Landtags* by Ein Rheinlander. First Article: *Debatten über Pressfreiheit und Publikation der Landständischen Verhandlungen.* MEGA, Pt. I, 1, i, pp. 179–229 (*q.v.* p. 212).

[2] *Die Verhandlungen* . . . Third Article: *Debatten über das Holzdiebstahls-Gesetz.* MEGA, Pt. I, 1, i, pp. 266–304.

[3] *Rechtfertigung des + + Korrespondenten von der Mosel.* MEGA, Pt. I, 1, i, pp. 355–83.

campaign against the Christian religion and the Christian State, this led to ever more serious trouble with the censorship, until finally in March 1843 the publication of the paper was forbidden by the government.

But in spite of its brief duration, this episode had a decisive effect on Marx's career. On the one hand, his preoccupation with economic and social questions led to an ever-increasing divergence from the Hegelian philosophy. The rapid strides made by science and industry were already making the Hegelian view of Nature, which depicted it merely as an external manifestation of Spirit, increasingly unplausible. On the other hand, the closer study of reality resulting from his journalistic activities led him to see the interconnection and relationship of facts and ideas in a new light. Hitherto, as a follower of Hegel, Marx had referred the process of history to the development of the Spirit. He now tends increasingly to invert the relationship, and to ascribe a much more decisive significance to material facts in determining the course of events. In this reversal of his position, Marx was notably influenced by Feuerbach's *Essence of Christianity*.

A further consequence of his work on the *Rheinische Zeitung* was that Marx also became progressively less friendly to Bauer's 'Criticism'. This period of his activity had shown him that the progress of the Idea was incapable of transforming reality, that facts are more powerful than theory. Marx therefore gradually drifted away from Bauer and the Berlin members of the Hegelian Left, who still clung to the abstract and fruitless programme of Criticism. This attitude of opposition to Bauer's 'Criticism' was later responsible for a joint work by Marx and Engels, *The Holy Family*.

The banning of the *Rheinische Zeitung* opened a new period in Marx's intellectual development, leading to the formulation of the materialistic conception of history and the gradual completion, under the influence of Hess, Weitling, Stein and Engels, of his conversion to communism.

What now preoccupied him was the problem of the State. His criticism of the debates of the Rhenish Diet had shattered Marx's Hegelian conception of the State as an instrument for the realization of a just and rational order of society. He was now inclined, rather, to see the power of government as a tool of private interests. This led him to undertake a critical examination of the Hegelian philosophy of the State, on which he had hitherto relied. The result was an essay, *The Critique of the Hegelian Theory of Constitutional Law*[1] which he probably composed in the summer of 1843.

[1] Edited by S. Landshut and J. P. Mayer in a collection of Marx's early writings, dating from the years 1837–48, entitled *Der historische Materialismus*. Kroners Taschenausgabe, Vols. 91/92. Leipzig 1932. *Cf.* also

Hegel's political philosophy had expounded the theory of the 'objective' or 'universal Spirit' as expressed in Law, Morality and Ethical Life. Hegel considered the ethical life to be realized in society, initially at a lower level, in the family and civil society, and then at a higher stage in the State. Just as, elsewhere in Hegelianism, the Idea constitutes the inmost essence of Nature and Spirit and thereby determines *a priori* the whole development of Being, so in the field of ethical life the State represents the highest realization of the Idea, previously incarnate in more imperfect fashion in the family and civil society, and now conscious of its own true essence in the State. The State is therefore in no sense a product of society; on the contrary, society and its political, legal and social arrangements are conditioned *a priori* by the State.

Marx protested against this point of view. For him it is the family and civil society that are primary, it is they that are the real components of the State, the latter existing only in so far as they do. In Hegel, on the contrary, the condition (family and civil society) figures as the conditioned, being governed by the Idea (of the State). The Idea becomes the only genuinely dynamic element, the subject, whereas the true subject, family and civil society, becomes the predicate, and merely appears as a further determination of the Idea. Marx's objection to Hegel is that he everywhere treats the Idea as subject, and converts what is actually the real subject into the predicate. Politics thereby becomes for him a branch of logic.

Marx calls this conversion of subject and predicate 'mystification'; and it leads him to set about 'inverting Hegel', whereby the latter, who is standing on his head, is to be set once more upon his feet.

In consequence of this 'mystification' Hegel puts State and civil society in opposition, as the collectivity in-and-for-itself (the State), versus the particular interests of private individuals (civil society). But such an opposition is irreconcilable, in Marx's view, with the true idea of collectivity and the true idea of the community. For in a 'true State' the collectivity should not be regarded as something over and above the domain of real individual life, as a special sphere of its own in addition to the private sphere of the individual; in a true State the real existent, the true subject, the citizen, should also appear at the same time as an embodiment of the collectivity, as a 'socialized human being'. In Hegel, however, the State becomes an 'abstract collectivity' which is ultimately not a genuine collectivity at all, but a thing apart, distinct from the life of the people and opposed to it as a governing institution and a bureaucracy. In contrast to the 'real', 'material' life of the individual, the State thereby

MEGA, Pt. I, 1, i, pp. 403–533 (*Aus der Kritik der Hegelschen Rechtsphilosophie. Kritik des Hegelschen Staatsrechts*, §§ 261–313).

becomes something 'external', 'alienated'. This 'alienation' from the true essence of man is responsible for the fundamental contradiction obtaining between reality as it now is, and the true idea of social life. In a true State this opposition between the private affairs of the individual and the public affairs of the community is transcended: each individual becoming a collective being, a 'socialized man', and man a genuine 'member of the species'. This is 'true democracy', in which man is no longer subjected to a social order that is alien to him; the 'political State' has vanished, withered away. Here we have the first foreshadowing of that idea of the 'classless society' which Marx was later to identify as the essence of 'true democracy'.

Marx also directed his criticism against a particular feature of Hegel's social philosophy. Hegel took the view that private property was the basis of civil society. Political and social inequality seemed to him both normal and necessary. Marx rebelled against this theory, being inclined, rather, to consider private property more and more as the basic evil of society and the modern State.

Marx's criticism of Hegel's theory of the State is therefore in the last resort a transference of Feuerbach's anthropologism into the political and social field; just as Feuerbach, in the field of religion, had seen in the idea of God an alienation of human nature, so Marx, in the social field, sees in the State an alienation of the collective nature of society, of social man. In order to regain possession of its own nature, therefore, humanity cannot rest content with abolishing religion. Along with religion it must also get rid of the (monarchical) State, to which society has given up its own substance and collective life and the people its powers and rights. It is a question once more of reversing the Hegelian order of things, and treating the people, civil society, as subject and the State as an attribute or object.

Here, however, Marx does not go on, as yet, to insist on communism; he poses the problem without offering a solution. His proposed reforms are still conceived, meanwhile, within the framework of a social democracy. He was merely demanding the abolition of the monarchy, without recognizing the State as such as an instrument for the establishment of class-oppression and tyranny.[1]

In the autumn of 1843 Marx settled in Paris in order to join Ruge in editing the periodical *Deutsch-Französische Jahrbücher* (Franco-German Annals). Only one number appeared, however, in which Marx published two articles, *Criticism of the Hegelian Philosophy of Right*,[2] and a review of two of Bauer's writings, *On the Jewish Question*.[3]

---

[1] *Cf.* Cornu: *Op. cit.*, p. 259.

[2] *MEGA*, Pt. I, 1, i, pp. 607–21. (Translated in H. J. Stenning: *Selected Essays by Karl Marx*, London 1926.)

[3] *MEGA*, Pt. I, 1, i, pp. 576–606 (also in Stenning: *Op. cit.*).

In the first article Marx once more applies Feuerbach's anthropological principle to the social field. Religion is created by man, according to Feuerbach, in that he sets up an illusory world into which he projects what the real world has denied him. Marx poses the problem as to *why* man creates an illusory world of this sort; and he finds his explanation in the fact that society as it stands at present is an inverted world. Man, to be sure, is 'no abstract being, squatting outside the world. Man is the world of men, the State, society'. And if society creates, in religion, such an inverted consciousness of the world, in which illusion becomes reality and reality illusion, this comes about because the world itself is upside down, alienated from its nature. Religion, in fact, is a spiritual mirror-image of the world and society, the 'general theory of this world'. It is the fantastic realization of human nature, inasmuch as the latter has no genuine reality. It is the 'opium of the people', because it holds out hopes of an illusory happiness and thereby diverts them from the struggle for their real happiness. The campaign against religion must therefore be enlarged in Marx's view, into a campaign against the inverted world which has brought religion into existence. The criticism of heaven must become the criticism of earth, of law and of politics.

As things stood in Germany at that time, however, the indictment of society and the State necessarily became, for Marx, an indictment of philosophy. Germany might be backward in the political and social sphere, but in the field of philosophy, the harbinger of the future, it yielded nothing to France and England, the most progressive countries in the world.

And yet a two-fold error has been committed in regard to this philosophy: in the present critical struggle between philosophy and the real world, one party cleaves to philosophy: their error consists in believing it possible to make philosophy actual without transcending it. The other party, the practical politicians, stand opposed to philosophy and seek to negate it. As against them Marx sums up his own position in a formula which affords a deep insight into the extent to which his intellectual outlook is still entirely under the Hegelian spell: 'You cannot transcend philosophy without making it actual.'

Now this 'actualization' of philosophy comes about, according to Marx, because criticism poses problems which can only be solved by practical activity, political action. For the weapon of criticism cannot replace the criticism of weapons; material force must be overthrown by material force. But 'theory, too becomes a material force, as soon as it takes hold of the masses'. In yet another sense, therefore, practice outweighs theory: the material circumstances decide the theory which is to achieve actualization.

'Revolutions in fact require a passive element, a material foundation. Theory becomes realized among a people only in so far as it represents the realization of that people's needs. . . . It is not enough that the thought presses towards realization; reality itself must press towards the thought.'[1]

We see how reality, in Marx's thought, comes increasingly to the fore at the expense of philosophy and the Idea, and tends to be regarded as the determining factor in historical development. The 'transcending of philosophy', its 'actualization', is not to be thought of, in Marx's sense, as the work of the philosophizing Spirit, but as the original handiwork of reality itself. At the bottom of this notion there still lies the idealist view, that it is the task of history itself to establish 'the truth of contemporary life', to 'actualize' philosophy, or the Idea, in the course of its own progress.

One other idea in this brief article is of cardinal importance in Marx's development of the materialistic conception of history. Owing to the special conditions obtaining in Germany, it is not possible there, as it was in France, to complete the transformation and emancipation of society in stages, by means of a partially political revolution. In Germany universal emancipation, brought about by a social revolution, is the *conditio sine qua non* of every partial emancipation. This total emancipation will be the work of that social class which is most sorely oppressed, robbed of all its rights and possessions and incapable of emancipating itself without thereby emancipating all other spheres of society as well, 'which represents, in a word, the complete loss of mankind, and can therefore only redeem itself through the complete redemption of mankind'[2]—namely, the proletariat. The proletariat will make the abolition of private property, which is in fact forced upon it, into a principle, and thereby emancipate the whole of society, so that egoism and social injustice are utterly eliminated.

The influence of Bakunin's antithetical dialectic is particularly in evidence here. Like Bakunin, Marx sees the proletariat as the moment of antithesis, the negative pole in the dialectical process of mankind's development. For Bakunin the negative is committed to the task of destroying the positive; in so doing it is itself transcended as a negative, undergoes a 'qualitative renewal', inasmuch as it becomes a being on its own account and an all-embracing principle, and thereby ushers in a 'young and splendid world' in which all discords are resolved in harmonious unity. So too with Marx: the opposites here are private property and the proletariat; the task of

[1] *MEGA*, Pt. I, 1, i, pp. 613, 615 f. (Stenning, pp. 26, 29—slightly modified).

[2] *MEGA*, Pt. I, 1, i, pp. 619 f. (English, p. 37).

the proletariat is to abolish private property; it thereby itself undergoes a qualitative change, ceases to be a proletariat, and in emancipating itself ushers in the ultimate and total emancipation of all mankind and hence a complete transformation of the entire world.[1]

Having imitated Feuerbach in overturning Hegel, and setting up Nature instead of the Idea as the primary reality, Marx already displays in this article an evident tendency to incorporate philosophy into history. For the moment, however, it still retains an independent significance. In the subsequent article, *On the Jewish Question*, he goes a step further and abandons the attempt to ascribe to philosophy a distinct and active rôle in social development.

Marx attacks the thesis of Bauer, who had held the political emancipation of the Jews to be contingent on their religious emancipation, their abandonment of Judaism. Both religious and political emancipation are insufficient from Marx's point of view; true emancipation must have a social character. It will come about through the political man, the citizen, returning to his fellows as a member of civil society, giving up his egoistic manner of life in order to achieve a collective, social life. Just as humanity must recover the ideal essence of itself it has projected upon heaven, so civil society must recover the ideal essence of itself it has located in the State. Hence, the social emancipation of Judaism becomes the emancipation of society from Judaism, whose nature Marx here equates with Capitalism:

'What is the secular basis of Judaism? Practical needs, egoism. What is the secular cult of the Jew? Huckstering. What is his secular God? Money. . . . The emancipation of the Jews in its last significance is the emancipation of mankind from Judaism.'[2]

The basic theme of both these articles is the application of Feuerbach's anthropological principle to society: religious and political emancipation alone are not enough; religious radicalism and political liberalism are powerless if they do not press on towards the transformation of society itself. The basic evil of the latter lies in the egoism engendered by private property. To such a society Marx opposes the ideal of a communistic society in which private property is eliminated and the aims of the individual coincide with those of the community. The transformation of society is thought of as occurring dialectically, by means of a total revolution, the decisive rôle being played by the proletariat. But although in the first of these two articles the thesis and antithesis of this dialectical process still appear in both logical *and* metaphysical form, in that philosophy still

---

[1] *Cf.* R. Lauth: *Op. cit.*, pp. 446 ff.
[2] *MEGA*, Pt. I, 1, i, p. 601 (English, pp. 88 f.).

plays an essential part, the thinker being regarded as an ally of the proletariat, in the second article the dialectic figures exclusively as an economic and social process; the development of the Idea is completely absorbed into the development of reality, and from now on philosophy no longer plays an independent or active rôle in the process of social development.

We are carried a step further towards the final notion of the materialistic conception of history in the *Economico-Philosophical Manuscripts of the Year 1844*,[1] in which Marx is no longer thinking of law, morality and the State in relation to society, but is already examining their economic basis and attempting to show that political economy is the key to all moral, political and social problems. This work represents to some extent a logical continuation of the two articles already referred to. In these Marx had argued that society must resume the nature which it has alienated to the State. It is now a question of showing how this alienation has come about, and the manner in which it is to be transcended. The attempt to grapple with these issues led him into the problems of political economy.

His procedure is founded once more on a criticism of Hegel—this time a critique of the Hegelian phenomenology: Hegel's great service is to have shown that all development has a dialectical character, proceeding by an alienation which is thereafter transcended. The Idea realizes itself by alienating itself, becoming estranged from its own content, only to recover it gradually once more by a progressive transcending of the alienation, through which it becomes aware of how its own substance is constituted.

In applying this dialectic to man, Hegel had rightly seen him as the product of a process of self-creation, resulting from the alienation of his substance into an object foreign and external to himself, and the transcending of this alienation through recognition of the object as an expression of his own activity, of himself. Hegel, in other words, had conceived of man as a product of his own exertions.

Marx points to a two-fold defect in this view of Hegel's. Its basic error is to represent the Idea as a genuine reality. Movement and activity are identified with the development of self-consciousness. The only exertions Hegel knows of are spiritual exertions, and he therefore knows nothing of the concrete, real activity of men, disclosed to the senses. Since man is essentially self-consciousness, the product of his activity, namely, the alienation of consciousness into the object and its subsequent transcending of this, remains, therefore, something abstract and unreal.

This involves a further deficiency in the Hegelian view. Since every opposition between subject and object remains within consciousness,

---

[1] *MEGA*, Pt. I, 3, pp. 29–172.

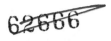

the Hegelian conception of dialectic is inherently liable to transcend the object itself by demonstrating it to be merely another aspect of consciousness. The recovery of what was alienated becomes not so much a matter of overcoming the estrangement of the object as of transcending the object itself. Instead of achieving a genuine synthesis between thought and being, the Hegelian philosophy tends towards a disavowal of being and reality, and their dissolution in consciousness.

Marx joins Feuerbach in once more turning Hegel upside down. Man conceived as self-consciousness can make nothing of his alienation beyond an abstract 'objectivity'; he never arrives at concrete material 'objects'. But if the real, concrete man, standing with his feet on the ground, alienates from himself, as external objects, his own substantial, real and material energies, the objective character of his being can equally be deduced from the objective character of these his activities. Only an objective being has objective efficacy. Man creates and constitutes objects only because he is himself constituted by objects, being himself in origin a part of *Nature*.

Hence again for Marx it is not the Idea that is primary, but Nature. Man himself is only a part of Nature, tied to her apron-strings. His primary activity is not spiritual, not cognitive, but a real material activity in which he produces real objects and puts his energies, himself in fact, into them. As an objective creature in Nature, man is in one sense an active being, equipped with natural vital forces; in another sense he is also a passive being, in so far as he is subject to numerous objects existing independently of himself and confronting him from without. A being having no objects external to itself is not an objective being; and a being that is not, in its turn, an object for some other being has equally little claim to objectivity. Thus there is no opposition in this respect between man and Nature, subject and object, but only a mutual interfusion and dependence; man becomes a product of Nature, and Nature a product of man.

The adjustment of Nature to human needs furnishes the content of history. Man's activity is at first instinctive, like that of animals; the objects of his activity simply exist outside him, though connected with him by the fact that he has need of them to supply his wants. Man, however, is not a natural being pure and simple, like an animal, which accepts Nature as it finds her. He exerts himself consciously upon her, struggles to bend her to his needs, and also, on the other hand, to adapt himself to hers. This two-fold adaptation constitutes the essence of labour, it is the stuff of 'practice', which from now on becomes a key-concept in the philosophy of Marxism.

The nature of 'practice' is further elaborated by Marx along the lines of Hegel's conception of 'knowledge'; in both cases the dialectical element is of cardinal importance.

As in the case of knowledge for Hegel, so labour, practice, for Marx consists essentially in an alienation of the subject. But this alienation differs from that implied in the Hegelian conception of knowledge in being concerned with the creation of real, externally existing objects, into which man puts his energies, alienates his own 'self'. And as in Hegel's knowledge, so in Marx's 'practice', this alienation must be followed by a recovery of that which is alienated. But while in Hegel the recovery tends, as Marx objected, to suppress the object itself, in 'practice' this recovery is supposed to be merely a matter of eliminating the 'estrangement' between subject and object, *i.e.*, overcoming the fact that man looks on the result of practice, the product of his labour, as something external and alien to him.

In this fashion, by a joint use of Feuerbach's anthropologism and Hegel's dialectic, Marx arrives at the materialistic conception of history and the demand for communism.

The social order based on private property is an order of estranged, alienated labour wherein the nature of man, which he has externalized in the product of his labour, is not recovered, but remains alienated from him. This accounts for the weakness of man's position in the present social order. Feuerbach's supposed discovery in the field of religion, namely, that man becomes ever weaker in himself, the more of himself he projects into an object independent of him, is confirmed by Marx in the social sphere: man becomes ever weaker, the more he produces; the labour which remains divided from man's nature becomes, in the shape of capital, a means to his enervation and oppression:

'The more wealth the worker produces, the greater the increase in the power and scale of his production, the poorer does he become. The more the worker exerts himself, the mightier grows the alien, outer world that he has raised up against him; the poorer he becomes in his inner world, the less it belongs to him for his own. So it is also in religion. The more man ascribes to God the less he retains for himself. The worker puts his life into the object; yet it now belongs, not to him any longer, but to the object. The greater his efforts in this direction the more destitute is he left. The product of his labour is something not himself; the greater the product therefore, the less he is in himself. The worker's alienation of himself in his product signifies not only that his work has become an object, an externally existing thing, but that it exists outside him, alien to him, independent of him, has become a selfsubsistent force opposing him, and that the life with which he has endowed the object is pitted in estranged hostility against him.' [1]

[1] *MEGA*, Pt. I, 3, p. 82 ff.

And Marx again draws the conclusion: neither the abolition of religion (Feuerbach), nor philosophical criticism (Bauer), are sufficient to restore human nature. This can only be done by a transformation of the social order, the abolition of private property and the removal of the material restrictions which are responsible for this estrangement. This will be the task of the social revolution which will be brought about through the development of the property-owning social order itself; for this presently dominant order is creating, in the proletariat, the instrument which is to effect its own downfall.

Communism, with its abolition of private property and removal of all alienation, represents the return of man to true human life. And just as this alienation has operated simultaneously in the sphere of consciousness and in that of concrete life, so the emancipation achieved by communism in the social and economic sphere will also bring about a religious emancipation and so give validity to atheism.

But this liberation will not come about through deliberate intervention; it will be effected rather, through the inner law of development of the present order itself, which already carries within itself the seeds of its own destruction.

In so saying, Marx has not only arrived at the demand for communism, but also approximates closely already to the final formulation of the materialistic conception of history. Whatever occurs in consciousness is merely a reflection of what is going on at the economic foundations of society; economic changes necessarily bring with them a transformation of political and social organization, and the moral and religious outlook. A two-fold legacy from his idealist Hegelian upbringing is still, however, traceable: firstly, the fact that criticism still plays a rôle, in that it serves, by discovering the contradictions in the social order, to indicate the road of historical development; and secondly the view that these contradictions are still to be thought of as proceeding from the idea of a moral defect, a discordancy between present-day reality and the true nature of man; a legacy from which neither Marx nor Marxism were ever able to free themselves entirely.

In Paris, Marx busied himself with an exhaustive study of the French Revolution and delved into the works of the classical political economists, Adam Smith and David Ricardo. In addition to these theoretical concerns he also continued his practical revolutionary activity. He launched into active propaganda among the German emigrants, kept in touch with the clandestine French trade unions, made the acquaintance of Proudhon, Bakunin, Louis Blanc, Cabet and others and became friendly with Georg Herwegh and Heinrich Heine. The all-too-revolutionary tone of the article he had published in the first number of the *Jahrbücher* led to a breach of relations with Ruge.

In Paris he also worked on the staff of *Vorwärts* (Forward), a German periodical appearing there, and published in it a series of articles in which he attacked Prussian absolutism and derided Frederick William IV.

In August and September 1844, Friedrich Engels, *en route* from England on one of his journeys, spent ten days in Paris, which marked the beginning of his intimate friendship with Marx. Both found themselves in complete agreement on all theoretical questions, and remained friends and collaborators for the rest of their lives.

After a discussion about the intellectual tendencies of their common friend Bauer they decided to work out a rejoinder to his theory. Engels hastily sketched out his ideas on the subject and left it to Marx to carry them out and complete them, and to prepare the work for the press. It grew under the latter's hand to two hundred pages. The original title was meant to be *A Critique of Critical Criticism*, but it was changed at the instance of the publisher to *The Holy Family or Critique of the Critical Critique. Against Bruno Bauer and Co.*;[1] the words 'Holy Family' are used by Marx and Engels as an ironical description of Bauer and his associates, because they had created out of Spirit and consciousness a transcendent entity, namely 'Criticism', which had been made incarnate in the members of the group.

If *The Holy Family* did not give Marx the opportunity of presenting his materialistic conception of history, the fruit of his labours in philosophy and political economy, in systematic form, it at least enabled him to give it precise application in certain concrete instances. As against Bauer's idealism he explains how the State, law, religion and morality are conditioned by the class-struggle.

Marx's articles in *Vorwärts* impelled the Prussian authorities to take steps with the French to have the author evicted from France. The French government were only too willing to comply, and Marx was obliged to leave France in January 1845. He went to Brussels, where he spent three years. Here, as in Paris, he pursued his theoretical and practical activities, working in conjunction with the trade unions and carrying on an intensive propaganda.

In the theoretical field he was especially anxious to put the finishing touches to his philosophical development in the years preceding. This he did, in the first instance, by laying down eleven briefly-stated theses against Feuerbach (*Theses on Feuerbach*[2]), and later by composing a more elaborate treatise, *The German Ideology*.

[1] *MEGA*, Pt. I, 3, pp. 173–388 (English version, Moscow–London 1956).

[2] Originally published by F. Engels as an appendix to the first inde-

The theses against Feuerbach were drawn up in March. They are not aimed at Feuerbach alone, since they also take issue against all earlier materialism, and idealism as well. Feuerbach's error, according to Marx, lies in his purely contemplative attitude to reality, which represents for him a mere object of sensuous contemplation, rather than positive activity. He treats man as an abstract entity, an isolated individual, not as a member of a concrete society.

Against Feuerbach's picture of man Marx again puts forward his own doctrine of practice. Man's primary attitude to the world is not one of passive contemplation, but a sensuous activity seeking to change the world, namely practice (Theses I and V). It is also a practical question 'whether objective truth can be attributed to human thinking', and it is in practice that 'man must prove . . . the reality and power, the this-sidedness of his thinking' (Thesis II); the subject of practice is not the abstract, isolated individual, but social man in the historical course of his social life (Theses VI and VIII); the result of this practice is the revolutionary transformation of the world (Theses I and IV), 'socialized humanity' (Thesis X). And Marx concludes: 'The philosophers have only interpreted the world, in various ways; the point however, is to change it.'

Engels having arrived in Brussels in 1845, Marx collaborated with him in an attempt to give an account of their philosophical development hitherto, in the shape of a criticism of the whole of post-Hegelian philosophy. The result was a comprehensive work entitled *The German Ideology. A Criticism of Recent German Philosophy as Represented by Feuerbach, Bauer and Stirner, and of German Socialism in the Works of its Various Prophets*, 1846.[1] It never found a publisher, and was first printed in the Soviet Union by Ryazanov, the German version in 1932 and the Russian in 1933. It contains criticism of Bauer, Feuerbach, Stirner, and the 'true socialism' of Grün, as well as of Proudhon's socialism and the popular communism of Weitling.

With this work the philosophical development undergone by Marx, from Hegelianism to historical materialism, can be regarded as ended. The very starting-point of the book is based on the materialistic conception of history: it sets out from man as a real, active being, and from his real life-process the development of the ideological reflexes and echoes of this process is likewise derived.[2] This approach is merely the application of a general law which dialectical materialism regards as basic to any materialistic view of

pendent edition of his *Ludwig Feuerbach* . . . (Stuttgart 1888), pp. 69–72, (Translated in *MESW*, II, pp. 365–7.)

[1] *MEGA*, Pt. I, 5, pp. 706. (Parts I and III translated by W. Lough and C. P. Magill as *The German Ideology* (ed. R. Pascal), London 1938.)

[2] *Ibid.*, pp. 17 ff. (English, pp. 18 ff.).

32   *Karl Marx and Friedrich Engels*

the world: 'Consciousness can never be anything else than conscious existence. . . . Life is not determined by consciousness, but consciousness by life.' [1] When the authors speak of 'life' in this context, it can be seen from subsequent passages that it is the concrete relationships of production that they have in view. The above-quoted formula therefore falls into place beside a later one, which ranks as the classic expression of the basic principle of historical materialism: 'It is not the consciousness of men that determines their being, but, on the contrary, their social being that determines their consciousness.' [2]

Marx and Engels subsequently go on to criticize earlier, and especially German, philosophy. They consider it the main fault of German thinkers that, instead of inquiring into men at work in reality, they concern themselves with abstract fabrications, so that their thoughts wander in the realm of 'pure Spirit', and they come to think of the 'religious illusion' as the moving force of history. In contrast to this the authors devote their entire energies to studying the actual history of man in his concrete activity on earth; they see in the process of material production the factor which conditions the whole of social life. This basic law gives rise to others—the law of division of labour, of the formation of classes, of the class-struggle, etc.—whose effect is to ensure that historical development will lead to the proletarian revolution and the establishment of communism.[3]

This work effectively represents the end of Marx's philosophical development. In 1847 he published in Brussels *The Poverty of Philosophy*,[4] containing a rejoinder to Proudhon's book: *Système des Contradictions Économiques, ou Philosophie de la Misère*, which had appeared in 1846. Marx here applies his materialistic theory of history to the explanation of social relationships, formulates the doctrine of the class-struggle and has already begun to lay the foundations of the theory of 'surplus value'.

His practical activities go hand in hand with his theoretical, being centred especially on the *Communist League*. The Second Congress of this organization, held in London in November 1847, entrusted

---

[1] *MEGA*, Pt. I, 5, pp. 15 f. (14 f.).

[2] Karl Marx: *Zur Kritik der Politischen Ökonomie*. First revised version, edited by K. Kautsky, of the work originally published in 1859. Stuttgart 1897, Preface, p. xi (translated in *MESW*, I (Preface only), p. 329).

[3] *Cf. Iz istorii filosofii XIX veka. Sbornik statey pod redaktsiey i s predisloviem I. K. Luppola* (The History of Philosophy in the 19th Century: a Collection of Essays, Edited with an Introduction by I. K. Luppol), 1933, pp. 70-7.

[4] *La Misère de la Philosophie. Réponse à la Philosophie de la Misère de M. Proudhon*, Brussels–Paris 1847; *MEGA*, Pt. I, 6, pp. 117–228 (English version, ed. C. P. Dutt and V. Chattopadhyaya, London 1936).

him with the task of drawing up a condensed account of their programme. The result was the *Communist Manifesto*,[1] published in German, in London, a few weeks before the revolution of February 1848; the French version appeared in Paris shortly before the June rising of the same year.

In this year a large part of Europe was convulsed by revolutionary movements. Beginning in Italy, they extended to France, Germany and as far as Hungary. Marx took an active part in these events. Having been expelled on that account by the Belgian authorities, he betook himself to Paris, and after revolution had also broken out in Germany, returned there in April, along with Engels, to take over control of the *Neue Rheinische Zeitung*, which appeared from 1st June 1848 to the 19th May 1849. After the suppression of the revolution in Germany Marx was put on trial, but was acquitted on 9th February 1849. Expelled once more, he first returned to Paris, but having been forbidden to remain there after the demonstration of 13th June 1849, took up residence in London, where he remained until his death.

He devoted himself to his literary labours, living in a state of penury, supported by his friend Engels. In 1859 he published his *Contribution to the Critique of Political Economy*,[2] of which the Introduction is particularly important for Marx's sociology and philosophy of history. This Introduction is the source of the quotation already described as the 'classical' formulation of historical materialism, which we shall have to discuss in more detail in another connection.

In the 'sixties Marx again took up practical activity. In 1864 he founded the International Working Men's Association, the so-called First International, of which he was the moving spirit. He himself composed the *Inaugural Address* of the Association to the workers of Europe, and drew up its *General Rules*.[3] His intention was to combine in this unitary organization the various forms of socialism that had emerged up to that time (Mazzini, Proudhon, Bakunin and Lassalle's German Socialist Movement). But the First International did not survive very long. It soon became involved in disputes, which were chiefly concerned with the authority of the General Council. The 'federalists' or 'anarchists' (Mikhail Bakunin), were opposed to a 'dictatorship' of the General Council; the 'centralists', on the other hand (Marx), were in favour of a council equipped with extensive powers, on the ground that only such a body could lead the international workers' movement to victory. After the suppression of the

[1] *MEGA*, Pt. I, 6, pp. 523–57 (*MESW*, I, pp. 21–61).
[2] *Cf.* p. 32, n. 2 above.
[3] First published in *Beehive*, 1864 (reprinted in *MESW*, I, pp. 342–353).

Paris Commune (1871) and the exclusion of Bakunin from the International (Bakunin had wanted to set up his anarchist International inside it, and was therefore excluded at the Hague Congress), the continuance of the First International in Europe became impossible. After the Hague Congress (1872) the General Council was transferred, at Marx's instigation, to New York, but soon afterwards the First International ceased to exist.

In addition to his organizational and revolutionary activities, Marx also carried on throughout this period with his theoretical work. 1867 saw the appearance of the first volume of his chief work, *Capital*. The second and third volumes were issued by Engels in 1885 and 1894. A fourth volume of Marx's posthumous writings was added by K. Kautsky in three parts in 1904, 1905 and 1910.

The strain of his practical activities on behalf of the First International, no less than his theoretical exertions in laboriously gathering material for *Capital*, had broken Marx's health. He died in London on 14th March 1883, and is also buried there.

In embarking, as we have, upon a somewhat lengthy and tedious analysis of Marx's early writings, we have not been animated by any belief in their close connection with the philosophy of Bolshevism. On the contrary, we are very much of Bocheński's opinion, that many critics of Bolshevism, in the effort to understand it 'more deeply', are much too ready to hark back to 'the youthful Marx'.[1] In the last resort these early writings of Marx are of interest to the student of Bolshevism in the Stalinist era only in so far as they contain the seeds of his later social doctrines, the abolition of private property, the classless society, communism, and so on, and in so far as they can be regarded 'in spite of their enclosure in the trappings of philosophy and their retention of Feuerbach's terminology' as the first significant sketches for the new point of view.[2] Since Stalin's death, however, there are signs of a new attitude in this respect. V. A. Karpushin, Lecturer at the University of Moscow, writing in *Voprosy filosofii*, gives expression to his regret that Marx's *Economico-Philosophical Manuscripts of the Year 1844* are no longer included

[1] I. M. Bocheński, O. P.: *Der Bolschewistische Katechismus*, in *Schweizer Rundschau*, XLVIII (1948/49), p. 237.

[2] *Cf.* V. M. Pozner: *Formirovanie teoreticheskikh osnov 'Kommunistiches-kogo manifesta' v rannikh rabotakh Marxa* (The Working-out of the Theoretical Basis of the 'Communist Manifesto' in Marx's Early Writings) in *Izvestiya Akademii Nauk SSSR, Seriya istorii i filosofii* (Bulletin of the Soviet Academy of Sciences: Historico-Philosophical Series; cited hereafter as *IAN*), V (1948), 6, pp. 489–502.

in the second impression of the (Russian) Collected Edition of the works of Marx and Engels.[1]

One by no means trivial advantage to be gained from a closer examination of the early philosophical writings can nevertheless be precisely that of demonstrating how little there is in common between Marx's speculations and the official philosophy of Bolshevism. For all his inversion of Hegel, Marx still remains, in his philosophical thinking, at the level of Hegelianism, and Soviet philosophy owes less to his dialectical materialism than it does to the more superficial and vulgar form of dialectic popularized by Engels. The main interest in considering this transition from Hegelianism to historical materialism, as exhibited in Marx's youthful thought, undoubtedly lies in its disclosure that the main concepts of Marxism—communism, revolution, the classless society, surplus value, etc., have a Hegelian origin; and the recognition that all this has its basis in the doctrine of the 'alienation' of man's nature through private property, and the 'recovery' of this nature which is to be effected by the revolution.

In conclusion we shall again review the salient features of this transition from Hegelianism to historical materialism. For Hegel the ultimate ground of all reality was the Idea: it conditions the entire process of development in the various fields of reality: that of Nature, which represents the Idea in alienation from itself, and that of Spirit, which represents the return of the Idea from its alienation back into itself. Feuerbach reversed this order; it is not the Idea, but Nature, that is the ground of all reality: Idea and Spirit represent a merely self-made distinction within the sensory, material individual; they are not entities but merely reflections. More particularly he applied these notions to the field of religion. Man alienates his own nature into the concept of God and sets it up as something alien over against himself; in order to restore the weakness in man so engendered, it is necessary to destroy the religious illusion, and to reinstate man's alienated nature back in himself.

Marx endorses this reversal of the basic concepts of Hegelianism. For him too, Nature, and man as a concrete constituent thereof, are the primary realities. Marx, however, transfers Feuerbach's anthropological principle from the sphere of religion to the theory of society. Just as, for Feuerbach, man alienates his nature in God, so for Marx it is society that alienates its specific nature, its collective life, in the State, and this too, is responsible in its turn for the anomalous, enfeebled, sickly condition of society. The egoism which

[1] V. A. Karpushin: *Razrabotka K. Marxom materialisticheskoy dialektiki v 'Ekonomichesko-filosofskikh rukopis'yakh' 1844 goda* (K. Marx's Working-out of the Materialist Dialectic in the *Economico-Philosophical Manuscripts of the Year 1844*), in *VF*, 1955, No. 3, p. 104.

finds expression in private property is a symptom of this sickness in present-day society (*Critique of the Hegelian Theory of Constitutional Law*).

In Marx's two articles in the *Deutsch-Französische Jahrbücher* and especially in the first, the *Contribution to a Critique of the Hegelian Philosophy of Right*, he takes a decisive step towards the formulation of the materialistic conception of history. The alienation of human nature that has occurred in the sphere of consciousness, in religion, is based on alienation in the social and economic field. Society, according to Marx, engenders religion, *i.e.*, an inverted consciousness of the world, because it is *itself* an inverted world. This is the first reasonably clear formulation of the basic idea of the materialistic conception of history, namely, that processes in consciousness must be construed as the reflection of economic and social processes in Nature.

In later writings, and above all in the *Economico-Philosophical Manuscripts*, Marx gives closer attention to the course of these processes occurring in the economic and social substratum: just as it is not the Idea, but Nature, and man as a concrete constituent thereof, that is the primary reality, so also it is not thought nor even the merely passive contemplation of Nature (Feuerbach) that represents man's primary activity, but rather 'practice', *i.e.*, concrete operations upon Nature for the production of material commodities, economic activity. It is this, in the last analysis, which determines the course of history. It represents, however, not merely an alteration of Nature, but at the same time an alteration of man himself. He creates himself, in the process, as a social being.

Conjoined with this there is also the fact that this 'practice' has a dialectical character, which Marx sets forth on the analogy of the dialectical character of 'knowledge' in the Hegelian scheme. In producing material goods man alienates his energies, *i.e.*, himself, into the goods so produced. Upon this alienation there must therefore supervene, as the third element in the dialectic, a recovery of the self so alienated, which takes the form of a transcending of the 'estranged' quality of the product, *i.e.*, of getting rid of the fact that man regards the product he has created as something that does not belong to him, as is so frequently the case under the régime of private property. The inmost essence of human labour, or 'practice', therefore requires as its normal condition a social order in which private property has been done away with.

To the dialectic of 'practice' there corresponds the dialectic of the whole historical development of mankind, for by practice is meant, not merely the labour of the individual man, but first and foremost the historical unfolding labour-process of man in society. In the social order based on private property the nature of man, which he has alienated into the product of his labour, remains estranged from him. This gives rise to that debilitation of man which reaches its ultimate limit in the formation of the proletariat, and becomes a negation of true humanity. But that in itself creates a historical necessity for a dialectical reversal of the historical process of development of social man: by social revolution the proletariat will smash the social order built up on private property, and so make possible the recovery of man's nature hitherto alienated in the product of his labour. This economic emancipation will necessarily lead to social and political emancipation as well: the realization of true social man, in whom the individual's private sphere of interests coincides with the public interests of society, also implies the elimination of the State. Social and political emancipation will in turn be followed, as a necessary consequence, by religious emancipation also.

All the elements of the materialistic conception of history are already present here in Marx's thought: the decisive factor in historical development is the economic one; it conditions social and political development; even man's intellectual activities are nothing more than a reflection of these economic and social processes in the consciousness of social man. This development has a dialectical character, leading to the formation of social contradictions which find expression in class-war. The class-struggle of the proletariat, however, implies the final removal of class-contradictions; in emancipating itself the proletariat will also be emancipating the whole of society.

In his other writings prior to the *Communist Manifesto*, Marx goes on to apply this conception, already complete in essentials, to specific issues arising in the course of polemics against other views, which gave him repeated opportunities to define his historical standpoint with ever-increasing precision.

By the time the *Communist Manifesto* came to be drafted, the materialist conception of history was already fully worked out. Engels, who despite his help with the drafting of the Manifesto, emphatically ascribes its basic principle to Marx, gives the following account of the matter:

'The "Manifesto" being our joint production, I consider myself bound to state that the fundamental proposition, which forms its nucleus, belongs to Marx. That proposition is: that in every historical epoch, the prevailing mode of economic production and exchange, and the social organization necessarily following from it, form the basis upon which is built up, and from which alone can be explained, the political and intellectual history of that epoch; that consequently the whole history of mankind (since the dissolution of primitive tribal society, holding land in common ownership) has been a history of class struggles, contests between exploiting and exploited, ruling and oppressed classes; that the history of these class struggles forms a series of evolutions in which, nowadays, a stage has been reached where the exploited and oppressed class—the proletariat—cannot attain its emancipation from the sway of the exploiting and ruling class—the bourgeoisie—without, at the same time, and once and for all, emancipating society at large from all exploitation, oppression, class distinctions and class struggles.' [1]

Marx's clearest and most detailed formulation of his materialistic conception of history was given in 1857 in the Preface to *A Contribution to the Critique of Political Economy*:

'In the social production of their life, men enter into definite relations that are indispensable and independent of their will, relations of production which correspond to a definite stage of development of their material productive forces. The sum total of these relations of production constitutes the economic structure of society, the real foundation, on which rises a legal and political superstructure and to which correspond definite forms of social consciousness. The mode of production of material life conditions the social, political and intellectual life process in general. It is not the consciousness of men that determines their being, but, on the contrary, their social being that determines their consciousness. At a certain stage of their development, the material productive forces of society come in conflict with the existing relations of production or—what is but a legal expression for the same thing—with the property relations within which they have been at work hitherto. From forms of development of the productive forces these relations turn into their fetters. Then begins the epoch of social revolution. With the change of the economic foundation the entire immense superstructure is more or less radically transformed. In considering such transformations a distinction should always be made between the material transformation of the economic conditions of production, which can be determined with the precision of natural science, and the legal, political, religious, aesthetic or philosophic—in short, ideological forms in which men become conscious of this conflict and fight it out. Just as our opinion of an individual is not based on what he thinks of himself, so can we not judge of such a period of transformation by its own consciousness; on the contrary, this consciousness must be explained rather from the contradictions of material life, from the existing conflict between the social productive forces and the relations of production. No social order ever perishes before all the productive forces for which there is room in it have developed, and new, higher,

[1] *Communist Manifesto* (Engels' Preface to the English edition, London 1888, *MESW*, I, p. 28).

relations of production never appear before the material conditions of their existence have matured in the womb of the old society itself. Therefore mankind always sets itself only such tasks as it can solve; since, looking at the matter more closely, it will always be found that the task itself arises only when the material conditions for its solution already exist or are at least in the process of formation.' [1]

There are good grounds for E. Bernstein's assertion that this passage may be reckoned among 'the most significant of all statements' of the materialistic conception of history. K. Kautsky describes it as 'classical', but to this it has been replied—and rightly, in our opinion —by Masaryk,[2] that if so it lacks the chief attribute of classicism, namely, clarity and exactness. 'Conditions' is a very indefinite expression which immediately raises the question whether it is a matter of true causality, and how such causality is to be properly understood; if Marx is intending to equate ideology and consciousness, this too is misleading and unclear, for here one immediately thinks of individual consciousness, whereas Marx has in mind the consciousness of social man, the nature of which remains, in any case, exceedingly doubtful.

The most deep-seated obscurity, however, concerns the problem as to the relationship of will and consciousness to the economic substructure, and whether the latter is really so independent of the former as the present formulation would seem to suggest. And in the event this very point has occasioned permanent modifications in the formulation of the materialistic conception of history. Marx himself, in a well-known passage from the first volume of *Capital*, was later to allow a much greater significance to intellectual activity in the production process:

'A spider carries on operations resembling those of the weaver; and many a human architect is put to shame by the skill with which a bee constructs her cell. But what from the very first distinguishes the most incompetent architect from the best of bees, is that the architect has built a cell in his head before he constructs it in wax. The labour process ends in the creation of something which, when the process began, already existed in the worker's imagination, already existed in an ideal form. What happens is, not merely that the worker brings about a change of form in natural objects; at the same time, in the nature that exists apart from himself, he realizes his own purpose, the purpose which gives the law to his activities, the purpose to which he has to subordinate his own will. . . . Apart from the exertion

[1] K. Marx; *Zur Kritik der Politischen Ökonomie*. Preface, pp. x ff. (*MESW*, I, pp. 328–9).
[2] T. G. Masaryk: *Op. cit.*, p. 94.

of his bodily organs, his purposive will, manifesting itself as attention, must be operative throughout the whole duration of the labour.'[1]

And in the third volume of the same work Marx expressly states that the political forces arising from the economic structure themselves in their turn have a determining influence in the economic sphere.

The criticisms of the materialist conception of history directed to this point were so forcible that, as we shall see, Engels, in later years, made other numerous qualifications of a far-reaching kind. And so far as concerns the bolshevik formulation of the materialistic conception we shall in due course have the opportunity of showing in more detail how very typical is its emphasis upon the retroactive influence of consciousness on the economic substructure.

In one other respect the formulation of the materialist conception of history never attained complete clarity, namely, as to what the 'substructure' actually consists of. Marx himself describes it differently on different occasions as 'productive and property relationships' or again as 'relationships of production and commerce'. Engels, in the aforementioned Preface of 1888 to the English edition of the *Communist Manifesto*, speaks of the 'mode of economic production and exchange'; in the *Anti-Dühring* he adopts a similar formula: 'The materialist conception of history starts from the principle that production, and with production the exchange of its products, is the basis of every social order.'[2] Stalin refers to the 'mode of production of material values'.[3]

The working-out of the materialist conception of history also entitles Marx to be considered as the founder of dialectical materialism. Nevertheless, his dialectical materialism differs considerably from the doctrine officially promulgated nowadays in the Soviet Union, which derives rather from Engels. Marx entertained the idea of undertaking a more thorough examination of the problems of dialectic on his own account. But he never got round to doing so. Only in the Preface to the second edition of *Capital* does he give an account of his dialectical method in a few short sentences which make it tolerably clear that since the production of his early works his philosophical thought has shed most of its Hegelianism:

'My own dialectical method is not only fundamentally different from

[1] K. Marx: *Capital* (translated from the fourth German edition by E. and C. Paul, London (Everyman) 1930), Vol. I, pp. 169–70.

[2] F. Engels: *Op. cit.*, p. 294.

[3] J. Stalin: *Voprosy leninizma*, 11th ed. 1947, p. 550 (*Problems of Leninism*, 11th edn., Moscow 1947, p. 583). The quotation is from the article *On Dialectical and Historical Materialism* (also incorporated as Ch. IV, 2, in *History of the C.P.S.U. (B)* (cf. below, p. 68, n. 1, p. 180, n. 1 and pp. 210–11) *q.v.* p. 119).

the Hegelian dialectical method, but is its direct opposite. For Hegel, the thought process (which he actually transforms into an independent subject, giving to it the name of "Idea") is the demiurge of the real; and for him the real is only the outward manifestation of the Idea. In my view, on the other hand, the ideal is nothing other than the material when it has been transposed and translated inside the human mind.' [1]

2. FRIEDRICH ENGELS [2]

Friedrich Engels came of a family of industrialists and was born in Barmen on 18th November 1820. Even before completing his secondary education he entered on a commercial career, originally learning the business in his father's firm, but later in the export house of a trade acquaintance, Heinrich Leupold, the Saxon consul in Bremen. In addition to this, he was soon taking an eager interest in the religious questions that were much debated at the time; he began by attaching himself to the democratic and literary movement known as 'Young Germany', but found only temporary satisfaction therein (till 1839). Later, the study of religious problems led him on from Schleiermacher and Strauss to Hegel. In the year 1841, in the course of his military service at Berlin, he joined Bruno Bauer's circle, and allied himself with the Hegelian Left. Even at this stage of his career, Engels attached great importance to philosophy, emphasizing the necessity of a bond between knowledge and life, philosophy and contemporary issues, 'Börne and Hegel'.

To this period belongs his critique of Schelling's philosophical outlook, which was set forth in a number of writings, more particularly in the essay *Schelling on Revelation*.[3] In this he defends the Hegelian philosophy against Schelling's Inaugural Lecture in Berlin. In 1842 Engels figured among Marx's collaborators on the *Rheinische Zeitung*.

[1] *Capital:* Preface to second German edition, 1873 (Paul, *Op. cit.*, Vol. II, p. 873. Also in *MESW*, I, pp. 413–14).

[2] On Engels *cf.* Gustav Mayer: *Friedrich Engels: Eine Biographie*. 2 vols. and supplement, Berlin 1920 (English translation, 1 vol., London 1935); K. Kautsky: *Friedrich Engels (Sein Leben, sein Wirken, seine Schriften)*, 2nd imp., Berlin 1908; E. Tsobel': *Osnovnye etapy politicheskoy deyatel'nosti Engel'sa* (Major Turning Points in Engels' Political Career) in *Bol'shaya Sovetskaya Entsiklopediya* (Great Soviet Encyclopaedia, cited hereafter as *BSE*), 1st edn., LXIV, cols. 239–77; M. Mitin: *Engels kak filosof* (Engels as a Philosopher), *ibid.*, cols. 277–89; V. Egorshin: *Engels i estestvoznanie* (Engels and Natural Science), *ibid.*, cols. 289–94.

[3] *Schelling und die Offenbarung. Kritik des neuesten Reaktionsversuchs gegen die freie Philosophie*, Leipzig 1842. *MEGA*, Pt. I, 2, pp. 181–227.

In the same year he came to England, to work in his father's business in Manchester. Here he became acquainted with the classical English economists and took up with the Chartists, the first independent workers' party in the country, which included a number of followers of Robert Owen, the utopian socialist. From England he contributed in 1844 an article, '*Outline of a Critique of Political Economy*',[1] to the *Deutsch-Französische Jahrbücher*. In their articles in this publication he and Marx arrived at similar conclusions, and this marks the beginning of their mutual influence and collaboration.

In the same year, 1844, in the course of a trip from England to Germany, Engels spent some days with Marx in Paris and communicated to his friend and ally his ideas concerning their joint publication already mentioned, *The Holy Family*. In 1845 he published a work already completed in Manchester, *The Condition of the Working-Classes in England*.[2] In this same year also he travelled with Marx to Manchester, where they established contact with the Chartists, and with the London organization of the German émigrés, the so-called 'League of the Righteous'.

In the years 1845 and 1846 he collaborated with Marx on their comprehensive work *The German Ideology*, to which reference has already been made.

Like his friend, Engels also took an active part in the revolutionary movements of the years 1848/9, acting as adjutant to Willich during the armed uprisings in Bavaria and the Palatinate. After the suppression of the revolution he returned to England by way of Switzerland and Italy, and resumed work in his father's business. This made it possible for him to support Marx from his own income. About this time Engels also began to busy himself with military matters. During the organization of the First International he supported Marx with advice merely, but in 1869 he became a member of the General Council and was actively engaged in the leadership of the International until its removal to the United States. He did not accompany it, remaining in London and lending his support to the workers' parties in the various countries concerned.

In the years that followed Engels devoted himself chiefly to theoretical concerns. Between 1878 and 1882 he was working on his treatise *Dialectics of Nature*;[3] in 1877 he published in *Vorwärts* the articles attacking Dühring, which subsequently appeared in book form in 1878.[4] After Marx's death he brought out, in 1885 and 1894,

---

[1] In *Deutsch-Französische Jahrbücher* 1844; *MEGA*, Pt. I, 2, pp. 379–404.

[2] *Die Lage der arbeitenden Klassen in England*, Leipzig 1845; *MEGA*, Pt. I, 4, pp. 5–186 (English version, London 1892; Preface reprinted in *MESW*, II, pp. 363–79).

[3] Regarding the posthumous editions of this work, *cf.* below, p. 44 n.

[4] *Anti-Dühring, Op. cit.* (1st edn., Leipzig 1878); *cf.* p. 16, n. 1.

the second and third volumes of the latter's *Capital*. Shortly before this, in 1884, he published *The Origin of the Family, Private Property and the State*,[1] an inquiry in which he set out to trace the origin of social classes and the State from the institution of private property. In 1886 there followed, in the periodical *Die Neue Zeit* (New Age), his articles on Feuerbach, which were later collected in a separate pamphlet.[2]

At the same time Engels worked energetically to revive the International. His efforts led to the calling of conferences at The Hague (1888) and Paris (1889) which resulted in the founding of the Second International. The years which followed were devoted to the building-up of workers' organizations in Austria, France and elsewhere. Engels died of cancer in England on 5th August 1895. In accordance with his own wishes his body was cremated and the ashes strewn to the winds over the open sea.

The friendship of Engels and Marx had a decisive influence, in each case, upon their philosophical development. In their joint works, *The Holy Family* and *The German Ideology*, they traverse together the road to dialectical materialism, though at this time it was Marx who was the more active in the philosophical sphere. Their later philosophical works also give evidence of close collaboration: Engels' polemic against Dühring, for example, was the product of co-operation with Marx.

This work, *Herr Eugen Dühring's Revolution in Science*, known for short as *Anti-Dühring*, gives an account, not only of the economic doctrines of Marxism, but also of the dialectical materialism which forms its philosophic basis. Dühring having sought to advance from supporting socialism to reforming it, the German workers asked Engels to pass criticism on this new doctrine. This was no easy task, for as Engels explains in his Preface, the new doctrine was the outcome of a new system of philosophy, so that it proved necessary to follow the philosopher step by step into that vast territory 'in which he dealt with all things under the sun and then a few more'.[3] The result was a series of articles which were first printed in *Vorwärts* and later appeared in book form.

Another work of great importance in the philosophical field is the pamphlet *Ludwig Feuerbach and the End of Classical German Philosophy*. Its origin derives from the period when Marx and Engels were collaborating in Brussels in an attack on post-Hegelian philosophy. The result of their labours, *The German Ideology*, could not

---

[1] *Der Ursprung der Familie, des Privateigentums und des Staates*, Hottingen–Zürich 1884 (English version in *MESW*, II, pp. 155–290).

[2] *Ludwig Feuerbach und der Ausgang der klassischen deutschen Philosophie* (English version in *MESW*, II, pp. 324–64; *cf.* p. 3, n. 3).

[3] *Anti-Dühring*, p. 10.

find a publisher at that time, and had to be consigned to the 'gnawing criticism of the mice'. During the forty years which elapsed before the publication of the pamphlet on Feuerbach there was no occasion to revert to the problem of the relationship of Marxism to Hegelian and post-Hegelian philosophy. With the world-wide growth and prestige of the workers' movements, however, the need again made itself felt. The appearance of a book on Feuerbach by Starcke occasioned Engels' decision to satisfy this need; he subjected the work in question to criticism in four successive articles in *Die Neue Zeit* (1886), which together make up the contents of *Ludwig Feuerbach and the End of Classical German Philosophy* (1888). It provides a systematic account of the relationship of Marx and Engels towards Hegel and Feuerbach.

Great importance, especially for his view of dialectic, is attached to Engels' book *Dialectics of Nature*, in which he criticizes the vulgar materialism of the day, contrasts it with dialectical materialism, and discourses, from this standpoint, on problems in natural science. This work, which was never completed, comprises a series of drafts dating from the years 1873–83.[1]

[1] The Preface to the Russian edition of 1948 has provided us with some exceptionally interesting details concerning the composition of these fragments and their subsequent literary vicissitudes. From 1873 onwards Engels had entertained the idea of writing a major work on the dialectic in Nature; he began collecting material and working on several chapters. The death of Marx (in 1883) compelled him, however, to postpone the work in favour of more pressing obligations (the publication of the second and third volumes of *Capital* and the organization of the international workers' movement), so that it remained unfinished until his death. The manuscripts subsequently came into the hands of the German social-democratic leaders 'who conspired for years on end to hide this extraordinarily valuable work from sight, and have continued to do so right up to the present day'. The *Dialectics of Nature* was first published in Moscow in 1925 (in the 'Marx-Engels Archive Series' of the Marx-Engels Institute), from photographic copies of the manuscript, in the German text with a Russian parallel translation. As is explained, however, in the Preface aforementioned, the execution of this task was utterly inadequate in point of scholarship, the deciphering of the manuscript having been done with extreme carelessness, such that a number of passages, including several directly concerned with the basis of Engels' theoretical views, were completely misrepresented. In spite of a certain amount of revision the German edition of 1927 and the Russian of 1929 still preserved all the major failings of the 1925 edition, as did all subsequent Russian editions. On the occasion of the fortieth anniversary of Engels' death (1935) the Marx-Engels Institute brought out a new version of the *Dialectics of Nature*, in the original, as part of its collected edition of the works of Marx and Engels. 'This edition represents a certain advance, both in its deciphering of the manuscript and in its more appropriate arrangement of the material in the

Engels' philosophical development begins, like Marx's, with Hegel, and proceeds by way of the young Hegelians to its termination, under the decisive influence of Feuerbach, in materialism. This reversal of his philosophical outlook, equally typical of Marx's case also, is vividly described by Engels himself in his tract on Feuerbach:

'Then came Feuerbach's *Essence of Christianity*. With one blow it pulverized the contradiction, in that without circumlocution it placed materialism on the throne again. Nature exists independently of all philosophy. It is the foundation upon which we human beings, ourselves products of Nature, have grown up. Nothing exists outside Nature and man, and the higher beings our religious fantasies have created are only the fantastic reflection of our own essence. The spell was broken. . . . One must himself have experienced the liberating effect of this book to get an idea of it. Enthusiasm was general; we all became at once Feuerbachians. How enthusiastically Marx greeted the new conception and how much—in spite of all critical reservations—he was influenced by it, one may read in *The Holy Family*.' [1]

Engels therefore concurs with Marx in turning Hegel 'upside down', but at a considerably deeper philosophical level, as may be seen from the following account of Hegel's dialectical method given by Engels in his *Ludwig Feuerbach*:

'According to Hegel, dialectics is the self-development of the concept. The absolute concept does not only exist—unknown where—from eternity, it is also the actual living 'soul of the whole existing world. It develops into itself through all the preliminary stages which are treated at length in the *Logic* and which are all included in it. Then

book. But it still suffers from very considerable deficiencies in both these respects as well as in the quality of its scholarly apparatus' (F. Engels: *Dialektika prirody* (Dialectics of Nature), Moscow 1948, p. vii). The latest Russian edition here referred to, also issued by the Marx-Engels-Lenin Institute, was based on the German text of 1935, reinforced by further collation with the photographic copies of Engels' manuscript (*ibid.*, p. xvi). It is curious, however, that so notable an academic foundation as the Marx-Engels Institute, headed by a scholar of world renown such as D. Ryazanov, should have been so far incapable of producing, from the very outset, a reasonably sound text from an Engels manuscript, that in the edition thus prepared 'a number of passages, including several directly concerned with the basis of Engels' theoretical views' should have later required correction. (The original English version by C. P. Dutt, with Preface by J. B. S. Haldane (London 1940), derives from the 1935 edition and is now superseded by the latest (1954) edition, based on the revised text.)

[1] *Ludwig Feuerbach, MESW*, II, pp. 332–3.

it "alienates" itself by changing into Nature, where, without consciousness of itself, disguised as the necessity of Nature, it goes through a new development and finally comes again to self-consciousness in man. This self-consciousness then elaborates itself again in history from the crude form until finally the absolute concept again comes to itself completely in the Hegelian philosophy. According to Hegel, therefore, the dialectical development apparent in Nature and History . . . is only a miserable copy of the self-movement of the concept going on from eternity, no one knows where, but at all events independently of any thinking human brain.' [1]

The essence of materialism, for Engels, consists in its inversion of this highly simplified view of the Hegelian relationship between thing and concept:

'This ideological perversion had to be done away with. We comprehended the concepts in our heads once more materialistically—as images of real things, instead of regarding the real things as images of this or that stage of the absolute concept. . . . Thereby the dialectic of concepts itself became merely the conscious reflex of the dialectical motion of the real world and thus the dialectic of Hegel was placed upon its head; or rather, turned off its head, on which it was standing, and placed upon its feet.' [2]

Even at this stage we may note in passing the confusion between materialism and realism which Engels perpetrates at this point, and which has pervaded dialectical materialism ever since.
    However, the inversion of the Hegelian dialectic did not mean that Hegel was simply 'cast aside'. Only the idealistic system was rejected; the dialectical method, on the other hand, whereby the entire world appears as an interconnected complex of processes, commended itself to Engels as the really valuable feature of Hegel's philosophy, which ought to be retained:

'Hegel was not simply put aside. On the contrary, one started out from his revolutionary side, described above, from the dialectical method. . . . The great basic thought that the world is not to be comprehended as a complex of ready-made *things*, but as a complex of *processes*, in which the things apparently stable no less than their mind-images in our heads, the concepts, go through an uninterrupted change of coming-into-being and passing-away, in which, in spite of all seeming accidentality and of all temporary regression, a progressive development asserts itself in the end—this great fundamental thought has, especially since the time of Hegel, so thoroughly

[1] *Ludwig Feuerbach*, *MESW*, II, p. 350.   [2] *Ibid.*, pp. 350–1.

permeated ordinary consciousness that in this generality it is now scarcely ever contradicted.' [1]

Such an 'inversion' of the Hegelian dialectic implies, for Engels, the primacy of motion and development in the objective world, though upon this primary motion there follows, in the second place, a corresponding movement in subjective human awareness:

'Thus dialectics reduced itself to the science of the general laws of motion, both of the external world and of human thought—two sets of laws which are identical in substance, but differ in their expression in so far as the human mind can apply them consciously, while in Nature and also up to now for the most part in human history, these laws assert themselves unconsciously, in the form of external necessity, in the midst of an endless series of seeming accidents.' [2]

Engels thereby distinguishes three different fields for the application of dialectics: Nature, history and human thought: 'Dialectics is nothing more than the science of the general laws of motion and development of Nature, human society and thought.' [3]

Having overturned Hegel, the first field in which Engels, like Marx, encountered a dialectical movement was that of the development of human society, namely history; and the result of this transference of the dialectical notion of development to history was, again as with Marx, the materialist conception of history. Engels repeatedly dwells on the fact that both he and Marx arrived at this conclusion independently of one another, though the chief credit for the final and definite formulation must nevertheless be ascribed to Marx:

'I cannot deny that both before and during my forty years collaboration with Marx I had a certain independent share in laying the foundations of the theory, and more particularly in its elaboration. But the greater part of its leading basic principles, especially in the realm of economics and history, and, above all, their final trenchant formulation, belong to Marx. What I contributed—at any rate with the exception of my work in a few special fields—Marx could very well have done without me. What Marx accomplished I would not have achieved.' [4]

We shall not go far wrong if we take it that the originality of each in working out the materialist conception of history consists in this, that Engels made his way to the idea chiefly on the strength of his work in political economy, whereas Marx approached it more from the philosophical angle, along the route we have endeavoured to

---

[1] *Ibid.*, pp. 350 and 351.   [2] *Ibid.*, p. 350.
[3] *Anti-Dühring*, p. 158.   [4] *Ludwig Feuerbach*, p. 349 n.

survey in the course of our analysis of his early writings in the previous section. This assumption receives its strongest support from the evidence expressly given by Engels himself in his Preface to the Third (1885) edition of Marx's *Revelations about the Cologne Communist Trial*:

'While I was in Manchester, it was tangibly brought home to me that the economic facts, which have so far played no rôle or only a contemptible one in the writing of history, are, at least in the modern world, a decisive historical force; that they form the basis of the origination of the present-day class antagonisms; that these class antagonisms, in the countries where they have become fully developed, thanks to large-scale industry, hence especially in England, are in their turn the basis of the formation of political parties and of party struggles, and thus of all political history. Marx had not only arrived at the same view, but had already, in the *Deutsch-Französische Jahrbücher* (1844), generalized it to the effect that, speaking generally, it is not the state which conditions and regulates civil society, but civil society which conditions and regulates the state, and, consequently, that policy and its history are to be explained from the economic relations and their development and not *vice versa*. When I visited Marx in Paris in the summer of 1844, our complete agreement in all theoretical fields became evident and our joint work dates from that time. When, in the spring of 1845, we met again in Brussels, Marx had already fully developed his materialist theory of history in its main features from the above mentioned basis, and we now applied ourselves to the detailed elaboration of the newly-won mode of outlook in the most varied directions.' [1]

Engels' own account of the materialist conception of history also provides abundant evidence of its origin in a concern with economic problems. In the tract on Feuerbach he enlarges in greater detail on his view of class antagonisms and class struggles as conditioned by economic factors. Even the origin of classes is ascribed to changes in economic relationships. Thus the transition from hand-craftsmanship to manufacture, for example, was responsible for the rise of the bourgeoisie, while the further advance from manufacture to large-scale industry based on steam and mechanical power, led to the emergence of the proletariat. As with the formation of classes themselves, so also the emergence of class antagonisms and their accompanying political conflicts was conditioned by economic developments:

'At a certain stage the new productive forces set in motion by the

---

[1] F. Engels: *On the History of the Communist League* (originally published in *Sozialdemokrat*, 1885; English version in *MESW*, II, pp. 311–12).

bourgeoisie—in the first place the division of labour and the combination of many detail labourers in one general manufactory—and the conditions and requirement of exchange, developed through these productive forces, became incompatible with the existing order of production handed down by history and sanctified by law, that is to say, incompatible with the privileges of the guild and the numerous other local and personal privileges (which were only so many fetters to the unprivileged estates) of the feudal order of society. The productive forces represented by the bourgeoisie rebelled against the order of production represented by the feudal landlords and the guildmasters. The result is known: the feudal fetters were smashed, gradually in England, at one blow in France. In Germany the process is not yet finished. But just as, at a definite stage of its development, manufacture came into conflict with the feudal order of production, so now large-scale industry has already come into conflict with the bourgeois order of production established in its place. Tied down by this order, by the narrow limits of the capitalist mode of production, this industry produces, on the one hand, an ever-increasing proletarianization of the great mass of the people, and on the other hand, an ever greater mass of unsaleable products. Overproduction and mass misery, each the cause of the other—that is the absurd contradiction which is its outcome and which of necessity calls for the liberation of the productive forces by means of a change in the mode of production.' [1]

Engels here conceives himself to have proved that, in modern history at least, all political struggles are class struggles aiming at economic emancipation, and hence that 'the state—the political order—is the subordinate, and civil society—the realm of economic relations—the decisive element'.[2] But if this holds good of the modern era with its gigantic means of production and communication, making it correspondingly easy for men to engage in production, it must be still more true of all earlier times, when a less fully developed technology compelled them to spend a much greater part of their time in satisfying their material needs.

'The State presents itself to us as the first ideological power over mankind. Society creates for itself an organ for the safeguarding of its common interests against internal and external attacks.' [3]

The State is 'only a reflex, in concentrated form, of the economic needs of the class controlling production'.[4] 'But once the State has become an independent power *vis-à-vis* society, it produces forthwith a further ideology'—law.[5]

---

[1] *Ludwig Feuerbach*, pp. 356–7.   [2] *Ibid.*, p. 357.   [3] *Ibid.*, p. 359.
[4] *Ibid.*, p. 358.   [5] *Ibid.*, p. 359.

Other ideologies, still further removed from the material, economic basis, are discerned by Engels in philosophy and religion. Here, however, the connection with the economic basis is obscured by the multitude of intermediate links and harder to recognize. Engels endeavours, for example, to depict the Renaissance and the new awakening of philosophy which then took place as a product of the towns and the burghers; to account for the rise of Christianity in terms of the need of the Roman world-empire for a world religion; and to contrast Protestantism, as the religion of the burghers, with the feudal character of Catholicism.

A very exact formulation of his materialistic view of history is to be found in the various Prefaces contributed by Engels to the *Communist Manifesto*, some of which have already been referred to.

It is essential to note, however, that in a number of letters written soon after the death of Marx, Engels goes some way towards qualifying the unconditional dependence of the ideologies on the relations of production, and even concedes them a rôle, albeit a secondary one, in determining the course of history.

'According to the materialist conception of history', he writes in a letter of 21st September 1890, 'the *ultimately* determining element in history is the production and reproduction of real life. More than this neither Marx nor I have ever asserted. Hence if somebody twists this into saying that the economic element is the *only* determining one, he transforms that proposition into a meaningless, abstract, senseless phrase.' [1]

In his application of dialectics to the field of history, and in his working-out of the materialist conception of history, Engels keeps closely in step with Marx; but his dialectical approach to the field of natural science is very much more his own work. Even so, the idea of such an approach would seem to have occurred to both of them together. Engels explains the situation in his Preface to the Second (1885) edition of the *Anti-Dühring*:

'Marx and I were pretty well the only people to rescue conscious dialectics from German idealist philosophy and apply it in the materialist conception of Nature and history. But a knowledge of mathematics and natural science is essential to a conception of Nature which is dialectical and at the same time materialist. Marx was well versed in mathematics, but we could only partially, intermittently and sporadically keep up with the natural sciences.' [2]

---

[1] Published in *Der Socialistische Akademiker*, V, 1, 10, 1895, under the title *Ein Brief von Fr. Engels. Zur Kritik der materialistischen Geschichtsauffassung* (English version, *Engels to J. Bloch* in *MESW*, II, p. 443).

[2] *Anti-Dühring*, p. 15.

Marx apparently never got beyond a preoccupation with mathematics, but from the autumn of 1870 onwards, Engels, having retired
from his merchant's business and moved from Manchester to
London, took up the study of natural science, to which he devoted
the best part of the next eight years. The death of Marx, which left
Engels with the task of editing the second and third volumes of
Capital, led to an interruption of these scientific studies. Their literary outcome is to be found in his preoccupation with the problems
of dialectics in Nature, both in the *Anti-Dühring* and in the unfinished
sketches and notes which were later published under the title of
Dialectics of Nature.

In pursuing this task, the goal which Engels had in mind was:

'to convince myself in detail—of what in general I was not in doubt—
that amid the welter of innumerable changes taking place in Nature,
the same dialectical laws of motion are in operation as those which
in history govern the apparent fortuitousness of events'. In this
'there could be no question of building the laws of dialectics into
Nature, but of discovering them in it and evolving them from it'.[1]

When Engels speaks of dialectics in Nature he has in mind the
discovery of pervasive interconnections in Nature, such as to call in
question the drawing of fixed boundaries between individual things
and phenomena. What Engels, following Hegel, describes as the
'metaphysical' method of thought and inquiry—adapted to the investigation of 'things' as fixed and essentially stable, given once and
for all—was justified in its own day: things had first of all to be
examined before it was possible to go on to inquire into the changes
going on in them and the 'processes' which link individual things
together. But now, it seems, the time has come in which natural
science has changed from a *collecting* to a *classifying* science,

'a science of the processes, of the origin and development of these
things and of the interconnection which binds all these natural processes into one great whole'.[2]

Three great discoveries are of crucial importance in this connection: first, the discovery of the cell as the unit from whose multiplication and differentiation the plant and animal body develops, and
whose capacity to change harbours the possibility of a more than
individual development; second, the law of the transformation of
energy, which demonstrates that all forces operative in the first
instance in inorganic Nature are different forms of manifestation of
universal motion, so that all motion and change in Nature can be
reduced to a process of incessant transformation from one form of
energy into another; and finally,

[1] *Ibid.*, pp. 15 ff.   [2] *Ludwig Feuerbach*, p. 352.

'the proof which Darwin first developed in connected form, that the stock of organic products environing us today, including mankind, is the result of a long process of evolution from a few originally unicellular germs, and that these again have arisen from protoplasm or albumen, which came into existence by chemical means'.[1]

The main business of the 'dialectics of Nature' according to Engels, is to demonstrate that, in spite of all antagonisms and distinctions, a thoroughgoing interconnection obtains among individual natural objects.

'The recognition that these antagonisms and distinctions are in fact to be found in Nature, but only with relative validity; and that on the other hand their imagined rigidity and absoluteness have been introduced into Nature only by our minds—this recognition is the kernel of the dialectical conception of Nature.'[2]

In his *Dialectics of Nature* Engels gives a more specific formulation of the three 'Laws of material dialectics', which were later to become the keystones of Soviet dialectical materialism: the law of the transformation of quantity into quality, the law of the mutual interpenetration of opposites and the law of the negation of the negation.

Just as reality, for Engels, is essentially in process, so that the singling-out of stable things has only a *prima facie* validity, so human knowledge also is essentially a process which never comes to an end, in that there are no final solutions or eternal truths. This is precisely what he considers to be positive in Hegel's philosophy,

'that it once for all dealt the death blow to the finality of all products of human thought and action. Truth, the cognition of which is the business of philosophy, was in the hands of Hegel no longer an aggregate of finished dogmatic statements, which, once discovered, had merely to be learned by heart. Truth lay now in the process of cognition itself, in the long historical development of science which mounts from lower to ever higher levels of knowledge without ever reaching, by discovering so-called absolute truth, a point at which it can proceed no further, where it would have nothing more to do than to fold its hands and gaze with wonder at the absolute truth to which it had attained.'[3]

Already, in dealing with Engels' proposed inversion of Hegel, we have seen how he treats the dialectic of concepts as merely the 'conscious reflex' of the dialectical motion of the real world,[4] and how both sets of dialectical laws, those of the objective process of

---

[1] *Ludwig Feuerbach*, p. 352.   [2] *Anti-Dühring*, pp. 18–19.
[3] *Ludwig Feuerbach*, p. 328.   [4] *Cf.* above, p. 46.

development in the world and those of the subjective process of knowledge, substantially coincide.

From this view of knowledge as a never-ending process reflecting the perpetual flux of development to be found in the objective world, Engels draws two conclusions: the first is the abandonment of the hope that any philosopher or philosophical system should ever attain to 'absolute truth', which implies, once it is fully thought out, the positivistic renunciation of philosophy.

'As soon as we have once realized—and in the long run no one has helped us to realize it more than Hegel himself—that the task of philosophy thus stated [*i.e.*, the claim of a system to have achieved absolute truth.—G. W.] means nothing but the task that a single philosopher should accomplish that which can only be accomplished by the entire human race in its progressive development—as soon as we realize that there is an end to all philosophy in the hitherto accepted sense of the word. One leaves alone "absolute truth", which is unattainable along this path or by any single individual; instead, one pursues attainable relative truths along the path of the positive sciences, and the summation of their results by means of dialectical thinking. At any rate, with Hegel philosophy comes to an end; on the one hand because in his system he summed up its whole development in the most splendid fashion; and on the other hand, because even though unconsciously, he showed us the way out of the labyrinth of systems to real positive knowledge of the world.' [1]

In Part Two we shall notice in greater detail how Leninism later renewed the attempt to make 'absolute truth' attainable for dialectical materialism and took issue against those Soviet philosophers who in this respect were more clear-headed in wishing to hold fast to Engels' point of view. We shall also have frequent occasion to observe how the strain of positivism which Engels here injected into dialectical materialism has repeatedly shown its effects, and how no complete accommodation has ever been reached between the anti-positivistic attitude which predominates in dialectical materialism and its periodic back-slidings into positivism.

The second conclusion drawn by Engels from his view of the nature of human knowledge is the denial of 'final solutions' and 'eternal truths'. He even goes beyond the Hegelian notion that the world is to be comprehended, not as a complex of ready-made things, but as a complex of processes,[2] inasmuch as he completely denies any element of stability in either process, whether it be the objective process of development in the world or the subjective process of knowledge: the objective world contains no inherently

[1] *Ludwig Feuerbach*, pp. 330–1.   [2] *Cf.* above, p. 46.

changeless entities underlying its development, and in the subjective process of knowledge there can be no ultimate concepts giving expression to such unchanging entities:

'If, however, investigation always proceeds from this standpoint, the demand for final solutions and eternal truths ceases once for all; one is always conscious of the necessary limitation of all acquired knowledge, of the fact that it is conditioned by the circumstances in which it was acquired. . . . One knows . . . that that which is recognized now as true has also its latent false side which will later manifest itself, just as that which is now regarded as false has also its true side, by virtue of which it could previously be regarded as true.' [1]

In the *Anti-Dühring* Engels enlarges in detail upon the problem of 'eternal truths'. He has to admit that it is not only in the sciences dealing with inanimate nature (mathematics, astronomy, mechanics, physics and chemistry) that such unalterable truths are to be found (*e.g.*, that twice two makes four, or that three angles of a triangle are equal to two right angles), for they also occur in biology, and even in the historical sciences (*e.g.*, that all men are mortal, or that Napoleon died on 5th May 1821); but he dismisses them as 'platitudes' and 'commonplaces'.[2]

Hegel's dialectic and Feuerbach's materialism would seem, therefore, to be the main pillars of the Marxian philosophical edifice. But contemporary Soviet philosophers have protested against this view, endorsed among others by Plekhanov, which regards Marx's dialectical materialism as a synthesis of Hegelian dialectic and Feuerbachian materialism. The socially conditioned motive of such a conception lies in the attempt to assimilate proletarian philosophy into bourgeois modes of thought.[3]

On the contrary it is initially a basic dogma of contemporary bolshevik teaching, formulated in particular by Zhdanov in the course of his intervention in the discussion on Alexandrov's book, *A History of Western European Philosophy*:[4]

'that Marx and Engels created a new philosophy differing qualita-

---

[1] *Ludwig Feuerbach*, p. 351.   [2] *Anti-Dühring*, p. 100.

[3] *Cf.* M. B. Mitin: *Dialektichesky materializm* (Vol. 1 of a two-volume work edited by M. B. Mitin and I. Razumovsky, *Dialektichesky i istorichesky materializm* (Dialectical and Historical Materialism): I. *Dialektichesky materializm*, ed. M. B. Mitin, Moscow 1933. II. *Istorichesky materializm*, ed. M. B. Mitin and I. Razumovsky, Moscow 1932), p. 101.

[4] *Cf.* below pp. 184 f.

tively from all previous philosophical systems however progressive they were;'

'the rise of Marxism was a genuine discovery, a revolution in philosophy'.[1]

The content of Marxism cannot be derived from previous philosophical systems on this account alone, that it represents

'a scientific and philosophical reflection . . . of the economic and political antagonisms of bourgeois society' and 'the objective necessity maturing in the womb of this society for its revolutionary transformation into socialism'.[2]

The essential novelty of this philosophy is seen in this, that with Marxism philosophy ceased to be the exclusive property of a select company of philosophers and their disciples, a privilege for intellectual aristocrats, and

'became a scientific weapon in the hands of the proletarian masses in their struggle for emancipation from capitalism'.[3]

Proletarian socialism, as Stalin emphasizes, is not just another philosophical doctrine.

'It is the doctrine of the proletarian masses, their banner; it is honoured and "revered" by the proletarians all the world over. Consequently Marx and Engels are not simply the founders of a philosophical "school" . . . they are the living leaders of the living proletarian movement, which is growing and gaining strength every day.'[4]

We can go no further here in tracing the later development of Marxism in Western Europe. But brief reference may be made to the 'Revisionism' which sprang up, especially in Germany, and is

[1] A. A. Zhdanov: *Vystuplenie na diskussii po knige G. F. Alexandrova 'Istoriya zapadnoevropeyskoy filosofii'* (Speech in the Discussion on G. F. Alexandrov's 'History of Western European Philosophy'), in *Bol'shevik. Teoretichesky i politichesky zhurnal TsK VKP(b)* (Bolshevik: Theoretical and Political Journal of the C.C. of the C.P.S.U. (B). Cited hereafter as *Bol'shevik*), 1947, 16, p. 9; (English version: *On Literature, Music and Philosophy*, London 1950, pp. 76-112, q.v. p. 80).

[2] V. Svetlov, T. Oyzerman: *Vozniknovenie marxizma—revolyutsionny perevorot v filosofii* (The Rise of Marxism —a Revolutionary Change in Philosophy), in *Bol'shevik*, 1948, 7, p. 30.

[3] A. A. Zhdanov: *Op. cit.*, p. 10 (*On Literature . . .*, p. 84).

[4] J. V. Stalin: *Anarkhizm ili sotsializm? Sochineniya*, I, Moscow 1946, p. 350 (English version, *Anarchism or Socialism? Works*, I, London 1953, p. 351).

particularly characteristic of the Marxism of the Second International; the tendency, that is, to subject the doctrines of Marxism to 'revision' or 'reform'. Philosophically it chiefly took the form of a desire to mitigate the uncritical dogmatism of Marx, and more especially Engels. In this connection particular attention was paid to the problem of knowledge. The main point insisted on was that Marxism was essentially a social and economic system without unconditional commitments to any particular type of philosophy. Some writers (among them E. Bernstein, K. Schmidt and H. Cunow) attempted, even, to establish it on neo-Kantian foundations.

It was not only the materialistic standpoint which came under revision, however, but the materialist conception of history itself. Eduard Bernstein objects to the excessive emphasis on necessity in historical development, insisting that non-economic factors also have their influence.

'No amount of historical materialism can get round the fact that history is made by men, that men have minds, and that mental dispositions are by no means so mechanical as to be entirely governed by the economic situation.' [1]

He admits not only 'the history of a country's political development' but also ethical codes and religious communities as factors influencing historical development, and even proposes to replace the term 'materialist conception of history' by 'economic conception of history'.

Nor was revision confined to theoretical concerns only, for it also extended to the sphere of political activity. It is characteristic of German social democracy that it no longer attempted to achieve its ends by means of a revolutionary upheaval, but adopted parliamentary methods instead. The German socialists were able, by constitutional methods, to gain an increasing number of seats in Parliament, while their registered supporters steadily multiplied. They achieved so much along parliamentary lines that the insurrectionary methods of 1848 came to be regarded as out of date. Engels himself, moreover, in the Preface to Marx's *Class Struggles in France*, written in the year of his death—it is dated 6th March 1895— abandoned the aim of violent revolution and advocated lawful methods of pursuing the campaign:

'But history has shown us too to have been wrong, has revealed our point of view of that time to have been an illusion. . . . The mode of struggle of 1848 is today obsolete in every respect.' [2]

---

[1] *Neue Zeit* (New Age), XVI, p. 749.
[2] K. Marx: *Die Klassenkämpfe in Frankreich 1848 bis 1850*. Introduction by Friedrich Engels and Foreword by August Bebel, Berlin 1895 (English version in *MESW*, I, p. 113).

Instead he hopes that parliamentary methods will bring decisive results to the working class.

'And so it happened that the bourgeoisie and the government came to be much more afraid . . . of the results of elections than of those of rebellion.'

'The irony of world history turns everything upside down. We, the "revolutionists", the "overthrowers"—we are thriving far better on legal methods than on illegal methods and overthrow. The parties of Order, as they call themselves are perishing under the legal conditions created by themselves. . . . And if we are not so crazy as to let ourselves be driven to street fighting in order to please them, then in the end there is nothing left for them to do but themselves break through this fatal legality.' [1]

[1] *Ibid.*, pp. 120 and 125.

CHAPTER III

Revolutionary Movements in Russia: The Origins of Russian Marxism

IN keeping with the struggle for primacy in all fields of culture, the Soviet historians of philosophy have striven, particularly during the Stalinist period, to establish a claim to Russian primacy in the philosophical sphere as well. They found this in the fact that even in the pre-Marxian period it was the Russian philosophers who by their own efforts came nearest to Marxist philosophy. Even so, the philosophy of Marx and Engels effected a revolutionary breach in the history of human thought which only became possible when the necessary economic and social conditions for it had been achieved. Owing to the economic and political backwardness of Russia and the lack of a revolutionary proletariat between the 'forties and 'sixties of the last century, the 'Russian revolutionary democrats' could not by themselves attain to the discovery of scientific socialism. Still, in this respect also, Russia achieved as much as was possible:

'Classical Russian philosophy, in fact, as exemplified in Belinsky, Herzen, Chernyshevsky and Dobrolyubov, represents the summit of philosophical thought throughout the world in the pre-Marxian era.'[1]

To this end the history of Russian science and philosophy is so presented as to suggest that materialism constituted the heart of Russian thought during the last century. As has been shown by Professor Zen'kovsky,[2] this is effected by means of a double artifice: in

[1] M. T. Iovchuk: *Leninizm i russkaya materialisticheskaya filosofiya* (Leninism and Russian Materialist Philosophy), in the collective work *Iz istorii russkoy filosofii* (From the History of Russian Philosophy), edited by I. Y. Shchipanov, Moscow 1951, p. 730.

[2] V. V. Zen'kovsky: *O mnimon materializme russkoy nauki i filosofii* (On

58

the first place, a number of outstanding Russian scientists and philosophers of the past are co-opted into the genealogy of Russian 'materialism' on the strength of having subscribed to particular opinions that are also upheld in dialectical materialism. Thus, evidence for the 'materialism' of Lomonosov, for example, is found in the fact that he regarded the material world as existing independently of consciousness.[1] Radishchev is recruited on similar grounds among the forefathers of materialism. Yet both of these men were believers. The enrolment of Herzen and Belinsky among the 'materialists' must also be definitely rejected. A further trick to make it appear that the basic achievements of Russian philosophy were materialistic in character, lies in the discounting of Russian thinkers opposed to materialism, either by not mentioning them at all, or by dismissing them as of no importance.

The genealogy of materialist philosophy in Russia is thereby reduced, in essentials, to such names as: Lomonosov, Lobachevsky, Radishchev, The Decembrists, Herzen, Ogarev, Belinsky, Chernyshevsky, Dobrolyubov, Pisarev, Sechenov, Mendeleyev, Umov, Pavlov, Timiryazev and others. The majority of really important philosophers, such as Vladimir Soloviev, L. Lopatin, B. Chicherin, N. Lossky, S. Frank, L. Karsavin, A. Losev and many others, are thus completely left out, and anyone who pays attention to them, as V. Zen'kovsky, N. Lossky and B. Schultze, for example, have done in their works on the history of Russian thought, is dismissed as a 'falsifier of the history of Russian philosophy'.[2]

Instead of entering further into this Soviet 'genealogy' we shall confine ourselves, in what follows, to a condensed account of revolutionary tendencies in Russia before the bolshevik revolution.

1. ORIGINS: RUSSIAN NIHILISM [3]

The revolutionary tradition in Russia reaches far back into the past. Already in the second half of the seventeenth century the revolt

the Fictitious Materialism of Russian Science and Philosophy), Munich 1956.

[1] G. S. Vasetsky: *Filosofskie vzglyady M. V. Lomonosova* (The Philosophical Opinions of M. V. Lomonosov), in *Iz istorii russkoy filosofii*, p. 104.

[2] *Cf* N. G. Tarakanov: *Fal'sifikatory istorii russkoy filosofskoy mysli* (Falsifiers of the History of Russian Philosophical Thought), in *VF*, 1955, No. 3, pp. 73–85; V. Malinin, N. Tarakanov, I. Shchipanov: *Protiv sovremennykh burzhuaznykh fal'sifikatorov istorii russkoy filosofii* (Against the Modern Bourgeois Falsifiers of the History of Russian Philosophy), in *Kommunist*, 1955, No. 10, pp. 62–76.

[3] The subject of this whole chapter is dealt with in greater detail in the

of the Cossack hetman Sten'ka Razin (1670) had given the lower orders of society in southern and south-eastern Russia the opportunity of venting their hostility towards the 'upper classes'. Similar disturbances recurred a hundred years later, again on social grounds, led on this occasion by a Don Cossack, the flighty Pugachev (1773). The nineteenth century saw a notable increase in Russian revolutionary activity. Contact with Western Europe in consequence of the Napoleonic Wars led to the social turmoil in Russia which brought about the Decembrist rising of 1825. From the forty-year-old schism in Russian society between 'Westerners' and 'Slavophiles' there emerged as chief protagonists of the revolutionary spirit the Russian revolutionary 'intelligentsia', which united adherents from every rank of society on the basis of a general dissatisfaction with existing conditions. The westerner, V. G. Belinsky (1810-48), whom Berdyaev describes as the 'father' of the Russian revolutionary intelligentsia, M. A. Bakunin (1814-76) and A. I. Herzen (1812-70) reacted violently against all oppression of human personality and fought for its liberation. Bakunin and Herzen also devoted themselves in person to revolutionary activity; at that time this was only possible outside Russia, but they exercised great influence through their writings even in their own country.

The conditions to which the peasants and common people were subjected under the régime of Nicholas I were such as to create a powerful revulsion and antagonism in all lovers of righteousness. Forced marriages among the peasants, military service which might last for twenty-five years and was imposed even on heads of families, floggings, which were often inflicted quite arbitrarily by their masters —such occurrences were anything but rare. Obviously such circumstances were bound to create in right-thinking people a desire for reform. Hence there began a movement for the liberation of human personality, conceived as an emancipation from any sort of higher authority. This outlook found its fullest expression, especially in the

following works: William H. Chamberlin: *Russian Revolution 1917–1921*, 2 vols., New York 1935; T. G. Masaryk: *The Spirit of Russia: Studies in History, Literature and Philosophy* (trans. E. and C. Paul), 2 vols., London 1919, II (New and revised edition 1955); N. Berdyaev: *The Origin of Russian Communism* (trans. R. M. French), London 1937. Reprinted 1948; K. Stählin: *Geschichte Russlands von den Anfangen bis zur Gegenwart*, IV, 1 and 2, Königsberg–Berlin, 1939; Jan Kucharzewski: *The Origins of Modern Russia*, New York 1948; R. Hare: *Pioneers of Russian Social Thought: Studies of Non-Marxian Formation in Nineteenth-Century Russia and of its partial Revival in the Soviet Union*, London–New York–Toronto 1951; Franco Venturi: *Il populismo russo*, 2 vols., Turin 1952; Peter Scheibert: *Von Bakunin zu Lenin. Geschichte der russischen revolutionären Ideologien 1840–1895*, 1 vol. so far, Leyden 1956.

years 1860–70, in Nihilism, of which the chief protagonists were
N. G. Chernyshevsky (1828–89), N. A. Dobrolyubov (1836–61) and
D. I. Pisarev (1841–68).

In the name of the liberation of the oppressed individual the nihilists not only denied all higher values, God, spirit and the soul, but were also opponents of culture in all its forms, which seemed to them a 'luxury'. Their thinking was governed by a single category only, that of 'utility'. Turgenev, in his novel *Fathers and Sons*, gives an example of the type in the person of Bazarov. The nihilistic standpoint is that of crude materialism. Even so, Berdyaev is right in pointing to an affinity between their views and those of Christianity. The nihilists' attitude is strongly reminiscent of the Christian ascetics, especially in the East, who utterly renounced the world and all its culture as 'lying in wickedness'. They also approach the Christian standard in their manifold and boundless capacity for sacrifice in pursuit of their own ideals. Berdyaev says of them:

'They did not understand the mystery of the Cross but they were in the highest degree capable of sacrifice and renunciation. In this respect they compared favourably with the Christians of their day who displayed very little capacity for sacrifice and so repelled men from Christianity.' [1]

Many of them carried this self-sacrifice so far as to volunteer to take the place of revolutionaries under sentence of death, lest the movement should be deprived of its leaders.

It is significant that many of these 'worldly idealists' were sons of priests (orthodox priests in Russia are allowed to marry) and had received their education in seminaries. It was there that they imbibed the Christian ideals of social justice which they saw so harshly trampled underfoot. Hence it came about that Russian orthodox seminaries repeatedly became the very hotbeds of revolution.[2]

The first intellectual leader of Russian Nihilism and a typical representative of these 'worldly idealists' was N. G. Chernyshevsky (1828–89). The son of a priest and educated in a religious seminary, he later became active as a writer. He was convicted of publishing incitements to sedition of which he was certainly not the author, the charge being based on false evidence and perjury. From 1862 to 1864 he was held prisoner in the Peter-Paul fortress and subsequently condemned to seven years' forced labour and transported to Siberia. Even after the end of this period he was forbidden to return, and had to remain in Siberia until 1883. When finally allowed to return

[1] N. Berdyaev: *Op. cit.*, p. 51.
[2] B. V. Titlinov: *Molodezh i revolyutsiya* (Youth and the Revolution), Leningrad 1924; André Mikhailov: *Les origines anticatholiques du bolchévisme*, in *Études*, LXVI (1929), Juillet–Septembre, pp. 14–43.

to European Russia he was confined to living in the town of Astrakhan until 1889, the year of his death. He endured exile and forced labour with remarkable strength and spiritual fortitude.

Chernyshevsky is the chief representative of Russian popular materialism. A disciple of Feuerbach, his materialism is directed, like that of his master, against man's inhumanity to man. But as Berdyaev rightly observes,[1] Chernyshevsky is also an idealist whose ideal is seated on earth. The motives of his materialism are ascetic; seeing the professional idealists and spiritual leaders of Russia, under pretence of pursuing noble aims, solely concerned for their own egoistic interests, these new men preferred in the name of a living idealism and social justice a coarsely utilitarian materialism to all ideas of a 'higher' character. In the economic field Chernyshevsky professed, as it were, a pre-Marxian and somewhat utopian form of socialism. He raised the question which so largely preoccupied Russian thought throughout the latter half of the last century, namely whether Russia, like the rest of Europe, was destined to go through a phase of capitalism or whether it would be able to move straight to socialism. His own view was that in Russia the capitalistic period could be curtailed to the furthest possible extent.

Chernyshevsky is also the author of a novel *What is to be done?* which had a great influence on the minds of the revolutionary generation, and was regarded as a catechism, a *vade-mecum* for revolutionists. It contains a portrait of the revolutionary Rakhmetov, who sleeps on a bed of nails in order to accustom himself to the endurance of pain and to strengthen his character.

2. *NARODNICHESTVO*

After the Nihilism of the 'sixties, the following decade in Russia saw the spread of a form of pre-Marxian socialism known as *Narodnichestvo*, which is of great importance for our inquiry, in so far as Russian Marxism grew up in opposition to it.

The influence of slavophile ideas had led to the common people becoming, not merely an object of pity, but a sort of ideal. Their capacity for suffering and for enduring injustice and hardship disclosed their greatness and strength of spirit. Thus many members of the Russian 'intelligentsia' came to see in the common people the guardians of a righteousness and a true way of life no longer known to the upper classes. But this truth preserved among the people was differently conceived according to the differing viewpoints of the thinkers concerned. Many, such as L. Tolstoy and F. Dostoyevsky, looked upon the people as primarily the guardians of religious truth,

[1] N. Berdyaev: *Op. cit.*, p. 56.

whereas others, such as A. Herzen, M. Bakunin and the revolutionary Friends of the People (*Narodniki*) of the 'eighties, saw in them a potential source of social truth.

It was the last-mentioned group who claimed to discern in the Russian *Obshchina* (village communes) the germ of a peasant collectivism which would enable Russia to achieve an immediate transition to socialism without the need of an intervening period of capitalism. The *Obshchina* represented a system of land tenure whereby the territory belonging to a village was considered the property of all members of the community, so that each individual had a right to the use of the common land, either in the form of a joint and simultaneous usufruct (as in the case of pasturage) or the temporary private use of a portion of the common property. The *Narodniki* looked upon the *Obshchina* as a peculiarly Russian economic institution, having no parallel in Europe, and felt that it also implied a special destiny for Russia herself. The main rôle in Russian economic development was ascribed to the peasant rather than to the worker or proletarian who dominated the scene in Europe.

As Berdyaev makes clear,[1] these Friends of the People all had the feeling that the intellectual class to which they belonged was divided by a great gulf from the common people—a feeling which often took the form of a sense of guilt in relation to them. The religious group felt the guilt of the intellectuals to lie in their estrangement from the religious convictions and customs of the mass of the people, whereas the revolutionary party saw the guilt of the 'intelligentsia' in the fact that it was only the toil and privations of the masses which enabled them to lead a life of superior culture.

This feeling of separation from the populace at large evoked in many Friends of the People the desire to be reunited with it, and led to a movement for 'going to the people'. Intellectuals, especially young students, took to the country in order to gain closer contact with the common folk, to 'enlighten' them and to be of service to them. Originally this movement was entirely peaceable in character but later, especially in the period from 1870 to 1880, it became a powerful revolutionary force.

Already in 1861 Herzen had called upon Russian students to 'Go to the people', and Bakunin had made a similar appeal to them in the following year to join the people, *i.e.*, the peasants, not in order to instruct them, for the people already had their own ideals, but in order to bridge the gulf between the common folk and the higher levels of society, to learn from them, and at the same time to arouse them to revolt (*bunt*).

A mass movement of this sort had already taken place in the

---

[1] N. Berdyaev: *Op. cit.*, p. 64.

latter half of the 'sixties, but it was not till 1876 that the revolutionary movements acquired their greatest impetus with the emergence of the organization known as *Zemlya i Volya* (Land and Liberty). It carried out a number of attacks on unpopular personages in high places and members of the government. In October 1879 it split into two parties, one radical, the *Narodnaya Volya* (People's Will) and the other more moderate, the *Cherny Peredel* (Black Earth Group).[1] *The Narodnaya Volya* devoted itself to the political struggle, by means of terrorism and attempts, particularly on the life of the Tsar, but also directed against other exalted personages, in order to create a situation which might prepare the way for social reform. The supporters of the *Cherny Peredel* had no confidence in political emancipation without prior social emancipation. A constitututon, in their opinion, would favour the emergence of a mercantile class, and hence of capitalism, while the people would derive no benefit from it; only on the basis of economic emancipation would political freedom have any advantages to offer. This would have to be achieved, not by the State, but by the people themselves, the State being based on Western, individualistic principles, whereas it was only in the Russian people and their peasant institutions, the *Mir* and the *Obshchina*, that the collectivist principles of an inbred solidarity were deployed to fullest effect. The West, with its individualistic traditions, would have to endure the purgatory of capitalism from which Russia would be spared, thanks to the inborn spirit of collectivism represented in the *Obshchina*.[2]

Among its forebears Bolshevism must reckon not Marx and Engels only, but also the Russian revolutionaries, particularly of the period from 1860 to 1880. In order to understand the special characteristics which Russian Bolshevism has inherited from its peculiar ancestry, and which distinguish it from other Marxist movements, we shall have to take a rather closer look at some of these forerunners.

The founder and leader of the terrorist organization *Narodnaya Volya*, A. I. Zhelyabov (1851–81), is a typical figure among the revolutionaries of the period 1870–80. Although the police arrested him two days before the event, he was chiefly responsible for organizing the successful attempt on the life of Tsar Alexander II (1st March 1881). After the assassination Zhelyabov wrote an account of his share in the business and demanded to be heard, since he wished to make use of the trial in order to explain the attitude of his party and to make its demands known to the authorities. In the course of the hearing he sought to exonerate his associates and take the

---

[1] According to W. H. Chamberlin (*op. cit.*) the name of this party derived from the demand they put forward, that the peasants should receive possession of the good 'black earth' which had been left, on their emancipation in 1861, entirely in the hands of the landed gentry.

[2] K. Stählin: *Geschichte Russlands*, IV, 1, p. 386.

responsibility entirely on himself. Asked if he was a Christian, he replied:

'I was baptized in Orthodoxy, but I repudiate it, although I acknowledge the essence of Christ's teaching. This essential teaching occupies an honoured place among my moral convictions. I believe in the truth and righteousness of that faith and I solemnly acknowledge that faith without works is dead and that every genuine Christian should fight for justice, for the rights of the oppressed and the weak, and if need be, also suffer for them. That is my faith.' [1]

Before his execution Zhelyabov kissed the Cross.

A kindred spirit of Bakunin in the propagation of anarchism is Prince Peter Alexeyvich Kropotkin (1842–1921).[2] Even as a young man, in the days of Nicholas I, he had been moved by the condition of the common people, especially the peasants, and from that time onwards his generous and responsive nature was marked for life: he became a revolutionary, but like so many others of the period, a revolutionary in the name of human dignity and social justice. He had already embarked with some distinction on a scientific career when he first began to play an active part in revolutionary circles. After a sumptuous dinner-party in some aristocratic mansion, Prince Kropotkin, Chamberlain to the Tsar, Secretary to the Geographical Society, would often repair to the outer suburbs of the capital, where, dressed as a labourer or peasant under the name of 'Comrade Borodin', he would visit his artisan friends. The latter listened with great attention to his accounts of the workers' movements in the West, and it was in their company that the Prince's happiest hours were spent. In 1874 he was arrested and imprisoned, but after two years succeeded in escaping and took refuge in Western Europe. In 1917 he was at last able to return to his native country.

The ideas he put forward represented an anarchist form of communism. The revolution must bring about the abolition of the State, written laws and private property, not only in the means of production, but also in consumer goods.

Towards intellectuals he adopted a hostile attitude, though he also

---

[1] Quoted from Berdyaev: *Op. cit.*, p. 85.

[2] Kropotkin's *Ethics* is the most interesting of his writings from the philosophical point of view. He could only complete the first volume, which was published posthumously by N. Lebedev: P. A. Kropotkin: *Etika, I. Proiskhozhdenie i razvitie nravstvennosti*, Petrograd–Moscow 1922 (*Ethics, Origin and Development*, trans. L. S. Friedland 1924). On Kropotkin, *cf.* also the following: *P. A. Kropotkin i ego uchenie. Pod redaktsiey i s primechaniyami G. P. Maximova* (P. A. Kropotkin and his Teaching. Edited with notes by G. P. Maximov), Chicago 1931; and Laurentius: *Kropotkins Morallehre und deren Beziehungen zu Nietzsche*, Dresden–Leipzig 1896.

wished to see facilities for higher education extended to the workers. By reducing the hours of labour to four or five a day the workers would have five or six hours at their disposal for their own pursuits. The 'scholars' and 'poets', however, he considered as debtors of the workers; in order to discharge their debt they would have to devote four or five hours a day to manual labour.

Sergey Gennadievich Nechaev (1847–82) is an embodiment of the alarmingly violent revolutionary spirit which took possession of so many in the years 1860–70. He attempted to stir up the students of St. Petersburg, who were agitating against the University authorities, into making a demonstration against the government; he also founded a revolutionary group, the *Obshchestvo Topora* (Fellowship of the Axe). After the murder of a student whom he suspected of treachery, Nechaev fled to Switzerland, but was handed over to the Russian authorities. From 1873 until his death he remained in the Peter-Paul fortress, where he was condemned to serve an exceptionally severe term of imprisonment. Even there, however, he succeeded in establishing relations with the *Narodnaya Volya* and in conveying to them a plan for liberating the revolutionaries held prisoner in the fortress. But on learning that the organization was engaged in plotting an attack on the Tsar he elected to remain in prison in order not to hinder the execution of the scheme.

The revolutionary organization favoured by Nechaev was in many respects an anticipation of the methods of the Bolshevik Party. Nechaev insisted on absolute centralization and despotic power for the organization. He envisaged the creation, throughout Russia, of cells which, though small, would be bound one to another by the most rigid discipline, and would be at liberty to use any means in order to achieve their aim.

Nechaev is also credited with the authorship of a characteristic document of the period, *The Revolutionary Catechism*, which preaches a quasi-religious, though atheistic, form of asceticism to which the revolutionary must dedicate himself. He is called to a genuine self-renunciation, a denial of the world, but in the name of the revolution he exists in order to serve.[1]

'The revolutionary is a doomed man. He has no personal interests, business, feelings, connections, property or even name. Everything in him is in the grip of one single interest, one single thought, one

---

[1] Berdyaev (*Op. cit.*, p. 70) attributes this catechism to Nechaev. According to K. Stählin, however (*Op. cit.*, p. 217), it is Bakunin who is generally regarded as the author. Hélène Iswolsky (*La vie de Bakounine*, Paris 1930, pp. 233 f.) considers it the work of Bakunin, though written under Nechaev's influence; elsewhere she maintains it to be a joint production of the two friends.

single passion: the revolution. In his inmost being, he has broken, not in words only, but in deeds, with all attachments to public order and the civilized world, with all laws, conventions and customs, and with every sort of morality. In all that concerns this civilized world he is its unrelenting enemy, and if he still continues to live therein, it is only to destroy it the more completely. . . . He knows but one science, that of destruction. . . . He despises public opinion, he loathes and execrates in all its motives and manifestations the social morality of the age. That alone is moral in his eyes which furthers the triumph of the revolution; everything which obstructs it is immoral . . .[1] Day and night he must have but one thought, one aim: the most implacable destruction. Deliberately and without ceasing he must work towards this goal and be ready to perish, and by his own hand to let everything perish, which stands in the way of achieving it.'[2]

Many, such as Berdyaev[3] and Stählin,[4] have seen a predecessor of Lenin in the revolutionist Peter Tkachev (1844–85). Although of aristocratic origin, he went over to the revolutionary side. Arrested as an adherent of Nechaev, he fled to Switzerland four years later, where he edited the revolutionary paper *Nabat* (The Tocsin). Unlike other revolutionaries, whose objects were primarily social and economic, he was a firm believer in political revolution, and as such, a forerunner of the *Narodnaya Volya*. He was opposed to the abolition of the State, as preached by Bakunin and the anarchists, and advocated the seizure of power by a strictly disciplined revolutionary minority. The socialist party must be well-disciplined and centrally organized. It must seize power and exercise it in despotic fashion. So too Lenin, in opposition to the Mensheviks, who wanted to recruit the largest possible membership for their party, was later to campaign for a party consisting only of confirmed, hand-picked and well-organized revolutionaries, a party capable of giving leadership to the proletariat in its struggle.

After the murder of Alexander II and during the reaction under Alexander III, another and more peaceful form of *Narodnichestvo* appeared on the scene. Its aim was to preserve the peasantry from the ruinous consequences of the emergence of capitalism, not by revolution, however, but by giving support to the smallholders. Various methods of assisting them were contemplated; Vorontsov, for instance, urging a policy of generous loans. This was the *Epokha mulykh del*, the 'period of petty measures' which occupied the penultimate decade of the 19th century.

---

[1] Lenin was later to express himself in similar terms. *Cf.* below, p. 268.
[2] Quoted in H. Iswolsky, *Op. cit.*, pp. 235 f. *Cf.* also M. Bakunin: *Sozial-politischer Briefwechsel mit Alexander Herzen and Ogarev*, 1895.
[3] N. Berdyaev: *Op. cit.*, pp. 80 ff.   [4] K. Stählin: *Op. cit.*, p. 231.

With the beginning of the 20th century there emerged a new type of *Narodnichestvo*, this time under the influence of the Marxist movement, namely the Social-Revolutionary Party, known from its initials (S.R.) as *Esery*, which continued until October 1917 to play an important part in Russian public affairs, especially during the 1905 revolution.

3. RUSSIAN MARXISM [1]

The first person to spread the knowledge of Marx's teaching abroad in Russia was N. Ziber (1844–88), Professor of Economics at the University of Kiev, who is mentioned by Marx in the Preface to the Second Edition of *Capital*, and whose writings in the 'seventies were based on Marx's economic doctrines. Thereafter the Marxist theory was gradually taken up by all the professors of political economy, though this did not as yet signify the emergence of Russian Marxism as a movement in the social life of the country.[2]

Russian Marxism in the proper sense originated abroad, beyond the boundaries of Russia itself.

In 1880 Plekhanov[3] fled to Western Europe, finally taking up permanent residence on the shores of Lake Geneva. He was impelled to flight, not so much by any danger to his life or liberty, as by the desire to find out about the differences of opinion which animated the Russian revolutionaries as the result of their contact with European socialism. He was still a *Narodnik* when he went to Europe; but the development he underwent there led to a breach with *Narodnichestvo* and carried him wholly into the Marxist camp. This took place in the years 1880–90.

Together with P. B. Axel'rod, L. Deutsch and Vera S. Zasulich, Plekhanov founded in Geneva in 1883 the first Russian Social-democratic organization, the *Gruppa, Osvobozhdenie truda* ('Liberation of Labour' group). At this time also, Plekhanov was busily engaged in translating the major socialist writings into Russian, besides dictating pamphlets, editing newspapers and giving lectures to the Russian exiles who were gathering in ever greater numbers in

---

[1] For this section *cf.* the article *Kommunisticheskaya Partiya Sovetskogo Soyuza* (The Communist Party of the Soviet Union) in *BSE*, 2nd edn., XXII, pp. 209–43. See also *Istoriya Vsesoyuznoy Kommunisticheskoy Partii* (*bol'shevikov*). *Kratky kurs*, Moscow 1945 (1st edn. 1938), pp. 10 ff. (English version: *History of the Communist Party of the Soviet Union* (*Bolsheviks*). *Short Course*, Moscow–London 1939, pp. 8–16); and K. Stählin: *Geschichte Russlands*, IV/1, pp. 379 ff.; IV/2, pp. 673 ff.

[2] *Cf.* N. Meshcheryakov: *Razvitie marxizma v Rossii* (Development of Marxism in Russia), in *Malaya Sovetskaya Entsiklopediya* (Little Soviet Encyclopaedia), IV. col. 913.

[3] For further treatment of Plekhanov *cf.* below, pp. 100 ff.

the towns of Switzerland. It was these lectures of Plekhanov's which furnished inspiration to the earliest propagandists of Marxian socialism in Russia.

Though revolutionary activity was virtually extinct in Russia in the 'eighties, the period saw the first growth of workers' organizations on a socialist basis. The first social-democratic organization came into being at St. Petersburg in 1885. This activity increased at the beginning of the 'nineties, when Lenin's influence also began to be felt.

In 1895 the latter succeeded in uniting some twenty different organizations already operating in St. Petersburg into the famous *Soyuz bor'by za osvobozhdenie rabochego klassa* (League of Struggle for the Emancipation of the Working Class). Soon afterwards organizations of the same type were also founded in other cities, such as Moscow, Kiev and Kharkov.

But it is not merely from the point of view of organization that this decade can be considered the hey-day of Marxism. Marxism also achieved great prominence in Russian affairs at this time in the sphere of literature and philosophy. These years saw the appearance of the most important writings in the Marxist campaign against *Narodnichestvo*, including those of P. Struve and G. Plekhanov. In the closing years of the decade Marxist newspapers also began to appear, though they were soon suppressed: *Novoe slovo* (The New Word) in 1897 and *Nachalo* (The Beginning) in 1899; in addition to these the Marxists also availed themselves of other legitimate journals, the periodical *Zhizn'* (Life), for example, in order to get their articles published.

In 1898 the Marxist organizations in the various cities attempted to unify themselves into a social-democratic party. For this purpose the 'First Congress of the Russian Social-Democratic Workers' Party' was held in Minsk. Nine members attended; Lenin was absent, having been banished to Siberia. They published a *Manifesto* drawn up by Struve, and elected a Central Committee, which can hardly be said to have operated, however, since all its members were arrested. The Congress therefore had no great practical consequences, being chiefly significant as a first attempt to unite the various Marxist groups. Even after it had taken place there was still no party programme or constitution, no common plan of campaign or leadership from any unitary centre.

The result was that considerable differences of opinion emerged at this period between individual Marxists, leading to a variety of schools and tendencies carrying within them the seeds of future schism.

The first of these groups, which declared itself Marxist in the last decade of the 19th century and fought with the Marxists against *Narodnichestvo*, though later seceding from orthodoxy around 190, was a group of intellectuals who recognized the inadequacy of Marxism, especially from the philosophic point of view, and moved from Marxian dogmatism to the critical standpoint of Kant, and thence, in some cases, to a mystico-religious form of idealism. The members of this group included, among others, P. Struve, N. Berdyaev, S. Bulgakov and M. Tugan-Baranovsky. Since these Marxists published their articles in legitimate journals (*Zhizn'* and others), they came to be known in bolshevik literature as 'legal Marxists'. They differed from Marx, not only on philosophical questions, but also on economic ones, a fact which exposed them in a special degree to the bitter antagonism of Lenin.

The final years of the century saw the emergence of yet another revisionist tendency in Marxism, that of 'Economism' so called. After Lenin's arrest (1897), a new set of men took over the leadership of the 'League'; as the party of 'youth' they had overthrown the previous leadership, which they referred to contemptuously as consisting of 'greybeards'. They maintained that the workers, in struggling to improve their economic position, should only make use of the strike, leaving the political battle against autocracy to be conducted by the liberal bourgeoisie. Hence they were unconditionally opposed to the organization of the proletariat into a political party, or were at least unwilling that it should be centralized and militant in character. They valued the unconscious elemental forces at work in the depths of the workers' movement, and decried the importance of being purposefully guided by theory—*stikhiynost'* (spontaneous impulses) being superior to *soznatel'nost'* (conscious control). These ideas were set forth by E. D. Kuskova in a programmatic work entitled *Credo* (1899).

At Lenin's instigation, seventeen of the Russian social-democratic revolutionaries living in exile in Siberia declared themselves against this form of 'Economism'. The 'Liberation of Labour' group also came out in protest. This was the signal for a campaign, under the leadership of Lenin and Plekhanov, to settle accounts between Economism and intransigent Marxism; the mouthpiece of the latter was the newspaper *Iskra* (The Spark), which was published abroad. The conflict ended with the defeat of Economism.

In the course of this controversy Lenin developed his ideas concerning the necessity for a party organization, and explained what its character, composition and objects should be. According to Lenin it must represent the advance-guard of the working-class, and must be centrally organized, strictly disciplined and composed of professional revolutionaries; its task being to unite the whole of the working-class and to take the lead in its battles. The ultimate objective must be to destroy capitalism and bring in socialism; the immediate aim, to destroy Tsarism and establish democracy.

In this demand for a strict and efficient party organization consisting of professional revolutionaries, Lenin was pursuing the traditional path of the Russian revolutionary, in which Nechaev and Tkachev had already preceded him.

In order that the foundation of the party should at last be put into effect, the Second Congress of the Russian Social-democratic Workers' Party was summoned in July 1903, and was attended by forty-three delegates from twenty-six local organizations. The Congress met secretly in Brussels, but was compelled under pressure from the Belgian police to remove itself to London. The party structure which Lenin had been advocating in *Iskra* for the past few years did not command universal assent (his followers were known as *Iskrovtsy*). Many were still mentally in tutelage to Economism, though they did not openly give themselves out as such, the economist movement having already been put down by then. But even the *Iskrovtsy* were by no means fully agreed among themselves.

The most serious difference of opinion arose in the discussion on the first clause of the constitution, concerning the membership of the party. According to Lenin's proposed formula, candidates for admission would be required to acknowledge the party programme, to give the party material support and also to be members of one of the local organizations already referred to. In the formula of Martov, a moderate member of the *Iskrovtsy*, this latter provision was dispensed with. This conflict on a matter of detail arose from a divergence in the conception of the party itself. Lenin envisaged the party as a strictly organized body whose members would not merely belong to it, as if to a club, but would be incorporated into the party organization and would therefore be subject to its discipline; from the administrative point of view he considered Martov's conception of the party a shapeless affair; the members would themselves decide on their own attendance, and hence would be under no particular party discipline, confining themselves to acceptance of the party programme and payment of their subscriptions.

At the Congress, Martov's formula was adopted by a narrow majority, but soon afterwards certain members who were not *Iskrovtsy* deserted the conference, so that Martov's group was left in a minority and Lenin's group predominated; hence the names Bolshevik (from *bol'she* = more) and Menshevik (from *men'she* = less); the consequence was that the remaining points in the constitution were settled in accordance with Lenin's formula, and that his candidates for the editorial board of *Iskra* were elected.

Hence this Congress, which is recorded in the party history as the Second Congress of the Social-democratic Workers' party of Russia, actually resulted, not only in the foundation of the party, but also in its simultaneous cleavage into a bolshevik and a menshevik faction.

The whole subsequent history of the party is filled with bickerings between these two groups. The position of the Mensheviks may be characterized as follows: in contrast to the *Narodniks* they considered the development of capitalism and bourgeois society a necessary condition for the creation of socialism, and rejected any 'peculiar path' of Russian development whereby Russia would be enabled to avoid the period of capitalism and make an immediate transition to socialism. They did not believe in the possibility of revolution proceeding from any but bourgeois sources; the proletariat must ally itself, not with the peasantry, but with the bourgeoisie. So far as the agrarian question was concerned they proposed to 'municipalize' the land, rather than 'nationalize' it, as the Bolsheviks wanted to do. When the Russian revolution of 1905 ended with the summoning of a parliament (*Gosudarstvennaya Duma*) a considerable number of Mensheviks favoured a dissolution of the illegal organizations and a resort to legal methods of campaigning; these *Likvidatory*, among whom Plekhanov was not, however, included, were ejected from the Party at the Prague Conference (1912). At this conference the Bolshevik wing established itself as an independent party. On the outbreak of the European conflict the Mensheviks favoured the war, in opposition to the tactics of Lenin, who preached the transformation of the imperialist war into a civil war. After the Revolution of 1917 the Mensheviks soon ceased to exist; many went over to those who were fighting against Bolshevism. Some of them emigrated abroad, where the paper edited by Martov, *Sotsialistichesky Vestnik* (The Socialist Bulletin: published in the U.S.A.), became the spiritual focus of Menshevism.

A further revisionist and reformist tendency within Russian Marxism may also be observed after 1903. Many of the Marxist intellectuals, in order to defend the more important aspects of the doctrine, were desirous of putting it on a different philosophical basis, and attempted to replace dialectical materialism by empirio-criticism (Bogdanov and others). Others again, such as Lunacharsky and Gorky, sought to create a new religion; they were known as *Bogostroiteli* (God-builders).

The October Revolution of 1917 brought about the complete triumph of Bolshevism, and put an end, not only to the bourgeois parties, but to any sort of opposition whatever, including that of the Social Democrats (Mensheviks) and Social Revolutionaries. The subsequent political history of Russia under the Bolsheviks must be taken for granted here as already known to the reader.[1]

[1] *Cf.* on this subject, Georg von Rauch: *Geschichte des bolschewistischen Russland*, Wiesbaden 1955.

CHAPTER IV

Philosophical Tendencies in Russian Marxism before the Revolution

---

1. THE PHILOSOPHICAL CONFLICT BETWEEN MARXISM AND *NARODNICHESTVO*

IT was against three points especially in the *narodnik* view of the world and of history that Russian Marxism directed its attack:

(a) the 'subjective method' in history and sociology;

(b) the positive conception of the rôle played by the individual in history;

(c) the idea of Russia as possessed of a peculiar historical destiny.

The Marxists and the *Narodniks* came into violent collision on this question of the application of the 'subjective method' to sociology and history: historical facts can be considered from alternative points of view, a theoretical and a practical one. In the first case the facts are considered as they are, as they present themselves objectively, it being merely a question of determining what they consist of, without praising or blaming them. In the second case they are considered in the light of some specific ideal, and tested as to whether or not they coincide with this and can or cannot serve as means to its attainment. To those who adopt the subjective method in sociology it is the subjective aspect, the 'ideal', the *desideratum*, the obligatory element which ranks the highest in importance. They see the distinction between the natural and social sciences as consisting precisely in this, that the latter consider their objects not only from the point of view of 'being' or 'reality' but also, and most importantly, from that of the 'obligatory' and the 'ideal'. Sociology has not merely to grasp the facts in their theoretical aspect, but must help to realize an ideal. In the words of P. L. Lavrov (1823–1900) 'theoretical truth'

73

(*pravda-istina*) is indissolubly bound up with 'practical truth' (*pravda-spravedlivost'*).

In the approach to history, too, in Lavrov's opinion, the subjective method is equally inescapable. Depending on the level of moral development of the historian himself, a moral ideal is adopted as a criterion whereby the facts are judged according to whether they promote or obstruct the realization of this ideal. History appears, therefore, as a struggle of the good principle against the evil, and so necessarily becomes a matter of 'progress'.

Lavrov shows himself in this a truly *Russian* positivist; he is not content with a cool or purely objective approach, being filled, rather, with a desire to enlist the aid of knowledge in order to transform the world in which he lives.

N. K. Mikhailovsky (1842–1904) makes a similar appeal for the use of the subjective method in the study of history. History is not, as the Marxists claim, a purely objective process, in which one period follows another under pressure of necessity. On the contrary, it is, for Mikhailovsky, a teleological process, in which individual men and groups pursue ends which they have themselves adopted as their own.

As for the rôle of the individual in history, the *Narodniks* were persuaded that the course of history is determined by individual outstanding personalities, by those 'heroes' whom Lavrov described as 'men of critical insight'. The people, the masses, the working-class, the plebs (*tolpa*, the mob, as the *Narodniks* contemptuously designated them), are merely the raw material of history and incapable of exercising any conscious control over events. They await their liberation at the hands of the 'heroes', and can only follow them blindly. As can be seen, this view is the diametrical opposite of the Marxist doctrine of the class-struggle and the historical rôle of the proletariat.

According to Lavrov the aim of history is progress, and the purpose of progress the full and comprehensive development of the individual. But since the individual can only develop himself within a well-organized society, the object of progress also consists in the establishment of *pravda* (the right, as truth and justice) in social life. Society has to secure the co-operation of each for the progressive advancement of all. And Lavrov envisages the aim of socialism as consisting precisely in the transformation of society into such a common co-operative effort in the interests of general advancement. Lavrov's socialism is therefore in no sense directed against the individual.

Progress, however, will only be achieved by virtue of the 'critical insight' whereby we determine the goals to be striven for and select the means to attaining them. Hence the predominant rôle assigned to the 'critical thinkers' in the *narodik* system of sociology; the intellectual minority has grave responsibilites to fulfil towards the uneducated masses:

'Any cultivated minority which refuses to exercise a civilizing influence in the widest sense of the word, bears a responsibility for all the troubles of its contemporaries, which it might remove from the world if it were prepared, not merely to sustain the rôle of representing and preserving culture, but also to take up the task of advancing and enlarging it.' [1]

As regards the special path of development in Russia itself, the *Narodniks* took the view that neither capitalism nor a proletarian class could come into existence there. They therefore sought to give their socialism an agrarian character, such as was already to hand, in embryo, in the Russian *Obshchina*, and worked for revolution and the introduction of socialism by way of a peasant revolt, in contrast to the Marxists, who regarded the industrial proletariat as the 'advance guard' of the revolution, whose task it would be to drag the peasantry along with them. Again, in accordance with their conception of the rôle of the individual in history, the *Narodniks* expected the destruction of absolutism to be brought about by acts of terrorism on the part of individual 'heroes'—this being the attitude from which the *Narodnaya Volya* originally sprang.

From 1890 onwards Marxism began to make itself felt in Russian public affairs, and spread very rapidly in 1893-4. Two books in particular, which constituted a violent attack on *Narodnichestvo* in the name of Marxism, had a powerful effect on public opinion: Peter Struve's *Critical Remarks on the Problem of Russian Economic Development*,[2] and Bel'tov's (*i.e.* Plekhanov's) *On the Question of the Development of the Monist View of History*.[3] Even Lenin entered the fray—albeit in his own fashion—again the *Narodniks*;[4] but it was Struve and Plekhanov who at this time sounded the key-note of Marxist criticism.

It was to orthodox historical materialism that the Marxists appealed in their polemic against the *Narodniks* and their philosophy of history. More especially they accused the *Narodniks* of adhering to an unscientific type of socialism, of ignoring the scientific laws

---

[1] P. L. Lavrov: *Istoricheskiya pis'ma* (Historical Letters), St. Petersburg 1905, p. 59.

[2] P. Struve: *Kriticheskie zametki po voprosu ob ekonomicheskom razvitii Rossii*, 1894.

[3] Bel'tov (G. V. Plekhanov): *K voprosu o razvitii monisticheskago vzglyada na istoriyu*, 1895 (translated as *In Defence of Materialism* by A. Rothstein, London 1947; another version, Moscow–London 1957).

[4] *Cf.* below, p. 112.

of economic and political development. They, the Marxists, on the other hand, stood for a logically consistent monistic theory of history: economic phenomena are the only effective basis for all social and political development. Political arrangements, philosophy, etc., are merely the various layers of a superstructure erected on economic foundations; once the foundations are altered the superstructure must necessarily change as well. As against the necessities of historical development, the individual consciousness counts for little or nothing. Marxist sociology 'knows nothing of personality as such, regarding it as a negligible quantity from the sociological point of view.[1]

The monism referred to is conceived in the form of a causal nexus between the economic phenomena and the superstructure. It is the class which is the real subject of economic development, the perennial warfare between the classes constituting the driving force behind economic change.

It will be evident that in tracing anything and everything back to economic sources these intransigent 'orthodox' Marxists were interpreting the materialistic conception of history in the strictest possible sense. As we saw, neither Marx nor Engels were invariably ready to push historical materialism to this length, and it is nowadays criticized and rejected in contemporary bolshevist doctrine as 'economic materialism'. The theorists of Soviet historical materialism are opposed to rigorous economism, on the ground that it conceives the economic factor to be the *sole* determining force in social development and attaches no significance to the ideological superstructure, as though this was merely a question of 'reflexes' pure and simple. They reject it because of the fundamentally fatalistic attitude involved, which implies a policy of passive endurance, awaiting the automatic effects of economic development, and therefore leaves no room for revolutionary action.

From this rigid standpoint the orthodox Marxists attacked the 'subjective method' in sociology, chiefly represented at this time by Mikhailovsky, who had renewed the campaign some twenty years after Lavrov. To this 'subjectivism' they opposed an extreme form of objectivism, according to which historical development pursues its course with inescapable necessity. The rôle of the individual is thereby reduced virtually to nothing. There is therefore no point in applying the category of 'justice' to history, or in postulating any sort of ideal and judging historical facts by reference to this ideal. They completely uproot the category of 'what ought to be' and replace it by that of 'what is'; ethics is superseded by logic. Rightness

[1] P. Struve: *Op. cit.* Quoted here from Ivanov-Razumnik: *Istoriya russkoy obshchestvennoy mysli* (History of Russian Social Thought), II. St. Petersburg 1911, pp. 357 ff.

and morality are thereby completely ruled out as categories of historical judgement.

'Only one thing has any meaning for us: that the social process is a necessary one; as to whether it is just or not, the question itself is absurd; for surely nobody bothers himself about whether lightning does well or ill when it strikes a man and kills him.' [1]

Sociology is thereby reduced to the level of any other of the natural sciences. It can no longer have the task of improving the world which Lavrov had claimed for it, but must be content to describe the laws of its development. Of Lavrov's synthesis of truth and justice (*pravda-istina* and *pravda-spravedlivost'*), only *pravda-istina*, logical truth, remains intact.

This actually led, for many Marxists, not merely to a straight-forward determinism, but to a genuine fatalism in the fullest sense of the word.[2] As Ivanov-Razumnik observes, many intransigent

[1] Quoted, without indication of source, in Ivanov-Razumnik (*Op. cit.*, p. 374).

[2] Plekhanov is especially anxious to rebut the charge of fatalism: 'Thus dialectical materialism not only does not strive, as its opponents attribute to it, to convince man that it is absurd to revolt against economic necessity, but it is the first to point out how to *overcome* the latter. Thus is eliminated the *inevitably fatalist* character inherent in *metaphysical materialism*' (*Op. cit.*, Rothstein, p. 244). But how does Plekhanov propose to escape fatalism? According to his view of history our 'anthropoid ancestors', like all other animals, were in complete subjection to Nature. But the evolutionary process led by physical necessity to their emancipation from the power of Nature. Ancestral man became a 'tool-making animal', by help of which he subjected Nature to himself. Consciousness dawned, and with it freedom. Increasing development of the means of production gave man a new authority over Nature, but gave rise correspondingly, to a new variety of human slavery. With the progressive 'development of the productive forces there become more complex the mutual relations of men in the social process of production. The course of that process completely slips from under their control, the producer proves to be the slave of his own creation (as an example, the capitalist anarchy of production).' So, once more, the relations of production, by the very logic of their development, bring man to realization of the causes of his enslavement by economic necessity, a cause which lies in the anarchy of production. Man organizes that production and thereby subjects it to his will. 'Then terminates the kingdom of *necessity*, and there begins the reign of freedom, which itself in turn proves *necessary*. The prologue of human history has been played out, history begins' (*Op. cit.*, Rothstein, pp. 242-4). In a pamphlet written in 1898, *The Rôle of the Individual in History* (*K voprosu o roli lichnosti v istorii*, Moscow 1948; translated in *Essays in Historical Materialism*, New York 1940), Plekhanov likewise sees in freedom nothing else than 'being conscious of necessity' (*Op. cit.*, p. 8, English, p. 16) and in free activity a *conscious* and

Marxists of the period exhibit in the highest degree of development
what Nietzsche describes as *amor fati*—they not only submitted to
the necessity of the historical process, but set themselves to love it.[1]
'Necessity' became a fetish with them, just as the category of 'utility'
had been to the previous generation, the Nihilists of 1860–70. Just
as the Nihilists had denied the subjective validity of ethics, so the
Marxists denied its objective validity. The former dismissed any
question of the morality of an *action*; sufficient that it was useful;
the latter refused to concern themselves with the justice of a *process*
—so long as it was necessary, that was good enough.

This outlook also determined their attitude to the problem of the
peculiar path of development in Russian history. In contrast to the
Narodniks, the orthodox Marxists strongly denied that the prospects
of development in Russia were any different from those of the West,
or that socialism could come into being directly on the basis of
the peasant commune, the *Obshchina*, holding that in Russia also
it would be necessary to pass through the capitalist phase of
development.

It is significant that on this point the intransigent Marxists were
contradicting everything that Marx himself had ever said on the
subject. In February 1881 Vera Zasulich, a *Narodnik* turned revolutionary, who later became a Marxist, had written direct to Marx
imploring him to give his opinion on this question which had been
so hotly disputed among the Russian revolutionaries, and to which
she herself attached extraordinary importance. For

'there are only two possibilities: it may be that the village commune,
once freed from the limitless impositions of the tax-gatherer, the
exactions of the landlords and the arbitrary interference of the police,
will be capable of development in the direction of socialism, capable,
that is, of organizing production and the distribution of its produce
on a collective basis. If so, it is evidently the duty of revolutionary
socialists to devote all their energies to the liberation and advancement of the peasant commune. But, if, on the other hand, the commune is destined to disappear, the only thing left for socialists is to
abandon themselves to more or less ill-founded speculations as to
how many decades it will take for the lands of the Russian peasant
to fall into the hands of the bourgeoisie, and how many centuries

free expression of necessity; he also attempts to show by appealing, among
other examples, to Islam, that a conviction of the inevitability of historical
development in no way restricts the impulse to practical activity. But this
account of human freedom is very far from removing the objections levelled
against these early Russian Marxists on grounds of fatalism; for it is really
no more than a restatement of their position.

[1] Ivanov-Razumnik: *Op. cit.*, p. 356.

may well elapse before Russian capitalism attains the same level of development as in Western Europe. In that case it will be the business of socialists to carry on propaganda amongst the urban workers only, who will be continually swamped by the mass of peasants thrown on the streets of the big towns and left to seek employment by the disintegration of the communes.' [1]

This letter takes a very pessimistic view of the hopes of the Russian revolutionaries, if events should prove the peasant commune incapable of providing for an immediate transition to socialism without an intervening period of capitalist development in Russia. And since those who regarded the peasant commune as an outmoded form of society, whose death-sentence had already been pronounced by history and scientific socialism, were continually appealing to the authority of Marx, Vera Zasulich beseeches him to give an answer to the question.

Marx answered on the 8th March 1881, explaining that the 'historical necessity' of which he had spoken in *Capital* was applicable only to Western Europe, since there alone was one form of property changing into another, namely, property based on individual labour into property derived from the exploitation of others. Under the peculiar circumstances prevailing in Russia, it would, however, be a case of changing from communal to private ownership. His own first-hand study of the sources had convinced him that the Russian peasant commune could serve to effect the social renovation of Russia once it was freed from the constraints which hampered it on every side.

In the following year, in the Preface to Vera Zasulich's translation of the *Communist Manifesto*, Marx expressed himself even more decisively to the same effect:

'If the Russian Revolution becomes the signal for a proletarian revolution in the West, so that both complement each other, the present Russian common ownership of land may serve as the starting point for a communist development.'

---

[1] Quoted in K. Stählin: *Geschichte Russlands*, IV/1, pp. 388 f. Both letters are also available in a Russian translation in the collection *Perepiska K. Marxa i F. Engelsa s russkimi politicheskimi deyatelyami* (Correspondence of K. Marx and F. Engels with Political Workers in Russia), Moscow 1947, pp. 240 ff.; (for a full, though somewhat unsatisfactory, English version *cf.* K. Marx–F. Engels: *The Russian Menace to Europe* (ed. Blackstock and Hoselitz), London 1953, p. 275; also contains (pp. 218 f.) a composite version of Marx's various drafts in reply).

[2] K. Marx–F. Engels: *Op. cit.*, Preface to second Russian edition, Geneva 1882 (*MESW*, I, p. 24).

But even these unequivocal expressions of dissent on the part of their master could not deter the intransigent Russian Marxists from obstinately proclaiming the validity of the law necessitating a capitalist interlude on the road to socialism in Russia as well. Plekhanov, for example, referring to a letter of Marx's dated 1877 and couched in similar terms, describes it somewhat ironically as a 'letter of condolence'. And by 1883, which saw the publication of his *Socialism and the Political Struggle*, Plekhanov was laying it down for a fact that Russia had already embarked on the road of capitalist development.[1]

On this point, therefore, the Russian Marxists were '*plus royalistes que le roi*'. In the teeth of the considered assertions of the master they continued to uphold the necessity for capitalist development and the formation of an industrial proletariat in Russia, before the country could go over to socialism.

This fatalistic determinism also led them to push to extremes another of Marx's theories, the so-called theory of collapse and impoverishment.[2] What matter if the village communes should be calmly sacrificed to the oppressive policies of the landed interest, the peasants be reduced to ruin and compelled to pour into the towns in the form of a proletariat, the resources of capital become concentrated in the hands of a few capitalists, and tens and hundreds of thousands of workers be thrown destitute on to the streets by economic crises? This is just what is needed to hasten the collapse of capitalism and the transition to socialism. The capitalist system is doomed to destruction by its own internal contradictions: hence it is not merely superfluous to oppose it—on the contrary, everything should be done to speed its growth, so far as anything *can* be done to influence the course of a natural and necessary process. Such were the self-contradictory conclusions arrived at by the more extravagantly optimistic among the orthodox Marxists.

[1] K. Stählin: *Op. cit.*, p. 391.

[2] The materialist conception of history and the doctrines of value and surplus value are the basis on which Marx then goes on to establish in detail the theory of the stages of capitalist development, according to which capitalism necessarily brings about its own downfall and the emergence of a socialist order of society. The theories of concentration, accumulation, crisis, impoverishment, collapse and revolution and finally the theory of socialization, are supposed to show how the constantly increasing use of machinery creates unemployment and depresses wages, thereby leading to an equally constant increase in the impoverishment of the proletariat. Over-production on the one hand, and on the other an insufficient consumption of the goods produced, owing to the impoverishment of the lower levels of society, are responsible for periodic crises within the capitalist system and ultimately for its collapse. *Cf.* J. Messner, article on 'Marxism' in *Staatslexikon*, III, pp. 1179 ff.

So it was that the intransigent Marxists came to adopt the slogan 'the worse things are, the better' (*chem khuzhe, tem luchshe*). Let the puny smallholder perish in want, the rich enlarge their fortunes still further—such things are inevitable, and heartening to see, since they open the road to the future happiness of society. 'Down with true personality, up with the necessity of the historical process and long live the abstract idea of man.' Such is Ivanov-Razumnik's summary of the position held by these Marxists.[1] The worse things go with actual men at the moment, the better it will be for society in the future.

The orthodox Marxists applied this principle to a variety of problems: the more a man's personal rights are restricted, the better, for his reaction will be all the more violent in consequence. There is indeed a grain of truth in the law so formulated, it being nothing more than an application, in the social field, of Newton's Third Law of Motion; but these Marxists propounded it, not merely as an objective axiom of sociology, but also as a subjective norm of personal conduct. And in this their error consists. For, as Ivanov-Razumnik rightly observes,[2] though a given cause must always produce the same effect, the same effect is by no means always due to the same cause. Thus, to apply this in the present connection, the Marxists should have shown that their 'better' (the future) was *only* attainable by way of the 'worse' (the present) and could not be achieved in any other way.

As it was, however, the intransigent Russian Marxists also took this objective sociological law as a subjective norm for their practical behaviour and thereby arrived at an extreme form of anti-individualism which is in fact exceedingly typical of Marxism generally. The actual welfare of the present generation is sacrificed to the highly problematical well-being of the generations to come; they envisage the present merely as a means, it being the future which constitutes the real goal. They are always dreaming of Dostoyevsky's 'Palace of Crystal'. The love of our neighbour is replaced, to borrow another expression from Dostoyevsky, by the 'love of them that are afar off'.[3]

This extreme anti-individualism also made itself felt in the attitude of the Marxists over the third point at issue between them and the *Narodniks*, the quarrel about the rôle of the individual in history. In their view, progress in history is attributable to the class-struggle,

[1] Ivanov-Razumnik: *Op. cit.*, p. 364.   [2] *Ibid.*, pp. 365 f.

[3] It is worth noting that Nietzsche, in his *Also sprach Zarathustra*, also teaches this 'love of them that are afar off': 'Higher than love of one's neighbour is love for the remote and for the future. . . . My brethren, I counsel you not love of your neighbour; I counsel you love of them that are farthest.' *Werke*, VII, Leipzig 1906, pp. 88 ff. (translated by A. Tille and M. M. Bozman, Everyman, London 1933, pp. 52–3).

not to the activities of isolated individuals. It is not ideas that condition historical development, but economic conditions, rather, which determine ideas. The effectiveness of 'outstanding personalities' in history amounts to nothing if their ideas and aspirations are not in accordance with the economic developments of their time; whereas people actually become outstanding personalities when their ideas and aspirations are fully and completely in harmony with the economic needs of society.

Against the claim advanced by the *Narodniks* in this connection, that the people were *tolpa* (a disorganized rabble or mob) and that only heroes made history and transformed the masses into a people, the Marxists maintained the opposite thesis, that it was not the heroes who made history, but history the heroes—not they who created the people, but the people that created them, it being the people itself that drove history onwards. Heroes can only be regarded as important insofar as they have rightly grasped the conditions of social development and brought their actions into line with these conditions; where this does not happen and they fail to reckon with the historical needs of society, they become ludicrous and impotent *Neudachniks* (bringers of ill-luck), which is what the Marxists considered the *Narodniks* to be.

For all that, the charge levelled by the Marxists against the *Narodniks*, that they failed to recognize the part played by the people in historical development and attributed all progress to the individual, is not entirely justified. The task which Lavrov, for example, ascribes to 'persons of critical insight', whom he adjures to bring to the peasantry that culture without which they remain incapable of recognizing their own rights, does not prevent him from urging that the social revolution should be carried out, not merely on behalf of the people, but also by their agency. If the Russian revolutionaries, after securing victory over the autocracy, should seek to endow the people with a new order, legally imposed upon them, this would merely constitute a renewal of tyranny. He had a clear intimation of the course that Russia was later to follow. By the same token Lavrov deemed it impossible to conjure up the revolution by artificial means, for a revolution is never brought about by the will of individuals or specific groups, but results from a complex set of historical antecedents.

In keeping with this doctrine of Lavrov's, the *Zemlya i Volya* had laid down, in principle, the following programme of action: 'The liberation of the people must be the people's affair'; which is nothing less, in fact, than a paraphrase of the corresponding point in the programme of the Marxist International: 'The liberation of the working-class must be the task of the working-class itself.' [1]

[1] *Cf.* K. Stählin *Op. cit.*, pp. 379 f.; on Lavrov, *cf. ibid.*, p. 210.

The closing decade of the last century was wholly taken up with this campaign of the orthodox Marxists against *Narodnichestvo*. We must take occasion here to refer to a remark of Struve's in which he compares, in passing, this controversy between Marxism and *Narodnichestvo* with that which had previously divided the Slavophiles and the Westerners. It is their belief in the absolute uniqueness of Russia's destiny which provides, in his view, the link between the Slavophiles and the *Narodniks*, whereas the Marxist campaign against this notion appears to be merely a continuation of that which the Westerners had waged against the Slavophiles. And a certain westernism of mind is indeed typical of Plekhanov's part in the struggle; far more than Lenin, he is a Westerner, a rationalist and a man of the Enlightenment.

Just as the conflict between Slavophiles and Westerners had been, in its day, a fruitful period for philosophy, so now the entry of Marxism into Russian life and thought served in its turn to reawaken an interest in theoretical and philosophical issues in Russian society, and to shake it out of the lethargy so characteristic of the 'eighties, the period of *Meshchanstvo* (philistinism) and the so-called 'petty measures'.

This influence had unfortunate repercussions upon Marxism itself, however, for a deeper study of philosophy revealed the inadequacy of its own philosophic foundations and speedily led to its decay.

In speaking of decay, however, a distinction must of course be drawn between Marxism as a socio-philosophical theory, and Marxism as a social-democratic policy of action and a working-class movement. The decay in question related to Marxism as a socio-philosophical theory, including as it did, much that was impracticable and doctrinaire. It had no effect upon Marxism as a workers' movement, as a Russian form of social democracy, in which capacity, indeed, it manifested great strength and vitality, though marked, as Berdyaev observes,[1] by a sinister damping-down of any sort of intellectual life or spirit of criticism.

2. CRITICISM IN RUSSIAN MARXISM

We have referred to Marxism as having rekindled an interest in philosophy in Russian society. But how this actually happened is something of a mystery. For Plekhanov's book *On the Question of the Development of the Monist View of History*, which together with

---

[1] *K istorii i psikhologii russkago marxizma* (On the History and Psychology of Russian Marxism) in *Polyarnaya Zvezda*, 1906, No. 10; *cf.* also N. Berdyaev: *Sub specie aeternitatis. Opyty filosofskie, sotsial'nye i literaturnye 1900–1906* (Philosophical, Social and Literary Essays, 1900–1906), St. Petersburg 1907, pp. 382–90, here p. 383.

Struve's did most to bring it about, is philosophically a mediocre work. As Ivanov-Razumnik says,[1] it is nothing more than a paraphrase of Engels' *Anti-Dühring*, with particular emphasis on the historical development of 'scientific socialism'. Moreover, Engels' own 'system' had already been dismissed by the German philosophical critics of the day as completely worthless from the philosophical point of view.[2] How, then, are we to account for the remarkable fact that such a philosophy should have been able, the moment it appeared on the scene, to effect a renewal and revival of philosophical thought in Russia?

The explanation lies in the character of the philosophy advocated in the book: Engels' philosophy (like that of the Russian Marxists who followed him) was dialectical materialism. The first factor, its materialism, serves to explain why Marxist philosophy should have gained such extensive currency in Russia, where a crude materialism and naive realism had already dominated the field for the previous thirty years. And the new doctrine, which accounted for the whole of life on earth in terms of a single principle, was a typical example of methodological monism on a materialistic basis.

The second factor is the dialectical character of this materialism. In this respect the new theory really did have genuine elements of novelty in it, as compared with popular materialism and old-style mechanism. Its dialectical character made it necessary to go more deeply into the sources of materialism. Students of philosophy felt themselves obliged to go back beyond the Hegel whom Marx and Engels had 'stood upon his head' to the real Hegel, and thereafter to Schelling and Fichte, and ultimately to the father of the whole of modern philosophy, Kant. In this fashion the new school of philosophy, having first expanded at large, was now compelled to plunge into the depths.

But this soon led to a division of opinion within Russian Marxism itself, between the orthodox and the critically-minded Marxists, of whom the most important among the latter were N. Berdyaev, S. Bulgakov and that same Struve whose *Critical Remarks on the Problem of Russian Economic Development* had been of such great importance in disseminating Marxism throughout Russia. They recognized the weakness of the philosophical basis of Marxism and reverted on that account to Kant, or, more precisely, identified themselves with the Neo-Kantianism which at that time prevailed in Germany, taking as their authority such writers as Lange, Schuppe, Riehl, Cohen, Windelband, Rickert and Stammler.[3]

[1] Ivanov-Razumnik: *Op. cit.*, pp. 449 f.

[2] *Ibid.*, p. 450; Gustav Mayer, however, in the work referred to above (p. 41, n. 2), takes a different view.

[3] T. G. Masaryk: *The Spirit of Russia*, II, p. 352.

Polemical exchanges began in 1896 and increased in bitterness in the years that followed. The orthodox Marxists were zealous in defence of the 'unshakable foundations' of dialectical materialism and accused their opponents of 'bourgeois philistinism'. Their mouthpieces were the Marxist newspapers *Novoe Slovo* (The New Word, 1897) and *Nachalo* (The Beginning, 1898), in which Neo-Kantianism was described as the 'mentality of the decadent bourgeois class'. Nevertheless they recognized the critical movement represented in the newspaper *Zhizn'* (Life, 1899–1901) as a serious and dangerous rival. Foremost in the fight against these opponents was Plekhanov in two series of articles, one dating from 1898 to 1901 directed against Bernstein, Konrad Schmidt and Struve and issued by himself in collected form under the title *Our Critics Criticized*;[1] the other, aimed at Struve, and published in the paper *Zarya* (Dawn, 1901–2); the same theme was pursued by L. Axel'rod (Ortodox) in a number of articles later collected under the title *Philosophical Studies*.[2]

The main difference which divided the critical outlook both from orthodox Marxism and also from *Narodnichestvo* was the philosophical theory of criticism which underlay it, and which rested on considerations drawn from logic and the theory of knowledge. By contrast, orthodox Marxism, together with its rival, *Narodnichestvo*, were both essentially positivistic doctrines. Nevertheless, and precisely in pursuit of its quarrel with the critical movement, orthodox Marxism did endeavour to pay more attention to the problem of knowledge, as we shall see in connection with Plekhanov's 'hieroglyphic' theory and the philosophy of Lenin; Lenin, in particular, is constantly recalling the fact that the dialectic is also a theory of knowledge. Other Marxists, however, in the course of their opposition to the critical school, attempted to couple Marxism with the empirio-criticism of Mach and Avenarius, of which more will be said when we come to deal with Bogdanov.

In reviewing, as we now propose to do, a number of doctrines which were the occasion of dispute between the two parties, we find yet another major topic of controversy in the economic materialism which considers changes in economic conditions to be the one and only basis for all political, social and cultural development. The critical group objected to this principle on the ground that economic and social progress were not identical, economics forming only one aspect of social phenomena. They did, however, acknowledge the great significance of the economic factor in social development, and therefore conceded to historical materialism the doctrine of the economic basis and the ideological superstructure, but as a

[1] *Kritika nashikh kritikov*, St. Petersburg 1906.
[2] *Filosofskie ocherki*, St. Petersburg 1906.

hypothesis only, a methodological principle, not as an account of reality.[1]

The exponents of criticism therefore dissented from the Marxist doctrine of economic primacy insofar as it postulated a *causal* dependence of the 'superstructure'—law, morality, philosophy, etc., on the economic factors. They admitted, indeed, the existence of close connections between economics and law, but only in the shape of a reciprocal correspondence, such as that between matter and form.[2]

They also considered it a major error of the 'superstructure' theory that it confused the abstract with the concrete. Concepts such as 'politico-social superstructure' or 'economic factor' are mere abstractions, which orthodox Marxism neglects to analyse into the concrete elements of which they are constituted.

'The material sphere of social phenomena is merely an abstraction, a collective concept for all those individual phenomena which stand to one another in causal relationships, and which can only operate singly and separately upon one another and upon outside happenings as well.'[3]

They thought that the 'economic factor' should be rendered more concrete, or, as they put it, 'purged of its abstractions' (*razotvlechenie*: the term derives from Mikhailovsky), after which it would become apparent that the alleged primacy was all too much a matter of hypothesis.

Struve was even more strenuously opposed to the 'superstructure' theory as applied to philosophy, and more especially in its particular application to Neo-Kantianism and those theories derived from contemporary philosophy in which orthodox Marxism saw an embodiment of a decadent bourgeois mentality:

'Between the concepts of "class" and "philosophical creation" there

---

[1] In this they approached the position of a number of Western sociologists, such as Max Weber, P. W. Schmidt and P. W. Koppers, who are prepared to acknowledge the materialist conception of history as a heuristic principle (*cf.* C. Hubatka: *Die materialistische Geschichtsauffassung*, Dissertation, Pont. Univ. Gregoriana, Rome 1942, p. 56).

[2] It is significant that Hubatka, adopting a scholastic approach, attaches more importance to the economic factor than these Russian critical Marxists, though conceiving it throughout as a contributory cause, and certainly not as the sole cause of historical development, as the orthodox Marxists do (*ibid.*, pp. 87 ff.).

[3] B. Kistyakovsky: *Kategorii neobkhodimosti i spravedlivosti pri izsledovanii sotsial'nykh yavleniy* (The Categories of Necessity and Justice in the Investigation of Social Phenomena), in *Zhizn'*, 1900, Nos. 5 and 6; quoted here from Ivanov-Razumnik: *Op. cit.*, p. 380.

stands for me a gulf so wide, and yet not empty, but filled with contents of the most various kind, that I find myself completely incapable of framing a proposition, with the one concept as subject and the other as predicate, to which it would be humanly possible to attach any sort of meaning. And if . . . it should ever come into my head to ask which class is to be held responsible for the metaphysics of Spinoza or Fichte, I confess—without being in the least ashamed of it—that in face of such a question my thinking would simply come to a standstill.' [1]

The critical school also objected strongly to yet another tenet of orthodox Marxism: the assimilation of the categories of 'is' and 'ought' (more precisely, of what 'ought to be': *sushchego i dolzhnogo*), and the exclusion of the category of 'justice' from sociology in favour of that of 'necessity'. The sociologist, it was pointed out, is not merely a professional expert, but first and foremost a man:

'The necessity of a social phenomenon in virtue of its natural causes in no way excludes it from judgement on grounds of equity.' [2]

In this connection the critical theorists also dissented from the celebrated principle that 'the worse things are, the better'. In 1897 Struve took issue against the fatalism of orthodox Marxism in his article *Freedom and Historical Necessity*,[3] in which he pointed out that the fatalistic ideal of an absolute necessity is a contradiction in terms. The supporters of the movement were thereby enabled to admit that individuals might exercise an influence on the historical process, and to think it possible to regulate the processes of production and distribution by means of planning. On every side there was opposition to the suppression of the individual, who was credited with an increasingly important part in the play of events.

In its later development the critical opposition struck out on two different paths, the one in the direction of scientific realism, the other towards a religious idealism. Once more that contradiction was revealed which, as Berdyaev notes,[4] was already latent in the dual aspect of classical Marxism, its scientific realism on the one hand, and its religious utopianism on the other. For classical Marxism was on one side a scientific system, insofar as it was concerned to discover the scientific laws of economic and social development; on the other

---

[1] P. Struve: *Protiv ortodoxal'noy neterpimosti—pro domo sua* (Against Orthodox Intolerance—*Pro domo sua*), in *Mir Bozhy*, 1901, No. 3; quoted here from Ivanov-Razumnik: *Op. cit.*, pp. 380 f.

[2] B. Kistyakovsky: *Op. cit.*, from Ivanov-Razumnik: *Op. cit.*, p. 381.

[3] P. Struve: *Svoboda i istoricheskaya neobkhodimost'* (Freedom and Historical Necessity) in *Voprosy filosofii i psikhologii* (Problems of Philosophy and Psychology), 1897, No. 1; *cf.* Ivanov-Razumnik: *Op. cit.*, p. 382.

[4] N. Berdyaev: *K istorii i psikhologii russkago marxizma, Op. cit.*

side, however, it could also be described at the same time as a pseudo-religious system, a utopian dream, especially in virtue of the messianic element contained in it, whereby the proletariat was credited with the task of liberating mankind, and leading it into a realm of freedom which would mark the end of the 'prehistory' of the human race and the beginning of its true career.

As leaders of the first party, reference may be made to such writers as B. Kistyakovsky and P. Struve whose names have been mentioned several times already. As early as 1894, the year in which his *Critical Remarks on the Problem of Russian Economic Development* was published, Struve had argued, against Marx, that the expropriation of smallholdings was certainly not the only way in which capitalism could come into existence. Towards the end of the century he finally broke away from orthodox Marxism in his articles *Against Orthodoxy* and *The Marxist Theory of Social Development*.[1] His subsequent course led him ever farther from dialectical materialism, first into transcendental, and later still into transcendent, idealism.

His example was followed by other intellectuals, such as N. Berdyaev, S. Bulgakov and S. Frank. But their development took on more of a religious turn and led them to an orthodox clerical idealism.

Two works of this period give an indication of Berdyaev's course of development. *Subjectivism and Individualism in Social Philosophy*,[2] with a Preface by Struve, is the first of them. It is typical of the transition from 'dialectic' to transcendental idealism (Berdyaev's position) and beyond it to the transcendent idealism espoused by Struve. Berdyaev conducts a campaign on two fronts: on the one hand against the philosophy of the *Narodniks*, and on the other against orthodox Marxism, in the course of which he draws attention to weaknesses, not only in the positivism of Mikhailovsky, but also in the dialectical materialism of Plekhanov. He still contemplates the possibility of reconciling historical materialism with a critical philosophy, but he is already antagonistic to a number of contentions of Marxist philosophy; thus he is firmly opposed to the conception of a 'legal superstructure' reared on an economic basis; he also objects to the fatalistic conclusions drawn by orthodox Marxists from historical materialism, namely to the necessity whereby historical development is allegedly bound to lead to the collapse of capitalism. So far as his own position is concerned, Berdyaev is a disciple of the Neo-Kantian Windelband. Struve, on the other hand, dissents, in his Preface, from transcendental idealism and aligns himself with transcendent idealism, holding the substance of the universe to be spiritual,

---

[1] *Protiv ortodoxii* in *Zhizn'*, 1899, No. 10; *Die Marxische Theorie der sozialen Entwicklung*, in *Braun's Archiv*, 1899, No. 14.

[2] *Subyektivizm i individualizm v obshchestvennoy filosofii*, St. Petersburg 1901.

and spirit the substance of the universe. He thereby makes known to Russian philosophy the 'bankruptcy of Kantianism' and ushers in the transition to a new period of independence.

Berdyaev goes a step further in his article *The Struggle for Idealism*,[1] published in the same year (1901). Though still professing adherence to socialism he is already attempting to prise it loose from its philosophical foundations; he now rejects historical materialism, the Marxist philosophy of history, and allies himself, under the influence of Kant, Nietzsche, Leo Tolstoy and V. Soloviev, with an idealism that is opposed to materialism in the philosophical and social sphere. Positivism, naturalism and hedonism have had their day, in Berdyaev's opinion, and idealism is on the march everywhere. In so saying, however, Berdyaev has no wish to deny the achievements of the 19th century in the field of positive science; he is merely attempting to combat the widespread prejudice to the effect that theoretical idealism must necessarily be associated with reactionary moods and forces, and materialism, by contrast, with progressive ones, a misconception which the careers of the Russian Revolutionaries of 1860–80—such men as Chernyshevsky, for instance, were especially liable to engender; but these men, who, for all their theoretical materialism, were so selfless in the fight against ignorance and entrenched prejudice, should really be regarded as practical idealists. And Berdyaev concludes:

'It seems to me that the time has come for the removal of a historical misunderstanding, and for theoretical and practical idealism to seek alliance in order to pit their united energies against the social and cultural philistinism of the bourgeoisie, and to prepare men's minds for the society of the future.' [2]

Bulgakov's separation from Marxism also took place in similar fashion at about the same period. In a dissertation of the year 1901, while still acknowledging the relevance of some of the Marxist laws to agricultural development, he had already come to reject the main assertions of Marxist philosophy: economic materialism, for instance, on the ground that it did not accord with reality, and more especially the positivistic doctrine of progress which went along with it. The utilitarian conception of progress errs in regarding the suffering humanity of today as merely a bridge leading to the happiness of the generations to come. On these lines Bulgakov eventually moved into the orbit of Soloviev's philosophy.

The individual stages of his development can also be followed out

[1] *Bor'ba za idealizm* in *Mir Bozhiy*, 1901; *cf.* also N. Berdyaev: *Sub specie aeternitatis*, pp. 5–34.
[2] *Ibid.*, p. 14; *cf.* Wolf Giusti: *Due secoli di pensiero russo*, p. 227.

in another of his writings, a collection of ten articles published in 1904 under the title *From Marxism to Idealism*.[1]

3. THE 'GOD-SEEKERS' AND THE 'GOD-BUILDERS'

The religious groups made up by these former Marxists, among whom others such as Merezhkovsky, Zinaida Hippius, Filosofov and Minsky may also be included, became known in Soviet literature under the name of the 'God-seekers' (*bogoiskateli*). Their activities centred upon the St. Petersburg 'Religio-Philosophical Society', in which, in addition to Berdyaev, Bulgakov and Merezhkovsky, Vyacheslav Ivanov and V. Rozanov also took a prominent part.

Plekhanov, in particular, took up the cudgels against them, discerning the origins of the movement in the pessimism prevailing among the Russian intelligentsia after the suppression of the 1905 Revolution; a pessimism which must necessarily overtake a person properly contemptuous on the one hand, of bourgeois philistinism, and yet incapable, on the other, of abandoning the bourgeois view of social relationships.

'Such a man, whether he wills it or not, is bound to become a pessimist in his view of society; he has, indeed, nothing whatever to hope for from social development. But the lot of a pessimist is a hard one . . . and hence the hater of "bourgeois philistinism" averts his gaze from earth, steeped as it is, forever and to the depths, in the ways of the "philistine", and turns his eyes . . . to heaven. . . . Taking all this into account, it is not difficult to discover the sociological counterpart of the religious impulses which manifest themselves so strongly in these circles, all of them verging more or less closely on decadence. Those who belong to them are seeking the road to heaven simply because they have lost their way here upon earth.' [2]

A few years later a similar tendency emerged within Russian Marxism, the exponents of which were dubbed by Russian writers the 'God-Builders' (*bogostroiteli*). This movement, half philosophical and half literary, is associated with the names of Lunacharsky, Gorky, Bazarov and others. These writers attempted to construct a religion without presupposing the existence of God. In this respect they differed from the God-seekers, who did indeed display a critical attitude towards current Christianity in wishing to set up a religion of the 'Third Testament', but acknowledged a transcendent deity. The God-builders, on the other hand, did not 'seek' God as an

---

[1] S. Bulgakov: *Ot marxizma k idealizmu*, St. Petersburg 1903; *cf.* K. Stählin: *Op. cit.*, p. 670.

[2] *BSE*, 1st edn., VI, col. 594.

already existing entity, but spoke of 'building' him, of the realization of deity in the collective achievement of mankind. These Marxists considered mysticism to be a necessary complement to scientific Marxism, which was too one-sided in this respect. Neither the demands of practical reason, nor even human aspirations to 'happiness', can be merely dismissed as non-existent, while science, as such, is unable to satisfy them. But to conclude from this that they must be cosseted by means of tales that are irrefutable only because they relate to a world beyond the senses amounts to a confession of man's spiritual incapacity.[1]

Lunacharsky shows no aversion, even, to the employment of traditional Christian symbols: for him the forces of production are the Father, the proletariat the Son, and scientific socialism the Holy Ghost. In describing the grandiose achievements of human thought and technology, he exclaims: 'In contemplating the handiwork of genius, do we not say to ourselves: What manner of man is this that even the winds and waves obey him? . . . Do we not sense the nascent power of the new-born . . . God?'[2]

The temper of Lunacharsky's atheism is no less religious than that of Feuerbach, who puts man in place of God. Man is himself God— here Lunacharsky is merely reiterating Feuerbach. To the God-builders, Marxian socialism represented the fifth great religion to have sprung from Judaism.[3]

In opposition to this, Plekhanov, in his article *On Religion*, points to the incompatibility of Marxism with any form of religion. Lenin also, in a letter to Gorky (November 1913), expresses a decided aversion to this sort of religion: 'God-seeking no more differs from god-building or god-making or god-creating or the like than a yellow devil differs from a blue devil.'[4]

At the 1909 Conference the Bolshevik Central Committee condemned this tendency in a special resolution, as 'a movement implying a breach with the very foundations of Marxism'.[5] The categorical declaration that even this sort of religion is irreconcilable with Marxism seems worthy of remark.

---

[1] A. Lunacharsky: *Religiya i sotsializm* (Religion and Socialism), St. Petersburg 1908; quoted in M. V. Vol'fson–G. M. Gak: *Ocherki istoricheskogo materializma* (Outline of Historical Materialism), Moscow–Leningrad 1931, p. 214.

[2] Quoted from Vol'fson-Gak: *Op. cit.*, p. 214.

[3] T. G. Masaryk: *Op. cit.*, pp. 358 f.

[4] V. I. Lenin: *Sochineniya*, 3rd edn., XVII, p. 81 (English version in *LSW*, XI, p. 675).

[5] Y. Royatov: Article *Bogoiskatel'stvo* (The God-Seekers Movement), in *BSE*, 1st. edn., VI, col. 595.

4. BOGDANOV'S EMPIRIO-MONISM

The defection of the aforementioned intellectuals, Struve, Berdyaev and Bulgakov, to the latest form of Western philosophy, namely Neo-Kantianism, had the effect of putting orthodox Marxism in a somewhat precarious position. In order to meet the attack on level terms a number of Marxists attempted to fall back on another contemporary trend in Western philosophy, the Empirio-Criticism of Mach and Avenarius. The leader of this school was Bogdanov, the founder of 'Empirio-Monism'.

Bogdanov (the pen-name of Alexander Alexandrovich Malinovsky, born 1873) was a doctor by profession. After joining the workers' movement in 1895, he was active in social-democratic circles in a number of cities. When the split in the party took place at the Second Congress, he aligned himself with the Bolsheviks, and took a zealous part in the work of the party in the years that followed. Differences of opinion on philosophical matters were already beginning to emerge at this time, though without arousing any particular interest as yet, the foreground being occupied by problems of action and campaign tactics. But after the suppression of the 1905/6 Revolution and the political reaction which then set in, increasing attention was paid to philosophical problems. In 1909 Bogdanov, together with Lunacharsky and Gorky, organized a bolshevik school of propaganda on the island of Capri. The Bolshevik Central Committee viewed this undertaking with a certain amount of suspicion. In the following year Bogdanov broke away from the party altogether. He took no part in the 1917 Revolution, though in 1918 we find him as organizer of the 'Proletarian University'. Later he was concerned in the founding of the Blood-Transfusion Institute. He died in 1928 from an unsuccessful experiment he conducted on his own body.

Three phases can be distinguished in Bogdanov's philosophical career: (*a*) the period when he was under the influence of Ostwald's dynamical philosophy, at which time he published his *Outlines of a Historical Approach to Nature*;[1] (*b*) the period of empirio-monism; (*c*) the period of 'Tectology'.

In his empirio-monism, Bogdanov takes as his starting-point the empirio-criticism most fully worked out by the Austrian physicist and philosopher Ernst Mach (1838–1916). Mach shares the positivistic anti-metaphysical outlook of his time, though he goes further than positivism in wishing to do away with any sort of distinction between appearance and reality. Like Berkeley before him, Mach maintains sensations and things-in-themselves to be one and the same. The

---

[1] *Osnovnye elementy istoricheskago vzglyada na prirodu*, St. Petersburg 1899.

whole world, the physical and material no less than the mental, is simply a mass of sensations. Physical objects, on this view, represent nothing more than relatively constant groups of visual and tactual sensations, and this is equally true of our own bodies, and of the self. The distinction between physics and psychology depends on the direction of our attention. Physics is concerned with the relationships of sensations as constituents of the external world, whereas psychology considers the interrelations of these sensation-complexes with reference to the human body, which is itself in turn merely a complex of sensations. The result is that Mach rejects the concepts of substance, causality, and so forth. The concepts of cause, matter, atoms and the like are devoid of any foundation in the elements of experience, having only a symbolical significance as working hypotheses. The object of thought is to grasp the stable interconnections between facts, and to order them according to the principle of economy, *i.e.*, to describe the constituents of experience as economically and as completely as possible. But since the facts are in a perpetual condition of change and flux, this can only be carried out in an approximate fashion, and it is for this very reason that our concepts have only a symbolic meaning.

Bogdanov perceives the inadequacy of empirio-criticism in the fact that it fails ultimately to abolish the dualism between the physical and the mental, and seeks on his own account to advance beyond this, to a monism whereby physical and mental phenomena are to be regarded as differently organized elements in one and the same experience. The mental consists of individually organized experience, the physical of socially organized experience. Hence the title of his system, *Empirio-Monism*.

The distinctive feature of the physical world is objectivity:

'The objective character of the physical world consists in the fact that it exists, not only for me personally, but for everybody, and has for everybody a particular significance which I take to be the same as that which it has for myself. The objectivity of a physical sequence consists in its universality. The "subjective" element in experience, on the other hand, is that which has no universality, having meaning only for one or more individuals.' [1]

But whence does the physical world derive its objectivity, universality and interconnection? Bogdanov takes this to be the result of a process whereby isolated individuals harmonize their experiences and share them one with another.

'The objectivity of the physical bodies which we encounter in our

[1] A. Bogdanov: *Empiriomonizm. Stat'i po filosofii* (Empirio-Monism. Essays in Philosophy), I, 3rd edn., Moscow 1908, p. 23.

experience depends in the last resort on the establishment of a common conviction and concordance between the assertions of different people. The physical world consists of nothing more than socially agreed, socially harmonized,—in a word, of socially organized experience.' [1]

The mental world, on the other hand, lacks this objectivity and universality:

'All these facts of "inner experience" are marked by the highest degree of certainty, but only for myself, only for the person actually acquainted with them. They are "subjective", *i.e.*, they are not brought into conformity with the mental processes, the experience, of other people, and therefore have no "objective" character from their point of view: they lack the social organization characteristic of physical experience.' [2]

This is not to imply, however, that mental facts are chaotic or lacking in organization. Mental experience also possesses coherence and order, though to a lesser degree. Its elements are associated together, and that in itself is a specific form of organization: acts of perception, representation or conation conjoin with one another in specific chains and complexes; eventually they are all absorbed into a complex mass of memories, feelings and conations, an especially stable and enduring complex designated by the word 'I'. In other words the mental is organized on an individual, not a social, basis: it consists of individually organized experience.[3]

Bogdanov describes this derivation of the material world from social experience as a 'universal substitution' (*vseobshchaya podstanovka*), inasmuch as objective and independently existing bodies are replaced by the social ordering of experience. The 'substitution' is made possible for empirio-monism in that it conceives of all being, the whole of reality, as a continuous chain of development, whose lowest members are still lost in a 'chaos of elements', while the highest represent human experience, mental and individual in the first place, and later social and physical. The highest point of development is reached in physical experience, since it requires, as already stated, the organization, not merely of individual, but also of collective experience. Bogdanov thereby thinks himself able to preserve that primacy of the physical over the mental order which is incumbent on any form of materialism.

In keeping with this view of reality, the concepts of space, time, causality and conformity to law lose their objective character and are taken, as in Kant, to be merely forms of organization.

[1] A. Bogdanov: *Empiriomonizm*, pp. 32 f.
[2] *Ibid.*, p. 35.   [3] *Ibid.*, pp. 35 f.

Bogdanov likewise repudiates the notion of objective truth, regarding as true whatever is 'socially accepted within a given period' (*sotsial'no znachimo dlya dannoy epokhi*). Truth is not, as it is taken to be on the conventional view, and also in Lenin's version of dialectical materialism, the conformity of our ideas to the object, since it is denied that there are any objects apart from our experience. Truth, for Bogdanov, is a 'mechanism, by aid of which reality is cut up, trimmed and tacked together'.[1] The aim of knowledge, therefore, is not the apprehension of the real, but a corresponding construction of our experience out of its elements, the creation of a world-picture.[2]

The idea already implicit in his empirio-monism, that it is only our own thinking, by means of the various forms of thought such as space, time, casuality, etc., which brings order into our experience, was carried further by Bogdanov in a later period of philosophical activity which gave rise to the 'Tectology' put forward in his *General Science of Organization*[3] and *Tectology*.[4]

In this new development Bogdanov sets out from one of the theses which Marx had advanced against Feuerbach: 'The philosophers have only interpreted the world in various ways; the point, however, is to change it.' Philosophy as a contemplative inquiry must be abandoned in favour of a constructive science of organization (or 'Tectology', from the Greek τεκταίνομαι), whose task consists, not in 'describing' the world as a whole, but in transforming it into an organized whole 'such as it never was before'. The material for this construction is again, as it was in empirio-monism, the 'chaos of elements' constituting experience.

Bogdanov distinguishes his 'Tectology' from philosophy proper. It is not concerned merely to 'explain' the world. Though it does in fact explain how elements of the most various kinds are combined in Nature, labour and thought, its primary concern is with the practical mastery of all these various possibilities of combination. It is wholly preoccupied with practice, knowledge itself being regarded as merely a special case of practical organization, the co-ordination of a special class of complexes. The present-day accumulation of scientific studies on particular aspects of the organization problem (in running a workshop, a business, an army, and so forth), has created an ever more urgent need for a general scientific theory of organization. But so long as the inquiry is not extended to the most general laws involved, all local investigations from a purely empirical point of view will continue to prove inadequate.

---

[1] '*Mashina, posredstvom kotoroy rezhut, kroyat i sshivayut deystvitel'nost'*.'

[2] *Cf.* S. Smolov: Article *Empiriomonizm* in *BSE*, 1st edn., LXIV, col. 221.

[3] *Vseobshchaya organizatsionnaya nauka*, 1913/17.

[4] *Tektologiya*, Berlin–Petrograd–Moscow 1922.

All human activity, whether in the technical, social, cognitive, artistic, or any other field, is an organizing activity. In all these activities, practical as well as theoretical, man does nothing else but unite or dissolve already present elements or complexes thereof. To denote this unification of complexes, Bogdanov borrows from biology the term 'conjugation'. It forms the basis of the ordering process which constitutes the essential nature of the entire world-process, both in Nature and history. Economic production is the ordering of things, just as thinking is the ordering of ideas. But both are no more than an imitation of Nature on the part of man. For Nature likewise confines itself to the exercise of an ordering activity, in providing animals with hair, for example, to enable them to withstand the cold.

Only through this 'tectological mode of apprehension'

'do we achieve a comprehensive and monistic view of the universe. It lies before us as a boundless unfolding network of forms of every kind and at every level of organization, ranging from the elementary constituents of the ether, of which we know nothing, to human societies and the systems of the stars.' [1]

The governing principle in this ordering process is the law of equilibrium. Whatever is organized is in equilibrium. But this equilibrium in the world is dynamic rather than static; it can be disturbed, and is in fact continually being abolished and restored, and this accounts for the changes that go on in the world. Every change represents a disturbance and restoration of equilibrium between the object (or 'complex' as Bogdanov calls it) and its environment. And this loss of equilibrium between object and environment is responsible in its turn for disturbing the equilibrium within the object itself and thereby arouses a conflict of opposing forces within the complex of which the object consists.

This also constitutes the essence of dialectic. For Bogdanov wishes to retain the dialectic, though he makes it a reproach to Marx and Engels that their conception of dialectic still contains a residue of idealism.

'Dialectic is nothing else but a process of organization which proceeds by way of contraries, or what comes to the same thing, by way of conflict between opposing tendencies.' [2]

Again:

'If this process has a beginning of any sort, there can clearly have

---

[1] *Tektologiya*, Berlin–Petrograd–Moscow 1922, p. 23.
[2] A. Bogdanov: *Filosofia zhivogo opyta* (Philosophy of Living Experience), p. 169; quoted from M. Z. Selektor: *Dialektichesky materializm i teoriya ravnovesiya* (Dialectical Materialism and the Equilibrium Theory), Moscow–Leningrad 1934, p. 7.

been no conflict, *till then*, between the two opposing forces involved in the process, and in this respect a certain *equilibrium* will have prevailed between them. If the process comes to an end in any way, then there is undoubtedly *no longer* any conflict between the two given forces and hence a *new equilibrium* will have been established between them both. We therefore have the complete triad: from equilibrium, *via* the conflict between two forces which disturb it, to a new equilibrium.'[1]

This mechanical conception of dialectic deserves notice, since it played an important part in the controversy which took place in Russia over the 'equilibrium theory'. While Engels, and still more Lenin, see the essence of dialectic in a contradiction inherent in the object or process itself, Bogdanov attempts to derive the whole essence of dialectic from an antagonism between distinct objects endowed with contrary forces. While Engels—in the *Anti-Dühring*, for example, sees the contradictoriness of life in the fact that every living creature at any given moment is at once the same and different, Bogdanov finds it in the fact that

'the organism is at war with its environment, continually transferring to it the energy it expends, and equally continuously drawing energy from it; so long as these two processes continue more or less in balance it remains "the same", but becomes different, "something else", insofar as one of them gains predominance over the other'.[2]

The philosophers of dialectical materialism accused empirio-monism—and not without reason—of idealism. In Berkeley's subjective idealism the whole of reality is effectively dissolved into perceptions; and Bogdanov is equally committed, in logic, to the conclusion that *esse est percipi*.

In accordance with his philosophical theory of the external world as a product of the organizing activity of communal experience, Bogdanov's social theory also attaches greater importance to consciousness than does that of orthodox Marxism: 'Social life', he maintains, 'is inseparable from consciousness. Social being and social consciousness are in the properest sense of the word identical';[3] this in opposition to Marx, who regarded social consciousness as a reflection of social being, based upon it and conditioned thereby.

In Bogdanov, therefore, the division of society is not based, as in Marx, on the ownership of the means of production, but on the possession of organizing experience. The dominant class is made up,

---

[1] A. Bogdanov: *Op. cit.*, p. 192; quoted from Selektor: *Op. cit.*, p. 7.

[2] *Ibid.*

[3] A. Bogdanov: *Iz psikhologii obshchestva* (Studies in Social Psychology), quoted from N. Karev: article *A. Bogdanov* in *BSE*, 1st edn., VI, col. 581.

not of those who own the means of production, but of those who organize it. The method of overcoming class divisions does not consist in seizing power and transferring the means of production into the hands of the working-class, but in socializing organizational experience by means of ideological education among the workers. Bogdanov aims, therefore, not at revolution but at raising the level of 'proletarian culture'. This is in complete contradiction to the Marxist conception of historical materialism, which considers the progressive energy of the historical process to reside, not in ideology, but in the development of the forces of production, whereby, on reaching a certain stage of development, they come into conflict with productive relationships and so bring about a transformation of society.

Apart from Bogdanov, its most important exponent among the Russian Marxists, empirio-criticism also had strong repercussions among other writers, such as Anatoly Vasil'evich Lunacharsky (1875–1933),[1] N. Valentinov (pen-name of Nikolay Vladislavovich Vol'sky, born 1878),[2] V. Bazarov (pen-name of Vladimir Alexandrovich Rudnev, born 1874)[3] and Yakov Alexandrovich Berman (born 1868).[4]

Pavel Solomonovich Yushkevich (born 1873, died at the end of

[1] A. V. Lunacharsky: *Etyudy kriticheskie i polemicheskie* (Critical and Polemical Studies), 1905; *Otkliki zhizni* (Echoes of Life), 1906; *Kritika chistago opyta* (Critique of Pure Experience), 1905. The last-mentioned work is a popular version of the book of the same name by Richard Avenarius.

[2] N. Valentinov: *Filosofskiya postroeniya marxizma* (Philosophical Speculations of Marxism), 1908; *E. Mach i marxizm* (E. Mach and Marxism), 1908.

[3] Bazarov was imprisoned at the end of 1930 in the course of the arrests made in preparation for the so-called 'Trial of the Menshevik Bureau' (January 1931). He seems not to have survived the interrogations, for his name does not figure in the trial. His main works are: *Avtoritarnaya metafizika i autonomnaya lichnost'* (Authoritarian Metaphysics and Autonomous Personality), in the collection *Ocherki realisticheskago mirovozzreniya* (Studies for a Realistic World-view), 1904; *Mistitsizm i realizm nashego vremeni* (Mysticism and Realism in our Time), in the collection *Ocherki po filosofii marxizma* (Studies in the Philosophy of Marxism), St. Petersburg 1908; *K voprosu o filosofskikh osnovakh marxizma* (On the Philosophical Foundations of Marxism), in the collection *Pamyati Marxa* (In Memory of Marx), 1908.

[4] Y. A. Berman: *Dialektika v svete sovremennoy teorii poznaniya* (Dialectic in the Light of Modern Epistemology), 1908; contains an interesting criticism of dialectic: the negation of a concept and the transition to its antithesis does not thereby give rise to a specific new concept; rather must the negation lead back to its starting-point; the Hegelian dialectic is based on a principle of conceptual ambiguity. By the same author: *Marxizm i machizm* (Marxism and Machism) in *Obrazovanie*, 1906, No. 11; *O*

World War II, probably in the winter of 1944–5), transposed empirio-criticism into an 'empirio-symbolism'.[1] He too sets out from a Machian conception of the universe as a complex of sensations, but Yushkevich regards these as also conditioned by the peculiarities of the perceiving organism. Hence reality is to be sought, not in elements (sensations) differing from one individual to the next, but, as it were, in their 'common multiple'. This alone constitutes the subject-matter of science, which endows it with conventional, simplifying symbols, namely concepts and laws, as a substitute for reality. Physics, for example, deals in absolutely rigid bodies, perfect fluids and gases, etc. It transforms the casual relationships found in experience among phenomena into exact unconditional relationships, namely natural laws. These 'empirical symbols' are the true reality.

'Being in itself is that infinite bounding system of symbols sought after by our knowledge. Being and thought coincide on the frontier, so that our thought about matter, for example, does not differ in any respect from extended, ponderous matter itself.' [2]

The various aspects of Russian empirio-criticism were eventually crystallized into three collective works, the joint production of Bogdanov and the other Russian members of the school: *Studies for a Realistic World View*,[3] *Studies in the Philosophy of Marxism*[4] and *Studies for a Philosophy of Collectivism*.[5]

Bogdanov's influence also had its effect on Bukharin, notably in the latter's *Historical Materialism: a System of Sociology*.[6] Though

dialektike (On Dialectic), in the collection *Ocherki po filosofii marxizma* (*cf.* preceding note); *Novya techeniya v nauke o myshlenii* (New Tendencies in the Science of Thought), 1911.

[1] P. S. Yushkevich: *Apriorizm, empirizm i empiriosimvolizm* (Apriorism, Empiricism and Empirio-Symbolism), in *Vestnik zhizni*, 1907, No. 3; *Filosofsky materializm i marxizm* (Philosophical Materialism and Marxism), in *Sovremenny mir*, 1907, No. 4; *Sovremennaya energetika s tochki zreniya empiriosimvolizma* (The Modern Theory of Energy from the Standpoint of Empirio-Symbolism), in the collection *Ocherki po filosofii marxizma* (*cf.* above), *Materializm i kritichesky realizm* (Materialism and Critical Realism), St. Petersburg 1908; *Novya veyaniya* (New Tendencies), St. Petersburg 1910; *Mirovozzrenie i mirovozzreniya* (World outlook and World-views), St. Petersburg 1912.

[2] *Cf.* M. A——v: *Filosofskiya techeniya russkago marxizma* (Philosophical Tendencies in Russian Marxism), in *Vestnik Evropy*, XLIV/3 (March 1909), pp. 355–63.

[3] *Ocherki realisticheskago mirovozzreniya*, 1904.

[4] *Ocherki po filosofii marxizma*, 1908.

[5] *Ocherki filosofii kollektivizma*, 1909.

[6] *Teoriya istoricheskogo materializma*, 1921 (English version, London 1926).

averse to empirio-monism as a philosophical theory, Bukharin thought it possible to take over Tectology as a general science of methods for organizing the world, having nothing at all to do with philosophy and containing nothing in the way of epistemological theory. Lenin took exception to this on the ground that Tectology and empirio-monism have a close connection one with another as elements of one and the same world-view.

The chief opponents of Bogdanov's empirio-monism were Plekhanov (*Materialism Militant*), Lenin (*Materialism and Empiriocriticism*), Deborin and Axel'rod.

5. PLEKHANOV

A survey of the various revisionist tendencies in Russian Marxism seems appropriate as a means to better understanding of the man who stood fast against them in defence of intransigent Marxism, and who is considered by many to be the most important philosopher of Russian Marxism. Lenin himself speaks highly of the significance of Plekhanov's philosophical achievement. After Plekhanov's death he wrote:

'It is *impossible* to become an intelligent, *real* communist without studying—precisely *studying*—all that Plekhanov wrote on philosophy, because that is the best there is in the whole international literature on Marxism,' [1]

and he went on to recommend their inclusion in the official handbooks of communism.

Georgy Valentinovich Plekhanov (1856–1918), the son of a fairly prosperous landowner, was originally intended for a military career. In 1875 he commenced revolutionary activities, and already by the following year had taken part in the founding of the *Zemlya i Volya* group. He soon left it again, however, on account of its predominantly terroristic inclinations, and after its division into the terroristic *Narodnaya Volya* and the more moderate *Cherny Peredel* he took over the organization of the latter. At this time his theoretical standpoint was that of a disciple of *Narodnichestvo*.

In 1880 Plekhanov was obliged to emigrate to Western Europe, where he was able to gain closer acquaintance with the socialist movements in the countries of their origin. After lodging, first in Geneva and later in Paris, he eventually settled for good on the shores of Lake Geneva, where he devoted himself to intensive study of the works of Marx and Engels, whose effect upon him was that

[1] V. I. Lenin: *Eshche raz o profsoyuzakh* (Once Again on the Trade Unions), in *Sochineniya*, XXXII, pp. 49–86 (here p. 73); English version in *LSW*, IX, p. 66.

of a revelation. In this he was following in the footsteps of those young men in the Russia of the 'thirties who had fancied themselves to have found a new revelation in the philosophy of Hegel. Just as Belinsky, thanks to a misunderstanding of Hegel's principle that 'the Real is the Rational and the Rational the Real', had once been persuaded of the rationality of Russian despotism, so now Plekhanov, having come to Europe as a *narodnik* believer in the Russian *Obshchina*, gave himself, with a corresponding enthusiasm, entirely over to Marxism.

Marx's materialistic dialectic, whose significance for mankind he rated equal to that of the theories of Copernicus and Darwin, became for him a key to every riddle of the universe. The progress it engenders represents a continual ascent of society to ever higher forms of life, till the reign of necessity to which the world is still subject is inevitably compelled to give place to the reign of freedom, at which point the prehistory of mankind is at an end and its true history begun.[1]

In Switzerland Plekhanov founded the first Russian Marxist organization, the 'Liberation of Labour' group, so that in a wider sense he may be considered the founder of the Bolshevik Party. From thence he carried on an energetic literary campaign, attacked *Narodnichestvo*, translated the major works of Western Marxism and gave lectures to instil the spirit of Marxism into the Russian revolutionaries abroad.

Of the writings of this period directed against *Narodnichestvo*, mention may be made of the pamphlet *Socialism and the Political Struggle*,[2] in which he criticizes the political programme of the *Narodnaya Volya* and points to the proletariat as the driving force of the revolution; also of his essay *Our Differences*,[3] and the polemical *Foundations of Narodnichestvo in the Works of Mr. V. Vorontsov*,[4] in which he takes his stand against the *narodnik* thesis regarding the peculiar path of Russia, and its peaceful transition to socialism through the development of the *Obshchina*, the *Artel*',[5] and so forth. He also maintained that the development of capitalism in Russia was already under way and that this fact, once established, makes it inevitable that the country should go through a period of capitalism.

These ideas found expression in his celebrated dictum on the

---

[1] *Cf.* p. 77, n. 2 above.   [2] *Sotsializm i politicheskaya bor'ba*, 1883.

[3] *Nashi raznoglasiya*, 1885.

[4] *Osnovanie narodnichestva v trudakh G. V. Vorontsova*, St. Petersburg 1896.

[5] *Artel'* is a form of consumers', producers' or banking co-operative. Prior to the Revolution the commonest form of it in Russia was the union for the provision of unskilled labour: thus there were *Artel's* of building workers, railway porters, etc.

occasion of the founding of the Second International, in which he participated:

'The revolutionary movement in Russia can triumph only as the revolutionary movement of the workers. There is no other way out for us, and cannot be',

an assertion which gave offence to a number of Russian revolutionaries.

After it had become possible, around 1895, for Marxist writings to be legally published in Russia, Plekhanov issued, under the pen-name of Bel'tov, his well-known *On the Question of the Development of the Monist View of History*,[1] (1895), in which he set forth the principles of historical materialism and subjected the *narodnik* doctrines, and more especially those of their chief exponent, Mikhailovsky, to severe criticism. The book had an important influence on the history of the Russian Revolution, having served, in Lenin's phrase, to rear a whole generation of Russian Marxists. Plekhanov also contributed a series of articles to *Novoe Slovo* (The New Word), the first Marxist newspaper in Russia, which began to appear towards the end of the century. At about the same time he published, in German, his *Essays in the History of Materialism*,[2] followed, in succeeding years, by two essays of some philosophical importance, *The Materialist Conception of History*,[3] and *The Rôle of the Individual in History*.[4]

After Lenin's arrival in Western Europe in 1900, Plekhanov joined him in editing the papers *Iskra* and *Zarya*, in which he showed himself especially hostile to economism.

From 1898 to 1902, in various sets of articles appearing in *Neue Zeit* and *Zarya*, later collected under the title of *Our Critics Criticized*,[5] Plekhanov carried on the fight against the philosophical revisionism of certain Marxists, such as Konrad Schmidt, Eduard Bernstein and P. Struve. Lenin speaks highly of these writings, declaring that Plekhanov was the only Marxist to have criticized the erroneous doctrines of the revisionists from the standpoint of a consistent dialectical materialism. Later bolshevik writers, however, having compared this critique of Plekhanov's with that which Lenin himself directed against the revisionists, have claimed that Plekhanov's typical failings can already be detected in it: his unduly abstract and academic treatment of problems, his appraisal of the

---

[1] *Cf.* p. 75, n. 3 above.

[2] *Beiträge zur Geschichte des Materialismus*, Stuttgart 1896 (English version by R. Fox, London 1934).

[3] *O materialisticheskom ponimanii istorii*, 1897 (translated, together with the following item, as *Essays in Historical Materialism*, New York 1940).

[4] *Cf.* p. 77, n. 2 above.   [5] *Kritika nashikh kritikov*, 1906.

revisionist movement as a fortuitous episode in the history of Marxism and his lack of interest in its social and economic origins; whereas Lenin had recognized revisionism as a deliberate and open campaign on the part of bourgeois elements against the theory of the revolutionary proletariat.

In the discussions which took place at the Second Congress of the Russian Social-democratic Party in London, Plekhanov had taken Lenin's side. But differences of opinion arose between them. These turned upon the peasant question. Lenin wanted to get the revolution going at once and was all for the immediate realization of socialism in Russia, but insisted that, thanks to the lowly state of capitalist development in Russia, the proletariat was as yet neither strong enough nor sufficiently class-conscious, and must therefore unite with the peasants; Plekhanov, on the other hand, having entirely abandoned his *narodnik* dreams of a Russian agrarian socialism, considered the immediate realization of socialism in Russia to be out of the question, since capitalism would first have to go through its complete development, and therefore urged a political alliance with the bourgeoisie against aristocracy and absolutism. Hence he did not approve of the 1905 Revolution. 'They should not have taken up arms,' he said.

Though Plekhanov thus became, and remained, a Menshevik, there were many issues, in the years that followed, on which he agreed with the Bolsheviks. After the 1905 Revolution, when legal parliamentary methods had become a possibility, the question arose whether illegal activities should be continued and their organizations kept in being. Plekhanov sided with the Bolsheviks against the 'Liquidators' in favour of keeping the illegal organizations in operation. At the same time he was campaigning in the theoretical field against the 'God-seekers' and 'God-builders', and Bogdanov's empirio-monism, against whom he published three letters in the form of a pamphlet under the title of *Materialism Militant*.[1]

Another important work of Plekhanov's deriving from this period was his *Fundamental Problems of Marxism*,[2] which deals, not so much with the economic as with the philosophical and methodological side of Marxism. The outlook of Marx and Engels is interpreted here by Plekhanov as the logical outcome of Feuerbach's materialism.

On the outbreak of the First World War he was strongly in favour of the war against Germany. The February Revolution of 1917 made

---

[1] Two of these open letters were published in 1908 in *Golos sotsial-demokrata* (Voice of the Social-democrat); the third was specially written by Plekhanov for the collective volume *Ot oborony k nastupleniyu* (From Defence to Attack), which appeared in 1910.

[2] *Osnovnye problemy marxizma*, 1910 (English version, trans. E. and C. Paul, London 1929).

it possible for him to return to Russia, where he supported the continuation of the war and endorsed the Provisional Government. He considered the October Revolution a great mistake, since he saw no possibility of introducing socialism into Russia at that particular moment, but he recognized it as a proletarian revolution and did not oppose it.

In the autumn of the same year he fell seriously ill, being removed in vain to a sanatorium in Finland, where he died on 31st May 1918. His body was taken to St. Petersburg and buried by the side of Belinsky, a spiritual kinsman of Plekhanov, both in his socialist ideals and in his westernizing tendencies.

The attitude of later Bolshevism towards Plekhanov's achievement as a thinker is not a unanimous one. On the one hand there can be no denial of his great services to the philosophy of Russian Marxism. They have to be acknowledged, if only because of the high praise that Lenin has bestowed on his works. Nevertheless, objection is taken to his menshevik outlook, which prevents him from ranking as a pillar of orthodox Marxism.

The result of this ambivalent attitude to Plekhanov is that, although editions of his works are issued by the official Institutes,[1] their introductions and annotations are zealously concerned to draw attention to his lapses from doctrinal purity and to the points on which he differs from Lenin.

We shall confine ourselves to indicating those major features in his philosophy which became the main target of subsequent criticism, there being no occasion to give a systematic account of his teaching, of which a detailed description is reserved for the second part of the present book.

The chief thing of which Plekhanov is repeatedly accused is that his campaign against *Narodnichestvo* and revisionism, especially the revisionism of Bernstein, is unduly abstract and academic in character; he is content with a merely theoretical analysis and fails to expose the social roots of the doctrines in question[2]—very differently from Lenin, who finds in Neo-Kantianism, for example, a pervasive expression of the consciousness of the decadent bourgeois class.[3]

[1] G. V. Plekhanov: *Sochineniya* (Works), ed. D. Ryazanov, 24 vols., Moscow 1922–7.

[2] V. A. Fomina: *Rol' G. V. Plekhanova v rasprostranenii marxistskoy filosofii v Rossii* (The Rôle of G. V. Plekhanov in the Diffusion of Marxist Philosophy in Russia), in the collective work: *Iz istorii russkoy filosofii*, ed. I. Y. Shchipanov, Moscow 1951, pp. 629–703, *q.v.* pp. 649, 657.

[3] *Cf.* V. Vandek and V. Timosko in the Introduction to their edition of Plekhanov's essays against the revisionists: G. V. Plekhanov: *Protiv filosofskogo revizionizma* (Against Philosophical Revisionism), Moscow 1935, pp. 7 and 20.

In general it is complained of Plekhanov that even in his genuinely Marxist period (*i.e.*, before he became a Menshevik) he failed to acknowledge the rôle of partisanship, of party spirit in science and philosophy. When he writes that 'strictly speaking there can be no such thing as a "partisan science",' [1] this is no accidental concession to revisionism on Plekhanov's part.[2]

So far as Plekhanov's specifically philosophical views are concerned, Lenin himself attacked his theory of knowledge, the so-called 'hieroglyphic' theory. According to this theory, sensations and impressions are not, as Lenin holds, images or copies (*kopii, otobrazheniya, snimki*) of things really existing outside us, but merely conventional signs or 'hieroglyphs'. Such a theory had already been worked out by the celebrated physicist and physiologist Helmholtz, and later by the Russian physiologist Sechenov, from whom Plekhanov actually took over the term 'hieroglyph'.

He first put forward this theory in the annotations to his Russian translation of Engels' pamphlet *Ludwig Feuerbach* (1892), and later in his articles against Konrad Schmidt, *Materialism or Kantianism*[3] and *Materialism Again*[4] (1898–9). In the notes on Engels he writes:

'Our sensations are a sort of hieroglyphs, which make us aware of what is happening in reality. These hieroglyphs bear no resemblance to the happenings which are conveyed by means of them.' [5]

And in the article *Materialism or Kantianism* he illustrates the relationship of our impressions to real things by the following analogy:

'Let us imagine a cylinder and a die. The cylinder is the subject, the die the object. The shadow thrown by the die on the cylinder is the impression. This shadow in no way resembles the die: the straight edges of the die appear broken in the shadow, and its flat surfaces curved. Nevertheless, to any change in the die there corresponds a change in its shadow. We may assume that something similar to this occurs in the formation of impressions. The sensations evoked in the subject by the efficacy of the object in no way resemble the object itself, any more than they resemble the subject, nevertheless, *to any change in the object there corresponds a change in its efficacy on the subject.*' [6]

Hence, in spite of the difference between the thing-in-itself and

---

[1] G. V. Plekhanov: *Sochineniya*, XI, 2nd edn., p. 60.
[2] V. A. Fomina: *Op. cit.*, p. 657.
[3] *Materializm ili kantianizm*, in G. V. Plekhanov: *Protiv filosofskogo revizionizma*, pp. 152–72.
[4] *Esche raz materializm; ibid.*, pp. 173–9.
[5] *Cf.* Plekhanov's notes to his (first Russian) translation of Engels' *Ludwig Feuerbach*, p. 118; quoted from M. B. Mitin: *Op. cit.*, p. 121.
[6] G. V. Plekhanov: *Protiv filosofskogo revizionizma*, pp. 168 f.

the impression it produces in the knower, a real knowledge of things is possible:

'The forms and relationships of things-in-themselves cannot be as they *appear* to us to be, *i.e.*, as they appear to us after having been "translated" in our heads. Our impressions of the forms and relationships of things are no more than *hieroglyphs*, but these hieroglyphs indicate these forms and relationships well enough, and that is sufficient for us to be able to study the effects which things-in-themselves produce in us, and to influence them in our turn.' [1]

In the second edition of his translation of Engels' essay on Feuerbach, published in 1905, Plekhanov does indeed abandon the ambiguous term 'hieroglyph', but in other respects he clings to his theory.

This theory of Plekhanov's was also adopted by several adherents of the movement in Soviet dialectical materialism known as 'Mechanism' (Axel'rod, Sarab'yanov *et al.*). Lenin, on the other hand, attacked it violently in his well-known work *Materialism and Empirio-Criticism*, opposing to it his so-called copy-theory, a completely realist position, of which more will be said in the sequel.

Lenin found Plekhanov's treatment of empirio-criticism unsatisfying; one of his objections to it was that it was conducted more from the standpoint of popular than dialectical materialism. He also considered it a fault that Plekhanov did not see this new philosophical movement in relation to the new situation in science which had been created by the discovery of sub-atomic particles.[2]

Of Plekhanov's conception of dialectic, Lenin, and later Soviet philosophy after him, complains that he pays insufficient attention to the law of the unity and conflict of opposites (or as Lenin calls it, the 'identity of opposites'), and that he altogether neglects the doctrine of dialectic as a theory of knowledge and a science of the laws of the objective world.[3] The bearing of all these objections will possibly become more intelligible in the course of the Second Part of this book.

In the field of historical materialism, Plekhanov is acknowledged to have rendered a major service in his theory of the rôle of the individual and the popular masses in history. He is also given full credit for having had a just appreciation, during his early days, of the great importance of revolutionary theory for the revolutionary movement. In his later menshevik period, however (after 1903), he showed himself strongly opposed to Lenin's doctrine of the importance of 'consciousness' (*soznatel'nost'*). In his article *The Working-*

---

[1] G. V. Plekhanov: *Protiv filosofskogo revizionizma*, pp. 178 f.
[2] *Cf.* V. A. Fomina: *Op. cit.*, pp. 660 f.   [3] *Ibid.*, pp. 669 f.

Class and the Social-Democratic Intelligentsia[1] he criticized Lenin's book *What is to be Done?* He thought that having once reached a certain stage of social development the workers would themselves arrive at socialism, whereas Lenin (and Stalin) maintained that the working-class was incapable of advancing in its spontaneous development beyond a trade-union state of consciousness, and that, on the contrary, socialist theory arises independently of the spontaneous workers' movement and must be imported into the latter.[2]

Plekhanov's conception of historical materialism has also been objected to on the ground that he presents it as an abstract sociology, too far divorced from concrete historical circumstances; he thinks of sociology as the 'algebra' and of history merely as the 'arithmetic' of social development.[3]

A crucial defect of Plekhanov's historical materialism is also discernible in the exaggerated significance he attaches to the geographical factor. The most extreme formulation of this 'geographical deviation' of his is to be found in his *Fundamental Problems of Marxism*:

'The peculiarities of the geographical environment determine the evolution of the forces of production, and this, in its turn, determines the development of economic forces and, therefore, the development of all the other social relations.'[4]

From this point of view Plekhanov eventually comes to regard Marxism as 'Darwinism in its application to social science',[5] *i.e.*, Marxism, for him, is the application to social development of the Darwinian theory of the adaptation of biological species to the conditions of the environment.

Plekhanov's 'geographical deviation' was also repudiated by Stalin in his *Dialectical and Historical Materialism*.

And finally, repeated criticism has been directed by later bolshevik authors against Plekhanov's well-known five-fold formulation of the materialist conception of history:

'If we wish to summarize the views of Marx and Engels on the relation between the famous "foundation" and the no less famous "superstructure", we shall get something like this:
1. The *state of the forces of production*;

[1] *Rabochy klass i sotsial-demokraticheskaya intelligentsiya.*
[2] *Cf.* V. A. Fomina: *Op. cit.*, pp. 682 f.
[3] Mitin-Razumovsky: *Dialektichesky i istorichesky materializm* (Dialectical and Historical Materialism), II, p. 33.
[4] G. V. Plekhanov: *Osnovnye problemy marxizma*, in *Sochineniya*, XVIII, p. 205; quoted in Fomina: *Op. cit.*, p. 672 (English, p. 34).
[5] G. V. Plekhanov: *K voprosu o razvitii . . .*, p. 200 n. (English version, Rothstein: *Op. cit.*, p. 244 n.).

2. *Economic relations* conditioned by these forces;
3. The *socio-political régime* erected upon a given economic foundation;
4. The *psychology of man in society*, determined in part directly by economic conditions, and in part by the whole socio-political régime erected upon the economic foundation;
5. *Various ideologies* reflecting this psychology.' [1]

This formula has been accused of exhibiting a certain degree of mechanism: the individual factors are piled on top of one another like separate storeys, but their unity and interaction are not brought out. The class-struggle and the dictatorship of the proletariat receive no mention whatsoever.[2] The concept of 'social psychology' could easily lead to idealistic notions, such as that of the 'unconscious', etc.[3]

As for the theory of the State, it is felt to be deplorable that even in the works of Plekhanov's 'Marxist' period, prior to 1903, there should be no clear account of the teaching of Marx and Engels on the dictatorship of the proletariat.[4]

The general estimate of Plekhanov current in the Stalinist era is typically expressed in the closing words of Fomina's essay on him, written in 1951:

'Plekhanov was not imbued with a creative Marxism. While clinging to the letter of a number of hackneyed formulae and isolated propositions of Marxism, he was unable to raise them to a new level . . . as was done by Lenin and Stalin, in accordance with the demands of the new epoch and the new conditions encountered in the class-struggle. Plekhanov showed himself unequal to mastering the new tasks incumbent on Marxist philosophy in the epoch of imperialism and proletarian revolution. The historic service rendered by Plekhanov during the best period of his career lay in fostering the spread of Marxism in Russia.' [5]

Stalin himself ranks Plekhanov among the 'peacetime' leaders, who though strong in theory are weak in matters of organization and practical work.[6]

Since then, however, the 'de-Stalinization' campaign appears to be opening the way to a new appreciation of Plekhanov. There are signs of this in V. A. Fomina's recently-published book *The Philosophical Opinions of G. V. Plekhanov* (1955),[7] and still more so in

---

[1] *Osnovnye problemy* . . ., p. 231 (*Fundamental Problems* . . ., p. 72; italics not in the English version).

[2] Mitin-Razumovsky: *Op. cit.*, pp. 36 f.

[3] V. A. Fomina: *Op. cit.*, p. 675.   [4] *Ibid.*, pp. 677 f.   [5] *Ibid.*, p. 703.

[6] J. V. Stalin: *Sochineniya*, IV, p. 314 (*Works*, IV, p. 326).

[7] V. A. Fomina: *Filosofskie vzglyady G. V. Plekhanova*, Moscow 1955.

a review of this work by M. Sidorov in *Kommunist*, April 1956.[1] Sidorov laments the fact that Plekhanov's philosophical legacy has not been sufficiently esteemed in recent years, that he has been more often criticized than studied; it is an error to regard him merely as a propagandist and popularizer of Marxism, for in his early days he was also of importance as a creative thinker.[2] Sidorov also seeks to correct a number of other ideas hitherto current about Plekhanov: in his early writings he did in fact defend the idea of the dictatorship of the proletariat; at the same period, too, he was already raising the question as to the proper relation between the working-class and the peasantry; and Lenin can be cited in disproof of the allegation that Plekhanov neglected to analyse the politico-social conditions giving rise to revisionism.

A revealing light is cast on the new valuation of Plekhanov by the remark with which Sidorov ends his review:

'It must also be pointed out that some of the faults of this book are attributable to the State Publishing House for Political Literature, which has held up the publication of V. Fomina's work for the past five years, has subjected it to repeated scrutiny, and has actually compelled the authoress into endorsing false opinions that were generally current at that time.'[3]

---

[1] M. Sidorov: *O filosofskom nasledii G. V. Plekhanova* (The Philosophical Legacy of G. V. Plekhanov), in *Kommunist*, 1956, 6, pp. 120–8.
[2] *Ibid.*, pp. 120, 124.   [3] *Ibid.*, p. 128.

CHAPTER V

Vladimir Ilyich Lenin

A S events proved in Russia, the doctrine which ultimately prevailed was not the revisionist Marxism of Struve, Berdyaev and
Bulgakov, which conceived it possible to detach the economic and
historical doctrine of Marxism from its philosophical foundations
and sought a new basis in the critical philosophy; nor was it the
menshevik Marxism of Plekhanov, which concentrated chiefly on the
scientific, deterministic and evolutionary side of Marxism; victory
went, rather, to a form of Marxism which relied to a greater extent
on its messianic element, which braced the wills of men to the highest
pitch, and was not content merely to propound a doctrine; a form of
Marxism mindful above all of the proletarian struggle to seize power,
in order to deliver it into the hands of a well-disciplined and strictly-
organized minority.

In its all-embracing, integral aspect this victorious form of Russian
Marxism was perfectly attuned to the all-or-nothing character of the
Russian people. A similar collectivist tendency had indeed already
emerged in the earlier phases of Russian philosophy, more especially
in the Slavophile doctrine of 'total knowledge' (tsel'noe znanie), which
exercised a great influence on the distinguished Russian philosopher
Vladimir Soloviev and still serves as an inspiration to the intellectual
endeavours of Russian religious philosophers at the present day.
Knowledge, according to this peculiarly Russian way of thinking, is
not the concern of individual, isolated human faculties, but of the
whole living man with all his powers of understanding, feeling and
will—a task incumbent on man as a whole, the entire personality.
Of all the schools of Russian Marxism, it was Bolshevism, with its
protest against the divorce of theory from revolutionary practice,
which came nearest to fulfilling this aspiration of the Russian mind.
It also satisfied the extremist character of the national outlook by its

demand for the immediate realization of socialism, without waiting till the development of society should have created the conditions for attaining it.

But that is neither the whole story nor a complete answer to the question why it was precisely the bolshevik form of Marxism that prevailed in Russia. The same conditions of social grievance coupled with well-meant efforts at relief had prevailed for centuries, and repeated attempts had been made to secure an immediate realization of the ideal of social justice, though admittedly without achieving any lasting result. Collectivist and maximalist schemes had also been proposed before, though hitherto without ever having found means for their practical attainment. Thus a new factor must have been present on this occasion to explain the success achieved, and this was obviously the powerful and extraordinary personality of Lenin, the man who by word and deed touched off the revolt of the anonymous masses, with an elemental violence which threw off the yoke of centuries, even though it was only to be forced into immediate submission to a new and still heavier yoke.

Lenin's personality and the course of his career have also had their effect at many points on the official philosophy of Soviet Russia. Many of the problems discussed in the dialectical materialism now exalted into an official state philosophy, can only be grasped in full when taken in conjunction with the life of Lenin and the battles which he and the Bolsheviks had to carry on against political and social tendencies of every conceivable kind.

1. LIFE AND PHILOSOPHICAL ACTIVITY

Vladimir Ilyich Ulyanov (Lenin)[1] was born in Simbirsk on the 10th (or, by the new reckoning, the 22nd) of April, 1870. His father, of petty bourgeois origin, was a school inspector, his mother the daughter of a doctor. In his early days Lenin had ample opportunities of living in the country among the peasants and so getting to know of their living conditions through first-hand observation. At that time he was very much influenced by his brother Alexander, who was executed for complicity in the murder of Tsar Alexander II (1st March 1881); as may be imagined, the event made a powerful impression upon the young Vladimir Ilyich. The death of his brother convinced him of the inadequacy and ineffectiveness of the campaign methods of the *Narodnichestvo*, which sought national emancipation by way of terrorism. 'No, we shall not take that road,' said Lenin, on learning that his brother had belonged to a terrorist organization.[2]

[1] For the life of Lenin *cf.* David Shub: *Lenin. A Biography*, New York 1949, pp. 438, and Gérard Walter: *Lénine*, Paris 1950, pp. 542.

[2] *Lenin: A Biography* (Marx-Engels-Lenin Institute), London n.d., p. 7.

After leaving high school in his native town (1887) he began studying law at the University of Kazan, but was expelled after a few months for having taken part in student disturbances and compelled to live at Kokushkino, a village near Kazan. In the years that followed he continued his law studies by himself, and finally qualified at the University of St. Petersburg in 1891. He only practised his profession for a very short time.

His first articles appeared about this time and were chiefly concerned with agrarian questions. Soon afterwards, however (1893), he embarked on revolutionary activity among the workers of St. Petersburg.

Lenin's philosophical career is divided by V. V. Adoratsky into three periods: the first embracing his early writings and continuing up to the Revolution of 1905, the second occupying the period from 1905 until the outbreak of the World War, and the third covering the years 1914–16.[1]

The first period is notable for his campaign against *Narodnichestvo* which he was one of the first among the Marxists to undertake. His pamphlet, *What the 'Friends of the People' Are and How they Fight the Social-Democrats*,[2] was written in 1894. It exhibits Lenin as already a Marxist, not only in economics, but also in philosophy. Already he shows a high regard for dialectic, contrasting the metaphysical method with the dialectical one. The former conceives of social conditions as an aggregate of mechanical linkages between social circumstances, whereas the latter sets out to comprehend the social structure in its totality as a living organism and endeavours to gain insight into its development.

Lenin's and Struve's[3] attacks on *Narodnichestvo* were both published in the same year. The coincidence of theme and timing is not, however, a sign of concerted action; Lenin, indeed, made clear from the beginning his opposition to the Marxist advocates of revisionism —unlike Plekhanov, who a year later was still hailing Struve as a valued ally against *Narodnichestvo*. In the autumn of 1894, Lenin, in a pamphlet characteristically entitled *Marxism as Reflected in Bourgeois Literature*, was accusing Struve of bourgeois philistinism. He later turned this into a longer work under the title *The Economic*

---

[1] V. V. Adoratsky : *O filosofskikh rabotakh Lenina* (On Lenin's Work as a Philosopher), Introduction to the First Edition in book form, edited by Adoratsky himself and V. G. Sorin, of Lenin's 'Philosophical Notebooks' (V. I. Lenin: *Filosofskie tetradi*, Moscow 1933), p. 8.

[2] V. I. Lenin: *Chto takoe 'druz'ya naroda' i kak oni voyuyut protiv sotsial-demokratov?*; *Sochineniya* (Works), I[4], pp. 111–313. (Excerpted at length in *LSW*, I and XI; the latter a fuller, and apparently revised, version.)

[3] *Cf. above*, p. 75.

Content of Narodism and the Criticism of it in Herr Struve's Book.[1] But the publication in which this was due to appear was burnt by the censor; only a few copies could be saved.[2] Thus at this time already, when all other Marxists were still making common cause with Struve, Lenin had entered upon his war on two fronts, against the *Narodniks* on the one hand, and on the other against the legal Marxists

'for whom the breach with *Narodnichestvo* represented the transition from bourgeois (or agrarian) socialism, not, as with us, to proletarian socialism, but to bourgeois liberalism'.[3]

In the spring of 1895 he set off for Western Europe where he established relations with the 'Liberation of Labour' group, but later returned to Russia, where he took a leading part in the founding and directing of the Petersburg Workers' Federation, the 'League of Struggle for the Emancipation of the Working Class'. He planned the publication of an illegal newspaper, the *Rabochaya Gazeta* (Workers' Gazette), but was arrested on 9th December 1895. Even in prison he continued his literary activities, producing a *Draft and Explanation of the Programme of the Social Democratic Party*,[4] and writing pamphlets and leaflets addressed to the workers, which were reproduced by friends on a clandestine printing press.

In February 1897 he was finally banished to Siberia, where he spent three years at the settlement of Shushenskoe on the Upper Yenisei. There he put the finishing touches to his large work *The Development of Capitalism in Russia*,[5] which had a powerful effect on the evolution of the socialist movement. While still in exile he also conducted a vigorous campaign against Economism. At his instigation the revolutionary groups in exile drew up a protest against the economist programme, *Credo*. In addition, Lenin was also working to perfect his philosophical training. Among the books he sent to his mother on returning from exile in 1900 the secret police noted works by Spinoza, Helvétius, Kant, Fichte, Schelling, Feuerbach, Lange and Plekhanov.[6]

---

[1] V. I. Lenin: *Ekonomicheskoe soderzhanie narodnichestva i kritika ego v knigo g. Struve*; *Sochineniya*, I⁴, pp. 315–484. (Excerpts in *LSW*, I and XI.)

[2] On its second printing in 1907 the work was again given the title of the original pamphlet: *Otrazhenie marxizma v burzhuaznoy literature* (Marxism as Reflected in Bourgeois Literature).

[3] V. I. Lenin: *Predislovie k sborniku 'Za 12 Let'* (Preface to 'Twelve Years', a collective work); *Sochineniya*, XIII⁴, p. 81.

[4] V. I. Lenin: *Proekt i obyasnenie programmy sotsial-demokraticheskoy partii*; *Sochineniya*, II⁴, pp. 77–104. (*LSW*, I, pp. 467–94).

[5] V. I. Lenin: *Razvitie kapitalizma v Rossii*; *Sochineniya* III⁴, pp. 1–535; also in numerous individual editions, *e.g.*, Moscow 1947. (Excerpts in *LSW*, I, pp. 219–385.)

[6] *Cf.* V. V. Adoratsky: *Op. cit.*, p. 13.

In the summer of the same year Lenin again returned to Western Europe in order to found there a newspaper which should serve as the organ of Russian socialism, and a germ-cell for the growth of the future party. He collaborated in this scheme with the émigrés Plekhanov, P. Axel'rod and V. Zasulich, and eventually published the paper in Munich. In the spring of 1902 the conduct of the paper was transferred to London. This journal, *Iskra* (The Spark), together with *Zarya* (Dawn), the theoretical mouthpiece of the Russian social-democrats, did in fact succeed in achieving its object, namely to prepare the way for the organization of the party. During the same period Lenin continued to wage energetic war on 'Economism' and the ideologists of the Second International (especially Bernstein) who were seeking to achieve socialism by peaceful methods. Lenin, on the contrary, was emphatic in stressing the doctrines of the class struggle, the dictatorship of the proletariat, and the necessity of creating a militant, strictly-disciplined party.

Lenin's ideas on the constitution of the party were explained in a work published in 1902, under the title which had already become traditional among revolutionaries when occasion arose for anyone to set forth his own ideas: *What is to be Done?*[1]

This work gives clear-cut expression to that activistic, anti-evolutionist, revolutionary spirit which Lenin instilled into the entire bolshevik movement, and which also set its stamp on Russian dialectical materialism. It may be seen how, in Lenin's person, the Marxism taken over from the West merges into unity with the Russian revolutionary tradition of Tkachev, Nechaev and the rest.

In *What is to be Done?* Lenin's chief emphasis is laid on the necessity for a policy of extreme centralization. Failing a small group of active and experienced leaders, exceptionally gifted professional revolutionaries operating as a disciplined unit in planning and action, there can be no hope, in modern society, of prosecuting a successful class-war. 'Give us an organization of revolutionaries, and we shall overturn the whole of Russia.' At the same time he lays down the principle which is to underlie the party organization: it is to consist of small but unified groups of experienced revolutionaries; only through the agency of these cells are the broadest contacts to be maintained thereafter throughout all levels of the proletariat and other classes of society.[2]

In a letter he elaborates on this proposed organization: a secret postal service must be set up, circular letters distributed, a watch must be kept for *agents provocateurs*, and so forth. It is a conspiratorial programme, such as had already been projected by many revolution-

[1] V. I. Lenin: *Chto delat'?*; *Sochineniya*, V[4], pp. 319–494 (*LSW*, II, pp. 27–192).

[2] *Op. cit.*, pp. 421 ff. (*LSW*, II, pp. 97 ff.).

aries before Lenin's day, though quite unlike that of the socialist parties at that time existing in the various countries of Western Europe.

No wonder, therefore, that Plekhanov, whose leanings were rather towards the Second International, should set himself against Lenin over this programme. 'In Lenin's views it is not Marxism we find, but —to use a term of ill-repute—peasant insurrectionism, a new version of the theory of heroes leading the rabble.' [1]

In the following year (1903), as we know already, the Second Congress of the Russian Social-Democratic Workers' Party took place in London, at which Lenin carried the day by a small majority. After the split between Bolsheviks and Mensheviks, Lenin became the leader of the bolshevik group. Together with Plekhanov, he had been nominated editor-in-chief of *Iskra*, the central organ of the Social-Democratic Party. But after Plekhanov had joined forces with the Mensheviks, Lenin resigned control of the paper, which became the mouthpiece of the menshevik group, and joined the Central Committee of the party, which consisted of bolshevik supporters. He wrote a pamphlet against the Mensheviks, *One Step Forward, Two Steps Back*.[2] It describes the differences of opinion which had arisen at the Second Party Congress. In December 1904 Lenin brought out a newspaper, *Vpered* (Forward), which after the Third, and (in the absence of the Mensheviks) exclusively bolshevik, Party Congress (April–May 1905) was renamed *Proletary* (The Proletarian).

In October 1905 Lenin returned to Russia, where he took a personal part in the revolutionary movement by means of his writings and public speeches, in which he campaigned against the Mensheviks in favour of an armed insurrection. He continued these activities into 1906, but was then obliged to take refuge in Finland, in order to escape the attentions of the police. Towards the end of 1907 he also had to leave Finland and emigrate abroad once more.

From thence he continued to direct the Bolshevik Party and to carry on revolutionary agitation. As leader of the party Lenin was against the so-called *Otzovisty* (derived from the verb *otozvat'*, to recall), who were demanding the recall of the social-democratic deputies from the Assembly (*Duma*) and were wholly opposed to the use of legal methods.[3] In opposition to them he pressed for participation in the *Duma*, for its use as a platform for agitation, for entry into

---

[1] In the above-mentioned article (p. 107), *Rabochy klass i sotsial-demokraticheskaya intelligentsiya* (The Working-Class and the Social-Democratic Intelligentsia). Quoted from M. B. Mitin: *Op. cit.*, p. 327.

[2] V. I. Lenin: *Shag vpered, dva shaga nazad*; *Sochineniya*, VII[4], pp. 185–392. Many individual editions. (*LSW*, II, pp. 407–466.)

[3] *Istoriya Vsesoyuznoy Kommunisticheskoy Partii* (*bol'shevikov*), *op. cit.*, pp. 130 ff., (*History of the C.P.S.U.(B)*, pp. 134 ff.).

the trade union organizations (*profsoyuzy*) and health insurance schemes, and for the publication of bolshevik newspapers and literature. On the other side he also entered the fray against those who objected to the simultaneous prosecution of illegal activity, the so-called *Likvidatory*, Mensheviks who numbered Trotsky among their supporters, and who were advocating the dissolution of the illegal party organizations. In 1910 Lenin founded a weekly, *Zvezda* (The Star), and in 1912 a daily paper, *Pravda*. In order to edit them more effectively he moved from Paris to Cracow. In the course of this period he took part as a Russian delegate in the international socialist congresses at Stuttgart (1907) and Copenhagen (1910), where he joined Rosa Luxemburg in endeavouring to form a revolutionary left wing.

In the earlier phase of his career Lenin had already shown an interest in philosophical problems. But he did not begin to study them seriously until after the 1905 Revolution, when empirio-criticism began to spread on a large scale among the Russian Marxists, especially after Bogdanov and his empirio-monism had appeared on the scene. Lenin joined Plekhanov in defending the purity of dialectical materialism. But Plekhanov's polemics gave him little satisfaction:

'Plekhanov is quite right in opposing them [the Machists] on principle, only he does not know how to, or he does not want to, or he is too lazy to say so *concretely* and in detail, simply and without any excessive frightening of the public by using philosophic subtleties. And whatever happens, I shall say this *in my own way*.' [1]

In fulfilment of this criticism there appeared in 1909 his well-known book *Materialism and Empirio-Criticism*.[2] Bolshevik writers have bestowed extravagant praise on this work. It has been described as 'an epoch-making work of genius';[3] Adoratsky considers it, together with Engels' *Anti-Dühring*, as the supreme philosophical achievement of Marxism.[4] The superiority of Lenin's critique to that of Plekhanov is discerned by these authors in the fact that, whereas the latter is content with a merely internal, theoretical critique, Lenin, without

---

[1] Letter to Gorky, 24th March 1908. V. I. Lenin: *Sochineniya*, XXXIV⁴, p. 338. (Translated in *Letters of Lenin* (ed. E. Hill and D. Mudie, London 1937), pp. 268–9.)

[2] V. I. Lenin: *Materializm i empiriokrititsizm; Sochineniya* XIV⁴, (English version: *Materialism and Empirio-Criticism. Critical Comments on a Reactionary Philosophy*, Moscow 1952. Also in *LSW*, XI, pp. 87–409. Cited hereafter as *ME*; page-numbers in brackets refer to the two English editions respectively).

[3] V. Vandek–V. Timosko: *Op. cit.*, p. 30.

[4] V. V. Adoratsky: *Op. cit.*, p. 14.

neglecting the immanent, logical aspect, prosecutes an inquiry into the social origins of this aberration, on the part of many Marxists, into the philosophy of empirio-criticism: since the 1905 revolution the bourgeoisie has realized that it is no longer possible to keep the masses under with the big stick, by main physical force. Even religion, which hitherto has at least served the purpose of keeping the masses in hand, and was, moreover, ideologically appropriate to the feudal system, has become increasingly ineffective and in need of modernization and adaptation to the new requirements of the age. Hence there has been need of a new ideological method of keeping the masses in check, and empirio-criticism has proved the very thing to come to the aid of the bourgeoisie and provide it, in Lenin's phrase, with 'an altogether new ideological cudgel, a spiritual cudgel'.[1]

The importance of Lenin's work rests upon its thoroughgoing treatment of two philosophical problems which were especially acute at this time. In the first place the development of modern philosophy subsequent to Marx and Engels had brought the problem of knowledge into the foreground of discussion. In the chapter on the various tendencies current among the Russian Marxists we have already noted the importance of Neo-Kantianism and empirio-criticism in this connection; Bogdanov's empirio-monism had likewise accorded a central position to the problem of knowledge, the problem of the relationship between sensations and reality. Hence it had become a matter of urgency to resolve the problem of knowledge in terms of dialectical materialism, in order to be able to maintain Marx's doctrine even in the field of philosophy.

Secondly, there was need to take account of the fact that since the time of Engels, the last great theorist of Marxism, the problem of matter had acquired fundamental significance in the natural sciences. In the days of Marx and Engels the concept of matter had appeared exceptionally simple, illuminating and clear. Science considered itself to have found, in the atom, the essential nature of matter. But the discovery of radio-activity in certain elements during the closing years of the previous century had compelled the assumption that the atom did not represent the utmost limit of divisibility in matter, but was a sort of miniature solar system, with negative electrons circulating about a positively charged nucleus. At this point the concept of the atom, previously so clear, had become distinctly obscure. Hence it came about that people had begun to talk of a crisis in physics, of the 'ruin' of the old principles (Henri Poincaré), of the 'dematerialization of the atom' and of the 'disappearance of matter'. (L. Houllevigue).[2]

[1] V. I. Lenin: *Nashi uprazdniteli* (Our Abolitionists); *Sochineniya*, XVII[4], p. 54; *cf.* V. Vandek–V. Timosko: *Op. cit.*, p. 33.

[2] *ME*, pp. 239 f., 245 (261, 267; 309, 315).

The result of this 'crisis' was that many physicists sought refuge in idealism (Poincaré: Everything that is not thought is sheer nothingness), and others again, notably many Russian Marxists, in empiriocriticism.

For this reason it is to these two problems above all that Lenin attaches great importance in his book. In the epistemological field, he proclaims the identity of dialectic with logic and theory of knowledge; expounds his own theory of knowledge, the so-called 'copy-theory', and the related problem of absolute and relative truth; criticizes Plekhanov's solution of the problem of knowledge (the 'hieroglyphic theory'); emphasizes the importance of practice as a criterion in epistemology; insists upon partisanship (*partiynost'*) in theorizing; and deals with the problem of space and time, the objectivity of which he defends against the idealists.

As regards the problem of matter, Lenin attempts to distinguish the philosophical and scientific conceptions of matter. The scientific concept is concerned with the physical structure of matter. For philosophy, on the other hand, matter is 'that which, acting upon our sense-organs, produces sensation; matter is the objective reality given to us in sensation'.[1] According to this view, 'the *sole* "property" of matter with whose recognition philosophical materialism is bound up is the property of *being an objective reality*, of existing outside our mind'.[2]

As can be seen here, and as we shall often have occasion to notice in what follows, Lenin conceives materialism to mean virtually the same thing as 'realism'; it is especially evident from the second quotation that matter, to him, simply means an objective reality independent of the knowing subject.

Materialism and Empirio-Criticism is the major philosophical product of the second period of Lenin's career as a thinker (1905–14). The outbreak of the World War marks the beginning of the third phase, the period of preparation for the Russian revolution (1914–16).

No sooner had war broken out than Lenin launched a furious attack on the socialist parties, who in each case supported the war along national lines. He prophesied the collapse of the Second International and began campaigning forthwith for the foundation of a new Third International. He also proclaimed the necessity of turning the imperialist war into a civil war.

Lenin took part, with a Russian delegation, in congresses of socialist opposition groups from the various belligerent countries, held at Zimmerwald (September 1915) and Kienthal (June 1916), at which he continually pressed for the foundation of a new International, though without making headway with this idea.

In Switzerland, during the war years, he also devoted himself to

[1] *ME*, p. 133 (145, 207).   [2] *ME*, p. 247 (269, 317).

an intensive study of philosophy. His notebooks are still extant, containing extracts from the works he read and the notes he made on them. Thus he made excerpts from Feuerbach's book on Leibniz, Hegel's *Logic, Philosophy of History* and *History of Philosophy*, Lassalle's essay on Heraclitus and finally Aristotle's *Metaphysics*. These notebooks were included after his death in the XIth and XIIth volumes of *Leninsky Sbornik* (Selected Writings) and issued in 1933 by V. V. Adoratsky and V. G. Sorin as an independent publication under the title of *Philosophical Notebooks*.[1] Lenin's whole manner and method of ordering this material makes it clear that he was getting it together to write a book, though he never succeeded in completing it.

The centre of his inquiries and interests was occupied by the problem of dialectic. Even in earlier years his attention had been particularly drawn to this topic, which he considered 'the essential element in Marxism'. And this explains his preoccupation with inquiry into the laws and essential nature of dialectic at this time of European conflict, in which his dialectical materialist outlook discerned the emergence of the contradictions inherent in the social structure of the bourgeois world, and perhaps also a presentiment of the impending proletarian revolution. The accelerated tempo, the abundance and pressure of incident, provided Lenin with rich sources for the study of those laws which govern the course of events.

The root of the matter is to be found in the 'unity of opposites', which he sees as the 'heart of the dialectic'.[2] The division of the one into its opposing elements, and the clash between them, is the immanent source of all activity and development. For all its abundance, complexity and variety, the objective world is none the less a unitary whole. Here we find in Lenin the same motive by which so many other Russian philosophers before him had already been drawn, with irresistible force, towards Hegel; the vision of the world as a universal web of connection and of a continuous process of development shaping its course through a clash of warring opposites. This notion comes out especially in a statement of the essential features of dialectic drawn up by Lenin in the course of his extracts from the chapter on the 'Absolute Idea' in Hegel's *Logic*. He there lists sixteen elements constituting the essence of dialectics:

"These elements may be represented in detail as follows:
(1) *Objectivity* of approach (no examples, no digressions, but the thing itself);

[1] V. I. Lenin: *Filosofskie tetradi*, Moscow 1933, pp. 475; last edition, Moscow 1947. German edition: W. I. Lenin: *Aus dem philosophischen Nachlass. Exzerpte und Randglossen*, Berlin 1949. Cited hereafter as *FT*; page numbers refer to the two last mentioned editions, those of the German in brackets. (*Cf.* also a brief excerpt, *On Dialectics*, in *LSW*, XI, pp. 81–5.)
[2] *FT*, p. 194 (145).

(2) the totality of this thing's manifold *interconnections* with other things;

(3) *development* of this thing (or phenomenon), its individual movement and life;

(4) the internally contradictory *tendencies* (*and* aspects) in the thing;

(5) the thing (phenomenon, etc.) as a sum and *unity of opposites*;

(6) *conflict* or disclosure of these opposites, contrariety of tendencies, etc.;

(7) union of analysis and synthesis—dissection of individual parts and the whole, the summation of all these parts together;

(8) the relationships of every thing (phenomenon, etc.) are not only manifold, but general, universal. Every thing (phenomenon, process, etc.) is bound up with *every other*;

(9) not only unity of opposites, but *transformation* of *every* degree, quality, feature, aspect, trait into *every* other (into its opposite);

(10) endless process of deducing new aspects, relationships, etc.;

(11) man engaged in endless process of deepening knowledge of things, phenomena, processes, etc., from appearance to essence, and from superficial to deeper layers of being;

(12) from coexistence to causality, and from one form of interconnection and reciprocal dependence to another, deeper, more general one;

(13) recapitulation of specific traits, properties, etc. on the lower level at the higher one, and

(14) apparent reversion to the old form (negation of the negation);

(15) conflict of content and form, and *vice versa*. Discarding of form, transformation of content;

(16) *transformation* of quantity into quality and *vice versa*. ((15) and (16) are *examples of* (9).) ' [1]

If this be compared with Engels' account of the 'materialist dialectic', it will be seen that Lenin is far more emphatic in putting the main accent on the unity of opposites, which Engels only mentions in second place, whereas the transition from quantity to quality, which Engels puts first of all, is here left to the last. And Lenin goes on to add, in doing so, that points 15 and 16 are merely examples of the unity of opposites.[2]

---

[1] *FT*, pp. 192 f. (144 ff.). The translation is based on the Russian original and departs on points of detail from the German version (Author's note).

[2] *FT*, p. 193 (146); *cf.* D. Chizhevsky: *Hegel bei den Slaven* (Hegel among the Slavs), Reichenberg 1934, p. 376.

Chizhevsky[1] remarks of this, that such a notion of dialectic on Lenin's part already implies an abandonment of naturalism. The 'unity of opposites' only makes sense when the question is no longer one of spatio-temporal being, but rather of an ideal reality. This argument seems, however, to presuppose an unduly atomistic conception of matter. If one ceases to think of the nature of matter in atomistic terms and bears in mind the knowledge that has been gained from atomic physics, it is not immediately obvious why there should be no possibility of a unity of opposites in the sphere of material, spatio-temporal being.

Dialectic, so understood, had a great attraction for Lenin, and enabled him to find much that was acceptable, and in many cases actually 'materialistic', in Hegel's 'logic'. Very typical in this respect is a note he appends in conclusion to his excerpts from Hegel's *Science of Logic*:

'It's a remarkable fact that the whole of the chapter on the "Absolute Idea" has hardly a word to say about God (except that a "divine" "concept" did slip out by chance on one occasion) and, moreover— mark *this*—that the chapter contains practically nothing specific about *idealism*, its main topic is the *dialectical method*. From start to finish the ultimate sum and substance of Hegel's logic is the *dialectical method*—that is extremely remarkable. One thing more: this predominantly idealist work of Hegel's has *very little* idealism, and a *great deal* of materialism about it. "Contradictory" maybe, but it is a fact.'[2]

That Lenin should think it possible to find even 'materialism' in Hegel is doubtless to be explained, on the one hand, from the fact that he interprets the dialectical method, the 'sum and substance of Hegel's logic', in terms of the unity of opposites, and could therefore transfer it without difficulty to matter and Nature; and on the other from the fact that, as we have already had occasion to observe, he frequently uses 'materialism' to mean 'realism', *i.e.*, the priority of the real in relation to the knowing subject. Now since Hegel's absolute idealism by no means resembles subjective idealism in attributing the external world to the activity of the individual knowing subject, but postulates, rather, a certain independence of the one from the other, the result is that Lenin, contrary to his expectations, finds much in Hegel to support his own realistic propensities.

All in all, Lenin has a very high opinion of Hegel's philosophy; its only failing lies, in his view, in its one-sidedness; it dwells too much on one particular aspect of knowledge:

'Philosophical idealism is *only* nonsense from the standpoint of

[1] D. Chizhevsky: *Op. cit.*, p. 376.
[2] *FT*, p. 205 (160); translated here from the Russian (Author's note).

crude, simple, metaphysical materialism. On the other hand, from the standpoint of *dialectical* materialism, philosophical idealism is a *one-sided*, exaggerated, extreme (Dietzgen) development (inflation, distension) of one of the features, sides, facets of knowledge into an absolute, *divorced* from matter, from Nature, apotheosized.' [1]

Even so, it was not through philosophical studies only that Lenin attempted to grasp the meaning of events during the years of the First World War. He also sought to prove on sociological grounds that the hour had come for the kindling of the proletarian revolution. After extensive preliminary studies and collection of material,[2] Lenin spent the months of January to June 1916 in Switzerland writing his book, *Imperialism, the Highest Stage of Capitalism*.[3] This treatise, which Soviet propaganda describes as a 'work of genius', a 'direct continuation and extension of Marx's *Capital*',[4] and which has achieved the highest publication-figures of all Lenin's works,[5] is in actual fact a work of little scientific originality. One of its main theories, the economic analysis of imperialism as originating primarily in the search for opportunities of investment, was taken over from an English author, J. A. Hobson. The theory of finance capital stems, on the other hand, from R. Hilferding, a German social-democrat. This does not, however, discourage Lenin from attacking both authors, in the course of the book, for their lack of radicalism.[6] Lenin endeavours in this book to prove that capitalism in its imperialist phase is already ripe for revolution. Whereas in the early stages of its career capitalism actually played a positive, 'progressive' part in stimulating economic development, in its imperialist phase it has become transformed into an inwardly rotten and parasitic economic system; hence imperialism is also the final phase of capitalism. The struggle for colonies, not only as new outlets for the export of commodities, but also more especially for the export of

[1] *FT*. p. 330 (288 f.); (*cf.* also *LSW*, XI, p. 84—cited here).
[2] These materials were published in 1939 as a comprehensive volume running to nearly 700 pages and containing extracts from 148 books and 232 articles. Cf. *BSE* (2nd edn.), XVII, p. 588.
[3] Reprinted as Vol. XXII of the *Collected Works* (English in *LSW*, V); the book originally bore the title 'Imperialism as the Latest Phase of Capitalism (A Popular Study)' and was first published in the middle of 1917 by the 'Parus' Press in Petrograd; the author's name was represented by both of Lenin's pseudonyms: 'N. Lenin (Vl. Ilyin)'.
[4] *BSE* (2nd edn.), XVII, pp. 587 f.
[5] Up to the beginning of 1954 it had gone through 174 editions in 42 languages, the total number of copies printed being 6,803,000! Cf. *Izdanie proizvedeniy Lenina v SSSR i za rubezhom* in *Kommunist*, 1954, 1, pp. 97–103.
[6] Cf. W. Theimer: *Der Marxismus*, Berne 1950, pp. 208 ff.

capital, leads to imperialist wars (among which Lenin included the First World War, then in progress) and hence to an internal weakening of the individual capitalist countries. This gives the proletariat the chance of severing the capitalist chain at its weakest link (law of the 'uneven politico-economic development of capitalism'). And that is precisely the task of the Russian proletariat at the present moment. Lenin went on to argue from this theory that socialism will triumph, not in every country simultaneously, but successively in one country after another. It was on this thesis that Stalin later founded his doctrine of the possibility of socialism in one country alone. And it is also appealed to today, chiefly for the purpose of depicting the slogan of 'peaceful coexistence' as a conclusion drawn from the inmost essence of Leninism.

On the outbreak of the February Revolution, despite the British and French refusal to allow Lenin the transit facilities to Russia which were nonetheless extended to other revolutionary émigrés, Germany permitted him to travel in a sealed train to Sweden, whence he returned to his native country. On the very day after his arrival (4th April 1917) he presented to a gathering of Bolsheviks his celebrated theses on *The Tasks of the Proletariat in the Present Revolution*.[1] In them we find once more a clear indication of Lenin's character, the personality which set its stamp on the movement he had created. He rejects the idea of collaboration with the provisional government, which other Marxists were anxious to promote under guise of 'defending the revolution', and demands the transference of power to the proletariat, nationalization of the land, reform of the party and the foundation of a Third International.

On this platform Lenin stood almost alone. Kamenev published the theses in *Pravda* as Lenin's own private opinions. But the latter immediately set to work, displaying ceaseless energy in making speeches, writing to his supporters and so on. At the All-Russian Conference of the Bolshevik Party which took place soon afterwards his theses were adopted, though Plekhanov ridiculed them with biting irony as fantastic ideas, completely out of touch with reality.[2]

In July a bolshevik uprising occurred in St. Petersburg. For three days the Bolsheviks were masters of the city, but the government succeeded in crushing the revolt. Lenin had to flee to Finland. There he wrote his book *State and Revolution*,[3] the contents of which are

[1] V. I. Lenin: *O zadachakh proletariata v dannoy revolyutsii; Sochineniya*, XXIV[4], pp. 1–7 (*LSW*, VI, pp. 21–6).

[2] *Cf.* M. B. Mitin: *Dialektichesky materializm* (Dialectical Materialism), Moscow 1933, p. 327.

[3] V. I. Lenin: *Gosudarstvo i revolyutsiya; Sochineniya*, XXV[4], pp. 353–462 (*LSW*, VII, pp. 3–112).

entirely directed against the Mensheviks, but which still retains its importance since it embodies Lenin's theory of the State.

The State, according to Lenin, is the product of the class struggle, the means whereby one class is able to dominate over the others. It is worth noting what Lenin says about the period of transition from capitalism to socialism: it is the period of the 'dictatorship of the proletariat'. This theory is taken to be the essence and foundation of Leninism. Pending the transition from capitalism to communism oppression is still necessary, except that now, in contrast to earlier times, it is the majority of those formerly oppressed who constrain the minority of former oppressors. The machinery of oppression, or in other words the State, is still needed, but only as a somewhat temporary arrangement, since oppression of the minority by the majority is assuredly a much easier, simpler, and more natural affair, which will not call for much bloodshed. Once the proletariat has finally achieved power the State will gradually disappear. Communism will remove the causes of crime from the world, and only a few individual crimes will then be possible, which the citizens themselves, once the State has disappeared, will be able to repress without difficulty.

Lenin distinguishes two phases in the development of communist society: during the first there is a common duty to work and each will be rewarded according to his labour; in the second, the phase of complete communism, in which there will be an unlimited abundance of goods, society will demand work from each in accordance with his capacities, while providing for each according to his needs. Stalin, in 1934, was still contrasting this as the 'communist' phase, with the first, which he described as 'socialist'.[1] The 12th article of the new constitution of 1936 adopted the first, or 'socialist' formulation.[2]

In the autumn Lenin returned illegally to St. Petersburg and preached the necessity for an armed insurrection. After its successful accomplishment in November 1917 he took over the office of Chair-

---

[1] *Otchetny doklad XVII syezdu partii o rabote TsK VKP(b), 26 yanvarya 1934 g.* (Report on the Work of the Central Committee to the XVIIth Congress of the C.P.S.U.(B), 26th January, 1934), in J. V. Stalin: *Voprosy leninizma*, 11th edn., Moscow 1947, p. 470. (*Cf.* J. Stalin: *Problems of Leninism*, Moscow 1947, p. 502.)

[2] V SSSR osushchestvlyaetsya printsip sotsializma: 'ot kazhdogo po ego sposobnosti, kazhdomu—po ego trudu.' (The principle applied in the U.S.S.R. is that of socialism: 'From each according to his ability, to each according to his work'. *Konstitutsiya (osnovnoy zakon) Soyuza Sovetskikh Sotsialisticheskikh Respublik*, Moscow 1950, p. 5 (English version: *Constitution (Fundamental Law) of the Union of Soviet Socialist Republics*, Moscow 1957, p. 18).)

man of the Council of People's Commissars and supreme control of the Party. The years that followed were filled with the most intensive labour. His health, however, was no longer of the best. On 25th May 1922 he suffered his first stroke, which he survived, together with a second. The third, on 21st January 1924, proved fatal. His funeral was of a splendour such as can scarcely ever have been seen in Russia before.

During the Revolution Lenin was far too busy to be able to give much time to his philosophical studies. But even at this period his interest in philosophical questions remained alive. In November 1920 he procured Labriola's *Historical Materialism* and *Letters to Sorel on Philosophy*. In June 1921 he provided himself with the Russian translations of Hegel's *Logic* and *Phenomenology of Spirit*. At about the same time he also wanted to read I. A. Ilyin's celebrated work, *The Philosophy of Hegel as an Exposition of the Concreteness of God and Man*.[1] It is said that he liked this book so much that he had the author released from jail. But despite this Ilyin was expelled from Russia in the following year.[2]

In forming a correct estimate of the importance which Lenin still continued to attach to philosophy at this period, account must be taken of his letter addressed to the editors of the Soviet philosophical periodical *Pod znamenem marxizma* (Under the Banner of Marxism) and published in that journal.[3] In it he dwells, precisely as he did in his writings of the 1914–16 period, on the great importance of dialectic. He calls on Soviet philosophers to study the Hegelian dialectic, since this has become necessary owing to the revolution which has lately been taking place in the field of natural science. Failing a profound philosophical development of Hegelian dialectics, the revolution in science will lead to idealism and clericalism. Only a materialistic interpretation of the Hegelian dialectic can be in a position to give an answer to the problems thrown up by contemporary science. In Lenin's view the editors and contributors of the journal should be a kind of 'Society of Materialist Friends of Hegelian Dialectics'.[4]

---

[1] *Filosofiya Hegelya kak uchenie o konkratnosti Boga i cheloveka*, 2 vols., Moscow 1918. D. Chizhevsky: *Op. cit.*, p. 367, describes this book as 'the best and most profound account of Hegel in Russian (and one of the best in any) literature'. A shortened German version appeared in Berne in 1946: I. Ilyin: *Die Philosophie Hegels als kontemplative Gotteslehre*.

[2] *Krasny ogonek*, 1929; D. Chizhevsky: *Op. cit.*, p. 374, n. 15.

[3] V. I. Lenin: *O znachenii voinstvuyushchego materializma* (On the Significance of Militant Materialism), *Sochineniya*, XXXIII[4], pp. 201–10 (*LSW*, XI, pp. 71–80).

[4] *Ibid.*, p. 187 (*LSW*, XI, p. 78).

2. LENINISM

The problem as to what Leninism consists in has been answered in a variety of ways.

Ryazanov sees the difference between Marxism and Leninism in the fact that the one is theory, the other practice.

Others see nothing in Leninism beyond an adaptation of Marxism to the particular circumstances prevailing in Russia.

Zinoviev finds the key to Leninism in the significance it attaches to the agrarian question; in his view Leninism is that theory of proletarian revolution which has evolved directly from a country in which the peasant element is the dominating one.[1]

Preobrazhensky distinguishes, within Marxism, between unchanging elements, those which have to be developed and completed, and ultimately those which have to be replaced by new and different elements. Its methodology, *i.e.*, dialectical materialism, constitutes, however, an essential feature under the first category, and the identity of this dialectical materialism in Lenin and Marx betokens the basic theoretical identity of Leninism and Marxism.

Bukharin, finally, makes a similar distinction between the aggregate of specific ideas, theses, etc., and the method whereby this aggregate is built up and analysed. If the term 'Marxism' is taken to denote, not the corpus of ideas to be found in Marx, but the methodology peculiar to Marxism, it follows that Leninism is not something which alters or disturbs the methodology of Marxian doctrine. On the contrary, Leninism in this sense represents a complete return to the Marxism formulated by Marx and Engels themselves.[2]

It will be clear from this that orthodox Bolshevism was unable to tolerate a view of Leninism which would depict it as a correction of Marxism. It was therefore necessary to find a definition which would safeguard both Lenin's Marxist orthodoxy and the originality of his work. In Stalin's opinion, Leninism is to be regarded as a further development of Marxism in all its constituent elements, philosophical, economic and so forth.

'Leninism is Marxism of the era of imperialism and of the proletarian revolution. To be more exact, Leninism is the theory and tactics of the proletarian revolution in general, the theory and tactics of the dictatorship of the proletariat in particular. . . . That is why Leninism is the further development of Marxism.'[3]

---

[1] *Cf.* M. B. Mitin: *Op. cit.*, p. 34.

[2] N. Y. Bukharin: *Ataka*, Moscow 1924, p. 225; *cf.*, M. B. Mitin: *Op. cit.*, p. 310.

[3] J. V. Stalin: *Voprosy leninizma*, 11th edn., Moscow 1947, p. 2 (English in *Problems of Leninism*, 11th edn., p. 14, *Works*, VI, p. 73).

In Stalin's view, however, such a further development of Marxism in the field of historical materialism (the doctrines of State and revolution, of the dictatorship of the proletariat, of Soviet structure, etc.), would not have been possible without a simultaneous extension and enlargement of Marxist methodology, *i.e.*, of dialectical materialism.[1]

Hence it was also necessary for Bolshevism to discover in Leninism a further development of the philosophy of dialectical materialism *as well*, and an adaptation of this to the new situation.

Lenin's contribution to the further progress of Marxist philosophy is held to lie chiefly in the following points: his deepening of the concept of matter, his establishment of the 'copy-theory', and his emphasis on the necessity of uniting theory and practice and on partisanship in philosophy. To this one might add that Lenin's outspoken enthusiasm for dialectic (interpreted primarily as a theory of the conflict of opposites), together with his great interest in Hegel generally, may well be responsible for the fact that dialectical materialism subsequently gained the upper hand over mechanism in the Soviet Union.[2]

[1] *Cf.* M. B. Mitin: *Op. cit.*, pp. 311 f.   [2] *Cf.* Ch. VI, below.

CHAPTER VI

Philosophical Developments in the U.S.S.R. prior to 1931

L ENINIST philosophy, after the victory of the Bolshevik Party, was not at first regarded as the only permissible view. In the early years of the Revolution considerable freedom did in fact prevail in the philosophical field, so that not only materialist philosophy, but a variety of idealist systems were put forward and allowed to be taught. It was not until the autumn of 1921 that the majority of the older professors of philosophy were removed from the universities.[1]

Even among the supporters of the Bolshevik Party, Lenin's dialectical materialism was not universally followed. The reason for this appears to have been that dialectical materialism was a platform on which revolutionaries of varying philosophical tendencies could find common ground. The two ingredients of this philosophy, materialism and dialectic, appealed equally to the exponents of a crude materialism—which had remained active in Russia since the time of the nihilists, especially among the revolutionaries, who considered it to be the only revolutionary and progressive doctrine—and also to those who were more inclined to speculation. To the latter it was the element of dialectic embodied in dialectical materialism which appeared to promise an advance in the direction of a true philosophy, which should lead to the downfall of crude popular materialism. Hence, at a time which required the concentration of all energies on

[1] Many of them, together with other professors—in all more than 100 intellectuals from various Russian cities—were arrested in August 1922 and exiled a few months later. Included among them were the philosophers S. Bulgakov, N. Berdyaev, S. Frank, I. Ilyin, L. Karsavin, N. Lossky and I. Lapshin. *Cf.* N. Lossky: *Filosofiya i psikhologiya v SSSR* (Philosophy and Psychology in the USSR) in *Sovremennyya Zapiski*, LXIX (1939), pp. 364f.

the struggle for power, the Bolshevik Party was able to enlist adherents of very diverse schools of thought in the common task. Once the revolution was over, however, and the transition to positive work of reconstruction had begun, differences of opinion on fundamental questions immediately came to light. Hence the remarkable way in which economic and political controversies in Soviet Russia have so frequently led to discussions on general questions of philosophy.[1]

Adherents of vulgar materialism were so numerous among the supporters of the Bolshevik Party, that in the early years after the Revolution this type of materialism became, as it had already done amongst the Russian nihilists of 1860–80, the dominating philosophy, and was reckoned the true philosophy of the Revolution. These materialists held that all higher-order phenomena can be accounted for in terms of lower-order phenomena: the organic being reducible to the chemical, the chemical to the physical, and the latter eventually to mechanical processes. Hence everything in the world, including the phenomena of consciousness and the social order, was explained in purely mechanistic terms.

Mention should here be made of a philosophical tendency, said by A. Stolyarov[2] to have been at one time 'fairly widespread among students, especially the younger party members'—the so-called theory of 'Enchmenism'. Emmanuel Enchmen, the founder of the school, preached a crude form of materialism, believing that only the tangible was real. Though acknowledging that he himself received mental impressions, he did not admit their occurrence in other people, since in their case he only perceived expressions or physical correlatives of mental phenomena (*e.g.* the facial expressions of a laughing or weeping man).[3] Enchmenism was vehemently assailed by Bukharin in the collective work *Ataka*.

About 1925, popular materialism gave place to the mechanist school, with whom we shall have to deal in greater detail.

In the early years after the Revolution there were many bolshevik theorists to whom even materialism of this sort was uncongenial, and who denied that philosophy had any title to existence whatever. The best known of them is O. Minin, whose article, *Overboard with Philosophy*, written in 1922, defends this position as follows:

'Both V. I. Lenin, and Plekhanov also, employ old-fashioned terms

[1] *Cf.* J. Danzas: *Sous le drapeau du marxisme* in *La Vie Intellectuelle*, 1936, pp. 422–45.

[2] A. Stolyarov: *Dialektichesky materializm i mekhanisty. Nashi filosofskie raznoglasiya* (Dialectical Materialism and the Mechanists. Our Philosophical Differences), Leningrad 1930, p. 28.

[3] *Ibid.*

such as "the philosophy of Marxism", "the philosophical implications of the natural sciences" and so forth, but these terms as used by Lenin and Plekhanov are merely slips of the pen and nothing more. In fitting out and trimming the ship of science we must take care to throw, not only religion, but also the whole of philosophy overboard.'[1]

This proposal was commended for its boldness by V. Rozhitsyn, in the Bulletin of the Central Committee of the Ukrainian Communist Party, and described as the 'true verdict of contemporary revolutionary Marxism'.[2]

The exponents of this popular materialism displayed the same contempt for aesthetic values as was typical of the Russian nihilists of 1860–80. Their attitude towards art was a utilitarian one, it being considered either as a 'means for the socialization of emotion' (Bukharin), or, to borrow a phrase from L. Tolstoy, as 'a means to the emotional infection of humanity'.[3]

This popular and mechanistic materialism, whose leading spirits were I. I. Stepanov and A. K. Timiryazev (son of the celebrated Russian physiologist K. A. Timiryazev) was offset, around 1925, by a strenuous reaction among the supporters of dialectical materialism, under the leadership of A. M. Deborin.

The controversy was occasioned, on the one side, by various publications on the part of Stepanov, calling for a revision of Engels' materialism and dialectics in the light of the electron theory; and on the other by the appearance (in 1925) of Engels' hitherto unpublished work *Dialectics of Nature*, which heartened the supporters of dialectical materialism.[4] Prokofiev praises the philosophical quality of this work on the ground that, unlike Engels' other philosophical writings, such as *Ludwig Feuerbach* and *Anti-Dühring*, it breathes the true spirit of Hegelianism.[5]

The dialecticians took yet further courage from the first publication, in 1929, of Lenin's *Philosophical Notebooks*,[6] which likewise represent an advance, philosophically speaking, on his *Materialism*

[1] O. Minin: *Filosofiyu za bort* in *Pod znamenem marxizma*, 1922, No. 11–12; quoted in P. Vostokov: *La philosophie russe durant la période post-révolutionnaire*, in *Le Monde Slave*, 1932, No. 11, p. 289.

[2] P. Vostokov: *Op. cit.*, p. 289.

[3] René Fülop-Miller: *The Mind and Face of Bolshevism*, London and New York 1927, p. 61.

[4] *Cf.* A. M. Deborin: *Dialektika i estestvoznanie* (Dialectics and Natural Science), Moscow–Leningrad 1930, pp. iii ff.

[5] P. Prokofiev: *Krizis sovetskoy filosofii* (The Crisis in Soviet Philosophy), in *Sovremennyya Zapiski*, XLIII (1930), p. 484; *cf.* also N. Lossky: *Op. cit.*, p. 366.

[6] *Cf.* above, p. 119.

and Empirio-Criticism and show how thoroughly he had grasped the nature of dialectic.[1]

The conflict reached a crucial stage around 1929. The main question at issue was as follows: Can phenomena of higher order (*e.g.* living organisms) be deduced from those of lower order (inorganic matter) or not? This led to a metaphysical problem: Can quality be completely deduced from quantity or not? The mechanists affirmed that it could, whereas the dialecticians denied it.

Deborin and the dialectical materialists attached great importance to the problem of quality:

'Either there is an absolute identity between inorganic and organic matter, and organic matter can be completely derived from the inorganic, in which case there is no sense at all in speaking of a transformation of the inorganic into the organic; or else, besides the unity of inorganic and organic, there is also a difference between them, in which case organic matter represents something qualitatively and specifically different from the inorganic.' [2]

The philosophical explanation of the appearance of new qualities was seen in the transformation, already asserted by Hegel, of quantitative changes into qualitative ones: all change and development operates initially in the direction of mere quantitative change; but once this has reached a certain stage, dependent on the nature of the thing concerned, and is continued beyond this limit, it no longer results in merely quantitative change; instead, by a sudden leap, a qualitative change takes place, and something new emerges. This transformation of quantity into quality, or more precisely, the transition from quantitative change into qualitative, was regarded as the essence of the dialectic. Such a 'leap' takes place in the transition from the inorganic to the organic, with the emergence of life, and also in the transition from organic matter to consciousness. A more detailed treatment of the laws of the materialist dialectic, which must be postponed to Part Two, will afford us a closer acquaintance with the significance of this train of thought.

The mechanists objected to this theory of the Deborinists on the ground that the dialectic is here employed in an abstract and *a priori* fashion. They emphasized, further, that the dialectic must be derived from Nature, that it must be sought as an outcome of exact scientific investigation, though they were strongly against the idea of using the dialectic as a method of discovery, by the application of already established general laws to new fields of inquiry.

Deborin, on the other hand, appealed to Engels and Lenin in support of his view that the dialectic must also serve as a method of

[1] P. Prokofiev: *Op. cit.*, pp. 478 and 485.
[2] A. M. Deborin: *Op. cit.*, p. 143.

discovery, which should govern our scientific inquiries.[1] This appeal did not, however, prevent the mechanists from accusing him of adopting a false methodology, which condemned the dialectic to idleness.

In general the mechanists objected to the Deborinists that their dialectic was idealist and Hegelian in character. A. Varyash, a Hungarian communist who emigrated to Russia after the suppression of the Hungarian Revolution, and who worked there at the Timiryazev Institute and as a joint editor of mechanistic publications, makes this point explicitly:

'We completely reject any comparison of the dialectic of Marx, Engels and Lenin with that of Deborin, which is nothing but a revival of Hegel's idealist dialectic.' [2]

The conflict was carried on with great intensity on both sides. For a time, fortune favoured the Deborinists. They gained control of the philosophical section of the State Printing House (*Gosizdat*), and were able, in consequence, to impose their censorship on the writings of their mechanist opponents. In 1929, moreover, the Timiryazev Scientific Institute was reorganized, and the Deborinist Y. Y. Agol appointed as its Commissar.

The Second Congress of the Marxist-Leninist Institutes of Science was held in April of the same year. Deborin emerged completely victorious. The Report of the Congress says of the mechanists:

'This movement is blatantly inconsistent with the tenets of Marxist-Leninist philosophy.' [3]

By the middle of 1929 the Deborinists had gained control of all philosophical posts in the U.S.S.R. and were also engaged upon the philosophical articles in the *Great Soviet Encyclopaedia*.

But this success was short-lived, for shortly after the triumph of the Deborinists over the mechanists, the positions of the victors began to come under fire from a third quarter. This was the work of a triumvirate, two of them, M. Mitin and P. Yudin, being directors of the communist cell in the Moscow Institute of Red Professors;[4] V. Ral'tsevich was the third member of the party.

The weapon against Deborin was put into their hands by Stalin,

---

[1] A. M. Deborin: *Op cit.*, pp. 350 f.
[2] P. Vostokov: *Op. cit.*, p. 295.   [3] *Ibid.*, p. 296.
[4] The 'Institute of Red Professors' (*Institut Krasnoy Professury*) was an institute of higher learning founded in 1921 with the object of providing Marxist-trained recruits for scientific research and teaching in senior schools. This Institute was regarded as the chief nursery for communist intellectuals.

in a speech delivered on 27th December, 1929, to the Conference of Marxist Students of the Agrarian Question. In this speech Stalin was severely critical of a number of theories at that time current in Soviet cultural life, for instance the mechanist theories of 'equilibrium' and '*samotek*', of which more will be said later, and complained of the theoreticians generally that theory had not kept pace with the practical and economic development of the Soviet Union. This was said to have led to a division between theory and practice, whereas theory must not only keep pace with practical work, but must keep ahead of it, so as to be able to equip the practical workers with weapons for their fight for the victory of socialism.[1]

Deborin's opponents made use of this speech in order to undermine his dominant position. They blamed him for having given the Party inadequate support in the fight against 'Rightist deviationism'; even after the latter had already been suppressed politically by the Party he had set about criticizing its philosophical foundation, mechanism, from a wholly abstract point of view.[2] He had separated theory from practice, and his version of the dialectic was wholly formalist in character. Moreover, he had not heeded Lenin's call for a campaign against religion.[3]

They were not, however, able to encompass their object of destroying Deborin right away. In the Joint Session of the Philosophical Institute of the Communist Academy and the Moscow Section of the Society of Militant Materialists, which took place on 24th April 1930, Deborin was still able to maintain his views. The report adopted by the participants still contains outspoken expressions of Deborinist lines of thought: it is asserted, against the mechanists, that the latest findings of the natural sciences transcend the existing boundaries of formal logic and the mechanist world-view. At the same time Deborin attempted to associate his battle against mechanism with the party campaign against 'Rightist deviationism' already in progress, mechanism being regarded as the theoretical foundation of the latter.

Nevertheless Deborin already appears to have been driven on to the defensive. Even at this stage the Deborinists find themselves compelled to reckon with the accusations lately levelled against them. Thus in answer to complaints of the idleness of philosophical inquiry the report recommends that every professor of philosophy should also cultivate some field within the special sciences. In answer

---

[1] J. Stalin: *Voprosy leninizma*, 11th edn., Moscow 1947, p. 275 (*Problems of Leninism*, 11th edn., p. 301).

[2] *Cf.* M. B. Mitin: *Op. cit.*, p. 347; as to how far mechanism is to be regarded as the philosophical basis of Rightist deviationism, more will be said later on.

[3] *Cf.* P. Vostokov: *Op. cit.*, p. 297.

to the objection that the Deborinist dialectic is formal in character, the report observes:

'We are strongly opposed to that conception of dialectic which would transform it into a lifeless schema, a collection of empty formulae having no connection with any concrete content and developing abstractly of its own accord without reflecting conditions in the material world.' [1]

The Deborinists also promise to take part in the anti-religious campaign. The only point on which they refuse to give in is on the condemnation of Plekhanov and his philosophical writings, which they still continue to value highly, as before.

The opposition to Deborin increased in strength in the months that followed. In May 1930, Yudin, in an article published in the Journal of the Collective of the Institute of Red Professors, complained particularly of Deborin that his theoretical work had lately held itself aloof from the great problems which the Party was called upon to solve. In the following month, on 7th June, 1930, *Pravda* published an article, *The New Problems of Marxist-Leninist Philosophy*, written by the above-mentioned triumvirate which, as Deborin put it, was struggling for power against him.

In defending themselves the Deborinists sought to hold fast to a number of positions which, by this time, had already become untenable in Russia. In May, the magazine *Pod znamenem marxizma* (Under the Banner of Marxism), published an article by 'ten authors', *The War on Two Fronts*. The work of philosophy, in their view, must continue to preserve its special character, and cannot be replaced by commonplaces such as 'socialist construction':

'The working-out of the materialist dialectic is, in fact, the chief service called for *from philosophy* by the class-struggle and the construction of socialism.' [2]

By September 1930, however, the opposition to Deborin had grown so strong that it had become practically impossible for him to continue the direction of the journal *Pod znamenem marxizma* any longer. He was not in fact removed from his post, but his activities were brought to an end, in that publication of the paper was suspended for the time being.

Finally, at the end of 1930, the whole affair reached a critical stage. In a discourse delivered on 9th December to the Bureau of the Cell of the Institute of Red Professors, Stalin gave vent to a strongly anti-Deborinist point of view. He described Deborin's doctrine as a form of 'menshevizing idealism', and called for a 'war on two fronts' in philosophy also, just like that which the Party was already con-

[1] *Cf.* P. Vostokov: *Op cit.*, p. 299.   [2] *Ibid.*, p. 300.

ducting against Leftist and Rightist deviation in the social and political sphere.

The effect of the interview was that the Cell immediately changed its attitude. Whereas, in a resolution adopted on 10th October, it had still maintained that recent philosophical developments in the Soviet Union had conformed, by and large, to the indications given by Lenin, it now confessed that the philosophical movement (of Deborinism) had been inadequately characterized as a 'formalist tendency', and represented, rather, a real idealist revision of Marxism.[1]

In this fashion the formal condemnation of Deborin was already being set afoot by the authority of the Party itself. On 25th January, 1931, in its resolution concerning the journal *Pod znamenem marxizma*, the Central Committee of the Party condemned both mechanism and Deborinism, and demanded of the new philosophical leadership a war on two fronts in philosophy also:

'In the field of philosophy the journal must wage a relentless struggle on two fronts: against the mechanist revision of Marxism, as the chief danger at the present time, and also against the idealist distortion of Marxism on the part of comrades Deborin, Karev, Sten and others.' [2]

The Deborinists were accused, above all, of having separated philosophy from politics, theory from practice. They were rebuked for not having understood that Leninism represents a new epoch in philosophy, a reproach directed at their high opinion of Plekhanov. All the same it is noteworthy that it was mechanism which was described as the 'chief danger' at the present time.

In consequence of this condemnation Deborin was removed from his position as responsible editor of the journal, though he remained on the board. Sten was completely excluded, Mitin and Yudin taking his place, of whom Mitin occupied the commanding position.

After the condemnation of the Deborinists the Soviet newspapers and journals also began to publish 'disclosures' about Deborin. He had taken Plekhanov, the theoretician, as a complement to Lenin, the man of action; he had constituted himself the uncritical apologist of Plekhanov's entire *œuvre*; he had taken over, lock, stock and barrel, the Hegelian dialectic; under his direction the Hegelianizing of Marxism had reached such a point that for three or four years the whole work of the philosophical section of the Institute of Red Professors had been devoted to Hegel's logic, and the last three or four courses had given no opportunity even for making acquaintance with the work of Feuerbach, let alone that of Marx and Engels. In conclusion, Deborin had failed to inquire into the social roots of the various philosophical systems.[3]

[1] *Pravda*, 26th Jan. 1931.   [2] *Ibid.*   [3] *Cf.* P. Vostokov: *Op. cit.*, p. 303.

It is typical of the intellectual atmosphere in which theoretical work is carried on in the Soviet Union, that in face of his condemnation by the highest authorities in the Party, Deborin made unconditional surrender. After a report of Mitin's to the Communist Academy, he made open acknowledgement of his lapses in the discussion, admitted that he had been too much addicted to menshevizing idealism and the separation of theory and practice, and publicly thanked the Central Committee 'and especially the leader of our Party, Comrade Stalin', for having 'restrained him just in time'.[1]

[1] *Cf.* N. Lossky: *Op. cit.*, p. 369.

CHAPTER VII

Mechanism

HAVING depicted the struggle between the two philosophical movements of mechanism and Deborinism, and their supercession by a *tertius gaudens*, we must now look more closely at their respective doctrinal contents.

As we have seen, Deborin thought to gain an advantage in his struggle with mechanism by representing it as the theoretical basis of that Rightist deviationism against which the Party, under Stalin's direction, was already carrying on an energetic campaign; he therefore endeavoured to couple his philosophical hostility towards mechanism with the Party's political struggle against 'Rightist deviationism'.

The expected success eluded him. Deborin had improvidently overlooked the fact that the Party was waging war, not only against Rightist deviation, but also against Trotsky, whose position was referred to as 'Leftist deviationism', and that hence it was possible for a given philosophical tendency to be linked with this other aberration, as its philosophical basis. He had thereby himself delivered the weapon into the hands of his opponents. Mitin, astutely making use of the conflict between Deborin and the mechanists, described mechanism as the philosophical basis of Rightist deviationism, and Deborin's 'menshevizing idealism' as the corresponding foundation of Leftist deviation. And since the Party was waging war 'on two fronts' against both aberrations, he set himself accordingly to waging a two-front war in philosophy against both mechanism and menshevizing idealism.

But though mechanism may be described as the theoretical foundation of Rightist deviation, and menshevizing idealism that of the Left, this is not to be regarded as an exclusive alternative (Mitin himself gives warning of this), as though Rightist deviation could only imply mechanism, and Leftist only idealism, without admixture of mechanism. Trotskyism, for example, which in politics ranks as a Leftist deviation, is 'steeped through and through' from the philosophical point of view 'with the commonest and most vulgar form of mechanism'.[1]

For contemporary Soviet philosophy, however, the essentials of a philosophical theory are only reckoned to have been grasped when its social and political roots have been exposed. Hence it was also incumbent on Mitin to point to the social origins of both aberrations. These, he considers, may be ascribed to the fact that even after the victory of the proletariat and the establishment of its dictatorship, many bourgeois views and habits had survived among the people without being given up immediately. Moreover the proletariat in its struggle for the revolution had been joined by numerous elements stemming from the bourgeoisie, who had not yet been able to emancipate themselves from their old opinions and attitudes. All this was bound sooner or later to lead to differences of opinion and deviations to Right or Left.

These two aberrations therefore give expression to the modes of thought of petty bourgeois elements, with this difference, however, that the Rightist deviation primarily exhibits the mentality of the bourgeois peasantry (*kulaki*), whereas the Leftist outlook is that of the ruined capitalist class, the petty bourgeois city-dweller.[2]

1. GENERAL CHARACTER OF MECHANISM

The primary characteristic of mechanism is its fundamentally hostile attitude towards philosophy, which, as in Minin's case, it often denies any title to existence. Hence the mechanists stand accused, in contemporary dialectical materialism, of a certain 'positivism', inasmuch as they deny the right to existence of any special discipline of philosophy over and above the positive sciences and refuse to recognize the dialectic (*i.e.*, philosophy) as a special science alongside the positive sciences. Stepanov's formula to this effect has become famous:

'The Marxist recognizes no special field of "philosophical activity" distinct from that of science; for the Marxist, materialist philosophy consists in the latest and most general findings of modern science.'[3]

'Does dialectic exist as a science on its own account, or is it merely a method?'—so the mechanists ask, and answer the question to the

[1] M. B. Mitin: *Op. cit.*, p. 236. [2] *Ibid.*, pp. 238 f.
[3] I. I. Stepanov: *Istorichesky materializm i sovremennoe estestvoznanie* (Historical Materialism and Modern Natural Science), 1927, p. 57; *cf.* M. B. Mitin: *Op. cit.*, p. 254.

disadvantage of dialectic. To profess to see in dialectic anything more than a method, to speak of the dialectic as present in reality, in Nature itself, to conceive of it as an independent science alongside the positive sciences, would amount, in their view, to scholasticism, logistic or even 'mysticism'. 'Science is itself philosophy' according to the mechanists, and in so saying they follow Minin's example.

In this positivism of theirs they come close to the position of certain theorists of the Second International, such as Adler, for whom Marxism is nothing else but a positive science, with no attached philosophy of its own; or Bernstein, Vorländer, and in Russia, Struve, whose view is that Marxism can be combined with any desired philosophy—in their case, for example, with Neo-Kantianism.

As against this mechanistic 'positivism', Mitin, the champion of Leninist orthodoxy, has pointed with some justice to the untenability of a position which seeks to deny philosophy any right to existence: no science is possible without a philosophical foundation. Every science must render an account of that which it investigates, whether it be a world independent of thought, or itself a product of thinking. Moreover, there can be no such thing as a positive science without a general theory of scientific thought or a grounding and establishment of its principles; for without thought it is impossible even to connect two facts of positive experience one with another, let alone to discover the permanent laws operative in Nature and society. No science can dispense with a clear answer to the question as to whether the world is knowable.[1]

In confirmation of his view Mitin cites a passage from Engels, drawn, not surprisingly, from the *Dialectics of Nature* (his maturest philosophical work, whereas elsewhere, for instance at one point in the *Anti-Dühring*, he inclines towards a form of positivism):[2]

'Natural scientists believe that they free themselves from philosophy by ignoring it or abusing it. They cannot, however, make any headway without thought, and for thought they need thought determinations. . . . Hence they are no less in bondage to philosophy, but unfortunately in most cases to the worst philosophy, and those who abuse philosophy most are slaves to precisely the worst vulgarized relics of the worst philosophies.'[3]

In like fashion Mitin also invokes the authority of Lenin on his behalf, appealing to that thesis 'which is binding on any party member who concerns himself with the study of natural science':[4]

[1] M. B. Mitin: *Op. cit.*, p. 255.
[2] *Cf.* T. G. Masaryk: *Die philosophischen und sociologischen Grundlagen des Marxismus*, Vienna 1899, p. 15.
[3] F. Engels: *Dialectics of Nature*, Moscow–London 1953–4, p. 279.
[4] M. B. Mitin: *Op. cit.*, p. 256.

'Unless it stands on a solid philosophical ground no natural science and no materialism can hold its own in the struggle against the onslaught of bourgeois ideas and the restoration of the bourgeois world-outlook. In order to hold his own in this struggle and to carry it to a victorious finish, the natural scientist must be a modern materialist, a conscious adherent of the materialism which is represented by Marx, *i.e.*, he must be a dialectical materialist.'[1]

A further difference between dialectical materialism and mechanism lies in the mechanists' conception of dialectic. They attribute all motion to impulses arriving from without, and thereby abandon that attribute of matter which the dialectical materialists regard as most essential, namely its inner liveliness, that spontaneity which they describe, in their Hegelian terminology, as the 'self-movement' of matter (*samodvizhnost'*). As we know already, dialectical materialism explains the origin of motion by means of the 'law of the unity of opposites', the chief law of the dialectic. Owing to the presence of internal contradictions—contradictions whose tendency is to break apart from one another—a thing, a phenomenon, a process is set in motion from within. According to the mechanist view, on the other hand, the origin of motion is ascribed to external impulses outside the thing. Lest they should be compelled, therefore, to acknowledge a First Mover, the mechanists, like the old French materialists of the 18th century, conceive of Nature as eternal and unchangeable.

As already indicated above, the mechanists see something mystical, teleological, in the notion of dialectic. Bukharin accused Marx and Engels of having bequeathed to the proletariat a world-outlook by no means free from 'a certain teleological flavour which inevitably clings to the Hegelian formula which speaks of a self-development on the part of "spirit"'.[2]

In spite of this the mechanists themselves make use of the term 'dialectic', though interpreting it in their own mechanistic fashion. Bukharin proposes, in place of the 'mystificatory' dialectic, to found Marxism on the 'theory of equilibrium', which 'would constitute a more general formulation, purged of idealist elements, of the laws governing material systems in motion'.[3] More will be heard of this equilibrium theory in dealing with Bukharin, its principal exponent.

One outcome of this basic conception is the denial of quality, and of the emergence of new qualities. The mechanists taught that

---

[1] V. I. Lenin: *O znachenii voinstvuyushchego materializma* (On the Significance of Militant Materialism); *Sochineniya*, XXXIII[4], pp. 201–10 (translated in *LSW*, XI, *q.v.* p. 77).

[2] N. I. Bukharin: *Ataka*, p. 118; quoted from M. B. Mitin: *Op. cit.*, p. 270.

[3] *Ibid.*

phenomena of higher order are attributable to those of lower order, and hence that everything can be explained by means of mechanical laws. Thus Stepanov maintains that all phenomena in the universe can be traced back to simple physical and chemical processes:

'To gain understanding of any organic phenomenon means, for modern science, to trace it back to relatively simple chemical and physical processes.' [1]

He seeks, therefore, to reduce physiology to physics and chemistry, and organic processes to physical and chemical ones of a highly complicated kind. By the same token, even mental activity is to be traced back to physical and chemical processes.

Stepanov was not alone in these assertions: he simply gave expression to a current mode of thought which was held in high regard even in so important an institution as the Moscow State Institute for Scientific Research, which bore the name of Timiryazev, the celebrated scientist. The publications of the Institute elaborated ideas akin to those of Stepanov. It was held that not only physical activities, but even phenomena of the social order, could be derived from physico-chemical processes:

'In theory and in fact, social phenomena may equally well be subjected either to qualitative, sociological investigation, or to quantitative analysis on chemical, physical and biological lines.' [2]

In their enterprise of deriving everything from simpler, and ultimately from mechanical phenomena, the protagonists of this school relied on the works of I. P. Pavlov (1849–1936),[3] the celebrated Russian physiologist and Professor at the University of St. Petersburg. The latter distinguishes between unconditioned and conditioned reflexes. Unconditioned (or stable) reflexes are those whose operation is immediately evoked by the stimulus: thus food entering

---

[1] I. Stepanov: *Op. cit.*, p. 26; quoted from M. B. Mitin: *Op. cit.*, p. 275.

[2] Quoted from P. Vostokov: *Op. cit.*, p. 291.

[3] Although Pavlov considered a mechanistic explanation to be the ideal aim of scientific research, he continued to be held in high regard even among the dialectical materialists, as may be seen from the warm tribute paid to him after his death by A. M. Deborin (*I. P. Pavlov i materializm* (I. P. Pavlov and Materialism), in *Vestnik Akademii Nauk*, 1936, No. 3, pp. 14 ff.). Deborin regards Pavlov's attempt to provide a physiological explanation for mental phenomena as of great service to materialism generally, even though one may still have doubts about what Pavlov calls the 'mechanistic ideal of scientific research'. Pavlov himself, in a speech delivered in 1931, described his outlook in the following terms: 'I am neither a materialist nor an idealist; I am a monist, or, if one must commit oneself, a methodological materialist.' (F. P. Mayorov: *O mirovozzrenii I. P. Pavlova* (On the World-Outlook of I. P. Pavlov), *ibid.*, p. 17.)

a dog's mouth induces salivation; reflexes are conditioned when their operation results, not immediately from the stimulus, but from the phenomena which accompany it; thus food enters a dog's mouth and at the same time a bell is sounded; when this is done repeatedly salivation is evoked by the mere sound of the bell. The mechanists saw in these conditioned reflexes the basis of association and thought. Every type of spiritual expression, up to and including the highest forms of cultural activity, science, art, philosophy and religion, was thought of as a mere product of physiological automatisms. This theory was also applied to the phenomena of social life.

In the social and political field, mechanism brought forward the theory of spontaneity.[1] The latter represents a radical economic determinism according to which socialism will come about automatically, spontaneously, by natural necessity, in the course of the social and politico-agrarian development of the national economy, in consequence of the socialization process in the towns (industrialization), without the intervention of the collective class-will, without class-warfare in the countryside, without an active struggle for the collectivization of the economy (*raskulachivanie*) and the introduction of the *kolkhoz* system.[2] The class-war and the dictatorship of the proletariat thereby lose their significance. In this respect the mechanists take their stand on the determinism of the early Russian Marxists, with their economic materialism, and of the Economists, with their conception of *stikhiynost'*.

In the mechanistic theory of *samotek* we may see the precise reason why mechanism finds no acceptance in Leninist Bolshevism: the mechanist thesis, which admits only of quantitative changes, leads to the denial of development by leaps and maintains that all such development is continuous. Evolution proceeds steadily, and not in jerks. Mechanism therefore implies the elimination of class-contradictions and avoidance of the class-struggle. Bukharin, the leading exponent of mechanism, was in fact accused of cherishing the hope that the larger peasants would move peacefully over to socialism.[3] Mechanism thereby set itself in direct opposition to the official Soviet theory, which was concerned to emphasize the class-struggle and the necessity of a central party organization to carry it through.

In addition, the authors reckoned as mechanists by the official

[1] In Russian *samotek*, pronounced *samotyok* (self-actuation).

[2] *Cf.* Stalin's criticisms in the speech already referred to, addressed to the Conference of Marxist Students of the Agrarian Question (II. The Theory of 'Spontaneity' in Socialist Construction), in J. Stalin: *Voprosy leninizma*, 11th edn., Moscow 1947, pp. 278 ff. (*Problems of Leninism*, 11th edn., pp. 304 ff.).

[3] *Cf.* N. Lossky: *Op. cit.*, p. 368.

philosophy themselves differed considerably in opinion one from another. Mitin himself acknowledges that it is not easy to bring them all in under one and the same title, since 'the mechanists of today represent an unprincipled coalition of revisionist groups'.[1]

The mechanists include both the vulgar materialists of the early years of the Soviet regime, such as Minin and Enchmen, and natural scientists such as Timiryazev and others of whom mention has been made already. Among the mechanist philosophers, the most prominent is Bukharin, who applied the philosophy of Bogdanov to historical materialism and political economy, and endeavoured to supplant the materialist dialectic by his well-known 'theory of equilibrium'. Finally, there are various other philosophers who are reckoned as mechanists, such as Axel'rod and Sarab'yanov, of whom the latter, however, is more of a positivist or subjective idealist, and Varyash, who ranks as a disciple of Freud.

All of them stand accused, according to the official philosophy, of seeking a revision of the fundamentals of dialectical materialism.

2. BUKHARIN

The most notable of the theorists of mechanism is Nikolay Ivanovich Bukharin (1888–1937).

The son of a municipal teacher in Moscow, he abandoned religion in early youth. While attending High School he felt deep sympathy for a time with the nihilism of Pisarev and joined the revolutionary organization for students in 1905. Having matriculated at Moscow University, he entered the Russian Social-Democratic Party in 1906 and became a convinced bolshevik revolutionary. Many times arrested, he was eventually exiled to Onega in 1910; but he succeeded in escaping to Western Europe, where he established contact with Lenin. His literary activities began about this time. He wrote a series of articles against the exponents of Marxist criticism and the 'legal Marxists' (Struve, Tugan-Baranovsky), which later appeared in collected form under the title *Attack*.[2]

In the winter of 1912/13 he attended Böhm-Bawerk's lectures on political economy in Vienna, and worked on his book *The Economic Theory of the Leisure Class*[3] which is considered in Marxist circles to be the best refutation of Böhm-Bawerk, the leader of the 'Austrian School'.

After the outbreak of the World War he was arrested by the Austrian police as a suspected spy and later expelled to Switzerland.

[1] M. B. Mitin: *Op. cit.*, p. 249.

[2] N. I. Bukharin: *Ataka*, Moscow 1924.

[3] N. I. Bukharin: *Politicheskaya ekonomiya rant'e*, Moscow 1919 (English version, London 1927).

There he joined the Bolsheviks in campaigning against those Marxists who supported the war under pretext of 'defending the Fatherland'. At the same time he wrote a new and larger work, *Imperialism and World Economy*.[1]

From Switzerland he emigrated to Sweden; driven out from there also, he moved to Norway and eventually arrived illegally in America. After the February Revolution of 1917 he travelled *via* Japan and Siberia to Moscow, and became a leading figure in the bolshevik movement. From December 1917 onwards he was editor of *Pravda*, but resigned this position in 1918, having fallen out with Lenin over the Treaty of Brest-Litovsk; Bukharin, in fact, was in favour of continuing the war against Germany. At that time he was at the head of a group of left-wing communists, but soon afterwards he acknowledged his conduct in this period of his career as an error, and in 1918 returned once more to his editorial position on *Pravda*.

From that time onwards, until 1927, he occupied a number of important party offices in the Central Committee and the Politburo. At the same time he was one of the most important leaders of the 'Communist International' (*Comintern*). In this capacity he made a number of trips abroad and took part in drafting the programme of the Third International.

In 1927 Bukharin was still an undisputed authority, as may be seen from the article on him in the *Great Soviet Encyclopaedia*, but already his star was on the wane. At this time Stalin opened his campaign for the socialization of agriculture, aimed at the abolition of private property in land and the expropriation of the larger peasants (*kulaki*). Bukharin was opposed to this policy: he was afraid that socialization would be harmful to agriculture, and took the view that the larger peasants could also be incorporated into the socialist state by peaceful means. On this account a violent campaign was set on foot against him and his followers, and their faction was condemned as a 'Right-wing deviation'; Bukharin himself and Rykov were officially regarded as the ring-leaders. At the Plenary Session of the *MK VKP(b)* (Moscow Committee of the C.P.S.U.(B)) in 1928, Stalin stressed the necessity of carrying on a war on two fronts. The 'Right-wingers' were denounced as '*kulak* agents' within the Party.[2]

In the years that followed the campaign against deviations to right and to left was carried on with increasing intensity. Eventually, in 1937, both opposition parties were finally liquidated, their leaders being tried and executed.[3]

[1] N. I. Bukharin: *Mirovoe khozyaystvo i imperializm*, Petrograd 1918 (English version, London 1929).

[2] *Istoriya Vsesoyuznoy Kommunisticheskoy Partii (bol'shevikov). Op. cit.*, p. 80 (*History of the C.P.S.U.(B)*, p. 295).

[3] *Ibid.*, pp. 331 f. (346 f.). A revealing light is cast upon the trial of

Bukharin's philosophical development was much influenced by empirio-criticism, especially of the Russian variety, and by Bogdanov's empirio-monism and Tectology. He himself admits, in his autobiography, that for a time he was 'possessed of a certain heretical leaning towards the school of empirio-criticism, and read everything that appeared on the subject in Russian'.[1]

The connection with empirio-criticism can be seen in Bukharin's conception of the nature of knowledge. Avenarius had previously maintained that the task of knowledge did not consist in gaining acquaintance with things-in-themselves, but in building up from individual 'elements', *i.e.*, sensations, a world-picture which should facilitate the struggle for existence with the minimum expenditure of energy. Hence concepts, logical categories and laws are nothing but a means of forming a world-picture in accordance with the principle of maximum economy.[2]

Bukharin rejects this theory of empirio-criticism, but the grounds of his dissent indicate that he had not entirely escaped its influence. He objects to exponents of the theory that they underestimate the *qualitative* difference which obtains between the product of cognitive activity and its sensory 'raw material,' 'just as a locomotive is qualitatively different from its metallic components, although it is "constructed" out of them'.[3]

He seeks to maintain the distinction between the 'product of cognitive activity' (concepts, general laws?) and the sensory elements of this knowledge (sensations). But his kinship with empirio-criticism shows itself in this, that he appears to derive the whole process of knowledge from the combination of sensations, and assumes that it is man himself who constructs his world from the chaotic mass of sensory elements. Science, according to this view, is concerned not with discovering general laws from among isolated facts, but merely with systematizing the products of knowledge:

'Science classifies, arranges, clarifies, eliminates the contradictions in, the thoughts of men; it constructs a complete raiment of scientific ideas and theories out of fragmentary knowledge.' [4]

[1] *Entsiklopedichesky slovar' Granat*, XLI, Pt. I, Appendix, pp. 54 f.; *cf.* M. Z. Selektor: *Op. cit.*, p. 10.

[2] G. V. Plekhanov: *Materialismus militans*, Moscow–Leningrad 1931, p. 113.

[3] N. I. Bukharin: *Etyudy*, p. 49; cited in M. Z. Selektor: *Op. cit.*, p. 10.

[4] N. I. Bukharin: *Teoriya istoricheskogo materializma*, Moscow 1921,

In making this claim Bukharin allies himself to empirio-criticism and especially to Bogdanov's version of it. For in Bogdanov's Tectology also, the unity of experience is not discovered beforehand, but 'created by positively organized activity'.[1]

Much more important than this epistemological standpoint is Bukharin's celebrated 'equilibrium theory', which was so violently attacked by the Russian dialectical materialists. It derives from the mechanistic view that Bukharin takes of the dialectic.

Like the mechanists in general, he takes over the term 'dialectical materialism' and explicitly describes himself as a dialectical materialist. Indeed he agrees with Lenin in defining the dialectic as 'a process of movement, the basis of which is the development of internal contradictions',[2] and the term 'internal contradiction' is repeatedly employed by him. But if one looks more closely a great difference can be noticed between the Leninist conception and Bukharin's materialistic view.

Lenin sees the heart of the dialectic in the unity of opposites,[3] and these dialectical opposites lie, moreover, in the inner nature of things and phenomena as such:

'Dialectic in the proper sense is the study of contradiction in *the nature of things as such*.' [4]

Hence it follows that things in dialectical opposition do not merely negate and exclude one another, but also presuppose and confirm one another; the bourgeoisie not only negates the proletariat but also presupposes it, for without the proletariat there can be no question of the bourgeoisie either.

Bukharin and the mechanists also speak of the unity of opposites, but among such opposites they recognize only mutual negation, and not mutual presupposition or confirmation. Bukharin thinks of 'opposites' in terms of 'antagonisms of opposing forces'.

Whereas for Lenin the internal unity of opposites gives rise to self-movement (*samodvizhenie*), a genuine movement *ab intra*, motion, for Bukharin, is the product of antagonisms between opposing forces. The origin of motion lies outside things, motion is conceived of mechanically as local motion, occasioned by an impulse supervening from without.[5]

This has the further consequence that every process is thought of as conditioned by equilibrium and the disturbance thereof.

According to Bukharin, every movement in the world proceeds

p. 215 (English version: *Historical Materialism; A System of Sociology*, London 1926, p. 189).
[1] *Cf.* M. B. Mitin: *Op. cit.*, p. 272.			[2] *Ibid.*, p. 77.
[3] *Cf.* above, p. 119.					[4] *FT*, p. 237 (188).
[5] *Cf.* M. V. Vol'fson–G. M. Gak: *Op. cit.*, p. 218.

from the operation of diverse opposing forces. If these forces did not operate on one another, the world would remain absolutely at rest. In the world it is 'the "conflict", the "contradiction", *i.e.*, the antagonism of forces acting in various directions (that) determines the motion of the system'.[1]

What sort of forces are intended here? They are those of the 'system' and its 'environment'. By 'system' is meant anything whatever, for everything in the world consists of diverse elements:

'Any object, a stone, a living thing, a human society, etc., may be considered as a whole consisting of parts (elements) related with each other; in other words, this whole may be regarded as a system.'[2]

But no system of this kind exists in empty space; it is surrounded by other things, which relative thereto may be termed its 'environment'. For man the primary environment is human society, for society, external Nature.[3]

Every movement in the world may be explained in terms of a disturbance of equilibrium between these two opposing forces.

'The world consists of forces, acting in many ways, opposing each other. These forces are balanced for a moment in exceptional cases only. We then have a state of "rest", *i.e.*, their actual "conflict" is concealed. But if we change only one of these forces, immediately the "internal contradictions" will be revealed, equilibrium will be disturbed, and if a new equilibrium is again established, it will be on a new basis, *i.e.*, with a new combination of forces, etc. It follows that the "conflict", the "contradiction", *i.e.*, the antagonism of forces acting in various directions, determines the motion of the system.'[4]

The process therefore runs its course from equilibrium to a state of motion resulting from the disturbance of equilibrium, and from thence to re-establishment of a new equilibrium, and so on:

'On the other hand we have here also the *form* of this process: in the first place, the condition of equilibrium; in the second place, a disturbance of this equilibrium; in the third place, the re-establishment of equilibrium on a *new* basis. And then the story begins all over again: the new equilibrium is the point of departure for a new disturbance, which in turn is followed by another state of equilibrium, etc., *ad infinitum*. Taken all together, we are dealing with a process of motion based on the development of internal contradictions.'[5]

The above applies, not only to the relations between the system

---

[1] N. I. Bukharin: *Teoriya istoricheskogo materializma*, p. 77 (English version, p. 74).
[2] *Ibid.*, p. 78 (75).   [3] *Ibid.*   [4] *Ibid.*, p. 77 (74).
[5] *Ibid.*

and its environment, but also to the internal structure of the system itself: here too, motion is the product of equilibrium-relations between the elements.

'Each system consists of its component parts (elements) united with each other in one way or another. Human society consists of people; the forests, of trees and bushes; the pile of stones, of the various stones; the herd of animals, of the individual animals, etc. Between them there are a number of contradictions, differences, imperfect adaptations, etc. In other words, here also there is no absolute equilibrium. If there can be, strictly speaking, no absolute equilibrium between the environment and the system, there can also be no such equilibrium between the elements of the system itself.' [1]

But where does the disturbance of equilibrium come from? Bukharin traces it to an alteration of the relationship between system and environment.

'It is quite clear that the internal structure of the system (its internal equilibrium) must change together with the relation existing between the system and its environment. The latter relation is the decisive factor; for the entire situation of the system, the fundamental form of its motion (decline, prosperity, or stagnation) are determined by this relation only. . . . Consequently, *the internal (structural) equilibrium is a quantity which depends on the external equilibrium (is a "function" of this external equilibrium).*' [2]

The dialectical materialists very properly object to this explanation that it makes it as impossible to continue to speak of 'internal contradiction' as it does of the origin of motion, since the former is in fact derived from the relation of the system to its environment. Moreover, this solution offers no answer to the question as to the actual origin of motion: for if motion be ascribed to the disturbance of equilibrium between 'system' and 'environment', the question still arises, as to how this disturbance comes about. Mitin is correct when he observes that, if Bukharin is to remain consistent, he has no alternative but to assume some sort of supernatural power, which has ordinarily been described hitherto as the 'First Mover', or simply as 'God the Creator'. [3]

It is in the threefold rhythm of motion: equilibrium, disturbance and re-establishment of equilibrium, that Bukharin discerns the true essence of the Hegelian dialectic.

The merit which Bukharin claims for his conception of dialectic

---

[1] N. I. Bukharin: *Teoriya istoricheskogo materializma* p. 81 (English version, p. 78).

[2] *Ibid.*, pp. 82 f. (79).　　　　　　　　[3] M. B. Mitin: *Op. cit.*, p. 276.

is that it frees the Hegelian dialectic from all mystical elements and makes it radically and consistently materialistic.[1] Hegel

'called the original condition of equilibrium the *thesis*, the disturbance of equilibrium the *antithesis*, the re-establishment of equilibrium on a new basis the *synthesis*. . . . The characteristic of motion present in all things, expressing itself in this tripartite formula (or triad) he called *dialectic*.' [2]

The equilibrium theory also had its effect, in the sphere of historical materialism, on Bukharin's sociological views. In this connection the dialectical materialists complain of him that he derives all social contradictions in the last resort from the relation between system (society) and environment (Nature). Historical development thereby becomes conditioned, not by the internal circumstances of society, but by the operation of natural forces.[3]

Hence his theory is also open to the objection that it is necessarily bound up with the bourgeois conception of society, which regards the capitalist order as one of 'harmonious co-operation between the classes' and devotes all its energies to preserving the equilibrium of capitalist society.[4]

3. AXEL'ROD (*ORTODOX*)

In the controversy between mechanists and Deborinists the mechanists were joined by a lady of high philosophical attainments, Lyubov' Isaakovna Axel'rod, who wrote under the pen-name of *Ortodox*. L. I. Axel'rod[5] was born in 1868. In 1887, after the attack on Alexander III, she was obliged to emigrate to Switzerland. There she completed her philosophical studies at the University of Berne and was awarded the Doctorate of Philosophy. About 1890 she joined the Social-Democratic Party. After the amnesty of 1906 she returned to Russia, where she belonged to a number of menshevik organizations. From 1918 onwards she stood outside the Party, but occupied herself intensively with the development of Marxist theory. She died in 1946.

Axel'rod's philosophical importance rests on her polemic against

[1] N. I. Bukharin: *Op. cit.*, p. 78 (75); M. B. Mitin: *Op. cit.*, p. 270.
[2] N. I. Bukharin: *Op. cit.*, p 77 (74 f.).
[3] M. V. Vol'fson–G. M. Gak: *Op. cit.*, p. 219.
[4] *Cf.* M. B. Mitin: *Op. cit.*, p. 278.
[5] Not to be confused with Paul Borisovich Axel'rod, a *Narodnik* who emigrated to Switzerland, where he joined Plekhanov in founding the 'Liberation of Labour' Group and later allied himself with the Mensheviks; nor with her sister, Ida Isaakovna Axel'rod, who also left for Switzerland in 1893 and subsequently belonged to the 'Liberation of Labour' Group.

the critical Marxists at the beginning of the century. As an orthodox Marxist she sided with Plekhanov in a highly effective defence of dialectical materialism. Her articles against various forms of Neo-Kantianism directed, among others, against Berdyaev and Struve, were published in collected form as *Philosophical Studies*.[1] Her later essays attacking empirio-criticism and Bogdanov also constitute a defence of dialectical materialism. After the Revolution they appeared, with other works, in a volume entitled *Against Idealism*.[2] She also published, after the Revolution, a collection of studies, *Marx as a Philosopher*,[3] and a work devoted to historical materialism, *Critique of the Foundations of Bourgeois Sociology and Historical Materialism*.[4] The pamphlet *In Defence of Dialectical Materialism. Against Scholasticism* [5] belongs to the period of controversy between mechanists and Deborinists. After the official condemnation of mechanism and menshevizing idealism she published a further pamphlet, *The Idealist Dialectic of Hegel and the Materialist Dialectic of Marx*,[6] which stands out favourably, for its penetrating account of the Hegelian system, above many of the Soviet philosophical publications of the period.

Axel'rod was an energetic opponent of the critical Marxists and their war-cry 'Back to Kant'—as if Marxism possessed no theory of knowledge its own. She accused them of confounding the critical theory of knowledge with epistemology in general, and pointed out that the latter was older than Kant and that many materialist systems of the 18th century had already possessed a theory of knowledge. All the more true is this of Marxist materialism, which is not metaphysical, but dialectical. Dialectical materialism, moreover, is by nature epistemological in character, since 'it acknowledges neither a closed metaphysical system nor fixed metaphysical substances'.[7]

It is precisely in this metaphysical conception of knowledge that Axel'rod sees the common failing of all the endeavours of modern philosophy—a conception which views all things as fixed, stable, isolated substances: this starting-point has given rise to the problem of knowledge and to a metaphysical interpretation of subject and object in the knowing-process as separate substances. It is the same mistake as that already found in Locke:

[1] *Filosofskie ocherki*, St. Petersburg 1906.

[2] *Protiv idealizma*, Petrograd 1922.   [3] *Marx kak filosof.*

[4] *Kritika osnov burzhuaznogo obshchestvovedeniya i istorichesky materializm*, Ivanovo–Voznesensk 1925.

[5] *V zashchitu dialekticheskogo materializma. Protiv skholastiki*, Moscow–Leningrad 1928.

[6] *Idealisticheskaya dialektika Hegelya i materialisticheskaya dialektika Marxa*, Moscow–Leningrad 1934.

[7] L. I. Axel'rod: *Filosofskie ocherki*, p. 96.

'He fails to conceive of our knowledge as a continuous uninterrupted process of development, in which consciousness has no function apart from the perception of external objects of experience, and hence cannot be divorced from them. . . . Locke thinks of consciousness, rather, as a form independent of the effect exerted by the object.' [1]

Consciousness divorced from the object of knowledge encounters in sensation a boundary, a limit:

'Between the object and consciousness sensation stands, therefore, as an impassable barrier. The result is that the influence of the object on our senses, instead of putting us in touch with it, cuts us off from it.' [2]

In consequence of this metaphysical method, Berkeley and Hume arrived at a total denial of the objective world.

Kant's critical philosophy, which endeavoured to reinstate the objective world and to provide a basis for the theory of scientific experience, suffers from the same Lockean defect. Here too, owing to the contradictory conception of the 'thing-in-itself', the influence of the object on the subject not only fails to effect any union between them, but sets up a severance of principle which makes the 'thing-in-itself' unknowable.[3]

These metaphysicians, in Axel'rod's opinion, have mistakenly isolated the thing from the knowing subject because they looked at knowledge from a metaphysical, not a historical point of view. Marx's dialectical materialism avoids this mistake.

For dialectical materialism, all knowledge derives from experience and is therefore knowledge *a posteriori*. The possibility of *a priori* knowledge is emphatically rejected. It does not follow from this, however, that knowledge has no necessary or universal characteristics. It is a metaphysical prejudice that *a priori* knowledge alone has necessary and universal validity.

'Truth acquired by way of experience is universally binding, real, indubitable and retains its full objective significance, so long as it does not itself contradict experience: a law inferred *a posteriori* serves therefore as an *a priori* guiding principle, so long as it is not confuted by practical reality.' [4]

And here Axel'rod appeals to the authority of Marx, who considered the question whether human knowledge could encompass reality to be not a theoretical, but a practical one, since it finds its solution in practice; and she continues:

'Our capacity for bringing about changes in the state of the object,

[1] *Ibid.*, p. 16.   [2] *Ibid.*   [3] *Ibid.*, p. 196.   [4] *Ibid.*, p. 83.

our ability to shape the material order in accordance with our purposes and to predict phenomena and their mutual relationships—
all this is a sufficient guarantee of the fact that material Nature
really exists and that we are acquainted with its characteristics.' [1]

For the same reasons as those she advances against Locke and
Kant, namely to prevent subject and object being separated in the
knowing-process by sensation, Axel'rod adheres to Plekhanov's
hieroglyphic theory and criticizes the Leninist copy-theory from this
point of view. In Lenin's conception she sees an inverted Platonism,
a dualism at variance with the materialist philosophy, which proceeds from a monistic principle. If sensations are copies of things,
then the things themselves are rendered superfluous and become
genuine examples of 'things-in-themselves', as they do in Kant.
But this is to open up an unbridgeable gulf between subject and
object.

Plekhanov's hieroglyphic theory avoids this pitfall:

'The symbolic theory, which asserts the existence of both subject and
object, unifies these two factors by treating the subject as a special
sort of object, and its sensations as a product of the interaction
between two objects of which one is at the same time the subject.' [2]

Hence, entirely in the spirit of the hieroglyphic theory, she concludes:

'But materialism adheres to the view that the sensations called forth
by the operation of the various forms of motion in matter do not
resemble the objective processes which give rise to them.' [3]

The Leninist dialectical materialists maintain that Axel'rod has
failed to grasp that in the copy-theory the relation between subject
and object is a dialectical one, and that subject and object are thereby
united, whereas in her view, as in that of Kant, 'knowledge does not
unite, it brings man no closer to Nature, but simply disintegrates
them both'. [4]

In the controversy between mechanism and Deborinism, Lyubov'
Axel'rod took the mechanist side and was vehemently attacked by
Deborin on that account. [5] He objected to her that she denied not

---

[1] L. I. Axel'rod: *Filosofskie ocherki*, p. 84.

[2] L. I. Axel'rod, in her introduction to Lenin's *Materialism and Empirio-
Criticism*; in V. I. Lenin: *Sochineniya*, XIII³, p. 330. In the fourth edition
of Lenin's Works this introduction has been omitted.

[3] *Ibid.*, p. 331.   [4] M. B. Mitin: *Op. cit.*, p. 260.

[5] Among other places, in Deborin's concluding speech to the Conference
of the Institute of Scientific Philosophy, 18th May 1925; reprinted, under
the title *Our Differences*, in A. M. Deborin: *Op. cit.*, pp. 242–94.

only the category of quality, but the dialectic itself,[1] turning it into a mere form of representation of scientific data, whereas in fact it must also be regarded as a science of the laws and objective forms of motion;[2] in general he accuses her of defending mechanistic materialism.[3]

Since most of the discussions between mechanists and Deborinists have not been made available to us in detail, we have, unfortunately, no means of deciding how far Axel'rod carried her mechanist views. Mitin[4] also numbers her among the mechanists. If he is right in doing so, she too must have altered her position after the suppression of mechanism in the U.S.S.R. In her pamphlet *The Idealist Dialectic of Hegel and the Materialist Dialectic of Marx* she adheres on all the main issues in dispute to the viewpoint of orthodox dialectical materialism. Thus she now sees dialectic as a science of motion in reality itself. Hegel's dialectic is described as 'formal',[5] since

'all transitions and distinctions, all forms of contradiction in the world-process, were elaborated down to the last detail by him "*within a framework of speculation*", so that these distinctions, being represented as *distinctions within substance itself,* bear no relation to the distinction between real things as such'; [6]

dialectical materialism, on the other hand, when it employs the dialectic as a method of inquiry, requires that the dialectical movement shall also be disclosed in the object under investigation itself.[7] Axel'rod also assumes here that this dialectical movement gives rise to new qualities in the world:

'new orders, in which the elements of the given order represent something more complex, something higher in comparison with previous orders, something constituting a new quality, which cannot be *immediately* traced back to the original elements of the starting-point'.[8]

[1] A. M. Deborin: *Op cit.,* p. 259.
[2] *Ibid.,* p. 283.   [3] *Ibid.,* p. 264.   [4] M. B. Mitin: *Op. cit.,* p. 249.
[5] L. I. Axel'rod: *Idealisticheskaya dialektika . . .,* p. 10.
[6] *Ibid.,* p. 79.   [7] *Ibid.,* p. 80.   [8] *Ibid.,* p. 68.

CHAPTER VIII

Menshevik Idealism

THE orthodox dialectical materialists see the theoretical origins of Leftist and Rightist deviation in a one-sided attitude on the part of both tendencies in relation to reality.

In both cases one of the elements actually present is separated from the other and erected into an absolute.

The Rightist deviation pays exclusive attention to the element of *continuity in development* and thereby slides into an evolutionism which allows only for continuous organic development and denies the possibility of leaps. The Leftist deviation, on the contrary, concerns itself only with the leaps occurring in history and makes them absolute. It denies any continuous organic development and maintains that everything takes place by means of revolutionary leaps.

But the truth, according to the orthodox view, lies in between, or rather in a dialectical synthesis of both elements. Development proceeds initially in a continuous fashion by means of purely quantitative increments, but this only extends up to a certain point. Once this is reached, the leap follows, and development or purely quantitative change passes over into a change of quality.

As we know already, in 1931 the Rightist deviation was accounted the number one danger to the internal politics of the Soviet Union, this being the time at which all the forces of public life were being concentrated by Stalin on the build-up of socialism, the complete industrialization of the U.S.S.R., and the collectivization of agriculture. But if the chief danger was seen at this time in the Rightist deviation, the previous generation, that of the New Economic Policy, the period of reconstruction after the devastations of the Revolution and the Civil War, had felt it to lie in the Leftist deviation, which was opposed to the temporary concessions made to certain capitalist modes of life.

154

1. GENERAL OUTLINES

The Deborinist wing took shape as a reaction against the vulgar and mechanistic materialism which held the field during the first decade after the Revolution. Its character was essentially governed by this controversy.

As we have seen, the mechanists endeavoured to reduce all higher-order phenomena to those of lower order, the phenomena of social and mental life to simple organic reflexes, and these in turn to chemical and physical processes. In the metaphysical field this implied a denial of the category of quality and the setting up of quantity as the sole category.

Their opposition to this view led the Deborinists into an intensive development of dialectic. As against the mechanists, they insisted with all possible emphasis on the independence of the category of quality, which can only be preserved through one of the so-called 'laws of dialectic', namely, that of the 'transformation of quantity into quality'. After reaching a certain level of intensity, quantitative changes are transformed by a sudden leap into a qualitative change and lead to the emergence of a new quality, whereby the preceding one is negated.[1] Hence it came about that the defence of quality drove them into the paths of dialectic.

In the development of the system of dialectical materialism, this Deborinist materialism falls pretty well into line with that promulgated after 1931, which will be dealt with in detail in Part Two; we may therefore confine ourselves here to indicating the main points of difference between the two.

A first such point of difference may be found in the accusation of Hegelianism which was levelled against menshevizing idealism, and which came to light in the course of its elaboration of the dialectic. Its opponents could not, indeed, deny that Lenin himself had laid especial stress on the necessity of studying the Hegelian dialectic. But Lenin—so the official dialectical materialists said—had prescribed a critical attitude towards the Hegelian dialectic, and called for it to be reformed on materialist lines and applied to the concrete reality of the proletarian struggle for existence.

Deborin, however, had done neither the one nor the other. In the first place the Deborinists had taken over the Hegelian dialectic as it stood, without transforming it into a materialist dialectic.[2] They had supposed that in Hegel's philosophy it was only the system that

[1] *Cf.* Part Two, Ch. III.
[2] *Cf.* the resolution of the Institute of Red Professors' 'Cell' for Philosophy and Natural Science, in *Pravda*, 26th Jan. 1931, also included in the anthology *Dialektichesky materializm. Marx, Engels, Lenin, Stalin*, Moscow 1933, pp. 538–44, *q.v.*, p. 541.

was idealistic, the method itself being a materialistic one. Deborin had thereby arrived at the assertion that dialectical materialism was merely a 'synthesis of Hegel's dialectical method and the materialist conception of Nature and history'.[1]

In addition to their unmodified acceptance of the Hegelian dialectic, the Deborinists had committed a further error in taking an entirely abstract view of the dialectic, without applying it to the concrete problems of Soviet reality. Their whole activity had been occupied almost exclusively with Hegel's *Science of Logic*, without taking any account of the questions of the day, the problems of politics and economics, the dictatorship of the proletariat and its struggle for the establishment of socialism. For them it was only the dialectic of logic that counted, not the dialectic of reality and the social struggle.

All this led to the complaint preferred against this school, that they separated theory from practice, philosophy from politics, and had given themselves up to a sort of formalism by making form prior to content.

But it was not only in this Hegelian conception of dialectic that the idealism of the Deborinists presented itself to the eyes of the orthodox dialectical materialists. Their conception of matter is almost equally erroneous.[2] They banish from it, indeed, everything which constitutes, in the Leninist view, the essential nature of matter, namely its character as an objective reality independent of our consciousness which gives rise to our sensations.[3] The nature of matter in this sense is misrepresented in the definition given by Deborin, whose book *Lenin the Thinker* begins by framing the concept of matter correctly enough, but then goes on: 'In the broader sense matter is the whole infinite concrete totality of "mediations", *i.e.*, ties and relationships'.[4]

Idealist views of this sort are still more palpably evident in Deborin's disciples. Hessen, for example, alleges that dialectical materialism conceives of matter as a synthesis of space and time.[5]

In the eyes of the orthodox, the error of such a standpoint lies in this, that it gives expression only to the form in which matter exists, and not to matter itself.

A still more extreme position in this regard is adopted by another

---

[1] A. M. Deborin: *Dialektika u Kanta* (Dialectic in Kant), in *Arkhiv K. Marxa i F. Engelsa*, I (1924), p. 14; *cf.* M. B. Mitin: *Op. cit.*, p. 288.

[2] *Cf.* the resolution cited in n. 2 above; *Op. cit.*, p. 541.

[3] *Cf.* Part Two, Ch. II.

[4] A. M. Deborin: *Lenin kak myslitel'* (Lenin the Thinker), Moscow 1929, p. 42; *cf.* M. B. Mitin: *Op. cit.*, p. 290.

[5] B. Hessen: *Osnovnye idei teorii otnositel'nosti* (The Basic Ideas of Relativity Theory), p. 69; *cf.* M. B. Mitin: *Op. cit.*, p. 291.

of Deborin's followers, Milonov, who considers the attribute of extension to be inessential to matter:

'There is absolutely no necessity for assuming extension to be everywhere present. A dialectical materialist is under no sort of unconditional obligation to insist on the attribute of extension.' [1]

Other supporters of Deborin again laid so much stress on the attribute of thought that the mechanistic materialists became seriously concerned about it. One of them, Perelmann, asks: What becomes of matter if we deprive it of the attribute of extension and leave it that of thought? The result is a moving thought, *i.e.*, spirit. The Deborinists, for their part, gladly invoked in their support against the over-simplified mechanist conception of matter the words of Lenin on the subject: 'An intelligent idealism stands closer to us than a stupid materialism.' [2]

The third main ground of complaint against the menshevizing idealists relates to their undue regard for the achievements of Plekhanov and their underestimation of Lenin's importance in philosophy.

So far as concerns Plekhanov, approval of him was not, as such, ill thought of, for Lenin himself had held him in regard, but the objection was that the Deborinists went too far in this respect and followed him uncritically. Deborin takes over from Plekhanov precisely what is least valuable in him, his apology for Feuerbach, the application of Feuerbach's anthropological principle to epistemology, the discounting of Lenin's theory of knowledge (the 'copy-theory'), the attempt to solve the epistemological problem of the subject-object relation in terms of purely metaphysical categories without regard for historical and revolutionary reality. The whole non-political, unrevolutionary spirit of Deborin's philosophy resembles that of Plekhanov's.

This attitude towards Plekhanov is paralleled, on the other side, by an inadequate appraisal of Lenin's significance in philosophy, a failure to understand the fact that he is actually the inaugurator of a new epoch, not only in political life, but also in philosophy.

The orthodox found Deborin's judgement on Lenin in his book *Lenin the Thinker* completely unacceptable:

'Both thinkers [Plekhanov and Lenin] are in a certain sense complementary to one another. . . . Plekhanov is essentially the theoretician, Lenin essentially the man of action, the politician, the leader.' [3]

Obviously such a judgement, which virtually installed Plekhanov as Lenin's teacher in matters of theory, was bound to arouse violent

---

[1] Quoted in P. Vostokov: *Op. cit.*, p. 295; *cf.* also P. Prokofiev: *Op. cit.*, p. 480.   [2] *Cf.* P. Vostokov: *Op. cit.*, p. 295.
[3] A. M. Deborin: *Op. cit.*, p. 26; *cf.* M. B. Mitin: *Op. cit.*, p. 283.

opposition. Elsewhere, in his Introduction to Volume IX of Lenin's *Selected Writings*, Deborin modifies his opinion to some extent, maintaining that Lenin and Plekhanov represented different stages in the development of Marxism:

'There is a difference between Plekhanov and Lenin which reflects what is peculiar to the historical phases of development in the revolutionary movement and the class-struggle of the proletariat.' [1]

To this the orthodox objected that the most important works of Plekhanov and Lenin, and not only the philosophical ones but also others, such as the polemic against the *Narodniks*, belong to the same period. Another well-known Deborinist therefore deals with the question in a rather different fashion. In an article in the magazine *Pod znamenem marxizma* he writes:

'Plekhanov and Lenin are representative . . . not of different periods in the workers' movement, but of different currents in it and in Marxism, a different type of insight into the same thing.' [2]

But even this approach found no acceptance from the orthodox point of view. To speak of different currents and tendencies in Marxism is to abandon Marxist-Leninism. It would mean reverting to the standpoint of the Second International, which looked on Marxism as an agglomeration of movements, tendencies, etc.

To sum up, we may say that menshevizing idealism is condemned by the orthodox, firstly as an *idealistic* tendency in that it offers too many hostages to Hegelianism, adopts the Hegelian dialectic without transforming it materialistically, separates form and content and misconceives the nature of matter; secondly, as a *menshevizing* tendency, in that it represents a revival of the traditions of the Second International, separates theory from practice, philosophy from politics, failing thereby to practise partisanship in philosophy, overestimates Plekhanov, and underestimates the importance of Lenin in the development of philosophy.[3]

In addition to Deborin, the main representatives of this group include B. Bykhovsky,[4] G. S. Tymyansky,[5] N. Karev,[6] I. Luppol, Y. Sten and others.

[1] *Leninsky Sbornik*, IX, p. 3; *cf.* M. B. Mitin: *Op. cit.*, pp. 283 f.

[2] *Pod znamenem marxizma*, 1930, No. 6, p. 35; *cf.* M. B. Mitin: *Op. cit.*, p. 284.   [3] *Cf.* M. V. Vol'fson–G. M. Gak: *Op. cit.*, p. 221.

[4] B. Bykhovsky: *Ocherk filosofii dialekticheskogo materializma* (Outlines of a Philosophy of Dialectical Materialism), Moscow–Leningrad, 1930.

[5] G. S. Tymyansky: *Vvedenie v teoriyu dialekticheskogo materializma* (Introduction to the Theory of Dialectical Materialism), 2nd edn., Moscow–Leningrad 1931.

[6] N. Karev: *Za materialisticheskuyu dialektiku* (For a Materialistic Dialectic), 2nd edn., Moscow 1930.

2. DEBORIN

The most important exponent of the philosophy of dialectical materialism in the period after Lenin is undoubtedly Abram Moiseyevich Deborin (Yoffe).

Born in 1881, he was first apprenticed as a locksmith in Kovno. In 1899 he entered the government service in Kherson, where he frequented illegal societies, was soon dismissed on that account, and returned to Kovno. Here too, however, he was arrested by the police in 1902 and placed under supervision; in 1903 he left Russia and emigrated to Switzerland where he studied philosophy at the University of Berne. He became an adherent of the Bolshevik group, but left it in 1907 to join the Mensheviks. In 1908 he returned to Russia. After the February Revolution of 1917 he abandoned Menshevism and remained without party ties until 1928; only then did he become a member of the Bolshevik Party. After the Revolution he devoted himself entirely to teaching and research, working at the Sverdlov University, the Institute of Red Professors, the Communist Academy and the Marx-Engels Institute. He took a leading part in the founding of the journal *Pod znamenem marxizma*, of which he became Chief Editor. In 1929 he was also nominated a full member of the Academy of Sciences of the U.S.S.R.

Since the above-mentioned condemnation of 'menshevizing idealism' by the Party Central Committee (25th January 1931), Deborin, having bowed to this decision and acknowledged his 'errors', has been able thereafter to occupy leading positions in the scientific work of the U.S.S.R. In November 1935 he was elected secretary of the Social Sciences division of the Academy of Sciences, in 1938 we find him on the Council of the Philosophical Institute of the same Academy of Sciences, while in 1939 he was elected to the Praesidium of the Academy itself. At present Deborin is a member of the editorial board of the *Vestnik*, the official organ of the Academy of Sciences of the U.S.S.R.

Throughout the years 1905 to 1917 he was one of the chief defenders of dialectical materialism against mechanism and Neo-Kantianism. This period saw the publication of one of his most important works, *Introduction to the Philosophy of Dialectical Materialism*;[1] in it he traces the development of empirio-critical ideas in the history of modern philosophy from Bacon onwards and presents at the same time a synthetic account of dialectical materialism. This work, to which Plekhanov contributed a Preface, played a major part in upholding the cause of dialectical materialism. But

[1] A. M. Deborin: *Vvedenie v filosofiyu dialekticheskogo materializma*, Petrograd 1916.

some things said in it no longer find favour nowadays with the Leninist philosophers. Lenin himself had already had to find fault with it on certain points.[1]

After the Revolution Deborin became intensely active in the philosophical field, making it his business to combat a variety of aberrations from dialectical materialism; he criticized the Hegelian interpretation of Marxism put forward by Lukács, opposed the theories of Freud and Spengler, which had found some response at this period even in Russia, and campaigned against ethical socialism and social-democratic Neo-Kantianism. In his book *Marx and Hegel*[2] he counters the attempt to interpret Marx, Engels and Lenin in a mechanistic sense. His next major work was *Lenin the Thinker*.[3] He devoted much attention, especially after the publication of Engels' *Dialectics of Nature*, to the problem of applying the dialectic to the natural sciences and published a series of articles which appeared in collected form under the title *Dialectics and Natural Science*.[4]

Under Deborin's supervision, editions of the works of Western materialist philosophers (Hobbes, Lamettrie, von Holbach, Diderot, Toland, Feuerbach) were put in hand, together with an edition of Hegel, for which he supplied an elaborate introduction, *Hegel and Dialectical Materialism*. He also directed publication of the series *Biblioteka ateizma* (Library of Atheism), containing translations of the works of celebrated atheists, such as Holbach, Helvétius and others.

Against the mechanists and vulgar materialists, who had little opinion of philosophy in general (Minin), or at best were unwilling to assign it any important or independent task, equating it throughout with the 'latest findings of the positive sciences', Deborin, like Engels, fought to preserve for philosophy an independent status over and above the positive natural sciences and sociology.

'Dialectical materialism exists as an independent discipline alongside

---

[1] *Cf.* Lenin's notes on this book in his *Filosofskie tetradi*, Moscow 1947, pp. 403–6; not included in the German edition.

[2] A. M. Deborin: *Marx i Hegel*, 1923/24.

[3] *Cf.* p. 156, n. 4 above.

[4] *Cf.* p. 130, n. 4 above. Apart from the works already cited, Deborin's philosophical writings include: L. *Feuerbach. Lichnost i mirovozzrenie* (L. Feuerbach, his Personality and Philosophy of Life), Moscow 1923; *Dialektika u Fichte* (Dialectic in Fichte), in *Arkhiv K. Marxa i F. Engelsa*, III (1927), pp. 7 ff.; a collection of essays under the title *Filosofiya i marxizm* (Philosophy and Marxism), Moscow–Leningrad 1926; *Ocherki po istorii materializma XVII i XVIII vv.* (Outlines of the History of Materialism in the 17th and 18th Centuries), Moscow–Leningrad 1929; *Lenin i krizis noveyshey fiziki* (Lenin and the Crisis in Modern Physics), Leningrad 1930.

the other positive sciences, more especially as the *methodology and theory of scientific knowledge.*[1]

Dialectical materialism, the Marxist world-outlook, is made up according to Deborin, of three main components:

'The *materialist dialectic*, as a general scientific methodology (including also the theory of knowledge); the *dialectic of Nature*, the methodology of the natural sciences (scientific materialism); and the *dialectic of history* (historical materialism).'[2]

Each of these three main factors has been sufficiently set forth by the founders of Marxism, though not to the same extent; particular stress has been laid on the third constituent, historical materialism; for this reason Deborin treats it less thoroughly than the other two.

The first component, the materialist dialectic, has been accorded only relatively minor interest; Engels, in his *Ludwig Feuerbach* and *Anti-Dühring*, deals with it only in passing. And Deborin takes the view that despite the works of Marx, Engels, Plekhanov and Lenin there is still a great deal to be done in the way of a theoretical working-out of the materialist dialectic. He and his disciples devoted themselves so exclusively to this task that Mitin, as we have seen, was able to make this a ground of objection against them.[3]

Deborin conceives of the materialist dialectic as an

'abstract science of the general laws and forms of motion, exemplified alike both in Nature and also in society and human thought.'[4]

The dialectic appears, therefore, as a universal methodology, and it is to this methodology that philosophy as a special science is confined, in the sense that the materialist dialectic, as Deborin sees it, represents a sort of 'algebra of the sciences' which must permeate the concrete sciences in order to provide them with internal coherence. But Deborin does not wish to be taken to mean by this that such coherence is introduced from outside; it is to be found, rather, within the things themselves, *i.e.*, it is objectively present and merely requires to be discovered in the course of our inquiry.[5]

The theory of dialectic as a methodology brought Deborin under heavy fire both from the mechanists and from the exponents of official dialectical materialism.[6] It was urged against him that his methodology was a system of concepts forcibly imposed upon the

---

[1] A. M. Deborin: *Dialektika i estestvoznanie* (Dialectics and Natural Science), p. 11.

[2] *Ibid.*, p. 23.

[3] *Cf.* above, p. 135.

[4] A. M. Deborin: *Op. cit.*, p. 27.

[5] *Ibid.*, p. 31.

[6] *Cf.* the above-mentioned resolution (p. 155, n. 2), *Op. cit.*, p. 541.

objective world. This objection is not entirely justified, however, for already in 1926 Deborin had roundly repudiated any account of dialectic

'depicting it as a sort of *a priori* conception which would enable scientific discoveries to be made on the strength of purely logical considerations and thereby exclude empirical inquiries or wholly supersede them'.[1]

He maintains, rather, that 'the dialectical method is intended, not to replace the concrete investigation of phenomena, but to guide it'.[2]

This task of guiding empirical scientific inquiry is subsequently defined by Deborin as follows: experience, practice, is the decisive test even in theoretical matters, but to methodology, *i.e.*, to theoretical reflection, there falls the extremely important task of filling in the gaps left in experience and empirical science. Methodology should guide our inquiries by indicating the direction in which to look for the answers to questions not yet solved by science.[3]

Dialectic therefore investigates those categories and laws which are operative throughout the whole of reality. These most general laws are exemplified and made concrete in various ways within the different spheres of reality, *i.e.*, one way in Nature and another way in society. Hence, in addition to such general, abstract, algebraic categories, it is also necessary to inquire into their specific concrete manifestations in Nature and society.

This is the task of the two other branches of dialectical materialism.

Deborin himself shows particular interest in the second of these, namely the dialectic of Nature, having been largely inspired in this by the publication of Engels' *Dialectics of Nature*, whose basic contentions he defends against the mechanists.

Following Engels, Deborin proclaimed the necessity of an alliance between empirical science and philosophy. There is a double danger and a double error to be avoided here: on the one hand we must prevent any revival of that philosophy of Nature, already repudiated by Engels in his *Ludwig Feuerbach*, which seeks to supply the as yet unknown connections between natural phenomena by means of *a priori* theories; on the other hand we must obviate the inadequacy of that purely empirical conception of natural science which rejects all philosophy and confines itself to the description of empirical facts.

Admitting then, what Engels had shown, that science is incapable of moving a step without philosophy, and hence the necessity of an alliance between them, it is with *dialectical* philosophy that science must ally itself, for this is the most progressive type. And the alliance is to consist in this, that science, which investigates individual facts,

[1] A. M. Deborin: *Op. cit.*, p. 270.   [2] *Ibid.*, p. 271.
[3] *Ibid.*, pp. 308 ff.

shall borrow from philosophy the dialectical method, by which alone it will be in a position to combine all these facts into a single whole.[1]

The history of human knowledge points towards such an alliance. The ancient Greeks already saw Nature as a whole; the universal connection of phenomena in the world was disclosed to them in immediate contemplation. But they were not in a position to demonstrate such a universal interconnection in concrete individual cases, or to discover, by analysis of Nature, the relationship of individual phenomena to the whole.

In contrast to this, modern natural science has achieved great success in dissecting Nature and accumulating knowledge of individual phenomena. But thanks to the traditional 'metaphysical' habit of thought it has hitherto proved incapable of discovering the road which leads from the apprehension of individual facts and phenomena to the apprehension of the entire universe, and the manner in which individual phenomena are connected with the whole.[2] If it now wishes to progress, however, it must seek alliance with dialectic:

'Dialectic provides the synthesis between the general and the specific and particular, between intuition and thought, practice and theory, the empirical and the theoretical sciences of Nature, namely "philosophy".'[3]

To justify the need for this alliance, Deborin relies upon his theory of the 'concrete concept',[4] which the student of Hegelian philosophy will have no difficulty in recognizing as Hegel's 'concrete universal'.[5]

Hegel had shown already that the weakness of empirical science arises from the fact that it apprehends the universal in an abstract, purely formal manner, as an abstract concept, having no determinations within itself, so that it fails to include in itself its multiplicity and particularity; the result being that the determinate content is left outside the universal and remains in consequence isolated, having no necessary internal connection with the universal itself.

In contrast to this, philosophical science, *i.e.*, dialectic, proceeds from the inner structure of things outwards, and looks upon Nature as a concrete unity, an organic whole. To the abstract universality of empirical science it opposes a dynamic unity. The philosophical or dialectical conception of the universal is of a universal which contains abundance in itself, in which specific differences and individual attributes are incorporated together into its indestructible

---

[1] *Ibid.*, p. 38.   [2] *Ibid.*, p. 21.   [3] *Ibid.*, p. 53.   [4] *Ibid.*
[5] For a fuller account of the 'concrete concept', see Part Two, Ch. VII.

unity. Concrete totality, the unity of universal and particular—that is the true philosophical category.[1]

From this Hegelian conception of the difference between natural science and the philosophy of Nature, Deborin, like Engels, deviates only to this extent, that he draws therefrom a further conclusion. Whereas Hegel was led into creating a special *philosophy of Nature*, Deborin joined Engels in demanding the replacement of all such philosophical fabrications by an introduction of the dialectical method into the positive natural sciences as such.[2]

In consequence, therefore, Deborin makes concrete application of the materialist dialectic to science itself and employs it in order to explain the real transitions from one form of motion (or order of being) to another. In opposition to the mechanists, he upholds the specific quality of each individual level of things in Nature, the specific difference between inorganic matter, the organism and consciousness:

'Being, Life and Consciousness represent three fundamental levels or stages in the development of matter. It is one and the same matter, as the substantial element in the process of development, which transforms itself into living matter, and this in turn into thinking matter.' [3]

Despite the emergence of higher forms from lower ones, Deborin still retains a qualitative distinction between them, so that living matter, for example, cannot simply be derived from the inanimate:

'The naïve mechanistic outlook considers it possible to effect a simple derivation of the phenomena, both of consciousness and life, from dead matter or "being", but in so doing the specific character of these phenomena, as particular "nodes" and "categories", is completely left out of account.' [4]

The mechanistic error consists in one-sidedly keeping only the unity, the continuity, of inorganic and living matter in view. But in

[1] A. M. Deborin: *Op. cit.*, p. 48.

[2] *Ibid.* It is interesting that L. I. Axel'rod (*Ortodox*) sees in the 'realism' which underlies Deborin's doctrine of the 'concrete concept' a danger to materialistic atheism. The central thesis of the Deborinists, whereby 'the universal concepts formed by our thinking represent merely a copy of the universal to be found in things themselves', must lead to the well-known ontological proof for the existence of God. 'The Deborinists are advancing with rapid strides into theodicy, or, to put it more plainly, into popery.' (Quoted from P. Prokofiev: *Op. cit.*, p. 484); Deborin himself outlines his doctrine of the 'concrete concept' in his *Dialektika i estestvoznanie*, pp. 243–9.

[3] A. M. Deborin: *Op. cit.*, pp. 142 f.   [4] *Ibid.*, p. 143.

reality such a 'continuous' development cannot be conceived of without interruptions (*pereryvy*).[1] For this reason the development must be seen as a dialectical one, *i.e.*, the continuous development gives place, dialectically, at a certain level, to discontinuity, a 'leap' occurs, and a completely new quality makes its appearance. This holds, in the first place, for the reducibility of organic phenomena to those of physics and chemistry:

'So far as its *origin* is concerned, *the living is descended from the inanimate*, but so far as its specific *form* is concerned it cannot be derived from inorganic matter.' [2]

The passage from the living to the conscious organism involves, in Deborin's view, a dialectical transition, no less than that from inorganic matter to the organic. At a certain stage in the development of living matter a new leap takes place, and consciousness, a new quality of matter, appears; the object becomes a subject.

Since living matter is also at the same time matter as such, and conscious matter also at the same time organic matter, the unity of object and subject is thereby realized:

'The subject appears to us, not as a spiritual centre, an abstract point, completely divorced from the object. It is also at the same time an object; the subject is above all an *organic whole, i.e.*, body, senses and brain. There can be no subject without an object.' [3]

From this standpoint, which discerns the unity of subject and object in the mode of being of the knowing subject himself, Deborin takes issue against the views of Axel'rod, already depicted above, according to which the unity of subject and object is realized in sensation.[4] Deborin describes this as an idealistic point of view. For the idealists do indeed consider both subject and object, together with their unity, to be merely given in representation.[5] But this argument appears to be wide of the mark, for Axel'rod does not at all maintain that such unity is *only* realized in representation. In her edition of Lenin's *Materialism and Empirio-Criticism* she expressly says:

'The theory of symbols, which upholds the existence of both subject and object, unifies both factors in that it views the subject as a special kind of object and its sensations as the product of interaction between two objects, of which one is also, at the same time, the subject.' [6]

Such, in outline, is the philosophical position of Deborin. Many of its elements were also incorporated into the official dialectical

---

[1] *Ibid.*   [2] *Ibid.*, p. 301.   [3] *Ibid.*, p. 256.   [4] *Cf.* above, p. 152.
[5] A. M. Deborin: *Op. cit.*, p. 256.
[6] V. I. Lenin: *Sochineniya*, XIII[3], p. 330.

materialism. The point on which Deborin was most strenuously attacked was his seemingly excessive emphasis on dialectic as a methodology. But as we have seen, this objection scarcely does him justice.

Mitin touches on a more important point when he makes it a further objection to Deborin that the latter's view of dialectic represents a reconciliation of opposites, not a struggle between them. In discussing Kant's antinomies, Deborin writes:

'Kant opposed the thesis to the antithesis and attempts to show that the thesis excludes the antithesis, and hence that they cannot be reconciled or resolved. The positive dialectic, on the other hand, sees in thesis and antithesis opposites which are not mutually exclusive, but reconciled one with another.' [1]

Mitin contrasts this view of dialectic with that of Lenin, according to which it is not the unity, but the opposition, which plays the primary rôle in the dialectic: the unity of opposites is relative, temporary, transient; whereas the conflict between mutually exclusive opposites is absolute, like development and movement itself.[2]

3. TROTSKY

Menshevizing idealism was designated by orthodox upholders of the 'party line' as the theoretical basis of Left-wing deviationism. But since these 'Leftists' included the celebrated figure of Leon Trotsky, it seems appropriate for us to inquire into the latter's philosophical opinions,[3] more especially since several of Deborin's pupils and followers (Sten, Karev) were expressly accused of Trotskyism.[4]

What constitutes the essence of Trotskyism? Stalin reduces Trotskyism to three essential points: the denial of the possibility of socialism in one country, the renunciation of the alliance between proletariat and peasantry, and the demand for a measure of 'democracy' within the party:

'The essence of Trotskyism is, first of all, denial of the possibility of completely building socialism in the U.S.S.R. by the efforts of the working class and peasantry of our country. . . . The essence of Trotskyism is, secondly, denial of the possibility of drawing the

---

[1] In *Arkhiv K. Marxa i F. Engelsa*, I (1924), p. 64; *cf.* M. B. Mitin: *Op. cit.*, p. 296.

[2] M. B. Mitin: *Op. cit.*, p. 296.

[3] Which at all events scarcely display much 'idealism', being marked, rather, by an outspoken mechanism.

[4] *Cf.* M. V. Vol'fson–G. M. Gak: *Op. cit.*, p. 228.

main mass of the peasantry into the work of socialist construction in the countryside. . . . The essence of Trotskyism is, lastly, denial of the necessity for iron discipline in the Party. . . . According to Trotskyism, the C.P.S.U.(B) must be not a single, united militant party, but a collection of groups and factions, each with its own centre, its own discipline, its own press, and so forth.' [1]

Lev Davidovich Bronstein (Trotsky) was born in 1879, the son of Jewish colonists in Kherson. Possessed of intellectual and literary gifts, it was as a student (at the University of Kiev) that he came, like most of his generation, into close contact with the social-revolutionary ideas of the day. In 1898 his participation in a workers' movement, the *Yuzhno-russky rabochy soyuz* (South Russian Workers' Union), led to his banishment to Siberia, whence he escaped to London. Here he joined Lenin in editing the periodical *Iskra*. At the Second Party Congress he took the side of the Mensheviks. In 1905 he returned to Russia, became a member of the Soviet of Workers' Deputies, and devoted himself to the publishing of a number of newspapers. Exiled with other members of the Soviet to Siberia once more, he escaped a second time and went to Austria, where he brought out the paper *Pravda* in Vienna. He succeeded in gathering round him a group who made it their object to pursue a 'non-factional' line, above party; a line, that is, of reconciliation between Mensheviks and Bolsheviks, though the latter, at all events, regarded it simply as a menshevik 'blind'. After the February Revolution of 1917, Trotsky returned to Russia and soon afterwards joined the Bolshevik Party. After the October Revolution he occupied a number of high positions: Commissar for External Affairs, Commissar for War, and later Commissar for Transport. On the question of the Peace of Brest-Litovsk he stood out against Lenin, his proposal being that there should be neither conclusion of peace nor continuation of the war.

In the years that followed he continued to disagree with Lenin on a number of questions, and still more so, after the latter's death, with Stalin. For this reason, from 1925 onwards, he was gradually deprived of his offices, and finally, in November 1927, expelled from the Party on account of a demonstration organized by the Trotskyist underground movement. Banished, after the Fifteenth Party Congress (December 1927), to Alma-Ata, and eventually (1929) sent into exile abroad, he died by assassination in Mexico on 21st August 1940.

[1] *Politichesky otchet Tsentral'nogo Komiteta XVI syezda VKP(b)* (Political Report of the Central Committee to the XVIth Congress of the C.P.S.U.(B)), in J. Stalin: *Voprosy leninizma*, 9th edn., pp. 557 f; omitted from the latest (11th) edition (English translation in *Works*, XII, pp. 364–6).

Defenders of the 'party line' in philosophy endeavour to ascribe Trotsky's political errors to his philosophical outlook; their chief concern is to show that his belief in the impossibility of confining socialism to Russia without a concurrent victory of socialism all over Europe is of a piece with his fatalist interpretation of history and historical materialism. Vol'fson and Gak[1] accuse Trotsky of sharing the belief held by the theoreticians of the Second International, that 'productive forces' are the decisive factor in the historical process. Whereas the official Soviet theory considers this decisive factor to embrace 'both the productive forces of society and men's relations to production',[2] in Trotsky's view productive relationships blindly follow the development of the productive forces, by which they are governed as if by mechanical causality. The new socialist relations of production appear automatically as the outcome of the productive forces; and since all Europe, Russia included, constitutes a single economic organism, socialism in Russia is impossible without a socialist Europe.

Trotsky—say Vol'fson and Gak—agrees with the German social-democrat Bernstein in regarding the determinism of Marx and Engels as a mechanistic determinism. The only difference between them is that Bernstein found this determinism a reason for turning against Marxism, whereas Trotsky, who gives himself out as a Marxist, is in fact a fatalist.[3]

Now it may well be true that Trotsky's historical materialism does at times recall the extreme and fatalistic formulae of the early Russian Marxists, who emphasized against the *Narodniks* the objective character of history, to which, in their opinion, only the category of necessity, not that of justice, could be made to apply:

'The Revolution'—says Trotsky in similar vein—'like history in general, can only be understood by regarding it as an objectively conditioned process. The development of peoples confronts them with problems which can only be solved by way of revolution. At certain periods the storm breaks with such violence that a whole nation gets swept into the tragic whirlpool. Nothing is more petty than to moralize about great social catastrophes. Then, above all, Spinoza's maxim is in season: neither to weep, nor to laugh, nor to hate, but to understand.'[4]

[1] M. V. Vol'fson–G. M. Gak: *Op. cit.*, p. 224.

[2] J. Stalin: *O dialekticheskom i istoricheskom materializme* (Dialectical and Historical Materialism), in *Istoriya Vsesoyuznoy Kommunisticheskoy Partii* (*bol'shevikov*), (*History of the C.P.S.U.(B)*)), p. 115 (English, p. 120); *cf.* also *Voprosy leninizma* 11th edn., p. 551 (English, p. 584).

[3] M. V. Vol'fson–G. M. Gak: *Op. cit.*, p. 225.

[4] L. Trotsky: *Istoriya russkoy revolyutsii* (History of the Russian Revolution), 3 vols., Berlin 1931; here I, pp. 7 f. (Preface to the Russian edition).

These remarks are not, however, to be understood in too extreme a sense. For as Wolf Giusti very rightly points out, Trotsky also lays continual stress on the anti-deterministic elements in Marxism:

'Dialectical materialism', he writes on one occasion, 'at any rate has nothing in common with fatalism.' [1]

In the same *History of the Russian Revolution* he expressly disclaims the view, later attributed to him by Vol'fson, that relations of production alter automatically, once the productive forces have attained a certain level of development:

'. . . But societies are not so rational in building that the dates for proletarian dictatorships arrive exactly at the moment when the economic and cultural conditions are ripe for socialism.' [2]

It is for this reason that Trotsky ascribes an essential rôle to the activity of an *élite*, who make the revolution:

' . . . The advance layers bring after them the wavering and isolate the opposing. The majority is not counted up, but won over.' [3]

Trotsky here stands close enough to Lenin in his account of the rôle played by consciousness in historical development.

Again, in evaluating the rôle of the individual in history, Trotsky shows a tendency to leave room for a certain amount of indeterminism, and to emphasize the subjective element in Marxism. Of Lenin's role in the Russian Revolution he says:

'He did not impose his plan on the masses; he helped the masses to recognize and realize their own plan. . . . If our exposition demonstrates and proves anything at all, we hope it proves that Lenin was not a demiurge of the revolutionary process, that he merely entered into a chain of objective historic forces.' [4]

On the other side, however, Trotsky also ascribes a crucial importance to Lenin in ensuring the success of the Revolution: he asks himself:

'Is it possible, however, to say confidently that the party without him would have found its road?' And he answers: 'We would by no means make bold to say that. . . . The rôle of personality arises before us here on a truly gigantic scale. It is necessary only to understand that rôle correctly, taking personality as a link in the historic chain.' [5]

[1] *Ibid.*, p. 366 (English version (tr. Max Eastman), 3 vols., London 1932, I, p. 341); *Cf.* Wolf Giusti: *Due secoli di pensioro politico russo*, Florence 1943, p. 269.
[2] L. Trotsky: *Op. cit.*, I, p. 356 (English version, I, p. 332).
[3] *Ibid.*, III, p. 197 (III, p. 178).
[4] *Ibid.*, I, pp. 362, 366 (I, pp. 337, 341).
[5] *Ibid.*, I, pp. 366 f. (I, p. 341).

Giusti therefore considers that Trotsky oscillates at this point between orthodox materialism and the urge to greater freedom of opinion.[1] But, as may be seen from the passages already cited, it would be better to speak, not so much of an oscillation, as of a standpoint which seeks to combine both elements, the significance of the masses and the rôle of the individual. Trotsky is indeed well aware of the fact that both elements play an essential part in history: whether it be the activity of individuals, or the unconscious and, as it were, subterranean development undergone by the whole of a people, or even the whole of mankind. The unconscious development of the masses occupies the same position in history as the head of steam in an engine, which in order to do its work, however, must first be fed into the cylinder so as to set the piston in motion. The cylinder and piston represent the factor of 'consciousness':

'Only on the basis of a study of political processes in the masses themselves, can we understand the rôle of parties and leaders, whom we least of all are inclined to ignore. They constitute not an independent, but nevertheless a very important element in the process. Without a guiding organization the energy of the masses would dissipate like steam not enclosed in a piston-box. But nevertheless what moves things is not the piston or the box, but the steam.' [2]

If these considerations, linked as they are with the first essential point in Trotskyism, seem strongly reminiscent of the controversies between the early Russian Marxists and the *Narodniks*, the same may be said of the arguments which Trotsky uses in support of another of his theories, that of the revolutionary rôle of the peasantry. His discussion bears upon the celebrated problem of the peculiar path in Russian history.

The conflict was occasioned by a book of Trotsky's entitled *1905*. In it he attempted to provide historical and theoretical justification for his watchword, the conquest of power by the proletariat, a slogan which he contrasted with two others, the menshevik proposal for a bourgeois-democratic republic and the bolshevik demand for a democratic republic of workers and peasants. These claims made a great stir, especially among the Mensheviks. Their counter-arguments ran as follows: The political dominance of the proletariat must necessarily be preceded by a bourgeois-democratic republic, for the proletariat requires to be educated through a long course of historical development. Any attempt to by-pass this stage would be to plunge into 'adventurism'. If even the proletariat of Western Europe is as yet in no position to seize power, the Russian proletariat must be considered far less capable still of doing so.

---

[1] W. Giusti: *Op. cit.*, p. 267.
[2] L. Trotsky: *Op. cit.*, I, p. 13 (I, p. 17).

Trotsky seeks to meet these objections by appealing to the deep-seated peculiarities of Russian historical development. He stresses

'that the indubitable and irrefutable belatedness of Russia's development under influence and pressure of the higher culture from the West, results, not in a simple repetition of the West European historic process, but in the creation of profound *peculiarities* demanding independent study.' [1]

These peculiarities arise from the fact that European capitalism has invaded Russia without giving the country time to pass through all those phases of development which it has itself undergone in reaching its present stage of evolution:

'Russian capitalism did not develop from handicraft through manufacture to the factory, because European capital, at first in the trade form and afterwards in the finance and industrial form, poured down on us during that period when Russian handicraft had not in the mass divided itself from agriculture.' [2]

The result of this is that Russia, though in one sense an exceptionally backward country, is in other respects an ultra-modern one:

'Hence the appearance among us of the most modern capitalist industry in an environment of economic primitiveness: The Belgian or American factory, and round about it settlements, villages of wood and straw, burning up every year, etc. The most primitive beginnings and the latest European endings.' [3]

This is the reason why Russia, which in many respects is so backward, is so far advanced in a number of fields, especially the political:

'Hence the political weakness of the Russian bourgeoisie, hence the ease with which we settled accounts with the Russian bourgeoisie; hence our further difficulties when the European bourgeoisie interfered.'

'And our proletariat? Did it pass through the school of the mediaeval apprentice brotherhoods? Has it the ancient tradition of the guilds? Nothing of the kind. It was thrown into the factory cauldron snatched directly from the plough. Hence the absence of conservative tradition, absence of caste in the proletariat itself, revolutionary freshness; hence—along with other causes—October, the first workers' government in the world.' [4]

The peculiarities of Russian historical development have therefore enabled her to by-pass the intermediate political forms which have

---

[1] L. Trotsky: *Op cit.*, I, p. 507 (I, p. 470).
[2] *Ibid.*, p. 512 (474).   [3] *Ibid.*   [4] *Ibid.*

first had to be traversed in Western Europe, and so made possible an immediate seizure of power by the proletariat. It is to this point especially that the exponents of the 'party line' have directed their criticism. Trotsky stands accused of a fallacious voluntarism. Marxism—so these critics say—by no means denies the rôle of personality in history, but the basis of volition, both in the individual and the class, is not choice, but knowledge of objective reality and of the economic class-needs that are rooted therein. To Trotsky's pure voluntarism they oppose a voluntarism based on 'objective logic' and mindful of the laws of development of objective reality. In Trotsky, however, voluntarism appears, not as the expression of a known objective necessity, but as something imposed, so to speak, on reality from without. This fallacious voluntarism leads him off into these attempts to overleap the necessary intermediate stages of development.[1]

This criticism deserves especial notice, in that it defines the position of the authors of the party line themselves as to the rôle which can be attributed to the will. It makes striking acknowledgement of the fact that the will must necessarily be governed by the cognitive capacities. Nevertheless, so far as it bears upon Trotsky's position, the criticism seems unfounded, for although he defends the possibility of an immediate seizure of power by the proletariat in Russia, he does not envisage this as a blind voluntarism, as these authors maintain. So much may be seen already from the declaration contained in the Preface to his *History of the Russian Revolution*, that he sees it as the object of his historical labours to give such account of events as will bring to light their conformity to law and the interconnection between them.[2] His view of the historical rôle of individual personalities tends, as we have already seen, in the same direction.

The artificiality, so apparent in this polemic and so typical of controversy between Soviet philosophers of opposing schools, in which politically objectionable opponents must at all costs be credited with false philosophical opinions—this artificiality also emerges in an objection levelled by Mitin against a passage in Trotsky's book. It is in fact just such a passage as to make it clearly apparent that Trotsky's voluntarism does not forsake the ground of objective reality. In the Preface to his *History of the Russian Revolution* Trotsky speaks of his political opinions, which he has no reason to conceal, and continues:

'But the reader does have the right to demand that a historical work should not be the defence of a political position, but an internally

---

[1] *Cf.* M. B. Mitin: *Op. cit.*, pp. 303 f.
[2] *Cf.* L. Trotsky: *Op. cit.*, I, p. 11 (I, p. 15).

well-founded portrayal of the actual process of the revolution. A historical work only then completely fulfils its mission when events unfold upon its pages in their full natural necessity.' [1]

Mitin assumes that Trotsky is here admitting the possibility of a contradiction between the political outlook of the proletariat and the actual process of history, which would be internally at variance with the thesis of partisanship in theory and philosophy. Trotsky concurs, in effect, with Plekhanov's remark that 'strictly speaking, there can be no such thing as a partisan science'.

This denial of partisanship in philosophy leads inevitably to a separation of theory from practice. Particular exception is taken to the tone of a speech on Mendeleyev, which Trotsky delivered to a conference of Soviet scientists, and in which he gave open expression to his own opinion, that theoretical inquiries must remain independent of the political partisanship of practice:

'It is perfectly possible for the individual researcher to pay no heed to the practical outcome of his inquiries. The freer, the bolder, the more independent the workings of his thought from the practical needs of the day, the better they will be.' [2]

Trotsky sees in such objectivism the essence of Marxism, which again indicates that this voluntarism is by no means so blind as his opponents would have us suppose:

'It is just in this that the essence of Marxism consists, that in the last resort it approaches society as an objective topic of inquiry and views the history of mankind as a gigantic laboratory record. . . . It is precisely such an objective attitude which gives to Marxism an irresistible power of historical foresight.' [3]

The separation of theory and practice underlying this 'false objectivism' is taken by Mitin as a highly typical feature of menshevizing idealism; and in this respect Trotsky approximates to Deborinism. But Mitin also draws attention to a further affinity on Trotsky's part towards mechanism, rightly detecting in him opinions symptomatic of mechanistic materialism. At the aforesaid conference on Mendeleyev Trotsky maintains phenomena of higher order to be deducible from those of lower order:

'Psychology, in our opinion, is reducible, in the last resort, to physiology, and the latter in turn to chemistry, physics and

[1] *Ibid.*, p. 15 (18).
[2] L. Trotsky: *Mendeleyev i marxizm* (Mendeleyev and Marxism), 1925, p. 6; *cf.* M. B. Mitin: *Op. cit.*, p. 301.
[3] *Cf.* M. B. Mitin: *Op. cit.*, p. 301.

mechanics. . . . Chemistry traces the nature of chemical processes to the mechanical and physical properties of the minute parts.'[1]

Nor do phenomena of a spiritual type form any exception:

'The soul is a complex system of conditioned reflexes, entirely rooted in the primary reflexes of physiology, which in turn trace their origins through the broad strata of chemistry into the underworld of physics and mechanics.'[2]

A similar derivation is extended even to society itself:

'The same may be said of sociology. In order to account for social phenomena there is no need whatever to invoke eternal or transcendent principles of any kind. Society is just as much a product of the development of primary matter as the crust of the earth or an amoeba. Thus it is that scientific thought, with its diamond-drill methods, can penetrate from the most complex phenomena of social ideology to matter and its constituent elements, the particles and their physical and mechanical properties.'[3]

On the strength of such opinions, others have also reckoned Trotsky among the mechanists,[4] and there is more justification for this, perhaps, than for contriving to connect him with menshevizing idealism.

[1] L. Trotsky: *Sochineniya* (Works), XXI, pp. 273 f., *cf.* M. B. Mitin: *Op. cit.*, p. 305.
[2] *Ibid.*, p. 275 (Mitin, p. 305).   [3] *Ibid.*
[4] *Cf.*, for example, P. Prokofiev: *Sovetskaya filosofiya* (Soviet Philosophy) in *Sovremennyya Zapiski*, XXXIII (1927), p. 495.

CHAPTER IX

Developments since 1931

1. CONSEQUENCES OF THE DECREE OF THE CENTRAL COMMITTEE OF 25TH JANUARY 1931

THE beginning of 1931, with its double condemnation, by the Central Committee of the Bolshevik Party, of mechanism and Deborinism alike, represents a decisive turning-point in the history of Soviet philosophy. Whereas previously there had at least been a continuing opposition between rival tendencies within Soviet philosophy, and a resultant conflict of schools and opinions, with discussion and controversy, all such contention is from this time forward abolished; the course of philosophy flows in the narrow channel of officially prescribed opinion; all controversy is now directed outwards merely, against the 'bourgeois' ideology, which is striven against as a class-enemy. To be sure, 'discussions' are still conducted within Soviet philosophy itself. But these are no longer concerned to promote the emergence of truth from an interchange of conflicting opinions, being devoted merely to discovering and 'rooting-out' deviations on the part of individual authors from the course laid down by the 'classics of Marxism', Marx, Engels, Lenin and Stalin.

For Deborin himself, the immediate consequence of the judgement on 25th January 1931 was that he was compelled to resign his post as Chief Editor of the journal *Under the Banner of Marxism*. The paper was entrusted to an editorial board composed of supporters of the 'party line' and distinguished for its party loyalty; the members of this board included Pokrovsky, Adoratsky, Mitin, Yudin and Maximov. But in spite of this, Deborin, who, as we have seen, made open acknowledgement of his 'error' and freely showed his remorse, continued to occupy leading positions on the 'philosophical front';

thus we later find him on the Council of the Philosophical Institute of the Academy of Sciences, on the Praesidium of the Academy of Sciences and even (as Deputy Chairman) on the editorial board of the *Vestnik* of the Academy of Sciences of the U.S.S.R.[1]

The leading philosopher of the 'thirties, who repeatedly occupies a prominent position, especially in the first half of the decade, is undoubtedly Mark Borisovich Mitin. On specifically philosophical questions the new movement sponsored by him remains faithful to the dialectical materialism already preached by Deborin himself against the mechanists; thus one of its main concerns, for example, is to uphold (against mechanism) the independent status of philosophy; it is also anxious to assert and establish on philosophical grounds the impossibility of reducing phenomena of higher order to those of lower order (*e.g.*, of life to physico-mechanical laws), and does so by giving prominence to the category of quality; this too was a major feature of Deborin's dialectical materialism.

The main respects in which the new movement is distinguished from that of Deborin are questions, rather, of method and form. Whereas it had been raised as an objection against Deborin, during the period of struggle, that his philosophical labours were too much divorced from concrete life, that he trespassed against the Marxist postulate of the unity of theory and practice, the attempt was now accordingly made to conform to this postulate by endeavouring after the greatest possible integration of philosophy with concrete life; one of the means to this end being the demand that nobody should be a philosopher who did not also cultivate one of the positive sciences. It having been a further and major complaint against Deborin that he neglected the need for 'partisanship' in philosophy, every effort was now devoted to keeping the work of philosophy in the closest possible contact with the life and work of the Party, and to providing the latter with philosophical support in its political struggle for the 'party line'.

This undoubtedly has a bearing on yet another main feature of the new trend in philosophy, namely its emphasis on the outstanding philosophical eminence accorded, not to Marx, Engels or Lenin only, but also to Stalin. Indeed, on looking through the philosophical works published during these years, one gets the impression that in the modern period of Soviet philosophy there is really only one productive philosopher, only one man capable of a creative advance in the subject, namely Stalin, while the philosophical task of all the

---

[1] *Cf.* p. 159 above. The *Vestnik* (Proceedings) is the main collective organ of the Soviet Academy of Sciences; in addition the various Departments and Institutes also issue special journals from time to time, which appear either under the traditional title of *Izvestiya* (Bulletin), or under particular titles of their own.

many professors and authors in the field consists merely in this, that they should expound what Stalin has spoken. Not Mitin alone, but all the other authors in question, seize every opportunity of setting in its proper light the whole unique and outstanding contribution of Stalin to the further development of Marxist philosophy. At the very beginning of this period Mitin had written:

'The further advancement of Marxist-Leninist theory in every department, including that of the philosophy of Marxism, is associated with the name of Comrade Stalin. In all Comrade Stalin's practical achievements, and in all his writings, there is set forth the whole experience of the world-wide struggle of the proletariat, the whole rich store-house of Marxist-Leninist theory.' [1]

This style of philosophical utterance grew steadily more typical as time went on.

The early years of the new régime in philosophy were relatively abundant in the production of philosophical work. From this period there date a considerable number of publications, including both comprehensive treatises, such, for example, as the two-volume textbook of Mitin and Razumovsky on dialectical and historical materialism, and also monographs on individual problems in Marxist-Leninist philosophy, among which particular mention should perhaps be made of P. Dosev's book *The Copy Theory. Studies in the Epistemology of Dialectical Materialism*,[2] described by Jakovenko as 'the most solid and fundamental philosophical product' of this period in Soviet philosophy.[3] In 1936, in the journal *Under the Banner of Marxism*, Mitin made a survey of the philosophical work done since the 'purge' of 1931: certainly no period in Soviet philosophy can have been so fruitful in philosophical literature as the years 1931–6; in addition to literary activity there has also been the pedagogic achievement of building up new, bolshevik-trained cadres, who have had to be reared up to the level of modern science and of the requirements laid down by the Party; this is attested by the list of contributors to the journal *Under the Banner of Marxism* who have received their training in the Institute of Red Professors.[4]

All these achievements, however, could not prevent a threatening storm gathering over Mitin's head also, such that even this very article takes on more the appearance of an apology than of a calm assessment.

---

[1] M. B. Mitin: *Op. cit.*, p. 347.
[2] P. Dosev: *Teoriya otrazheniya. Ocherki po teorii poznaniya dialektiches-kogo materializma*, Moscow–Leningrad 1936.
[3] Boris Jakovenko: *Dějiny ruské filosofie*, Prague 1938/9, p. 484.
[4] *Cf.* B. Jakovenko: *Op. cit.*, p. 486.

This may well have been connected with the politico-social upheaval marked by the adoption of the new Constitution in November
1936, the

'Constitution embodying the victory of socialism and workers' and
peasants' democracy'.[1]

From this time on there was much talk of democracy, parliamentary
institutions and the liberation of human personality; the example
of the Soviet Union in introducing true Soviet parliamentarianism
was said to have revealed to the eyes of the world's workers that
the only road to true socialism and true democracy was the dictatorship of the proletariat, the road, that is, of Marx, Engels, Lenin and
Stalin. Leninist-Stalinist socialism alone redeems human personality;
the true humanism of Marxist-Leninism finds its expression in love
for oppressed humanity; and the relentless prosecution of the class-
struggle for the classless society is the indispensable condition for the
victory of proletarian humanism throughout the entire world.

This new spirit may well have also had its repercussions in the
fields of culture and philosophy. At all events the fact is that even
the latest phase of Soviet philosophy (Mitin *et al.*) now suddenly
began to be described as 'out of date' and senile and subjected to
vehement abuse. Despite the loud assurances of Mitin and company
that Marxist-Leninist philosophy represented the summit of all philosophical thought, that Lenin had inaugurated a new epoch in philosophy, that the presence of Stalin guaranteed the further development of philosophy along the right path, despite the emphasis on
partisanship in philosophy and the indissoluble unity of theory and
practice, it was charged against them that their writings of the years
1932–4 were in every respect outdated and completely useless owing
to their 'abstract and scholastic presentation of the subject'. The
complaint was raised that their books were polluted 'with quotations
from the execrable writings of Trotsky and Zinoviev' and were full
of 'crass political illiteracies'.[2]

It throws a revealing light on the atmosphere in which philosophical life is carried on in the Soviet Union, that Mitin hastened to
acknowledge that his latest writings had transgressed against the
line laid down by the Party for the 'philosophical front'.[3] This may
be the reason why, despite the attacks launched against him, Mitin
has remained to this day one of the leading philosophers and theoreticians in the Soviet Union; in later years we find him as deputy
director of the Philosophical Institute of the Academy of Sciences,

[1] *Istoriya Vsesoyuznoy Kommunisticheskoy Partii (bol'shevikov). Kratky
kurs*, p. 331 (English version: *History of the C.P.S.U.(B). Short Course*,
p. 346).
[2] B. Jakovenko: *Op. cit.*, pp. 486 f.   [3] *Ibid.*

at whose General Assembly on 28th–29th January 1939 he was elected to ordinary membership.[1] Nor again did the attacks on the work of Mitin and his collaborators imply that any fundamental change had taken place in the philosophical teachings of Bolshevism. If we compare the later publications with those of the years 1931–6, we find no difference in the doctrines contended for.[2] The differences are chiefly concerned with the formal aspect: ordering of the subject-matter, alignment of philosophy to the political activities of the Party (which is mainly evinced in the choice of illustrative material), insistence on the partisan character of philosophy, emphasis on the significance of Stalin to philosophy, and the like—in a word, an accentuation of the 'dictatorship of the proletariat' even in the sphere of philosophy. In addition, one may also note in the years immediately following a lessening in the actual number of philosophical publications. Lossky's opinion, dating from 1939, that 'in the last six years there has been a striking decline of philosophical literature in the U.S.S.R.',[3] is particularly true of the years after 1936, at least so far as quantity is concerned.

[1] On the occasion of his nomination to ordinary membership of the Academy of Sciences, Mitin's services to Soviet philosophy were appraised by the *Vestnik* of the Academy as follows: Mitin is 'one of the foremost researchers in the field of philosophy. For the past 10 years he has been engaged in investigating the problems of dialectical materialism and of the history of philosophy. Among the deepest inquiries devoted to the problems of dialectical materialism are works such as his *Boevye voprosy materialisticheskoy dialektiki* (Burning Questions of Materialist Dialectics), *Engels i dialektichesky materializm* (Engels and Dialectical Materialism), *Materialisticheskaya dialektika—filosofiya proletariata* (Materialist Dialectic—the Philosophy of the Proletariat), *Stalin i materialisticheskaya dialektika* (Stalin and the Materialist Dialectic). As regards the history of philosophy, particular importance attaches to those works of Mitin which outline the interrelation of ideas between Marxism and classical German philosophy, more especially the philosophy of Hegel (*Hegel i materialisticheskaya dialektika* (Hegel and the Materialist Dialectic), *Istoriya filosofii Hegelya* (Hegel's History of Philosophy), *Filosofiya prava Hegelya* (Hegel's Philosophy of Right). Translations of a number of Hegel's greatest works are appearing under M. B. Mitin's editorship (*Science of Logic*, *History of Philosophy*). In combination with his scholarly activities, Mitin pursues a thorough-going campaign against mechanist and idealist theories in the field of philosophy. In addition to his academic work, Mitin displays great activity as a lecturer and publicist. He is in charge of the philosophical and socio-political journal *Under the Banner of Marxism* and is at present Director of the Marx-Engels-Lenin Institute.' (*Vestnik Akademii Nauk SSSR*, 1939, No. 2/3, p. 181.)

[2] This is also the reason why the publications of 1931–6 still retain their importance at the present day.

[3] N. Lossky: *Op. cit.*, p. 369.

A quite special importance for all subsequent work in the ideological field attaches to the *History of the C.P.S.U.(B). Short Course* which appeared in 1938. Although described as 'edited by a Commission of the Central Committee of the C.P.S.U.(B)', it was generally attributed, especially after 1948, to the personal authorship of Stalin.[1]

1936 saw the introduction of the new 'Stalin' Constitution in the Soviet Union, whereby the socialization of the country was held to be completed. The next step to be taken was the transition to communism, and hence the creation of the preliminary conditions for this transition became a question of urgency in every quarter, notably in matters of economics, politics and administration. In the economic field the prerequisite for communism was held to be an abundant surplus of material goods; in the political field 'the communist education of the workers', together with 'abolition of the survivals of capitalism in the consciousness of the people', and 'further reinforcement of the power of the Soviet State'; in the administrative field the crucial task was seen in the creation of cadres, the problem of effecting a

'scientific organization of effort towards the propagation and training of cadres for Party and State'.[2]

For their ideological equipment it was said, Stalin and the Party had now sought, by this *Short History*, to put into the hands of the cadres awaiting formation a book which should present them with a history, not only of 'great deeds', but also of 'great ideas'. The history of the Party was meant to be depicted in this handbook as an unfolding of the fundamental ideas of Marxist-Leninism, as 'Marxist-

[1] The official Russian (and English) editions, already frequently cited, contain on the title-page the legend '*Pod redaktsiey komissii TsK VKP(b)*' ('Edited by a Commission of the Central Committee of the C.P.S.U.(B)'); only the Italian translation (*Storia del partito comunista (bolscevico) dell' URSS*, Rome 1944) is more explicit in this respect, mentioning Stalin, Kalinin, Molotov, Voroshilov, Kaganovich, Mikoyan, Zhdanov and Beria as authors, and adding in a special note '*sotto la redazione di Stalin*'. The practical work of editing was not in fact done by any of the Soviet politicians above-mentioned, but by the party historian E. M. Yaroslavsky, as may be gathered from an article by the Soviet woman historian A. M. Pankratova (*Sovetskaya istoricheskaya nauka za 25 let* (25 Years of Soviet Historical Science) in a collective work published by V. P. Volgin, E. V. Tarle and A. M. Pankratova, *Dvadtsat' pyat' let istoricheskoy nauki v SSSR* (25 Years of Historical Science in the U.S.S.R.), Moscow–Leningrad 1942, p. 35).

[2] '*Kratky kurs istorii VKP(b)*'—*Moguchee ideynoe oruzhie bol'shevizma* (The *History of the C.P.S.U.(B)*—A Powerful Ideological Weapon of Bolshevism), in *Bol'shevik*, 1948, No. 17, p. 2.

Leninism in action'. Having received the approval of the Party Central Committee, the *Kratky Kurs* thereupon became an officially prescribed work, or as Zhdanov expressed it, an

'encyclopaedia of basic knowledge in the field of Marxist-Leninism, a guide, laying down the official interpretation of basic problems in the history of the C.P.S.U.(B) and of Marxist-Leninism, as verified by the Party Central Committee, and in no way allowing of arbitrary interpretation.' [1]

Throughout all the years that followed, until Stalin's death, this book was now destined to exercise an absolute dictatorship in the ideological sphere.

2. THE PHILOSOPHICAL INSTITUTE OF THE ACADEMY OF SCIENCES

The further development of philosophy in the Soviet Union is intimately connected with the Philosophical Institute of the Academy of Sciences of the U.S.S.R. This Institute has been part of the Academy of Sciences only since 1936. In February 1936, in fact, by decree of the Central Committee of the Bolshevik Party and the Council of People's Commissars, the Communist Academy, founded in June 1918, was incorporated into the Academy of Sciences of the U.S.S.R.; this meant that the Philosophical Institute which had existed, since 1928, within the Communist Academy, was also transferred to the Academy of Sciences. On this occasion it was considerably enlarged and placed under the direction of V. V. Adoratsky, M. B. Mitin (who at that time was not even a member of the Academy) being nominated as his deputy.[2] In 1939 the General Assembly of the Academy of Sciences selected P. F. Yudin (who was merely a corresponding member) as Director of the Institute; on the Council we find, among others, names already known to us, or such as we shall meet again in what follows: A. M. Deborin, M. B. Mitin, I. K. Luppol, B. E. Bykhovsky, E. M. Yaroslavsky, A. A. Maximov, F. I. Khaskhachikh and others.

The work done by the Philosophical Institute in the pre-war years was not very extensive. The main tasks assigned to it were the issue of a six-to-seven-volume history of philosophy, of which the first volume was printed in 1939 and the second in 1940 (under the editorship of Mitin, Yudin, Alexandrov and Bykhovsky), together with the preparation of a two-volume dictionary of philosophy, of which the first volume (under the editorship of Mitin, Yudin, Alexandrov, Konstantinov and Cheremnykh) appeared in print in 1939. Great

---

[1] From the Decree of the Central Committee of the C.P.S.U.(B), 14th Nov. 1938; *ibid.*, p. 4.   [2] *Vestnik AN SSSR*, 1936, No. 2, pp. 57 f.

importance was attached to the bringing-out of a textbook of dialectical materialism. As early as January 1938, at the council-meeting of the Social Science Section of the Academy of Sciences, Mitin produced a report 'On the Plan for a Textbook of Dialectical Materialism'; but this plan, like the history of philosophy, remained a project for years afterwards. As preliminary makeshifts there appeared in 1939 a second edition of V. M. Pozner's *Outline of Dialectical Materialism*, and in 1940 A. V. Shcheglov's one-volume *Short Outline of the History of Philosophy*.[1] Besides this, a start was made upon editions, in Russian, of the works of Western European philosophers, such as Bacon, Helvétius, Condillac, Rousseau and Fourier, and the Russian translation of Hegel was continued (*Lectures on Aesthetics*). From among the writings of Russian forebears of Bolshevism there appeared a volume of *Selected Philosophical Essays* by N. G. Chernyshevsky.[2] But the output of original monographs is relatively small.

A special and peculiar task still assigned to the Institute was the campaign against religion. In 1938 the Praesidium of the Academy of Sciences complained that the Institute was not doing justice to this task. Two years later the Praesidium again returned to the subject and recommended the Institute to enlist specialists in the natural sciences for the purpose of its anti-religious work and to carry on the campaign in the closest possible association with the League of Militant Atheists.[3]

It is an evident proof of the great importance which has continued to be assigned to philosophy in the Soviet Union, that not even the major crisis of the Second World War, calling as it did for all efforts to be concentrated on military tasks, was sufficient to extinguish interest in the work of philosophy, either among the 'philosophical workers' themselves or on the part of the party authorities. In 1944 a decree was issued by the Central Committee of the C.P.S.U.(B) on shortcomings in the scientific work being done in philosophy, which points to serious errors in the exposition and assessment of German philosophy contained in Volume III of the *History of Philosophy*, which had meanwhile appeared. The authors of Volume III were held to have sinned by passing over in silence the reactionary attitude of Hegel, his nationalism and his deification of the Germans as a 'chosen people'. [4]

---

[1] A. V. Shcheglov: *Kratky ocherk istorii filosofii*, Moscow 1940.

[2] N. G. Chernyshevsky: *Izbrannye filosofskie sochineniya*, Moscow 1938, pp. 588 (English version, Moscow 1953, pp. 610).

[3] *Vestnik AN SSSR*, 1940, No. 8/9, p. 105; No. 10, p. 89.

[4] *Cf.* M. A. Leonov: *J. V. Stalin o preobrazuyushchey roli dialekticheskogo materializma* (J. V. Stalin on the Transforming Rôle of Dialectical Materialism), in *Voprosy filosofii*, 1949, 2, p. 181.

3. THE 'PHILOSOPHICAL DISCUSSION' OF 1947
AND ITS AFTERMATH

With the end of the Second World War, philosophical activity in
the Soviet Union received a powerful new impulse—an impulse
wholly in keeping with that same spirit of partisanship in philosophy
which even before the war had already lent its peculiar cast to Soviet
philosophy, and which now, redoubled in strength and equipped
with certain new features, again makes its presence felt. Among
'workers on the philosophical front' we still encounter a proportion
of the same names as before the war: Deborin, Mitin, Alexandrov and
Bykhovsky; but a number of new names have also gained importance: Kedrov, Leonov, Iovchuk and others.

One of the leading philosophical personalities at the moment is
Georgy Fedorovich Alexandrov (born 1908), sometime Director of
the Philosophical Institute. When the General Assembly of the
Academy of Sciences elected him, on 30th November 1946, to its
ordinary membership, the *'Vestnik* of the Academy of Sciences' presented him to its readers with the following account of his services to
philosophical scholarship:

'Georgy Fedorovich Alexandrov (born 1908), Stalin prize-winner,
Head of the Propaganda and Agitation Section of the Central Committee of the *C.P.S.U. (B)*, Professor of the History of Philosophy
in the Academy of Social Sciences. G. F. Alexandrov is widely known
in the U.S.S.R., and also abroad, as a gifted exponent of Marxist-
Leninist philosophy. The scope of his theoretical interests is extremely
broad, ranging from the philosophy of antiquity to that of modern
times, from the history of the rise and development of Marxist
philosophy to criticism of contemporary philosophy and bourgeois
sociology. In each of these fields G. F. Alexandrov has distinguished
himself by a considerable number of original publications, displaying
a high level of scientific research and making a new contribution to
our philosophical knowledge. We are also indebted to the pen of
G. F. Alexandrov for a series of works dealing with the history of
social theories, together with a number of books, pamphlets and
articles directed against Fascism. The most important of his scientific
treatises are: *Aristotle's Conception of the Philosophy of Nature* (1936),
Aristotle's Conception of Social and Political Theory, a study entitled
Aristotle (1940), and *A History of Western European Philosophy*
(1946). In 1942 G. F. Alexandrov was awarded the Stalin Prize for his
scientific work. For his outstanding achievements, G. F. Alexandrov
has been decorated with the Order of Lenin, the Order of the Banner
of Labour, the Order of the Patriotic War, 1st Class, and with the

medals "For the Defence of Moscow" and "For Heroic Service in the Great Patriotic War, 1941–45".' [1]

The name of Alexandrov is associated with what is easily the most important philosophical event in the Soviet Union since the end of the war, namely the discussion arranged by the Central Committee of the Party in June 1947 on his *History of Western European Philosophy*: this being the occasion of the celebrated intervention on the part of A. A. Zhdanov in which he pilloried a number of Alexandrov's failings and deviations from orthodoxy. A discussion on this book had already taken place in the Philosophical Institute in January 1947. But this having turned out, as Zhdanov put it, a 'pale' and 'ineffective' affair, [2] the Central Committee of the C.P.S.U.(B) ordered the organization of a new discussion on a much more extensive scale. [3] If Alexandrov has in fact achieved wide fame abroad as well, he owes this not so much to his works as to this discussion on his book, and its official condemnation by the Secretary of the Central Committee of the Bolshevik Party.

What had happened? How are we to account for this sudden reversal in the evaluation of Alexandrov's scientific achievements? How did it come about that Alexandrov, who only six months previously had received such praise from the Academy of Sciences, the first (1945) edition of whose book had been commended, by decree of the Council of Ministers of the Soviet Union, as worthy of the Stalin Prize and had received in *Bol'shevik*, the theoretical and political journal of the Party Central Committee, an extremely appreciative notice in which its 'high theoretical standard, depth of content and clarity of presentation' were approvingly referred to, [4]—how did it come about that this same Alexandrov and this very same book were made the occasion for the Central Committee's incursion upon the philosophical front?

The reasons for this procedure are not entirely clear. But if one looks more closely at Zhdanov's intervention in the debate, [5] one

[1] *Vestnik AN SSSR*, 1947, No. 1, p. 56. Very interesting biographical details, and an estimate of Alexandrov's importance in relation to the course of official ideology in the Soviet Union, are provided in N. Gradoboyev: *G. F. Alexandrovs dialektische Laufbahn*, in *Ost-Probleme*, III (1951), No. 28, pp. 855–8.

[2] In *Voprosy filosofii*, 1947, No. 1, p. 5. Cited hereafter as *VF*.

[3] *Cf. Izvestiya AN SSSR. Seriya istorii i filosofii*, VI (1949), p. 507. Cited hereafter as *IAN*.

[4] P. Vyshinsky: *Nauchny trud po istorii filosofii* (A Scientific Work on the History of Philosophy), in *Bol'shevik*, 1946, No. 13/14, pp. 65 ff. By 1946 the second, enlarged edition of the book had already appeared.

[5] A. A. Zhdanov: *Vystuplenie na diskussii*, etc. (*cf.* above, p. 55, n. 1) (*On Literature, Music and Philosophy*, pp. 76–112).

gets the impression that the whole of this noisy discussion was dragged in only in order to give the Central Committee the opportunity of delivering an attack on the 'philosophical front' and of achieving a corresponding emphasis in laying down new norms for philosophical work. This interpretation is confirmed by the relative triviality of the shortcomings censured in Alexandrov's book, by the fact that only a part of Zhdanov's speech is devoted to the book itself, the whole second part of it being given over to an indictment of conditions on the 'philosophical front' in general, and lastly by the consideration that this attack on the 'philosophical front' represents but one link in a chain of similar incursions into the ideological field on the part of the Central Committee: into literature (1946), into music (1948) and also into biology (1948).

The discussion held in Moscow was attended by more than 90 'workers in philosophical science' from Moscow and the Union republics, including Mitin, Svetlov, Kedrov, Iovchuk and others. The book itself was criticized for its lack of party spirit, evinced in its objective manner of presentation, its inadequate investigation of the social roots of philosophical systems; there were also loud protests against its manner of dealing separately with Western European philosophy, without giving a simultaneous account of the history of Russian philosophy as well.

Zhdanov's speech laid particular stress on the fact that in Alexandrov's book the history of philosophy appears as a smooth continuous process of development; Marxist philosophy does not emerge clearly as a revolutionary eruption into philosophy.

'The author obviously does not understand that Marx and Engels created a new philosophy, differing qualitatively from all previous philosophical systems, however progressive they were.' [1]

The revolutionary novelty introduced by Marxism consists in the fact that it 'supersedes the old philosophy' which 'was the property of a small élite, the aristocracy of the intellect', and marks

'the beginning of a completely new period in the history of philosophy, when it became a scientific weapon in the hands of the proletarian masses in their struggle for emancipation from capitalism'.[2]

The main weakness of the book which Zhdanov censures is its 'objectivist' spirit: the exposition is abstract, neutral, and Alexandrov sees in every philosopher first of all a professional associate and only secondarily an opponent. Moreover, the author violates the basic position of scientific materialism as regards the dependence of the development of ideas upon the material conditions of social life;

[1] *Ibid.*, p. 9 (80).   [2] *Ibid.*, p. 10 (83–4).

this deprives the book of a large part of its scientific character. Zhdanov also sees it as a fundamental failing of the book that it is only carried up to the rise of Marxism (1848), and more especially that it leaves Russian philosophy completely on one side, which implies a belittlement of the latter and an endorsement of the bourgeois distinction between 'Western' and 'Eastern' culture.

Zhdanov then goes on in the second part of his speech to deal with the general situation on the 'philosophical front'. 'The fact that the book did not evoke any considerable protest, that it required the intervention of the Central Committee, and particularly Comrade Stalin, to expose its inadequacies'—this is a proof, for Zhdanov, that serious misconceptions are abroad on the philosophical front.[1] The philosophical front is no longer a real front; philosophical work does not manifest either a militant spirit or a bolshevik tempo. The Philosophical Institute presents a particularly unsatisfactory picture; only in name does it represent an institution of an All-Union character; in reality it is completely out of touch with the periphery, with the philosophical institutes and chairs in the individual republics, regions and territories; the work of the Institute is scarcely directed at all to contemporary problems, being still far too much orientated upon the past.

Zhdanov sees the reason for these deficiencies in the fact that the workers in philosophy have not yet taken to heart the lessons inculcated by the Central Committee in its injunctions against lack of ideas and an unpolitical character in ideological work, against the divorce of the latter from contemporary issues, against the deification of all things foreign, and in favour of a militant bolshevik party spirit; the philosophers have supposed that all this is none of their concern. There has also been a lack of true bolshevik criticism and self-criticism. At this point Zhdanov makes it a complaint against Alexandrov personally that he overestimates his own powers and relies on a far too narrow circle of intimate collaborators and admirers. In this way the work of philosophy has become to some extent the monopoly of a small group of philosophers. All these failings can only be put down to the lack of true bolshevik criticism and self-criticism.

'In summing-up at the end of the discussion Comrade Alexandrov admitted that serious faults and failings had been disclosed, both in his book and in the organization of scientific work in the philosophical field. Comrade Alexandrov then went on to discuss how a course in the history of philosophy ought to be arranged if it was to do justice to what had been said in the discussion, and what conse-

[1] A. A. Zhdanov: *Vystuplenie na idskussii*, etc., p. 18 (*On Literature* . . . , p. 100).

quences must be drawn from the debate for the organization of scientific work in the field of philosophy.' [1]

In an article in *Bol'shevik* devoted to this discussion, these consequences are summarized in the following terms:

'The substance of the discussion constitutes a serious warning to workers in philosophy, that it is their duty to uphold the banner of Leninist-Stalinist partisanship throughout their scientific work—by theoretical elucidation of the problems of the Soviet system and all-round exposition of its great virtues, by treatment of the problems of Soviet culture and all-round demonstration of its superiority to bourgeois culture, by energetic campaigning against all manifestations of servility towards bourgeois culture and against any and every residue of capitalism in the mentality of the people. . . . It must be the task of the Soviet philosophers to put themselves at the spearhead of the struggle against the decadent and horrible ideology of the bourgeoisie and to deal out devastating blows against it.' [2]

War upon non-party 'objectivism', war upon servility towards bourgeois culture, war upon 'cosmopolitanism', and cultivation of Soviet-Russian patriotism—these are the watchwords that the 'philosophical discussion' was evidently employed to proclaim.

In order to draw out the practical consequences of this discussion, Alexandrov delivered a lecture a few months later in the Philosophical Institute on the programme of the Institute's scientific work during the next two or three years. Zhdanov had dwelt on the fact that the philosophers were lagging far behind in their work and were not fulfilling their part in the collective plan for communist education of the workers; Soviet philosophy must not remain the exclusive property of a small parcel of professors— it must be made available to the entire Soviet intelligentsia and must serve the interest of the Party. In order to do justice to the great rôle which Marxist-Leninist philosophy has always played, and must continue to play, in the Party's struggle, the Philosophical Institute must needs organize its scientific work in such a fashion that the lost ground is made up and philosophical back-slidings are avoided in the future; a true philosophical front must be created, filled with militant zeal, whose business it must be to further the progress of science, and to deal out devastating blows against ideologies hostile to communism. For this purpose the Philosophical Institute must establish contact, not only with all the other Institutes in the Academy of Sciences, but also

---

[1] *Cf. Bol'shevik*, 1947, No. 15, p. 56. A verbatim account of Alexandrov's concluding speech is contained in *VF*, 1947, 1, pp. 288 ff.; extracts, in German, are available in I. M. Bocheński: *Op. cit.*, pp. 171 f.

[2] G. Gak–A. Makarovsky: *Zhurnal 'Voprosy filosofii'* (The Journal *Problems of Philosophy*), in *Bol'shevik*, 1947, No. 15, p. 58.

with all qualified professors of philosophy throughout the entire Soviet Union and endeavour to provide effective aid to theoretical workers on the periphery; the habit of individual working must cease, and a beginning must be made towards solving the great theoretical problems by combined effort. The lecturer ended with a proposal to begin publication of a philosophical library, in which the works of the most outstanding philosophers, and especially of Russian authors, would be made available to a wider public.[1]

The first visible result of this great self-searching was the philosophical journal *Voprosy filosofii* (Problems of Philosophy), replacing the periodical *Under the Banner of Marxism* which disappeared in 1944. It appears three times a year, each number consisting of about 400 double-column pages,[2] and contains systematic articles dealing with individual aspects of Soviet philosophy (dialectical and historical materialism, philosophy of science, history of philosophy in Russia and in the other nations of the Soviet Union), copious polemics against 'bourgeois' philosophy, reviews of new publications and a chronicle of Soviet philosophical life. It is issued by the Philosophical Institute of the Academy of Sciences of the U.S.S.R. and is dedicated to

'carrying on an active and unrelenting struggle against the philosophy of bourgeois reaction and bourgeois objectivism, in the interests of the basic Leninist thesis of partisan spirit in philosophy and of a militant materialism. . . . The watchword of the journal is the wise saying of Stalin: To be master of Marxist-Leninist-theory is to understand it, to develop it and to carry it further.' [3]

The original Chief Editor was B. M. Kedrov, who was later supersided by D. I. Chesnokov.

At its first beginning, *Voprosy filosofii* brought once more a breath of fresh air into Soviet philosophy. Several notable essays appeared, fundamental discussions were initiated, and so on. Particularly worthy of note is an article by M. A. Markov, *On the Nature of Physical Knowledge*[4] (which will occupy us in more detail in Part Two), in which the author is so bold as to say something new which had never been said before by any of the 'classics' of Marxist-Leninism, and which actually seeks to explain physics in complete independence from Leninism. This article provoked a lively discussion to which the Editors readily gave space.[5] Similar controversies

---

[1] *Vestnik AN SSSR*, 1948, No. 3, pp. 124 f.

[2] Since 1951, six numbers a year have been issued, on a somewhat diminished scale.

[3] *VF*, 1949, 1, third endpaper.

[4] M. A. Markov: *O prirode fizicheskogo znaniya*, in *VF*, 1947, 2.

[5] *Diskussiya o prirode fizicheskogo znaniya. Obsuzhdenie stat'i M. A.*

arose out of an article by Z. A. Kamensky, *On the Problem of Tradition in Russian Materialist Philosophy of the 18th and 19th Centuries*,[1] and from the publication of the draft programme for a course on *The Foundations of Marxist-Leninist Aesthetics*.[2]

It seems, however, that under Kedrov's leadership the Stalinist motto about furthering the development of Marxist-Leninist theory must have been taken too seriously by the Editorial Board. Hardly had the fourth number appeared before Kedrov was relieved of his post and the journal reorganized. In the leading article of the first number put out by the new editorship the previous incumbents are charged with having published a series of defective articles: the article by Markov, which Kedrov must have taken under his wing, as appears both from his notes to the discussion and from the 'tendentious' choice of the contributions published therein; the article *Concepts of the Whole in Modern Biology* by I. I. Schmalhausen, which contradicts the principles of Michurinist biology from beginning to end (*cf.* below); and the article by Kamensky, which ought not to have been discussed, since it

'raised questions which are not open to dispute, and sought to revise the positions of Marxist-Leninism in relation to the history of Russian social thought'.[3]

4. FROM THE 'PHILOSOPHICAL DISCUSSION' TO THE DEATH OF STALIN

An even greater sensation, and still more lasting consequences, were occasioned by a further event on the 'theoretical front', which although directly related to another sector on this front, had repercussions also in the philosophical sphere and must therefore be briefly mentioned, namely a similar incursion on the part of the Central Committee of the Bolshevik Party into the territory of biology.[4] The issue here related to the classical Mendel-Morgan

Markova (Discussion on the Nature of Physical Knowledge. Further Opinions on the Essay by M. A. Markov), *VF*, 1948, 1, pp. 203–32; 3, pp. 222–35.

[1] Z. A. Kamensky: *K voprosu o traditsii v russkoy materialisticheskoy filosofii XVIII–XIX vekov*, in *VF*, 1947, 1; discussion thereon in *VF* 1948, 1, pp. 184–202.

[2] V. F. Berestnev–P. S. Trofimov: *Proekt programmy kursa 'Osnovy marxistsko-leninskoy estetiki'* in *VF*, 1948, 2, pp. 338–48; discussion thereon, ibid., 3, pp. 327–39.

[3] *Za bol'shevistskuyu partiynost' v filosofii* (For a Bolshevik Partisanship in Philosophy), in *VF*, 1948, 3, pp. 11 f.

[4] The 'biological discussion' was made the subject of propaganda on a particularly large scale and has therefore attracted greater attention abroad

theory of inheritance. This, it will be remembered, accounts for the fact that the descendants of an organism exhibit the same structure as their ancestors by reference to 'genes', which function as the material carriers of morphological and physiological characteristics. In opposition to this a new theory of inheritance was set up by a number of Soviet scientists, notably Michurin (d. 1935) and more recently Lysenko. This theory denies the existence of 'genes' and asserts the heritable transmission of characteristics acquired by the organism during its own lifetime, thereby in principle allowing for the possibility of using artificial regulation of the living conditions of organisms in order to guide the development of Nature in accordance with human desires. Now since this theory, with its denial of fixed unalterable species, was in striking accord with one of the basic principles of dialectical materialism, which rejects all unchangeable entities as 'metaphysical', it met with the approbation and active support of the Party Central Committee. In order to break the opposition to this new biological theory and to expose the supporters of the classical theory of inheritance which, prior to its condemnation by the Central Committee, was still accepted in Soviet biology also by a number of scientists (notably by the President of the White-Russian Academy of Sciences, Professor A. Zhebrak, the Director of the Institute of Developmental Morphology, I. I. Schmalhausen and others), an elaborately-mounted Session of the Lenin Academy of Agronomic Sciences was arranged from 31st July to 7th August 1948.[1] The entire session was devoted to discussion of Lysenko's report, *The Situation in Biological Science*. Once Lysenko had declared: 'The Central Committee of the Party examined my report and approved it',[2] the fate of the opposition was sealed: many erstwhile adherents of the Mendel-Morgan theory went over to Michurinism. In a letter to the Editors of *Pravda*, Professor Zhebrak declared:

'So long as two schools of thought in Soviet genetics were recognized

as well. But 'discussions' of very much the same type were also instituted within a number of other scientific and cultural fields. The measures for self-purging and renewal undertaken in literature and music are well known; those in the field of historical writing and research are less familiar. The latter, as it happens, which originated in the condemnation of a work by the Soviet historian N. L. Rubinstein, *Russkaya istoriografiya* (Russian Historiography), are tolerably closely connected with the 'philosophical discussion'.

[1] *O polozhenii v biologicheskoy nauke. Stenografichesky otchet sessii vsesoyuznoy akademii sel'sko khozyaystvennykh nauk imeni V. I. Lenina, 31 iyulya–7 avgusta 1948 g.*, Moscow 1948, pp. 534 (English version: *The Situation in Biological Science*, Moscow 1949).
[2] *Pravda*, 10th August, 1948; *O polozhenii . . .*, p. 512 (English, p. 605).

by the Party, and controversies between them were reckoned to constitute a fruitful discussion of theoretical problems, I have been obstinate in defending my own views. . . . But now, having convinced myself that the principles of Michurinism in Soviet genetics have been approved by the Central Committee of the C.P.S.U.(B), I no longer find it possible for myself, as a party-member, to persist in these opinions, which have been declared erroneous by the Central Committee of our Party.' [1]

This session was of absolutely crucial significance, not only in Soviet biology, but also far beyond its frontiers for the situation all along the 'theoretical front' in the Soviet Union. The Philosophical Institute of the Academy of Sciences itself held a session on 15th August 1948, which was attended not only by members of the Institute, but also by other philosophical workers in Moscow and adherents of Michurinism in biology, and in which counsel was taken on the value of what had emerged in the historic session of the Academy of Agronomic Sciences. In his opening speech, Alexandrov, the Director of the Institute, underlined the great significance of this session of the Academy of Agronomic Sciences. It has shown how the Party Central Committee guides the development of Soviet science, supporting everything progressive and cutting away everything reactionary in it; so far as the Philosophical Institute is concerned, Soviet philosophers are indeed for the most part supporters of the Michurinist view; only a few of them, such as P. P. Bondarenko for example, have taken up an attitude of indecision. The Michurinist school of biology is in full keeping with the spirit of Marxist-Leninist philosophy, whose radical uniqueness lies precisely in its pursuit of revolutionary changes in reality in the name of the victory of communism.

Two years after the 'discussion' on Alexandrov's book a collective 'heart-searching' on the state of philosophical studies was again instituted. From 8th to 15th July 1949 an 'All-Union Conference of Holders of Chairs of Marxist-Leninism and Philosophy in Institutions of Higher Education' was gathered together in Moscow from all quarters of the Soviet Union. The focal point of the conference was occupied by the report delivered by S. V. Kaftanov, Minister of Higher Education, 'On the State of Instruction in Marxist-Leninism and Philosophy in Institutions of Higher Education, and Measures for its Improvement'.[2] The Minister conceded that in consequence of

[1] *Pravda*, 15th August, 1948; a full account of the antecedents, course and consequences of this crisis in Soviet biology will be found in the author's article *Sowietwissenschaft. Der Sieg T. D. Lysenkos über V. Vavilov*, in *Wort und Wahrheit*, IV (1949), pp. 570–86.

[2] S. Kaftanov: *Vsemerno uluchshat' prepodavanie osnov marxizma-leninizma v vysshey shkole* (An All-out Drive to Improve the Basic Teaching of Marxist-Leninism in Higher Education), *Bol'shevik*, 1949, No. 12, pp. 22–33.

the discussions on problems of biology the chairs of Marxist-Leninism and Philosophy had found themselves obliged to enter into closer collaboration with teaching departments in the special sciences, and that their influence on the ideal conduct of instruction in these departments had thereby sensibly increased. In spite of this, however, Kaftanov also pointed to failings in the work of the chairs of General Philosophy: there is still evidence in many quarters of an objectivist attitude, of inadequate adherence to the principle of partisanship, of a lack of penetrating criticism and self-criticism; nor have a number of chairs been entering with sufficient energy into the controversy over Michurinism in biology. Many teachers of philosophy have not been doing enough, in the course of their work, as militant party propagandists; as is witnessed by the fact that they have not been sufficiently forward in uncovering the reactionary character of the theoretical prevarications of bourgeois philosophers in England, and more especially America, nor have they sufficiently exposed the dependent and servile attitude of these latter, directed as it is to upholding the order of imperialist tyranny.

Interesting sidelights on the Soviet practice of philosophy are also thrown by the individual speeches of participants in this conference, which are frequently critical of the work of the Philosophical Institute of the Academy of Sciences; particular offence was caused by the fact that Alexandrov could not find time to take part. Short résumés of the individual contributions to the discussion have been published in *Voprosy filosofii*.[1]

In the unanimously adopted Address to 'Our leader and teacher, Josef Vissarionovich Stalin', the participants in this conference promised, among other things:

'We shall let ourselves be infallibly guided by your directions as to the strict preservation of the unity of theory and practice, philosophy and politics, as to the principle of bolshevik partisanship in theory. . . . We promise you, dear Comrade Stalin, to take a leading part in the struggle against idealist, reactionary doctrines. . . . We promise you to transform our chairs into militant party collectives, exercising a continuing influence on the entire process of pedagogic teaching and displaying bolshevik vigilance and intolerance against every manifestation of bourgeois objectivism and cosmopolitanism. We shall fight unceasingly and untiringly against the reactionary ideology of Anglo-American imperialism. By wielding the sharp sword of bolshevik criticism and self-criticism we shall raise our work of

[1] *Vsesoyuznoe soveshchanie zaveduyushchikh kafedrami marxizma-leninizma i filosofii vysshikh uchebnykh zavedeniy* (All-Union Conference of Holders of Chairs of Marxism–Leninism and Philosophy in Institutions of Higher Education), in *VF*, 1949, 1, pp. 366–79.

teaching, scientific research and party propaganda to a higher level, consonant with the tasks of the struggle for communism.' [1]

Pravda, too, in its issue of 7th September 1949,[2] again turned its attention to the philosophical front. In a review of the third number of *Voprosy filosofii* for 1948, the first to appear under the new editorship, the organ of the Communist Party Central Committee concedes that under the new board a gratifying improvement has certainly occurred. For all that, attention is again drawn to a number of deficiencies, notably the fact that the leading article of the number in question

'fails to provide any deep analysis of the situation on the philosophical front in the period that has elapsed since the philosophical discussion'.[3]

The new Editors thereupon hastened to repair the omission in their next issue (No. 1, 1949). They open in self-critical fashion with the admission

'The Editors of the journal *Voprosy filosofii* acknowledge the observation made in *Pravda* to be completely justified and accept them as a guide to which they will unfailingly adhere.' [4]

They then go on to deal with the situation on the philosophical front. There has certainly been something of a revival during the last two years. But in spite of this, the lag on the philosophical sector of the ideological front has not yet been disposed of. Now, as before, the further development of philosophical thought is being carried on outside the precincts of professional philosophy. Many publications still contain errors of an objectivist, nationalist, cosmopolitan and idealist character. All these shortcomings are particularly evident in the work of the Philosophical Institute. The plan of scientific research for the year 1948 has not been fulfilled; work on the production of important current monographs is only progressing slowly. Alexandrov has still not contrived to free himself from his 'academic', bloodless style of exposition. The Institute is also failing in its task of co-ordinating the work carried on in the outlying Institutes: the Philosophical Institutes of the Ukraine, White Russia, Georgia . . . confine themselves exclusively to the history of philosophy in their respective countries and are content to leave the working-out of

[1] *Ibid.*, p. 379.
[2] *Za boevoy filosofsky zhurnal* (For a Militant Philosophical Journal), in *Pravda*, 7th September 1949, also in *VF*, 1949, 1, pp. 7–10.
[3] *Ibid.*, p. 7.
[4] *Korennym obrazom uluchshit' rabotu Instituta filosofii* (The Work of the Philosophical Institute must be Radically Improved!), in *VF*, 1949, 1, p. 12.

contemporary problems of Marxist philosophy as a 'monopoly' to the Philosophical Institute of the Academy of Sciences of the U.S.S.R.

All these criticisms obliged the Praesidium of the Academy of Sciences to dedicate a Session held on the 19th January 1950 to consideration of 'the scientific activities, the present state of affairs, and the training of cadres in the Philosophical Institute'. The Praesidium drew particular attention to the fact that the Institute had failed to fulfil its plan either in 1948 or 1949, and to the excessive disproportion obtaining between the number of tasks assigned to the Institute by the Academy (13 projects) and the programme devised by the Institute itself (62 topics). The works published continue to exhibit ideological errors and frequently suffer from an 'academic' mode of presentation. There is too little recourse to criticism and self-criticism. And concern for the training of cadres does not form a central preoccupation of those in charge. The Praesidium called on the Director of the Institute, Alexandrov, to see that these deficiencies were remedied, failing which, the question of the headship of the Institute would be put upon the agenda. As regards the further activities of the Institute, the Praesidium laid it down, among other things, that works ready for the press must be subjected to thoroughgoing discussion before publication, and the results of this discussion made public through the medium of the learned journals.

After this series of weighty criticisms on the part of the 'All-Union Conference', *Pravda*, *Voprosy filosofii* and now finally the Praesidium of the Academy of Sciences, something had at last got to be done within the Institute itself. The Council of the Institute, together with the 'entire collective of its staff', therefore assembled to review the situation in the light of the directive issued by the Praesidium on 19th January 1950. The committee subjected the work of the Institute as a whole and of its individual sectors and collaborators, but more especially that of the Directors, to a searching inquiry. The *Vestnik* of the Academy of Sciences contains a detailed account of the resolutions adopted at the session,[1] which provide us with such a vivid picture of philosophical work in the Soviet Union that at this point we shall quote its report verbatim.

'The Council began by acknowledging the complete justice of the profound and comprehensive criticism of the work of the Institute by the Praesidium of the Academy of Sciences of the U.S.S.R. . . .

'Having regard to the criticisms made, the Council confirmed the plan put forward by the Directors for the scientific work of the Institute during 1950, but instructed all sector-leaders in the Institute to lose no time in drawing up individual daily schedules of work

[1] *V Institute filosofii* (In the Philosophical Institute), in *Vestnik AN SSSR*, 1950, No. 3, pp. 109 f.

for each particular worker in the sector concerned, setting a precise finishing-date for work on every single chapter or section in the projects under preparation. The Directors are called upon to exercise strict control over the work-plan of the Institute as a whole, and also over that of each individual worker. Special control is to be kept over works undertaken on themes prescribed in the plan of the Academy.

'The resolution of the Council then goes on to specify in more detail the method of controlling the fulfilment of the plan. Sector-leaders are instructed to keep the progress of scientific works under thorough daily supervision, and to be prompt in submitting their co-workers' progress reports to sessions of the sector.

'The Council then made it clear that the reason for the low quality of ideal content in books already published was chiefly that these works had not previously been made the subject of bolshevist criticism, and decided that for the future no single work prepared by the Institute should be permitted to appear without having first been subjected to discussion within a wide circle of the scientific public.[1]

'Discussions were envisaged, in the first instance, on the already-completed chapters of the collective "History of Philosophy", namely those on the history of Russian philosophy and that of the peoples of the U.S.S.R., the foundation and development of historical and dialectical materialism by Marx and Engels, the further extension of Marxist philosophy by Lenin and Stalin, and more especially the chapters devoted to setting forth the history of Marxist-Leninist philosophy in the Soviet epoch. Similar discussions were projected on works prepared under the auspices of the Academy plan: "Lenin and Natural Science" (by A. A. Maximov, Corresponding Member of the Academy of Sciences of the U.S.S.R.), "On the Socialist Soviet State" (by D. I. Chesnokov), the logical textbooks (by A. A. Chudov), "Philosophical Problems of Modern Biology" (a collective work), and individual chapters of the collective production "Studies in the History of Russian Philosophy". . . .'

It is an elaborately concocted document, bringing vividly to life the conditions under which philosophical work is carried on in the Soviet Union, with its atmosphere of planning, control, governmental pressure and collectivization, in which all free creative endeavour must inevitably be stifled.

In all these incursions of the Party into the ideological sphere which have hitherto concerned us, the blow has always been struck by subordinate personalities or party institutions (Zhdanov, the Central Committee). But the summer of 1950 produced yet another

---

[1] In the Preface to the comprehensive text-book published at the beginning of 1951 on Historical Materialism (*Istorichesky materializm*, ed. F. V. Konstantinov, pp. 747) it is expressly emphasized, for the first time, that an all-round preliminary examination of this sort has taken place.

intervention, in which Stalin, for the first time in twelve years, again found it necessary to take pen in hand on his own account, and to lay down the law on matters of ideology. The topic in question here was the seemingly innocent subject of linguistics, and the effect of this intervention was to put a sudden end to the work of Marr and his school, who had hitherto held uncontested sway in the field of Soviet linguistics.

Nikolay Yakovlevich Marr (1864–1934) was the son of a Scottish father and a Georgian mother. After the Revolution he was converted to Marxism and endeavoured to establish linguistics on a Marxist basis. In so doing, Marr sets out on the assumption that language must be regarded as a form of 'ideology' and therefore belongs to the category of the 'superstructure'. He distinguishes, in this connection, between 'simple ideologies' (language and thought) and 'higher ideologies' (religion, art, ethics, law, politics, science and philosophy). Like all ideologies, language, including grammar, has a class character. Since language, which is intimately bound up with thought, is regarded as an ideology, Marr maintains that its development does not exhibit the characteristics of a gradual evolution, but unfolds by stages (*stadial'noe razvitie*) with sharply-separated qualitative distinctions between each successive language-system: a process reflecting the dialectic of social development. In the concrete, these qualitative leaps are realized in the form of 'language-crossings', which follow in the train of transformations in the economic basis of society and do not constitute an anomaly, but rather the normal mode of origin of new types of language. Owing to his conception of language as an ideology, Marr attaches particular importance, not only to the form of language, but also to its content, semantics, or the meaning of words. So far as concerns the inner connection of language and thought, in Marr's account of the matter, present-day spoken language corresponds to the thinking of formal logic; this is the thought of a society split up into classes. For thousands of years before the rise of articulate speech there prevailed a system of hand-signals or gesture-language. Formal logical thinking, with its articulated language, is due in turn to be superseded by dialectical materialist thinking, the mode of thought of the proletariat, of the classless society. Whereas, under present conditions, articulate language has the upper hand over formal logical thought, in the classless society

'thought gains the upper hand over language, and will continue to gain it, until in the new classless society not only will the system of spoken language be done away with, but a unitary language will be created, as far, and even farther, removed from articulate language as the latter is from gesture'. [1]

---

[1] N. Y. Marr: *Izbrannye raboty* (Selected Works), III, p. 118.

In this new, unified world-language, 'thanks to the latest discoveries', thought will no longer be in any way dependent on its phonetic expression in language; thought itself will replace language.

'The language of the future is thought, growing out of technique free from the use of natural materials. No language will be able to resist it, certainly not spoken language, forever bound as it is to the norms imposed by Nature.' [1]

Up till quite recently, Marr's theory of language still ranked as *the* Soviet linguistics. Especially after the discussion on biology, when similar 'battles' were staged between true 'materialist' doctrines and old 'reactionary' tendencies in every branch of science, Marr's linguistics was paraded alongside Michurin's genetics as a true Soviet science. An Academician by the name of Meshchaninov even had the idea of drawing a parallel between the theory of the *Ursprache*, denounced by Marr and his school, and the 'mythical unalterable units of inheritance' of Mendel-Morgan-Weismann genetics.[2]

All at once, a 'free discussion' on linguistic problems was opened in *Pravda* on 9th May 1950, with an article by Professor A. S. Chikobava, *On Certain Problems in Soviet Linguistics*. On 20th June, Stalin himself intervened in the discussion, contributing a letter *Concerning Marxism in Linguistics*. This was followed by four further letters, the first dated 29th June, published in *Pravda* on 4th July, *Concerning Certain Problems of Linguistics. Reply to Comrade E. Krasheninnikova*, then three letters, headed *Reply to Comrades*, published in *Pravda* on 2nd August (*To Comrade Sanzheyev*, of 11th July, *To Comrades D. Belkin and S. Furer* of 22nd July, and *To Comrade A. Kholopov*, of 28th July 1950).[3]

[1] *Ibid.*, p. 121. V. V. Vinogradov: *O lingvisticheskoy diskussii i rabotakh J. V. Stalina po voprosam yazykoznaniya* (On the Linguistic Discussion and the Works of J. V. Stalin on Problems of Linguistics), in *Bol'shevik*, 1950, 15, pp. 7–23; *cf.* the collective work, *Voprosy dialekticheskogo i istoricheskogo materializma v trude J. V. Stalina 'Marxizm i voprosy yazykoznaniya'* (Problems of Dialectical and Historical Materialism in J. V. Stalin's *Marxism and Problems of Linguistics*), 2 vols., Moscow 1951/52; G. F. Alexandrov: *Trudy J. V. Stalina o yazykoznanii i voprosy istoricheskogo materializma* (J. V. Stalin's Writings on Linguistics and the Problems of Historical Materialism), Moscow 1952.

[2] V. K. Nikol'sky–N. F. Yakovlev: *Osnovnye polozheniya materialisticheskogo ucheniya N. Y. Marra o yazyke* (Basic Principles of N. Y. Marr's Materialist Theory of Language), in *VF*, 1949, 1, pp. 265–85, *q.v.* pp. 277 ff.

[3] These articles were not only reprinted from *Pravda* in professional journals of a philosophical and general kind, such as *Voprosy filosofii* (1950, No. 1, pp. 3–20; No. 2, pp. 3–8). By August 1950 an edition in book form under the title *Marxizm i voprosy yazykoznaniya* (Marxism and

Stalin's first point against Marr is that language is not to be assigned to the superstructure. It is not the product of a basis, a particular social structure, itself temporarily conditioned and relatively short-lived, but the outcome of society as a whole. Nor, again, can it be assigned to the superstructure, if for no other reason than because it stands in direct relation to production, whereas the superstructure is only indirectly dependent on production, *i.e.*, by way of the basis (the economic structure of society). But language cannot, on the other hand, be reckoned part of the basis either. And that means that there are social phenomena belonging neither to the basis nor the superstructure.

It follows further from this, that language is not conditioned by the class-structure, as Marr had maintained it to be. It is the creation, not of any single class, but of the whole of society; it is created as a whole for society in general, not in the interests of any one class at the expense of others, but in the same fashion for all. One should therefore beware of confusing language with dialect or jargon. Class-conditioned words peculiar to jargon constitute barely one per cent of the total vocabulary.

There is a special interest and significance in what Stalin has to say against Marr on the subject of linguistic development. The latter is governed by the developmental laws of society as a whole (the people), not those of the superstructure. This means that language develops, not by way of sudden eruptions (*vzryvy*—'explosions'), but by way of a gradual accumulation of new elements and an equally gradual dying away of old ones; in general, the law of transition from one quality to another by way of leaps continues to hold in the sphere of social development only for the society divided into mutually hostile classes, not for the socialist classless society; here this law emerges in a new form.

As for Marr's doctrine of 'language-crossings', Stalin maintains for his part, that when different languages encounter one another they do not mingle to form a new one, but one prevails over the other; this is particularly observable in the history of the Russian language, which has always emerged victorious from encounters of this kind.

Stalin finally goes on to accuse Marr of idealism, on account of his doctrine of the unitary world-language of the future, which will in fact no longer be a 'language' at all, but rather a soundless and immediate communication of thoughts. Stalin regards this as implying a separation of language and thought; his view, on the contrary, is that thought is essentially bound up with language; there can be no

Problems of Linguistics, pp. 114), had already been issued by the State Publishing House for Political Literature. (English version, Moscow 1955, pp. 71).

thought without a material basis in language; the instance of deaf-mutism only appears to constitute an argument against this, for even in their case thoughts are associated with sense-impressions (visual sensations and impressions of touch, taste and smell).

To these factual objections Stalin adds a last accusation, that Marr and his 'disciples' have set up an 'Arakcheyev régime' within the field of linguistics,[1] which has hitherto blocked all free expression of scientific opinion and which now, thanks to the discussion opened in *Pravda*, has at last been exposed and demolished. For no science can prosper without conflict of opinion and freedom to criticize.

These articles of Stalin's again produced a shattering effect, not only in the sphere of linguistics, where Marr, hitherto a star of the first magnitude, is now described as the 'Don Quixote of linguistics' and his 'new theory' of language, like his 'school' and his 'disciples', referred to only in quotation marks, but also in every department of theoretical enquiry. The articles have been discussed in innumerable sessions of learned bodies, and the new doctrines have been disseminated in books and articles by the score.[2] The Editors of *Voprosy filosofii* expressed their regret at having published in recent numbers of the paper (Nos. 1 and 3, 1949), fallacious articles propagating the 'anti-Marxist' doctrines of Marr and endorsing the Arakcheyev régime of his supporters; at the same time they announced publication of further articles promulgating the 'Marxist' theory of language and illuminating the problems raised by Stalin in his articles within the fields of dialectical and historical materialism.[3]

Even before all five of Stalin's articles had yet appeared, the Philosophical Institute of the Academy of Sciences had already held two sessions, on 18th and 27th July 1950, dedicated to consideration

[1] Count Alexey Andreyevich Arakcheyev (1769–1834), the favourite of Alexander I; as Minister of War he showed reckless brutality in implementing Alexander's universally unpopular scheme of 'military colonies', which enforced life-long military service upon some 750,000 members of the population in the frontier provinces of Russia and subjected their entire economic life, and to a large extent their private life as well, to a rigid system of discipline. In the last decade of Alexander's reign especially (d. 1825), Arakcheyev enjoyed the unlimited confidence of the monarch, so that in practice the whole conduct of the régime was in his hands. (*Cf.* K. Stählin· *Geschichte Russlands*, III, pp. 258 ff.)

[2] We may cite as an instance a leading article in *Izvestiya Akademii Nauk, Otdelenie ekonomiki i prava* (Bulletin of the Academy of Sciences, Economics and Law Section), under the title: 'The Works of Comrade Stalin on Problems of Linguistics and their Significance for the Development of Economic and Legal Science' (*Trudy tovarishcha Stalina po voprosam yazykoznaniya i ikh znachenie dlya razvitiya ekonomicheskikh i pravovykh nauk*), 1950, pp. 331–9.

[3] *VF*, 1950, 2, p. 350.

of Stalin's intervention in the linguistic field and its consequences in relation to the work of philosophy. A number of speakers, foremost among them Alexandrov, expatiated on the various philosophical problems raised by this latest of Stalin's works. In the field of historical materialism Stalin has clarified the doctrine of the basis and the superstructure, and more especially has enlarged the theory of the active rôle of the superstructure and the conception of the nation; in the sphere of dialectical materialism the law of the transition from quantity to quality, together with that of the unity of opposites, has been 'deepened' in certain very important respects; his arguments against Marr's language of the future have given Stalin the opportunity of dealing with problems of epistemology, particularly the question of the relation of thought and being. Great attention was also paid to Stalin's demand for freedom in science. Kedrov in particular, the erstwhile Chief Editor of *Voprosy filosofii*, whose reprimand had given him a personal taste of the blessings of an 'Arakcheyev régime' in the field of science, was insistent on the fact that Stalin's articles pointed to a campaign against vulgar Marxism not only in linguistics, but also in other fields, such as those of logic and natural science.[1]

All speakers were in agreement that these articles of Stalin's represented a 'new, world-historical contribution to the treasury of Marxism'.[2] And this time they were not mistaken. Stalin's last personal intervention in the realm of Marxist theory far outweighs in importance the incursions of the Party Central Committee in previous years and may yet perhaps establish itself in fact as of 'world-historical significance'. For whereas the previous attacks were chiefly directed against the formal aspects of bolshevik doctrine ('partisanship', 'pseudo-objectivism', 'cosmopolitanism', etc.), Stalin has on this occasion shaken the pillars of Marxist theory itself (in his amplifications of historical materialism) and the main positions of dialectical materialism as such, as understood in the Soviet Union (the basic laws of the materialist dialectic concerning the transition from quantity into quality and the unity of opposites). Indeed one almost has the impression that Stalin deliberately chose so harmless a field as that of linguistics for purposes of his attack, in order to correct certain fundamental points in bolshevik doctrine. The seeming concern with linguistics in this connection was intended to lessen the impact which would otherwise have been produced by an open realignment of the basic tenets of Marxist-Leninist doctrine as hitherto understood. The real meaning of this *démarche* of Stalin's

[1] *Stat'i tovarishcha Stalina po voprosam yazykoznaniya i zadachi v oblasti istoricheskikh i filosofskikh nauk* (Comrade Stalin's Article on Problems of Linguistics and the Tasks in the Field of Historical and Philosophical Science), in *IAN*, VII (1950), pp. 322–59, *q.v.* p. 349.   [2] *Ibid.*, p. 345.

seems to us to lie in the fact that the new course, which Stalin had been pursuing for at least sixteen years in the field of bolshevik politics, was now at last to find a theoretical anchorage also in 'Marxist-Leninist theory'. We shall return to this subject again in the course of the following chapter.

From this time on, Stalin's booklet on linguistics was to occupy a central position in all the subsequent activities of the Soviet philosophers. On the first anniversary of the appearance of the letters (June 1951) a conference was held at the Philosophical Institute, attended by more than 1,200 scholars. As was indicated in the speeches, it had been a year of strenuous toil; in the course of it, the academic co-workers of the Institute had published more than 50 articles in various journals and delivered over 350 lectures on the significance of what Stalin had said. It had also given birth to a collective work, published by the Institute: *Problems of Dialectical and Historical Materialism in J. V. Stalin's 'Marxism and Problems of Linguistics'*.[1] The second anniversary of the appearance of this work of Stalin's was similarly observed at the Philosophical Institute by an augmented session of the academic council (as was also the case in other Institutes).[2]

Meanwhile, five years had also elapsed since the philosophical 'Discussion'. *Pravda* took advantage of the occasion, in its issue of 12th March 1952, to inform 'workers on the philosophical front' that, although some improvements had been effected in the course of these years, the philosophers were still 'under heavy obligations to the Soviet public' and were only slowly fulfilling the Party's directives. The Editors of *Voprosy filosofii* just found it possible to refer to *Pravda's* criticism in the leading article of their second number, which was already in the press, applying it self-critically to themselves and calling on Soviet philosophers to make this momentous fifth anniversary the occasion 'for an active display of creative criticism and self-criticism'.[3]

The results of these heart-searchings are disclosed in the leading article of the following issue: in the course of the last five years a certain advance has certainly been achieved: the themes treated of in philosophical writings have in general become more topical, contact with the periphery has been restored, efforts have been made towards training cadres and improving the quality of philosophical production, as can be seen from the fact that a number of works have been awarded the Stalin Prize. But in spite of this, philosophical productivity remains extremely poor in comparison with what is

[1] *VF*, 1951, No. 5, pp. 195 f.; *cf*. also *IAN, Seriya istorii i filosofii*, 1951, No. 4, pp. 315–22.
[2] *Vestnik AN SSSR*, 1952, No. 8, p. 17.
[3] *VF* 1952, 2, p. 13.

required. The textbook situation is still exceptionally bad: the two-volume *History of Philosophy* is only just being completed, the textbook on dialectical materialism is still bogged down in the preliminary stages. Among topics of discussion, the problems of dialectical materialism and of communist ethics and aesthetics are unduly neglected. The disproportion between the number of dissertations defended and the number published is still too great, and must be regarded as an indication of lowered quality.[1]

In September 1952, Stalin's last important work, *Economic Problems of Socialism in the U.S.S.R.*, was published in the periodical *Bol'shevik*. This was followed by the XIXth Party Congress at the beginning of October, both of these events being also of crucial importance for the development of philosophy in the years that followed.

The publication of Stalin's work on the eve of the XIXth Congress was a clear indication that it was intended as Stalin's message to the Congress, at which on this occasion the general report was no longer to be delivered by himself, as hitherto, but by his favourite pupil, Malenkov. In its external trappings this work purports to consist of Stalin's concluding comments on an economic discussion convened, in November 1951, to consider the plan of a textbook on political economy. The records of this discussion were submitted to Stalin, who now in this pamphlet delivers his final oracular judgement on a number of the issues in dispute. The book consists of four independent sections. The first, 'Remarks on Economic Questions Connected with the November 1951 Discussion', bears the date of 1st February 1952 and sets out Stalin's own position *vis-à-vis* the discussion. As in the case of *Marxism and Problems of Linguistics*, it is supplemented by various additional documents bearing on the subject, namely 'Reply to Comrade A. I. Notkin' (21st April 1952), 'Concerning the Errors of Comrade L. D. Yaroshenko' (22nd May 1952), and 'Reply to Comrades A. V. Sanina and V. G. Venzher' (28th September 1952).

The most important part of it, philosophically speaking, is the first section of the 'Remarks on Economic Questions', which bears the subtitle 'Character of Economic Laws under Socialism'. Stalin here rebukes the impatience of certain youthful party-members, who have supposed that the Soviet régime 'can do anything', that it is bound by no objective economic laws and can 'create' new laws of its own; they have repudiated the notion that economic laws have an objective character, independent of the will of man. And according to Stalin they have fallen into grave error. He stresses that even under socialism economic laws retain their objective, necessary character,

[1] *VF* 1952, 3, pp. 3 ff.

just as the laws of Nature do. As with the latter, so also with the former, man can do nothing else but recognize them, utilize them by guiding their operation into the particular channels willed by him, and 'impart a different direction to the destructive action of some of the laws'; but to destroy them or create new economic laws is not within his power.[1] In this work of Stalin's, the leaders of the economic movement he condemns are not referred to by name. But from other Soviet publications we may gather that a certain N. Voznesensky is held to be chiefly responsible. In his book *The Soviet War-Economy during the Great Patriotic War*, which met with an exceptionally warm welcome, on publication, from the party press, Voznesensky had propounded the thesis that the socialist economy is determined by the State planning agencies, that the State is the 'source of motion and development' in such an economy, and that the State's planning activities constitute its law of development. Fedoseyev, Iovchuk and Alexandrov also stand accused of the same heresy.[2]

For the rest, Stalin deals with other questions of less philosophical interest: the problems of commodity-production and the law of value under socialism, the abolition of the antitheses between town and country and mental and physical labour, the disintegration of the single world-market and the deepening crisis of the world capitalist system, the inevitability of wars between capitalist countries, the basic economic laws of modern capitalism and socialism, and 'other questions'. In conclusion he speaks of the international importance of the proposed textbook of political economy and points out ways of improving the draft textbook in question.

Among all these problems, the most frequently discussed in Soviet philosophical literature are those of abolishing the antitheses between town and country and mental and physical labour, and of the basic laws of modern capitalism and socialism.

As for the remaining documents in this booklet of Stalin's, the most important passage they contain is one in which he corrects Yaroshenko's views on the transition to communism and lays down the following three conditions for this transition: firstly, the expansion of all social production, with a relatively higher rate of expansion of the production of means of production; secondly, the raising of collective-farm property, by means of gradual transitions, to the level of public property; and thirdly,

'such a cultural advancement of society as will secure for all members of society the all-round development of their physical and mental abilities',

---

[1] J. V. Stalin: *Ekonomicheskie problemy sotsializma v SSSR* (Economic Problems of Socialism in the U.S.S.R.), Moscow 1952, pp. 10 ff. (English, p. 8).   [2] *Cf. Kommunist* 1953, No. 2, pp. 6 ff.

and this on two counts:

'so that the members of society may be in a position to receive an education sufficient to enable them to be active agents of social development, and in a position freely to choose their occupations and not be tied all their lives, owing to the existing division of labour, to some one occupation'.[1]

The XIXth Party Congress of the C.P.S.U.(B), which took place at the beginning of October 1952, was another important event in the further development of Soviet philosophy. Stalin's essay on the economic problems of socialism in the U.S.S.R., and more especially his remarks on the preconditions for the transition to communism, formed the ideological basis for its resolutions, and in particular for the congressional directives relating to the fifth Five-year Plan.[2] The Congress also decided to set up a commission for the purpose of working out a new programme for the Communist Party, and called upon it to adopt Stalin's *Economic Problems of Socialism in the U.S.S.R.* as the basis of its work.[3]

In his Report to the XIXth Party Congress, Malenkov made frequent and copious reference to the problems of intellectual life. He outlined what the Party had done to further the causes of popular education, science, culture, literature and art, and was particularly critical in this connection of certain deficiencies in the fields of literature and art: complaining of the many colourless, empty and tedious works still being produced. He again confronted Soviet artists and writers with the ideal of socialist realism, whose strength and meaning lie in the fact that it reveals the 'higher inner qualities and typical positive character-traits of the ordinary man'. But 'typical', here, must be understood to mean, not merely 'that which is most frequently in evidence', but rather 'that which corresponds to the nature of the given social and historical phenomena', instead of just

'the most widely-distributed, most frequently-recurring, most commonplace. . . . The problem of the typical is in every case a political problem.'[4]

In the course of this he attacks those who champion the theory of 'absence of conflict', who believe, or at least behave as if they believed, that there are no contradictions in Soviet reality, and calls for the cultivation of satire:

'It would be false to suppose that our Soviet reality offers no material

---

[1] J. V. Stalin: *Op. cit.*, p. 161 (English, p. 76).

[2] *Cf.* M. D. Kammari: *O novom vydayushchemsya vklade J. V. Stalina v marxistsko-leninskuyu filosofiyu* (On J. V. Stalin's Latest Outstanding Contribution to Marxist–Leninist Philosophy), in *VF* 1952, 6, p. 40.

[3] *Pravda*, 14th Oct. 1952.   [4] *Pravda*, 6th Oct. 1952.

for satire. . . . Our Soviet art and literature must be bold in depicting the contradictions and conflicts of life and in learning to employ the weapon of criticism as one of the most effective means of education.' [1]

Towards the end of his Report, in speaking of the Party, Malenkov deplores the fact that ideological work is too little regarded in many party circles, even at the highest level. Although Soviet society no longer provides any class-basis for the dominance of bourgeois ideology, there are still extremely persistent residues of this, which do not die out of their own accord, but must be fought against. The ideological training of cadres is particularly neglected.

'The deepening of political knowledge among party members and candidates is an essential condition for strengthening their leading rôle in all spheres of life.' [2]

Nor has the Arakcheyev régime in many scientific institutions been altogether eliminated:

'In some branches of science . . . the monopoly of particular groups of intellectuals, who repress the growth of fresh influences, insulate themselves from criticism, and attempt to solve scientific problems by administrative methods, has not yet been altogether liquidated. No branch of science can flourish effectively in a stifling atmosphere of mutual incense-burning and concealment of errors.' [3]

Malenkov had already insisted energetically in another connection on the need for continual recourse to criticism and self-criticism.

These directions, emanating from the two highest sources of authority, Stalin and the Party Congress, laid a most pressing burden of obligation upon the Soviet ideologists to revise their work and to draw the necessary conclusions from what had been said. At its annual general assembly, from 3rd January to 2nd February 1953, the Academy of Sciences of the U.S.S.R. applied itself to the tasks created for it by the resolutions of the XIXth Party Congress. The President, A. N. Nesmeyanov, delivered an address on 'The Tasks of the Academy of Sciences of the U.S.S.R. in the Light of the Resolutions of the XIXth Congress of the Communist Party of the Soviet Union'. He began by assigning to the philosophers the general duty of providing a

'theoretical generalization of the experience gained in the construcstruction of socialism and of the prospects for the construction of communism in our country'.

With reference to Stalin's latest work he then laid down the following

----

[1] *Ibid.*   [2] *Ibid.*   [3] *Ibid.*

programme of philosophical endeavour in the years to come: In view of Stalin's observations on the objective character of economic laws, the philosophers must pay greater attention to the laws of social development and their employment in the interests of society, and to overcoming subjectivist conceptions of the laws of development in Soviet society; fuller consideration must also be given to the relation between general sociological laws and the specific laws of development of individual groupings, and similarly to the relation between objective laws and the conscious activity of men. Still other problems thrown up in Stalin's essay must in future be adopted by Soviet philosophers as topics of inquiry: the elimination of the essential distinctions between town and country, and between mental and physical labour; and likewise the problem of the all-round development of personality under socialism and communism, and of the cultural advancement of society as one of the most essential preconditions for the transition to communism. Probably with Malenkov's Report in mind, the President of the Academy of Sciences also enjoined on the philosophers the working-out of a Marxist aesthetics, a vigorous struggle against contemporary bourgeois ideology, and the laying bare of the connection between this ideology and the basic laws of present-day capitalism.[1]

The campaign against 'subjectivist' interpretations of the laws of development, which Nesmeyanov calls for in the present context, was very energetically pursued by the Party in the months which followed the publication of *Economic Problems of Socialism in the U.S.S.R.* This is particularly evident in connection with the 'Fedoseyev affair'.

P. Fedoseyev, a former Chief Editor of *Bol'shevik*,[2] the theoretical organ of the Party Central Committee, had published two articles in the newspaper *Izvestiya*, on 12th and 21st December 1952, in which he commented on Stalin's new book and expressed orthodox disapproval of Voznesensky's position, as failing to do adequate justice to the objective character of the laws of social development. In spite of this he was violently attacked in *Pravda* three days later by M. Suslov, a member of the Praesidium of the Central Committee. Since Fedoseyev, when still Chief Editor of *Bol'shevik*, caused articles to be printed in that paper wherein Voznesensky's 'un-Marxist' views

[1] *Zadachi Akademii Nauk SSSR v svete resheny XIX syezda Kommunisticheskoy partii Sovetskogo Soyuza* (The Tasks of the Academy of Sciences of the U.S.S.R. in the Light of the Resolutions of the XIXth Congress of the C.P.S.U.), in *Vestnik AN SSSR*, 1953, No. 3, pp. 18 f.

[2] Since the XIXth Congress, this periodical has appeared under the name of *Kommunist*, the name 'Communist Party of the Soviet Union (Bolsheviks)' having been altered at this Congress to 'Communist Party of the Soviet Union'.

are lauded to the skies, he has exercised a damaging influence on the education of party functionaries, administrative officials and scientific workers, and committed a no less grievous offence in the eyes of the Party. Hence it should now have been his duty to acknowledge this openly. Seeing that he has let slip this golden opportunity for self-criticism, one can only wonder if his present assertions coincide with his own inner convictions, or whether he is not in fact playing a double game.

On the following day, *Izvestiya* reprinted Suslov's article, together with an editorial note declaring that it had been gravely in error in publishing Fedoseyev's un-self-critical articles. Fedoseyev himself drew similar conclusions from Suslov's attack and made a clean breast of the matter in *Právda* on 2nd January.

'Having thought over the errors of the articles I published in *Izvestiya* and become conscious of them, I acknowledge unreservedly the justice . . . of the criticism passed on them by Comrade M. Suslov. I have to admit that in publishing my work . . . I failed to display . . . a self-critical attitude towards my own mistakes. At the time when I was Chief Editor of the paper [*Bol'shevik*; G. W.], I permitted a number of authors to print articles in which Voznesensky's un-Marxist work *The Soviet War-Economy during the Great Patriotic War* was praised to the skies. . . . Having failed to recognize the anti-Marxist core of the subjectivist position . . . I allowed the journal *Bol'shevik* to be used for the dissemination of these extremely pernicious ideas and thereby did harm to the Party's ideological work. When, in my articles, I explained Stalin's theses as to the objective character of the laws governing society, I should have made it my duty . . . to be openly critical of my own false, uncritical and fundamentally complacent attitude. In neglecting to do this, I failed to do my elementary duty and did not apply the Party's demand for self-criticism to my own case. My articles on the laws of social development are therefore inadequate and can justly be regarded as an attempt to gloss over my own failings. I shall draw the necessary lessons from the criticism in *Pravda*, and will do everything to remedy and overcome my faults.'[1]

This article of Suslov's also caused alarm among the Editors of *Voprosy filosofii*. They hunted through all the back numbers of the periodical, right back to the year of its foundation in 1947, and fortunately discovered two articles, one written in 1949 and the other in 1947, in which theories were propounded that were no longer tenable after the appearance of Stalin's latest work. In the leading article of the final 1952 number, which luckily had not yet gone to press, they

---

[1] *Pravda*, 2nd Jan. 1953.

therefore hastened to add yet another self-critical admission of guilt:

'As M. A. Suslov has shown, it is "the elementary duty of every party member not to gloss over past mistakes, not to sidle round them, but rather to confess them openly and honourably and to remedy them". This observation also has an immediate application to *Voprosy filosofii*, which has given space to a number of articles containing erroneous assertions about the laws of development of socialist society.' [1]

[1] *XIX syezd Kommunisticheskoy partii i voprosy ideologicheskoy raboty* (The XIXth Congress of the Communist Party and Problems of Ideological Work), in *VF* 1952, No. 6, p. 12; this number was printed on 18th January 1953.

CHAPTER X

Stalin as a Philosopher

FROM the account just given of philosophical life in the Soviet Union it will be clearly evident that throughout the whole of the Stalinist period Stalin himself was the only person in the Soviet Union who could ever dare to say anything new. In his lifetime, therefore, his contributions to the progress of Marxist philosophy were hymned in the highest superlatives by the Soviet philosophers. His short pamphlet on *Dialectical and Historical Materialism* was then reckoned as a

'creation . . . marking an epoch in the development of Marxist–Leninist philosophy, and of world-historical significance'.[1]

This makes it necessary for us to inquire whether Stalin did in fact contribute to the development of Marxist philosophy, and in what sense he can be called an original thinker.

It must certainly be said of the eulogies which Soviet authors bestowed during his lifetime on Stalin's services to philosophy, that they are altogether too flattering to him. But here one must also guard, on the other hand, against an over-simplified manner of approach. For owing to the principle of the unity of theory and practice, and also to that of partisanship, practice, *i.e.*, concrete social and political life, becomes an essential factor in the process of gaining knowledge of truth. Truth is discovered, on this view, in the concrete conduct of life. The leader of the Party, in giving direction to the

---

[1] M. B. Mitin: *Rol' i znachenie raboty tovarishcha Stalina 'O dialekticheskom i istoricheskom materializme' v razvitii marxistsko-leninskoy filosofskoy mysli* (The Rôle and Significance of Comrade Stalin's Work *Dialectical and Historical Materialism* in the Development of Marxist–Leninist Philosophical Thought), in *Bol'shevik*, 1949, No. 1, p. 22.

proletarian class in its practice, thereby necessarily contributes to theory as well.

This will explain, for example, how, on the occasion of Stalin's seventieth birthday, the Editors of the philosophical journal *Voprosy filosofii* were able to bring off the *tour de force* of packing virtually the whole of a 334-page number of the paper with articles on Stalin. For 'philosophy', in Soviet terminology, includes not only dialectical but also historical materialism. Hence we find that this issue contains, besides a number of properly philosophical articles, a variety of essays on social and political topics as well.[1]

Stalin's not very extensive literary output began as early as 1901 and consists for the most part of articles published in various newspapers. Particular importance attaches to a series of essays, *Anarchism or Socialism?* (1906/07)[2] and to a pamphlet dating from 1912/13: *Marxism and the National Question*.[3] A number of articles written in 1917 appeared in book form in 1925, together with an Introduction, *The October Revolution and the Tactics of the Russian Communists* under the title *On the Road to October*.[4] In April 1924 Stalin delivered a series of lectures at the Sverdlov University in Moscow on *The Foundations of Leninism*, which later formed the nucleus of the celebrated collection of his writings, *Problems of Leninism*.[5] Very wide circulation has also been given to his report *On the Draft Constitution of the U.S.S.R.*, delivered on 25th November 1936 to the Extraordinary VIIIth Congress which was summoned to ratify the new Constitution.[6]

A peculiarly outstanding importance among Stalin's works was attributed in its day to the *History of the C.P.S.U.(B). Short Course*, which from 1948 onwards was ascribed to Stalin himself. Although Stalin's authorship of this work, published as 'Edited by a Commission of the Central Committee', is only to be understood in a some-

[1] *VF*, 1949, 2; some of these articles, together with others, were subsequently made available to a wider public as a collective volume under the title *Voprosy marxistsko-leninskoy filosofi* (Problems of Marxist–Leninist Philosophy), Moscow 1950.

[2] J. V. Stalin: *Anarkhizm ili sotsializm?* in *Sochineniya*, I, pp. 294–392 (English, *Works*, I, pp. 297–391).

[3] J. V. Stalin: *Marxizm i natsional'ny vopros*, in *Sochineniya*, II, pp. 290–367 (English, II, pp. 300–81); often reprinted separately.

[4] J. V. Stalin: *Na putyakh k oktyabryu*; the individual articles are now reprinted in Vol. III, the Introduction in Vol. VI of the collected works.

[5] J. V. Stalin: *Voprosy leninizma*, 1st edn. 1926; latest (11th) edn. (somewhat altered in content), Moscow 1947 (the English edition, Moscow 1947, is based on this; for *Foundations* . . ., cf. also *Works*, VI).

[6] J. V. Stalin: *Voprosy leninizma*, 11th edn., pp. 507–34 (English, pp. 540–68).

what indirect sense, meaning that Stalin himself may have laid down the main ideas and the 'interpretation' to be put upon events, there seems little doubt, however, that he was actually the author in a much more immediate fashion of what would certainly have been the most responsible and hazardous portion of the book for any of his subordinates to have undertaken, namely, Section 2 of Chapter 4: *On Dialectical and Historical Materialism*. Of this short, 27-page account it is said, in what was then the ultra-official biography of Stalin, that it *'raises dialectical materialism to a new and higher level'* and 'is one of the pinnacles of Marxist–Leninist philosophical thought'.[1]

Of Stalin's later works, his book *On the Great Patriotic War of the Soviet Union*[2] enjoyed a particularly large circulation; it is a collection of his reports, speeches and orders during the period of World War II. A very fundamental importance for the subsequent development of Soviet philosophy attaches to his two last works, *Marxism and Problems of Linguistics* (1950), which set the ideological tone during the closing years of the Stalinist era, and *Economic Problems of Socialism in the U.S.S.R.* (1952), which was written shortly before his death and continued to dominate the field until his second burial at the XXth Party Congress in February 1956.

By decree of the Central Committee of the C.P.S.U.(B), the publication of Stalin's *Collected Works* was put in hand from 1946 onwards. Sixteen volumes were planned, but only thirteen of these have seen the light of day. The Russian edition was paralleled by editions in fifteen other languages of the peoples of the Soviet Union. N. Gradoboyev has described the desperate exertions required of the Commission of the Central Committee, entrusted, under the presidency of Molotov, with the issue of these collected works;[3] in order to fill up the volumes as ordained, they not only collected the articles Stalin had published in the various newspapers, but also tracked down all his letters and telegrams, the records of his telephone conversations, and every scrap of paper that had ever been written on, or at least signed by him. When even this proved insufficient to make up the prescribed number of volumes, they found themselves compelled to credit Stalin with works that he had never written: Gradoboyev designates as such the dissertation on *The National Question*

---

[1] *Josif Vissarionovich Stalin (kratkaya biografiya)* Moscow 1945, etc., p. 69 (English version: *Stalin: A Short Biography*, London 1943, p. 56). Western biographies of Stalin include: I. Deutscher: *Stalin. A Political Biography*, London–New York–Toronto 1949; A. Ouralov: *Staline au pouvoir*, Paris 1951; L. Fischer: *The Life and Death of Stalin*, London 1953.

[2] (*Cf.* also *War Speeches*, London 1946.)

[3] N. Gradoboyev: *Stalins gesammelte Werke*, in *Ost-Probleme*, Vol. 3, No. 32 (11th Aug. 1951), pp. 982–4.

and Leninism, contained in Volume XI of the collected works, which is alleged to be the first published version of a work written as early as 1929.

The publication-figures of works by Stalin are truly enormous. Up to 1949 the 11 editions of *Problems of Leninism* had been 238 times reprinted, in 52 languages, to a total of 16,980,000 copies. The short *History of the C.P.S.U.(B)* was first published in a series of articles in *Pravda* and reproduced in a great many other newspapers and periodicals; incomplete estimates have put the total circulation of papers and periodicals in which it was reprinted at 85 million. In book form it went through 234 impressions in 11 years (1938 to the end of 1949), being published in 66 languages with a total of 35,762,000 copies, of which 27,567,300 were in Russian, 6,405,500 in other languages spoken in the Soviet Union and 1,789,200 in foreign languages. The brochure *On the Draft Constitution of the U.S.S.R.* had by 1949 achieved a total of 58,878,000 copies. The Russian version of Stalin's *Collected Works* appeared in an edition of 500,000 copies.[1]

Now what did the Soviet philosophers of the Stalinist period consider to be Stalin's outstanding contribution to philosophy? We shall examine this question firstly in regard to the field of dialectical materialism. It was no easy task to extract anything epoch-making from Stalin's meagre literary output, more especially from the small pamphlet on *Dialectical and Historical Materialism*. The effort was therefore made to discover something important in the very fact that in this work Stalin had accomplished what fate had not spared any of his classical predecessors the time to achieve. Engels was unable to bring his projected *Dialectics of Nature* to completion, nor was Lenin able to turn to account the materials gathered together in his *Philosophical Notebooks*. To Stalin alone it had been reserved to give the first comprehensive, systematic account of the doctrine of the materialist dialectic.[2]

It was deemed a highly significant fact that in the above-mentioned work Stalin deals first of all with the theory of the 'Marxist dialectical method' and only later with that of 'Marxist philosophical materialism', rather than in the reverse order, as had previously been customary (and as would also have been more appropriate to the matter in hand, since, as will be shown later, 'dialectic', for dialectical

---

[1] *Cf.* T. Zelenov: *Izdanie i rasprostranenie proizvedeniy J. V. Stalina* (Editions and Circulation Figures of the Works of J. V. Stalin), in *Bol'shevik*, 1949, No. 23, pp. 85–96, and T. Zelenov–R. Savitskaya: *Izdanie proizvedeniy V. I. Lenina i J. V. Stalina v zarubezhnykh stranakh* (Foreign Language Editions of the Works of V. I. Lenin and J. V. Stalin), in *Bol'shevik*, 1951, No. 4, pp. 61–7.

[2] *Cf.* M. B. Mitin: *Rol' i znachenie . . ., Op. cit.*, p. 19.

materialism, means not a method only, but primarily a rhythm of development in reality itself).[1]

Further distinctive services to philosophy on Stalin's part were seen in the fact that, in this work, he had raised the principle of philosophical partisanship to a higher level; and that, at a time when a variety of idealistic conclusions were being drawn from the striking advances in atomic physics, he had again defended the materiality of the world.[2] In the field of logic he had once more upheld the knowability of the world against the 'physical idealism' and agnosticism of 'Weismann–Morganism'; he had demonstrated the dialectical character of the process of cognition;[3] and in so doing had preserved dialectical logic against the errors of abandoning precision and concreteness of thought and violating the law of contradiction.[4]

So too, after the appearance of the letters on linguistics and Stalin's last work, the Soviet philosophers were again to be found zealously engaged in setting forth the fundamental importance of these writings for the further development of Marxist philosophy.[5] So far as the letters on linguistics were concerned, the going was somewhat easier for them, since the Stalinist notion of a violent upheaval (*vzryv*—an 'explosion') docs indeed represent a novelty in the history of dialectical materialism. For till then it had been the leap of transition from one quality to another which was held to be sudden and violent, it being this which constituted the radical difference between the revolutionary and evolutionary phases in the process of development. Now, however, Stalin was teaching that this leap itself may take place not only in the form of a violent upheaval or 'explosion', but also 'in the form of a gradual transition'.[6]

We can see, therefore, that it was no easy task for the Soviet philosophers to be called on to inflate these three small works of

[1] M. A. Leonov: *Stalinsky etap v razvitii dialekticheskogo materializma* (The Stalinist Stage in the Development of Dialectical Materialism), in *IAN*, VI (1949), p. 508.
[2] M. B. Mitin: *Rol' i znachenie* . . ., p. 30.
[3] A. V. Vostrikov: *Voprosy teorii poznaniya v trudakh J. V. Stalina* (Problems of Epistemology in the Works of J. V. Stalin), in *VF*, 1949, 2, pp. 184 ff.
[4] M. A. Leonov: *Stalinsky etap* . . ., pp. 513 ff.
[5] Cf. *Voprosy dialekticheskogo* . . ., *Op. cit.;* D. Chesnokov: *Voprosy marxistskoy filosofii v trude J. V. Stalina 'Ekonomicheskie problemy sotsializma v SSSR'* (Problems of Marxist Philosophy in J. V. Stalin's *Economic Problems of Socialism in the U.S.S.R.*), in *Kommunist*, 1952, No. 21, pp. 24–48.
[6] V. S. Molodtsov: *Voprosy dialekticheskogo materializma v trude J. V. Stalina 'Marxizm i voprosy yazykoznaniya'* (Problems of Dialectical Materialism in J. V. Stalin's *Marxism and Problems of Linguistics*), in *VF*, 1951, 5, pp. 3–17; *q.v.* p. 13.

Stalin's, helped out by his relatively scattered references to philosophical topics in earlier writings, into something of epoch-making novelty.

From what has been said above, the reader will doubtless already be in a position to draw his own conclusions about Stalin's philosophical importance. Stalin was very far from having the degree of philosophical culture that Lenin possessed. His philosophical training was that required of any highly-placed communist: a basic knowledge of dialectical materialism and a certain adroitness in applying it to political and social questions. One may certainly grant him a special mastery of this art. On purely philosophical questions, however, he is less at home. His incursions into this field are therefore often very sketchy, nor does he evince in them any great power of precise expression or really consecutive argument. In one of his earliest works, *Anarchism or Socialism?* Stalin attempts, in speaking of the cognitive act, to demonstrate that the external world is prior to human consciousness, and alleges that the materialist theory says

'that our conceptions, our "self", exist only in so far as external conditions exist that give rise to impressions in our "self" '.[1]

Here he simply fails to notice how he identifies 'our self' with the act of cognition.

We find a similar short-cut in his tract on *Dialectical and Historical Materialism*, the 'pinnacle of Marxist-Leninist philosophical thought', where he is seeking to prove the dependence of ideologies (philosophy, legal and moral opinions, social attitudes, etc.) on the economic life of society, by reference to the conditioning of consciousness by the (material) object in the individual act of cognition:

'If Nature, being, the material world, is primary, and mind, thought, is secondary, derivative; if the material world represents objective reality existing independently of the mind of men, while the mind is a reflection of this objective reality, it follows that the material life of society, its being, is also primary, and its spiritual life secondary, derivative, and that the material life of society is an objective reality existing independently of the will of men, while the spiritual life of society is a reflection of this objective reality, a reflection of being.'[2]

Apart from the fact that in this argument Stalin (like Lenin) assumes, without attempting to justify it theoretically, a parallel between the individual consciousness and a social consciousness and 'spiritual life' which are quite different from this, he also proceeds without

[1] J. V. Stalin: *Sochineniya*, I, p. 318 (*Works*, I, p. 321).
[2] J. V. Stalin: *Voprosy leninizma*, 11th edn., p. 545 (English, p. 578; *cf.* also *History of the C.P.S.U.(B)*, p. 115). Cited hereafter, as *DHM*, from both English sources (in brackets) as well as the original.

further ado to carry over what is true of the former and apply it to the latter: just as individual awareness is conditioned by the (material) world existing apart from our awareness, so too with social awareness. Here Stalin slips in the course of his argument into a mistake which goes right back to Marx, in that he supposes social consciousness to be conditioned wholly by *social* (material) being, whereas individual consciousness is conditioned by (material) being *simpliciter*. What the argument is supposed to prove is the Marxian thesis, that different economic and social arrangements go together with different ideologies, and that the inherently vicious social being of the capitalist order of society is also accompanied by symptoms of vice in its social consciousness, its ideologies, which can only be removed by the restoration of health to the being of society, after the socialist revolution. Even if it be assumed that there is a social consciousness in addition to that of the individual, and that the same laws apply to both, this argument from the parallel between them would only hold water if individual consciousness were conditioned, not by (material) being as such, but by the actual material being of the knowing individual himself, or, in more concrete terms, not by the (material) external world, but by the degree of maturity and state of health of the knowing individual. These examples may suffice to indicate the sort of philosophical level on which Stalin's arguments operate, and what becomes of his often wondrously 'convincing' demonstrations when they are subjected to genuine philosophical criticism.

If Stalin's 'epoch-making significance' in the field of dialectical materialism crumbles, on closer inspection, into nothing, the same can hardly be said of his importance in the sphere of historical materialism, where he is much more in his element.

Here too, the Soviet philosophers' first concern was to discover in anything and everything some further significant achievement on Stalin's part: Marx and Engels had worked out the laws of the origin, growth and decline of capitalist society; Lenin had discovered the principles governing imperialism and also those of socialist revolution and the dictatorship of the proletariat; Stalin was now credited with having disclosed the laws of development of socialism after its victory in the U.S.S.R., and with having established the road to communism. By way of preliminary to the attainment of socialism, he had first of all begun by laying down a strictly scientific, practical and theoretical programme of socialist industrialization. Secondly, he was responsible for having worked out in theory and implemented in practice the plan for the collectivization of agriculture.

He was also held to have improved upon Leninism in regard to a number of problems, such as those of the State, social classes, labour, the driving-forces of social development, and the position of nationalities under socialism and communism. On the subject of the State,

Stalin had shown that although Engels' formula about its 'withering-away' is correct in principle, it presupposes the victory of socialism throughout the whole world; so long as 'capitalist encirclement' continues, the machinery of government must also be retained; but it is nevertheless possible, under these circumstances, to achieve communism in one country alone. In the theory of social classes, Stalin had been the first to give an account of the class-structure under socialism in the U.S.S.R. The establishment of socialism in the U.S.S.R. implies the complete destruction of all the exploiting classes (the last of them being that of the *kulaks* on the land); socialist society in the Soviet Union now consists of two classes only, though there is no antagonism between them, and their nature has undergone a radical transformation: the workers and the peasantry; the Soviet intelligentsia no longer represents a class on its own. Only in days to come, under communism, when the antitheses between town and country and between mental and physical labour have at last been overcome, will class-distinctions be entirely done away with.[1]

There are, however, three points in particular to be emphasized, wherein Stalin did indeed show some originality in his conception of historical materialism and in which—though following, to some extent, in Lenin's footsteps—he does make considerable departures from the original Marxian view. They are: (*a*) the exceptional significance he attaches to the retroactive influence of the super-structure, *i.e.*, the intellectual factor of consciousness, on the basis in the course of historical development; (*b*) the solution of two individual problems concerning the developmental laws of the socialist classless society (that of its 'driving-forces', and that of the 'leaps' in the development of a socialist society); (*c*) the ever-increasing importance he comes to assign to the national factor.

As regards the retroactive influence of the superstructure on the economic basis, Stalin's underlining of

'the tremendous organizing, mobilizing and transforming value of new ideas, new theories, new political views and new political institutions'

is no more than a renewal of Lenin's campaign on behalf of *soznatel'nost'* (consciousness) against the Economists, who derived the whole process of historical development from the economic factor alone. Marxism may indeed have traced the *origin* of these ideas and institutions to the conditions of material life in a given society, but it by no means follows from this that these ideas, once

[1] M. B. Mitin: *J. V. Stalin—korifey marxistsko–leninskoy nauki* (J. V. Stalin—A Coryphaeus of Marxist–Leninist Science), in *VF*, 1949, 2, pp. 17–39.

arisen, cannot react in turn upon the material basis, social being, and contribute powerfully to its further development:

'New social ideas and theories arise only after the development of the material life of society has set new tasks before society. But once they have arisen they become a most potent force which facilitates the carrying out of the new tasks set by the development of the material life of society, a force which facilitates the progress of society. . . . New social ideas and theories arise precisely because they are necessary to society, because it is *impossible* to carry out the urgent tasks of development of the material life of society without their organizing, mobilizing and transforming action. . . . Thus social ideas, theories, and political institutions, having arisen on the basis of the urgent tasks of the development of the material life of society, the development of social being, themselves then react upon social being, upon the material life of society. . . .' [1]

Stalin subsequently dwelt on this point once more in the first of his letters on linguistics.

This is bound up with the fact that the Leninist–Stalinist view of historical materialism also leaves more room again for the rôle of the individual. In theory, Stalin abides by the Marxian conception of the subordinate part assigned to the individual as a factor in history. Just as in his early work *Anarchism or Socialism?* he had found the main difference between anarchism and socialism to be that the one builds upon the individual, the other on the masses, so also he insisted in his *Dialectical and Historical Materialism* that in viewing the historical process one must rely

'on the concrete conditions of the material life of society, as the determining force of social development; not on the good wishes of "great men" '.[2]

But this did not alter the fact that, especially after the posthumous dethronement of the one-time leading Soviet historian Pokrovsky (of whom more will be heard anon), the individual was in fact increasingly reinstated in his old rights. Whereas, in the orthodox Marxist picture of history provided by Pokrovsky, the focus of interest lay in demonstrating the efficacy of Marx's 'iron laws' in history, and the individual was regarded only as an exponent of the economic factors setting history in motion, the patriotism which spread throughout the Soviet Union from 1934 onwards also had the effect of redirecting interest upon the great figures in the country's history on their own account. Ivan the Terrible, tsarist generals such as Kutuzov, and even Alexander Nevsky, who is venerated as a saint by the Russian church,

[1] *DHM*, pp. 546 f. (580, 116 f.)   [2] *DHM*, pp. 545 f. (579, 115 f.)

were resurrected in literature and on the stage and screen. At the same time this provided an opportunity for turning the bolshevik leaders themselves, Lenin, and Stalin even while he was still alive, into objects of an open, unconcealed cult.

The same tendency to reassign a more decisive significance to the superstructure, *i.e.*, the intellectual factor, can also be seen in Stalin's method of solving the problem of the two laws of development aforementioned, which are supposed to govern the progress of the classless socialist society.

Marx had pointed to class-contradictions as incentives to social development, in that they give rise to class-war. But since, in the socialist society, there are no longer supposed to be any class-antagonisms, it was necessary to discover new driving-forces of social development, if the attainment of socialist society (officially promulgated in the 1936 Constitution) was not to bring the course of history to a stop.

Moreover, Marx had also pointed out that historical development is dialectical in character, in that at certain nodal points the social contradictions are resolved in revolution; the continuous evolution hitherto prevailing is replaced by a dialectical leap, a radical break in social development. But now even according to Marx, the proletarian revolution is supposed to be the last concluding stage of the process. Hence, therefore, the problem which, though less pressing for Marx himself, required to be settled by Stalin once the new constitution had been introduced: how can social development continue thereafter to have a dialectical character, if there are to be no more revolutions?

To take this latter question first, Stalin found the answer in his letters on linguistics, by distinguishing different types of dialectical leap. As already mentioned, the leaps are only supposed to take the form of 'explosions' in an antagonistic class-society; in socialist society they are alleged in the first place to occur much more 'gradually'; secondly, and by no means less importantly, they no longer lead to the collapse of the existing régime. Stalin found examples of such novel leaps in social development in the Stakhanov movement, and more particularly in the collectivization of agriculture. Since the latter, however, was not effected without resistance on the part of the peasantry, he coined for this process the euphemistic term 'revolution from above', because

'the revolution was accomplished on the initiative of the existing power with the support of the bulk of the peasantry'.[1]

We are not so much concerned at this point with the cynicism

[1] J. V. Stalin: *Marxizm i voprosy yazykoznaniya* (Marxism and Problems of Linguistics), Gospolitizdat 1950, p. 59 (English, p. 39.)

implicit in Stalin's reference to 'the support of the bulk of the peasantry' (he is himself obliged to admit in the *History of the C.P.S.U.(B)* that the peasants resisted collectivization and attempts to palm off responsibility on the party agencies in charge for having pressed the matter too forcibly; though as he once confided personally to Churchill, ten million *kulaks* lost their lives in the process).[1] What is much more important to us here is the concept of a 'revolution from above': for in this instance the initiative proceeds from the State power, *i.e.*, from the superstructure, and from the Party, which must also be assigned to the superstructure, and in Lenin's view is held to represent the organized consciousness of the working-class.

We have already referred to Stalin's enumeration of the new driving-forces in the development of socialist society: the moral and political unity of Soviet society, friendship among the peoples of the Soviet Union, Soviet patriotism and criticism and self-criticism. We shall return to these principles at greater length in Part Two. Here we merely wish to observe briefly that these factors also are exclusively mental in character: the first three must be ascribed to the field of volition, while criticism and self-criticism belongs to that of the understanding.

Nowhere in Stalin's teaching is his departure from the original intention of Marx's historical materialism more evident than it is at this point. Marx would literally turn in his grave if he were to learn of this complete reversal of his materialist conception of history, or were to get wind of the fact that in the socialist order of society, social development is to be primarily determined by wide-ranging moral and spiritual factors, and that motivating forces in history are again to be supplied by that very 'criticism' which he explicitly attacked (in his polemic against 'Bruno Bauer and Co.' and their wish to see philosophical 'criticism' installed as the determining factor in history), at the period when he was striving to establish his own materialist conception of history.

This contradiction of the Marxian formulation of historical materialism is supposedly glossed over by saying that the question here is concerned merely with a *retro*active effect which emerges as a secondary result of the influence of the economic basis and merely assists the latter 'to take shape and consolidate itself'.[2] But this is a purely formal solution. The importance assigned by Stalinism to the moral and subjective factor in historical development is altogether too large for it to be reckoned as merely 'assisting' the process. The closer this process of development approaches to communism the greater the significance ascribed by Stalinism to the 'subjective

---

[1] *Cf. Ost-Probleme*, Vol. 8, No. 25/26 (22nd June 1956), p. 900.
[2] J. V. Stalin: *Op. cit.*, p. 13 (English, p. 9).

factor', *i.e.*, to factors such as consciousness, organization, will and determination,—indeed they actually become a 'decisive' force in history! [1]

It is, moreover, of cardinal importance here to observe that there has probably been little or no change in official Soviet doctrine on this point as a result of the 'de-Stalinization' policy. For in the first place the whole Stalinist conception of the 'organizing, mobilizing and transforming' significance of the superstructure is already laid down in principle in Lenin's theory of *soznatel'nost'*; and besides, all four of the new driving-forces that Stalin unearthed to propel the development of socialist society are also found cropping up again in Khrushchev's Report to the XXth Party Congress.

A still more striking alteration of the Marxian view of history is effected by Stalin in relation to the national question: it was indeed merely a corollary of the reinstatement of the individual, and the enhanced significance allotted to the subjective factor, that the importance of the national issue should also have come increasingly to the fore. But although the rehabilitation of subjective moral and ethical values could be effected with at least a semblance of preserving Marx's materialist conception of history, by speaking of a 'reciprocal action' of the superstructure upon the basis, it was no longer so easy, in the course of a positive treatment of the national factor, to remain within the categorical framework of basis and superstructure; Stalin eventually found himself compelled, therefore, in his letters on linguistics, to embark on a thoroughgoing 'extension' of this framework and to construe it in somewhat relative fashion, by explaining that not all social phenomena can be reduced to the categories of basis and superstructure.

The national question had long been a field in which Stalin was especially interested. His earlier writings on the subject were unambiguously committed to the view that social interests take precedence over national ones. While allowing certain formal concessions (languages, schools, etc.) to the different national cultures, he did so only in order that these national cultures might be the more readily imbued with a socialist spirit. A classic example of his views in this connection may be found in his observations to the XVIth Party Congress of 1930, at which he coined the celebrated formula that national cultures must be 'national in form but socialist in content'. We shall venture to quote here a fairly lengthy excerpt from the speech in question, the more so as it is somewhat difficult of access for the English-speaking reader, being no longer included in the 11th edition óf *Problems of Leninism*, on which the English translation is

[1] M. A. Leonov: *Klassiki marxizma-leninizma o predmete dialektich-eskogo materializma* (The Classics of Marxist-Leninism on the Content of Dialectical Materialism), in *IAN*, VI (1949), pp. 297–312, *q.v.* p. 308.

based. At the same time this passage is also a good example of the way in which Stalin treats of social problems against a background of dialectical materialist philosophy.

Against the 'deviation towards Great-Russian chauvinism', which had cited Lenin in support of its view that the slogan of national culture was a bourgeois slogan, Stalin defends the right of national minorities to cultural development:

'Lenin did indeed qualify the slogan of national culture *under the rule of the bourgeoisie* as a reactionary slogan. But could it be otherwise? What is national culture under the rule of the national bourgeoisie? It is culture that is *bourgeois* in content and national in form, having the object of doping the masses with the poison of nationalism and of strengthening the rule of the bourgeoisie. What is national culture under the dictatorship of the proletariat? It is culture that is *socialist* in content and national in form, having the object of educating the masses in the spirit of socialism and internationalism. How is it possible to confuse these two fundamentally different things without breaking with Marxism? Is it not obvious that in combating the slogan of national culture under the bourgeois order, Lenin was striking at the bourgeois *content* of national culture and not at its national form? It would be foolish to suppose that Lenin regarded socialist culture as *non-national*, as not having a particular national form. . . .

'Those who are deviating towards Great-Russian chauvinism are profoundly mistaken in believing that the period of building socialism in the U.S.S.R. is the period of the collapse and abolition of national cultures. The very opposite is the case. In point of fact, the period of the dictatorship of the proletariat and of the building of socialism in the U.S.S.R. is a period of the *flowering* of national cultures that are *socialist* in content and national in form.'[1]

Here, however, the question arises as to how this proposed flowering of national cultures is to be reconciled with the socialist ideal of a unified socialist culture of the future. In the solution of this problem, Stalin proves himself as nimble in dialectics as he had previously shown himself adept at splitting philosophical hairs in his distinction between the socialist content of a culture and its national form:

'It may seem strange that we who stand for the future *merging* of national cultures into one common (both in form and content) culture, with one common language, should at the same time stand for the *flowering* of national cultures at the present moment, in the period

[1] J. V. Stalin: *Politichesky otchet* . . . (*cf.* p. 167, n. 1), pp. 565 f. (English version, *Works*, XII, pp. 378 f.)

H*

of the dictatorship of the proletariat. But there is nothing strange about it. The national cultures must be allowed to develop and unfold, to reveal all their potentialities, in order to create the conditions for merging them into one common culture with one common language in the period of the victory of socialism all over the world. The flowering of cultures that are national in form and socialist in content under the dictatorship of the proletariat in one country *for the purpose* of merging them into one common socialist (both in form and content) culture, with one common language, when the proletariat is victorious all over the world and when socialism becomes the way of life—it is just this that constitutes the dialectics of the Leninist presentation of the question of national culture.' [1]

At this point Stalin expressly addresses himself to the problem of Marxist dialectic and defends it against the charge of contradiction, drawing a parallel as he does so between the future coalescence of national cultures and the promised withering-away of the State:

'It may be said that such a presentation of the question is "contradictory". But is there not the same "contradictoriness" in our presentation of the question of the State? We stand for the withering away of the State. At the same time we stand for the strengthening of the dictatorship of the proletariat, which is the mightiest and strongest state power that has ever existed. The highest development of state power with the object of preparing the conditions *for* the withering away of state power—such is the Marxist formula. Is this "contradictory"? Yes, it is "contradictory". But this contradiction is bound up with life, and it fully reflects Marx's dialectics. . . .

'Anyone who fails to understand this peculiar feature and "contradiction" of our transition period, anyone who fails to understand these dialectics of the historical processes, is dead as far as Marxism is concerned." [2]

Although here (in theory at least) the national element is still clearly and decidedly subordinated to the socialist, national culture being valued only as a preparation for the common socialist culture of the future in which individual national cultures are due to merge and disappear, from 1934 onwards there was a definite and surprising shift of emphasis on this point in favour of the national factor, and in actual fact predominantly in favour of the Russian national element. Klaus Mehnert, in his very important and illuminating study *Stalin versus Marx*,[3] has brought together a mass of evidential

---

[1] J. V. Stalin: *Op. cit.*, p. 566 (English, p. 380).
[2] *Ibid.*, pp. 566 f. (380–1).
[3] K. Mehnert: *Stalin versus Marx: The Stalinist Historical Doctrine*, London 1952.

material throwing light on the details of this change-over. It began quite suddenly with a decree, issued on 16th May 1934, and signed by Stalin and Molotov, concerning the teaching of history, which condemned the whole of Soviet historiography up to that date, and especially its most prominent representative, M. N. Pokrovsky, who died in 1932. Pokrovsky, whose chief work, *The History of Russia*, had received the highest praise from Lenin, considered it the task of the historian to demonstrate from the example of every individual nation the correctness of Marx's materialist conception of history; what matters are the general laws of Marxism, the particular affairs of individual peoples appearing merely incidental by comparison; at the same time he made it his business to show off the Soviet Union in the best possible light, and this was the more effectively accomplished by painting the darkest possible picture of Russia as it had been before.

Even so, the full scope of the new conception of history did not become visible right away. Admittedly, certain happenings, such as the rehabilitation of the words 'homeland' and 'patriotism' and the energetic working-up of Soviet patriotism, gave an indication of the quarter in which to look for this new historical view. But it was not until the early 'forties that its main contours began to emerge in full: the Soviet Union was depicted therein as the heart and backbone of human history, in which everything that had ever taken place within the present territories of the Soviet Union is ranked as part of its history, beginning, therefore, not with the year 1917, but with the ancient Chaldeans and Assyrians of the second or even third millenium 'before our (calendar) era'. Everything occurring outside this region is reckoned as a more or less marginal phenomenon in world history. It therefore becomes a chief task of the Soviet historian to vindicate the primacy of the Soviet Union in every field of culture, and more especially when dividing history into periods to give proof that the Russians were ahead of other peoples in the inauguration of each historical epoch. And since the Russian people are the leading nation in the Soviet Union, this patriotism, which had originally taken the form of a Soviet patriotism, emerges more and more as an officially-inspired Russian national patriotism.[1]

The official ideological background ultimately achieved this full development in Stalin's letters on linguistics during the summer of 1950. What chiefly strikes the eye in these letters is, in the first place, the shift of emphasis from class-antagonisms to that which serves to unify the different classes within society. The language of a people is the bond which unifies all members of society, whose function consists 'not in serving one class to the detriment of other classes' but in

[1] *Cf.* Part Two, Ch. I.

serving 'the entire society, all the classes of society',[1] if it is not to 'degenerate' into 'the jargon of some social group',[2] and create 'the threat of the disintegration of society';[3] but language appears here, not merely as the bond unifying any sort of society, but more especially as that which unites all the members of a nation together: national languages 'are not class, but common languages, common to all the members of each nation'.[4]

A further characteristic change of emphasis may also be noted, from the discontinuity of social development to its continuity. In dealing with the development of language, Stalin is especially insistent on the continuity of its evolution, which takes place, not by means of leaps or 'explosions', but by the gradual emergence of new elements and the dying away of old ones. In this connection he makes the pregnant observation that even in the case of social development the element of discontinuity should not be overstressed, for it applies only within a class-society, not in the classless Soviet society, where leaps (revolutions) no longer occur. In this way language becomes a bond of unity, not only between the members of a present-day society or nation, but also between the different generations, past and to come.

This automatically gives rise, without need of assertion on Stalin's part, to an additional readjustment of the balance in favour of the national element. Though it may seem a trifle exaggerated to go on, as Professor V. V. Mavrodin did in a speech at Leningrad,[5] and affirm, on the strength of this new Stalinist 'line', that the people is 'eternal', the nation, thanks to its greater longevity than the class, does at all events take on a greater degree of importance in comparison with the latter. For whereas class-antagonisms are already destined to disappear during the period of realizing socialism in one country (the Soviet Union), the merging, which is still insisted on, of national cultures and languages into a common culture and language, is only due to begin after the victory of communism all over the world.[6] The threatened supersession of nationalism is thereby postponed to the Greek calends.

And finally, there is yet a fourth shift of position to be detected in these letters of Stalin's: the dominant status accorded therein to the Russian language, which has emerged victorious from all previous encounters with other languages.[7] Zaslavsky,[8] indeed, already dis-

---

[1] J. V. Stalin: *Marxizm i voprosy yazykoznaniya*, p. 15 (English, p. 10).
[2] *Ibid.*, p. 17 (11).　　　　　　[3] *Ibid.*, p. 21 (14).
[4] *Ibid.*, p. 27 (17).　　　　　　[5] *Cf.* K. Mehnert: *Op. cit.*, p. 29.
[6] G. E. Glezerman: *Klass i natsiya* (Class and Nation), in *VF*, 1950, I, pp. 259–75; *q.v.* pp. 273 f.
[7] J. V. Stalin: *Op. cit.*, pp. 61 f. (40).
[8] D. Zaslavsky: *Veliky yazyk nashey epokhi* (The Great Language of our Epoch), in *Literaturnaya Gazeta*, No. 1 (2488) of 1st Jan. 1949.

cerns the dawn of the period in which Russian will become the international world-language: just as Latin was the world-language of antiquity, French that of feudalism, and English that of imperialism, so we already see Russian emerging as the world-language of socialism.

Now what is the deeper significance of all this? The primary reason for it was doubtless the endeavour to provide a Marxist justification for the rehabilitation of the national factor. Klaus Mehnert considers that Stalin had learnt from Hitler to put a high value on the importance of the national element; hence the fact that the inauguration of the nationalist policy in the Soviet Union should have coincided with the seizure of power by National Socialism in Germany. Hitler's example may indeed have had great influence in accelerating the adoption of the course in question. But too much stress should not be laid, in our opinion, on the novelty of this policy that has prevailed in Russia since 1934. For in the first place the tendency to make the Soviet Union the be-all and end-all of history is already discernible in Russia a good ten years before 1934. The transformation of the Comintern into a docile instrument of the Soviet government and the Russian Communist Party was already beginning in Lenin's lifetime; even then the complaint was heard that Russia was no longer the vanguard of the communist world-revolution, but rather that the international communist movement was being turned into the rearguard of the Soviet Union.[1] And so far as the ever-increasing insistence on *Russian* patriotism is concerned, it is noteworthy in the extreme that even Lenin himself should have complained of Stalin's pursuit of Great-Russian nationalism in his attitude towards the Georgian communists, and that a quarrel would have broken out between them on this very point if Lenin's illness had not put a sudden end to any further control, on his part, of the affairs of the régime.[2]

[1] *Cf.* Branko Lazitch; *Lénine et la III Internationale*, Neufchâtel 1951.

[2] This was occasioned by Stalin's recalcitrant attitude towards the constitutional reform of 1922, which transformed what had hitherto been the 'Russian Soviet Federative Republic' into the Union of Soviet Socialist Republics, with equal rights granted to all the participating nations; also by Stalin's brutal measures in the Caucasus, not only against the Georgian Mensheviks, who dreamed of a sort of new Switzerland between Europe and Asia, but even against the Georgian Bolsheviks, who favoured immediate entry into the Union as an independent Soviet republic, and not an indirect adherence as part of Stalin's projected Transcaucasian Federation. When Lenin came to hear of the violence practised in the Caucasus, on Stalin's orders, by Ordzhonikidze and Dzerzhinsky, he was highly incensed, accused Stalin and Dzerzhinsky, who were neither of them Russian-born, of 'pure-Russian' nationalism, and remarked that russified products of other nations were often worse chauvinists than Russians by

In addition to this, the significance of the letters on linguistics has often been seen in the fact that they transform linguistics into an 'instrument of Russian imperialism'.[1] It is true enough that in this work Stalin not only sought to effect a theoretical rehabilitation of the national factor, but also endeavoured to harness Russian nationalism to his car, and therefore gave the Russian people the leading rôle among the nationalities of the Soviet Union. But an appeal was also intended to the national feelings of the other peoples, inasmuch as they are assured of the fullest development of their national cultures under the leadership of the Russian people, and insofar as the 'friendship of the peoples of the Soviet Union' is designated as an incentive to the development of socialist society. But besides this, it also appears, as N. Gradoboyev has pointed out, that Stalin's appeal to national feelings was directed above all to the colonial peoples. He obviously hoped that the establishment of communism on a world scale would be more readily attained by mobilizing the national struggles for liberation of the colonial and oppressed peoples than by stoking the embers of the class-war. Stalin would therefore seem to have been concerned here with the cultivation of a Soviet rather than a Russian brand of imperialism.[2]

No less significant, however, than the stress laid on the national factor, is the pronounced conservative tendency which runs through Stalin's letters on linguistics and is evinced in all the shifts of emphasis already referred to. The function of language is to serve as a unifying bond for the whole of society, in order to prevent it from falling to

---

birth; he ended by giving orders that they should both be called to account 'for this Great-Russian nationalist campaign'. In a note of 4th January, 1923, Lenin sums up Stalin as follows: 'Stalin is too rude, and this fault, though entirely supportable in relations among us communists, becomes insupportable in the office of General Secretary' and goes on to consider whether the dangers of a split owing to differences of opinion between Stalin and Trotsky might be obviated by putting in someone else instead of Stalin as General Secretary of the Party. After Lenin had got wind of renewed acts of violence by Stalin in Georgia, his secretary reported on 6th March, 1923, 'Vladimir Ilyich is preparing a bomb for Stalin at the Congress'. And his widow, Krupskaya, tells us, of the last letter that Lenin was able to dictate, 'Vladimir has just dictated to the stenographer a letter to Stalin, breaking off all relations with him'. *Cf.* on this subject Boris Souvarine: *Stalin. A Critical Survey of Bolshevism*, London 1939, pp. 307 ff.; also *Le 'Testament de Lénine'*, in *Est et Ouest* (B.E.I.P.I.), Vol. 8, No. 151 (1st–15th May 1956), pp. 14–16.

[1] *Cf.* Lucien Laurat: *Staline, la linguistique et l'impérialisme russe*, Paris 1951, pp. 61 ff.

[2] N. Gradoboyev: *Stalin depolnyaet marxizm* (Stalin Augments Marxism), in *Vestnik instituta po izucheniyu istorii i kul'tury SSSR*, 1951, No. 1, pp. 38–50.

pieces; after so much earlier talk of the class-struggle, one cannot but be struck by this insistence on a unifying bond for the whole of society. In the theory of the various types of dialectical leap, and of the 'revolution from above', the conservative impulse is plainly visible: the poison-fangs must be drawn from the dialectic, lest its leaps should one day operate also to the disadvantage of the communist power-machine. The rehabilitation of the national factor again sounds an unmistakably conservative note.

A similar conservative tendency and a corresponding retreat from a too unguarded extension of Marxist doctrines is likewise observable in Stalin's last work, *Economic Problems of Socialism in the U.S.S.R.* It was Stalin himself who in earlier years had put forward the theory of the retroactive influence of the superstructure on the basis and had dwelt on 'the tremendous organizing, mobilizing and transforming value of new ideas . . . new political institutions' (*i.e.*, above all the institutions of the Communist Party and the Soviet State). But in so doing he had inspired certain hotheads with the idea that the Party could do anything. And the great clamour raised about the Michurin–Lysenko theory of inheritance was bound to encourage a similarly misguided view. Indeed it was precisely for this reason that the theory had found such high favour with the Party authorities, since it appeared to offer men the power to dominate Nature in the most complete fashion and themselves to control the development of organic life at their own behest, without being bound in this endeavour by limits due to the immutability of species. Stalin was now obliged to stress that the power of the Party was not unlimited, and that it was confronted, not only by the laws of Nature as an objective datum, but even by the laws of social development as well. In this connection Bertram D. Wolfe[1] makes interesting reference to the note of pessimism which sounds through these essays of Stalin's. It is not just that he credits man only with the power of discovering and making use of natural laws, without being able to suspend them or to create new ones; in the foreground of Stalin's interest in Nature there now stands above all the concern to cope with 'the destructive action of some of the laws', to limit their field of operation, to take precautions against natural disasters, floods and inundations.

We observed earlier that Stalin's conservative tendency emerges, *inter alia*, from the letters on linguistics, in his view of language as a bond unifying the whole of society. In his last work he goes still further in this respect and uncovers many other more deep-lying bonds uniting society in all ages and among all nations. Against Yaroshenko, who had denied the need for a single political economy applicable to all levels of social development, Stalin points out that

[1] *The New Gospel of Stalinism*, in *Problems of Communism*, Washington, January 1953.

there are also laws of social development common to all social formations, feudalism, capitalism and socialism alike, such as *e.g.*, 'the law of the unity of productive forces and the relations of production', and concludes from this:

'Hence, social formations are not only divided from one another by their own specific laws, but also connected with one another by the economic laws common to all formations.' [1]

In replying here to Yaroshenko, Stalin speaks only of a 'law of the unity of productive forces and the relations of production'. But at the outset of his essay he refers to it as the 'law that the relations of production *must necessarily conform* with the character of the productive forces'. Whereas in Marx's Introduction to the *Critique of Political Economy* this law is purely *descriptive* in character, it is here transformed under Stalin's hand, as H. Chambre has pertinently observed,[2] into a *normative* law, or postulate. This carries on the conservative trend which in both his previous writings was implicit in the theory of the active rôle of the superstructure (meaning by this in particular the Communist Party and the Soviet Government). Just as this latter theory was already able to justify, in the Soviet Union, the prior erection of the political structure of socialism (the Soviet State), before the creation of the socialist economic basis, so now the law of the 'necessary' conformity of productive forces and relations of production also made it possible to justify the undisguised and extremely vigorous intervention of the State when, immediately after the Revolution, and particularly during the collectivization of agriculture, the new relations of production were imposed by force: in so doing, it was merely proceeding in accordance with its knowledge of objective economic law!

As in the case of the objective character of social laws of development, so Stalin also beats a similar retreat with regard to the elimination of the distinctions between town and country and mental and physical labour. Hitherto the impression had been given that in the Marxist Utopia—the classless society of the future—the antitheses between town and country, industry and agriculture, mental and physical labour would be completely done away with. It was supposed, not only that labour in general would be transformed from a burden into a primary necessity of life, but that, in consequence of the use of technology, more or less the same working conditions would prevail everywhere, and moreover that owing to the high cultural level of mankind everyone would be capable of performing any kind of work.

---

[1] J. V. Stalin: *Ekonomicheskie problemy* . . ., pp. 167 f. (English, p. 79).

[2] H. Chambre: *Le marxisme en Union Soviétique. Idéologie et Institutions. Leur évolution de 1917 à nos jours*, Paris 1955, pp. 472 ff.

On this point also Stalin found himself obliged to damp down the expectations placed upon the ideal communist society of the future. The promised elimination of the distinctions between town and country and mental and physical labour, signifies merely the removal of the *opposition*, which is an essential feature of capitalism, and consists in a *conflict of interests*, and likewise the removal of the *essential* distinction, which still holds good even in the socialist society. So far as the antithesis of town and country is concerned, this consisted under capitalism in the exploitation of the country by the town, in the

'ruin of the majority of the rural population by the whole course of development of industry, trade and credit under capitalism'.[1]

The antithesis between mental and physical labour (between physical workers and the managerial personnel in industry) has similarly been based on exploitation of the physical workers by the representatives of mental labour. In the socialist society of the Soviet Union, according to Stalin, the basis of the opposition between town and country has at length been removed, by the liquidation of the property-owners and the alliance between workers and peasants, who are now supposed to share the same interests. The same is also held to be true of the antithesis between mental and physical labour.

For all that, an essential distinction between town and country still remains, for the time being, even in Soviet society. It consists in this, that public ownership of the means of production prevails generally in industry, whereas group-ownership (the *kolkhoz*) still continues to be the rule in agriculture. Not till this group-ownership has been converted into public ownership will the essential distinction between town and country also disappear. The same applies to the distinction between mental and physical work. It will only be removed when the physical workers have attained the cultural and technical level of the technicians.

But this will serve only to remove the essential distinctions involved, and not every sort of distinction. Some such contrast will always remain, if only because of the difference in working conditions between industrial and agricultural labour, and likewise mental and physical labour. And Stalin stresses that 'some distinction, even if inessential' will always remain, even in the future, and this 'because the conditions of labour of the managerial staffs and those of the workers are not identical'.[2]

Finally, Stalin is not only concerned to tone down the expectations reposed in the communist ideal society, but also to put off the redemption-date of the innumerable promises secured upon it to the remotest

[1] J. V. Stalin: *Op. cit.*, p. 61 (English, p. 29).
[2] *Ibid.*, pp. 69 f. (English, p. 34).

possible future. Having laid down against Yaroshenko the three basic conditions for the transition to communism (continuous expansion of all social production, with a relatively higher rate of expansion of the production of means of production; raising of collective-farm property to the level of public property; advance in the cultural standard of the members of society), he follows this up with the ineffably cautious and non-committal remark that:

'These are the basic conditions required to pave the way for the transition to communism.' [1]

Furthermore, in order to realize these 'basic conditions', Stalin also goes on in this work to list a number of preconditions, *e.g.*, for raising the level of culture: the working-day to be reduced, first to six, and later to five hours; universal, compulsory, polytechnical education to be introduced (which itself will require a series of preparatory phases); housing conditions to be radically improved; and finally, the real wages of workers and employees to be at least doubled, 'if not more'. Only when all this has been achieved will the 'basic conditions' have been realized, and even then there will always be the possibility, if need be, of interpolating further 'subsidiary conditions'. And supposing these also to be established, we are still no further forward than the possibility of being able to begin 'preparations' for the transition to communism. Stalin could take his departure with confidence: the danger of any premature fulfilment of communist promises had been banished, for his successors, to an immeasurably remote future.

He had left them, in this work, a veritable 'testament', in which the main features of the Stalinist era of communism are again highlighted, and also supposedly fixed for the future: the progressive increase in the production of capital goods is to ensure that in future also the populace will be subjected to an extreme privation of consumer goods; the 'raising' of collective-farm property to the 'level' of public property will serve to complete the disinheritance of the peasantry by depriving them of the last semblance of roots in the ownership of land; the announcement that even in days to come 'the conditions of labour of the managerial staffs and those of the workers' will not be 'identical', is intended to sanction once and for all the privileged status of the main props of the Stalinist régime, namely the 'technical personnel', and to gild and render it palatable by appealing to the developmental laws of socialism.

[1] J. V. Stalin: *Op. cit.*, p. 163 (English, p. 77).

CHAPTER XI

Since the Death of Stalin

THE ideological evaluation of Stalin's last work, *Economic Problems of Socialism in the U.S.S.R.*, together with the resolutions based on it at the XIXth Party Congress, had scarcely got under way before Stalin died on 5th March 1953. In view of the absolute dictatorship he had established, not only in the political, but also in the ideological sphere, it might have been expected that this event would have very decided repercussions in matters of ideology. But Stalinism did not expire with the death of Stalin. This explains why, immediately after his death, there was scarcely any change to be observed in the ideological field. The struggle for power within the Party which broke out among his successors soon after the dictator's death, together with the experiences undergone by 'workers on the philosophical front' after the conclusion of the struggle for the succession to Lenin, must have made it seem prudent for the latter to begin by adopting a waiting rôle. Thus, when in course of time a certain change in regard to ideology did become apparent, it was as a by-product, partly of the changed political strategy pursued by Stalin's heirs (the 'policy of thaw', for example), and partly of the general weakening of discipline within the country resulting from the struggle for power among the heirs themselves.

First among the external events affecting the further progress of philosophy must be mentioned the two Plenary Sessions of the Party Central Committee in September 1953 and January 1955. It seems that after Stalin's death the authorities were seriously concerned lest the hopes of the populace for a betterment of their condition—hopes that had been dashed once already, after the end of the Second World War—might declare themselves with such violence that the régime would no longer be able to control the situation. It is no accident that two such alarm-signals should have been sounded in these first few months after Stalin's death: the 17th July rising in the Soviet Zone of Germany, and as an echo of this, the strike of prisoners in the coalmines of Vorkuta on the Arctic Circle. However that may be, the Plenary Session of September 1953 deemed it necessary, at all events, to take measures for a 'rapid upswing' in the production of consumer goods. This was based on the consideration that whereas production of capital goods had increased 55-fold in the previous 28 years, the production of consumer goods had risen only 12-fold in the same period. In general it is Malenkov who must be reckoned the originator of this policy.

But such a course had powerful opponents within the Party, who were able to muster ever-increasing strength. At the same September Plenum which decided to raise the production of consumer goods, Malenkov had to yield the General Secretaryship of the Party to N. S. Khrushchev. The latter made such headway thereafter that at the Plenary Session of January 1955 the course adopted in September 1953 was broken off once more and a rise in the production of capital goods again announced as the main objective. Notwithstanding all the din of propaganda surrounding the slogan of 'peaceful co-existence', the underlying background of this decision is very clearly reflected in the decree of the Plenum itself:

'As before, the Party considers its main task to lie in the further development of heavy industry, which forms the firm foundation of the whole economy, the unshakeable basis of the defensive capacity of our homeland, and the source of the continual increase in the wellbeing of the Soviet people'.[1]

A number of changes are also observable during these years among the learned institutions of Soviet philosophy. By a resolution of the Praesidium of 10th August 1953 philosophy was removed from the hitherto existing History and Philosophy Section of the Academy of Sciences of the U.S.S.R. and attached to the Economics and Law Section, which was now entitled 'Section of Economics, Philosophy and Law'. The Philosophical Institute has since been subject to the latter.[2]

At the General Assembly of the Academy of Sciences of the U.S.S.R. held on 22nd–26th October 1953, a number of philosophers were among those newly elected to membership of the Academy, P. F. Yudin becoming an Ordinary Member, and M. D. Kammari, F. V. Konstantinov and V. S. Kruzhkov Corresponding Members. On this occasion the *Vestnik* of the Academy of Sciences presented the new member to its readers in the following terms:

'Yudin, Pavel Fedorovich (born 1899), elected Member of the

[1] *Kommunist* 1955, No. 3, p. 23.
[2] *Vestnik AN SSSR*, 1953, No. 6, p. 226; *cf.* also No. 9, p. 54.

Academy in the special field of Philosophy. P. F. Yudin graduated in 1924 from the Communist Stalin-University of Leningrad and in 1931 from the Institute of Red Professors. From 1932 to 1938 he was Director of the Institute of Red Professors, and from 1938 to 1944, Director of the Philosophical Institute of the Academy of Sciences of the U.S.S.R., while carrying on at the same time an extensive range of activities in Party and State. In 1939 P. F. Yudin was elected a Corresponding Member of the Academy of Sciences of the U.S.S.R. A notable proportion of P. F. Yudin's researches have been dedicated to the working-out of such important problems of historical material-ism as those of the State and law, of the laws of development of socialist society and the transition from socialism to communism, and of the position of science, literature and art in the building-up of socialism. P. F. Yudin can boast of major works, such as *The Materialistic and the Religious World-Outlook, Marxist–Leninism on Culture and the Cultural Revolution,* and *Soviet Culture.* A number of his scientific writings have been devoted to examining the rôle and significance attaching to the classic works of Marx, Engels, Lenin and Stalin in relation to the development of philosophical science. P. F. Yudin's activities as a Marxist philosopher have been distinguished by energetic opposition to menshevizing idealism and also to bour-geois theories of the State and law, and of literature and art. In 1948 P. F. Yudin received the Stalin Prize for his part in the preparation of Volumes I and II of the collective *History of Philosophy.* A member of the Communist Party of the Soviet Union from 1918 on-wards, P. F. Yudin was elected at the XIXth Party Congress to the Central Committee of the C.P.S.U. P. F. Yudin is a Deputy of the Supreme Soviet of the U.S.S.R. and has been decorated with the Order of Lenin, two Orders of the Red Banner of Labour, and medals of the U.S.S.R.' [1]

At the end of 1953, therefore, the following Soviet philosophers were members of the Academy of Sciences of the U.S.S.R.: Ordinary Members: G. F. Alexandrov, M. B. Mitin and P. F. Yudin in the Section of Economics, Philosophy and Law, and A. M. Deborin, who had stayed behind in the Historical Sciences Section; Corresponding Members: M. T. Iovchuk, M. D. Kammari, F. V. Konstantinov, V. S. Kruzhkov, A. O. Makovel'sky, A. A. Maximov, P. N. Fedoseyev and (for Psychology) S. L. Rubinstein.[2]

Significant changes have also taken place among the personnel of the Philosophical Institute. To begin with, from October 1953 on-wards, F. V. Konstantinov figured as Chief Editor of *Voprosy filosofii,* his predecessor, D. I. Chesnokov, having been relieved of the

---

[1] *Vestnik AN SSSR,* 1954, No. 2, p. 91.
[2] *Ibid.,* 1953, No. 6, p. 230.

post, according to the Academy *Vestnik*,[1] 'on being transferred to other duties'. The reason for this may well have been that at the XIXth Party Congress Chesnokov was elected to the Praesidium of the Central Committee of the C.P.S.U. Two years later, however, Konstantinov also relinquished office 'on being transferred to other employment',[2] and was replaced by Kammari.

On G. F. Alexandrov's appointment as Minister of Culture in April 1954, the Praesidium of the Academy of Sciences released him from his responsibilities as Director of the Philosophical Institute and Secretary of the Section of Economics, Philosophy and Law, though he remained on the Praesidium of the Academy itself.[3] The Praesidium, however, preserved no very fragrant memory of his achievements as head of the Institute. When, in the summer of 1955, it reviewed the work of the Institute over the years 1951–5, and in so doing found it behindhand with the tasks assigned to it, the Praesidium expressly emphasized that this was the fault of the leadership, and especially of Alexandrov, who had occupied the post of Director for many years past and must be held responsible, not only for a variety of deficiencies in the organization of the Institute, but also for a series of ideological errors that had crept into its work.[4] The position of Director was not filled again until a year after Alexandrov's demission of office, and then by P. N. Fedoseyev.[5]

Actual happenings in the philosophical life of the Soviet Union included the appearance of the long-awaited textbook on dialectical materialism, produced by an authors' collective under the general editorship of G. F. Alexandrov, and the publication of the second edition of the textbook on historical materialism, issued under the general editorship of F. V. Konstantinov. Both books appeared in 1954 and were thereafter subjected to discussion on a very extensive scale in the various scientific institutions of the Soviet Union. We shall be returning to many of the reports of these discussions, since they provide a very graphic picture of the present state of philosophy in the U.S.S.R. and also give clear evidence of the shifts of emphasis and 'atmospheric' changes which have taken place since Stalin's death.

As regards these changes in Soviet philosophical life after the death of Stalin, they are primarily discernible in the fact that the person of Stalin has been promptly relegated to the background. Hardly had the official lamentations and ritual elegies died away, than his name was shrouded in a mysterious silence. Whereas in the year preceding his death, eight articles in *Voprosy filosofii* had been devoted to Stalin, there is but one further article to be found on him afterwards, and

---

[1] *Vestnik AN SSSR*, 1953, No. 2, p. 53.   [2] *Ibid.*, 1955, No. 1, p. 104.
[3] *Ibid.*, 1954, No. 7, p. 65.   [4] *Ibid.*, 1955, No. 9, pp. 88 f.
[5] *Ibid.*, 1955, No. 7, p. 104.

in only one other title is he mentioned along with the other three 'classics'; and these in the first two numbers compiled after his death. Since then his name no longer occurs in any title.

The present endeavour is to install the Communist Party, and especially the Central Committee, in the position previously occupied by Stalin. Very fortunately for the purpose, it so happened that Stalin's death occurred in the very year of the fiftieth anniversary celebrations of the founding of the Communist Party of the Soviet Union. In the speeches and publications which greeted this jubilee there was a striking tendency to credit the Party with achievements previously attributed to Stalin alone, and to refer to the Central Committee at points where Stalin's name would formerly have been mentioned. The journal *Voprosy filosofii* celebrated the occasion in the leading article of its fourth number of 1953, which went to press at the end of August, hardly six months after Stalin's death. In the course of this article, which bears the title 'The Communist Party— the Leading and Guiding Force of Soviet Society',[1] Lenin is very frequently referred to, whereas Stalin is only mentioned on two occasions. The first of these is a quotation from Malenkov's speech to the XIXth Party Congress; the second names Stalin as leader of the Central Committee in a context which must have remained for many an abhorrent memory, namely as organizer of the bloodthirsty liquidation of the partisans of Trotsky, Bukharin and Zinoviev.[2] The new Constitution adopted in 1936 and commonly referred to in earlier days as the 'Stalin Constitution', is now described as the 'new Constitution';[3] the winning of the Great Patriotic War, unfailingly attributed to Stalin on former occasions, is now 'a triumph of the inspiring leadership and political wisdom of the Communist Party';[4] even the principle of the 'tremendous mobilizing and transforming value of the socialist ideology'—a typically Stalinist formula'- is ascribed, in a leading article in *Voprosy filosofii* on 'The Great Philosophical Heritage of Lenin', to Lenin himself.[6]

It was not enough, however, merely to keep silent on the subject. There soon began a violent campaign also against the 'cult of personality' as 'alien to the spirit of Marxism–Leninism'. 'Collective leadership' was proclaimed to be the only truly Marxist form of government, and stress was laid on the importance of the people as 'creators of history'.

'The "cult of personality" is irreconcilable with the principle of collective leadership. This cult, which is alien to the spirit of Marxist–Leninism, disparages the rôle of the Communist Party and its central leadership and depreciates the activity of the party masses and the

---

[1] *VF*, 1953, 4, pp. 3–17.   [2] *Ibid.*, p. 10.   [3] *Ibid.*, p. 11.
[4] *Ibid.*   [5] *Cf.* above, p. 216.   [6] *VF* 1955, 2, p. 8.

Soviet people. The "cult of personality" has nothing in common with the Marxist–Leninist appreciation of the high importance attaching to the guiding activity of leading institutions and personalities. The Party sets out from the consideration that only the collective experience and collective wisdom of the Central Committee, founded on Marxist–Leninist theory and the broad initiative of the leading cadres, are able to guarantee the correct leadership of Party and country.'[1]

The 'struggle against the un-Marxist cult of personality', the principle of collective leadership, the historical rôle of the masses, now become no less recurrent themes in Soviet ideological writing than the 'struggle against cosmopolitanism' and the like had been in the years preceding.

Lest the break with the immediate past should appear too obvious, this struggle against the cult of personality is frequently based on an appeal—to Stalin himself. On the occasion of the Fiftieth Anniversary of the Party, the Economics, Philosophy and Law Section of the Academy of Sciences held a joint session, in conjunction with the Historical Sciences and Literature and Language Sections, on 19th October 1953. All three speakers, the President of the Academy, A. S. Nesmeyanov in his opening address, and P. N. Pospelov and F. V. Konstantinov in their respective contributions, took issue against the cult of personality. Pospelov referred in doing so to a remark made by Stalin himself about a work entitled 'Tales of Stalin's Childhood', which had been got ready for the press in 1938 by the Publishing House for Juvenile Literature. Stalin sent a letter instructing that the manuscript should be burnt, on the ground that this work was liable to implant in the minds of Soviet children and Soviet citizens generally the cult of personalities, the cult of infallible 'heroes'—a dangerous and pernicious undertaking, since the theory of 'heroes' and 'masses' represented an unbolshevik theory of social-revolutionary origin.[2] On reading this, we might almost be tempted to suppose that Stalin was really not to blame for the emergence of the personality cult, were we not aware that the universal and blatant adulation customary in the last years of his life would not have been possible without his consent.

No less elegant is the artifice employed by V. S. Kruzhkov in order to avoid associating his attack on the personality cult with a too-obvious disavowal of Stalin. In an article, 'V. I. Lenin—Genius of Creative Marxism',[3] he contrives to represent matters as if indulgence in the cult of personality were at least equally chargeable against those heads of scientific institutes who have established an 'Arak-

[1] *VF* 1955, 2, pp. 15 f.   [2] *VF* 1953, 6, p. 227.
[3] *Vestnik AN SSSR* 1954, No. 1, pp. 3–20.

cheyev régime' in their departments, have stifled free criticism and prevented the forces of youth from coming into play.[1]

The extent to which, soon after his death, the authority of Stalin had lost its character of absolute infallibility, can also be seen in the reviews accorded to the textbook on 'Dialectical Materialism'. In his pamphlet on *Dialectical and Historical Materialism* Stalin had begun by expounding the 'Marxist dialectical method' under four heads, and thereafter devoted a further three to 'Marxist philosophical materialism'.[2] Since then, the content of the textbooks had also followed a similar plan of arrangement, including the one under review. But very many reviewers now declared that it would have been more to the purpose if the exposition had begun, not by dealing with problems of method, but with a description of Marxist philosophical materialism, for

'it is not possible to throw light on the manner and method of investigating the material world without having previously explained what this material world itself consists in'.[3]

B. M. Kedrov of the Moscow Academy of Social Sciences actually went so far as to say that the textbook would have done better to dissociate itself entirely from the structure of Stalin's booklet, with its four dialectical and three materialistic clauses, since on this plan a whole series of important problems of dialectical materialism, such as the 'law of the negation of the negation', etc., were left completely unprovided for.[4] Many of the participants in this discussion also urged that the various categories of the materialist dialectic should have been dealt with in a chapter on their own. In slavish adherence to the pattern of Stalin's book they have not in fact been treated separately in recent years, as was formerly the case, but have been tacked on to one or other of the seven basic theses enunciated by him.[5]

Even in the attitude towards non-Marxist philosophy, a certain change is observable. An editorial article in *Kommunist* for March 1955, in yet another examination of the state of philosophical work, reproaches the authors' collective engaged in producing the two-volume 'History of Philosophy' on the ground that those responsible for the chapters in question have not dealt adequately with pre-Marxian philosophy. Whereas Zhdanov, in the 1947 Philosophical Discussion, had accused Alexandrov's book of depicting the emergence of Marxism as a purely evolutionary continuance of earlier philosophical systems, there is now a tendency to fall into the opposite extreme: no notice is taken of the fact that the 'leap', the

---

[1] *Ibid.*, p. 13.   [2] *Cf.* above, p. 212.   [3] *VF* 1954, 5, p. 199.
[4] *VF* 1954, 4, p. 202.   [5] *Ibid.*, p. 203; No. 5, p. 199.

'revolution' in philosophical development inaugurated by Marxism, was the legitimate outcome of the development that preceded it. Whereas previously the Russian philosophers were neglected, it is now the importance of Western European philosophy that is under-rated, and this represents an equally undesirable extreme.[1] In very much the same spirit, a reviewer of the textbook on 'Dialectical Materialism' objects that the criticism of bourgeois philosophy there-in is content with a bare negation.[2] Another reviewer expostulates vehemently at the fact that it dismisses Hegelian philosophy as 'unscientific'. This charge of being unscientific recoils, rather, upon the authors' collective, for it betrays a 'metaphysical', unhistorical attitude and fails to grasp that in its day the Hegelian philosophy had a progressive significance.[3] Even the editors of *Voprosy filosofii* exclaim against the nihilistic attitude of those many Soviet philo-sophers who confine themselves merely to assertive and vociferous outcries against bourgeois philosophy and sociology, instead of sub-jecting the opposing positions to serious analysis, and reminds them of Lenin's admonition,

'that one cannot be a true Marxist until one has appropriated the philosophical heritage of the past'.[4]

At a conference of provincial and metropolitan philosophers, held at the Philosophical Institute in January 1955, a number of speakers in the discussion made the very revealing observation that what was needed to overcome this failing was that philosophers should pay more attention to mastering foreign languages, and that the libraries should be better supplied with bourgeois philosophical literature.[5]

A certain change in the 'atmosphere' of Soviet philosophy also emerges clearly from other criticisms advanced against the textbook on 'Dialectical Materialism', or the practice of philosophy generally. The textbook is further objected to on the ground that it contains a great many 'resounding phrases'; the scientific character of dialectical materialism is established by mere repetition of the assertion that the dialectical method is the 'only scientific one'.[6] The authors behave as if

'in Soviet science, and Soviet philosophy in particular, all problems were already solved and all answers already discovered'.[7]

In a survey of the philosophical dissertations defended during the

[1] *Nasushchnye voprosy filosofskoy nauki* (Salient Problems in Philo-sophical Science), in *Kommunist*, 1955, No. 5, pp. 18 f.
[2] *VF* 1954, 3, p. 182.   [3] *VF* 1954, 5, p. 198.
[4] *Velikoe leninskoe filosofskoe nasledstvo* (The Great Philosophical Heritage of Lenin), in *VF* 1955, 2, p. 9; *cf.* also p. 6.
[5] *VF* 1955, 2, p. 232.   [6] *VF* 1954, 5, p. 201.   [7] *VF*, 1954, 3, p. 182.

last two years in the various institutions of higher learning, the journal *Voprosy filosofii* remarks that the dissertations on the history of Marxist–Leninist philosophy all suffer from one major defect:

'they allow the history of philosophy to become merged in the history of Marxist–Leninism, and do not reveal the process whereby real philosophical problems develop.' [1]

It is openly admitted that in most of the philosophical dissertations there is too much politics and too little philosophy.

'Many dissertations have been written on the history of philosophy among the peoples of the U.S.S.R., and some of them are good ones. But on closer inspection all these dissertations turn out, for the most part, to be too little philosophical in character. They deal with the history of political doctrines, the history of social thought—but the basic problems of the history of philosophy, the problems of epistemology or logic in any given thinker, remain in the shadows, or are treated "in a general way" and often by reference to one and the same stereotype. No matter who may be under discussion, the same old formulae are universally repeated: "he came very close [to materialism]", "at bottom he is a materialist", "he surpassed all pre-Marxian thinkers", and so on and so forth. The result of such levelling mania is that all dissertations look alike and all thinkers are portrayed in the same colours." [2]

Of other dissertations it is observed that all the revolutionaries in Russian history are forcibly converted into Marxists:

'Energetic steps must be taken to end the still prevalent custom of modernizing the views of the Russian revolutionary democrats, of attempting to squeeze them into Marxism by force.' [3]

Even the long-standing reproach of 'dogmatism', so frequently raised against the Soviet philosophers, now takes on a rather new tone.

'Many questions', says Instructor V. A. Stoff in complaining of the textbook, 'are dogmatically dealt with, according to the formula: "Marxism teaches", "the Marxist–Leninist theory tells us", "science has proved", etc.' [4]

No less striking and candid is the criticism levelled by Instructress A. T. Fedorova during the above-mentioned conference at the 'dogmatism' of many philosophers:

'Dogmatism is so deeply rooted in the minds of many philosophers,

---

[1] *VF* 1955, 3, p. 195.　　　　[2] *Ibid.*　　　　[3] *Ibid.*
[4] *VF* 1954, 3, p. 182.

that even now they have not yet succeeded in shaking it off; they recoil from any new solution of a question as from a fire, for fear lest they should somehow offend against an established canon.' [1]

In general the Soviet philosophers have often been rebuked of late for timidity.

'Timidity, superficiality, the perpetual dishing-up of threadbare truisms, abject flattery, are not infrequently to be encountered in scientific works on political economy and problems of historical materialism.' [2]

One result of this timorousness is that many philosophers retreat into the innocuous field of commentating on the classic writers.

'We must overcome the very dangerous tendency to be observed among a certain number of philosophers, who specialize in commentating on the works of the Marxist–Leninist classics. They take it for granted that the advancement of philosophical knowledge is not their affair. They are afraid of the difficulties involved in generalizing the exceptionally rich store of practice relating to the building of communism in our country. . . .' [3]

'Whence this theoretical cowardice and superficiality?' asks the author of the article. This question, posed only a year after the above-mentioned *affaire* Fedoseyev, may divert us by its almost tragi-comic air. But the author is ready with his answer: such cowardice arises

'from ignorance of life, from a divorce between scientific work and practice, from a bookish, cliché-ridden approach to scientific questions. The investigator can be bold in setting and solving theoretical problems only when he is completely equipped with the latest facts, when he has seen a great deal for himself and has tested and examined it.' [4]

A further feature of the development of philosophical life in recent years, as of Soviet cultural and scientific life generally, has been the earnest endeavour to establish scientific contact with the outside world. There has lately been a marked increase in the number of Soviet delegations dispatched to scientific congresses abroad, and of foreign delegations invited to visit the Soviet Union. On the philosophical side, a very large Soviet delegation attended the Congress of the *Union Internationale de Philosophie des Sciences* (UIPS) at Zürich from 23rd–28th August 1954. Conversely, a party of English academics toured the Soviet Union from 17th September to 5th October, and their leader, Professor J. D. Bernal, delivered an

[1] *VF* 1955, 2, p. 231.
[2] *Edinstvo teorii i praktiki* (Unity of Theory and Practice) in *VF* 1954, 2, p. 12.　　　　[3] *Ibid.*, p. 14.　　　　[4] *Ibid.*, p. 12.

address at the Philosophical Institute on the present state of scientific studies in Britain.[1] In May 1954 a French communist, Roger Garaudy, defended a doctoral dissertation on 'The Problem of Freedom and Necessity in the Light of Marxism' at the Philosophical Institute of the Academy of Sciences of the U.S.S.R.[2]

All these developments make it perfectly clear that things have altered to some extent in the last few years. The discussions have somehow become more interesting, there is not such exclusive reliance as before on appeal to the authorities—instead, there is real discussion, and by using the opportunities afforded by the ever-repeated injunction to 'criticism and self-criticism' the participants have actually dared, on frequent occasions, to put a finger on genuine and characteristic grievances felt under the Soviet system.

Even so, it would be a mistake to be too optimistic in drawing conclusions from this. In spite of everything, Stalinism has not expired along with Stalin. All the genuinely interesting and apposite criticisms above-mentioned are still embedded in a flood of the usual complaints: philosophy is not fulfilling the tasks set to it by the Party and rightly expected of it by the Soviet public; Zhdanov's injunctions at the Philosophical Discussion have still not been adequately complied with, there is too little campaigning against bourgeois objectivism, too little observance of the demand for partisanship.

Although less has been said of Stalin in recent years, and that little in less obtrusive fashion, he nonetheless remains one of the foremost authorities, and is still reckoned among the 'classics'. The problems thrown up by him, especially in his last work, continue to dominate the foreground of philosophical inquiry. One of the most central topics is the question of the objective character of the laws of social development, and the theme of overcoming the antitheses between town and country, mental and physical labour, is very frequently dealt with.

The Party likewise remains, as in Stalin's lifetime, the highest authority, even in cultural and scientific matters. Indeed it might well be said that this applies to an even greater extent of the period since Stalin's death, in so far as the calling-off of the Stalin cult has thrust the Party Central Committee into the vacuum left behind him. The resolutions of the Communist Party must be regarded by Soviet philosophers as 'an inexhaustible fount of Marxist–Leninist wisdom',[3] and are to be made the basis of all their research activity. In order to

---

[1] *Vestnik AN SSSR* 1953, No. 11, pp. 83 ff.

[2] *VF* 1954, 5, pp. 216 ff.; this dissertation has since been published under the title *La liberté*, Paris, 1955, pp. 469.

[3] *Za tvorcheskuyu razrabotku voprosov dialekticheskogo materializma* (For a Creative Working-Out of the Problems of Dialectical Materialism), in *VF* 1954, 5, p. 7.

make this easier for them, a collection of party resolutions was issued in two volumes, shortly after Stalin's death, the purpose of which was evidently to replace the heritage of the short-course *History of the C.P.S.U.*, which, even before its withdrawal from circulation at the XXth Party Congress, had lately been enveloped in a curious silence. It is still the Party that watches over the purity of dialectical materialist philosophy.[1] Although 'criticism and self-criticism' are often conducted in lively fashion, it still remains the custom for criticism to proceed 'from above' and thereafter to waken a 'self-critical' echo 'from below'. The leading article just quoted from *Voprosy filosofii* is no more than an echo, in this sense, of an article in *Kommunist*.[2]

This insistence on making the party resolutions the basis of their theoretical inquiries has also met with very speedy compliance from the Soviet philosophers. In November 1953, after the September Plenum of that year had decided on a policy of expansion in agriculture and the production of consumer goods, A. F. Okulov, addressing the Academy of Social Sciences, under the auspices of the Central Committee of the C.P.S.U., on 'The Tasks of Soviet Philosophers in the Light of the Resolutions of the September Plenum', drew the appropriate conclusions for philosophical research, and particularly enjoined the treatment of such questions as: the ties between workers and peasantry, the problem of correctly combining private and social interests, the principle of material interest in regard to labour, etc.

It is expressly emphasized, moreover, that all the 'criticisms' and 'free discussions' so repeatedly called for are subject to certain limitations which must not be overstepped:

'It should not be forgotten that the whole of Soviet science develops on the ideal basis of Marxist–Leninism, namely dialectical and historical materialism. . . . Attacks on Marxist–Leninism, whatever the banner they are conducted under—"freedom of opinion" or "freedom to criticize"—are really in every case attacks on true freedom and true science. When reference is made, therefore, to the free exchange of opinions . . . what is envisaged is a clash of opinions conducted on the basis of Marxist–Leninism, as the scientific worldview prevailing amongst us. We cannot and must not tolerate those "schools" and "movements" which attempt a revision of Marxist–Leninism and follow in the wake of bourgeois ideology.'[3]

---

[1] *Za tvorcheskuyu razrabotku . . .*, p. 7.

[2] *Za tvorcheskoe izuchenie marxistsko-leninskogo ucheniya* (For a Creative Study of Marxist–Leninist Theory), in *Kommunist* 1954, No. 14, pp. 3 ff.

[3] *Velikoe leninskoe filosofskoe nasledstvo*, VF 1955, 2, p. 15.

All the above-mentioned indications of the new philosophical atmosphere prevailing after Stalin's death are primarily related to the formal aspect of contemporary philosophizing in the Soviet Union. But it remains to ask how things stand in regard to its content, and whether here too there are new tendencies to be noted.

It is in keeping with the basic character of Soviet philosophy as a State-controlled system of thought, that so far as content is concerned there should as yet be nothing essentially new to report, and that efforts to modify the content of dialectical materialism, even within the framework of 'Marxist–Leninism', should have declared themselves only in a wholly provisional fashion. The Soviet philosophers have too often had to apologize for opinions expressed at a time when they could not foresee that one day the opposite view would be officially promulgated, for them to risk taking up new positions in the ideological field before the political situation has settled down and a decision been reached in the struggle for power among Stalin's successors.

For all that, there are several changes to be noticed even in the content of Soviet philosophy since the death of Stalin. Some of these primarily reflect the after-effects of Stalin's last work and the resolutions of the XIXth Party Congress. In addition to numerous investigations into the objective character of the laws of social development in general, they also include a series of studies on individual problems connected with this, such as the problem of freedom and necessity, etc. Other changes, already referred to at greater length above, have an immediate connection with Stalin's death, for instance those relating to the struggle against the personality cult and in favour of collective leadership in Party and State.

Two other features, however, appear to sound a new note at a considerably deeper thematic level. On looking through recent numbers of the Soviet learned journals, one is struck by the repeated hostility displayed towards a group of philosophers who either neglect dialectical logic or repudiate it altogether. But now even in Stalin's lifetime there was a discussion, occasioned by the appearance of the letters on linguistics, as to the respective merits of formal and dialectical logic,[1] which ended by conceding them both a title to existence. The resurrection of this question seems to suggest the presence of tendencies seeking to utilize the *détente* occurring after Stalin's death in order to withdraw again from positions previously occupied. In other directions too there is complaint against deviation from established positions: many are showing signs of a 'positivistic' tendency to merge philosophy into the concrete sciences, leaving the

---

[1] *Cf.* Part Two, Ch. VII, Sec. 2.

natural sciences to work out their own methodology; others again exhibit a 'Kantian' tendency to restrict philosophy to the theory of knowledge.[1]

If such outbursts from exponents of the official doctrine give evidence of a new outlook on the part of individual philosophers and groups, indications of a possible change of front can also be detected, on the other hand, within the official doctrine itself. This comes out most clearly in the accusation levelled against certain philosophers (notably Alexandrov and the textbook on dialectical materialism edited by him), that they pay no regard to the Leninist epoch in philosophy. Very revealing in this respect is an article by Kedrov and Gurgenidze in the September 1955 number of *Kommunist*, the theoretical organ of the Central Committee of the C.P.S.U.[2] Although the discussion on the textbook of dialectical materialism had already been concluded in the previous year, the authors think it necessary to revert once more—and in a tone of considerable acerbity —to the prime failings of this book, since up to 1st November 1954 the authors' collective has not fulfilled its pledge to subject the work in question to thoroughgoing revision. The disregard of the Leninist heritage emerges most clearly in this book from its failure to abide by Lenin's principle of the unity of dialectic, logic and epistemology. It receives verbal acknowledgement, but does not underlie the presentation of Marxist philosophy as a whole. As Lenin saw it, dialectic and epistemology (together with logic) were to form a unity; epistemology (the copy-theory) was to be nothing but an application of the laws of dialectic to the field of human knowledge. But in Alexandrov's textbook, dialectic and epistemology are severed one from another. Dialectic spends itself in proving Stalin's four principal features to be the fundamental laws of objective reality, but fails to appear also as the fundamental law of human thought. Logic too is separated from dialectic. The Leninist principle of the unity of the historical and the logical in the process of development of human knowledge receives no application. The individual categories are artificially tacked on to one or other of the 'principal features', instead of being depicted, as Lenin wished, as 'nodal points' and 'stages' in the history of the development of human knowledge, by virtue of which man detaches himself from Nature. The use made of the natural sciences is likewise confined, in the textbook under discussion, to an incoherent assemblage of examples to illustrate the various principal features, instead of following up Lenin's indications and showing how the different forms of materialism correspond to different stages in the develop-

[1] *Cf. VF* 1955, 1, p. 16; 2, p. 233.
[2] B. Kedrov, G. Gurgenidze: *Za glubokuyu razrabotku leninskogo filosofskogo nasledstva* (For a Thorough Study of Lenin's Philosophical Remains), in *Kommunist* 1955, No. 14, pp. 45–56.

ment of the natural sciences. These criticisms, which gain greatly in authority from the periodical in which they were published, are extraordinarily suggestive. If effect were to be given to them, Soviet philosophy would actually be released from its ossified adherence to Stalin's seven basic theses and would again be compelled to adopt a new approach to the philosophical problems most fundamental to dialectical materialism.

This picture of the state of philosophical studies in the U.S.S.R. during the last few years would be incomplete without reference to the very special attention that has lately been given to the philosophical problems arising from modern science. A number of discussions have been held in these years on problems of this kind in relation to cosmogony, quantum mechanics and relativity theory (at the last of which attacks were made on those Soviet philosophers accustomed to reject the valuable physical conclusions drawn from this theory on the ground of their seeming inconsistency with dialectical materialism, an objection particularly directed against Maximov); in addition, there have also been discussions on the philosophical problems of psychology, on the reconstruction of psychology on the basis of Pavlov's teaching, and the like.

In 1951 already, while Stalin was still alive, a large-scale collective work was put in hand: 'Dialectical Materialism and Modern Natural Science'. This work was intended to deal with all the borderline questions involving philosophy and natural science in all its branches, beginning with cosmogony and relativity theory, and proceeding by way of atomic physics, chemistry, the origin of life, and biology, to Pavlovian psychology, the whole being carried out in collaboration between philosophers, and scientists competent in the various individual fields. It would appear, indeed, that progress on the above work has lately come to a standstill. But in the meantime, three collective works have appeared on particular aspects of this group of problems: *Philosophical Problems of Modern Physics* (1952), *Philosophical Problems of Modern Biology* (1951), and *The Teaching of I. P. Pavlov and the Philosophical Problems of Psychology* (1952).

And finally, we must also note a renewed insistence on the necessity for the struggle against religion. In an article, *The Rôle of Socialist Ideology in the Struggle against the Survivals of Capitalism*, M. T. Iovchuk points out that 'religious prejudices' constitute 'one of the most tenacious survivals of capitalism'. Anyone who believes the freedom of conscience guaranteed by the constitution to mean an abandonment of atheistic propaganda, has fallen into error and is setting himself against the policy of the Party, which aims at 'doing away with the remnants of the old order, including the religious remnant'.

'An intensification of scientifico-atheistic propaganda is needed in order to raise the cultural level of Soviet citizens and to further their education for communism.'

But as was pointed out by the Central Committee of the C.P.S.U., in their directive 'On Mistakes in the Conduct of Scientifico-Atheistic Propaganda among the People', this must not give rise to administrative interference with the activities of the churches, or to affronts against priests and believers, the majority of whom now adopt a loyal attitude towards the Soviet regime.[1]

After all that we have learnt in the present chapter about the ideological developments in the Soviet Union since the death of Stalin, there can be nothing to surprise us in the de-Stalinization policy inaugurated at the XXth Party Congress (14th–25th February 1956). The campaign against the cult of personality, which had already been in progress throughout the three years since Stalin's death, had left no doubt as to whom it was aimed at. And even the discussion on the textbook of *Dialectical Materialism* put out by Alexandrov had for the most part been really more a criticism of Stalin than of Alexandrov himself. The novelty of the situation created by the XXth Party Congress consisted primarily in the fact that Stalin was now openly referred to by name.

The charges made against Stalin in the ideological field are mostly concerned with minor issues and are mainly confined to the sphere of historical materialism (the acknowledgement of the possibility of achieving socialism by parliamentary methods, etc.). As against this, a number of points in Khrushchev's Report continue to provide clear evidence of typically Stalinist modes of thought (possibility is not the same thing as reality; the moral and political unity of the Soviet people, friendship among the nationalities of the Soviet Union and Soviet patriotism as incentives to the development of socialist society). The measures adopted by the Congress to further the advance towards communism are also just the same as those advocated by Stalin in his last book.

The elements of novelty which have made their appearance in the field of dialectical materialism since the XXth Party Congress consist primarily in a reversion to the three laws of the materialist dialectic, and more especially in the rehabilitation of the Law of the Negation of the Negation, and in an extension of the theory of categories, which had been very much neglected in Stalin's day.

[1] *VF* 1955, 1, p. 7.

PART TWO

The System of Soviet Philosophy

CHAPTER I

Conception of Philosophy

1. PHILOSOPHY AND THE SPECIAL SCIENCES

IT is to the credit of official Soviet philosophy that despite a variety of attempts–even within Bolshevism itself–to deny philosophy any title to continued existence, it has preserved the concept of philosophy as an independent intellectual discipline. This was the outcome of its struggle against the mechanists, the 'positivists' of Soviet philosophy.[1]

Again, in specifying the *object* of philosophy in relation to the natural sciences, it was in the course of its struggle against mechanism and 'menshevizing idealism' that the official Soviet philosophy worked out its adopted position.

Whereas the mechanists wanted to get rid of all philosophy and to see the entire Marxist 'world-outlook' embodied in the latest findings of the positive sciences, the menshevizing idealists were accused of having degraded Marxist philosophy to a mere methodology and robbed it of any positive 'content'; philosophy having become, in their hands, a system of empty concepts and abstract categories, divorced from the concrete historical development of the natural and social sciences.[2] How far this objection may legitimately be urged against Deborin has already been discussed in Part One.[3]

In the view of official Soviet philosophy, dialectical materialism is neither exclusively a methodology nor yet a general theory of the world built up on the basis of the natural sciences, but both of these, a combination of world-outlook and methodology.

In the first place it is certainly a world-outlook, a theory of reality, and as such deals, in the material sense, with the same subject-matter as the special sciences. But if this is so, the question arises, how then

[1] *Cf.* above, p. 138 ff.
[2] *Cf.* V. Ral'tsevich: article on *Dialektichesky materializm* (Dialectical Materialism) in *BSE* (1st edn.), XXII, col. 133.   [3] *Cf.* above, p. 160 f.

is philosophy possible as a truly scientific discipline alongside the special sciences?

B. M. Kedrov dealt with this question in considerable detail in his address to the Zürich Congress of the International Union for the Philosophy of Science, in August 1954. In antiquity, so he began, philosophy was the sole science, and as such also included material appropriate to the natural and social sciences. The relation between philosophy and all other branches of knowledge consisted in an absolute subordination of the one to the other. This viewpoint has also survived in those later systems of natural philosophy, some of them very recent, which have attempted to incorporate into philosophy all branches of human knowledge. Here philosophy figures as a 'science of sciences' or the 'queen of the sciences'. The individual is swallowed up in the general.

Since the Renaissance, however, one field of knowledge after another has separated itself from philosophy as an independent science, and hence there arose in the 19th century the positivistic attitude towards philosophy, which refused to allow it any title to existence at all, since once the individual sciences had detached themselves it was no longer left with any subject-matter of its own. Here the relation between philosophy and the special sciences consists in a complete antagonism. The individual has swallowed up the general.

It was Marx and Engels, according to Kedrov, who first found the true solution. The process of differentiation among the sciences did not remove the foundations of philosophy, but led to a more exact determination of its proper subject-matter: whereas the special sciences confine their inquiries to a particular portion of reality and investigate the laws operative in that field, philosophy's inquiries are directed to the laws operative in reality as a whole and in all fields in common. Hence the mutual relations of philosophy and the special sciences no longer consist in subordination of one to the other, or in antagonism, but in a mutual interfusion and supplementation: philosophy provides the general method of scientific knowledge and a philosophical interpretation of the detailed information furnished by the sciences; the sciences supply the concrete factual material which serves philosophy as a starting-point in its task of generalization.

'The foundation for this view of the mutual relation between philosophy and the other sciences consists in the true, dialectical solution of the problem of the mutual relation between general and particular in scientific knowledge: these two opposites form a unity, interfuse with one another, without either destroying or dividing themselves from one another.' [1]

[1] B. M. Kedrov: O *klassifikatsii nauk* (On the Classification of the Sciences), *VF*, 1955, 2, pp. 49–68, *q.v.* p. 51.

Thus the subject-matter of dialectical materialism consists, according to Soviet philosophy, in

'the most general laws of motion, change and development in Nature, society and knowledge, investigation of which gives rise to a unitary, scientific world-picture'.[1]

It is precisely because dialectical materialism investigates the most general laws applicable to reality as a whole, that it is able to provide a 'closed all-comprehensive world-picture'.[2] It becomes 'a total world-outlook which generalizes the findings of all the sciences'.[3]

In this conception of philosophy the Soviet philosophers make a definite break with that anti-philosophical attitude which is here and there to be encountered in Engels. For despite Kedrov's attempts to cite the latter as a crown-witness to the correctness of this intermediate position in regard to the scope of philosophy, there is no mistaking a markedly positivistic element in Engels' point of view.

'As soon as each separate science is required', he writes in *Anti-Dühring*, 'to get clarity as to its position in the great totality of things and of our knowledge of things, a special science dealing with this totality is superfluous. What still independently survives of all former philosophy is the science of thought and its laws—formal logic and dialectics. Everything else is merged in the positive science of Nature and history.' [4]

Similarly, in another passage:

'It is in fact no longer a philosophy, but a simple world-outlook which has to establish its validity and be applied not in a science of sciences standing apart, but within the positive sciences.' [5]

It may be admitted, indeed, that Engels' attitude on this point is not unambiguous. In certain passages he interprets the 'dialectics' which, apart from logic, he is alone ready to leave standing of all previous philosophy, as

---

[1] *Dialektichesky materializm, pod obshchey redaktsiey akademika G. F. Alexandrova* (Dialectical Materialism, compiled under the editorship of Academician G. F. Alexandrov) Moscow 1954, p. 9. (Cited hereafter as *DM.*)

[2] M. A. Leonov. *Klassiki marxizma-leninizma o predmete dialekticheskogo materializmu* (The Classics of Marxist-Leninism on the Content of Dialectical Materialism) in *IAN*, VI (1949), pp. 297–312; *q.v.* p. 308.

[3] V. Svetlov–T. Oyzerman: *Vozniknovenie marxizma—revolyutsionny perevorot v filosofii* (The Rise of Marxism—a Revolutionary Upheaval in Philosophy), in *Bol'shevik*, 1948, 7, pp. 28–41, *q.v.* p. 34.

[4] *Anti-Dühring*, p. 31. [5] *Ibid.*, p. 155.

'the science of the general laws of motion and development of Nature, human society and thought',[1]

and hence as a discipline which includes not only the supreme laws of thought, but also the most general laws of being (a sort of 'ontology'). But at other times he confines 'dialectics' to the residue of philosophy, ejected from Nature and history and confined to the field of thought:

'For philosophy, which has been expelled from Nature and history, there remains only the realm of pure thought, so far as it is left: the theory of the laws of the thought-process itself, logic and dialectics.'[2]

Thus whereas Engels, in many passages of his writings at least, attempts to limit philosophy purely to the field of thought, the official Soviet philosophy reappears as a science of the most general laws of being as well.

Precisely because dialectical materialism, as a doctrine of the most general laws of motion and development within the world, aspires to the making of assertions about reality, it also lays claim to consideration at the same time as a universal methodology, without which no single science could subsist. Zhdanov advanced this claim in the discussion on Alexandrov's *History of Western European Philosophy*:

'Marxist philosophy, as distinguished from preceding philosophical systems, is not a science above other sciences; rather, it is an instrument of scientific investigation, a method, penetrating all natural and social sciences, enriching itself with their attainments in the course of their development.'[3]

Inasmuch as Soviet philosophy claims to 'equip' all branches of science with a single unitary method, 'the method of dialectical and historical materialism', it would appear, in spite of Zhdanov's assurances to the contrary, to figure once more in relation to the special sciences as a science of sciences standing above them and considerably restricting these sciences in their freedom of manœuvre.

'The Marxist method provides all the sciences with general principles of operation, shows them how they should approach the phenomena, and in what manner they are to investigate them.'[4]

[1] *Anti-Dühring*, p. 158; *cf.* also *Dialectics of Nature*, pp. 83, 271, 353.
[2] F. Engels: *Ludwig Feuerbach* . . . (*MESW*, II, p. 363).
[3] *Bol'shevik*, 1947, 16 (English version in *On Literature, Music and Philosophy*, p. 84).
[4] M. A. Leonov: *Ocherk dialekticheskogo materializma* (Outline of Dialectical Materialism), Moscow 1948, p. 65.

How this leadership of the special sciences by dialectical materialism, the Marxist method, functions in practice, we have already discovered in Part One from a concrete example in the field of biology.

At a later stage, in the chapter on 'Dialectical Materialism and Modern Science', we shall see how even after Stalin's death it still comes about that dialectical materialism not only shows the way to the sciences as a method, but also commits them *a priori* to specific positions, as an assertion about reality.

In virtue of the above-explained relation between dialectical materialism and the special sciences, the philosophers are obliged to familiarize themselves so far as possible with the findings of these sciences. And there is a correspondingly rigorous insistence that the scientists also should not be content to specialize in their own particular fields, but should equally be well acquainted with Marxist philosophy. This demand is justified on the ground that

'Individual laws are simply manifestations of the general laws: apart from the fact that the general law manifests itself in various fields in a variety of ways, all these different manifestations themselves contain an element of generality. Hence a profound grasp of the individual law presupposes acquaintance with the general law on which it is based.' [1]

Voprosy filosofii cites as a shining example the Sverdlovsk branch of the Academy of Sciences, which organized philosophical seminars for high school teachers in the various departments of science, one on philosophical problems in chemistry, for example, others for physicists, geologists and biologists, and even one for mathematicians. [2]

It is noteworthy that in recent years, since the death of Stalin, voices have again been raised in criticism of the above definition of the concept of dialectical materialism and its relation to the individual sciences. In the discussion on the new textbook of dialectical materialism, issued under Alexandrov's editorship, V. Karpushin and N. Dimchevsky, of the University of Moscow, attacked the idea that it was the business of dialectical materialism to provide a 'unitary, scientific world-picture'. [3] The difference between Marxist philosophy and the other sciences lies, not in the fact that the former investigates the world as a whole instead of mere individual ranges of phenomena, but

'above all in the fact that it represents a tool of scientific inquiry, a method permeating all the natural and social sciences'. [4]

[1] *Ibid.*, p. 309.
[2] *VF*, 1952, 5, pp. 250 ff.
[3] *DM*, p. 9.
[4] *VF*, 1954, 4, p. 203.

2. INDIVIDUAL PHILOSOPHICAL DISCIPLINES

We have just seen evidence of Engels' propensity to limit the scope of philosophy so far as possible in favour of the special sciences. Of all the manifold specialized disciplines in philosophy which generally form the subject of philosophical inquiry (epistemology, general theory of being or ontology, cosmology, psychology, anthropology, ethics, aesthetics, the philosophies of history and law, and natural theology or theodicy), Engels was only prepared to leave room for epistemology.

His first step was to exclude Nature and history from the sphere of philosophy. So far as the philosophy of Nature was concerned, this was only possible, in Engels' view, so long as the natural sciences were not yet in a position to provide a comprehensive picture of the interconnections in Nature, an *a posteriori* account of the ties linking both individual phenomena in the various fields of inquiry and also the various inquiries one with another. The philosophy of Nature attempted what science was not yet able to provide,

'by putting in place of the real but as yet unknown interconnections ideal, fancied ones, filling in the missing facts by figments of the mind and bridging the actual gaps merely in imagination'.[1]

Thanks to the three great discoveries already referred to,[2] which have disclosed the totality of events in Nature as a single, interconnected, dialectically advancing process of development,

'we have now arrived at the point where we can demonstrate the interconnection between the processes in Nature not only in particular spheres but also the interconnection of these particular spheres on the whole, and so can present in an approximately systematic form a comprehensive view of the interconnection in Nature by means of the facts provided by empirical natural science itself'.[3]

This however, signifies the end of the philosophy of Nature:

'To-day, when one needs to comprehend the results of natural scientific investigation only dialectically, that is, in the sense of their own interconnection, in order to arrive at a "system of Nature" sufficient for our time . . . to-day natural philosophy is finally disposed of. Every attempt at resurrecting it would be not only superfluous but a *step backwards*.' [4]

Engels also cut out the philosophy of history in a similar fashion:

'But what is true of Nature, which is hereby recognized also as a

[1] F. Engels: *Ludwig Feuerbach . . . (MESW*, II, p. 353).
[2] *Cf.* above, p. 51 f.   [3] F. Engels: *Op. cit.*, pp. 352–3.
[4] *Ibid.*, p. 353.

historical process of development, is likewise true of the history of society in all its branches human (and divine). Here, too, the philosophy of history, of right, of religion, etc., has consisted in the substitution of an interconnection fabricated in the mind of the philosopher for the real interconnection to be demonstrated in the events'— this having appeared to consist in the realization of some Idea, or in a 'mysterious providence'.

'Here, therefore, just as in the realm of Nature, it was necessary to do away with these fabricated, artificial interconnections by the discovery of the real ones—a task which ultimately amounts to the discovery of the general laws of motion which assert themselves as the ruling ones in the history of human society.' [1]

This task has now been completed, in Engels' opinion, by the working-out of the Marxist materialist conception of history, which makes any sort of philosophy of history superfluous from now on.

The outcome of all these reflections was that all that was left, for Engels, of the whole of philosophy, was logic and the theory of knowledge.

In Soviet philosophy, however, we find in the course of time an ever more obvious retreat from this position of Engels, and a gradual reinstatement of the individual philosophic disciplines in their rightful places.

Whereas Engels, having driven philosophy out of Nature and history, had sought to restrict it to the realm of pure thought, 'logic and dialectics', Soviet philosophy interprets the dialectic in the sense elsewhere conceded to it by Engels, namely as a 'science of the general laws of motion and development of Nature, human society and thought'.[2] The result has been that in this way Nature and history have again been smuggled back into the jurisdiction of philosophy, from which Engels wished to exclude them. In addition to epistemology, a general theory of being, *i.e.*, ontology, has again appeared as part of the content of dialectical materialism, although the term 'ontology' is avoided in Soviet philosophy. As we shall see in due course, the basic laws of the materialist dialectic (law of the unity and struggle of opposites, etc.), together with the categories of dialectical materialism, have a meaning that is not only or even primarily epistemological, but is ontological instead.

Apart from this, moreover, the last few years of philosophical development in the Soviet Union have shown an evident tendency towards the gradual incorporation of an increasing number of individual disciplines into the system of Soviet philosophy. The Philosophical Institute of the Soviet Academy of Sciences includes sections

[1] *Ibid.*   [2] *Anti-Dühring*, p. 158.

devoted to the following subjects: Dialectical Materialism, Historical Materialism, History of Philosophy and Philosophy of Science, to which three further sections were added in 1956, for Psychology, Aesthetics and Atheism, respectively.[1] What is particularly astonishing about this revival of the individual philosophic disciplines is the reintroduction of the philosophy of science after Engels had so emphatically dismissed it. In order to make the resultant contradiction of Engels less obvious the title 'Philosophy of Science' has, however, been rather shamefacedly adopted, instead of simply calling it 'Philosophy of Nature'. Lenin himself had already felt that the rise of modern science, so far from rendering the philosophy of Nature superfluous, had created, on the contrary, a pressing necessity for such a field. Later Soviet philosophy has followed his example, especially in the controversy over Michurin's biology. But the implied departure from the traditions of Marxist philosophy was very properly recognized by Professor Maslennikov (of the Bashkir Pedagogical Institute), who already in 1949 at an All-Union Conference of Philosophy Professors was moved to protest against the introduction of this 'so-called Philosophy of Science': firstly, it was in principle impossible to give a satisfactory definition of this specialism, and secondly it meant a reversion to the past, a transformation of philosophy into a 'science of sciences'.[2] From the standpoint of traditional dialectical materialism he was indeed absolutely right, but his words produced not the slightest echo of response.

Hardly less astonishing, even, is the return to psychology. For Marxist philosophy hitherto, concerned as it was solely with Nature, society and man as a social being, had been characterized by a notable lack of interest in man as an individual. And here it was not just a question of a merely experimental psychology based on scientific methods, but of a philosophical discipline founded on the dialectical materialist thesis that the mental is something essentially distinct from the physical and the physiological. We shall see in more detail later what difficulties the Soviet philosophers have had to contend with, lest they should be compelled also to postulate a spiritual substance, essentially distinct from matter, as a substratum for mental activity so understood.

3. THE UNITY OF THEORY AND PRACTICE

There are two methodological principles in particular which to a large extent give Soviet philosophy a special stamp of its own in Marxist philosophy: the insistence on preserving the unity of theory and practice, and the insistence on party spirit, the partisan character

---

[1] *VF*, 1956, 4, p. 238. [2] *VF*, 1949, 1, p. 375.

of philosophy. In the polemic, not only against revisionism, but also, and most violently, against a variety of deviations within Soviet philosophy itself, it is these two methodological principles that have come to be ever more strongly emphasized as the distinguishing characteristics of genuine Marxist–Leninism.

The demand for a unity of theory and practice goes back in origin to Marx himself. The whole of his early philosophical development is indeed dominated by the idea that philosophy must be 'transcended' by being 'actualized'. The seemingly complete reconciliation of Idea and reality in the self-enclosed theory of the Hegelian system has proved a sham to his disciples. It stands in harsh contrast to the contradictory reality of everyday public life in State and society. Under present conditions there, it would be truer to say that man has reached his extreme point of 'self-alienation': in the social field this is represented by the formation of the proletariat; in politics, by the fact that in the 'political State' the sphere of public, communal affairs, embodied in the constitution and the bureaucracy, stands as something special on its own, in opposition to the private concerns of the individual and of bourgeois society; in the field of spiritual life, man's state of 'self-alienation' shows itself in his creation of an illusory consciousness of the world in the shape of religion.

Marx sees the way out of this situation in a theory advanced by Count von Cieszkowski, namely that the age of thought is to be followed by an age of will, a transformation of reality by way of action.

'It is a psychological law, that once the theoretical spirit has been liberated it turns to practical energy, emerging as *will* from Amenthes' kingdom of shades and rounding upon the independently existing world of reality.' [1]

But philosophy thereupon ceases to exist, its actualization is at the same time its defeat, and its transcendence correspondingly implies its actualization.

But what does Marx mean by the 'actualization' of philosophy? It means for him the transference of the Idea out of the realm of pure thought into that of practice. The cleavage between Idea and reality must not merely be overcome (as with Hegel) in philosophical cognition, it must also be transcended in concrete, perceptible practice.

But this real conquest of man's self-alienation and the inauguration of 'true reality' can only be the work of the historical process itself. The transcending of man's *real* self-alienation is possible only by way

---

[1] Karl Marx: *Die Frühschriften*, ed. S. Landshut, Stuttgart 1953, p. 16 (from the *Doctoral Dissertation*; for Amenthes, the Egyptian Hades, *cf.* Plutarch: *De Is. et Os.*, § 29—Tr.).

of his *practical* self-realization. Theoretical cognition thus takes on the rôle of 'criticism'. Starting from the idea of a true determination of man, it shows up the existing state of affairs as defective. But at the same time it must also discover in reality itself the factors responsible for man's self-alienation, and so is likewise able to point out the conditions for transcending them and enabling man to 'realize himself'. By discovering this contradiction, theoretical cognition, itself a factor in the contradictoriness of reality, becomes a factor making for progress.

In spite of this, however, the establishment of a 'rational reality' must, as already said, be the work of the historical process itself, which therefore always bears within itself already the seeds of rationality:

'Reason has always existed, but not always in rational form. The critic can therefore start from any form of theoretical or practical consciousness and develop out of its *own* form of existing reality, the true reality as its ideal and ultimate goal.' [1]

According to this notion of Marx's, therefore, the business of criticism is not to 'bring' truth into reality, but as it were to stand by reality itself, in the rôle of a midwife, to deliver it of the truth, and that simply by

'making the world aware of its own consciousness, awakening it from its dreams about itself, *explaining* its own actions to it. . . . It will then appear that the world has long been dreaming of something which it only needs to become aware of in order to possess it in reality.' [2]

What is required, therefore, is not merely 'that thought presses towards realization; reality itself must press towards the thought'.[3] In this case it is sufficient that theory should sing to the world its 'own melody' [4] in order itself to become a 'material force' by 'taking hold of the masses'.[5] Whereas Lenin was later to require a special organization in order to 'bring' a revolutionary consciousness to the proletarian masses, it is enough for Marx merely, that somehow the spark should leap across from thought pressing towards reality into reality pressing towards thought, in order to kindle the fires of revolution:

'Just as philosophy finds in the proletariat its *material* weapons, so the proletariat finds in philosophy its *intellectual* weapons, and as soon

---

[1] Letter to Ruge of Sept. 1843; *ibid.*, p. 169.   [2] *Ibid.*, pp. 170 f.
[3] *Die Frühschriften*, p. 218 (English in H. J. Stenning: *Selected Essays*, p. 29; here slightly modified—Tr.).
[4] *Ibid.*, p. 211 (English, p. 18).   [5] *Ibid.*, p. 216 (p. 26).

as the lighting of thought has penetrated into the flaccid popular soil, the elevation of *Germans* into *men* will be accomplished.'[1]

There is a further factor of importance in Marx's early thought on this topic of the unity of theory and practice: We have seen above that the reason why man, in his view, creates an 'inverted picture of the world' (in religion) is because present-day society itself by nature represents an 'inverted world'. But once the 'weapon of criticism' has been replaced by the 'criticism of weapons', the effect of this social and political emancipation of human society will also be to amend its state of mind. Only under communism, therefore, is it possible to apprehend reality in its true colours.

Now the Marxian standpoint here outlined also forms the initial starting-point for the Soviet theory of the unity of theory and practice, even though the latter is far from attaining the philosophical level of Marx's speculations. For a classical formulation of the Soviet view of this doctrine, it is still possible even now to refer to a passage from Stalin's lectures on the *Foundations of Leninism,* delivered at the Sverdlov University in 1924:

'Theory is the experience of the working-class movement in all countries taken in its general aspect. Of course, theory becomes purposeless if it is not connected with revolutionary practice, just as practice gropes in the dark if its path is not illuminated by revolutionary theory. But theory can become a tremendous force in the working-class movement if it is built up in indissoluble connection with revolutionary practice; for theory, and theory alone, can give the movement confidence, the power of orientation, and an understanding of the inner relation of surrounding events; for it, and it alone, can help practice to realize not only how and in which direction classes are moving at the present time, but also how and in which direction they will move in the near future.'[2]

The unity of theory and practice is also supposed to exhibit a dialectical character, emphasis being laid in this connection on the 'decisive rôle of practical activity in this unity, the primacy, the preeminence of practice in relation to theory'; this primacy is based on the fact that

'practice—the foundation for the development of theory, is also the criterion for its truth, and that the tasks created by theory can only find their solution in practice'.[3]

[1] *Ibid.,* p. 223 (pp. 38 f.).

[2] J. V. Stalin: *Voprosy leninizma,* 11th edn., p. 14 (English, p. 26; also in *Works,* VI, p. 92).

[3] M. N. Rutkevich: *Praktika—osnova poznaniya i kriteriy istiny* (Practice as the Foundation of Knowledge and Criterion of Truth), Moscow 1952, p. 193.

In Lenin and Leninism, however, in contrast to Marx, a momentous shift of accent may be noted in the relation between theory and
practice, namely that Lenin lays great stress on the necessity of
'bringing' socialist consciousness into the proletarian movement from
without. This contrast with Marx becomes all the more significant
here in that this 'from without' is actually taken by Lenin to mean
that such a consciousness has arisen outside the working-class, from
within that bourgeois intelligentsia to which Marx and Engels belonged, *i.e.*, the very class who, on Marx's theory of alienation,
represent the main exponents of the inverted view of the world.

'We have said', wrote Lenin, '*that there could not yet be* social-
democratic consciousness among the workers. This consciousness
could only be brought to them from without. The history of all
countries shows that the working-class, exclusively by its own effort,
is able to develop only trade-union consciousness, *i.e.*, it may itself
realize the necessity for combining in unions, for fighting against the
employers and for striking to compel the government to pass necessary labour legislation, etc. The theory of socialism, however, grew
out of the philosophic, historical and economic theories that were
elaborated by the educated representatives of the propertied classes,
the intellectuals. According to their social status, the founders of
modern scientific socialism, Marx and Engels, themselves belonged
to the bourgeois intelligentsia.' [1]

It may be said, indeed, that even in Marx consciousness enters into
the movement of reality 'from without'. But here it is the wellnigh
spontaneous passage of a spark which kindles the fires of revolution
and thereby allows the truth, already latent, as in a charmed sleep,
within reality, to emerge in full blaze in and from the latter. But in
Lenin (and still more in Stalin) there is need of a mighty, organized
effort in order to bring a socialist consciousness to the workers'
movement. And it was precisely for this purpose that Lenin founded
the Communist Party. The elaboration of a socialist ideology and the
'bringing' of this into the workers' movement figures even to this day
as one of its most important tasks:

'Throughout its glorious history of more than half a century, the
Communist Party of the Soviet Union has regarded it as of first-rate
importance to develop the socialist ideology and to bring this into
the workers' movement and into the consciousness of the working-
class.' [2]

[1] V. I. Lenin: *Chto delat'?* (What is to be Done?); *Sochineniya*, V[4], p. 347
(*LSW*, II, p. 53).

[2] M. T. Iovchuk: *Rol' sotsialisticheskoy ideologii v bor'be s perezhitkami
kapitalizma* (The Rôle of Socialist Ideology in the Struggle with the
Survivals of Capitalism), *VF*, 1955, 1, pp. 3–16, *q.v.* p. 3.

Socialist consciousness here is not something which awakens almost of its own accord; it has to be laboriously brought to the workers first.

The unity of theory and practice is therefore an artificial creation:

'The unification [even the terminology here is characteristic; not "unity" merely, but "unification"—G. W.] of socialist ideas with the workers' movement is brought about by the revolutionary *party* of the proletariat.' [1]

Now it is interesting to see *how* the Party effects this unity of theory and practice. It becomes evident in the course of this how the differing conceptions of the translation of theory into the reality of the proletarian movement, as entertained by Marx, on the one hand, and by Lenin and Stalin on the other, contain the root from which the latter have evolved an image of the Party which might well have filled Marx with dismay.

As a postscript to Stalin's declaration about the 'tremendous organizing, mobilizing and transforming value' of political ideas and theories, Rutkevich attempts the following description of the manner and method whereby the Party introduces theory into the workers' movement. The first thing, having regard to theory and the party programme, is to

'draw up a plan of action, a correct political line of behaviour for each strategic phase', so as 'to know how to ensure that the political line shall take concrete shape in clear-cut *slogans* (rallying-cries) and *directives* (rules and regulations) intelligible to the masses.' [2]

Since, as Stalin says, 'great energy is aroused only for a great objective', one must put this great objective before the masses as a completely concrete call to immediate action. It is in this way that the ideas of Marxist–Leninism acquire their gigantic *mobilizing* power.[3]

But the conceptual indoctrination of the masses is not sufficient by itself;

'the mobilizing power of progressive ideas must be supplemented by their *organizing* power'.[4]

In his report to the XVIIth Party Congress, Stalin very definitely underlined the necessity for organizational intervention, if ideas were to be translated into reality:

'Good resolutions and declarations in favour of the general line of the Party are only a beginning; they merely express the desire for victory, but not the victory itself. . . . After the correct political line

---

[1] M. N. Rutkevich: *Op. cit.*, p. 198.　　[2] *Ibid.*　　[3] *Ibid.*
[4] *Ibid.*, p. 199.

has been laid down, organizational work decides everything, including the fate of the political line itself, its success or failure.'[1]

Here Stalin considers two factors in particular to be of crucial importance: the first essential for success in organization is the correct choice of the most highly conscious elements and their continual supervision during the carrying-out of directives,[2] but this must be coupled with a flexible and sensitive attitude towards the claims of the masses, which implies that

'in issuing slogans, directives and regulations and in drawing up plans, the objective conditions of social development and the level of mass-consciousness should be taken into account'.[3]

Marx had supposed it enough to awaken the world from its dream of itself and to make it conscious of the thing dreamt of, in order for it already to possess this thing in reality. Stalin had doubtless learnt better than that from experience. It had taught him that the awakening of the proletariat is by no means so simple a matter as Marx would have it appear. It needs a well-thought-out, tightly-knit organization, which keeps even the better-informed elements under continual pressure and control, and beguiles the less-informed by an elastic deference to their more limited awareness.

Thanks to the mobilizing and organizing power already described, the ideas of Marxist–Leninism also come to have 'a gigantic *transforming* power'.[4] With the liquidation of the exploiting classes in the Soviet Union, an ever-increasing importance has come to be attached to the subjective factor, *i.e.*, to Marxist–Leninist theory, to party policy, and to the communist consciousness of the masses.

'The colossal economic achievements of the Soviet people during the post-war years would have been impossible without the everyday work on communist education of the masses, carried out by the Communist Party and the Soviet State. In its world-historical significance, the latest victory of the Soviet people—the considerable over-fulfilment of the post-war Five Year Plan for reconstruction and development of the national economy—represents a material incarnation of the ideas of Marxist–Leninism and a living testimony to the mighty rôle played by revolutionary theory. The nearer Soviet society approaches to communism, the greater becomes the rôle of communist consciousness among the masses, the rôle of the ideas of Marxist–Leninism.'[5]

From this conception of the unity of theory and practice it follows

[1] J. V. Stalin: *Sochineniya*, XIII, pp. 365 f. (*Works*, XIII, p. 373).
[2] J. V. Stalin: *Sochineniya*, IX, p. 158 (*Works*, IX, p. 162).
[3] M. N. Rutkevich: *Op. cit.*, p. 200; *cf.* J. V. Stalin: *Op. cit.*, p. 162 (166).
[4] M. N. Rutkevich: *Op. cit.*, p. 201.   [5] *Ibid.*, pp. 202 f.

that each is dependent on the other, that practice cannot get on without theory, nor theory without practice.

In the first place, the Communist Party has need of theory, in its practice, because of its 'organizing, mobilizing and transforming rôle'.

'Marxist–Leninist theory serves the Party and the people as a trustworthy compass; it equips them with knowledge of the laws of socialist construction, with an understanding of the interconnection of events and phenomena; it enables them to discover the underlying processes in life, it points out the course of development, the shortest way of advance to the goal; it gives warning of danger, and by its aid the intrigues of the enemies of socialism are detected, serious mistakes are opportunely averted, and the masses are inspired with faith in the victory of socialism.' [1]

But in particular the Communist Party also cherishes its theory as a means of 'scientifically' foreseeing the broad outlines of future development, and thus of being able to pursue a 'scientifically' grounded policy.

'Dialectical materialism is able to provide a theoretical generalization, not only of past facts, but also of the present, and even to foresee the future in a scientific manner.' [2]

As Lenin, too, had already emphasized (in 1902):

'Without a revolutionary theory there can be no revolutionary movement.' [3]

But theory itself requires, in Soviet opinion, to be intimately connected with practice. The general laws of social development have admittedly been discovered by the classical authorities of Marxism. But society is continually developing, and it is the task of the communist theoretician to provide a theoretical generalization of the new experiences of the proletariat in its struggle for communism.

'What a multitude of new things are occurring in the life of the socialist society! What great deeds are being accomplished by our Soviet people! . . . New ties are coming into being, new forms of cooperation and mutual aid among men, of creative initiative on the part of workers, collective-farm peasants and the intelligentsia, new forms of growth of communist consciousness. All these processes are

---

[1] *Edinstvo teorii i praktiki* (The Unity of Theory and Practice), *VF*, 1954, 2, pp. 2–14, *q.v.* p. 6.
[2] G. F. Alexandrov: *DM*, p. 27.
[3] V. I. Lenin: *Op. cit.*, p. 341 (*LSW*, II, p. 47).

of world-historical significance. Our country is pointing all other countries towards the new day, it is opening the road to communism for the whole of mankind'; all these experiences 'therefore call for diligent study and theoretical generalization.' [1]

All this betokens the *creative character of Marxism*. Hence, especially in recent years, there has been a determined campaign against 'dogmatism', 'pedantry' (*nachetnichestvo*) and 'talmudism'. Even today the classic justification for this struggle is still derived from Stalin's letters on linguistics:

'As a science, Marxism cannot stand still, it develops and is perfected. In its development, Marxism cannot but be enriched by new experience, new knowledge—consequently some of its formulas and conclusions cannot but change in the course of time, cannot but be replaced by new formulas and conclusions, corresponding to the new historical tasks. Marxism does not recognize invariable conclusions and formulas, obligatory for all epochs and periods. Marxism is the enemy of all dogmatism.' [2]

Only

'the dogmatists and talmudists regard Marxism and separate conclusions and formulas of Marxism as a collection of dogmas, which "never" change, notwithstanding changes in the conditions of the development of society'.[3]

The charge of separating theory from practice is directed above all at the social-democrats. They have turned Marxism into a rigid dogma, and use it to justify their political opportunism. Within Soviet philosophy the same objection was also levelled especially against mechanism and 'menshevizing idealism'. The mechanists paid altogether too little regard to theory and thereby lapsed into a narrow-minded activism and myopic officiousness. The 'menshevizing idealists', on the other hand, neglected practice; their activity was stifled in abstract theorizing, from which all living class-antagonism had been strained away.[4]

Till the present day, indeed, even since Stalin's death, and in spite of the de-Stalinization campaign, the Soviet ideologists are continually being accused of separating theory and practice, and of 'talmudism', 'pedantry' and dogmatism. Khrushchev set the tone in his

[1] *Edinstvo teorii . . .*, p. 7.

[2] J. V. Stalin: *Marxizm i voprosy yazykoznaniya*, p. 55 (English in *Marxism and Problems of Linguistics*, p. 71).

[3] *Ibid.*, p. 54 (p. 70).

[4] *Cf.* L. Zvonov: *Partiynost' filosofii* (The Partisanship of Philosophy), Moscow–Leningrad 1932, pp. 27 f.

Report to the XXth Party Congress, when he declared of the state of ideological work: 'The main shortcoming at present is that it is largely divorced from the practice of communist construction.' And almost in Stalin's own words he continues:

'Marxist–Leninism teaches us that a theory isolated from practice is dead, and practice which is not illumined by revolutionary theory is blind.' And in order to avoid 'slipping into talmudism and dogmatism', the theory of Marxist–Leninism must be translated into action by 'practical day-to-day effort to increase production and raise the well-being of the working people'.[1]

In the leading article of the second number of the 1956 volume, the editors of *Voprosy filosofii* point out the lessons to be learnt by the philosophers from these statements of Khrushchev's, with particular reference to the link between 'talmudism and dogmatism' and the 'cult of personality':

'The personality cult and pedantry, dogmatism, always go hand in hand.'[2]

And in this connection they paint a very striking picture of ideological work in Stalin's day:

'Instead of allowing themselves to be guided by Marxist–Leninism and its method, and generalizing independently upon the living experience and historical development of the present day, many workers in the social sciences thought it their main business to parrot quotations, to reiterate commonplaces enunciated by a person in authority, to enthuse over talmudically interpreted utterances.'[3]

The chief symptom of this personality cult was that, in flat defiance of the materialist conception of history, it forgot the Marxist axiom concerning the decisive rôle of the masses in history and imputed the main source of progress to the activity of a 'superhuman' personality. A further consequence of the cult was to be seen in a limitation of philosophical inquiry to the particular group of problems dealt with in Stalin's essay *Dialectical and Historical Materialism*.

'The erroneous idea got about that this work, which gives a condensed account of the foundations of dialectical and historical materialism, was actually the "summit" of Marxist philosophy.'

[1] *Pravda*, 15th Feb. 1956 (English version, *Soviet News* booklet, No. 4, pp. 89–90).
[2] *XX syezd KPSS i voprosy ideologicheskoy raboty* (The XXth Party Congress of the C.P.S.U. and Questions of Ideological Work), *VF*, 1956, 2, pp. 3–18, *q.v.* p. 15.
[3] *Ibid.*, p. 14.

Owing to this cult of personality, a series of dogmas arose in Marxist philosophy,

'dogmas which put thought in chains and hampered independent creative work in the field of dialectical and historical materialism and also on the history of philosophy'.

Such a dogma, too, was the false idea that Stalin's 'principal features' of the dialectical method and of philosophical materialism exhausted all the problems of dialectical materialism; many logicians had 'concluded' from this that there was no need to work out a dialectical logic, and that formal logic was the only logic—in complete contrast to Lenin, who had called for the creation of a 'greater', *i.e.*, a dialectical logic; this same dogma was also responsible for the low estimation accorded to the categories of the materialist dialectic, since nothing was said about them in Stalin's essay.[1]

From all the foregoing discussion of the principle of the unity of theory and practice it emerges that from the Soviet standpoint it is absolutely impermissible to try to discern the essence of Marxism merely in a socio-economic doctrine, or in some sort of positive science of the transformation of society, or to suppose that its socio-political programme has no intrinsic connection with the world-outlook of materialism. Just as dialectical and historical materialism form a monolithic structure, so theory and socio-political practice likewise constitute an indivisible unity:

'Dialectical materialism is the theoretical foundation of the practical activity of our party. The party of Lenin and Stalin has solved, and continues to solve, all problems of its programme, its strategy and its tactics in complete accordance with the teaching of dialectical and historical materialism. The politics of our party are founded on the bedrock foundation of the dialectical materialist world-outlook.' [2]

Thus, although the idea may lately have gained currency in certain communist circles outside Russia, that communism is not essentially a materialist doctrine, and even that it has nothing whatever to do with a world-outlook, such opinions, from the point of view of Soviet philosophy, are either heresy, or merely temporary concessions, deviations to be tolerated for the moment for the sake of some practical advantage, but liable, when the time comes, to be ruthlessly wiped out again.

It would equally be a dangerous delusion to expect that, in pursuit of a policy of 'coexistence', Soviet communism may somehow liberalize itself to the extent of permanently tolerating another world

[1] *XX syezd KPSS* . . ., p. 15.
[2] M. A. Leonov: *Ocherk* . . ., p. 46.

view in addition to its own within its sphere of control. To do such a thing would imply an abandonment of the principle of the unity of theory and practice, and hence of Marxism itself. In his Report to the XXth Party Congress, Khrushchev expressly warns his hearers against transferring the slogan of coexistence into the ideological sphere, describing it as a 'harmful mistake' to attempt to carry the principle of coexistence out of the political sphere into that of ideology:

'It does not at all follow from the fact that we stand for peaceful coexistence and economic competition with capitalism, that the struggle against bourgeois ideology, against the survivals of capitalism in the minds of men, can be relaxed.' [1]

Our discussion of the unity of theory and practice shows yet another aspect of Soviet affairs in an entirely new light, namely the Five-Year Plans. The latter are more than merely attempts to rationalize the economy on a gigantic scale. They are regarded much more as that 'actualization of philosophy', that extension of philosophy into real life, of which Marx himself spoke. This conviction, that the Idea must be realized in life, that truth must be conceived, not in a theoretical sense merely, but as a living aspect of practical endeavour, accounts for the pathos, the pseudo-religious ceremony with which labour is invested under the bolshevik régime.

'The basic tenets of Marxist philosophy, made concrete in the politics of our party, have become guiding principles for the activities of tens of millions of Soviet citizens who are creating a new life';[2]

these principles have evoked a powerful response among the masses of the people,

'who are purposefully rebuilding their way of life, on the basis of knowledge of the laws of reality as disclosed by Marxist philosophy. . . .' [3]

With this *motif* of truth as something to be realized, Marxism was bound, in Russia at least, to fall on fertile soil. For the notion of *pravda*, as a truth to be realized and a true reality, is none other than the age-old Russian ideal that has long since served as a beacon to the minds of the Russian people, inspiring both the researches of the thinker and the humble quest of the *strannik*, the simple pilgrim among the people, who traversed the endless Russian plains, making his way from one shrine to the next, eternally seeking a higher truth and a more perfect way of life.

---

[1] *Pravda*, 15th Feb. 1956 (English, *Op. cit.*, p. 92).
[2] V. Svetlov–T. Oyzerman: *Op. cit.*, p. 41.   [3] *Ibid.*

4. THE PARTISAN CHARACTER OF PHILOSOPHY

The demand for unity of theory and practice is intimately connected with another requirement of the greatest significance in Soviet philosophy: the demand for partisanship in philosophy, for the exercise of party spirit in philosophical activity.

The classic formulation of this, to which Soviet philosophers are constantly recurring, was given by Lenin in his polemic against Struve:

'Materialism includes, so to speak, partisanship, in that it enjoins the direct and open adoption of the standpoint of a definite social group in any judgement of events.'[1]

Peter Struve, as we have seen in Part One, had contended, in the course of his polemic against the early Russian Marxists, that it would be nonsensical to talk of any kind of party philosophy.[2]

The Leninist demand for a party affiliation in philosophy stands in such direct contrast to the objectivity which we are accustomed to regard as the first prerequisite of scientific thought, that we are utterly at a loss to understand how it can have been put forward by a thinker in all earnest. But the matter becomes intelligible as soon as we take our stand upon the materialist conception of history. For within a class-society, on this view, every form of social consciousness, including philosophy in particular, appears as class-determined, as an expression of the interests of one or another class.

'A non-party, neutral philosophy, indifferent to the interests of this or that class, does not exist and cannot do so, so long as there are classes and a class-struggle.'[3]

Party-mindedness is therefore a characteristic, not of proletarian philosophy only, but also of the bourgeois variety. The difference lies only in this, that the former openly admits the fact, whereas the latter endeavours to conceal its partisanship under a mask of 'objectivity'.

'In bourgeois society, absence of partisanship merely signifies a hypocritical, wrapped-up, passive expression of membership of the party of the well-fed, the party in power, the exploiters' party.'[4]

This alleged hypocrisy of bourgeois philosophy explains why it can never be really objective, and why its subjectivism is bound to yield a

---

[1] From a work dating from 1895, *Ekonomicheskoe soderzhanie narodnichestva i kritika ego v knige g. Struve* (The Economic Content of Narodism and its Critique in Herr Struve's book), *Sochineniya*, I⁴, pp. 380 f. (*LSW*, XI, p. 616; translation slightly amended—Tr.).

[2] *Cf.* above, p. 68 f.   [3] *DM*, p. 28.

[4] V. I. Lenin: *Sochineniya*, X⁴, p. 61.

distorted account of reality. Since the practice of the bourgeoisie consists in exploitation, the function of its theory is to cover up this situation.

There is also a further reason why bourgeois philosophy can never be really objective. For it seems that the bourgeoisie has an interest in representing reality in a distorted form:

'It is to their interest, because the true interpretation of reality foreshadows the downfall of the bourgeoisie. Their efforts to perpetuate their dominant position arouse in the bourgeoisie a conflict between their own desires and reality, since the course of history is in process of putting an end to the dominating position of the bourgeoisie. Hence the bourgeois dread of looking into what is, for them, a bleak future. The bourgeois ideologists, to borrow a phrase from Marx, find enchantment in contemplating the past, uncertainty in face of the present, and dread at the thought of the future.' [1]

In complete contrast to bourgeois partisanship, it is held to be characteristic of proletarian partisanship that its subjectivism reflects reality, not in a distorted form, but as it really is, and hence that its subjectivism is at the same time truly objective in character. How can this be so? Dialectical materialism attributes it to the fact that the subjective interests of the proletariat coincide with the objective laws of development:

'Present-day social life develops by virtue of objective laws, independent of the human will; and develops in the direction of an inevitable collapse of the old, capitalist society and the victory of the new, communist society. . . . The class-interests of the working-class not only do not conflict with the objective laws of social development, but completely coincide with them. . . . Hence it must be the object of the working-class and their ideologists to achieve an all-round grasp of the developmental laws of Nature and society and to provide a correct, undistorted, philosophical account of the world. The more completely the interests of the working-class find expression in philosophy, the more exactly, completely and profoundly will it render the objective laws of the world about us.' [2]

This principle of partisanship is based on the notion that, so far as knowledge of truth is concerned, the proletariat is in a privileged position; it appears to some extent as the bearer of a new kind of 'relevation'. And hence –granted, of course, the validity of the materialist conception of history—it will readily be seen that one has

---

[1] M. A. Leonov: *Marxistsko–leninskaya nauka — osnova nauchnogo predvideniya* (Marxist–Leninist Science—The Foundation of Scientific Prediction) in *Bol'shevik*, 1946, 1, p. 28.

[2] *DM*, pp. 29 f.

to adopt the standpoint of the proletariat in order to know reality aright.

But the demand for partisanship means more than this: in virtue of this principle the philosopher is not merely bidden to adopt the standpoint of proletarian class-interest; he must also be guided above all in his work by the *Communist Party*, the 'vanguard' of the working-class:

'A persistent struggle to carry through the policies of the Communist Party, a relentless warfare against all enemies of the proletarian world-outlook—this is the most essential meaning of the Marxist–Leninist principle of party-mindedness in philosophy.' [1]

In the concrete, this partisanship of philosophy must show itself in the philosopher's loyal adherence to the party line throughout his work. According to the political tasks to be accomplished by the Party at any time, we therefore find endlessly renewed variations on the summons to partisanship. At the end of the 'twenties and beginning of the 'thirties, when the Party was carrying on a campaign against right- and left-wing deviations in the political field, it became a duty for the philosophers, in the name of the call to partisanship, to engage in a similar 'war on two fronts' against the theoretical foundations of these deviations, namely mechanism and menshevizing idealism. In the years after the Second World War, roughly until the death of Stalin, and especially during the period of so-called *Zhdanovshchina* (the 'Zhdanov policy', which found its clearest epitome in the latter's speech in the course of the philosophical discussion of 1947), the main watchwords of partisanship were: war on 'objectivism', war on 'cosmopolitanism', war on 'servility towards bourgeois culture', and the display of a symbolic 'Soviet patriotism'. The nature of objectivism may be gathered from the charge levelled by Zhdanov against Alexandrov: it is objectivism when Alexandrov:

'before criticizing some bourgeois philosopher, pays "tribute" to his merits and burns incense to him'.[2]

Cosmopolitanism is said to be distinguished from proletarian internationalism in that the latter (in virtue of the Stalinist formula of cultures as 'national' in form and 'socialist' in content) does not imply the rejection of one's own culture, whereas cosmopolitanism 'preaches complete indifference towards the fate of one's homeland'.[3]

[1] *DM*, p. 38.   [2] *Bol'shevik*, 1947, 16, p. 13 (*On Literature* . . ., p. 88).
[3] F. Chernov: *Burzhuazny kosmopolitizm i ego reaktsionnaya rol'* (Bourgeois Cosmopolitanism and its Reactionary Rôle), in *Bol'shevik*, 1949, 5, p. 34. The ideological approach extends even to orthography. Thus the Russian text of the above-mentioned article departs from orthodoxy in this respect by spelling the words 'homeland' (*Rodina*) and 'fatherland' (*Otechestvo*) with a capital.

'Soviet patriotism' has very frequently degenerated, however, into blatant Great-Russian nationalism. The excuse for this was doubtless provided by Stalin's well-known toast to the virtues of the Great-Russian people, delivered at the Kremlin, after the victory over Hitler, on 24th May 1945.[1] The many and often grotesque claims to cultural priority, on behalf on the Russian people, that have been advanced in connection with this, are common knowledge. But it may not be so generally realized that an acknowledgement of Russian dominance was demanded, as proof of a true 'proletarian' outlook, not only among the other peoples of the Soviet Union, but also from the international workers' movement as a whole.[2]

Since the death of Stalin, the precept of partisanship has acquired a somewhat different concrete content. The necessity of the struggle against cosmopolitanism is still to be heard of, indeed; but in line with the new approach to 'bourgeois' philosophy and science which we have already had occasion to notice,[3] there are now warnings against a 'nihilistic' attitude towards Western culture:

'The Leninist principle of partisanship in philosophy consists not only in uncompromising criticism of the reactionary interpretations given by bourgeois intellectuals to the latest discoveries in science, but also in the demand that everything of real value produced by science in the modern capitalist countries shall be taken over and carefully preserved.'[4]

[1] 'Comrades! Permit me to propose one more, last toast. I should like to propose a toast to the health of our Soviet people, and in the first place, the Russian people. I drink in the first place to the health of the Russian people because it is the most outstanding nation of all the nations forming the Soviet Union. . . . I propose a toast to the health of the Russian people not only because it is the leading people, but also because it possesses a clear mind, a staunch character, and patience. . . . It trusted the correctness of the policy of its Government, and it made sacrifices to ensure the rout of Germany. . . . Thanks to it, to the Russian people, for this confidence! To the health of the Russian people!' J. V. Stalin: *O Velikoy Otechestvennoy voyne Sovetskogo Soyuza* (On the Great Patriotic War of the Soviet Union), Moscow 1947, pp. 196 f. (English in *War Speeches*, London 1946, pp. 138–9).

[2] 'Love for the Russian people, which is marching together with the other peoples of the Soviet Union in the vanguard of the common proletarian struggle for communism, is not only one of the most important aspects of Soviet patriotism; it is a characteristic feature of every genuinely proletarian movement, even in capitalist countries.' *Za bol'shevistskuyu partiynost' v filosofii* (For a Bolshevik Partisanship in Philosophy), *VF*, 1948, 3, pp. 1–15, q.v. p. 7.

[3] *Cf.* above, p. 238.

[4] *Velikoe leninskoe filosofskoe nasledstvo* (The Great Philosophical Heritage of Lenin), *VF*, 1955, 2, p. 6.

According to Iovchuk, the struggle against cosmopolitanism does not call for a purely negative attitude towards Western European philosophy and science; it presupposes, rather,

'a deep respect for the cultural heritage, not only of one's own people, but also that of others'.[1]

The elasticity of the principle of partisanship is very clearly shown in a recent leading article in *Voprosy filosofii*, written after the events of October 1956 in Poland and Hungary had already taken place. The philosophers are again enjoined, in the spirit of the XXth Party Congress, to cast off the relics of 'dogmatism and pedantry' so often induced by the Stalinist cult of personality, and exhorted to 'independent study of life', albeit 'under the leadership of the Party'.[2] But immediately there comes a reminder of all those who had been only too literal in their acceptance of such exhortations:

'The Leninist principle of partisanship must be made the foundation of all our work in developing and propagating the communist world-outlook.'[3]

This is aimed in the first place at those who, with a view to the effective development of the materialist world-outlook, had also demanded freedom on behalf of idealist philosophy; secondly at those who

'have interpreted the task of developing Soviet democracy, as laid down at the XXth Party Congress, in a bourgeois-anarchist sense, as freedom from party leadership';[4]

and finally at a certain current of opinion among the artists, who were finding party leadership in the arts an oppressive affair. When B. A. Nazarov and O. V. Gridneva, for example, insist on the major rôle of popular opinion in artistic development,[5] there is certainly something in what they say; but they tend to lose sight of the fact that the official viewpoint develops at all times under the influence of the various social ideas worked out by the ideologists of different classes.

'Public opinion among the Soviet people is formed and developed under the leadership of its most progressive part, its *avantgarde*—the

---

[1] M. T. Iovchuk: *Op. cit.*, p. 12.

[2] *Za leninsky printsip partiynosti v ideologicheskoy rabote* (For the Leninist Principle of Partisanship in Ideological Work), *VF*, 1956, 6, pp. 3–10, *q.v.* p. 3.

[3] *Ibid.*, p. 4.   [4] *Ibid.*, p. 5.

[5] In their article: *K voprosu ob otstavanii dramaturgii i teatra* (On the Problem of Stagnation in Dramatic Criticism and the Theatre), *VF*, 1956, 5, pp. 85–94.

Communist Party—under the guiding, organizing and inspiring influence of the great ideas of Marxist–Leninism.'[1]

If, after all that we have just heard about the principle of partisanship, we now return to what was said earlier about the unity of theory and practice, we can see that the Party has a dual rôle in bringing about this unity. In the first place it figures as the organ which brings forth the Idea, consciousness, from out of reality. It is the Party which 'generalizes' the experiences of the working-class in their struggle, and thereby continuously promotes the development of Marxist–Leninist theory:

'The Communist Party and its Central Committee are not only the collective organizers, but also the collective centre for the development of Marxist theoretical thought';[2]

its strength is seen precisely in the fact that it not only conducts its practical activity in accordance with Marxist–Leninist theory, but also, conversely,

'boldly brings theory itself into line with the new data of historical development'.[3]

The resolutions of Party Congresses and Conferences, together with those of Plenary Sessions of the Central Committee, must therefore be regarded accordingly as

'classical examples, not merely of the application of Marxist–Leninist theory to life . . . but also of the creative advancement of Marxist–Leninist theory'.[4]

The Party is also supposed, on the other hand, to be the organ whereby socialist consciousness is again 'brought to' the workers' movement. We have had evidence above of the amount of energy expended by the Party in order to imbue the workers' movement with socialist consciousness. This Janus-aspect of the Party is governed by the dual character assigned by Stalinism to the ideological superstructure: on the one hand the various social theories and political institutions emerge from the basis; but on the other, they are also supposed, once they have arisen, to react vigorously upon it.

Hence it is the Party which causes the Idea to arise out of reality. And it is also the Party which, once the Idea has arisen out of reality, again applies it thereto, brings about its 'incarnation', and thus transfigures reality into the shape of the Idea:

'The history of the C.P.S.U. represents an organic unification of

---

[1] *Za leninsky printsip* . . ., p. 8.   [2] *XX syezd KPSS* . . ., p. 7.
[3] *Ibid.*   [4] *Edinstvo teorii i praktiki*, p. 5

revolutionary theory and revolutionary practice, the *visible incarnation of the ideas of Marxist–Leninism.*' [1]

'The policy of the Communist Party and the Soviet government is Marxist–Leninism in action.' [2]

Hegel remarked on one occasion:

'The march of God in the world, that is what the State is.' [3]

When one considers the all-commanding status of the Communist Party, and how it underlies the principle of partisanship just described, one may feel inclined to rewrite Hegel's epigram and to say: 'The march of God in the world, that is what the Communist Party is.'

5. THE PHILOSOPHICAL 'ATMOSPHERE' IN THE U.S.S.R.

After all that has been said of 'partisanship' in the previous section, we should now be in a position to understand the peculiar 'atmosphere' in which philosophy is carried on in the U.S.S.R.

The principle of 'partisanship' means, as N. Berdyaev very rightly remarks, that Soviet philosophy is really no longer philosophy at all, since genuine philosophy presupposes freedom of thought.

'Soviet philosophy is . . . more a sort of godless "theology". It depends on revelation and the "holy scriptures"; it bows before the authority of a "church" and the opinions of the "fathers"; it distinguishes between "orthodoxy" and "heresy" . . . Philosophical discussion here implies no free pursuit of truth, no clash of diverse opinions matched in argument; it consists in the unmasking of heresies and the excommunication of those convicted of them.' [4]

The expression 'godless theology' is a very apt description of Soviet philosophy. For despite its repudiation of God and revelation, the Soviet method in philosophy is a typically theological one: the basic assumption of 'Soviet philosophizing' is precisely that found in theology, namely the existence and continuously felt presence of an 'infallible' source of doctrine.

'The organizer and leader in the workers' struggle for communism,

---

[1] *Za tvorcheskoe izuchenie marxistsko–leninskoy teorii* (For a Creative Study of Marxist–Leninist Theory), *Kommunist*, 1954, 14, p. 6 (our italics —G. W.).

[2] *Edinstvo teorii . . .*, p. 5.

[3] G. W. F. Hegel: *Philosophy of Right* (tr. T. M. Knox), Oxford 1945, p. 279.

[4] N. Berdyaev: *Wahrheit und Lüge des Kommunismus*, Lucerne, 1934, pp. 62 f.

the organizer of all ideological and political activity in the Soviet State, is the Bolshevik Party. The Central Committee of the Bolshevik Party represents not only the political but also the theoretical nerve-centre of the country.'[1]

In contrast, however, to a truly theological method, which remains strictly confined to the field of revelation, *i.e.*, to matters of faith and morals, and is invoked in other fields of inquiry, such as philosophy, at most as a 'negative norm',[2] the bolshevik 'source of infallible doctrine' extends, as we have already seen from the foregoing, and shall see further in the chapter on 'Dialectical Materialism and Modern Science', into every field of knowledge and culture. This constant endeavour to demonstrate the conformity of party doctrine to the sciences, or rather, of the sciences to party doctrine, often verges on the grotesque. When a certain Comrade Zaytsev, for example (of the Moscow Engineering Institute), complains at the All-Union Conference of High-School Professors of Marxist–Leninism that some of the students at his Institute have not yet grasped 'that physics can be a partisan science',[3] we feel ourselves back in the darkest days of Tsarist cultural politics under Nicholas I, in which, for fear of 'injurious influences' from Western European philosophy, an official 'curriculum of philosophy' was prescribed, whence it came about, for example, that a professor at the University of Kazan was led to expatiate at length on the 'complete conformity of mathematics with Christian doctrine'.[4]

A further characteristic feature of Soviet philosophy, which it owes to the principle of 'partisanship', is its militancy of manner. Berdyaev very aptly describes the Soviet philosophers as 'warriors of *philosophia militans*'.[5] In reading the products of Soviet philosophy It is perhaps this very militancy, the almost military character of their terminology, which chiefly strikes the eye. There is talk of a 'philosophical front', of the training of 'philosophical cadres' whose task it is to carry on a 'war on two fronts', and more especially of late, to deliver 'annihilating blows' in a 'relentless struggle' against bourgeois ideology. The first number of *Voprosy filosofii* after the reorganization of the Editorial Board was reviewed by *Pravda* under the significant

---

[1] *Za bol'shevistskuyn partlynust* . . ., p. 7

[2] Meaning by this that even from a purely scientific standpoint there can be no possibility of ever demonstrating the truth of anything contradictory of revelation, since no contradiction can obtain between natural and supernatural truth.

[3] *VF*, 1949, 1, p. 375.

[4] A. Vvedensky: *Sud'by filosofii v Rossii* (The Vicissitudes of Philosophy in Russia), in *Filosofskie ocherki* (Philosophical Studies), Prague 1924, p. 22.

[5] N. Berdyaev: *Op. cit.*, p. 62.

title 'For a Militant Philosophical Journal'.[1] The reader will already
have noticed how even today the Soviet philosophers very frequently
preface the titles of their articles with the words 'For' or 'Against',
and also how the word 'struggle' repeatedly crops up in these head-
ings. In the philosophical discussion on Alexandrov's book, Zhdanov
depicted, in graphic phrases, the conception of a 'philosophical
front'.

'We have often used in our discussion the term "philosophical front".
But where is this front? The philosophical front does not exactly
resemble our notion of a front. When we speak of the philosophical
front, it immediately suggests an organized detachment of militant
philosophers, perfectly equipped with Marxist theory, waging a
determined offensive against hostile ideology abroad and against the
survival of bourgeois ideology in the consciousness of Soviet people
within our country. . . . But does our philosophical front resemble a
real front? It resembles rather a stagnant creek, or a bivouac far from
the battle-field. The field has not yet been entered, for the most part
contact with the enemy has not been established, there is no recon-
naissance, the weapons are rusting, the soldiers are fighting at their
own risk and peril; while the commanders are either intoxicated with
past victories, or are debating whether they have sufficient forces for
an offensive or should ask for aid from outside, or are discussing to
what extent consciousness can lag behind daily life without appearing
to lag too far.' [2]

A final expression of the demand for partisanship in philosophy is
to be found in the collective character of Soviet philosophizing, and
in the fact that it is thought possible to apply norms and planning to
philosophical no less than to industrial production.

'Their thinking', says Berdyaev of the Soviet philosophers, 'has become completely impersonal: philosophical research is conducted by
an anonymous collective, guided by the party line and governed by
the ideological requirements of revolutionary economic construction.
One cannot help being reminded of the words of Verchovensky in
Dostoyevsky's *The Devils*: "We shall stifle every genius in the
cradle".' [3]

Ample illustration of this collective character of philosophical activity
has already been assembled in Part One; we have seen how it is
repeatedly insisted that party directives must be loyally adhered to in
ideological work; how philosophical productions have to be sub-

---

[1] *Cf.* above, p. 193.
[2] *Bol'shevik*, 1947, 16, p. 19. *On Literature . . .*, p. 103 (third sentence
lacking in the text).
[3] N. Berdyaev: *Op. cit.*, p. 62.

mitted for collective discussion prior to publication; how whole 'collectives' of philosophical workers engage in producing individual works, and so on.

The thing that makes creative philosophical work especially difficult, however, is the planning and setting of norms for philosophical production.

The plans are drawn up by the Praesidium of the Academy in conjunction with representatives of the interested ministries and other institutions, particular attention being paid in every case to the directives handed down at the last Party Congress or the last Plenary Session of the Central Committee. In previous years the individual Institutes of the Academy of Sciences also worked out their own plans. But in 1952 'Institute plans' were done away with.[1] Responsibility for the Institute's fulfilment of the plans laid down by the Academy falls upon the Bureau of the section subordinated to the Institute in question. Thus in the Philosophical Institute's Report on its activities for 1953, the Bureau of the Section for Economic, Philosophical and Juridical Sciences complains that up to the present the habit of duplicated planning still persists in the Institute, in that the directors have failed to enlist all its members into fulfilment of the official plans of the Academy. As a result, the work of a section of the membership has eluded the control of the bureau.[2] At a Co-ordinating Conference of the Philosophical Institute, held in January 1955, A. M. Bogoutdinov was critical of the failing

'that the thematic programmes on dialectical materialism . . . are very often drawn up in accordance with the particular interests of this or that specialist, and do not take as their starting-point the demands of Soviet science and the tasks of communist construction'.[3]

This atmosphere of planning, supervision and pressure from above, with its restriction of any sort of free initiative, is sufficient to explain the evident barrenness of philosophical achievement which emerges so plainly from the account given in Part One, and the way in which even so elementary a matter as the compiling of a philosophical textbook can become an affair of state, and one which even now awaits a satisfactory solution. The situation betrays a disastrous misunderstanding of the nature of mental work, namely the belief that it can be subjected to norms in exactly the same way as material production.

The account just given of the philosophical 'atmosphere' in the Soviet Union certainly found its most clear-cut expression in the Stalinist era, especially during the period of so-called *Zhdanovshchina*.

---

[1] Cf. *Vestnik Akademii Nauk SSSR*, 1953, p. 81.
[2] *VF*, 1954, 1, pp. 244 f.   [3] *VF*, 1955, 2, p. 299.

D.M.—K

Since Stalin's death, as we have had occasion to note in Part One, there have admittedly been signs of a certain relaxation of party dictatorship in the theoretical sphere. But the decisive fact, for us is that no *fundamental* change has occurred.[1] So long as liberty of expression is ultimately restricted to opinions current within Marxist–Leninism, it is impossible to talk of a genuine freedom of thought.

Nor is this picture of the way in which philosophy is actually carried on in the U.S.S.R. included merely for purposes of illustration; a grasp of the facts is really essential in order to form an opinion on the Soviet conception of philosophy. Without such awareness of how this conception operates in practice, all that has been said about the reinstatement of philosophy in its old rights, the determination of its subject-matter in relation to the special sciences, the gradual readmission of a range of philosophical disciplines discarded by the older type of Marxism, and above all the campaign for the unification of theory and practice, for the realization of philosophy in everyday life—all this might otherwise create a sort of optical illusion and give the impression that the Soviet Union had been the first to bestow upon the world the true conception of philosophy. In actual fact the over-refined interpretation put by Lenin and Stalin on the Marxist notion of the unity of theory and practice has led directly to a new and exceedingly unhealthy separation of the two fields. Philosophy ceases, in consequence, to be thought of as an unprejudiced pursuit of truth; no longer bound in the first instance, to 'the service of truth', it is subordinated instead to practical interests, and ultimately to politics. Its first duty is no longer to find out what is true. It is obliged to proceed, rather, from certain propositions, deemed 'incontestable'[2] in virtue of having been laid down by the 'classical authorities', and to 'instill them into the consciousness of the masses', in order to lend 'security' and a 'sense of direction' to the revolutionary movement. This indifference to truth has led Soviet theory into a new and marked separation of theory from practice: it has become, in effect, a sort of arsenal of euphemistic slogans, serving to cloak realities of a very different and often decidedly brutal sort. There is talk, for instance, of a

'colossal mass-movement among the people, who are purposefully rebuilding their way of life on the basis of knowledge of the laws of reality',[3]

whereas in actual fact the conjuring-up of this 'movement' has required the incarceration in forced labour camps of approximately

[1] *Cf.* above, p. 241. [2] *Za bol'shevistskuyu partiynost'* . . ., p. 11.
[3] V. Svetlov–T. Oyzerman: *Op. cit.*, p. 41.

one-seventh of the adult male population;[1] the 'friendship of the peoples of the Soviet Union' is described as a spur to the development of the new Soviet society, whereas it is to be feared that certain smaller nations under the Soviet hegemony are actually in process of extermination (as witness, for instance, the mass deportations from the Baltic territories and from Hungary after the crushing of the revolution of October 1956; the Soviet action in Hungary was indeed twice branded by the General Assembly of the United Nations, on 9th and 22nd November 1956, as a breach of the convention, to which the Soviet Union was also a signatory, 'for the prevention and punishment of the crime of genocide'). There is talk of 'criticism and self-criticism', though in, fact, as we have seen so clearly in Part One, this invariably means criticism from above. The complete practical ineffectiveness and purely decorative character of this 'genuine bolshevik criticism and self-criticism' is plain enough from the mere fact that, as has already been shown in detail, 'criticism from above' has repeatedly felt itself obliged to reprove the very lack of such 'criticism and self-criticism'. Measured against reality, all the theories erected on catch-words of this sort, such as those of 'friendship among the peoples of the Soviet Union', 'Soviet patriotism', 'criticism and self-criticism', etc., emerge as a system of empty concepts leading a life of their own, completely divorced from the real situation, over which they are required to throw a veil of extenuation and euphemism.

[1] David J. Dallin and Boris I. Nicolaevsky (*Forced Labor in Soviet Russia*, New Haven 1947) estimate the number of those condemned to forced labour camps at 12 millions, *i.e.*, 16 per cent of the adult male population.

CHAPTER II

The Theory of Matter

HAVING dealt with the formal side of Soviet philosophy in the last chapter, we may now apply ourselves to the intellectual content of Soviet dialectical materialism. In the present chapter, therefore, we shall consider the problems raised by this system, insofar as it purports to be a form of *materialism*. In the following chapter we shall then be concerned with the *dialectical* character of this materialism.

In taking matters in this order we are making a conscious departure from the scheme laid down by Stalin, whose essay on *Dialectical and Historical Materialism* (like his early work, *Anarchism or Socialism?*) begins with the 'Marxist dialectical method' and only then goes on to 'Marxist philosophical materialism'—an arrangement tacitly accepted, up to the time of his death, as obligatory in all published Soviet accounts of the system of dialectical materialism. Leonov, who adheres to this scheme in his *Outline of Dialectical Materialism*, published in 1947, and who was praised on that account in the discussion on his book arranged by the Academic Council of the Philosophical Institute on 23rd and 25th December 1948,[1] has indeed attempted to provide a theoretical justification for this procedure: it gives better expression to the revolutionary change in philosophical thought which Marxism has brought about.[2] To this it must be replied that the scheme is an illogical one. For dialectic, in the Soviet view, is not just a method, merely, but also, and in the first place, itself a property

[1] M. I. Sidorov: *Ob itogakh obsuzhdeniya knigi M. A. Leonova 'Ocherk dialekticheskogo materializma'* (On the Findings of the Examining Committee on M. A. Leonov's book *Outline of Dialectical Materialism*), in *VF*, 1948, 3, pp. 315–23, *q.v.* p. 316.

[2] M. A. Leonov: *Stalinsky etap v razvitii dialekticheskogo materializma* (The Stalinist Stage in the Development of Dialectical Materialism), in *IAN*, VI (1949), pp. 501–20, *q.v.* p. 508.

of the motion of matter. Before discussing this property of matter it is therefore incumbent on us to discover first of all what matter, the substratum of this dialectical movement, itself consists in. In any case, this latter order of treatment coincides with that found in such Soviet accounts of dialectical materialism as were written before 1938, *i.e.*, prior to the dictatorship established by Stalin's tract on *Dialectical and Historical Materialism*. Since Stalin's death there has again been a return to the earlier style of arrangement. At the discussion on *Dialectical Materialism*, the textbook edited by Alexandrov which appeared in 1954, the majority of those taking part expressed themselves in favour of a reversion to the original method of presentation.[1]

1. MATERIALISM OR REALISM?

The Soviet interpretation of the concept of 'materialism' is governed by a fatal misunderstanding, first given currency by Engels in his pamphlet on *Ludwig Feuerbach*.

'The great basic question of all philosophy, especially of more recent philosophy', says Engels, 'is that concerning the relation of thinking and being'.[2]

But he immediately goes on to confuse this epistemological question with another, quite different, ontological one:

'The question of the relation of thinking to being, the relation of Spirit to Nature—the paramount question of the whole of philosophy . . . which, by the way, played a great part also in the scholasticism of the Middle Ages, the question: which is primary, Spirit or Nature? —that question, in relation to the church, was sharpened into this: Did God create the world or has the world been in existence eternally?'[3]

On this question, according to Engels, the whole of philosophical thought has split into two camps:

'Those who asserted the primacy of Spirit to Nature and, therefore, in the last instance, assumed world creation in some form or other . . . comprised the camp of idealism. The others, who regarded Nature as primary, belong to the various schools of materialism.'[4]

Thus, according to Engels' way of putting the problem, the question of the relation of Spirit and Nature (God and the World) appears

---

[1] *VF*, 1954, 4, p. 203.

[2] F. Engels: *Ludwig Feuerbach* . . . (*cf.* above, p. 3, n. 3); *MESW*, II, p. 334.

[3] *Ibid.*, pp. 334–5.   [4] *Ibid.*, p. 335.

as an aspect of the question of the relation of thinking and being; there is yet another side to this also, however:

'The question of the relation of thinking and being has yet another side: in what relation do our thoughts about the world surrounding us stand to this world itself? Is our thinking capable of cognition of the real world? Are we able in our ideas and notions of the real world to produce a correct reflection of reality?' [1]

As can be seen, Engels in effect equates the two problems: that of the relation of thinking and being and that of the relation of Spirit and Nature: the question 'of the position of thinking in relation to being' means the same, to him, as the question: 'which is primary, Spirit or Nature'—the same, indeed, as the further question: 'Did God create the world or has the world been in existence eternally?' At best the specifically epistemological application of the question as to the relation of thinking and being represents, for him, merely the 'other side' of the problem, whereas the first and most important aspect of it from his point of view is, which is primary, Spirit or Nature?

To this ambiguous and muddled statement of the problem there corresponds in consequence an equally ambiguous and muddled classification of the systems which claim to resolve it, one way or the other. Engels describes them as idealism and materialism, meaning by idealism a solution which asserts 'the primacy of Spirit to Nature', whereas those that regard 'Nature as primary' are assigned to the camp of materialism. It is here that the concept of 'materialism' acquires that hybrid meaning so typical of all later Soviet philosophy: insofar as it designates that system which maintains the primacy of Nature (matter) over Spirit, it signifies 'materialism' in the true sense of the word; but insofar as this same system is set in opposition to idealism and represented as a solution of the epistemological problem of the relation of thinking and being, the word 'materialism', in Engels' usage, comes to mean the same thing as 'realism'.

This confusion of the concepts of 'materialism' and 'realism' has had a decisive effect on all later Soviet handling of the concept of 'materialism'. We find it again in Lenin and Stalin, who invariably set out from the above-quoted passage in Engels' *Ludwig Feuerbach*,[2] with increasing emphasis on the 'realist' sense of the term.

'Materialism in general'—so Lenin proclaims against Bogdanov— 'recognizes objectively real being (matter) as independent of con-

---

[1] F. Engels: *Ludwig Feuerbach . . .*, p. 335.

[2] V. I. Lenin: *Materialism and Empirio-Criticism, Op. cit.* (p. 116, n. 2, above); cited, as *ME*, from *Sochineniya*, XIV[4] and, in English, from the Moscow 1952 edn. and *LSW, XI*, respectively; *q.v.* p. 87 (94 f., 163 f.)

sciousness, sensation, experience, etc., of humanity. . . . Consciousness is only the reflection of being, at best an approximately true (adequate, perfectly exact) reflection of it.' [1]

This realistic strain in Lenin's definition of the concept of 'materialism' will occupy us further in due course.

In Stalin too, the concepts of 'materialism' and 'realism' merge into one another. In his essay on *Dialectical and Historical Materialism* he lists three 'principal features' of Marxist philosophical materialism:[2] The first asserts
'
that the world is by its very nature *material*, that the multifold phenomena of the world constitute different forms of matter in motion', that 'the world develops in accordance with the laws of movement of matter' and therefore 'stands in no need of a "universal spirit" to explain it';

in this respect Marxist philosophical materialism stands in opposition to idealism,

'which regards the world as the embodiment of an "absolute idea" a "universal spirit", "consciousness".' [3]

Although the meaning implicit in this first principal feature is that of 'materialism', Stalin's formulation of the second feature immediately confounds it once more with that of 'realism', and does so by relying yet again on the passage from Engels' *Ludwig Feuerbach*:

'Contrary to idealism, which asserts that only our mind really exists, and that the material world, being, Nature, exists only in our mind, in our sensations, ideas and perceptions, the Marxist materialist philosophy holds that matter, Nature, being, is an objective reality existing outside and independent of our mind; that matter is primary, since it is the source of sensations, ideas, mind, and that mind is secondary, derivative, since it is a reflection of matter, a reflection of being. . . .' [4]

As his third principal feature of Marxist philosophical materialism, Stalin cites the knowability of the world, and this again

'contrary to idealism, which denies the possibility of knowing the world and its laws, which does not believe in the authenticity of our knowledge, does not recognize objective truth, and holds that the

---

[1] *ME*, p. 312 (340, 377).

[2] J. V. Stalin: *Op. cit.*, cited, as *DHM*, from *Voprosy leninizma, Problems of Leninism* (11th edn.) and *History of the C.P.S.U.(B)* respectively; *q.v.* pp. 541–4 (575–7, 111–14).

[3] *DHM*, p. 541 (575, 111). [4] *DHM*, p. 542 (575–6, 112).

world is full of "things-in-themselves" that can never be known to science. . . .' [1]

It will be seen from this that in Stalin also 'materialism' has the two-fold meaning of materialism and realism, and that he too lays most of his emphasis on the second of these, since two of his three 'principal features' formulate the realist thesis, and only one the typically materialist view. 'Idealism' likewise, as the counterpart of materialism, has no unitary meaning, but appears each time as the opposite pole of 'materialism' in its various senses and includes the most heterogeneous things, from Hegel's absolute idealism, *via* Kant's transcendental idealism, to agnosticism and even scepticism!

Such a confusion of 'materialism' and 'realism' is not so harmless as might perhaps at first sight appear, for it has momentous consequences. Anyone who rejects idealism as a theory of knowledge is subpoenaed as a crown-witness for materialism, and arguments tending to prove the existence of a reality independent of the knowing subject are seized upon without further ado as arguments in favour of the materialist thesis as such, though this entails an assertion about the *nature* of objective reality, and does in fact proclaim it to be exclusively material. Thanks to fallacies of this sort the philosophically untutored reader is often left with the impression that materialism is nothing other than the philosophy of ordinary commonsense, directed merely against 'cranky' idealist beliefs.

When Stalin lays it down as his first principal feature 'that the world is by its very nature *material*',[2] this means in the first place 'that the multifold phenomena of the world constitute' nothing other than merely 'different forms of matter in motion'. This, in effect, is to maintain the material unity of the world in the sense that there is nothing in the world besides matter in motion, however diverse such motions may be. But this thesis as to the 'material nature' of the world then takes on the further sense, that the world is not to be regarded 'as the embodiment of an "absolute idea", a "universal spirit", "consciousness" ', and 'stands in no need of a "universal spirit" '.[3] This is also to maintain a form of materialistic monism, in the sense that the material world is the sole existent, leaving no room for any additional spiritual principle:

'Matter, in its perpetual change and motion', says Alexandrov's textbook, 'is the ground and essence of all the multiplicity of the world. There is no other world but that of matter in an infinite process of development. Materialism decisively rejects all idealist and religious hypotheses as to the existence of another world.' [4]

---

[1] *DHM*, p. 543 (576, 113).   [2] *DHM*, p. 541 (575, 111).
[3] *DHM*, p. 541 (575, 111).   [4] *DM*, p. 282.

This thesis has been an essential constituent of dialectical materialism ever since the days of Engels. Against Dühring, who considered the unity of the world to be given in its being, Engels maintains:

'The real unity of the world consists in its materiality, and this is proved . . . by a long and protracted development of philosophy and natural science.' [1]

The Soviet philosophers are nowadays attempting to carry through in detail Engels' suggested proof of the material unity of the world from the 'protracted development of natural science'. They argue more or less as follows: Copernicus' establishment of the heliocentric system provided the first step towards proving the material unity of the world; at the same time his theory shattered the prevailing religious conception of the world as divided into two separate parts, the view, namely, that 'Earth' represents a material, sensuous, and at the same time unclean and sinful world, in which everything is transient and perishable, whereas 'Heaven' on the contrary is a 'spiritual', supersensory and inaccessible sphere;[2] thanks to the heliocentric system, the earth has become one planet among others, and the contrast between earthly and heavenly has thereby fallen to the ground. Galileo, too, produced a similar effect by proving that celestial bodies are not ideally spherical, as the theologians had maintained, claiming to perceive in this a radical difference between such bodies and the material, 'sinful earth'. Further stages in the establishment of the proof of the material unity of the world are marked by Newton's general law of gravitation, and above all by spectrum analysis, which has demonstrated the presence in celestial bodies of the same elements as are found on earth.[3] Stoletov also ends by referring, in this connection, to modern physics, which is already in process of transmuting the elements, and can even transform the various constituent parts of the atom (electrons, protons, positrons, etc.) into one another. What physics has already accomplished in the realm of inorganic matter, Michurinist biology, based on the Marxist–Leninist principle of the material unity of the world, is also attempting in the organic sphere: the mutation of biological forms into one another. But here Stoletov is obliged to admit that so far as it involves not merely the transmutation of forms within the same species, but the transformation of one species into another, this goal has not yet been reached.[4] All the same, it is not very easy to see why

[1] *Anti-Dühring*, p. 53.
[2] M. A. Leonov: *Ocherk* . . ., p. 410; *cf. DM*, pp. 279 ff.
[3] M. A. Leonov: *Op. cit.*, pp. 410 f.
[4] V. N. Stoletov: *Rabota V. I. Lenina 'Materializm i empiriokrititsizm' i voprosy biologii* (Lenin's *Materialism and Empirio-Criticism* and the Problems of Biology), in *VF*, 1949, 1, pp. 85–108, *q.v.* pp. 96–8.

the Soviet philosophers should make their task such a difficult one. In order to demonstrate the 'material unity of the world' there is really no need to make out that biology is capable of assimilating one species into another; it would be quite sufficient for the purpose to point to the simple fact that cats are capable of assimilating mice.

By appealing, therefore, to certain findings of the natural sciences which point to the identity of matter throughout its elementary constituents and to the fact that the various forms of matter can be changed into one another, the Soviet philosophers believe themselves to have proved the thesis formulated by Stalin concerning the 'material unity of the world'; in the sense, that is, that there is nothing else in the world except matter. But it will be immediately evident that this is a fallacy. Even non-materialist philosophers are patently aware of the fact that the self-same matter is to be found in the various celestial bodies, and that different kinds of matter can be transformed into one another. Scholasticism itself recognizes a *mutatio substantialis*, in which one material substance is changed into another. The question is simply whether it follows from this that there is nothing else in the world except matter, and whether everything that exists must be seen as constituting merely different forms of matter; and the arguments brought forward do nothing whatever to prove this.

2. THE LENINIST CONCEPT OF MATTER

We have seen above,[1] how Lenin attempted to resolve the crisis in philosophical materialism conjured up by the development of atomic physics, by laying down a 'philosophical concept of matter' from a dialectical materialist point of view. In order to evade discussion of the problem as to the structure and nature of matter, in view of the difficulties presented in this field, Lenin defined matter in purely epistemological terms:

'Matter is a philosophical category denoting the objective reality, which is given to man by his sensations, and which is copied, photographed and reflected by our sensations, while existing independently of them.'[2]

Or, as he says elsewhere:

'Matter is that which, acting upon our sense-organs, produces sensation; matter is the objective reality given to us in sensation.'[3]

The philosophical concept of matter is therefore essentially bound up, for Lenin, with the problem of the *origin of our knowledge*, i.e.,

[1] *Cf.* above, p. 118.   [2] *ME*, p. 117 (127, 192).
[3] *Ibid.*, p. 133 (145, 207).

with the question as to the relation between knowledge and reality, between subject and object, and has no intrinsic concern with that of the *structure* or inner *nature* of matter:

'Materialism and idealism differ in their respective answers to the question of the *source* of our knowledge and of the relation of knowledge (and of the "mental" in general) to the *physical* world; while the question of the structure of matter, of atoms and electrons, is a question that concerns only this "physical world" '.[1]

Lenin thereby believes himself to have overcome this 'crisis' in philosophical materialism. For it had consisted in the fact that certain scientists and philosophers had supposed either that matter was reducible to electricity (Augusto Righi) or that it had disappeared altogether (Houllevigue). But according to Lenin, the new discoveries in physics had created a crisis only for 'metaphysical', anti-dialectical materialism, based as it was on the 'recognition of immutable elements, "of the immutable substance of things" and so forth'.[2]

As Soviet philosophy sees it, metaphysical materialism of this kind is exemplified, for instance, in the position of Descartes, who identified matter with extension; and likewise in the doctrines of the French 18th-century materialists and their 19th-century successors in Germany (Vogt, Büchner and Moleschott), who supposed the essence of matter to consist in certain mechanical properties. The Russian mechanists, who then came to see the ultimate essence of things in the electron, are also of this company. Thus Stepanov, for example, wrote:

'Matter as such exists as sensibly perceptible to us in the form of negative electrons and positive nuclei.' [3]

But since dialectical materialism, with its philosophical concept of matter, does not set out from the structure or specific properties of the latter, it cannot be affected by perennial fluctuations in the scientific notion of matter:

'The *sole* "property" of matter with whose recognition philosophical materialism is bound up is the property of *being an objective reality*, of existing outside our mind.' [4]

But here, indeed, the aforementioned confusion between materialism and realism becomes particularly clear. For the definition thus given of the philosophical concept of matter is in itself so broad as to be

---

[1] *Ibid.*, pp. 246 f. (268, 316).   [2] *Ibid.*, p. 248 (269, 317).
[3] I. I. Stepanov, in the journal *Pod znamenem marxizma*, 1925, Nos. 8/9; *cf.* M. V. Vol'fson–G. M. Gak: *Ocherki istoricheskogo materializma* (Outline of Historical Materialism), Moscow 1931, p. 21.
[4] *ME*, p. 247 (269, 317).

capable of embracing all being whatsoever and taken literally could even include a spiritual being; for the latter, too, is an 'objective reality' and exists 'outside our mind'. But in the definitions of matter already offered, Lenin again converts this realism into an unambiguous materialism, in that he confines the notion of 'reality' to that which affects our sense-organs; this is also the case insofar as the 'objective reality' described as 'material' is restricted to a reality existing in space and time.

From this point of view Lenin also regards it as inadmissible, now that the atom can no longer be represented as the ultimate 'essence' of matter, to look for the latter in the electron (the same would also hold nowadays, from the Leninist angle, for the other elementary particles that have since been discovered, and is in fact so applied to them by the Soviet philosophers):

'The "essence" of things, or "substance", is *also* relative; it expresses only the degree of profundity of man's knowledge of objects; and while yesterday the profundity of this knowledge did not go beyond the atom, and today does not go beyond the electron and ether, dialectical materialism insists on the temporary, relative, approximate character of all these *milestones* in the knowledge of Nature gained by the progressing science of man. The electron is as *inexhaustible* as the atom, Nature is infinite. . . .' [1]

In this fashion Lenin fancied himself to have insured his philosophical materialism against all doubts arising from the further progress of the sciences: the discovery of subatomic particles, even supposing that these again should turn out not to be the smallest ultimate constituents of matter—supposing, indeed, the possibility of probing further *ad infinitum*—all this would in no way signify that 'matter has disappeared':

' "Matter is disappearing" means that the limit within which we have hitherto known matter is vanishing, and that our knowledge is penetrating deeper; properties of matter are likewise disappearing which formerly seemed absolute, immutable, and primary (impenetrability, inertia, mass, etc.), and which are now revealed to be relative and characteristic only of certain states of matter.' [2]

Since the appearance of the first edition of this book a very considerable shift has occurred on this topic within Soviet philosophy. Until 1951 it was generally taken for granted that a distinction had to be drawn between the 'philosophical' and the 'scientific' or 'physical' concepts of matter, and this distinction was commonly attributed to Lenin.

[1] *ME*, p. 249 (271, 318–19).   [2] *Ibid.*, p. 247 (269, 317).

But at the end of 1951, *Voprosy filosofii* published an article by F. T. Arkhiptsev,[1] in which a number of authors were hotly attached to making this distinction. Some weeks later the 'Bulletin of the Academy of Sciences of the U.S.S.R.' also brought out an article on similar lines by I. V. Kuznetsov.[2] In it the responsibility for introducing this distinction between the two concepts of matter, was ascribed to the 'menshevizing idealists', and notably to A. M. Deborin.[3] Among the younger 'professional philosophers' A. A. Maximov,[4] M. A. Leonov,[5] M. E. Omel'yanovsky[6] and others were singled out as exponents of this view. But it is evident that the above authors were merely acting as scapegoats here; for until 1951 the distinction was part of the generally accepted stock of dialectical materialist theory; in the first edition of the *Great Soviet Encyclopaedia* it was described as a 'necessary presupposition for the consistent tenure of a materialistic line in philosophy';[7] it was also generally upheld, and not by Leonov only, in all the textbooks of dialectical materialism.[8]

In distinguishing between the philosophical and scientific concepts of matter, the former was taken to include what has just been said of Lenin's account of matter, while the scientific concept represented the picture of the internal *structure* of matter answering to the current position in science; whereas the former was regarded as immutable, the latter was treated as a merely 'relative truth', to be improved upon periodically with the advance of the sciences.

According to the new theory, however, there is only one concept of matter, namely the philosophical. The latter is exceedingly broad: it covers all types of matter, known and unknown, everything that has been, is being, or has yet to be found out from Nature. Scientific concepts, on the other hand, reflect individual aspects and properties of objective reality; the special sciences, physics, chemistry and

[1] F. T. Arkhiptsev: *Leninskoe uchenie o materii—obrazets tvorcheskogo marxizma* (The Leninist Theory of Matter as an Example of Creative Marxism), *VF*, 1951, 6, pp. 41–59.

[2] I. V. Kuznetsov: *Protiv putanitsy v voprose o ponyatii materii* (Against Confusion over the Concept of Matter), *IAN*, IX (1952), 3, pp. 251–72.

[3] F. T. Arkhiptsev: *Op. cit.*, p. 51; I. V. Kuznetsov: *Op. cit.*, p. 251.

[4] A. A. Maximov: *Materiya i massa* (Matter and Mass), in *Pod znamenem marxizma*, 1939, 9, p. 128; also *Marxistsky filosofsky materializm i sovremennaya fizika* (Marxist Philosophical Materialism and Modern Physics), *VF*, 1948, 3, pp. 105–24.

[5] M. A. Leonov: *Ocherk dialekticheskogo materializma*, 1948.

[6] M. A. Omel'yanovsky: *V. I. Lenin i fizika XX veka* (V. I. Lenin and Twentieth-Century Physics), 1947.

[7] *BSE* (1st edn.), XXII, col. 134.

[8] *Cf.* for example, the textbook by M. B. Mitin: *Dialektichesky materializm* (Dialectical Materialism), Moscow 1933, p. 107.

biology, investigate different types of matter, their physical, chemical and biological properties, etc.;[1] hence there cannot be different concepts of matter, but only different concepts of the various forms and types of matter.[2]

The philosophical concept of matter is also said to be obligatory for the sciences: it represents the only possible basis for the solution of concrete physical problems, such, for example, as that of the nature of the electron; a scientist who bases himself on this concept will be committed in advance to the rejection of certain theories held by 'physical idealists', such as the conclusion drawn from quantum mechanics, that micro-objects are less real than objects of the macroscopic world; the Leninist philosophical concept of matter is also of service to physicists in helping them to dispose of certain still unsolved problems, such as the question as to the nature of electronic motion, etc.[3]

And here already we slowly begin to catch sight of the deeper background which accounts for this sudden rectification of a hitherto acknowledged dogma of dialectical materialism: the distinction between the two concepts of matter might have led to an emancipation of the sciences from their dialectical materialist tutelage:

'The notion of a dual concept of matter implies a divorcement of dialectical materialism from the living process of inquiry into Nature and leads to a dissolution of the creative force and *guiding rôle* of Marxist–Leninist philosophy in gaining knowledge of the world.' [4]

Moreover, this separation of the two concepts might accentuate still further the scornful treatment of materialist philosophy on the part of certain scientists and lend countenance to an 'objectivist' blurring of the opposition between Soviet and bourgeois science, the former developing on the basis of Marxist–Leninist philosophy, and the latter tied to the apron-strings of a reactionary idealism.[5] Kuznetsov likewise accuses adherents of the dual concept of matter of contravening Lenin's clear and explicit recommendations by espousing a 'neutral' and 'non-party' line for science in the struggle against idealism.[6]

The doctrine of the two concepts of matter has thus been done away with; the authors' collective of the new textbook on *Dialectical Materialism*, edited by Alexandrov, already adheres to the new line

[1] F. T. Arkhiptsev: *Op. cit.*, p. 52.
[2] I. V. Kuznetsov: *Op. cit.*, p. 261.
[3] F. T. Arkhiptsev: *Op. cit.*, pp. 47 f.
[4] I. V. Kuznetsov: *Op. cit.*, pp. 260 f. (our italics—G. W.).
[5] F. T. Arkhiptsev: *Op. cit.*, pp. 50 f.
[6] I. V. Kuznetsov: *Op. cit.*, p. 259.

and considers the Leninist philosophical concept to be the only concept of matter. [1]

We have seen how this Leninist concept defines matter solely from an epistemological standpoint, and tells us nothing of what matter is in itself; above all there is no unambiguous answer to be had either from Lenin or the later Soviet philosophers to the really important question: is matter in the last resort a substance, or is it not?

Lenin was not enamoured of the term 'substance'; in his opinion the 'professors' preferred this expression 'for pomposity's sake' and used it instead of the much 'clearer' concept of 'matter'. Nevertheless, he distinguishes clearly between processes occurring in reality and the medium in which they inhere. Commenting on empirio-criticism, which denied any substantial basis to reality, Lenin remarks that this comes to the same thing as supposing a sensation without matter or a thought without a brain. In his *Materialism and Empirio-Criticism* Lenin devotes a special section to the question 'Is motion without matter conceivable?' and answers it with a decided negative, in emphatic contrast to those 'consistent idealists' who say ' "It moves" —and that is all.' [2] And despite his distaste for the concept of 'substance', Lenin notes at one point in Hegel's *Logic*, where the latter is maintaining that substance is only real as cause:

'On the one hand it is a question of reaching down from the knowledge of matter to the knowledge (the concept) of substance. . . . On the other hand, however, the real knowledge of causes is a reaching of knowledge beyond the external aspect of phenomena and down into their substance.' [3]

Elsewhere, however, Lenin more often appears to take it as if there were no ultimate substantial basis to Nature in general. This being the case where he speaks of matter as 'infinite in depth'. As we know already, he was prepared to reckon with the possibility that even the electron might prove in turn to be composed of still smaller particles, and that Nature indeed might be infinite also on the microscopic scale. At one point in Hegel's *Logic*, where the latter is discussing the dialectic of finite and infinite, Lenin observes:

'Apply this to the atom versus the electron. Matter throughout infinite in depth. . . .' [4]

If such a descent 'into the depths' is nowhere to light upon an

---

[1] *DM*, pp. 287 f.   [2] *ME*, p. 254 (276, 322).

[3] V. I. Lenin: *Filosofskie tetradi* (Philosophical Notebooks), *Op. cit.*, (p. 119, n. 1 above); cited, as *FT*, from the Russian and German editions respectively; *q.v.* p. 134 (78).

[4] *FT*, p. 86 (29).

ultimate substantial foundation, then the question as to the ultimate substratum of motion in matter remains unsolved.

This view of matter as 'infinite in depth' is also to be met with among later Soviet philosophers; Kedrov, for example, is exceptionally clear on the point:

'Just as the relations between things, and their modes of change, are endless, so too is the number of stages leading *into the depth* of things, *into the depth* of their being. For any particle of matter represents merely a stage in the infinite series of qualitatively distinct forms of matter in motion, a series which has neither beginning nor end; however simple and elementary a given particle of matter may appear to us, in reality it can never be absolutely simple, absolutely elementary, there can never be any sort of ultimate building-stone, any sort of mythical *materia prima*, from which the whole world might seem to be built up. "Man's thought", says Lenin, "probes ever deeper into the infinite, from the phenomenon to its essential nature, from its first-order nature, as it were, to its second-order nature, and so on without end." ' [1]

Rozental' and Yudin's *Short Philosophical Dictionary* gives the following definition of 'substance':

'In pre-Marxist philosophy' it denotes 'the immutable basis of all that exists, in contrast to the changeable properties of individual things. . . . For Marxist philosophical materialism, substance, *i.e.*, essence, the ground of all things, consists in self-moving and eternally developing matter.' [2]

Here it is assumed that Marxist philosophy is alone capable of furnishing a dynamic concept of substance, and that all other philosophies are compelled to conceive it in terms of the notorious 'inert lumps of reality'. In addition to this concept of substance, we also encounter another in Soviet literature, deriving rather from Spinoza, and holding that it must necessarily be regarded as *causa sui*. It is employed in this sense, for example, by I. B. Novik, in a controversy with A. I. Uemov about relativity theory. Against Uemov's theory that space-time and matter interact in much the same way as form and content, Novik objects that this contravenes the substantiality of matter, which entails

'that matter is cause of itself, and hence that nothing can act upon it,

[1] B. M. Kedrov: *Leninsky vzglyad na elektron i sovremennaya fizika* (Lenin's View of the Electron and Modern Physics), in *Bol'shevik* 1948, 2, pp. 44–61, *q.v.* p. 45.

[2] M. Rozental', P. Yudin: *Kratky filosofsky slovar'*, 4th edn., Moscow 1955, p. 467. Cited hereafter as *KFS*, and if not otherwise indicated, from the 4th edn. (English version announced, but not yet available—Tr.).

since there is nothing in the universe apart from self-moving matter and its forms of appearance'.[1]

But, as with Spinoza, it is mistakenly inferred from this that the autonomy characteristic of substance implies an absolute independence.

There have, however, been other attempts in dialectical materialism to define matter without reference to the epistemological problem. Engels, in doing so, could find no better definition of the concept of 'matter' than that it is an 'abstraction' or 'abbreviation' used in place of the endless multiplicity of concrete existing manifestations of matter.

'Matter is nothing but the totality of material things from which this concept is abstracted, and motion as such nothing but the totality of all sensuously perceptible forms of motion; words like matter and motion are nothing but *abbreviations* in which we comprehend many different sensuously perceptible things. . . .' [2]

We have already noted how, in furtherance of this notion of Engels', the concept of matter is sometimes taken in Soviet philosophy to be simply the most general concept of all, like the concept of *ens* in scholasticism. Mitin gives a particularly clear formulation of this idea:

'Matter is the entire world existing independently of us. The concept of matter is the most general of all concepts. Everything that exists is matter in one form or another, though matter itself cannot be defined as falling under any other class.' [3]

Just as with the scholastic *ens*, Mitin, too, conceives it impossible to 'assign a specific difference' to the concept of matter.[4]

Mitin also goes on, moreover, to make use of this universality of the concept of matter in order to deduce from it the material character of knowledge:

'We distinguish matter from mind and oppose them one to another; *but this opposition is nonetheless relative, and has meaning only in relation to the "epistemological" problem*, insofar as we find in matter itself a specific property, namely mind, as a property of highly organized matter. The contrast between knowledge and being is a

[1] I. B. Novik: *O sootnoshenii prostranstva, vremeni i materii* (On the Reciprocal Relations of Space, Time and Matter), *VF*, 1955, 3, pp. 140–6, q.v. p. 142; *cf.* A. I. Uemov. *Mozhet li prostranstvenno-vremennoy kontinuum vzaimodeystvovat' s materiey?* (Can the Space-Time Continuum Interact with Matter?), *VF*, 1954, 3, pp. 172–80.

[2] F. Engels: *Dialectics of Nature*, Moscow–London 1953/4, pp. 312–13.

[3] M. B. Mitin: *Op. cit.*, p. 107.   [4] *Ibid.*

contrast between *knowing* matter and *known* matter, and nothing else. The wholly proper and legitimate contrast between subject and object loses its meaning outside the theory of knowledge. If we were to begin contrasting matter, from the scientific point of view, with spirit, this would amount to a betrayal of materialistic monism and a defection to a dualistic position. The only thing that exists is matter and its appearances. The subject also is material. Man the knower is himself one of the manifestations of matter.' [1]

Mitin only succeeds here in this reduction of mind to matter at the cost of employing a purely deductive procedure, in that he first makes the arbitrary assumption that matter is the most general concept and then concludes from this that it must also embrace thought and consciousness; any other approach is ruled out with the warning that it would mean a 'betrayal' of materialistic monism.

In itself there is some justification for Lenin's attempt to distinguish the philosophical concept of matter from the physical and biological concepts framed by the sciences. There are also grounds for a further viewpoint advanced in the controversy about the two concepts of matter: namely that the sciences could not wholly renounce philosophy, even if the 'claim to leadership' which dialectical materialism makes upon them had not gone so far as frequently to impose specific positions on them *a priori*, within their own spheres of competence.

But Lenin's philosophical concept of matter has very serious drawbacks. First to be mentioned here is the quite arbitrary limitation of all reality to material reality which is tacitly presupposed in his definition, though without any theoretical justification.

A further major defect is that Lenin's philosophical concept, adapted as it is for purely epistemological purposes, has nothing to say about matter as such—what it is in itself; and more especially, that Lenin and Leninism deal so confusedly with the problem of substance, which is of such importance in philosophy. When Lenin, and still more plainly the Leninists, refer to matter as 'infinite in depth', and understand this to mean that in the process of dissecting matter into molecules, atoms, sub-atomic particles, etc., no end, no 'ultimate building-stone' is ever reached, such a view shows striking affinities with those very opinions of certain modern scientists which Lenin, for his part, attacked so fiercely: the view, namely, that

'the concept of substance . . . has been superseded by those of the field and conformity to law. . . . The "states" or "processes" in Nature are . . . self-sufficient, not states *of* anything or processes *in*

[1] M B. Mitin: *Op. cit.*, p. 107.

anything. Modern physics is not a physics of substance, but a physics of the "field" '.[1]

Lenin, who devoted such energy to belabouring these same scientists for assuming the possibility of motion without anything that moved, should have had every reason, therefore, for paying more attention to the concept of substance, and for defining it philosophically with greater precision.

There is one final objection to be raised against the use made by Lenin and the Soviet philosophers of the philosophical concept of matter. If it implies matter to be that which exists independently of consciousness and acts upon our sense-organs, this independence and priority of matter in regard to consciousness can be understood in two different ways: firstly, as an *epistemological* priority, in that the material world is not created by the knowing consciousness (of man), but conditions the latter; secondly, however, as an *ontological* priority, in that the being of matter (Nature) presupposes no consciousness of any kind (such as an intelligent first cause outside it), but on the contrary, itself gives rise to consciousness out of its own being. Now both Lenin and the Leninists infer, from an intrinsically correct belief in the epistemological priority of matter, to its ontological priority, which constitutes an obvious misuse of the 'philosophical concept of matter'. We have already noticed a passage from Mitin in which this misuse is plainly evident. But it also emerges very clearly from the second of the three theses in which Stalin summarizes Marxist philosophical materialism:

'Contrary to idealism . . . the Marxist materialist philosophy holds that matter, Nature, being, is an objective reality existing outside and independent of our mind; that matter is primary, since it is the source of sensations, ideas, mind, and that mind is secondary, derivative, since it is a reflection of matter, a reflection of being; that thought is a product of matter which in its development has reached a high degree of perfection, namely, of the brain. . . .'[2]

The claim that thought is a product of matter and has no need of any substantial mental principle, cannot be justified by representing thought as conditioned in its content by an external world that is independent of it.

---

[1] M. Schlick: *Naturphilosophie* in *Lehrbuch der Philosophie* (ed. Dessoir), Berlin 1925, II, pp. 422, 426 (parts of this work translated in M. Schlick: *Philosophy of Nature*, New York 1949).

[2] *DHM*, p. 542 (575-6, 112).

3. MATTER AND MOTION

Although the Leninist philosophical concept of matter offers us no answer to the question as to what matter is in itself, Soviet philosophy does have some things to say about certain properties of matter. More especially there are three theses which serve to specify the properties of matter: (1) Matter is eternal, uncreated and indestructible; (2) Matter is essentially in motion; (3) This motion in matter is not a circular motion, from which nothing emerges, but essentially an upward movement, an evolution or history.

As to the first thesis concerning the eternity of matter, there is not very much to be said. In Soviet dialectical materialism it constitutes an axiom which is presupposed without much trouble being taken to justify it in any way. There is no lack of attempts, however, to find 'corroborations' of this thesis in modern natural science. Ever since Engels' day, the main argument put forward for the eternity of matter has been the 'Law of Conservation and Transformation of Energy'. This law states that in all conversions of qualitatively different forms of motion into one another the numerical quantity of the energy remains conserved.

'Although ten years ago the great basic law of motion, then recently discovered, was as yet conceived merely as a law of the *conservation* of energy, as the mere expression of the indestructibility and uncreatability of motion, that is, merely in its quantitative aspect, this narrow, negative conception is being more and more supplanted by the positive idea of the *transformation* of energy, in which for the first time the qualitative content of the process comes into its own, and the last vestige of a creator external to the world is obliterated.' [1]

And just as motion is taken, on the strength of this law, to be uncreatable, so matter is also; we know from experience and from theory, according to Engels,

'that both matter and its mode of existence, motion, are uncreatable'.[2]

This first thesis stands in strange contrast to the third, whereby the world-movement is to be thought of, not as an endless cycle, but as an ascending process of development, an evolution, and therefore presupposes a beginning. But since the philosophical elaboration of this idea requires that the dialectic shall play an essential part in the process, discussion of this thesis is best deferred to the chapter on dialectic.

[1] *Anti-Dühring*, p. 18.
[2] *Dialectics of Nature*, p. 337 (included in some editions as *Notes to Anti-Dühring*).

The second thesis gives expression to a most important feature in the doctrine of dialectical materialism, the thesis of the unity of matter and motion. Motion is conceived of as an *attribute* of matter, *i.e.*, its one essential and indispensable property. Engels had already proclaimed as much:

'*Motion is the mode of existence of matter*. Never anywhere has there been matter without motion, nor can there be. . . . Matter without motion is just as unthinkable as motion without matter.' [1]

Lenin follows him:

'Whether we say the world is moving matter, or that the world is material motion, makes no difference whatever.' [2]

But does not this thesis of the inseparability of matter and motion conflict with the obvious fact that the world also contains bodies at rest? Dialectical materialism does not deny the occurrence of rest, but explains it to be relative. One may speak of rest if one separates the body in thought from the whole web of things and conceives of it in isolation; but there is no possibility of finding a single body at rest, which could not be incorporated in one moving system or another.

'All rest, all equilibrium, is only relative, and only has meaning in relation to one or other definite form of motion. A body, for example, may be on the ground in mechanical equilibrium, may be mechanically at rest; but this in no way prevents it from participating in the motion of the earth and in that of the whole solar system, just as little as it prevents its most minute physical parts from carrying out the oscillations determined by its temperature, or its atoms from passing through a chemical process.' [3]

Thus rest, for dialectical materialism, is simply a moment of motion, conditioned by the relative stability of some one or other of its appearances. As such it possesses, indeed, an essential importance for matter in motion: in fact for Engels 'the possibility of bodies being at relative rest' is actually 'the essential condition for the differentiation of matter and hence for life'.[4] Motion and rest, in the doctrine of dialectical materialism, constitute a dialectical unity, a unity of opposites.

'Each separate movement strives towards equilibrium, and the motion as a whole puts an end to the equilibrium.' [5]

The opposition is only relative, however, for rest itself is relative, limited in time, and motion alone is absolute and eternal.

[1] *Anti-Dühring*, p. 70.
[2] *ME*, p. 257 (279, 326).
[3] *Anti-Dühring*, p. 70.
[4] *Dialectics of Nature*, p. 326.
[5] *Anti-Dühring*, p. 73.

The thesis of the inseparability of matter and motion is of extreme importance to dialectical materialism because it shows the motion of matter to be essentially 'self-movement'. If this unity is broken, however, as it might be by supposing matter without motion, or motion without a material substratum, there is no possibility, so exponents of dialectical materialism believe, of avoiding a relapse into 'idealism'. For if matter is thought of without motion, its normal state is one of rest, from which it can only be set in motion by the operation of an external force (Newton). This must logically lead to the assumption of a First Mover, a conclusion also drawn by Descartes, the chief defender in modern philosophy of the belief in matter as an absolutely static mass. It was in his polemic against Dühring, who had likewise presupposed an initially motionless state of matter, that Engels therefore postulated the unity of matter and motion. In this manner he hoped to avoid the difficulties arising from the problem as to

'how we are to get from absolute immobility to motion without an impulse from outside, that is, without God'.[1]

Lenin's main opponents in the controversy over this thesis of dialectical materialism were those, however, who like Bogdanov and others, had relied upon Ostwald's 'energetics' as a way of envisaging motion without matter. Such

'attempts to think of motion without matter, force with nothing material behind it, are the beginning and true essence of philosophical idealism and clericalism (*popovshchina*)'.[2]

and are so because, in Lenin's view, motion divorced from matter gets imperceptibly transformed into a movement of ideas and as such very soon gives rise to the danger of spiritualism.

'What is essential is that the attempt to *think* of motion without matter smuggles in *thought* divorced from matter—and that is philosophical idealism.'[3]

In addition to Kant and Ostwald,[4] the Soviet philosophers also condemn Bergson as a champion of dynamism among bourgeois

---

[1] *Anti-Dühring*, p. 70.   [2] M. B. Mitin, *Op. cit.*, p. 111.
[3] *ME*, p. 255 (277, 324).
[4] Not that we wish to maintain, however, that Ostwald's 'energetics' should actually be regarded as 'dynamism', *i.e.*, as a doctrine of accidents without a substance. The fact is, rather, that Ostwald conceived of energy as itself a substance, a view that has lately found acceptance also among many scholastic writers. 'In view of the overall significance that energy has for the whole conception of natural phenomena, it might well be described in accordance with its own law of conservation as a *substance in the truest sense*.' (W. Ostwald: *Vorlesungen über die Naturphilosophie*, 2nd edn.,

philosophers, since he too accepted the possibility of motion without
an underlying medium.[1] In the Soviet Union itself, similar views
were upheld by the menshevizing idealists, of whom Tymyansky, for
example, maintained that motion is 'self-governed, self-inclusive,
self-moving' and that 'the concept of the motion of motion . . . is not
alien to us',[2] and the same thing has lately occurred among certain
physicists who were led by the influence of Einstein's relativity
theory into postulating motion without matter.[3]

When dialectical materialism speaks of motion as an attribute of
matter, it is nevertheless wary, in doing so, lest motion should be
understood in this context in a purely local, mechanical sense, as was
done by 'metaphysical materialism', in that it reckoned only with
unchangeable material particles moving in space; in Soviet philosophy
this was the standpoint of mechanism (Timiryazev, Zeitlin *et al.*). But
the official Soviet philosophy understands motion in a wider sense, as
equivalent to change in general. This too goes back to Engels:

'Motion is not merely change in place, in fields higher than mechanics
it is also change in quality.' [4]

In detail, Engels lists the following as major forms of motion:

'Motion in cosmic space, mechanical motion of smaller masses on a
single celestial body, the vibration of molecules as heat, electric tension, magnetic polarization, chemical decomposition and combination, organic life up to its highest product, thought—at each given
moment each individual atom of matter is in one or other of these
forms of motion.' [5]

Leipzig 1902, p. 280.) Among scholastic authors who argue for the substantiality of energy we may mention: Zeno Bucher, O.S.B. (*Die Innenwelt
der Atome*, Lucerne 1946, p. 192), Gerard Esser, S.V.D. (*Cosmologia*,
Techny 1939, p. 113), Stanislaus V. Dunin-Borkovski, S. J. (*Neue philo-
sophische Strömungen*, in *Stimmen der Zeit*, 1912, pp. 215 f.), Albert Mit-
terer (*Wandel des Weltbildes von Thomas auf heute*, II, Bressanone 1936,
p. 133). *Cf.* also Julius Seiler: *Philosophie der unbelebten Natur*, Olten 1948,
pp. 379 83.
    [1] M. A. Leonov: *Ocherk . . .*, p. 440.
    [2] *Cf.* M. B. Mitin: *Op. cit.*, p. 111.
    [3] As Frenkel' was, for example. On whom, *cf.* M. E. Omel'yanovsky:
Fal'sifikatory nauki. Ob idealizme v sovremennoy fizike (Falsifiers of Science.
Concerning Idealism in Modern Physics), in *VF*, 1948, 3, pp. 143-62, *q.v.*
p. 161, and P. Y. Steinman: *O reaktsionnoy roli idealizma v fizike* (On the
Reactionary Rôle of Idealism in Physics), *ibid.*, pp. 163-73, *q.v.* p. 172.
    [4] F. Engels: *Dialectics of Nature*, p. 334.
    [5] From Engels' *Preparatory Writings for Anti-Dühring*, printed as an
appendix to the latest (1954/5) Edition of *Anti-Dühring*, Moscow–London,
p. 470.

In so saying, Engels and his disciples in Soviet dialectical materialism go out of their way to emphasize that the higher forms of motion cannot simply be reduced to those of lower order:

'This is not to say that each of the higher forms of motion is not always necessarily connected with some real mechanical (external or molecular) motion; just as the higher forms of motion simultaneously also produce other forms, and just as chemical action is not possible without change of temperature and electric changes, organic life without mechanical, molecular, chemical, thermal, electric, etc., changes. But the presence of these subsidiary forms does not exhaust the essence of the main form in each case.' [1]

We see, therefore, that thought and consciousness are likewise regarded simply as properties of matter, as special forms of its motion. In their day, the Deborinists were accustomed to speak of a two-fold attribute of matter, thereby coming very close to Spinoza's view: in opposition to the mechanists they introduced a special attribute of consciousness (thought) in addition to that of extension.[2] Since then, however, this has again been rejected by the official Soviet philosophy, which now speaks of matter as having only one attribute, that of motion in general, within which thought is also included as a special form.

As for the question whether the principle of the 'inertia of energy' ($E = mc^2$) as propounded in special relativity theory, affords evidence for or against the dialectical materialist thesis of the indissoluble unity of matter and motion, we shall return to this in the chapter on 'Dialectical Materialism and Modern Science'.[3]

In this dialectical materialist doctrine of motion there is one point which immediately calls for further examination, namely, its decided aversion to the mechanist point of view, and its Aristotelian concep-

---

[1] *Dialectics of Nature*, p. 328.

[2] Deborin differs, however, from the Spinozistic view, in that he conceives the relationship of the two attributes, extension and thought, not as a static relation, but as a dynamic, evolutionary one. Although the attribute of thought is certainly taken to be an essential and necessary property of matter, in the earlier stages of the latter's development this attribute is present merely in the potential form; only later does it emerge as an actual reality, once matter, in the course of its evolutionary process, has reached a sufficiently high level of internal organization. *Cf*. W. Sesemann: *Die bolschewistische Philosophie in Sowjet-Russland*, in *Der Russische Gedanke*, 1931, 2, p. 179.

[3] *Cf*. below, pp. 422 ff.

tion of motion, not as change of place merely, but as including any sort of qualitative change whatsoever.

As regards the favourite thesis of dialectical materialism, that motion is inseparable from matter, and hence that absolute rest (in the sense of absolute lack of change) is nowhere to be found in the universe, there is nothing further to be said against it.

The question arises, however, whether it follows from the conception of the motion of matter as 'self-movement', that matter is eternal and has no need of a supernatural first cause (or creator) in order to exist. And both these assertions must be denied.

In the first place, it by no means follows from the notion of 'self-movement' that its possessor should exist without beginning or end. Even the law of the conservation of energy merely states that the total sum of energy remains constant *so long as* the system, within which the energy-transactions occur, continues in being. But nothing can be concluded from this law as to the absolute duration of the process as a whole.

But even if the material world and its motion are taken to be eternal (uncreated), and especially if motion is understood in the Aristotelian and dialectical materialist sense as 'change' in general, the existence of a 'First Mover' is by no means rendered superfluous; only so, indeed, does he appear in his true rôle, not as a being who gives the whole world-mechanism a first push and thereby sets it going, but as a necessarily existing being having the ground of his existence in himself, who thereby first makes it intelligible how the 'movement' and change in the universe betrays it as contingent being. For the decisive ground for postulating a creator-God lies, not in the fact that the world requires a temporal *beginning*, but in its existentially *conditioned* character, to which the fact of change bears witness. Why can a changing world not be absolute (*i.e.*, 'unconditioned')? The following argument may help to make this clear: it follows from the principle of sufficient reason that everything existing must have a sufficient reason for doing so. If this principle were to be rejected, it would cut the ground from under all science and all understanding whatsoever, and there would be equal justification for any proposition one cared to maintain. Now this sufficient reason may either lie outside the thing in question, in which case we speak of its cause; or else in the thing itself, in which case it can be none other than the fact that this thing exists *from inner necessity*, that unlike contingent things (which do not so exist), it cannot just be or not be, but necessarily *is*. But if so it must be immutable and independent of all becoming in time. For if it changes, it will be evident that neither its state at moment A, nor again at moment B, C, . . . etc., is a necessary one. A being thus existing from inner necessity is unconditioned, absolute. Now since our world changes through time, this shows that it does not exist by necessity and hence is not absolute. But seeing that it does exist, and even if it had no beginning in time, the sufficient reason for its existence must lie elsewhere, and ultimately in the absolute.

In and by itself, therefore, the assumption of the material world as uncreated still offers no sort of threat to a theistic point of view. Though anyone who is content with mere ideas as a substitute for thought may well fail to be entirely convinced by arguments to this effect. But that our world did in fact have a beginning in time is not only a matter of Christian faith, but also a doctrine which commands increasing support within contemporary science. Without entering in detail at this point upon certain astronomical findings, we shall be content merely to refer to the conclusion drawn by Clausius from the second law of thermodynamics, namely that our universe must eventually end up in a condition of 'heat-death'. Radio-active processes, nuclear reactions in the interior of the stars, the expansion of the universe, cosmic radiation, all imply a debasement of energy. This process of decay is thought of as occurring violently to begin with, but later slowing down and ultimately tending towards a final state. But there is no need, on that account, to picture this state as one in which movement of any sort will have come to a standstill, or in which all forms of energy will have been wholly converted into heat. Present-day science is of the opinion, rather, that in such a final state there will simply be no more irreversible processes. Such irreversible, non-returning processes—reactions, that is, in which the energy converted can no longer be returned to the system in its original form, so that a part of the energy has become debased, with a consequent increase of entropy[1]—are a feature of the present course of evolution in the universe and give it a specific direction. In the end-state to which this course is tending there will seemingly be no more irreversible processes of this sort, though even then it will still be possible to conceive of reversible processes, such as cosmic rotation, for example.

The world's history proves, therefore, to be a non-reversible process tending towards a specific final state, even though the latter need not necessarily turn out to be a state of absolute rest. It follows from this, moreover, that we are entitled to infer the existence of an initial state, characterized by a maximum of potential energy and a minimum of entropy. But this rules out the possibility of an eternal cyclical recurrence. Thus Eddington was able to say:

'Whoever wishes for a universe which can continue indefinitely in

---

[1] Such an irreversible process would be represented, *e.g.*, by the swing of a pendulum, where the energy appears alternately as potential (at the top of the swing) and kinetic (at the bottom), and in which energy is gradually transferred to the air and the pendulum-shaft, so that the movement eventually comes to a standstill.

activity must lead a crusade against the second law of thermodynamics. . . . At present we can see no way in which an attack on
the second law of thermodynamics could possibly succeed.' [1]

A. Vislobokov, who has devoted a curious monograph to the
problem of the unity of matter and motion, attempts to evade the
implication of a 'heat-death' by attributing to the first law (that of
the conservation of energy), the status of an 'absolute and eternal law
of Nature', while denying this of the second; it holds neither for very
small volumes nor for the universe as a whole, which in virtue of its
infinity (as postulated by dialectical materialism), cannot be described
as a 'closed system'; but finally he has to admit:

'Though we do not know at present how the heat-energy dissipated
into space is converted into other forms of energy, science will undoubtedly be able to show in the future how this comes about.' [2]

But this recourse to the future gains nothing in credit from the fact
that Vislobokov appeals to the authority of Engels, who likewise left
it to the future to show how the heat radiated into space is again
transformed into higher forms of energy,[3] or that he conjures up the
spectre of the class-struggle:

'The class-character of this "theory" is manifest: if, after a certain
period, the universe is going to be "dead", what is the point, then, of
struggling for a better life on earth? The theory of the "heat-death"
of the universe defends the interests of the imperialists, disarms the
workers in capitalist countries and diverts them from the class-
struggle.' [4]

It is unfortunate that Vislobokov did not read the above-mentioned
passage from Engels to the end. For he would then have seen that the
theory of an 'eternal cycle' in the evolution of the universe, which
Engels there develops, also defends the class-interests of the imperialists and inhibits the workers from the class-struggle; for as Engels
sees it, it is only matter in all its changes which remains eternal, and
not our planet or the life upon it:

'We have the certainty that matter remains eternally the same in
all its transformations, that none of its attributes can ever be lost,
and therefore, also, that with the same iron necessity that it will

[1] A. S. Eddington: *The Nature of the Physical World*, London (Everyman) 1935, p. 92.
[2] A. Vislobokov: *O nerazryvnosti materii i dvizheniya* (On the Inseparability of Matter and Motion), Moscow 1955, pp. 45 f.
[3] F. Engels: *Dialectics of Nature*, p. 53.
[4] A. Vislobokov: *Op. cit.*, p. 42.

exterminate on the earth its highest creation, the thinking mind, it must somewhere else and at another time again produce it.'[1]

The idea that the history of our universe had a beginning in time is so far open to discussion among contemporary physicists, that attempts have often been made to arrive at an approximate value for the age of the cosmos, in which the various methods employed for the purpose have led to strikingly similar conclusions, namely that the universe came into existence some five to ten thousand million years ago.

'Summing up the knowledge obtained so far it may be said that we have not encountered any celestial object whose age has proved to be more than about 10,000,000,000 years.'[2]

4. SPACE AND TIME

The problem of motion is intimately connected with that of space and time. In determining the nature of space and time, dialectical materialism dissociates itself alike from the excessive realism of Newton, for whom space and time were realities independent of matter,[3] and from the subjectivism of Kant, who took them to be subjective forms of intuition. A further antagonist, whom Lenin particularly had in view, was empirio-criticism, which regarded space and time as means of ordering experience.

'Dialectical materialism teaches that space and time are objective forms of existence of matter.'[4]

This definition is intended to bring out the objective character of space and time as well as their inseparable connection with matter. There is nothing which is not spatially extended; but nor, on the other hand, is there any space which is not occupied by matter. 'All space is filled with matter.'[5] The same applies to time. Nothing can be located out of time, nor yet, conversely, 'can there be any time with nothing in it'.[6]

Matter therefore exists in space and time as its modes of existence, but is not on that account to be identified with them. This is

[1] F. Engels: *Op. cit.*, p. 54.

[2] Pascual Jordan: *Die Physik des 20. Jahrhunderts*, Brunswick 1939[3], p. 148. It may be observed here that by no means all of these methods rely upon relativity theory, as Zhdanov implies in his ironic remarks about attempts to determine the age of the cosmos: cf. *Bol'shevik*, 1947, 16, p. 22; (*On Literature . . .*, p. 110). Also below, p. 437, n. 3.

[3] A. A. Maximov: *Bor'ba Lenina s 'fizicheskim' idealizmom* (Lenin's Fight against 'Physical' Idealism), in *Bol'shevik* 1949, 2, pp. 21–33, q.v. p. 28.

[4] *DM*, p. 303.   [5] M. A. Leonov: *Ocherk . . .*, p. 448.   [6] *Ibid.*

emphasized in opposition to the attempt of a Deborinist, Hessen, who was ready to see in matter merely a 'synthesis of space and time';[1] the official Soviet philosophy insists, on the contrary, that this means reducing objective reality itself to its own modes of existence.[2]

Space and time are not merely modes in which being exists, but—owing to the identification of being and matter—modes in which *all* being exists. This principle had already been laid down by Engels in his polemic against Dühring:

'The basic forms of all being are space and time, and existence out of time is just as gross an absurdity as existence out of space.' [3]

And Lenin gives it as a reason for this, that

'there is nothing in the world but matter in motion, and matter in motion cannot move otherwise than in space and time'.[4]

In dealing with the problem of many-dimensional space, Soviet philosophy is steadfast in maintaining three-dimensional space to be uniquely applicable to the real world: 'Real space is three-dimensional.' [5] All attempts to credit it with more than three dimensions can lead only to 'spiritualism and mysticism'.[6] In introducing the concept of a 'four-dimensional world', modern physics is seeking merely to express the fact that three-dimensional space and one-dimensional time form an inseparable unity. As for the non-Euclidean geometries, it is quite in the spirit of Soviet patriotism that the opportunity does not pass without an express reminder of the fact that a Russian, Lobachevsky, played a notable part in their development.

As with the doctrine of space, so also with that of *time*, the starting-point is the contention that it constitutes a 'form of existence of matter':

'Time is a form of existence of matter, which represents the duration and succession of material processes and expresses the objective connectedness of material motion.' [7]

Time, like space, is a basic form of all being, and existence outside it is as unthinkable as existence out of space.[8]

As a form of existence of matter, time is considered to be infinite, like matter itself. Things have always existed and always will. Time also, which owes its entire reality to things, accordingly has neither beginning nor end.

[1] B. Hessen: *Osnovnye idei teorii otnositel'nosti* (Basic Ideas of Relativity Theory), p. 69; quoted from M. B. Mitin: *Op. cit.*, p. 291.
[2] F. T. Arkhiptsev: *Op. cit.*, p. 51.   [3] *Anti-Dühring:* p. 62.
[4] *ME*, p. 162 (177, 236).   [5] *DM*, p. 307.
[6] *Ibid.*, p. 308.   [7] *Ibid.*, pp. 303 f.
[8] *Cf.* n. 3 above.

As in the case of space, dialectical materialism is again concerned here to occupy a middle position between a subjective conception like that of Kant and an unduly realistic, 'abstract', 'metaphysico-mechanical' view of time as absolute empty duration, constantly identical with itself and indifferent as regards the matter it contains.[1]

A further essential property of time is its non-reversibility: past, present and future cannot be interchanged. Ral'tsevich, to be sure, went so far in his day in stressing the concrete character of time as objective duration, that he even tried to prove from this that it was reversible after all. If time is conceived in the abstract, so he argued, as flowing unbroken from the past, through the present, into the future, it plainly appears to be irreversible. But if it is viewed concretely, there can be no denying that it exhibits a certain reversibility. For the development of reality, both in Nature and history, does not present itself as a completely straightforward process, having no deviations or regressions; on the contrary, it is often possible to observe certain retrograde tendencies towards stages of evolution which have already been traversed; in Nature, for instance, in the form of simplifications in the biological structure of organisms and the functioning of organs, and in history, in the shape of reversions from a more advanced period to a more primitive one. Admittedly, these retrogressions are only relative in character, the main tendency throughout being a progressive one; but they indicate nonetheless a certain 'reversibility of time'.[2] It is obvious, however, that such regressions in the development of reality, whose objective *duration* is the basis of time, imply no reversibility of *time* as such. More recently, it has been customary to refer simply to the non-reversibility of time; its course runs in one direction only, from the past into the future.[3]

Space and time are two different forms in which matter exists, but their difference does not exclude their dialectical unity. The latter is already apparent from the study of simple mechanical motion, where the velocity is expressed in terms of spatial and temporal co-ordinates. But this inseparable connection is more particularly evident in dealing with very high velocities (as in relativity theory).[4] Here, however, we must postpone treatment of the space-time problem in connection with relativity theory; we shall return to the subject in Chapter V.

So long as the doctrine of the two concepts of matter still held the field, a number of authors, among them Leonov, in his textbook on dialectical materialism[5] and the university teacher V. I. Svidersky,[6]

---

[1] *Cf. DM*, pp. 304 ff.
[2] V. Ral'tsevich, in *BSE* (1st edn.), XXII, cols. 137 f.
[3] *BSE* (2nd edn.), IX, p. 273.   [4] *Cf. DM*, pp. 306 f.
[5] M. A. Leonov: *Ocherk . . .*, pp. 450 f.
[6] V. I. Svidersky: *O filosofskom i estestvenno-nauchnom ponyatiyakh*

attempted also to distinguish a philosophical and a scientific concept of space and time; but this view was hotly contested.[1] In his more recent and thoroughgoing study of the space-time problem[2] Svidersky accordingly avoids this distinction.

Some very interesting discussions are to be found in recent Soviet literature on the relation between space and time as *form* and self-moving matter as *content*. Svidersky summarizes this relationship under three heads:

'In the first place, space and time as such are the basic, objectively real forms of existence of self-moving matter; secondly, as forms, their properties are conditioned by their content, self-moving matter; thirdly, as forms, they possess a specific character of their own, distinct from that of their content, self-moving matter'.[3]

Basing himself on general relativity-theory, the eminent Soviet nuclear physicist D. D. Ivanenko regards space-time and the 'stuff' in motion therein as the two subordinate concepts to the generic concept of 'physical reality':

'Physical reality has long been divided into two categories: space-time on the one hand, and on the other the stuff, "embedded" in space, as it were, and in motion therein.'

Each of these, according to Ivanenko, can be transformed into the other.[4] Uemov seeks to avoid such an excessively sharp division of the two and regards space-time as a form which enters into interaction with its content, matter, as form and content generally do. He finds corroboration for this view in general relativity theory, according to which the metric of space-time is governed, on the one hand, by the presence of large masses, while on the other, the mutual attraction of bodies is dependent on the degree of curvature of space-time.[5] I. B. Novik attempts a correction of this position, arguing that what is required is an interaction, not between space-time and matter, but

prostranstva i vremeni (On the Philosophical and Scientific Concepts of Space and Time), in *Uchenye Zapiski Leningradskogo Gosudarstvennogo Universiteta, seriya filosofskikh nauk*, 2, No. 109, 1948.

[1] I. V. Kuznetsov: *Op. cit.*, pp. 262 f.

[2] V. I. Svidersky: *Filosofskoe znachenie prostranstvenno-vremennykh predstavleniy v fizike* (The Philosophical Significance of Spatio-Temporal Conceptions in Physics), Leningrad 1956.

[3] V. I. Svidersky: *Op. cit.*, p. 112.

[4] D. D. Ivanenko: *Elementarnye chastitsy i ikh vzaimodeystviya* (Elementary Particles and their Interactions), in *Uspekhi khimii XVII*, 5, 1948, p. 545.

[5] A. I. Uemov: *Op. cit.*, p. 175.

between space-time and the *motion* of matter, in other words an interaction between the different attributes of matter.[1]

It may be granted at once to dialectical materialism that the basic premiss of its conception of space and time, namely that of preserving a middle course between a purely subjective view (Kant) and an unduly realistic approach, conceiving of space and time as a pair of realities independent of the material world, is perfectly justified. We may agree with the Soviet philosophers when they inveigh against the 'abstract' 'mechanical' conception of time which turns it into an empty reality, independent of the actual world, and when they treat space and time as intimately bound up with matter. In this sense we may accept the dialectical materialist definition of space and time as forms of existence of matter. Admittedly, in its philosophical treatment of space and time, dialectical materialism never gets beyond this definition; it is incapable of specifying more exactly how this unity and difference of space and time on the one hand, and matter in motion on the other, is to be understood in detail.

The dialectical materialist conception of space and time is basically in agreement with that of scholasticism, which considers them to be creations of the mind on a factual basis (*ens rationis cum fundamento in re*) and therefore as a combination of subjective and objective. The objective aspect, the factual basis of the concept of space, consists in extended material objects; that of the concept of time in the succession of states in things. Yet these concepts are subjective, mind-made entities inasmuch as we conceive, or rather picture, spatial juxtaposition and temporal succession as existing in themselves and independent of things.

How closely the Soviet conception of space and time approaches this doctrine may be seen, for example, from the polemic of the Soviet mathematician A. D. Alexandrov against the manner in which Eddington, and among Soviet philosophers, Terletsky, interpret the notion of a 'frame of reference', which is central to relativity theory. Alexandrov accuses them of envisaging the latter as a merely conceptual affair, a fictitious network imposed on the world by the observer. He concedes to this view that initially the frame of reference does *also* function as a mode of representing space-time. But

'the task of the materialist in regard to the concepts of a frame of reference or system of coordinates is to discover and establish their *objective basis*, what they reflect in reality, and thereby to show that they are *not merely* modes of representation'.[2]

[1] I. B. Novik: *Op. cit.*, pp. 142–4.
[2] A. D. Alexandrov: *Po povodu nekotorykh vzglyadov na teoriyu otno-*

As we shall see below,[1] Alexandrov discerns this objective basis of the space-time frame of reference in the fact that it represents an objective co-ordination of things and phenomena in space and time, whose existence is independent of our consciousness.

Ral'tsevich, too, comes very near to this view when he makes time, the duration of a thing, depend on its inner structure and organization. But here he identifies time too closely with its factual basis, duration, more especially when he seeks to infer from this that 'time is reversible'. Nevertheless, the idea of ascribing a difference of duration to different things according to their various natures is basically a very sound one, and that in a much deeper sense than that of Ral'tsevich, who seemingly thinks of difference of duration only in a purely quantitative sense, according to its length. But a different type of duration may also be ascribed to different things according to the degree of perfection of their being: inorganic matter, such as a stone, having one type of duration, plants or animals another, and man with his spiritual nature, and ultimately God, having others still.[2]

But the chief error of the dialectical materialist doctrine of space and time consists once more in the wholly unjustified assertion of Engels and Lenin, that space and time represent basic forms of 'all being', and that a being independent of space and time would be an absurdity. Behind it there lies the usual materialist assumption that all being must be material; but this we have already dealt with earlier, and have therefore no need to enter upon further here.

sitel'nosti (Concerning Certain Interpretations of Relativity-Theory), *VF*, 1953, 5, pp. 225–45, *q.v.* p. 232 (our italics in the first instance—G. W.).

[1] *Cf.* below, p. 421.

[2] On the analogy of the time-concept, in the sense of concrete duration, *cf.* August Brunner, S. J.: *Die Grundfragen der Philosophie*, Freiburg-i-B. 1933, p. 151.

CHAPTER III

The Materialist Dialectic

I N the foregoing chapters we have been engaged in examining the dialectical materialist conception of matter. In the course of this it has appeared that dialectical materialism considers matter to be essentially mobile. Motion represents an essential attribute of matter, the term 'motion' here being understood in its widest sense, as change of any kind whatever.

We must now take a more searching look at the nature of the motion so conceived. As has already been made clear, dialectical materialism is firmly opposed to the vulgar materialist and mechanistic point of view in its insistence that the course of motion in matter gives rise to qualitative changes therein. This motion is conceived, therefore, as an ascending process whereby matter raises itself to ever higher forms of existence. The theoretical justification for the emergence of new and ever higher qualities is held to be provided by the dialectic itself, in that it shows how qualitative changes are brought about in matter in the course of its evolution.

It must be noted beforehand, that the term 'dialectic' has no very precise connotation in Soviet usage. This is in keeping with the account of the concept outlined above, which is broad in the extreme, including as it does 'the general laws of motion and development of Nature, human society and thought'.[1] Hence it has come about that in Soviet philosophy 'dialectic' often has precisely the same meaning as the concept of a 'dynamic' or even simply a 'historical' approach to reality, in contrast to a static view thereof, which is designated as 'metaphysical' in character. 'Metaphysics' thereby becomes a collective term for all systems opposed to dialectical materialism, though these may often have very little to do with metaphysics proper.

[1] *Cf.* above, p. 252.

310

Where, then, are we to discern the essence of the materialist dialectic? Is it to be found, perhaps, in the celebrated triad of thesis-antithesis-synthesis? Hegel himself hardly considered this triad to be anything more than the external aspect of the dialectic. Still more so is this the case with Lenin: 'No other rôle remains for the triads than as a lid and a skin';[1] his own attempt to define the essential elements of dialectic resulted, as we have seen, in a list of 16 items.[2]

The views of Soviet philosophy on this subject were long governed by Engels' mode of treatment, which summed up the essence of the materialist dialectic in three basic laws: the law of the transformation of quantity into quality and *vice versa*; the law of the mutual inter-penetration of opposites; and the law of the negation of the negation.[3] Until the appearance of Stalin's essay on *Dialectical and Historical Materialism*, this formulation of the essence of the materialist dialectic was common property in Soviet philosophy, with the solitary exception that Engels' second law was placed first, in deference to the overriding importance attached by Lenin to the unity of opposites as an explanation of motion in the world.

The significance of this first law (by the new reckoning) lies in the fact that it is held to account for the origin of motion in things and in the world at large; motion accordingly, is not to be attributed to an external mover lying outside things; still less does the explanation of motion in the world as a whole require the postulation of a 'First Mover' existing outside the latter; the origin of motion in things and in the world is held to lie, rather, in the inner 'contradictions' residing in the nature of every single thing and phenomenon as such; these contradictions struggle for release and thereby set the thing in motion. The business of the second law is therefore to explain how this motion gives rise to the emergence of new qualities, essentially different kinds of being. It is supposed that, up to a certain point, the motion has the character of a purely quantitative addition or subtraction; but that once the quantitative change goes beyond this limit, conditioned as it is by the nature of the object in question, the mere alteration of quantity gives place to a change in quality and a new characteristic emerges by way of a 'leap', which signifies, in the terminology of dialectical materialism, that the thing is essentially altered and be-comes something different. This law is held to provide philosophical justification for the evolutionist thesis of dialectical materialism, by showing how it could come about that in the course of the world's

---

[1] V. I. Lenin: *Suchinenlya*, I[1], p. 150 (in the pamphlet *Chto takoe 'druz'ya naroda' i kak oni voyuyut protiv sotsial-demokratov?* 'What the "Friends of the People" Are and How They Fight the Social-Democrats'; *LSW*, XI, p. 447).

[2] *Cf.* above, p. 119 f.

[3] F. Engels: *Dialectics of Nature*, p. 83.

process of development life should have emerged from the development of inorganic matter, and mind and consciousness in turn from that of the organic.

Stalin's essay on *Dialectical and Historical Materialism* sets the matter out in an altogether different fashion. In place of Engels' three basic laws of the materialist dialectic, he lays down four 'principal features of the Marxist dialectical method':

1. The general connection between phenomena in Nature and society;
2. Movement and development in Nature and society.
3. Development as a transition from quantitative changes into qualitative;
4. Development as a struggle of opposites.

Stalin omits the 'law of the negation of the negation'. Until his death, this arrangement was slavishly followed by Soviet authors. It still underlies the textbook on *Dialectical Materialism*, edited by Alexandrov, which appeared only in 1954. As already noted, it was only after Stalin's death that voices were to be heard urging the abandonment of this scheme and a revival of the law of the negation of the negation.

But since we still lack any new account of the theory of the materialist dialectic which can claim to be an interpretation of the official point of view, the solution adopted in the present work will be in the nature of a compromise: in our opening section we shall deal with the first two laws formulated by Stalin as 'principal features' of the materialist dialectic; the two sections that follow will be concerned with the pair of laws to be found in both Stalin and Engels; and the last section of this chapter will then be devoted to Engels' law of the negation of the negation, which Stalin omitted to mention.

1. STALIN'S ACCOUNT OF THE FIRST TWO 'PRINCIPAL
FEATURES' OF THE MARXIST DIALECTICAL METHOD

It may be noted in advance that Stalin mistakenly refers to principal features of the Marxist dialectical *method*. In point of fact, all four of the propositions he lays down are not just methodological guiding principles for the proper study of reality, but themselves, in the primary sense, already assertions about reality.

'Contrary to metaphysics', says Stalin, expounding the first principal feature of the Marxist dialectical method, 'dialectics does not regard Nature as an accidental agglomeration of things, of phenomena, unconnected with, isolated from, and independent of, each other, but as a connected and integral whole, in which things, phenomena are organically connected with, dependent on, and determined by, each other.

'The dialectical method therefore holds that no phenomenon in Nature can be understood if taken by itself, isolated from surrounding phenomena, inasmuch as any phenomenon in any realm of Nature may become meaningless to us if it is not considered in connection with the surrounding conditions, but divorced from them; and that, *vice versa*, any phenomenon can be understood and explained if considered in its inseparable connection with surrounding phenomena, as one conditioned by surrounding phenomena.' [1]

In this first principal feature, Stalin formulates the ideas underlying nos. 2, 7, 8 and 10, especially, of the 16 'elements' of dialectic distinguished by Lenin. But even in Engels we already find this notion of universal connection throughout the world as a presupposition of the dialectical approach:

'the first thing that strikes us in considering matter in motion is the interconnection of the individual motions of separate bodies, their *being determined* by one another'.[2]

Stalin's statement, which is no more than the pathetically solemn enunciation of a platitude, is customarily supported by the production of a whole string of more or less plausible examples from the fields of science and social life, in order to create in the philosophically untutored reader or hearer the impression that this endorsement of a single thesis constitutes a dazzling scientific confirmation of dialectical materialism as a whole—a procedure we have often had occasion to observe in action already. It is pointed out that the totality of Nature represents a vast interconnected whole, whose individual departments exhibit a manifold mutual dependence on one another; thus the earth itself exists, not as an isolated body in space, but in common with the other planets as part of the solar system, the latter again as part of the galaxy, and so forth; the work of the Russian biologist K. A. Timiryazev on photosynthesis has likewise brought out the connection between inorganic and organic matter.[3]

But it is not only in the world as a whole that such pervasive interconnections are manifested; in every single thing and phenomenon a similar set of elements may be distinguished, standing in interconnection and reciprocity one with another; moreover, all such elements in things and phenomena are bound together in such a way that change on the part of any *one* of them gives rise to change in the others. As dialectical materialism sees it, this has a special significance for

---

[1] *DHM*, p. 536 (570, 106).
[2] F. Engels: *Dialectics of Nature*, p. 304.　　　　　[3] *DM*, p. 70.

Darwin's theory of evolution. Engels makes a direct appeal to this law of functional dependence in organisms in order to elucidate the process of evolution from ape to man: the employment of tools, the labour performed by their aid, led, in the course of evolution, to the perfecting of the hand, and parallel with this the foot became adapted to the needs of an erect gait; both must then have given rise to subsequent changes in other parts of the organism.[1]

The same reciprocal dependence is also observable in social life: society, too, represents an organism, whose elements are in mutual dependence on one another; it is just this that is brought out by the materialist conception of history, when it points to the means of production as the basis on which the whole of social development everywhere depends.[2]

Now 'metaphysics' is accused of ignoring all this. Thus 'exponents of the idealist philosophy of so-called existentialism' maintain, for example, that there is no sort of lawful connection among phenomena, that historical facts can only be described as accidental and meaningless. Even where reactionary bourgeois philosophy has succeeded in advancing to the concept of wholeness, as in the 'Holism' of Smuts, 'the field-marshal of the English army, who for many years oppressed the South-African peoples', this concept is distorted in that the wholeness of the organism is attributed to the presence of a special 'factor of wholeness' which differs in no essential respect from a creator-God.[3]

There is naturally no neglect of the opportunity so presented for adverting likewise to the social and political significance of these bourgeois creeds; the denial of law in general, and of social law in particular, is allegedly intended solely for the purpose of conjuring out of existence the laws governing the decline of the capitalist order and the emergence of a new socialist society.[4]

The second 'principal feature of the Marxist dialectical method' is formulated by Stalin as follows:

'Contrary to metaphysics, dialectics holds that Nature is not a state of rest and immobility, stagnation and immutability, but a state of continuous movement and change, of continuous renewal and development, where something is always arising and developing, and something always disintegrating and dying away.

'The dialectical method therefore requires that phenomena should be considered not only from the standpoint of their interconnection and interdependence, but also from the standpoint of their movement,

---

[1] F. Engels: *Op. cit.*, p. 228 f.   [2] *DM*, p. 72.
[3] *Ibid.*, pp. 68, 7. 1.   [4] *Ibid.*, p. 68.

their change, their development, their coming into being and going out of being.'[1]

Of the sixteen elements in Lenin's account of dialectic, this formula corresponds above all to the third; and it is precisely this element that has been responsible for the dialectical materialist habit of forthwith equating 'dialectical' and 'dynamic'. This can be seen in Engels, for whom dialectics is always that which grasps

'things and their images, ideas, essentially in their interconnection, in their sequence, their movement, their birth and death'.[2]

This point of view is represented by Engels and all his successors as opposite to that of 'metaphysics'; indeed, in dialectical materialist usage the postulation of unchanging entities, and more generally the disregard of movement and change in Nature and history, is reckoned the essence of metaphysics. Thus in regard to the observation of Nature, Leonov cites, as examples of such 'metaphysics', Voltaire, who believed the marine fossils discovered in the Alps to have been left there by travellers, or Linnaeus, who took them for an idle game on the part of Nature; or again the Mendel-Morgan theory of an unchanging inheritance, localized in the genes. In social theory, similarly 'metaphysical' views are exemplified by the utopian socialists, whose socialism was built on the idea of an unchanging 'human nature'; by bourgeois sociology, which imagines the doctrine of private property to be an eternally-given 'natural phenomenon'; and more especially by the opinions of present-day reactionary bourgeois philosophers and historians, who look upon capitalism not as a transitory phase but as an eternal and unchangeable form of production. The political significance of all these theories is said to be merely that of undermining the popular belief in a better social order in the future, and of persuading the public that the present order can never be shaken.[3]

'This means that in present-day society the metaphysical view of development, and the dialectical conception opposed to it, reflect the radical conflict between the bourgeois world-outlook and that of the proletariat.'[4]

In setting up motion and development as a general law, dialectical materialism has no wish to discount the element of rest, which lends a relative degree of constancy to things and phenomena. Without such an element of constancy there would indeed be no qualitative definiteness in the world and no specific concrete subjects of development. But the materialist dialectic recognizes rest and constancy as

---

[1] *DHM*, p. 537 (570 f., 106 f.).   [2] *Anti-Dühring*, p. 29.
[3] M. A. Leonov: *Ocherk . . .*, pp. 177 ff.   [4] *DM*, p. 117.

316   *The Materialist Dialectic*

relative merely, not as something 'absolute'; to think otherwise would be 'metaphysics'.[1]

Since, therefore, everything in the world is in a state of movement and development, it must naturally be of crucial importance to become acquainted with the laws of this development, and this is precisely where the Marxist dialectic comes in. From this point of view it is first and foremost the *foundation of a scientific knowledge of the past*. The first thing required in the investigation of any occurrence is the historical mode of approach; only by virtue of its connection with preceding developments does any event become intelligible. Inquiry into the past should not, however, be confined merely to establishing and describing the facts; what matters, rather, is to discover the circumstances and meaning of events. Nor again should a scientific investigation of history consist in accumulating facts in order to pass judgement on the past from the standpoint of the present; it is a question, rather, of making clear which classes were in conflict with one another and thereby determining the content of history in any given period, and of evaluating the activities of these classes from the standpoint of the subsequent historical developments. Here it becomes evident that classes which are nowadays reactionary may have played a progressive part in earlier times. And finally, the historical scrutiny of development must abstract from everything that is irrelevant or contingent in events in order to bring out the decisive factors, the major line of development; this too can only be done with the aid of the dialectic, which points the way to a 'generalization' of historical events. The theory of any given subject, for dialectical materialism, is nothing other than its history in a generalized form. Thus in the sequence of categories of capitalism, for example, as stated by Marx in *Capital*, one may see reflected the historical development of capitalism. All sciences are at bottom concerned with the history of their development in a generalized form: so it is in astronomy, in geology, in chemistry even, and so on.[2]

By its discovery of the laws of development the Marxist dialectic also provides, however, the *wherewithal for a scientific prediction of future developments*, and for communism this is by far its most important achievement. The possibility of scientific prediction is based on knowledge of the laws of development, but above all on knowledge of the fact that events repeat themselves, which represents an essential aspect of developmental law. From the extreme historicism outlined above we might have expected, rather, that emphasis would be laid on the unique and unrepeatable character of history. Stalin, however, surprisingly declares: 'History repeats itself, though on a new basis.'[3] Science can therefore disclose a certain invariance

[1] *DM*, pp. 125 ff.   [2] M. A. Leonov: *Ocherk . . .*, pp. 180 ff.
[3] J. V. Stalin: *Voprosy leninizma*, 11th edn., p. 180 (English, p. 203).

in development, which is expressed in the form of law; 'Law is the permanent (the enduring) element in phenomena.'[1] Hence law may give expression, not only to what was or already is the case, but also, in broad outline, to the future situation emerging from present tendencies of development. Lenin points out that it was this lawfulness of historical development which gave Marx the opportunity of showing that communism

'*has its origin* in capitalism, that it develops historically from capitalism, that it is the result of the action of a social force to which capitalism *has given birth*. There is no trace of an attempt on Marx's part to conjure up a utopia. . . . Marx treats the question of communism in the same way as a naturalist would treat the question of the development of, say, a new biological species, if he knew that such and such was its origin, and such and such the direction in which it was changing.'[2]

In order to achieve a sound prognosis of future development it is particularly important to distinguish correctly, in the present, between what is arising and what is in process of dying away. This is not always easy, since the novel element often appears quite insignificant at the outset and can easily be overlooked.

'The dialectical method regards as important primarily not that which at the given moment seems to be durable and yet is already beginning to die away, but that which is arising and developing, even though at the given moment it may appear to be not durable, for the dialectical method considers invincible only that which is arising and developing.'[3]

That the element of novelty in the complex of developmental factors may be the more readily identified, the Soviet authors provide a number of criteria for its recognition.

To begin with, novelty represents a negation of the old. The struggle between old and new therefore signifies in the first place a denial of the one and an affirmation of the other. But between old and new in this process there prevails a specific interconnection of law. For the old, which is negated, does not change into anything else you please, but into a quite specific new thing, whose character is an outcome of its own past. A is transformed, not into any completely arbitrary not-A, but into some other quite definite thing, a quite definite B. Every phenomenon has its own perfectly specific manner of undergoing negation. A grain of wheat does not give rise to an

---

[1] *FT*, p. 126 (German, p. 69).
[2] V. I. Lenin: *Gosudarstvo i revolyutsiya, Sochineniya* XXV[4], p. 430 (English version: *State and Revolution, LSW*, VII, p. 77).
[3] *DHM*, p. 537 (571, 107).

animal, nor does the embryo of a horse become a wolf. Negation thereby shows itself to be internally contradictory in character; it contains within itself a moment in which the old is conserved.

A further distinctive feature of the new is its progressive character, *i.e.*, the fact that it aims at reaching a higher level of development. Thus even capitalism, at the time of its inception, was by origin progressive and new in relation to the feudalism which preceded it.

And finally, the essentially typical feature of novelty is the very fact of its invincibility, governed as this is by the laws of development, *i.e.*, by the fact that the new corresponds to newly-arisen needs of social development and incorporates everything positive in the development that has gone before. The old order may sometimes put up a despairing resistance. But that, as was long since noted by Chernyshevsky, is precisely a symptom of the vitality of the new:

'Is it not clear, that the more brutal the means to which the old order must resort in order to preserve itself against the onset of new interests, the more plainly does it bear witness to the strength of these new interests? Brutal measures are only resorted to against a powerful and dangerous enemy.' [1]

In his article, *The Struggle between New and Old under the Conditions of Life in Soviet Society*, Fedorov goes on to point out the essentially different character taken by this struggle in a society ridden by class-antagonisms and in the socialist classless society. In a class-society the old can only be conquered by a 'liquidation' of the reactionary classes; in the atmosphere of moral and political unity prevailing in Soviet society, however, the conquest of the old is primarily effected by means of education, persuasion, the transformation of human consciousness, and the like.[2]

The assertions embodied in Stalin's first two 'principal features', namely that the things and phenomena in the world are all multiply interrelated, and all involved in a continuous process of coming-to-be and passing-away, are obvious commonplaces, at least if one stops short, as dialectical materialism does, at the mere factual assertion, without attempting to inquire philosophically as to how such a multiplicity can also be one, and how the changeable can likewise exhibit constancy.

[1] N. G. Chernyshevsky: *Frantsiya pri Lyudovike Napoleone* (France under Louis Napoleon), in the collection *Shestidesyatye gody* (The Sixties), issued by the Academy of Sciences of the U.S.S.R. 1940, p. 17; cited in M. A. Leonov: *Op. cit.*, p. 194.

[2] G. Fedorov: *Bor'ba mezhdu novym i starym v usloviyakh sovetskogo obshchestva*, in *Bol'shevik* 1947, 19, pp. 36–49, *q.v.* p. 48.

It is precisely this last-mentioned aspect that has always interested 'metaphysics' and incited it to inquiry. As a further criticism of these 'principal features', we must therefore draw attention to the peculiar notion of 'metaphysics' which dialectical materialism exhibits in this connection. To be a metaphysician is in no way to discount the occurrence of change and decay *in the empirical world*; nor does it imply any denial of interconnection among the changing objects of our experience. The sole concern of metaphysics is to infer *in thought* beyond the world of experience, insofar as it is subject to *physis*, i.e., change and decay, to the realm of the in*experienceable* (not to be confused with the un*knowable*), and thereby to penetrate into that sphere of reality where it is possible to discern the unity behind multiplicity and the constancy behind change. To this end, metaphysics begins by investigating what is common to everything real, that is to say, it views everything in its most general aspect, as being, and inquires into the nature, properties and laws thereof. Thus it is metaphysics which alone makes it possible to discover the necessary connections within the manifold contiguity and succession of empirical reality, and so to establish those real connections within spatial contiguity and temporal succession, whose existence is alleged in these first two 'principal features' of dialectical materialism.

Of the second of these, in particular, it may also be observed that a merely 'relative' stability and rest, amid the absolute flux of movement and change, do not suffice to make possible the differentiation and emergence of 'qualitatively determinate' things and phenomena in the course of this process of development in matter. Failing the *absolute* validity of certain laws, such as the principle of sufficient reason, the causal law, the law of contradiction and other equally fundamental principles, themselves in turn grounded upon unchanging essential properties of being and existence, there could be no determinacy of any kind whatever. We have seen, too, in the previous chapter, how dialectical materialism itself describes certain laws, such as that of the conservation of energy, as 'absolute and eternal', though in doing so it acts in strange contrast to its own basic principles.

2. THE LAW OF THE TRANSITION FROM QUANTITY TO QUALITY

We have already had occasion to point out that dialectical materialism conceives of the motion dealt with in the previous chapter, not as a cyclical motion, but as having the character of development, in which elements of novelty, new 'qualities', are continually coming to light.

'Contrary to metaphysics,' so Stalin formulates this third principal feature of the Marxist dialectical method—'dialectics does not regard the process of development as a simple process of growth, where quantitative changes do not lead to qualitative changes, but as a development which passes from insignificant and imperceptible quantitative changes to open, fundamental changes, to qualitative changes; a development in which the qualitative changes occur not gradually, but rapidly and abruptly, taking the form of a leap from one state to another; they occur not accidentally but as the natural result of an accumulation of imperceptible and gradual quantitative changes.'[1]

The content of this law is as follows: The development of things and phenomena in the world proceeds up to a certain point in the form of a gradual, merely quantitative change, by successive addition or subtraction. But once this quantitative change advances beyond the limits set by the nature of the thing in question, a sudden shift from quantitative to qualitative change occurs; the thing ceases to be what it is and becomes something else; a new 'quality' makes its appearance.

'Quality', in dialectical materialist usage, 'is the essential determinacy of an object, the determinacy of its organic properties, features and characteristics, by virtue of which it is this object and no other, and is thereby distinguished from other objects.'[2]

Quality is in the first instance something inseparable from the thing in question, indissolubly bound up with it, and secondly also, something characteristic of the thing, peculiar to it alone, something which radically differentiates a given thing from every other thing.[3]

Dialectical materialism follows Hegel in distinguishing between quality (*kachestvo*) and property (*svoystvo*). Hegel defined quality as 'the immediate determinateness of the something', whereas he reckoned the properties of an object to comprise its

'determinate relations to Other; Property is given only as a mode of attitude of one towards an Other'.[4]

Hence, for dialectical materialism also, quality represents an inner determinateness intrinsic to the object, whereas property signifies this determinateness in its relation to other things:

[1] *DHM*, p. 537 (571, 107).
[2] *KFS*, p. 190.
[3] B. M. Kedrov: *O kolichestvennykh i kachestvennykh izmeneniyakh v prirode* (On Quantitative and Qualitative Changes in Nature), Moscow 1946, p. 13.
[4] G. W. F. Hegel: *Science of Logic*, II, p. 116.

'A property is the manifestation of a quality through its relation to another quality.'[1]

Thus the quality of gold, for example, is determined by its inner structure, whereas its properties, such as malleability, weight, sheen, freedom from rust, etc., depend upon this.[2] Unlike qualities, properties are not inseparable from the object: an object may lose a property without ceasing to be what it is: rubber, for example, loses its elasticity at low temperatures and becomes rigid and brittle like glass, but without therefore ceasing to be rubber.[3]

The category of quality is connected with that of quantity.

'Quantity is a determinacy of objects and phenomena that is characterized by number, size, rate, degree, extent, etc.'[4]

In specifying the relationship dialectical materialism again falls back upon Hegel, who formulates the distinction between quality and quantity as follows:

'Quality may be described as the determinate mode immediate and identical with Being— as distinguished from Quantity . . . which, although a mode of Being, is no longer immediately identical with Being, but a mode indifferent and external to it.'[5]

Dialectical materialism likewise sees in quantity an 'external mode of the object',[6] whose changes (at least within certain limits) have no effect upon the quality of the thing in question. Thus whereas quality gives expression to the relative stability of the thing, its inner wholeness and unity, quantity expresses its capacity for change while leaving its qualitative determinacy undisturbed.

This invariance of quality in the course of quantitative change is but relative, however, for it extends only up to a certain limit; once the quantitative change goes beyond this limit, there is a sudden transition, in the form of a leap, from the previous quality of the thing to a new one. This 'organic unity of qualitative and quantitative determination' is described by dialectical materialism as *measure*. 'Measure denotes the limits within which quantitative changes do not evoke qualitative'; the points of transition from one measure to another are referred to as 'nodes'.[7]

This doctrine also goes back to Hegel.

[1] B. M. Kedrov: *Op. cit.*, p. 15.
[2] V. Ral'tsevich in *BSE* (1st edn.) XXII, col. 155.
[3] B. M. Kedrov: *Op. cit.*, pp. 14 f.   [4] *DM*, p. 158.
[5] *The Logic of Hegel* (Wallace), pp. 170 f.
[6] B. M. Kedrov: *Op. cit.*, p. 26.   [7] *DM*, pp. 160 f.

'Measure now is immediate unity of the Qualitative and the Quantitative.' [1]

'We have here a Measure-Relation, an independent reality, qualitatively different from others. Such a Being-for-Self is also essentially a relation of Quanta, and therefore open to externality and variation of Quantum: it has some play, within which it remains indifferent to this change and does not alter its Quality. But there comes a point in this quantitative change at which Quality changes and Quantum shows itself as specifying; so that the altered quantitative relation is turned under our hands into a Measure and thereby into a new Quality and a new Something.' [2]

For Hegel too the quantitative change goes on gradually, whereas the qualitative emerges '*per saltum*'.[3] And he adduces a series of examples from mathematics, from music, and above all from the field of chemistry, where such 'nodal lines of measure' are exemplified with especial clarity.

Dialectical materialism gives Hegel the credit for having been the first to formulate the law of transition from quantity to quality; but he did so, however, in a regrettably 'idealist' fashion, in that quantity and quality figure as determinate stages in the development of the Absolute Idea, but are not related to material objects of any kind.[4] This error of Hegel's has now been corrected by the founders of Marxism, in that they have given 'a deeply materialist interpretation' [5] to the Hegelian formula. Engels puts it as follows:

'For our purpose, we can express this by saying that in Nature, in a manner exactly fixed for each individual case, qualitative changes can only occur by the quantitative addition or quantitative subtraction of matter or motion (so-called energy). All qualitative differences in Nature rest on differences of chemical composition or on different quantities or forms of motion (energy) or, as is almost always the case, on both. Hence it is impossible to alter the quality of a body without addition or subtraction of matter or motion, *i.e.*, without quantitative alteration of the body concerned.' [6]

Like Hegel, Engels also finds particular confirmation of this law in chemistry, in which it celebrates 'its most important triumphs':

'And indeed the various proportions in which oxygen combines with nitrogen or sulphur, each of which produces a substance qualitatively

[1] G. W. F. Hegel: *Science of Logic*, I, p. 348.
[2] *Ibid.*, p. 387.   [3] *Ibid.*, p. 388.
[4] M. A. Leonov: *Ocherk* . . ., p. 221.
[5] M. B. Mitin: *Op. cit.*, p. 160.
[6] F. Engels: *Dialectics of Nature*, p. 84.

different from any of the others! How different is laughing gas (nitrogen monoxide N_2O) from nitric anhydride (nitrogen pentoxide N_2O_5)! The first is a gas, the second at ordinary temperatures a solid crystalline substance. And yet the whole difference in composition is that the second contains five times as much oxygen as the first, and between the two of them are three more oxides of nitrogen (NO, N_2O_3, NO_2), each of which is qualitatively different from the first two and from one another.'[1]

This law is reinforced by means of a number of more or less happily-chosen examples. The classic instance from physics is the periodic system of the elements, in which a change of atomic number tends also to coincide with a new qualitative state of the element. In chemistry, for example, the quantitative division of a substance below the molecular level leads to qualitative changes (individual atoms have different properties from those of the molecule they comprise). In the field of biology there is constant recourse to Darwin and the proof he is alleged to have given, that initially insignificant quantitative changes in plants and animals eventually lead by accumulation and inheritance to the formation of new species. In the field of social theory the reference is to Marx and his example of how a master-craftsman becomes a capitalist as soon as his capital exceeds a certain level.[2] Lenin, too, sees a similar transformation of quantity into quality realized in the transition from bourgeois to proletarian democracy.

'Democracy, introduced as fully and consistently as is generally conceivable, is transformed from bourgeois democracy into proletarian democracy; from the state . . . into something which is no longer really a state.'[3]

And lastly, this law also holds good of human mental processes. Zhdanov sees it at work in the creation of Marxism, which betokens a revolution in philosophy: here, as in every other sort of leap, the discovery was prepared for by a previous accumulation of quantitative changes, in this particular case by the assembled findings of philosophical inquiry prior to Marx and Engels; but these then gave rise to a new type of philosophy, different in quality from all the philosophical systems that had gone before.[4] Even nowadays, however, there are still repeated references to a less happy example originally put forward by Engels, and later quoted by Stalin, namely that if a liquid is heated or cooled beyond a certain point there is

[1] *Ibid.*, p. 88.   [2] M. A. Leonov: *Ocherk . . .*, p. 223.
[3] V. I. Lenin: *Gosudarstvo i revolyutsiya* (State and Revolution), *Sochineniya*, XXV[4], p. 391 (*LSW*, VII, p. 41).
[4] *Cf. Bol'shevik*, 1947, 16, p. 9; (*On Literature . . .*, p. 80).

a change in the 'aggregate state';[1] Kedrov does not even boggle at employing the following example: if the dimensions of a writing-table, say, are reduced below a certain minimum, it ceases to be a table and become a toy.[2]

The law of the transition from quantity to quality figures, there-fore, as one of the main pillars in the philosophical edifice of dialectical materialism; it is taken to provide theoretical warrant for the assumption of an unbroken rule of transformation operating throughout the entire course of the world-process. In contrast, how-ever, to the world-view of mechanistic materialism, there is no immediate elimination of the essential, qualitative differences between the various realms of being: the atom certainly consists of electrons, but despite this its laws are not reducible to electronic laws; so too, the molecule is made up of atoms, but its nature is not exhausted by the laws prevailing in the atomic sphere. The same applies to the cell, the organism, mind, society, etc. In general, three main fields of reality are distinguished: inorganic matter, the organic world (where-in, in turn, the emergence of mind itself represents a transition of the highest importance), and the sphere of social life. The 'forms of motion' governing each of these spheres are basically irreducible one to another, each retaining its own specific quality. But despite this *formal* irreducibility of the higher levels to the lower, dialectical materialism insists that they are *genetically* derived from the latter.[3] And it is the law of the transition from quantity to quality which is supposed to provide the theoretical basis for this claim.

Quantitative and qualitative changes condition two essentially different kinds of development, *evolution* and *revolution*:

'And so the dialectical method says that movement has two forms: the evolutionary and the revolutionary form.' [4]

It is characteristic of the first that it is gradual, whereas the second takes place in a sudden, sweeping, violent manner:

'Movement is evolutionary when the progressive elements spontane-ously continue their daily activities and introduce minor *quantitative* changes into the old order.' [5]

Conversely:

'Movement is revolutionary when the same elements combine,

¹ *DHM*, p. 538 (572, 109); *DM*, p. 162.
² B. M. Kedrov: *Op. cit.*, p. 35.
³ *Cf.* N. O. Lossky: *Dialektichesky materializm v SSSR* (Dialectical Materialism in the U.S.S.R.), Paris 1934, p. 35.
⁴ J. V. Stalin: *Anarkhizm ili sotsializm?* (Anarchism or Socialism? 1906/7). *Sochineniya*, I, p. 300 (*Works*, I, p. 303).
⁵ *Ibid.*, p. 301 (303).

become imbued with a single idea, and sweep down upon the enemy camp with the object of uprooting the old order and of introducing *qualitative* changes in life, of establishing a new order.'[1]

Evolution and revolution are mutually correlated according to law:

'Evolution prepares for revolution and creates the ground for it; revolution consummates the process of evolution and facilitates its further activity.'[2]

The correlation resides, however, not only in the fact that the quantitative changes lead up to and prepare the way for qualitative ones, but also and conversely in the fact that the qualitative changes are followed by a new increase on the quantitative side. The cultivation of qualitatively new and better agricultural land also assists the production of quantitatively better crops, the breeding of new strains of cattle yields greater quantities of milk, meat, etc.[3]

The transition from quantitative to qualitative changes therefore implies a breach of continuity; it takes place by means of a *leap*. But this theory of dialectical leaps harbours a danger to the Soviet system itself. For the doctrine that all development includes a moment of both evolution and revolution lends itself to the conclusion that even the Soviet order of society must in turn be advanced by way of a qualitative dialectical leap, *i.e.*, by a revolution in the social field, if history is not to be admitted to have come to a complete standstill.

In order to avoid this conclusion, a distinction of exceptional importance was introduced into Marxist–Leninist theory by Stalin, in his letters on linguistics, where he differentiates between leaps that occur suddenly (*vzryv*, literally an 'explosion' or violent upheaval) and those that take place gradually. Only in antagonistic forms of society does the transition from one form to another take the shape of an 'explosion'; whereas in the development of the classless Soviet society these 'leaps' occur

'by way of a gradual accumulation of elements of the new quality and a dying-away of the old one'.[4]

The relevant passage in the first of these letters is outwardly most unimpressive, having the air of a casually interpolated remark à propos the question whether the development of language takes place by way of violent upheavals:

'It should be said in general for the benefit of comrades who have an infatuation for explosions (*vzryv*) that the law of transition from an

---

[1] *Ibid.*   [2] *Ibid.*, (304).   [3] M. A. Leonov: *Ocherk* . . ., pp. 239 f.
[4] *DM*, p. 171.

old quality to a new by means of an explosion is inapplicable not only to the history of the development of languages; it is not always applicable to other social phenomena of a basis or superstructural character. It applies of necessity to a society divided into hostile classes. But it does not necessarily apply to a society which has no hostile classes. In a period of eight to ten years we effected a transition in the agriculture of our country from the bourgeois, individual-peasant system to the socialist, collective-farm system. This was a revolution which eliminated the old bourgeois economic system in the countryside and created a new, socialist system. But that revolution did not take place by means of an explosion, that is, by the overthrow of the existing government power and the creation of a new power, but by a gradual transition from the old bourgeois system in the countryside to a new system. And it was possible to do that because it was a revolution from above, because the revolution was accomplished on the initiative of the existing power with the support of the bulk of the peasantry.' [1]

In an article on *Basis and Superstructure*, published on 5th October 1950, *Pravda* describes these opinions of Stalin's as 'of tremendous importance':

'Comrade Stalin is the first in the literature of Marxism to have shown that in the socialist society, where antagonistic classes no longer exist, the operation of a basic dialectical law, the law of transition from an old quality to a new, takes on a new form. Comrade Stalin has destroyed the vulgar notion that qualitative changes must always and under all circumstances take place by way of explosions. Comrade Stalin has shown that the law of transition from an old quality to a new by means of explosions only applies to a society divided into hostile classes. But this law by no means applies to a society where there are no antagonistic classes.' [2]

Stalin's 'solution' of the problem of the fateful dialectical 'leaps' amounts, therefore, to this, that the new term 'explosion' is now introduced in place of 'leap'. Leaps are still allowed moreover, it is only 'explosions' that are forbidden.

In a report, *The Further Development of Dialectical and Historical Materialism in J. V. Stalin's 'Marxism and Problems of Linguistics'*, delivered by Alexandrov at a session of the Academic Council of the Philosophical Institute of the Academy of Sciences, the distinction between the old and the new types of 'leap' is formulated as follows: In the antagonistic class-society, the decisive rôle in the 'leap' from an

[1] J. V. Stalin: *Marxizm i voprosy yazykoznaniya*, p. 58 (English, pp. 38 f.).
[2] *O bazise i nadstroyke*, in *Pravda*, 5th Oct. 1950; *cf.* also *Ost-Probleme*, II (1950), No. 44.

old to a new quality is taken by an initiative 'from below', *i.e.*, by a revolutionary uprising amongst the masses, accompanied by furious resistance on the part of the ruling classes; hence the characteristic feature of this leap, the fact that it develops into an 'explosion' (*vzryv*) involving the liquidation of the old order of society and its replacement by a new one.

Matters are otherwise in the classless Soviet society.

'In effecting the transition from one stage of development of socialist society to another, higher one, from an old quality to a new, the leading part is played by the *initiative from above, the initiative of the Soviet State*. The masses of the people *actively support* such a revolutionary initiative from above. . . . And it is precisely this which gives rise to the *peculiarity* of the transition occurring under such conditions *from an old quality to a new, namely that here the leap no longer takes on the character of an explosion* and a liquidation of the established order of society, *and cannot possibly do so*'.[1]

This is doubtless enough to provide a formal solution of the difficulty; the only trouble is that, having ceased to be an 'explosion', the 'leap' also loses its sudden character, takes on the character of a *gradual* transition, and therefore ceases to be a 'leap' at all.

There is yet another 'deepening' of previous understanding which Alexandrov ascribes to Stalin's letters on linguistics—this time concerning the relationship of evolution and revolution; and typically enough it again tells in favour of continuity. Stalin has here rectified an erroneous account of social development to be found in a number of works on historical materialism, whereby the individual stages in the development of society are made to appear as separated by an absolute break and the history of society reduced to a succession of isolated situations having no connection one with another. In contrast to this, Stalin has made it clear that although the development of particular bases and superstructures certainly occurs by way of leaps and breaches of continuity, there are other social factors, notably those of technology and language, whose development does not follow the irregular progress of basis and superstructure, but rather ensures by its continuity the continuous character of the history of social development.[2]

The theory of the different kinds of leap has since become one of the generally prescribed doctrines of dialectical materialism.

'The Marxist dialectical method teaches us to approach the analysis of leaps in a concrete, historical manner, and to recognize their qualitative diversity and variety.'[3]

Kedrov has devoted a special study, *Gradualness as a Form of*

---

[1] *Cf. VF*, 1950, 2, p. 356.   [2] *Ibid.*   [3] *DM*, p. 169.

Transition from an Old Quality to a New,[1] to an analysis of changes of this type. Gradualness, he argues, should not be attributed only to quantitative changes; it is also a feature of many qualitative transitions, and this not only

'as a form of quantitative preparation for the leap, an evolutionary prelude to revolution, but also as a form in which the leap or revolution takes place, a form of qualitative change'.[2]

He illustrates the point with a series of examples from Nature and history: in astronomy, cosmogonical theories are based on the idea of a gradual evolution among cosmic objects and a correspondingly slow transition to qualitatively new conditions. In geology, and especially in soil science, gradual leaps of this sort are to be found in the theory of Dokuchaev and Williams. In biology, such qualitative transitions occur in the formation of new species. In a later work Kedrov appeals to this fact in defending Darwin against the charge of 'flat evolutionism'; those who object to Darwin on this score are confusing gradual qualitative transitions with purely quantitative ones.[3] In the fields of anthropology and physiology, another example is provided by the process of human evolution; in the development of language, 'explosions' are altogether absent, and so too in the history of technology, science and production.[4]

Above all, however, Kedrov endeavours to prove that the transition from socialism to communism is a slow and gradual process of this kind; he demonstrates this by an analysis of the three 'basic conditions' for the transition to communism, as laid down by Stalin in his last book, *Economic Problems of Socialism in the U.S.S.R.*[5]

But when reference is made to the gradual transition to a new quality in the course of social development under socialism, this must not be taken to imply that the process will necessarily be a slow one; on the contrary

'Thanks to the many . . . special features and advantages of a socialist system, the productive forces are developing there at an accelerated rate.'[6]

The true purport of all these speculations is really quite obvious: the revolutionary sting in the law of transition from quantity to quality is to be drawn, and in the interests of preserving the existing Soviet system the accent is again to be placed increasingly on the 'continuity' of the developmental process: the 'leaps' are no longer

[1] B. M. Kedrov: *Postepennost' kak odna iz form perekhoda ot starogo kachestva k novomu kachestvu*, *VF*, 1954, 2, pp. 50–70.
[2] *Ibid.*, p. 55.   [3] *Cf.* below, p. 462.
[4] B. M. Kedrov: *Op. cit.*, pp. 67 f.
[5] *Ibid.*, p. 57; *cf.* above, pp. 229 f.   [6] *DM*, p. 178.

permitted to assume the character of 'explosions', *i.e.*, as Alexandrov sees it, they no longer imply the overthrow of the existing state power; and if, for the sake of theory, revolutions continue to be envisaged in the future, what is intended is that they shall consist only of revolutions 'from above', conducted by the established régime. And in order to anchor this newly-discovered conservatism of continuity still more firmly into the nature of social development, it is pointed out that the sphere of operation of the dialectical leaps is by no means so extensive as might appear, since there are factors in social life (technology and language) which remain wholly unaffected by this law.

The emergence of new qualities in the course of the developmental process is also bound up with a belief in their progressive character, *i.e.*, the optimistic conviction that development takes its course from the lower to the higher and better.

Here too the 'metaphysicians' are of a different opinion, more especially the adherents of a cyclical theory of development in Nature and society, which brings forth nothing new, but merely repeats the stages already traversed before; this was the view of Giambattista Vico at the beginning of the 18th century, who supposed all societies and civilizations to run through the same cyclical course of youth, maturity and decay. In modern bourgeois ideology of the epoch of imperialism, Oswald Spengler, the 'ideologist of the German imperialists, and intellectual forerunner of Fascism' represents a similar point of view, namely that society must run through three stages in the course of its development—growth, maturity and decadence.[1]

In despite of all such notions, dialectical materialism proclaims its belief in progress, in the idea

'that the process of development should be understood, not as movement in a circle, not as a simple repetition of what has already occurred, but as an onward and upward movement, as a transition from an old qualitative state to a new qualitative state, as a development from the simple to the complex, from the lower to the higher'.[2]

There is no need on that account to picture this progressive development as an uninterrupted triumphal march in which there are no occasional setbacks and regressions. Just as biology is acquainted with the phenomena of so-called regressive evolution, *i.e.*, a certain reversion to evolutionary stages already traversed, so social evolution also is familiar with periods of defeat and retrogression.

'The revolution normally develops, not in a directly ascending line . . . but on a zigzag path, a series of offensives and defensives, of ebbs

[1] *DM*, p. 179.   [2] *DHM*, p. 537 (571, 107).

and flows, which in course of development steel the forces of revolution and prepare the way for their ultimate victory'.[1]

But in spite of all such occasional regressions, the historical development of human society represents on the whole an upward process, leading finally, by whatever devious ways, to its invariable culmination in socialism:

'We live in an age when all roads lead to communism.'[2]

The socialism which has already been realized in the Soviet Union represents, however,

'not only a progressive stage in historical development, but also a qualitatively new system of society'.[3]

The liquidation of exploiting classes and of class-contradictions has brought it about that even the upward development has acquired a novel character, in that it now no longer pursues the earlier zigzag path or exhibits regressions, but takes the form, rather, of an *uninterrupted* advance.

'The most important feature of the upward development of Soviet society lies in the fact that this development is continuous in character.'[4]

This novel manifestation of what has hitherto been one of the most fundamental laws of the world's development, namely that with the advent of the socialist order of society there is no longer any discontinuity, but only a perfect continuity of social development, is exceptionally worthy of remark. In broad outline it is held that in future there is to be nothing but a pure and unbroken ascent. This fact, this expectation that the world is to be fundamentally transformed down to its innermost laws of being, does more than almost any other to bring out clearly the messianic aspirations which underlie Marxism, and more especially Marxism in its Soviet form.

The dialectical materialist law of transition from quantitative changes to qualitative undoubtedly gives expression to a situation actually to be met with in real life: namely the emergence of essential

---

[1] J. V. Stalin: *Ob oppozitsii* (On the Opposition), p. 172.

[2] V. M. Molotov: *Tridtsatiletie Velikoy Oktyabr'skoy revolyutsii* (Thirtieth Anniversary Celebration of the Great October Revolution), Moscow 1947, p. 31.

[3] N. Dzhandil'din: *Ob osobennostyakh postupatel'nogo razvitiya sotsialisticheskogo obshchestva* (On the Distinguishing Features of the Upward Development of Socialist Society), in *VF*, 1950, 1, pp. 58–76, *q.v.* p. 60.

[4] *Ibid.*, p. 65.

changes in the course of a gradual process of inessential change—so long, at least, as 'essential' is understood in the everyday sense, whereby water, say, is taken to be 'essentially' different from *e.g.*, salt. In this sense the law is by no means peculiar to dialectical materialism. We need only refer to the fact that Thomism, for example, employs a similar notion when it treats of *substantial change* (transformation of essence) as in many cases the result of a more or less lengthy process of *accidental change*.[1]

In the present state of physics it is, however, very difficult to decide whether genuine transformations of essence, or 'qualitative' changes, as they are called in dialectical materialism, actually occur in the inorganic world, or whether this should not be confined only to the transition from inorganic to organic matter and the various transitions of organisms one into another. Thus a first reservation to be made against the dialectical materialist doctrine on this point is that it ought to distinguish more clearly between 'qualitative' and essential changes. It is certainly quite a different matter whether water is transformed into steam, or whether its atoms are assimilated by an organism. For in the latter case these atoms are subjected to new laws, which although describable in physico-chemical terms, are not explicable from them alone,[2] whereas the differences in behaviour of the individual atom inside and outside the molecular bond can be completely accounted for in terms of the quantum-physical laws operative within its electronic 'shell'. Now it is indeed possible to find in dialectical materialism an inclination to differentiate more precisely between the 'qualitative distinctions' separating the three great orders of reality (inorganic matter, life and mind), and those occurring among the various phenomena within these orders (such as that between water and oxygen). This is the case, for example, when the Soviet authors, in dealing with the origin of life, refer to matter, hitherto governed solely by the 'physico-chemical form of motion', as having now acquired a new, 'biological form of motion'; a further distinction is often drawn in this connection, moreover, between separate 'chemical' and 'physical' forms of motion.[3] Even from the dialectical materialist standpoint, it would be more consistent, therefore, to employ some term such as 'essential change' to distinguish those changes in which a new structural principle emerges ('form of motion' or 'form' in general), from those in which this does not occur, as when a molecule is split into atoms. And even if it should be

---

[1] *Cf.* P. Hoenen, S.J.: *Cosmologia*, Rome 1936, pp. 281 ff.; J. Gredt, O.S.B.: *Die aristotelisch-scholastische Philosophie*, I, Freiburg-i-B 1935, pp. 148, 267.

[2] Further details in Chapter V, *à propos* the problem of the origin of life.

[3] In *DM*, for example, p. 157.

possible in principle to account for molecular properties entirely in terms of the quantum-physical laws prevailing in the sub-atomic field, *i.e.*, to reduce them to quantitative changes, there might still be some justification, perhaps, for speaking of a 'qualitative' distinction between the molecule and its atoms, and between molecules of different substances; insofar, that is, as there are specific laws still operative in the macrophysical field, in contrast to the quantum-physical laws of microphysics; and insofar as it is possible, despite the statistical character of the latter, to arrive at truly dynamical laws in the macrophysical sphere.

This leads us to a further and more important reservation in regard to the dialectical materialist doctrine on this subject. The main thing it aims at in this law is to provide some sort of philosophical possibility that in the course of the world's evolution the 'higher' phenomena should have arisen of their own accord from the 'lower'. Now the explanation for this is said to be that, at certain 'nodal points', the hitherto purely quantitative changes necessarily become qualitative. This may indeed happen in qualitative transitions involving no 'essential change' in the sense just explained, as when a radio-active element having one quality changes into another of a different 'quality' by emission of alpha-particles. But even 'qualitative' changes of this kind are not always capable of occurring spontaneously, on their own, without the intervention of an 'efficient cause'. To return to the example, so frequently cited in this connection, about the change in aggregate state: water does not spontaneously change into steam of its own accord, but requires a cause to make it do so, namely a source of heat.

Moreover, there is an absolute necessity for such influence on the part of an extra-mundane cause as soon as it is a matter, not just of changes within the same order of reality, but of ascending to a higher one, as with the emergence of life or conscious mentality. In dealing with this law the Soviet authors proceed as if the supposition that life, for example, has arisen spontaneously from inorganic matter, were a scientifically established fact, to be taken as a starting-point in any philosophical treatment of the question and laid down as a datum for 'philosophical generalization'. We shall see in Chapter V that Soviet science is far from having provided any such proof. From the philosophical point of view, however, it must be urged against this thesis that it involves a repudiation of the principle of causality —which dialectical materialism is elsewhere resolute in defending against a variety of indeterministic tendencies in modern physics itself. For this principle not only demands a cause in general for the emergence of anything new, but also an *adequate* cause; and if we were to assume a spontaneous generation from the less perfect, the 'gain' in perfection would lack any corresponding cause, and must in fact have arisen out of nothing. But to postulate such a generation would be to credit the less perfect, which is incapable of creating out of nothing, with a genuine power of creation; and this is impossible. To ascribe such creative power to an infinite, perfect world-creator, as is done in theism, where the greatest wealth of being is situated at the world's beginning, is a notion which straightway lends itself to completion. But to set what is poorest in being, lifeless, mindless matter, at the world's beginning, and to endow it with genuine creative power, is an assumption that can only be filled out in idea, but not in thought. For it would mean surrendering the basic principles on which all thought is founded, the causal law, for example, the principle of sufficient reason and the law of contradiction; and with their abandonment, there would be equal justification for maintaining any proposition whatsoever, and all science and philosophy would be rendered impossible.

In conclusion we shall venture to refer to a matter which is not without a certain flavour of irony: Engels sought to exclude the philosophy of Nature from the system of dialectical materialism, remarking contemptuously that it replaced the real but as yet unknown interconnections in Nature by ideal, fancied ones.[1] But now it is the dialectical materialists themselves, armed with the law of transition from quantity to quality and following, moreover, in Engels' own footsteps, who plunge on impatiently like bold philosophers of Nature ahead of the advance of the positive sciences; for they not only inform us of the fact *that* higher beings have arisen by evolution from lower ones, but are also already prepared to tell us *how* this has come about— namely, by the transformation of quantity into quality.

3. THE LAW OF THE UNITY AND STRUGGLE OF OPPOSITES

Among his 'principal features' of the Marxist dialectic, Stalin assigns only fourth place to the struggle of opposites, though Engels lists it in second position and although in accounts of Soviet dialectical materialism published before 1938 it always figured first.

'Contrary to metaphysics, dialectics holds that internal contradictions are inherent in all things and phenomena of Nature, for they all have their negative and positive sides, a past and a future, something dying away and something developing; and that the struggle between these opposites, the struggle between the old and the new, between that which is dying away and that which is being born, between that which is disappearing and that which is developing, constitutes the

---

[1] F. Engels: *Ludwig Feuerbach* . . ., *MESW, II*, p. 353.

internal content of the process of development, the internal content of the transformation of quantitative changes into qualitative changes.

'The dialectical method therefore holds that the process of development from the lower to the higher takes place not as a harmonious unfolding of phenomena, but as a disclosure of the contradictions inherent in things and phenomena, as a "struggle" of opposite tendencies which operate on the basis of these contradictions.' [1]

But though Stalin actually puts this law in last position, it is still credited even nowadays with supreme importance 'as the main feature of the whole dialectical process of development'.[2] Though the law of transition from quantitative changes into qualitative may have made it clear how the evolutionary process gives rise to new and higher qualities, it still remains to be explained from whence in general the entire process of development derives its origin, and what it is that sets it in motion. To account for this, and to do so without calling on the aid of a supernatural cause, a supernatural 'First Mover', is the point and purpose of the thesis concerning the struggle of opposites.

Dialectical materialism solves the problem of where to look for the origin of motion in the world by conceiving of all motion as ultimately a 'self-movement' whose origin is supposedly derivable from the 'internal contradictions' lying hidden in each individual thing.

According to Lenin there are essentially two views of development to be found in the history of philosophy:

'The two basic (or two possible? or two historically observable?) conceptions of development (evolution) are: development as decrease and increase, as repetition, *and* development as a unity of opposites (the division of the one into mutually exclusive opposites and their reciprocal relation).' [3]

On the first view, things undergo no real inner change, but remain at bottom always the same. Their whole development, whether we are dealing with plants or animals, man or society, is reducible to a purely quantitative addition of various properties and aspects which they already possessed beforehand to a more limited extent, or at least in embryonic form. The weakness of this conception lies in its inability to account either for the origin of motion or the emergence of novelty in the process. But this is precisely what the second view does provide for:

'In the first conception of motion, *self*-movement, its *driving* force,

---

[1] *DHM*, p. 539 (English pp. 572 f., 109).   [2] *DM*, p. 195.
[3] *FT*, pp. 327 f. (*cf. On Dialectics, LSW*, XI, p. 82).

its source, its motive, remains in the shade (or this source is made *external*—God, subject, etc.). In the second conception it is to the knowledge of the *source* of *"self"*-movement that attention is chiefly directed. The first conception is lifeless, poor and dry. The second is vital. The second *alone* furnishes the key to the "self-movement" of everything in existence; it alone furnishes the key to the "leaps", to the "break in continuity", to the "transformation into the opposite", to the destruction of the old and the emergence of the new.' [1]

For Lenin, therefore, and for dialectical materialism generally, motion in the world is not to be thought of in mechanical terms— that would call for the assumption of an origin lying outside it, and eventually lead to the further assumption of a 'First Mover', a divine first cause; no—motion is to be understood in terms of 'self-movement', whose source must be looked for in the internal oppositions or 'contradictions' inherent in all things and phenomena.

In this Lenin really does nothing more than follow the lead of Engels in giving a materialistic turn to the Hegelian doctrine of 'contradiction' and 'self-movement'. Hegel deals with the theory of contradiction in the Second Book of his *Science of Logic*, and it made an extremely lasting impression on Lenin's mind.

'But it has been a fundamental prejudice of hitherto existing logic and of ordinary imagination that contradiction is a determination having less essence and immanence than identity; but indeed, if there were any question of rank, and the two determinations had to be fixed as separate, contradiction would have to be taken as the profounder and more fully essential. For as opposed to it identity is only the determination of the simple immediate, or of dead being, while contradiction is the root of all movement and life, and it is only in so far as it contains a contradiction that anything moves and has impulse and activity.' [2]

On entering this passage into his notebook, Lenin embellished it with heavy strokes in the margin and underlined the reference to contradiction as the root of all movement, so as to emphasize it further still.[3]

Thus already in Hegel we find that notion of a certain primacy of contradiction over identity which held such a fascination also for the Russian revolutionaries of an earlier generation. No less a person than Mikhail Bakunin conceived it his business to prove the primacy of the negative to the positive in the dialectic, and to end his celebrated essay *Reaction in Germany*, in the Left-Hegelian *Deutsche Jahrbücher*, with the fiery summons:

'Let us put our trust, therefore, in the eternal spirit, who shatters and

---

[1] *Ibid.*, p. 328 (82).   [2] G. W. F. Hegel: *Science of Logic*, II, pp. 66 f.
[3] *FT*, p. 113 (German, pp. 54 f.).

destroys only because he is the unfathomable and eternally creative source of all that lives. The desire to destroy is itself a creative desire.'[1]

Lenin also took over the concept of self-movement from Hegel.

'And similarly internal or self-movement, or impulse in general . . . is nothing else than the fact that something is itself and is also deficiency or the negative of itself, in one and the same respect. Abstract self-identity has no life; but the fact that the positive in itself is negativity causes it to pass outside itself and to change. Something therefore has life only in so far as it contains contradiction, and is that force which can both comprehend and endure contradiction.'[2]

The concept of 'self-movement' here established and expounded by Hegel inspired Lenin with ardent enthusiasm. After having copied out this passage he added:

'Movement and "*self*-movement" (N.B. this! An autonomous [independent], spontaneous, *internally necessary* movement), "change", "movement and being alive", "principle of all self-movement", "impulse" ("instinct") towards "movement" and "activity"—opposite to "dead being"—who would have thought that this is the core of "Hegelism", the abstract and abstruse (dreary, absurd?) business of Hegelizing? This core has had to be discovered, grasped, "rescued", peeled out, purified, and Marx and Engels have actually accomplished it.'[3]

'Metaphysics' is declared to be incapable of grasping such a conception of motion. It can only envisage motion as beginning with a push from outside, and this leads in turn to the assumption of a First Mover, an intervention on the part of a divine First Cause, who sets the world as a whole in motion by means of an incursion effected from without, as Newton required Him to do. The French materialists took a similar view of motion and thereby admitted the logical possibility of assuming a First Mover, however much they themselves rejected the idea.

And metaphysics, moreover, is incapable of rising to this conception of self-movement because it cannot grasp the existence of real contradictions inherent in things, and sides with Dühring in describing such assumptions as 'the apex of absurdity'.[4] The impossibility of real contradiction also supplies the basis for Zeno's celebrated paradoxes against the possibility of motion: a moving body can only be

---

[1] M. Bakunin: *Reaktion in Deutschland*, in *Deutsche Jahrbücher*, vol. 17, 21 Oct. 1841, p. 1002; quoted in D. Chizhevsky: *Hegel bei den Slaven*, Reichenberg 1934, p. 203.

[2] G. W. F. Hegel: *Op. cit.*, pp. 67 f.   [3] *FT*, p. 116 (57).

[4] Quoted by Engels, *Anti-Dühring*, p. 134.

in one place at any given moment—but this means that it is at rest; now since this contradiction is impossible, motion itself is impossible also. Various 20th-century Russian 'metaphysicians', such as P. Struve and V. Chernov, attempted to resolve this antinomy by asserting that there is actually no contradiction at all: if one divides up the whole course traversed by the moving body into a series of minute sections, or points, the moving body occupies a point in space at each single point in time; at one moment it is at one point, at the next moment it is at the next point, and so on. Lenin repudiated this sort of argument: it derives motion, which is continuous, from a sum of states of rest.[1]

A deviant form of the 'metaphysical' concept of motion is held to be represented by the 'equilibrium theory' (Comte, Spencer, Dühring, *et al.*), which considers a state of rest to be the normal situation and ascribes to motion only a transient, occasional significance. The source of motion, on this view, is the struggle between conflicting forces externally opposed to one another; the aim of motion, the restoration of equilibrium. The same is also supposed to hold good in the field of social development, where this equilibrium theory is exploited by opportunists in order to preach the reconciliation of class-antagonisms; the dissemination of such fallacies in Russia is especially laid by Soviet philosophy at the door of Bukharin, who relied on the equilibrium theory in accepting the possibility of peaceful coexistence between the socialist and capitalist sectors of the economy and advised waiting until 'the larger peasants have grown up into socialism'.

Now in opposition to all these 'metaphysical'' systems dialectical materialism maintains that motion in the world has the character of self-movement; its essence consists in the fact that it rests upon 'real contradictions' which find concrete expression in the fact that every individual thing and phenomenon is internally divided against itself and contains different aspects and elements in mutual opposition to one another, which impel the thing into change and motion.

Self-movement accordingly implies in the first place the presence of real contradiction, which

'is objectively present in things and processes themselves and so to speak appears in corporeal form'.[2]

Against Dühring, who had roundly described this notion as absurd, Engels argues that we fail to run up against contradictions only so long as we

'consider things as static and lifeless, each one by itself, alongside of

[1] *FT*, p. 242 (194 f.); *cf.* M. A. Leonov: *Ocherk* . . ., p. 273.
[2] *Anti-Dühring*, pp. 135 f.

and after each other. . . . We find certain qualities which are partly common to, partly diverse from, and even contradictory to each other',

but which betoken no contradiction in the things themselves, since we find them distributed among different objects. But the position is altered

'as soon as we consider things in their motion, their change, their life, their reciprocal influence on one another'.[1]

On adopting this 'dialectical' mode of approach we immediately encounter real contradictions inherent in the things themselves.

'Motion itself is a contradiction: even simple mechanical change of place can only come about through a body at one and the same moment of time being both in one place and in another place, being in one and the same place and also not in it. And the continuous assertion and simultaneous solution of this contradiction is precisely what motion is.'[2]

So too Lenin:

'Motion is the union of continuity (of space and time) and discontinuity (of space and time). Motion is a contradiction, a union of contradictions.'[3]

But this applies not only to spatial movement, but also to motion of any kind in the sense of change in general. All development is therefore a contradiction, implying as it does a union of mutability and constancy.

'When anything comes into being it does not yet exist, for it is only beginning to do so; but if we were only to say that, it would not be correct, for once it has started it is already beginning to be, *i.e.*, already exists. This means, therefore, that of anything coming into being we must maintain simultaneously both that it exists and that it does not exist. In coming-to-be there is a simultaneous union of being and not-being, *i.e.*, of opposites which directly exclude one another.'[4]

Motion and contradiction are therefore inseparable from one another. And since, as we have seen already, motion is to be understood in its broadest sense as becoming in general and also appears, in this dialectical materialist conception of it, as an essential attribute of matter (which is to say, of being in general), the presence of internal contradictions thereby becomes an ontological law of the

---

[1] *Anti-Dühring*, p. 135.   [2] *Ibid.*   [3] *FT*, p. 241 (193).
[4] M. A. Leonov: *Ocherk . . .*, p. 277.

highest and most general kind: real contradictions constitute the innermost essence of things:

'In its proper meaning, dialectics is the study of contradiction in the essence of objects as such.' [1]

In the concrete, these inner contradictions are revealed in the fact that every thing, phenomenon or process is divided within itself and has two opposite sides. Such pairs of opposites are to be met with in every sphere of reality: in mathematics—positive and negative quantities, differential and integral; in mechanics—action and reaction; in astronomy—the determination of planetary motions by centrifugal and centripetal forces; in physics—the atom as a complex unity of opposites: electrons repel one another, and so do protons, while electrons are attracted by them; positive and negative electricity and magnetic polarity are further examples of opposites bound together in unity. But it is in the field of biology especially that life presents itself as a 'contradictory process' of this type, featuring a continual cycle of accretion and destruction, assimilation and dispersal. These two opposite tendencies—the building-up of cells on the one hand and their decay on the other—constitute the basis, the condition, for the process of life.

'Life is therefore also a contradiction which is present in things and processes themselves, and which constantly asserts and solves itself; and as soon as the contradiction ceases, life too comes to an end, and death steps in.' [2]

Similarly, in Pavlov's physiology of higher nervous activity, the activity in question represents a unity of the phenomena of excitation and inhibition.[3] In the sphere of thought also, Engels remarks

'that for example the contradiction between man's inherently unlimited faculty of knowledge and its actual realization in men who are limited by their external conditions and limited also in their intellectual faculties finds its solution in what is, for us at least, and from a practical standpoint, an endless succession of generations, in infinite progress.' [4]

In the field of social life, there is the contradiction between productive forces and relations of production in the capitalist order of society, giving rise to crises and class-struggles; even such social phenomena as war participate in this all-pervading dualism, for it is the opinion of Soviet philosophy that war too, like everything else in life, has a positive side as well as a negative one: the Second World War, for

[1] *FT*, p. 237 (188).
[3] *DM*, p. 204.
[2] *Anti-Dühring*, p. 136.
[4] *Anti-Dühring*, p. 136.

example, served to exhibit governments, states and parties in their true colours, and also operated as a sort of trial by ordeal and security-test for the Soviet system itself.[1]

Dialectical materialism lays stress on the fact that this two-fold inter-relation of opposites is to be conceived, not 'eclectically', as a mere conjunction or succession, but dialectically, in the sense that these opposites are so far intertwined that the one cannot exist without the other. Not only do they not exclude one another, they presuppose and reciprocally condition each other. In the capitalist order of society, bourgeoisie and proletariat are in hostile opposition; yet they are so tied up with one another in the economic structure of capitalism, that the one class represents a condition for the other's existence. Lenin also sums up the dialectical relationship of contradiction in yet another fashion, as representing a transition from one member of the opposition into the other:

'*Dialectics* is the theory of how *opposites* can be and commonly are *identical* (how they become so)—under what conditions they remain identical when changing into one another.' [2]

But although opposites or real 'contradictions' form a dialectical unity, Lenin expressly emphasizes that in the dialectical relationship of material presupposition and exclusion so constituted, it is the conflict rather than the unity which takes first place:

'The unity (coincidence, identity, resultant) of opposites is conditional, temporary, transitory, relative. The struggle of mutually exclusive opposites is absolute, just as development and motion are absolute.' [3]

It is noteworthy that here too Stalin's letters on linguistics have recently brought about a shift of emphasis in favour of the stable factor of unity. As we have already seen earlier, Stalin is unequivocally of the opinion that language is a bond uniting the whole of society, which ought not to serve any one class to the detriment of the remainder. In this connection he then goes on to maintain that in general the class-struggle does not imply a disintegration of society. So long as capitalism exists the bourgeoisie and the proletariat are bound together and made dependent on each other by a mass of

[1] J. V. Stalin: *Rech' na predvybornom sobranii izbirateley Stalinskogo izbiratel'nogo okruga g. Moskvy 9 fevralya 1946*, p. 8; (English in *Speeches Delivered at Meetings of Voters of the Stalin Electoral District, Moscow*, Moscow 1950, pp. 25 f.); on contradiction, as dealt with in this section, *cf.* also V. I. Lenin: *FT*, pp. 327 f. (*On Dialectics, LSW*, XI, pp. 81 f.), F. Engels: *Anti-Dühring*, pp. 134 ff., M. V. Vol'fson–G. M. Gak: *Ocherki* . . ., p. 43, *DM*, pp. 195 ff.
[2] *FT*, p. 83 (26).   [3] *FT*, p. 328 (*On Dialectics, LSW* XI, p. 82).

economic ties. The removal of these ties would mean a cessation of all economic production, and hence the collapse of society and of the classes themselves:

'Consequently, however sharp the class struggle may be, it cannot lead to the disintegration of society.' [1]

When Stalin's letters on linguistics were discussed at a meeting of the Academic Council of the Philosophical Institute of the Academy of Sciences, V. P. Chertkov amplified this by observing that Lenin's words on the conditional character of unity had lately been misunderstood by a number of philosophers. It had clearly been forgotten

'that in dealing with the law of unity and conflict of opposites the unity (of opposites) represents a philosophical category just as much as the struggle between them'.

The hushing-up of unity and the absolute status accorded to the struggle of opposites does not lead, as is supposed by thinkers and revolutionaries of a primitive-anarchist turn of mind, to a strengthening of the idea of development, but on the contrary makes the latter quite impossible. For if, in the course of development, the given unity is not continually displaced by a new one, the contradiction too remains perpetually one and the same. A deeper penetration into the course of Stalin's argument shows clearly, moreover, that this powerful emphasis on the reality of unity in no way points to any preaching of conciliation between the opposites. [2]

To sum up, we can do no better than cite the conception of 'self-movement' formulated by Vol'fson and Gak as follows: every phenomenon in the various orders of being contains in itself opposing elements which are mutually exclusive, and yet also presuppose and interpenetrate one another; the conflict between them conditions all development; within the bounds of the unity of any given thing a continuous accentuation of the contradiction between the opposites is always going on; once this opposition has reached a certain level, conditioned in each case by the specific quality of the thing in question, the contradiction is resolved, and the previous quality is thereupon replaced by a new one, with new internal contradictions. [3]

As may easily be seen from the foregoing, the true meaning of the law of the unity and struggle of opposites consists in providing a

---

[1] J. V. Stalin: *Marxizm i voprosy yazykoznaniya*, p. 39 (English, p. 26).

[2] *VF*, 1950, 2, p. 364. More recently, too, since Stalin's death, a number of Soviet philosophers have several times been accused of leaving the 'unity' out of the formula of the 'Unity and Struggle of Opposites'; *cf. VF*, 1954, 3, p. 181; 1954, 4, p. 205; 1954, 5, p. 9.

[3] M. V. Vol'fson–G. M. Gak: *Ocherki . . .*, p. 47.

philosophical justification for the social phenomena of class-war and revolution discovered by Marx. What was originally regarded by Marx as a law of social development has here been transformed into an ontological law of being having universal application.

But in the process, this law also becomes a thorn in the side of bolshevik theory itself. For if it possesses the universal character of a general law of being, it must now apply in the social field, not only to capitalism, but also to the socialist and communist orders of society. Their development too must proceed at the instigation of inner 'contradictions', unless we are prepared to conclude that with the onset of communism all development completely ceases, and that human history itself, and not merely the prologue thereto, has come to an end. There was need, therefore, to draw the sting from this law and discover new incentives to social development, new forms of the 'conflict' of opposites which should at the same time be a conflict no longer. This was effected by the *distinction of 'antagonistic' from 'non-antagonistic contradictions'*.

In the discussion on Alexandrov's book, Zhdanov asserted, among other things:

'In our Soviet society, where antagonistic classes have been eliminated, the struggle between the old and the new, and consequently the development from the lower to the higher, proceeds not in the form of struggle between antagonistic classes and of cataclysms, as is the case under capitalism, but in the form of criticism and self-criticism, which is the real motive force of our development, a powerful instrument in the hands of the Party. This is incontestably a new form of movement, a new type of development, a new dialectical law.' [1]

The law of the unity and conflict of opposites therefore operates differently in a society composed of antagonistic classes to the way it does in a society where class-antagonisms no longer exist.

'Antagonistic contradictions' are taken to be 'contradictions founded on the irreconcilable interests of hostile classes, groups and forces', whereas 'non-antagonistic contradictions' are those 'which have no hostile classes with directly conflicting interests behind them, contradictions, not on fundamental issues, but on current points of detail'.[2]

The first include the conflicts between the bourgeoisie and the proletariat, or between the various imperialist powers. During the period of transition in the Soviet Union, such antagonisms existed between the workers and smallholders on the one side, and the urban bour-

---

[1] *Bol'shevik*, 1947, 16, p. 21 (*On Literature . . .*, pp. 107 f.).
[2] *KFS*, p. 15.

geoisie and the wealthier peasant class (the *kulaks*) on the other. Prior to the establishment of socialism in the Soviet Union (1936), there were non-antagonistic contradictions between the workers and the smallholders, who still possessed some property; and since that time there have also been other such conflicts, between the more and the less progressive elements, for example, or between men's socialist way of life and certain survivals of capitalism in their consciousness. All contradictions can be resolved only by a struggle; but while the first type can be dealt with only by the violent methods of war or revolution, it is characteristic of the second that they do not necessarily have to develop to the point of hostile opposition, and that the struggle between the parties does not rise to the level of open conflict.[1]

The question of contradictions in the socialist society has lately been the subject of an animated discussion among the Soviet philosophers, touched off by an article in *Voprosy filosofii* by Ts. A. Stepanyan: *Contradictions in the Development of Socialist Society and the Means of Resolving Them.*[2] Stepanyan begins his account with a definition of the concept of 'contradiction' which he differentiates from various fallacious conceptions of it:[3]

'Contradiction is a division within unity and a struggle between the various internally connected aspects and tendencies of objects and phenomena in the objective world.'[4]

Difference, contrariety and conflict are separate manifestations of contradiction. Every concrete contradiction goes through three stages in its development: origin, growth and resolution.[5] Stepanyan allows for the possibility of conflict in both antagonistic and non-antagonistic contradictions. It is the error of the 'no-conflict theory' that it fails to take this into account. But he considers that there is a most essential difference between these two types of conflict. Those in antagonistic forms of society express the fundamental economic

---

[1] *Ibid.*
[2] Ts. A. Stepanyan: *Protivorechiya v razvitii sotsialisticheskogo obshchestva i puti ikh preodoleniya*, VF, 1955, 2, pp. 69–86.
[3] Of particular interest here is the notion attributed to the 'menshevizing idealists', namely that all development goes through four stages: identity, difference, contradiction and contrariety; Stepanyan rejects this view, since in this case contradiction cannot be the source of motion, at least in the first two stages. It is interesting to note that one participant in the discussion was prepared to defend this view, provided it was rightly understood. (*Cf.* I. S. Perlov: *Neobkhodim konkretny podkhod k voprosu o protivorechiyakh* (The Problem of Contradictions must be Approached Concretely), VF, 1956, 4, pp. 164–9).
[4] Ts. A. Stepanyan: *Op. cit.*, p. 73. [5] *Ibid.*

and political interests of social groups; they are more enduring and are resolved in violent collision; in non-antagonistic societies, however, they relate, not to the economic interests of whole groups, but to the attitude of the individual towards society or to other individuals; they are therefore very easily resolved, thanks to the unity of the people as a whole.[1]

As for the special case of contradictions within the socialist society, Stepanyan distinguishes them according to the following three features: (a) they are non-antagonistic; (b) they are contradictions of growth, occurring throughout the whole formation of the socialist order, and not merely at the beginning, as is the case with capitalism; (c) they do not lead, as happened under previous social orders, to an eventual collapse of the production-relations of the existing (socialist and communist) order, but to a continual perfecting of the same.

These three traits are paralleled by the specific manner in which such contradictions are resolved under socialism: (a) they are settled, not by a violent upheaval ('explosion'), but gradually, by means of a planned development of social production; (b) they are disclosed and dealt with, not by way of the class-struggle, but through criticism and self-criticism and the establishment of new driving-forces for the development of Soviet society; (c) they are eliminated, not as in capitalism, by a revolutionary destruction of the existing order, through mass pressure from below, but by degrees, without 'explosions', the initiative proceeding from above, from Party and government.[2]

So far as the socialist mode of production is concerned, it too, according to Stepanyan, is subject to the general law of contradiction between the tendency to continuous advancement on the part of the productive forces, and the tendency to relative inertia and self-sufficiency on the part of the relations of production. But whereas under capitalism the result is that at a certain stage in the development of the productive forces they necessarily become fettered by the existing relations of production, this no longer happens under socialism, thanks to social ownership and correct leadership, based on an understanding of the laws of economic development:

'The progressive advance of Soviet society towards communism gives assurance that impending contradictions in the development of the socialist mode of production will be promptly discovered and disposed of.'[3]

Stepanyan also raises the question as to what constitutes the fundamental contradiction in socialist society. Contrary to the

[1] Ts. A. Stepanyan: *Op. cit.*, pp. 73 f.			[2] *Ibid.*, pp. 74 ff.
[3] *Ibid.*, p. 81.

opinion of certain Soviet authors who had sought to dismiss this issue, he argues that socialism, like capitalism, also has its underlying contradiction. It is generally agreed in Soviet circles that under capitalism it is the contradiction between the social character of production and the private character of ownership. Under socialism, according to Stepanyan, it is the

'contradiction between the limitless expansion in the requirements of the population as a whole, and the level of development attained at any given time in the production of material and cultural goods'.[1]

It is this contradiction which provides a continual spur to economic development. The intention here is to keep in line with the Stalinist formulation of the basic economic law of socialism:

'the securing of the maximum satisfaction of the constantly rising material and cultural requirements of the whole of society through the continuous expansion and perfection of socialist production on the basis of higher techniques'.[2]

It would carry us too far to enter in detail into the various rejoinders provoked by Stepanyan's article.[3] Much of what was said has more to do with historical materialism and political economy. And many of the criticisms and amplifications brought forward, though often of great interest, are more in the nature of personal opinions; the whole controversy appears to be still too fluid to allow even the statements generally agreed upon to be treated as representing the main current in Soviet philosophy. As it is, Stepanyan's observations coincide, at least in broad outline, with what have long been generally accepted points of view.[4]

Among non-antagonistic contradictions in the socialist Soviet society, chief importance is still assigned to the antitheses between town and country, and between mental and physical labour. Only under capitalism, according to Stalin, did these antitheses genuinely obtain. Under present conditions in the Soviet Union it is more a matter of 'essential distinctions'; where the mutual relations of town and country are concerned, it is the prevalence in industry of communal ownership of the means of production, whereas group-ownership is still the rule in agriculture. But with the transfer to communal ownership in agriculture, the 'essential' distinction between town and country will also be overcome, and all that will remain is an inessential distinction, exemplified in the difference

[1] *Ibid.*, p. 82.
[2] J. V. Stalin: *Ekonomicheskie problemy* . . ., p. 95 (English, p. 45).
[3] *Cf.* especially the essays in *VF*, 1955, 6, pp. 179–190; 1956, 2, pp. 171–183; 1956, 4, pp. 157–73.
[4] *Cf.* M. A. Leonov: *Ocherk* . . ., pp. 293 ff.; *DM*, pp. 215 ff.

of working-conditions. The same applies to the division between mental and physical labour, where with the raising of the cultural level of the manual worker the 'essential' difference still remaining is supposed to disappear.[1]

In accordance with this doctrine of the non-antagonistic nature of the contradictions in socialist society, Soviet authors are continually taking issue against supporters of the 'no-conflict theory'. This was an attitude particularly widespread among writers and artists and founded on the belief that in Soviet society the only possible difference lay between good and better, and hence that there could be no contradictions or conflicts between the old and the new. This theory led to neglect of the growth-factor, and of the struggle against the survivals of capitalism in human consciousness, and thus had a harmful effect.[2]

It has already been mentioned, that the chief method of revealing and overcoming non-antagonistic contradictions consists in 'criticism and self-criticism'. It therefore becomes one of the most important *driving-forces* in the development of Soviet society. Three others are referred to by Stalin in his Report to the XVIIIth Party Congress, in which he draws a comparison between capitalist society, with its division into exploiting and exploited classes, and Soviet society with its workers, peasants and Soviet intelligentsia united in friendly collaboration:

'It is this community of interest which has formed the basis for the development of such motive forces as the moral and political unity of Soviet society, the mutual friendship of the nations of the U.S.S.R., and Soviet patriotism.' [3]

The solution of criticism and self-criticism was originally put forward by Stalin purely for the doings of the Party, especially after the XVth Party Congress, when, thanks to the final victory over the opposition, a situation had arisen which might subsequently have exposed it to the danger of resting complacently on its laurels.

'What does it mean, however, to rest on one's laurels? It means to put paid to our forward advance. In order to prevent this happening we have need of self-criticism, not the malignant and essentially counter-revolutionary criticism practised by the opposition, but an honourable, upright bolshevik self-criticism.' [4]

A more concrete expression of criticism and self-criticism in economic life is to be found in socialist emulation, the nature of

---

[1] *Cf.* J. V. Stalin: *Op. cit.*, pp. 60 ff. (pp. 32 ff.).   [2] *DM*, pp. 226 f.
[3] J. V. Stalin: *Voprosy leninizma*, 11th edn., p. 589 (English, p. 621).
[4] *Lenin i Stalin o partiynom stroitel'stve* (Lenin and Stalin on the Construction of the Party), II, p. 490; quoted in G. Fedorov: *Bor'ba . . .*, p. 45.

which is fundamentally different from the capitalist principle of competition; whereas the latter betokens a struggle of every man for himself and against the remainder, socialist emulation implies a general fellowship of the community in the struggle towards common achievement and comradely assistance for the weaker brethren on the part of the stronger, thereby giving evidence of the advance of socialist consciousness. In general, the transition from socialism to communism calls not only for increased production, but also for a transformation of consciousness, a high level of 'communist awareness',[1] which is itself to be attained by way of criticism and self-criticism. Hence the enormous importance attached to criticism, particularly in the ideological field, a fact which has been sufficiently clearly manifested in the various incursions of the Central Committee upon the theoretico-ideological front.[2]

Criticism and self-criticism are also of the greatest importance in the life and work of the Party; this is especially connected with the fact that the Bolshevik Party is the only party and must therefore itself bear the burden of discovering its own failings. Such criticism provides a safeguard against dogmatism, against the unthinking acceptance of traditional doctrines without testing them to see if they still answer to changed circumstances (this also applies, in Stalin's opinion, to the classics of Marxism; they too, he insists, must be regarded with a critical eye).[3] Lastly, criticism and self-criticism protect the tender shoots of the still emergent new against bureaucratic rough-handling on the part of the old.[4]

There is far less evidence, however, for the dialectical character of the other driving-forces in Soviet society. The first of these, as laid down by Stalin in the passage already mentioned, is the 'moral and political unity of Soviet society'. By moral and political unity is meant:

'a state of Society in which there are no social antagonisms, and in

---

[1] M. A. Leonov: *Kritika i samokritika—zakonomernost' razvitiya sovetskogo obshchestva* (Criticism and Self-Criticism—a Law of the Development of Soviet Society), in *Bol'shevik*, 1948, 5, pp. 24–36, *q.v.* pp. 29 f.

[2] *Ibid.*, pp. 30 f.

[3] *Ibid.*, p. 32. 'One cannot advance'—says Stalin in reply to the letter of a certain Comrade Razin—'and one cannot further the progress of science, without bringing critical analysis to bear on old-fashioned views and assertions on the part of certain authorities in the field. This applies not only to authorities on warfare, but also to the classics of Marxism' (cited by Leonov from *Bol'shevik*, 1947, 3, p. 7).

[4] I. S. Sharikov: *Kritika i samokritika—dvizhushchaya sila razvitiya sovetskogo obshchestva* (Criticism and Self-Criticism—a Driving-Force in the Development of Soviet Society), in *VF*, 1950, I, pp. 35–57, *q.v.* p. 45.

348 The Materialist Dialectic

which social contradictions are overcome, not in the throes of the class-struggle, but within the framework of a consciously directed policy carried through by the leading power in this society—the Bolshevik Party'.[1]

The next driving-force referred to by Stalin is 'friendship of the peoples of the Soviet Union'. The solution of the national question in the U.S.S.R., the blossoming of national and socialist cultures (cultures, that is, which are national in form and socialist in content), has given the mass-millions of all nationalities a share in the culture and leadership of the State.

'There are millions upon millions of men engaged in furthering the course of historical development, and the more there are taking an active part in this development, the more rapidly and fruitfully will the process go on.' [2]

The last of the driving-forces listed by Stalin as contributing to socialist development is that of 'Soviet patriotism'. He himself has given the 'classic' definition of Soviet patriotism in his book *On the Great Patriotic War of the Soviet Union*:

'The strength of Soviet patriotism lies in the fact that it is based not on racial or nationalistic prejudices, but on the people's profound loyalty and devotion to their Soviet motherland, on the fraternal partnership of the working people of all the nationalities in our country. Soviet patriotism harmoniously combines the national traditions of the peoples and the common vital interests of all the working people of the Soviet Union.' [3]

The influence of this factor upon historical development lies in the fact that it is the source of heroism and creative energy; the victory of the Soviet Army in the Great Patriotic War was no less due to this cause than were the cultural advances and the successful progress made in all spheres of life in the years after the war.[4]

It is significant that even after 'de-Stalinization' these incentives have remained unaltered. In his address to the XXth Party Congress, Khrushchev declared it a major task of domestic politics in the years ahead to strengthen friendship among the peoples of the Soviet Union and the moral and political unity of the Soviet people as a

---

[1] M. B. Mitin: *J. V. Stalin, korifey marxistsko–leninskoy nauki* (J. V. Stalin, a Coryphaeus of Marxist–Leninist Science), in *VF*, 1949, 2, pp. 17–39, *q.v.* p. 32.

[2] *Ibid.*

[3] J. V. Stalin: *O Velikoy Otechestvennoy voyne Sovetskogo Soyuza*, Moscow 1947[5], pp. 160 f. (English in *War Speeches*, London 1946, p. 109); *cf.* M. B. Mitin: *Op. cit.*, pp. 32 f.

[4] *Cf.* M. B. Mitin: *Op. cit.*, p. 33.

whole, as also to educate the mass-millions of the workers in the spirit of Soviet patriotism.[1]

The Communist Party itself is also reckoned among the decisive motivating forces of the Soviet society:

'It is impossible to grasp the effectiveness of the driving-forces in socialist society without stressing the quite special rôle played in the development of this effect by the Communist Party. The Party is the leading and guiding power in socialist society. It coordinates the effect of all the driving-forces in socialist society, guides them towards a single goal and uses them to strengthen and extend the development of the socialist order.' [2]

In attempting a philosophical appraisal of this basic tenet of dialectical materialism it will be advisable to deal separately with two different questions: the problem as to whether 'real contradictions' actually obtain in the world, and the problem as to the significance attaching to these real contradictions as the origin of 'self-movement' and the source of change and movement in the world.

In his study *Über die dialektische Methode*, Eduard von Hartmann sets out a series of typical fallacies which lead to the seeing of 'contradictions' where none in fact exist; the commonest are as follows:

(a) allegedly contradictory opposites fail to conflict, because they do not characterize the subject in the same respect;
(b) unity is confused with identity;
(c) the correlative character of concepts (*e.g.*, cause and effect) is confused with the notion that one is subordinate to the other.[3]

What von Hartmann here observes of the Hegelian dialectic is true to a very much greater extent of the dialectic of dialectical materialism.

Even in the examples already given[4] of the presence of real contradictions in the world, it will be evident that in the majority of cases there is really no contradiction at all. Often it is a matter of contrary opposites (positive and negative qualities in mathematics), or again the alleged contradictions do not pertain to the same subject (attraction and repulsion between sub-atomic particles: repulsion holds between electrons, attraction between protons and electrons),

---

[1] *Pravda*, 15th Feb. 1956, p. 9 (English, p. 77).

[2] F. V. Konstantinov: *Istorichesky materializm* (Historical Materialism), Moscow 1954, pp. 460 f.

[3] Berlin 1868; cited by N. O. Lossky: *Dialektichesky materializm v SSSR.*, p. 23.

[4] *Cf.* above, pp. 339 f.

or at least not in the same respect (growth and decay of cells in a living organism); polar opposites (north and south magnetism), and even the banal observation that a phenomenon (such as war) may have positive and negative consequences, are likewise designated as 'contradictions'. The confusion of 'contradiction' with 'opposite' gives pause even to the reviewer of Leonov's textbook in *Voprosy filosofii*, and he puts this error right by explaining that 'contradictions' (such as that between the social character of production and the individual character of appropriation) constitute the 'basis' of 'oppositions' (such as that between the bourgeoisie and the proletariat).[1] But this confusion between the two concepts on the part of a second- or third-rate author is no longer matter for surprise when we observe how Lenin, a 'classic' of Marxism, himself equates the concepts of 'unity' and 'identity', as may be seen from his fragment *On Dialectics*:

'The identity of opposites (their 'unity', perhaps it would be more correct to say?—although the difference between the terms identity and unity is not particularly important here. In a certain sense both are correct) is the recognition (discovery) of the contradictory, *mutually exclusive*, opposite tendencies in *all* phenomena and processes of nature (*including* mind and society).'[2]

If the majority of the examples adduced to prove the thesis that there are 'real contradictions' present in the world can therefore be excluded, there still remain the classical examples—the contradictory character of motion in space, which is supposed to lie in the fact that a body in motion both is and is not at a given 'here' at the same moment;[3] and the contradiction involved in all becoming generally, insofar as it is regarded as a unity of being and non-being. But in point of fact these arguments are nothing but a repetition of the old fallacies of Zeno, directed against the possibility of motion. The error consists in presupposing that a line is made up of points. The path of motion is a line continuously extended in one dimension; but a point has no extension in any dimension. Even if an infinite number of points be set beside one another, we do not obtain the smallest degree of extension. Hence a line is not made up of points, but belongs to a different order altogether. But for this reason also, a moving body cannot be said to be, or not to be, at any given point. There are therefore no grounds for alleging it as a 'contradiction' that a moving body both is and is not at a particular point.

The contradiction between being and non-being supposedly present in becoming, also dwindles, on closer examination, into nothing.

[1] V. P. Tugarinov, in *VF*, 1948, 2, p. 310.
[2] *FT*, p. 327; (*LSW*, XI, p. 81).   [3] *Cf.* above, pp. 336 f.

Contradiction would arise only if becoming actually were both being and non-being *simpliciter* at one and the same time, or exhibited a (restricted) being and non-being in the same respect. But the former is impossible in becoming, for being *simpliciter* is infinite being, which cannot become, since it contains no non-being from which it could come into being (*i.e.*, become); while non-being *simpliciter* is nothing, from which nothing can come; becoming always presupposes a something that becomes; the transition from nothing into being occurs, not by way of becoming, but through a *creatio ex nihilo*, an act of creation.

It follows that becoming is possible only when what becomes has being and non-being merely in a certain respect. But in this case it cannot exhibit them both *in the same respect*, which is the only way in which a contradiction could arise. For the becoming is non-being in respect of that which lies just ahead of it, and being in respect of what it has already become.

It is clear, therefore, that becoming involves no real contradiction between being and non-being, but merely a transition from a relative non-being into a relative being, from the not-yet of possibility into the being of relative reality. And this also makes it clear that the source of motion cannot lie in 'contradiction'.

But now how does this dialectical materialist thesis fare if the term 'contradiction' is taken, not in its commonly accepted sense (as in the law of contradiction, which rules out the possibility that one and the same thing should simultaneously be and not be in the same respect), but in the sense of an 'opposition'? What is to be said of those pairs of opposites which dialectical materialism produces from the various fields of reality, and by which it attempts, as already noted, to prove that 'self-movement' is everywhere prevalent in the universe? We shall disregard those examples which may definitely be pronounced ill-chosen, such as the opposition between the north and south poles of a magnet; for here there can be no question of self-movement, but at best only movement from elsewhere.

The first thing to be said of this thesis, that all motion in the world is ultimately 'self-movement' is that it does not follow, since many of the examples adduced do nothing to prove it.

It must further be objected, that dialectical materialism does not make it sufficiently clear as to whereabouts in the world we are ultimately to look for that unity of the subject which is presupposed in 'self'-movement. If the contradictions, or oppositions, from which motion results are supposed to be internal, and if the motion is taken to proceed from within the subject moved, rather than being evoked in it by an 'other', this presupposes that the subject in which motion is thus located represents a substantial unity. Thus if all motion in the world is to be regarded as 'self-movement', this would imply that the world as a whole forms a substantial unity and that all the things in it not only stand in some sort of relation to one another, thereby forming a unity of system merely, but together constitute the substantial unity of a single subject; and hence that not only the whole of inorganic Nature, but organisms also—men included—are not separate entities, but merely various determinations of the one world-substance. But does dialectical materialism really wish to maintain this? No definite answer is vouchsafed to this question. There is talk, indeed, of the 'material unity of the world', but as we have already pointed out, unity here means likeness, merely, rather than identity. The thesis of universal connection is also put forward as the first principal feature of the dialectic, but the unity there referred to does not extend beyond a unity of system, in which the various inter-co-ordinated objects retain their substantial individuality, so that the changes they produce in one another do not have the character of 'self-movement', but rather of movement from elsewhere, a causal operation of one thing upon *another*.

There is yet a third point to be dealt with. We may begin by leaving it an open question, whether and where self-movement occurs in the world, to what extent it may be attributed to the behaviour of living organisms (though the external influences of light, air, soil, etc., certainly play an essential part in this), and whether true self-movement is also to be found in inorganic Nature (as in radioactive breakdown, for example). But philosophically speaking one thing is certain: if there can in fact be true self-movement, it assuredly applies only to those changes where no enhancement of being is involved, as in change of position, etc.—not to any true process of becoming in the above-defined sense of a transition from relative non-being into relative being. By 'relative non-being' here we refer to being that in certain respects is already actualized, but in others, *i.e.*, in respect of the perfection of being it has still to attain, is 'not yet in being', or—in dialectical materialist terms, which are also those of Aristotle—is still in a state of 'possibility'. Now it is clear—and we shall see in the next chapter that this is also the express teaching of dialectical materialism—that the possible cannot become actual of its own accord, since non-being cannot of itself provide the being which it lacks; to maintain otherwise would be to dispense with the causal law and the principle of sufficient reason, which, as already shown, would amount to intellectual suicide. In this sense, therefore, the old rule still holds good: Everything that moves (or changes) is moved (or changed) by something else (*Quidquid movetur, ab alio movetur*).

It follows from this, that though the opposition between being and non-being, conceived as an opposition of the real principles of being, possibility and actuality, certainly makes motion (= change) internally possible, it cannot give rise to the latter. For this purpose we also require the operation of an efficient cause distinct from these two.

This leads us to a further conclusion of great importance: given that this efficient cause in turn is not a being existing from its own inner necessity, but the actualization of a possibility, it points us to a further being to which it is indebted for its emergence from possibility into actuality, and so on. But this chain of dependence cannot be prolonged indefinitely, since otherwise we should nowhere find an origin for this repeated multiplication of being, and that would imply that being in general did not exist. In pursuing this chain of dependence one must therefore arrive somewhere at a cause which has no need of being lifted into actuality by another one, since it exists by virtue of its own inner necessity and is pure actuality, pure reality, without intermixture of possibility. And such a cause we describe, in fact, as the 'First Mover' or God.

In other respects also, philosophical investigation of this key feature of the materialist dialectic will be found to lead us beyond materialism. For a philosophical analysis of this very law shows us, in fact, that there is more in material Nature than meets the eye of the materialist, namely being in space and time alone, and that on the contrary, it must also be presumed to embody ideal principles of being which are thus essentially inaccessible to all empirical methods of knowledge or to any sort of sensory experience and hence (though not intellectual in their own being) can only be grasped in intellectual cognition—principles, that is, which go to make up the inner constitution of 'matter' as it figures in spatio-temporal appearance. That the law of the 'unity of opposites' only makes sense with reference to a sphere of being untrammelled by space and time, and therefore with reference to a sphere of ideal being, has also been noted by Chizhevsky in his book *Hegel Among the Slavs*.[1] And Prokofiev likewise draws attention to this fact: if this formula of the unity of opposites is not to be reducible to the banal assertion that 'here' is one thing and 'there' another, 'now' one thing and 'then' another, 'the unity of opposites is possible *solely* and *exclusively* as a unity outside the bounds of space and time. But given the reality of such a unity, then *eo ipso* the possibility of an *ideal being* is given thereby. Thus the doctrine of the unity of internal opposites—once it is seriously thought out to the bottom—ends by demolishing the entire intellectual system of dialectical *materialism*.'[2]

And this is more than just a matter of chance. For in actual fact

---

[1] D. I. Chizhevsky: *Hegel bei den Slaven*, p. 376.

[2] P. Prokofiev: *Krizis sovetskoy filosofii* (The Crisis in Soviet Philosophy), in *Sovremennyya Zapiski*, XLIII (1930), p. 486.

the law of the unity of opposites is none other than the doctrine, inherited by German idealism, of the *Coincidentia oppositorum*, the core of German mysticism and the philosophy of Nicolas of Cusa, and the starting-point of the philosophy of identity (Schelling). There are historical reasons why this doctrine should have found such acceptance specifically on Russian soil. For idealism here looks back to neo-Platonism, with which the spiritual culture of Russia has long been intimately connected, primarily by way of the Byzantine liturgy but also through the Patristic literature. A fondness for paradox, a strongly developed feeling for the mystery of the world, are frequently to be met with, not only in Russian *philosophy*, but also in the literature and other achievements of the Russian spirit. Chizhevsky makes particular mention of the Areopagitic writings as having been a favourite spiritual text among the Russian people ever since the 14th century.

'Along with many other ideas, the writings of the Areopagite awakened again and again in the mind of the Russian reader an awareness of the paradoxical, contradictory and dynamic quality of the higher forms of being. Through these writings the Russian reader gained access to the most important of the forerunners of Hegel, Proclus, with his ideas of the dynamic character of true being and the mystical dialectical movement of the spirit. Even the triple rhythm of this dynamic, and its counterpart in true being, can be extracted by an attentive reader from the Christianized Proclus of the Areopagitica.' [1]

A strange fate for dialectical materialism! It took refuge in this law of the unity of opposites so as to be able to explain the motion and development in the world from the world itself without appealing to any higher principle, and thereby to 'liberate' mankind from all 'mysticism' and religious faith.

'The acceptance of self-movement frees us from the idealist notions of a God, a World-Spirit, a World-Soul, etc., as the source of motion and development.' [2]

And yet in fact this law lies at the heart of a centuries-old mystical tradition, and leads not only to the acknowledgement of ideal principles in the world, but more especially also to the recognition of a 'First Mover', God the Creator; or does so, rather, provided only that it is logically followed out to the end, and that philosophy is not compelled, from motives which lie outside philosophy, to shut its

---

[1] D. I. Chizhevsky: *Hegel v Rossii* (Hegel in Russia), Paris 1929, pp. 10 f.
[2] I. Razumovsky, in *BSE* (1st edn.), XXII, col., 149.

eyes and desist from further philosophical inquiry as soon as it runs up against limits of a certain kind.

4. THE LAW OF THE NEGATION OF THE NEGATION

This doctrine of dialectical materialism has had a checkered history. Engels devoted a whole chapter to it in *Anti-Dühring*; Lenin lists it as nos. 13 and 14 of the 16 elements of dialectic; and until 1938 it also figured in Soviet accounts of dialectical materialism. But for some reason or other it then fell out of favour. Even in Alexandrov's textbook on *Dialectical Materialism*, which was not published until after Stalin's death, we still find a somewhat uncertain attitude towards this law. It is mentioned in connection with the thesis as to the upward character of development, but it is emphasized that in Hegel it took an avowedly mystical form, that Hegel's idealist dialectic was sharply criticized by Marx and Engels, and hence that when they too, are frequently found using the expression 'negation of the negation', its content, in their case, is essentially different. Nowadays there are open references to a 'rehabilitation' of this law.[1] Vorobiev draws attention to an interesting 'evolution' in its treatment throughout the successive editions of Rozental'-Yudin's *Short Philosophical Dictionary*: in the first two editions (1939 and 1940), it is the *form* of ascending development (motion in a spiral) which constitutes the essence of the law, whereas in the 4th and 5th the (spiral) form has disappeared and it is the *content* (ascending development) that is chiefly referred to.

'In short, the development proceeds "in Hegelian fashion" from one extreme to the other. To begin with, on account of the form, there is insufficient attention given to the content, and then, for the sake of the content, the form is lost sight of. The restoration of the law of the negation of the negation at the present day requires that both these one sided approaches should be overcome.'[2]

This law can only be understood, however, in the opinion of the Soviet philosophers, on the basis of Engels' first two laws: the law of the unity and struggle of opposites, the central principle of the materialist dialectic, is concerned with the nature and origin of

[1] M. F. Vorobiev: *O soderzhanii i formakh zakona otritsaniya otritsaniya* (On the Content and Forms of the Law of the Negation of the Negation), in *Vestnik Leningradskogo Universiteta*, 1956, 23, pp. 57–66, *q.v.* p. 58. The tug-of-war which took place between supporters and opponents of this reintroduction of the law of the negation of the negation is fully described in H. Dahm: *Ontologische Aspekte der sowjetischen Dialektik*, in *Osteuropa*, vol. VII, No. 4 (April 1957), pp. 233–44.

[2] M. F. Vorobiev: *Op. cit.*, p. 58.

development; the second expresses the form of development as a transition from quantitative to qualitative change; while the third, the law of the negation of the negation, relates to the tendency and direction of development. The first tells us *why* development occurs, the second *how*, and the third *whither* it is going.[1]

The content of the law of the negation of the negation is briefly as follows: The sudden change to a new quality, as depicted in the law of the transformation of quantity into quality, necessarily implies the negation of the previous quality. But such a negation is not the end of the matter. The new quality also becomes in turn the starting-point for a process of development which again leads to its negation; the first negation is 'transcended' into a new one. Thus the total rhythm of the dialectical process is concluded by the negation of the negation.

This law is supposed to show how it is that, despite the negation, the dialectical process of development retains its connection with the past, does not immediately abolish or annihilate what has gone before, does not open up any 'metaphysical' gulf between past and present. Just as, in Hegel, the synthesis represents a 'transcending' of thesis and antithesis, in the dual meaning of the word, as at once a 'supersession' and a 'conservation', so likewise in dialectical material-ism, the negation of the negation' implies no immediate cancellation of the past, but a denial which preserves all that is positive in what had previously been attained.

'It is not flat negation' says Lenin, 'nor casual, thoughtless negation, nor yet the wavering, doubting negation of the sceptic, that is characteristic and essential in dialectic . . ., but negation as a moment of conjunction, as a moment of development, in which the positive is conserved'.[2]

The process of dialectical development therefore takes the form of an ascending spiral: the return to the starting-point is in each case only an apparent one; the movement may well appear to be reverting to its starting-point, but in reality it invariably regains its original position on a higher level. This peculiarity of dialectical development is numbered by Lenin under items 13 and 14 of his list of the elements of dialectic:

'Recapitulation of specific traits, features, etc., on the lower level at the higher one, and . . . apparent reversion to the old form (negation of the negation)'.[3]

Engels seeks to prove the universality of this law by pointing out

[1] M. F. Vorobiev: *Op. cit.* p. 57.
[2] *FT*, p. 197 (150).   [3] *Ibid.*, p. 193 (145); *cf.* above, p. 120.

numerous examples of such triads in Nature and history: the seed-grain which falls into the soil and passes away brings forth the plant (negation) which in turn produces new seed-grains (negation of the negation); similarly, human society develops from an original state of common ownership in land, *via* private property (negation) to a new type of common ownership under communism (negation of the negation); Engels even claimed to detect a triple rhythm of this sort in the development of human thought: from the original material-ism of Greek philosophy, by way of idealism, to dialectical material-ism, which is not just a straightforward return to the original materialism, but a return enriched by all the positive ideas worked out in the course of the history of philosophy.[1] Lenin applies the same law to an episode in the development of the Russian Social-Democratic Party; this is also worth mentioning here, since it typifies the habit, frequently observable among bolshevik writers, of dealing with political questions against a background of philo-sophical problems. At the London Congress of the Party in 1903 (at which the discussion, more especially on the first paragraph of the draft party constitution put forward by Lenin and Plekhanov, gave rise to the split between Bolsheviks and Mensheviks), it was Lenin's opinion that the development of the controversy exhibited the three-fold rhythm at work in reality: the disputes on the first paragraph (conditions of party membership; Lenin and Plekhanov were initially in a minority on this issue), became a starting-point from which the discussion turned towards other, more secondary matters (on which Lenin and Plekhanov secured a majority), only to return, enriched by the outcome of the whole debate, to its original point of departure:

'In a word, not only do oats grow according to Hegel but the Russian Social-Democrats wage war among themselves according to Hegel.' [2]

Dühring had accused Marx of erecting on the basis of this Hegelian law an *a priori* historical framework in which socio-economic conclusions were drawn from the Hegelian formula of the negation of the negation. Engels replies to this:

'It is obvious that in describing any evolutionary process as the negation of the negation I do not say anything concerning the *particular* process of development, for example, of the grain of barley from germination to the death of the fruit-bearing plant. For, as the integral calculus also is a negation of the negation, if I said

[1] *Anti-Dühring*, pp. 152 ff.
[2] V. I. Lenin: *Shag vpered, dva shaga nazad* (One Step Forward, Two Steps Back); *Sochineniya VII*[4], p. 380 (*LSW*, II, p. 463).

anything of the sort I should only be making the nonsensical statement that the life-process of a barley plant was the integral calculus or for that matter that it was socialism. That, however, is what the metaphysicians are constantly trying to impute to dialectics. When I say that all these processes are the negation of the negation, I bring them all together under this one law of motion, and for this very reason I leave out of account the peculiarities of each separate individual process.' [1]

In Russia a similar objection to Marxism had been put forward by Mikhailovsky, who insisted against Marx that his arguments for the inevitability of communism were all supported 'exclusively on the end of the three-fold Hegelian chain'. [2] In his *What the 'Friends of the People' Are and How they Fight the Social-Democrats,* Lenin stresses

'that Marx never even thought of "proving" anything by means of Hegelian triads, that Marx only studied and investigated the real process, and that he regarded the conformity of a theory to reality as its only criterion. If, however, it sometimes transpired that the development of any particular social phenomenon conformed with the Hegelian scheme, namely, thesis—negation—negation of the negation, there is nothing at all surprising in this, for it is no rare thing in Nature generally.' [3]

After Marx's inversion of the Hegelian dialectic, Lenin no longer regards the triads as having any important part to play; they are merely a 'lid' and a 'skin'. [4]

Within Soviet philosophy the mechanists were accused in their day of having interpreted the negation of the negation to signify a restoration of equilibrium; [5] Bukharin, for example, thought of synthesis, not as the negation of the negation, but as a 'reconciliation' of opposites:

'a unifying position, in which contradictions are reconciled'. [6]

The same objection was also brought against 'menshevizing idealism', Deborin, for example, having seen in dialectical materialism a reconciliation of empiricism and rationalism, [7]

Since the rehabilitation of this law in Soviet philosophy, a number of authors have made very interesting attempts to give it a deeper philosophical meaning. The Leningrad University journal (*Vestnik Leningradskogo Universiteta*) devoted the whole philosophical

---

[1] *Anti-Dühring*, pp. 157 f.
[2] Quoted in *BSE* (1st edn.), XXII, col. 165.
[3] V. I. Lenin: *Socheniniya*, I, p. 146; (*LSW*, XI, p. 443).
[4] *Cf.* above, p. 311.   [5] *Cf.* above, p. 147.
[6] Quoted in *BSE* (1st edn.), XXII, col. 165.   [7] *Ibid.*, col. 166.

section of its 23rd number in 1956 to an examination of the law. In the essay by M. F. Vorobiev it is declared to operate in a two-fold form. A notable feature of this inquiry is that the author sets out from a statement by a new classic authority—Mao Tse-Tung:

'Of the two contradictory aspects, one must be the principal and the other secondary. The principal aspect is that which plays the leading rôle in the contradiction. The quality of a thing is mainly determined by the principal aspect of the contradiction that has taken the dominant position.' [1]

Thus in Hegel, for example, the process of coming-to-be is a unity of being and non-being under the form of being, whereas passing-away is a unity of the same determinations under the form of non-being. Mao Tse-Tung infers from this that qualitative change in a thing is bound up with change in the dominant aspect of the contradiction. Vorobiev concludes, in consequence, that in the qualitative leap the previously dominant aspect becomes subordinate, and *vice versa*,

'which produces a radical change in the old qualitative determination and likewise conditions its transition into a new, higher and thus *opposed* qualitative determination'. [2]

The leap therefore appears in regard to the previous qualitative determination as a negation. Since the latter is an intrinsically contradictory process, a unity of destruction of the old and construction of the new, a two-fold phase or moment must be distinguished within it: destructive and constructive negation. Vorobiev bases this distinction on a passage in Hegel's logic:

'Here the *first* negation (negation in *general*) must carefully be distinguished from the second, the negation of negation, which is concrete and *absolute* negativity, while the first is only *abstract* negativity.' [3]

This leap of negation, in the unity of its two moments, abstract and concrete negation, represents the intervening link between two qualitative determinations, the transition from the old form to a new one. Vorobiev illustrates this by concrete examples drawn from the history of the Russian revolution. The dissolution of the old form of marriage and the family led, immediately after the Revolution, to a brief phase of total negation for both, when certain left-wing radical elements wanted to abolish marriage and the family altogether

[1] Mao Tse-Tung: *Selected Works*, II, London 1954, p. 37; quoted in M. F. Vorobiev: *Op. cit.*, pp. 58 f.
[2] M. F. Vorobiev: *Op. cit.*, p. 60.
[3] G. W. F. Hegel: *Science of Logic*, I, p. 128.

'in the name of what were held to be genuinely free and truly socialist relations between the sexes'.[1]

But Vorobiev also thinks he can show that here there is bound to be that apparent reversion to the old, albeit at a new level, which Lenin regards as characteristic of this law:

'The result of the leap, as a fundamental qualitative change, is a transition of the object into its opposite and the emergence of a new qualitative determination. The transition of a phenomenon into its opposite not only presupposes a distinction, but also an interconnection, a historical continuity, and hence a certain similarity of the higher stage to the lower.'[2]

From this first form of the law, Vorobiev distinguishes a second, in which the mediating factor, the transitional phase, is realized, not in the leap merely, but in a particular qualitative determination. This second form exhibits the 'reciprocal transition' of the opposites into one another, as well as the repetition of the initial stage at a higher level. As such it is the truest and most important form of the law, for here its characteristic feature, the repetition of previous stages on a higher footing, is particularly clearly manifested. Both forms bring out the character of ascending motion as movement along a spiral; but the first only exhibits individual segments of this spiral, whereas the second embraces it as a whole.[3]

The problem of how negation can give rise to a new positive determination also preoccupies the two authors of another contribution, Kazakevich and Abolentseva. Following Hegel, they trace this positive determination of the new content to the fact that it results from a *determinate* denial, the denial of a determinate content.

Unlike 'metaphysical' denial, the dialectical variety does not come from without, or originate outside the process in question.

' "Naked" denial is therefore characteristic of metaphysics: here "not-A" annihilates "A"; but in dialectical denial, "not-A" signifies the next stage of development, which certainly negates "A", but also arises from it in doing so. Negated and negating are conjoined and mutually conditioned. The one emerges from the other, the other passes over into the one. Socialism emerges from capitalism, and could not, as Fourier, for example, maintained, have come into being thousands of years earlier; capitalism is replaced by socialism in accordance with law.'[4]

---

[1] M. F. Vorobiev: *Op. cit.*, p. 61.　　[2] *Ibid.*, p. 62.　　[3] *Ibid.*, pp. 62 ff.

[4] T. A. Kazakevich, A. G. Abolentseva: *Nekotorye voprosy zakona otritsaniya otritsaniya* (Some Problems concerning the Law of the Negation of the Negation), *Vestnik Leningradskogo Universiteta*, 1956, 23, pp. 67–76, *q.v.* p. 69.

Here too, negation reveals itself, not as a destructive factor merely, but also as a factor in the build-up of the new, whereby the old is 'transcended' (and conserved) therein. But, relying on Lenin's *'Left-Wing' Communism, an Infantile Disorder*, the authors relate this 'transcendence" not only to the content, but also to the form of such processes, and draw from this an extremely topical conclusion:

'The problem of utilizing old forms is of exceptional theoretical and practical importance nowadays, in regard to the possibility, referred to at the XXth Party Congress, of utilizing the parliamentary form in the transition from capitalism to socialism.' [1]

El'meyev and Kazakov are also concerned in their essay with the problem of how negation can give rise to historical continuity (*preemstvennost'*). They find the answer to this in the dialectical doctrine that

'a thing does not pass over into any other whatsoever, into any sort of opposite, but into *its own opposite*'.

In confirmation they quote a marginal note from Lenin's *Philosophical Notebooks*:

'Very true and important, the "other" as *its own* other, development into *its own* opposite.' [2]

This doctrine likewise enables the two authors to point a very topical moral: the Soviet professions of coexistence cannot be insincere, and the Soviet Union cannot possibly harbour any of the designs imputed to it for exporting the revolution, since such ideas spring from a 'metaphysical' conception of negation.

'As a process of dialectical negation, the socialist revolution cannot be "exported" from without [*sic*—G. W.], but is the outcome of the internal development of capitalism.' [3]

In conclusion, two points of detail: what is the meaning of the two-fold negation in this law? Why is it called the 'law of the negation of the negation'? Does this duality have any real significance? According to Kazakevich and Abolentseva it certainly has. For dialectical movement is not a pure negation in which everything that arises promptly disappears again without a trace. In form, the negation of

[1] *Ibid.*, p. 68.
[2] V. Y. El'meyev, A. P. Kazakov: *Zakon otritsanlyu otritsaniya i preemstvennost' v razvitii* (The Law of the Negation of the Negation and the Continuity of Development), *Vestnik Leningradskogo Universiteta*, 1956, 23, pp. 77–84, *q.v.* p. 78; *cf. FT*, p. 245.
[3] *Ibid.*, p. 79.

the negation is meant to express the transcendence of the first negation, and in content, the conservation of all that is positive in the previous development.[1]

A further question concerns the role of the triad: starting-point—negation—negation of the negation (with some sort of reversion to the starting-point). According to our authors, all that needs stressing is that nothing can be proved by the triad.

'Marxism by no means rejects the triad, but nor is it regarded as a universal master-key which can be used to prove everything. As understood in dialectical materialism, the triad is above all an expression of the path of double negation pursued by all natural and social phenomena, as well as our knowledge, in the course of their development. The triad reflects the triple rhythm of development.'[2]

We can enter no further, unfortunately, into all the other ideas to be found in the various contributions to this number of the Leningrad University journal. Many of them are doubtless the uncommitted opinions of the authors concerned, and the whole controversy was assuredly arranged in advance. But we have sought to present some specimens from these essays in order to give an idea of the breath of fresh air which distinguishes these writings from Leningrad.[3] They have an agreeable freshness, these articles—at last one again has the sense of personal thought; for all their adherence to the basic theses of Marxist–Leninism, which here too is naturally the starting-point for philosophizing, one still has the impression that the authors have to some extent succeeded in freeing themselves from the customary stereotype. Even the frequent references back to Hegel are worthy of note. In comparison with *Voprosy filosofii*, one feels that the Leningrad writers have been able to allow themselves to strike out more boldly, whereas the central organ of the Philosophical Institute of the Academy of Sciences must naturally be more concerned with upholding the official 'line'. To be sure, even *Voprosy filosofii* has become a great deal more interesting in the last few years; but in the writings of the Leningrad philosophers one senses, in effect, a different 'style'. One astonishing thing, however, is the extraordinarily limited circulation of the *Vestnik Leningradskogo Universiteta*: whereas *Voprosy filosofii* prints 50,000 copies an issue, and even the *Vestnik Moskovskogo Universiteta*, the organ of Moscow University,

[1] T. A. Kazakevich, A. G. Abolentseva: *Op. cit.*, pp. 70 f.
[2] *Ibid.*, p. 76.
[3] We shall be able to note it again in the chapters to follow, especially in the treatment of the categories, and in the discussion on relativity theory.

at least reaches the figure of 3,300, the Leningrad University journal only runs to 1,810 copies.

To return once more to the law of the negation of the negation, the first thing that strikes us is that it should again have been hauled out of obscurity since the death of Stalin. The decisive reason for this is quite openly specified in the articles considered above:

'The nihilistic attitude towards the science and culture of bourgeois society, which has long been in evidence, was having a negative effect upon various aspects of our own practical work. The Plenum of the Party Central Committee of July 1955 forcibly condemned such an approach to the achievements of the capitalist countries, and called for an application of the best of these achievements in the fields of science and technology in the interests of communist construction.' [1]

And since such a 'nihilistic attitude' rests upon a denial of continuity in development, and betrays a 'metaphysical conception of negation', this law is at present of particularly topical significance.[2]

In all this philosophical discussion of the law, the chief interest lies, for us, in what is said as to the special character of 'dialectical negation', whereby our authors seek to explain the upward course of development. Two things are maintained in this connection: firstly, dialectical negation is supposed to give rise to a new *determination*, and then, thanks especially to the negation of the negation, to bring about an *ascent* in development, in that there is no immediate return to the starting-point, but rather a repetition of the previous stage of development at a *higher* level. But is this possible?

This must definitely be denied. For in the first place, negation, whether 'metaphysical' or 'dialectical', can do nothing more than negate, and can never produce a new determination on its own account. Negation alone merely leads from 'A' into the boundless expanse of 'not-A', but not to a determinate 'B' or 'C', etc. When Kazakevich and Abolentseva maintain in their article that in dialectical negation 'not-A' signifies the 'next stage in development', which negates 'A' and at the same time arises from it, it is misleading to designate this next stage as 'not-A', when strictly speaking it should be denoted by a *determinate* letter of the alphabet ('B', or 'C', or 'E' . . .). Moreover, it owes this new determination, not to negation, but to the previous determination of 'A'. It is equally evident that it is not 'dialectical' negation which brings about historical continuity, by transforming a thing into 'its own' opposite (El'meyev and Kazakov). If its 'own' opposite emerges, this is not the outcome of negation as such, even when qualified to some extent by the little

---

[1] V. Y. El'meyev, A. P. Kazakov: *Op. cit.*, p. 77.   [2] *Ibid.*

word 'dialectical'; it is the upshot rather, of the first determination itself, or else of some third thing.

This is still more plainly to be seen in the work of Vorobiev, in whose analysis the transition of an object into its opposite and the emergence of a new qualitative determination appears as the result of a 'leap of negation'. From his own previous analysis (founded on Mao Tse-Tung) as to how the 'leap' comes about, it follows that it is not negation as such which gives rise to a new determination, but on the contrary, that both determinations are already present from the beginning, and merely change places as a result of the 'leap of negation': the dominant becoming the subordinate, and the subordinate the dominant.

We see, therefore, that the new determination is not the product of 'negation', but is due to the first determination (or attributable to the action of a third thing). No less arbitrary is the claim that evolution moves upward on the basis of the negation of the negation. Here our first complaint must be that no sort of criterion is provided by which to assess the 'lower' and the 'higher'. The repetition of certain features of an already-traversed stage of development, plus some new features, does not necessarily imply a move *upwards*, for it might also represent a purely quantitative increase. So if an ascent should in fact be observable in evolution, some further explanation must be found for this. In point of fact, the 'negation of the negation' does not serve to *explain* even the apparent 'reversion in some respects to the old'. The Soviet authors suppose that a development, when twice transformed into its opposite, must again lead back to its starting-point. But it is arbitrary to assume that the negation of a determination must necessarily imply its transformation into its opposite; for a determination *different* from the first might also supervene, which does not require to be the *opposite* of the first. Whatever sort of determination should happen to replace the first, it would still be a negation of the latter. Hence it is clear that a twofold negation by no means necessarily lands one back at the starting-point (even at a higher level).

This law of the negation of the negation therefore provides at best a *description*, in highly general terms, of certain evolutionary processes in the world, but is in no sense an *explanation* of this evolution, nor yet, as is maintained, an explanation of the 'tendency and direction' of evolution.

As with the other three laws of the materialist dialectic already discussed, so here, too, we see how questionable is this union of materialism and dialectics. For if the subject of dialectical development is ultimately assumed to be matter, this is to treat the development in question, with its postulated progress from lower to higher, as in the last resort a process unfolding *in time*: at the outset there is *only* the poorest kind of being, and *only* at a later stage does the greater perfection appear. Any sort of proleptic influence on the part of the greater perfection thereby becomes impossible, unless one is prepared to credit the latter with some sort of real pre-existence. But in that case the whole process of development would be an illusion.

At the outset, therefore, according to dialectical materialism, we have lifeless and mindless matter, which, with the assistance of the 'materialist dialectic' and its three basic laws, is then supposed to conjure up all the higher determinations. Analysis of these laws has shown us, however, that they are none of them equal to this task. The opposition of non-being (possibility) and being (actuality) certainly makes becoming internally possible, but this alone is insufficient to bring it about; even if quantitative changes may be assumed to lead to the emergence of an essentially higher 'quality', this too is impossible without a correspondingly higher cause; and the negation of the negation, whether 'dialectically' or 'metaphysically' set forth, can never of itself give birth to a new determination, let alone, therefore, a higher one: if, on negation, a new determination arises, it is conditioned by the nature of its predecessor; and if it should belong to a higher level of being, the ascent itself is equally unthinkable without the intervention of a third factor, on a level of being at least as high as that which the 'negation of the negation' is supposed to lead up to.

The position of dialectical materialism is essentially more unfavourable, in this respect, than that of Hegel. In Hegel's logic, the unfolding of the Idea into its categories is not a temporal process. Since, on the one hand, this process is not external to the Idea, as a result thereof, but is preserved and incorporated within it, as part of its own self-realization, so too, on the other, the result of each stage in the process is always present already. But this is not the case with dialectical materialism. Since here it is matter, necessarily bound up with space and time, which figures as the subject of development, the process is a temporal one. And this rules out any sort of pre-existence or proleptic influence of the result upon the process that is yet to come.

CHAPTER IV

The Theory of Categories

THE laws of the materialist dialectic dealt with in the preceding chapter merely reproduce the most fundamental patterns of development. They require to be supplemented by the categories of this dialectic, which enrich the Marxist dialectical method with new features and aspects.[1]

In Soviet accounts of dialectical materialism appearing prior to 1938, the theory of categories normally followed, as a separate chapter, after the treatment of the basic laws of the materialist dialectic.[2] In the textbooks published after 1938, which adhered slavishly to the structure of Stalin's *Dialectical and Historical Materialism* (in which the theory of categories was omitted), the main categories were dealt with under one or other of the 'principal features' of the dialectical method, wherever they seemed, on the whole, to fit in best.[3] After Stalin's death, as people began to emancipate themselves from the authority of the above-mentioned work, the theory of categories featured as one of the most important points which were now rehandled in great detail.[4]

[1] *Cf.* M. M. Rozental', G. M. Shtraks: *Kategorii materialisticheskoy dialektiki* (The Categories of the Materialist Dialectic), Moscow 1956, p. 5.

[2] *Cf.*, for example, M. B. Mitin: *Dialektichesky materializm* (Dialectical Materialism), Moscow 1933, pp. 171 ff.; *BSE*, 1st edn., XXII, cols. 167 ff.

[3] See, for example, the textbook by M. A. Leonov: *Ocherk dialekticheskogo materializma* (Outline of Dialectical Materialism), Moscow 1948, and also that edited by G. F. Alexandrov under the title *Dialektichesky materializm*, Moscow 1954.

[4] Among the more important discussions are: *Kategorii dialekticheskogo materializma* (The Categories of Dialectical Materialism), Uchenye Zapiski Yaroslavskogo gosudarstvennogo pedagogicheskogo instituta im. K. D. Ushinskogo, vyp. XVI (XXVI), edited by G. M. Shtraks, N. V.

The concept of 'category' is not very accurately formulated. The *Short Philosophical Dictionary* gives the following definition: Categories represent:

'the basic logical concepts reflecting the most general and essential properties, aspects and relations of things and phenomena in reality'.[1]

Tugarinov likewise asserts:

'The philosophical categories are concepts designating the most general objects, properties, aspects and connections in reality.'[2]

If these definitions are compared with that generally employed in philosophy: The root-concepts or highest genera, from which all other concepts are derived, and which cannot themselves be referred to any higher genus, the vague nature of the Soviet definition of a 'category' immediately becomes clear.

Soviet authors commonly distinguish between the categories employed in the special sciences and philosophical categories, which retain their validity in every field of knowledge. The categories of physics, for example, include mass, substance, light, energy, atom, etc.; those of biology, life, species, inheritance, etc.[3] The basic categories of dialectical materialism, as listed by the *Short Philosophical Dictionary*, are: matter, motion, time, space, quality, quantity, reciprocal connection, contradiction, causality, necessity, form and content, essence and appearance, possibility and actuality, 'etc.' Those of historical materialism: mode of production, socio-economic formation, productive forces, production-relations, basis and superstructure, classes, revolution, etc.[4] Rozental' and Shtraks deal, in their monograph, with the following categories: appearance and essence, cause and effect, necessity and contingency, law, content and form, possibility and actuality, singular, particular and general, abstract and concrete, and historical and logical.

This catalogue of fundamental categories creates an impression of great arbitrariness. In his day, the Deborinist Gonikman had proposed 'a closed system of dialectical categories', which was to begin

Pilipenko and N. V. Medvedev, Yaroslavl' 1954; D. P. Gorsky: *O kategoriyakh materialisticheskoy dialektiki* (On the Categories of the Materialist Dialectic), *VF*, 1955, 3, pp. 17–31; V. P. Tugarinov: *Sootnoshenie kategoriy dialekticheskogo materializma* (The Correlation of the Categories of Dialectical Materialism), Leningrad 1956; and the work of Rozental'–Shtraks referred to in footnote 1 above.

[1] *KFS*, p. 186; for a similar account, see M. M. Rozental'–G. M. Shtraks: *Op. cit.*, p. 12, n. 1.
[2] V. P. Tugarinov: *Op. cit.*, p. 4.
[3] M. M. Rozental'–G. M. Shtraks: *Op. cit.*, p. 12.   [4] *KFS*, p. 186.

and also to conclude with the category of being. This point of view was at that time rejected by a resolution of the party-cell in the Institute of Red Professors.[1] Obichkin on this occasion protested against such a view, on the ground that:

'In the materialist dialectic there is no closed or complete system of categories, nor can there be such a thing. All that can be spoken of is a systematic account of the laws and categories which truly reflect the dialectic of reality, a further working-out of these, and the exploration of new categories, representing hitherto unknown forms of material motion.' [2]

This standpoint is also echoed in the latest edition of Rozental' and Yudin's *Short Philosophical Dictionary*:

'The categories of dialectical and historical materialism, like those of any other science, do not constitute a closed and unalterable system of basic concepts.' [3]

This same Rozental' insists, however, in the first chapter which forms part of his contribution to the already oft-quoted collection *The Categories of the Materialist Dialectic*, that:

'The connection and interaction of the categories, their reciprocal transitions, require us to approach them, not as a mechanical series of concepts, but as a unitary *system* of categories, having a definite inner structure and a definite order of transition from one category to another.' [4]

But how we are to imagine a 'unitary' system with a 'definite inner structure', without it also having a certain degree of closure, is not immediately evident.

Rozental' bases his demand for a 'unitary', internally structured system of categories on a passage from Engels, who in his *Dialectics of Nature* had argued that dialectical logic requires a subordination of the forms of judgement and conclusion:

'Dialectical logic, in contrast to the old, merely formal logic, is not, like the latter, content with enumerating the forms of motion of thought, *i.e.*, the various forms of judgement and conclusion, and

---

[1] *Itogi diskussii na filosofskom uchastke teoreticheskogo fronta* (Findings of the Discussion on the Philosophical Sector of the Theoretical Front), *Pravda*, 26th Jan. 1931.
[2] G. Obichkin: *Osnovnye momenty dialekticheskogo protsessa poznaniya* (The Chief Moments in the Dialectical Process of Knowledge), Moscow–Leniningrad 1933, p. 80.
[3] *KFS*, p. 186.   [4] M. M. Rozental'–G. M. Shtraks: *Op. cit.*, p. 48.

placing them side by side without any connection. On the contrary, it derives these forms out of one another, it makes one subordinate to another instead of putting them on an equal level, it develops the higher forms out of the lower.' [1]

What Engels here insists on for the forms of judgement and conclusion, Rozental' also applies to the theory of categories. They must in some way reflect the historical development of human knowledge. The question as to the part played by one or other of these categories in the various stages of this process is of first-rate importance for the theory of knowledge. When Kant opens his table of categories with those of quantity, this is already a mistake, since both the development of science and the experience of the individual in his own thinking provide evidence of the fact that qualitative relations are grasped earlier than quantitative ones: thus the qualitative differences between colours, for example, leap to the eye at once, whereas their quantitative basis, the various wave-lengths, are only grasped at a relatively late stage.[2]

A more interesting attempt, and one that is original within Soviet philosophy, to classify the categories on the basis of their subordination, has been undertaken by Professor V. P. Tugarinov of Leningrad University.[3] Like Descartes, Spinoza and Locke, and Aristotle before them (who, in addition to his well-known list of 10 categories, also postulated a threefold division into things, properties and relations), Tugarinov divides the categories into three groups:

'the group of object- or substratum- categories (Nature, being, matter, appearance), the group of categories reflecting the most general properties of Nature (motion—change—development, space—time, objective—subjective, consciousness—thought), and the extensive group of categories which give expression to the ties and relations between phenomena and the properties thereof (such as necessity—contingency, content—form, causality—purposiveness, possibility—actuality, general—particular—singular, etc.). We shall call the first group substantial, the second attributive, and the third relative (correlative) categories. Subordination also occurs among the categories of any one group within the above threefold division of the objects that make up reality.' [4]

Within the third group, according to Tugarinov, subordination

---

[1] F. Engels: *Dialectics of Nature*, p. 296.

[2] M. M. Rozental'–G. M. Shtraks: *Op. cit.*, pp. 48 f.

[3] Initially in his article, *Sootnoshenie kategoriy dialekticheskogo materializma*, in *VF*, 1956, 3, pp. 151–60, and later in expanded form in the monograph of the same title (Leningrad 1956), already listed in n. 4, p. 366 above.

[4] V. P. Tugarinov: *Sootnoshenie . . .*, Leningrad 1956, p. 17.

appears in the fact that the categories most closely associated are ordered in definite 'nests'; among these he lists:

'Quality—quantity—gradualness—leap; substratum—essentiality—appearance; content—form; general—particular—singular; identity —unity—difference—opposition—contradiction—conflict; causality — necessity — contingency — possibility — probability — actuality; necessity — purposiveness — goal — freedom; law — regularity; and objective—relative—absolute truth.' [1]

The alleged impossibility of setting up a 'closed' system of categories is defended, in the *Short Philosophical Dictionary*, on the ground that

'the number and content of the scientific categories becomes enriched in accordance with the development of objective reality and the progress of scientific knowledge', and that 'as an expression of the essential connections in reality' the categories 'must necessarily be as mobile, elastic and coherent as the objects and processes of the material world itself'.

Thus production of goods, for example, is one thing under capitalism and another under socialism. It engenders capitalism only where there is private ownership of the means of production; but where, as in the Soviet Union, the means of production are socially owned, commodity-production helps to reinforce the establishment of socialism.[2] Tugarinov is more far-sighted on this point, in that he freely acknowledges the correlation of categories to be 'stable', even though it is not absolutely stationary and immobile.

'In conformity with the demands of practice and the development of science, new categories emerge, new connections are disclosed within them, and the mutual relations of one to another grow richer and more complex.' [3]

At this stage we may leave open the question whether, with the development of science, new categories require to be added to the current list of high-level concepts (in order, for example, to take account of the facts discovered by modern quantum physics); there may be some point in supposing the theory of categories to be capable of alteration in this respect. But when such possibilities of alteration are understood to mean that one and the same category, possibility, say, has one meaning today and may perhaps have a different meaning a thousand years hence, this is a view that must be rejected as absurd. One day, perhaps, we may recognize things that are nowa-

[1] V. P. Tugarinov: *Sootnoshenie* . . ., Leningrad 1956, p. 19, n. 1.
[2] *KFS*, p. 186.   [3] V. P. Tugarinov: *Op. cit.*, p. 9.

days thought possible to be impossible, and conversely, many things will prove to be possible which are nowadays regarded as impossible. But the situation referred to under the concept of 'possible' will always remain the same, meaning by this, roughly, 'something that under given conditions can become, or be thought of as, actual'. Of the example of commodity-production it may be said that no internal change is implied in an object or phenomenon by the fact that it produces different effects under differing external circumstances.

1. APPEARANCE, ESSENCE AND LAW

The first pair of categories dealt with in the collective volume, *The Categories of the Matérialist Dialectic*, is that of 'appearance and essence'. But since the category of law presupposes that of essence, we shall discuss it here along with the other two. In Stalin's day the categories of appearance and essence were normally treated as part of the theory of knowledge.

In the knowing process and in practical activity man is primarily concerned with the individual. But scientific knowledge cannot be content with this, for its task is to detect the general and permanent, the essence, in the individual and in concrete phenomena. In practical activity man proceeds

'from knowledge of the appearance to knowledge of its essence, from the immediate and external to the mediate and internal'.[1]

The definitions which dialectical materialism attaches to the concepts of 'essence' and 'appearance' are again very inexact, being descriptions, in effect, rather than definitions:

'Essence is the internal, relatively stable aspect of objective reality, hidden under the surface of appearances and finding expression therein.'[2]

'Essence gives expression to the main features characterizing objects, their inner and most important aspects, the underlying processes that go on in them.'[3]

'Essence is the element of generality presented in appearances', it is 'the unity of the appearances'.[4]

But in order to eliminate the conception of essence as an inner substantial principle, Tugarinov locates it in a purely external similarity among things:

'Essence is the common factor exhibited in the external aspect, and in no sense an inner substance of any kind.'[5]

---

[1] M. M. Rozental'–G. M. Shtraks: *Op. cit.*, p. 63.   [2] *Ibid.*, p. 64.
[3] *KFS*, p. 472.   [4] V. P. Tugarinov: *Op. cit.*, p. 54.   [5] *Ibid.*

The category of appearance is similarly defined:

'Appearance is the outer, more mobile and changeable aspect of objective reality, and represents a form in which essence is expressed.'[1]

'Appearance is the outward expression of essence, the external form presented on the surface by the objects and processes in reality.'[2]

This distinction between essence and appearance, the conception of essence as something hidden behind the phenomena, has pervaded human thought throughout its entire history, indeed, according to dialectical materialism, a similar tendency is already to be found in the animal kingdom; the images which animals form of their own kind already manifest a rudimentary capacity for abstraction, while in cracking nuts and so forth they likewise exhibit a certain proficiency in analysis. In the course of labour, man has since released himself from the embrace of Nature and developed the ability to recognize natural laws and thereby dominate over Nature. As soon as there was anything at all resembling philosophic thought (the Eleatics), it endeavoured to seize on the essence of all things. In the Middle Ages, however, the doctrine of 'unchanging essences' endowed the concept of essence with a 'metaphysical' character, and Kant, with his doctrine of 'things-in-themselves', later opened up a deep metaphysical rift between essence and appearance, which was only bridged by Hegel's repudiation of an unchanging, immobile, otherworldly essence, and his theory of the essence as manifesting itself in the phenomena. Even so, Hegel's doctrine of essence was still an idealistic one.[3]

The category of essence first took on a 'profoundly materialistic sense' in the writings of Marx, who differed from the vulgar materialists in that he by no means rejected this category. In the Third Part of *Capital* he says quite explicitly that if the phenomenal form and the essence of things were to coincide exactly, all science would be superfluous.

Herewith some examples of this 'profoundly materialist conception' of the categories of essence and appearance: the basic contradiction in the capitalist order of society between the social character of production and the individual character of appropriation is seen as the essence which finds expression in a variety of phenomena: in the struggle between capital and labour, in economic crises, unemployment, war, etc. Labour is to be regarded, in like fashion, as the common essence in which the diversity of goods finds its unity. A further example is provided by Lenin in his polemic against Kautsky:

---

[1] Rozental'–Shtraks: *Op. cit.*, p. 64.   [2] *KFS*, p. 472.
[3] M. B. Mitin: *Dialektichesky materializm*, Moscow 1933, p. 171; *cf.* Rozental'–Shtraks: *Op. cit.*, pp. 64 ff.

'The forms of the bourgeois state are extremely varied, but in essence they are all the same: in one way or another, in the last analysis, all these states are inevitably the *dictatorship of the bourgeoisie*.'[1]

This unity of essence and appearance is conceived, however, as a 'dialectical', 'contradictory'[2] unity: the appearance is, and is not, identical with the essence, it expresses it adequately, and again it does not. Moreover, this dialectical unity of the two is realized in a mutual transformation of one into the other:

'We see the transition, the overflow, of one into the other: the essence appears, the appearance is essential.'[3]

Hence it is not enough to discover the essence merely by freeing the core from inessentials; one must also examine the motion of the essence, its becoming, its transformation into the appearance, which is also at the same time its 'actualization'.[4] Thus the essence appears, not as an immovable dead abstraction, but as the 'inner connection of appearances according to law'.[5]

The category of essence is connected with that of law. For

'law is the reflection of what is essential in the motion of the universe'.[6]

In elaborating this category, dialectical materialism sets out from the Hegelian formula: 'Law . . . is essential Appearance',[7] a definition which Lenin takes over word for word.[8] In appealing thus to the Hegelian concept of law, which represents it as a relation between the essences of things, dialectical materialism is seeking to stress that law must not be regarded as an external force standing in opposition to appearance, but as an inner tendency on the part of the phenomena themselves.

This category, too, exhibits a dialectical character. This comes out, in the first place, in the fact that law is in one respect superior to the phenomena, but in another is subordinate to them.

Law only has regard to what is constant in phenomena, the universal element; it leaves out of account the whole multitude of individual peculiarities which in fact are always bound up with particular phenomena. As Lenin therefore puts it:

'Law seizes on the constant—and hence law, any law, is narrow,

---

[1] V. I. Lenin: *Gosudarstvo i revolyutsiya* (State and Revolution), 1917; *Sochineniya*, XXV[4], p. 385; (*LSW*, VII, p. 34).
[2] Rozental'-Shtaks: *Op. cit.*, p. 71.   [3] *FT*, p. 237 (188).
[4] In Russian *osushchestvlenie* (actualization) echoes *sushchnost'* (essence).
[5] M. B. Mitin: *Op. cit.*, p. 177.   [6] *FT*, p. 127 (70).
[7] G. W. F. Hegel: *Science of Logic*, II, p. 133.
[8] *FT*, p. 127 (70).
       D.M.—N

374   *The Theory of Categories*

incomplete, approximate',[1] and 'the phenomenon is richer than the law'.[2]

On the other hand, however, the law is superior to the phenomenon, since it covers and expresses a multitude of individual instances, is necessarily realized in them, and represents the constant features of phenomena. In this sense law expresses a *deeper* knowledge of the world.[3]

Before the appearance of Stalin's last work, *Economic Problems of Socialism in the U.S.S.R.*, it was still customary to follow Engels in laying great stress on another aspect of the 'dialectical' character of law, namely on the relative, 'historical' character of both natural and social laws. As we have seen already, Engels is firmly opposed to all final solutions and eternal truths.[4] By the same token, there is a corresponding repudiation of any 'fetishistic', simple-minded view of the absolute character of law. Marx is referred to as having shown, in his *Capital*, that there are no permanent economic laws, valid for all time. And Engels has done the same for the laws of Nature, having demonstrated that

'even the universal, absolute, eternal laws of Nature . . . are essentially historical laws, historic in the sense that they emerge in different ways, under different conditions, at different stages in the development of Nature'.[5]

Thus the laws governing the life and development of plants and animals cannot be eternal, if only for the reason that it is not until organisms have arisen and the conditions for their life are present, that these laws come into play;[6] even the law that water remains fluid at a temperature from 0°–100° C. depends on the earth's state of geological evolution, and might well be subject to modification on the moon or the sun.[7]

Since the publication of the above-mentioned work of Stalin's, however, there has been little further said on this point; instead, the emphasis has all been put upon the objective character of the laws of Nature and social development, and their independence of the

---

[1] *FT*, p. 126 (70).
[2] *Ibid.*, p. 127 (71).
[3] M. A. Leonov: *Ocherk* . . ., p. 134.
[4] *Cf.* above, p. 52.
[5] V. M. Kaganov: *O svyazi i vzaimnoy obuslovlennosti yavleniy v prirode* (On the Interconnection and Interdetermination of Phenomena in Nature), in *VF*, 1949, 1, pp. 128–46, *q.v.* p. 132.
[6] *Ibid.*, pp. 132 f.
[7] F. Engels: *Dialectics of Nature*, pp. 315 f.

human will. Even the socialist society develops in accordance with objective laws.[1]

In the definition of the categories of 'essence' and 'appearance' we are again forcibly struck by that imprecision, not to say ineptitude, in the formulation of concepts, which is typical of Soviet philosophy. This is partly bound up with the fact that dialectical materialism never draws any precise distinction between thing and process, 'thing' and 'phenomenon' being frequently mentioned in the same breath as if they were synonymous. But, above all, this confusion is due to the basic attitude of dialectical materialism in consciously denying the element of stability in reality. Given such an assumption, it is naturally not easy to provide for the concepts of 'essence' and 'law'.

This is also connected with the existence of an evident conflict within dialectical materialism on precisely this point, namely between the measure of positivism already injected by Engels, and a truly philosophical treatment of the question. When Marx observes that essence and phenomenon cannot coincide, since otherwise all science would be superfluous; when dialectical materialism insists that scientific research must involve penetrating behind the external appearances into the 'depth' of things and phenomena, they are both evidently swayed, unconsciously, by the idea of something resembling a world accessible only to thought, a sort of *kosmos noetos*. But in order to avoid having to assume the existence of such ideal principles in the world, spasmodic efforts are then made to iron out this 'deeper level' on purely empirical lines, into the sum of the relations obtaining between individual things.

As for Engels' assertion that all laws are relative and have only a historically conditioned validity, the answer to that is that the absence of conditions for the application of á law offers no ground whatever for concluding that the law is invalid. The fact is, in any case, that science always takes great pains to incorporate into the formulation of its laws a statement of the conditions under which they hold good (as for instance in defining the boiling-point of water).

2. CAUSALITY AND FINALITY

One of the most important categories involved in the problem of universal connection, and the most important form of connection between phenomena in Nature and society, is that of causality.

[1] N. E. Ovander: *Ob obyektivnom kharaktere zakonov razvitiya sovetskogo sotsialisticheskogo obshchestva* (On the Objective Character of the Laws of Development in the Soviet Socialist Society), *VF*, 1953, 4, pp. 40–9.

By cause is meant 'a phenomenon which precedes another and gives rise to the latter';[1] an effect, on the other hand, is 'a phenomenon which follows upon another and constitutes its outcome'.[2] Friction causes heat, private ownership of the means of production and exploitation—causes the class-struggle. It should be noted, in this connection, that Leonov conceives the linkage of cause and effect to be a necessary one: 'The causal nexus between phenomena consists in this, that one phenomenon necessarily gives rise to another.'[3]

A distinction must be drawn between the prime cause (the deciding or determining cause), the immediate cause and the occasion, the rôle of the latter being to accelerate the emergence of the effect. If the prime cause of economic crises under capitalism is the contradiction between the social character of production and the individual character of appropriation, the immediate cause of such crises must be seen in a chronic failure of demand, while the occasion may lie in the bankruptcy of some individual bank or trust.[4]

Particular importance is also attached to the concept of 'condition'. Leonov understands by a condition 'a complex of phenomena, in whose absence a given phenomenon can neither arise nor continue to exist', 'a totality of circumstances which prepare the way for the emergence of this or that object, and determine its existence'.[5] Although these definitions are not particularly clear, and scarcely bring out the difference between a condition and a cause, Leonov nevertheless asserts quite plainly that the connection between condition and conditioned is not the same as that between cause and effect, and also produces an example to illustrate the point (air is a condition, not a cause, of human life).[6]

Dialectical materialism does indeed allow that for purposes of exact research into natural connections, cause and effect must necessarily be considered in isolation and picked out from the total web of appearances; but this has only relative significance and is permissible only on condition that, in doing so, the totality of connections and the reciprocal interaction prevailing among individual phenomena should not be left out of sight. For Engels, indeed, interaction is. the most fundamental of all categories. In dialectical materialism, Nature as a whole is seen as a vast organism, determining itself without requiring an impulse from outside. Matter is substance, and substance is *causa sui* very much as it is in Spinoza, who is consciously echoed at this point.[7] All the things in the world are in mutual con-

---

[1] M. A. Leonov: *Ocherk* . . ., p. 140.
[2] *Ibid.; cf.* Rozental'–Shtraks: *Op. cit.*, p. 93.
[3] *Ibid.;* Rozental'–Shtraks, p. 98.
[4] *Ibid.*, pp. 147 f.; Rozental'–Shtraks, p. 119.
[5] *Ibid.*, p. 124; Rozental'–Shtraks, p. 95. [6] *Ibid.*, p. 149.
[7] *Cf.* V. Ral'tsevich in *BSE* (1st. edn.) XXII, col. 187.

nection and condition one another. Here too, however, as so often before, we must again draw attention to the lack of any clear definition of the concepts involved; nowhere is it exactly stated what interaction is supposed to cover, and the term is frequently applied to situations where there is really no true interaction at all.

'It is just the same', says Engels, 'with cause and effect; these are conceptions which only have validity in their application to a particular case as such, but when we consider the particular case in its general connection with the world as a whole they merge and dissolve in the conception of universal action and interaction, in which causes and effects are constantly changing places, and what is now or here an effect becomes there or then a cause, and *vice versa*.' [1]

Owing to this fugitive character of relations of dependence within the world's interconnectedness, it is difficult to discover the causal connections operative in an individual case. Leonov gives the following rules for doing so:

(*a*) In the first place, the causal nexus between two phenomena may be indicated by their temporal succession. Here Leonov goes so far as to maintain that the cause *always* precedes its effect; to suppose it possible for cause and effect to be simultaneous would amount to allowing the entire world-process to shrivel up into a single instant. From the necessary temporal successiveness of cause and effect, Leonov goes on to infer that the cause–effect relation is not a reversible one: the effect which follows from the cause cannot be the cause of the phenomenon which precedes it; he simply fails to notice that in so saying he rules out the possibility of any true 'interaction' of the kind which dialectical materialism so emphatically declares to be of supreme importance in explaining the world-process.

(*b*) It is not every temporal succession, however, that betokens a causal nexus. Dialectical materialism is by no means disposed to argue *post hoc, ergo propter hoc*. That is taken to be the view adopted in contemporary 'bourgeois' philosophy, which thereby calls in question the ideas of causality and law and gives encouragement to every kind of superstition. Only superstitious peasants would attribute a fall of rain to a church procession, for example, and only blockheads would try to connect the appearance of the comet of 1812 with Napoleon's invasion of Russia which occurred soon afterwards. The constant succession of two phenomena may indeed point, on occasion, to a cause common to them both, as for instance with the regular succession of day and night, but even when two phenomena regularly occur together at the same time, this is no ground for presuming them to be causally connected.

[1] *Anti-Dühring*, p. 29.

(*c*) Such successions on the part of two phenomena can only be regarded as instances of causal connection where one not only precedes the other, but also gives rise to it.[1]

In addition to the category of cause, dialectical materialism is also a staunch upholder of the universal validity of the causal principle. We shall be seeing in the following chapter how energetically the latter is defended against certain exponents of modern physics. If we ask, however, for a theoretical justification of its validity, we do not get much of an answer. At best it is held sufficient to appeal, with Engels, to the mere fact of human activity, in the sense, that is, that human activity makes it possible to demonstrate the fact of causality;[2] as for instance, when we strike a match and observe that the friction first produces heat and then flame.

In developing its doctrine of causality, dialectical materialism is chiefly concerned with two views which it considers to be erroneous. One is that held by those philosophers who seek to construe causality as a purely subjective category, whether it be a question of Kant's idealism or Mach's empirio-criticism, or of the attempts made by many modern physicists to replace the causal law, like all other laws of Nature, by functional relationships, and thereby reduce them to differential equations.[3]

The other view of causality attacked by Soviet philosophy is that of the mechanists, who sought to reduce all causality to the mechanical variety. As against this, Soviet philosophy very properly insists that mechanical causality (by external impulse) is only the lowest form of causality in general, and that besides this the world also contains a whole series of other types of causal linkage, such as the chemical, the biological or the social, which differ from mechanical causality in producing qualitative changes.[4] Lenin is surprised that in Hegel's logic the problem of causality, which plays such a large part in the history of philosophy, is not treated at greater length. He finds the explanation of the fact in this, that 'causality, as we ordinarily understand it' is 'only a small portion of the universal interconnection between things'.[5]

The problem of causality also confronts the Soviet philosophers with the problem of finality: does the world contain efficient causes only, or are there final causes as well?—or, to retain the terminology of dialectical materialism, is there causality merely (this being conceived solely in terms of efficient causes), or is there also finality?

Here too, Soviet philosophy takes issue against two opposing

---

[1] M. A. Leonov: *Ocherk* . . ., pp. 143 ff.; *cf.* Rozental'–Shtraks: *Op. cit.*, pp. 97 f.
[2] F. Engels: *Dialectics of Nature*, pp. 304 f.
[3] M. A. Leonov: *Op. cit.*, p. 462; *cf. BSE* (1st edn.), XXII, col. 191.
[4] M. A. Leonov: *Op. cit.*, p. 141.   [5] *FT*, p. 136 (80).

factions and proclaims the inseparable connection of cause and purpose, bourgeois philosophy being again accused of disregarding this connection.

On the one hand there is a further assault on mechanism, which completely denies the existence of finality in the world and seeks to explain everything in terms of causality (efficient causes).

On the other, however, objection is also taken to the attempt to separate finality from causality, or even to prefer it to the latter; this being precisely what is complained of in idealism, that in contrast to the materialist conception of objective causality it brings forward the concept of 'purpose' as apparently holding sway throughout the whole of Nature. From this teleological standpoint, every phenomenon is the realization of a purpose urging it to development and completion. This is taken to be yet another relic of the religious conception of 'providence', this having been replaced, in course of the progressive development of productive forces, by the teleological mode of apprehension; the latter no longer locates the purpose outside the things themselves, but reposes it in them, a theory originally deriving from Aristotle, which subsequently gained special favour in Leibniz's monadology and theory of pre-established harmony, and has lately found expression in vitalism (Driesch).[1]

As against these conceptions, dialectical materialism puts forward its own doctrine as the 'sole scientific explanation of finality', claiming that it unifies the causal and the final modes of approach and in such a manner as to bring out the primacy of the causal mode and to offer scope for finality only as a special manifestation of causality. Dialectical materialism is

'strenuously opposed to finality in Nature and teaches that everything takes place by virtue of the operation of objective causes. Goal-seeking is only present in human behaviour, and even there it depends on man's objective conditions of existence, especially on the material living-conditions of society.'[2]

In the realm of Nature, therefore, all finality is repudiated. Admittedly, Nature furnishes a mass of examples of startling purposiveness. But since Darwin such purposiveness has been held to be causally explicable, as an outcome of 'natural selection': chance variations in organisms, which improve their adaptation to the struggle for existence, get handed down by inheritance to their descendants, whereas the less resistant individuals perish in the struggle for existence. In Soviet opinion this theory of Darwin's deals a devastating blow

---

[1] *Cf.* M. A. Leonov: *Ocherk* . . ., p. 460; M. B. Mitin: *Op. cit.*, p. 197.
[2] M. A. Leonov: *Op. cit.*, p. 458; *cf.* Rozental'–Shtraks: *Op. cit.*, pp. 108 ff.

against the teleological point of view; Engels, indeed, had already waxed ironical at the expense of the Wolffian teleology,

'according to which cats were created to eat mice, mice to be eaten by cats, and the whole of Nature to testify to the wisdom of the Creator'.[1]

In the realm of human activity, however, and especially in the social field, dialectical materialism is by no means inclined to dispute the validity of final causes. Marx and Engels considered the conscious pursuit of goals as the characteristic distinction between social activity and natural processes. We have already had occasion to notice how Marx finds in purposeful activity the essential factor which ultimately distinguishes the work of the most incompetent architect from that of the best of bees.[2] One of the most important doctrines of Marxism is actually built on the validity of final causes in the social sphere, namely the theory of the class-struggle. This is particularly true of Lenin, who fought with the utmost energy against the beliefs of certain Russian Marxists, that social development would automatically lead to socialism, the theory of *stikhiynost'* or passive waiting, and on behalf of a conscious, purposeful struggle (*soznatel'nost'*) for the socialist order of society. It was precisely this which led him to the most individual creation of his career: the Bolshevik Party, whose task it was to import consciousness and purpose into the spontaneous process of social evolution.

In appraising the dialectical materialist doctrine of causality we may again begin by acknowledging some positive merits. More especially we must applaud its defence of the objective validity of the causal concept against any sort of subjectivism, and of the universal validity of the causal law against certain tendencies in modern quantum physics, even though nothing is done to provide a theoretical justification of the causal law.

In general, too, we may accept the definitions given of the concept of cause, in spite of the fact that they not infrequently exhibit that inaccurate manner of framing concepts, so typical of Soviet philosophy and already long since familiar. The separating-out of essentially distinct types of causality in different fields of reality (mechanical, chemical, social, etc.) is also quite correct.

Finally, we must acknowledge the moderation displayed by dialectical materialism, unlike other forms of materialism, in that it does not do away at once with final causes, and does at least allow them validity in the field of human activity.

[1] F. Engels: *Dialectics of Nature*, p. 36.
[2] K. Marx: *Capital* (Everyman), I, p. 170; *cf.* above, p. 39.

Here, however, we encounter the crucial point at which dialectical materialism breaks down, in that it believes it possible to account for these evident proofs of purposiveness within the realm of Nature in purely causal terms (by reference to efficient causes only). Here it appeals to the Darwinian law of natural selection. But since the category of 'contingency' plays a part in this explanation, we must postpone examining it in greater detail for the time being.

In contending that finality is also operative in the realm of Nature, we are by no means wishing to maintain by this that it somehow replaces causality or makes it superfluous. Even where finality is at work it realizes itself by way of efficient causes. When organisms acquire a particular form adapted to their environment, when roots grow downwards, whereas the stem and branches grow up, this all takes place by virtue of the operation of efficient causes. But these efficient causes are not in themselves sufficient to explain the purposiveness in Nature. We may therefore agree with Mitin when he protests against the separation of the question 'why', from the question 'wherefore'. But we cannot accept the conclusion he draws from this:

'Any complete account of a given phenonemon, any explanation of "why" it occurs, also contains in itself the explanation of "wherefore", to what purpose the given phenomenon occurs. Once we have explained how the eyes are adapted to a purpose we have also made clear in the process "wherefore" they are so constructed.'[1]

This is simply untrue. The causal explanation of the origin of the eye tells us nothing whatever, as yet, about the purpose it serves in the organism. Nor again does a causal explanation as to the physiological changes in the organism of a migrant bird which induce it to seek a warmer climate, throw any greater light on the purpose for which it does so, namely to secure its own preservation.

3. NECESSITY AND CONTINGENCY. THE PROBLEM OF FREEDOM

In dealing with this category, dialectical materialism is confronted with a problem that has always had notably ominous implications for Marxist philosophy, since it has invariably led to the disclosure of an underlying contradiction in Marxism; this is the problem of determinism. Soviet philosophy shows itself not unskilful, however, in evading the full weight of the problem, in that it follows the example of Hegel's logic in contrasting the necessary with the 'accidental'

[1] M. B. Mitin: *Op. cit.*, p. 197.

rather than with freedom. 'Accidental', for Hegel, meant the same thing as 'contingent':

'Accordingly we consider the contingent to be what may or may not be, what may be in one way or in another, whose being or not-being, and whose being on this wise or otherwise, depends not upon itself, but on something else.' [1]

This way of putting the matter effectively reduces the problem of determinism to that of necessary and contingent being. And the Soviet philosophers' definitions of the concept of necessity are in accordance with this. The *Short Philosophical Dictionary* takes necessity to be

'that which is rooted in the essence of phenomena and processes as such, which proceeds from the inner connections and relations among things and in its fundamental aspects cannot be other than it is'.[2]

Stranger still is the definition given in the collective *Categories of the Materialist Dialectic*:

'By necessity, dialectical materialism understands that which has its cause in itself, which arises inevitably and lawfully from the essence itself, and from the inner connection among things, processes and events, and which must, in the main, inevitably occur in this fashion and not in any other way.' [3]

But when I let go of a stone and it falls to earth, this is certainly a necessary occurrence, even though the cause does not reside in the stone itself.

The concept of contingency is similarly defined:

'Contingency is that which has its ground and cause, not in itself, not in the essence of phenomena, processes, events and things as such, but in something else; something which does not arise from inner connections and relations, but from ancillary or external connections, and hence may either be or not be, may occur in this or in some other way.' [4]

The concept of necessity is a presupposition of all science: Where necessary connection is absent, says Engels in the *Dialectics of Nature* science comes to an end.

Such determinism should not, however, be interpreted too strictly. That would conflict with Lenin's campaign against the *stikhiynost'* of

[1] G. W. F. Hegel: *Encyclopaedia*, I, Logic, § 145; (*The Logic of Hegel* (tr. W. Wallace), p. 263.
[2] *KFS*, p. 325. [3] Rozental'–Shtraks: *Op. cit.*, p. 142.
[4] *Ibid.*, p. 143; repeated almost *verbatim* in *KFS*, p. 325.

the earlier Russian Marxists, whose position is denounced by the official Soviet philosophy as 'fatalism', in that it leaves no room for man's conscious activity or the proletarian struggle for emancipation.[1] In order, therefore, to provide a certain scope within Marxist determinism for the Leninist notion of *soznatel'nost'*, Soviet philosophy distinguishes between a 'mechanistic' and a 'dialectical' determinism,[2] and holds it a reproach to 'metaphysics' that it ascribes exclusive validity either to the category of necessity or else to that of contingency, whereas dialectical materialism proclaims a 'dialectical unity' of them both.

The 'abstract' mechanistic type of determinism recognizes only necessity. Such was the position of Democritus in antiquity, who asserted that men had set up the idol of chance in order to conceal their own lack of understanding. Spinoza, too, like the 'metaphysical' materialists of the 18th century, rejected the notion of contingency. The hot-bloodedness of a conqueror, the dyspepsia of a monarch, were regarded as sufficient to account for the outbreak of wars, the onset of famines and the like; the course of history hung upon the beauty of Cleopatra or the cold in Napoleon's head. Engels derided such 'metaphysics' in the *Dialectics of Nature*:

'That a particular pea-pod contains five peas and not four or six, that a particular dog's tail is five inches long and not a whit longer or shorter, . . . that last night I was bitten by a flea at four o'clock in the morning, and not at three or five o'clock, and on the right shoulder and not on the left calf', these facts are all supposedly 'produced by an irrevocable concatenation of cause and effect, by an unshatterable necessity of such a nature indeed that the gaseous sphere, from which the solar system was derived, was already so constituted that these events had to happen thus and not otherwise'.[3]

The manner in which mechanism introduced an 'abstract' determinism of this sort into Soviet philosophy was somewhat different from this, in that it supposed 'contingent' to mean 'uncaused' and therefore treated contingency as a purely subjective category, a mere product of thought, having no counterpart in objective reality.

The opposing 'metaphysical' faction, on the other hand, denies necessity and will hear of nothing except contingency; but in so doing it also denies the presence of objective law in Nature and society.

Hegel is given great credit for having attempted to bridge the gulf between necessity and contingency and to view these two categories in their dialectical unity. His idealism, however, prevented him from attaining the complete success eventually granted, for the first time,

---

[1] *Cf.* above, p. 380.   [2] *Cf.* Rozental'–Shtraks: *Op. cit.*, pp. 144 ff.
[3] F. Engels: *Dialectics of Nature*, p. 290.

to Marx and Engels. Their dialectical materialism has resulted in a truly dialectical concept of determinism, in which necessity does not exclude contingency, but combines with it to form a dialectical unity; each category presupposes the other and each transforms itself into the other. Hence contingency too has become an objective category, an objective form of the causal nexus; it is both a completion and a manifestation of necessity. For contingency does not mean, as the mechanists held, the absence of causation. Even the contingent is causally conditioned and in this sense necessary.

If that is the true state of affairs, where then does the real difference between contingency and necessity lie?

In their own day the Deborinists drew this distinction in the following manner: everything is contingent which proceeds, not from the inner nature of a thing, but as a result of 'a conjunction of the fundamental law of this thing with special laws of another order'. Thus the fact that the leader of the Russian Revolution was born in Simbirsk is not a consequence of the inner laws of development of the Russian Revolution, but a purely external and contingent fact in relation to them.[1] In this the Deborinists are following Plekhanov, who likewise allows contingency 'only at the point where necessary processes intersect'.[2]

Later Soviet philosophy does not, indeed, reject this account, but lays emphasis, rather, on the inner connection between necessity and contingency and their mutual transformation into one another.

This inner connection between necessity and contingency resides in the fact that the contingent represents a manifestation, or as Engels puts it, a completion, of necessity. Necessity pursues its course through an endless host of accidents,[3] it issues as a general tendency or pattern of evolution from out of a mass of aberrations from the main line of development, it 'emerges statistically from these contingencies, *i.e.* as the mean of a large number of facts which deviate from this mean'.[4] This concept of necessity is based on a remark made by Marx in the third volume of *Capital*, where he asserts that under capitalist conditions of production general laws only manifest themselves as prevailing tendencies. But it is not disputed that this

---

[1] Y. Sten in *Malaya Sovetskaya Entsiklopediya* (Little Soviet Encyclopaedia), V, cols. 708 f.

[2] *Cf. BSE* (1st edn.), XXII, col. 185. A similar concept of 'contingency' is frequently to be met with in modern philosophy. Heinrich Schmidt defines chance as 'the occurrence of unforeseen, unintended events, themselves causally conditioned; their causally unconditioned encounter with other events; the "intersection of one causal nexus with another" (Eisler)' (H. Schmidt: *Philosophisches Wörterbuch*, Leipzig 1934, p. 747).

[3] *Cf.* F. Engels: Letter to Bloch, 21–22 Sept. 1890 (*MESW*, II, p. 443).

[4] M. A. Leonov: *Ocherk* . . ., p. 155.

concept of necessity also holds good of the Soviet order of society; even a socialist, planned economy is not immune from accidents (harvests, for example, are necessarily governed by meteorological conditions). To be sure, the mutual relationships of necessity and contingency within Soviet society are held to be fundamentally different from those under capitalism; for under socialism economic necessity operates, not as a blind, elemental force, but as a necessity consciously taken into account.[1]

The internal connection of necessity and contingency is also seen in this, that under specific conditions the contingent becomes necessary. Darwin has shown how, in the evolution of organisms, chance variations may under certain circumstances come to figure as essential changes which can actually lead to the formation of a new type. If such originally accidental deviations prove useful to the organism in the struggle for existence, these chance effects are preserved in the course of the evolutionary process by natural selection, are hereditarily transmitted, and indeed may eventually become essential attributes. This theory of Darwin's provides, in Engels' opinion, a practical proof of the correctness of the Hegelian view that necessity and contingency are internally connected.[2] Marx makes a rather similar observation in *Capital* with regard to social life: originally, under a barter economy, the exchange of commodities between individual members of the clan was largely a matter of chance; in time, however, it became increasingly frequent and eventually developed into a necessary form of human relationship, while at the same time the system of bartering dropped out of sight as a contingent feature, a relic of a bygone age.

In many accounts of Soviet dialectical materialism the problem of freedom is also dealt with in this connection.[3] Engels concurs with Hegel's notion of freedom as 'the appreciation of necessity'.

'Freedom does not consist in the dream of independence of natural laws, but in the knowledge of these laws, and in the possibility this gives of systematically making them work towards definite ends.'[4]

'Freedom of the will therefore means nothing but the capacity to make decisions with real knowledge of the subject.'[5]

[1] *Ibid.*, pp. 155 f; *cf.* also Rozental'–Shtraks, pp. 167 ff.
[2] F. Engels: *Dialectics of Nature*, pp. 292 f.
[3] Particularly in the earlier versions. It is worth noting that both in Alexandrov's 1954 textbook on *Dialectical Materialism* and in the collective *Categories of the Materialist Dialectic*, the problem of freedom is left out of account. Tugarinov, as we have seen, relegates freedom to the category-'nest' of necessity—purposiveness—goal—freedom.
[4] *Anti-Dühring*, p. 128. [5] *Ibid.*

Plekhanov calls this definition of freedom as consciousness of necessity 'one of the most brilliant discoveries ever made by philosophic thought';[1] this concept can only be grasped by those who are really capable of thinking philosophically, and even they will do so only

'when they have cast off dualism and realize that, contrary to the assumption of the dualists, there is no gulf between the subject and the object'.[2]

This ontological unity of subject and object leads Plekhanov to the conclusion that in the consciousness of the acting subject necessity coincides with freedom and freedom with necessity; the consciousness of a lack of free-will presents itself only in the form of a

'complete subjective and objective impossibility of acting differently from the way I am acting, and when, at the same time, my actions are to me the most desirable of all other possible actions, then, in my mind, necessity becomes identified with freedom and freedom with necessity; and then, I am unfree only in the sense that I cannot disturb this identity between freedom and necessity . . . cannot feel the restraint of necessity. But such a lack of freedom is at the same time its fullest manifestation.'[3]

Plekhanov begins the exposition of his concept of freedom by observing that history shows how theories which have held human conduct to be wholly governed by necessity, and even outspokenly fatalistic doctrines, have not only been no hindrance to exceptionally energetic action in practical life, but have actually been a psychologically necessary basis for such action. He points, for example, to the followers of Mohammed, who in a short space of time subjugated an enormous part of the globe stretching from India to Spain, to the Puritans, who in energy excelled all the other parties in England in the 17th century, to Calvinism, to men like Cromwell, who regarded his actions as the fruits of the will of God, etc. By the same token the Marxist doctrine, that the due development of capitalism must necessarily lead to its own collapse and the setting-up of a socialist order of society, in no way serves as a psychological obstacle to energetic action and free participation in the process. On the contrary. The revolutionary feels himself an instrument of historical necessity and consciously puts himself at its service; he cannot help doing so, in fact, owing to his social status and his mental and moral tempera-

---

[1] G. V. Plekhanov: *K voprosu o roli lichnosti v istorii*, Moscow 1948; (English version: *The Rôle of the Individual in History*, in *Essays in Historical Materialism*, New York 1940), *q.v.* p. 9 (16).

[2] *Ibid.*, p. 9 (16 f.).   [3] *Ibid.*, pp. 8 f. (16).

ment. He passionately desires to serve as an instrument of necessity and cannot help desiring to do so. This was the psychological mood expressed in Luther's 'Here I stand, I can do no other', a mood in which lack of freewill is tantamount to a complete incapacity for inaction.

'This is an aspect of freedom, and, moreover, of freedom that has grown out of necessity, *i.e.*, to put it more correctly, it is freedom that is identical with necessity—it is necessity transformed into freedom',

this being wholly in keeping with the Hegelian conception of freedom:

'Necessity does not become freedom because it vanishes, but only because their (as yet inner) identity is manifested.' [1]

A freedom so conceived leads to liberation from that moral restraint which curbs the energy of those who have not yet been able to cast off dualism, who are unable

'to bridge the gulf between ideals and reality. Until the individual has won *this* freedom by heroic effort in philosophical thinking he does not fully belong to himself, and his mental tortures are the shameful tribute he pays to external necessity that stands opposed to him. But as soon as this individual throws off the yoke of this painful and shameful restriction he is born for a new, full and hitherto never experienced life; and his *free* actions become the *conscious and free* expression of *necessity*';

Plekhanov also appeals in this connection to Hegel, who in another passage 'very finely' remarks:

'Freedom is just this, namely, the . . . willing of nothing except itself.' [2]

Plekhanov believes the synthesis of free action and necessity in this historical process to be realized in this, that the free activity of the historical individual represents an inevitable link in the chain of inevitable events: the more the individual is imbued with consciousness of this fact, the less he wavers and the more resolute are his actions.[3] Plekhanov does not, indeed, exclude the possibility that the

---

[1] *Ibid.*, p. 10 (17) and *passim*; *cf.* G. W. F. Hegel: *Science of Logic*, II, p. 204 (slightly adapted—Tr.); on the 'transfiguration of necessity into freedom', *cf.* also *The Logic of Hegel*, pp. 282–3.

[2] G. V. Plekhanov: *Op. cit.*, pp. 10 f. (18); *cf.* G. W. F. Hegel: *Philosophy of Religion* (trans. E. B. Speirs and J. B. Sanderson), London 1895, II, p. 227.

[3] G. V. Plekhanov: *Op. cit.*, p. 6 (12).

individual may weaken and fail to do his share in realizing the inevitable process; but he is optimistically convinced that in such a case another individual, aroused perhaps by the very apathy of the first, will take his place, determined to perform what necessity requires;[1] the general course, the over-all tendencies in history, transcend the influence of historical accidents and the collaboration or non-participation of particular individuals, since they are determined by forces of an entirely different kind (economic relationships); the personal element can alter the individual shape and particular details of the historical process, but not its general course.[2]

These Plekhanovian speculations about freedom are philosophically the most important that Soviet dialectical materialism has so far produced on this subject. For the rest, the doctrine of freedom in dialectical materialism is not primarily concerned with the freedom of the individual. Just as, in the total structure of Marxist philosophy generally, the individual human personality retires into the background, the discussion being confined solely to Nature and society, so too the Marxist ideal of freedom refers, not to the private freedom of the isolated individual, but to the 'freedom' of social man in relation to Nature and the laws of his own social development. The entire historical process constitutes, in the Marxist view, a continuing ascent of humanity to an ever more perfect freedom. Man's ancestors, originally in total subjection to Nature, began, by the employment of tools, to subdue Nature to themselves, and to free themselves from her tutelage. The continued improvement of the means of production has meant a progressive liberation of mankind from their enslavement to Nature, but has led, nonetheless, to a new enslavement of men at the hands of one another. With increasing complexities of production the social relationships of production and the laws of social development have also become more complicated. The consequence has been that productive relationships have slipped out of man's control, this being particularly true of the capitalist order of society. The result is an anarchy of production leading to economic crises, unemployment, wars, etc. But Marxism will also serve to liberate mankind from this final form of slavery. By uncovering the laws of social development it offers social man the means of consciously guiding his own development.

'The seizure of the means of production by society puts an end to commodity production, and therewith to the domination of the product over the producer. Anarchy in social production is replaced by conscious organization on a planned basis. . . . And at this point, in a certain sense, man finally cuts himself off from the animal world,

---

[1] G. V. Plekhanov: *Op.* cit., p. 11 (19).   [2] *Ibid.*, p. 33 (40 ff.).

leaves the conditions of animal existence behind him and enters conditions which are really human. . . . The laws of his own social activity, which have hitherto confronted him as external, dominating laws of Nature, will then be applied by man with complete understanding, and hence will be dominated by man. . . . The objective external forces which have hitherto dominated history, will then pass under the control of men themselves. It is only from this point that men, with full consciousness, will fashion their own history. . . . It is humanity's leap from the realm of necessity into the realm of freedom.' [1]

It will be seen that dialectical materialism conceives of the problem of freedom in a purely social sense. The question which properly belongs under this head, namely the free-will of the individual as a personality, does not interest it, and is dismissed in contemptuous phrases; and here it is not only the philosophical problem that is thrust aside, but even the thing itself, namely individual freedom. The manner in which the individual is thereby unconditionally delivered over to the community emerges very clearly from a recent Soviet study on the problem of freedom and necessity:

'Dialectical materialism unmasks the typical view of contemporary bourgeois philosophy, which regards personality as something supposedly free from social and national conditions, absolutely enclosed in itself, tragically alone and retaining its pure individual content independently of the social environment. The nature of man consists, not in any sort of abstraction ("free-will", etc.), belonging to the isolated individual, but in the totality of social relations. As Lenin says, one cannot live in society and be free from it. But just as it is impossible for a personality to exist in isolation, so also is it impossible for the will to exist as something purely individual, absolutely and exclusively "mine". The Marxist–Leninist solution of the problem of the mutual relations of personality and society reveals the social content of the personal. The materialist conception of the real individual in his real community with other men does away with any sort of idealist or metaphysical notion of the freedom of the will. . . . It is not from itself alone that the human will acquires the capacity for freedom, for this will also, says Engels, itself becomes what it is by virtue of a mass of particular vital circumstances. Unlike the legendary Münchhausen, man cannot pull himself out of the water by his own hair; his consciousness reflects the social being of the class to which he belongs. Here, the dialectic of the personal and the social lies in the fact that the more a personality constitutes himself a conscious and active member of the progressive class, the more he grows

[1] *Anti-Dühring*, pp. 311–12.

in individuality and becomes capable of freedom, being in no way levelled down by this, as the reactionary sociologists attempt to show.' [1]

The problem of determinism has long been one of the most puzzling features of the Marxist system of thought: how is the preaching of 'iron laws of development' to be reconciled with the demand that all energies be enlisted in the 'last decisive struggle' for the emancipation of the working-class and the abolition of all class-distinctions? The conflict between these two factors was still further exacerbated by the personality of Lenin, the outspoken man of action, who laid the greatest emphasis on *soznatel'nost'*, which implies not merely 'consciousness' in the sense of an act of the cognitive faculty, but rather 'deliberation', conscious willing, a deliberate striving and fighting unswervingly directed towards definite goals.

Dialectical materialism attempts to break the sovereign sway of determinism by propagating a 'dialectical' determinism, in which necessity and contingency are bound together in dialectical unity; on the one hand, the contingent is necessary, since it is causally conditioned; on the other, necessity results, not from an unalterable essence, but as a statistical law based on the contingency of individual instances. On closer examination it appears, however, that 'contingency' alone is of no avail in setting limits to the domain of 'necessity', or determinism, since such contingency does not, in fact, represent an exercise of freedom.

The accidental and the necessary can only be contrasted in one of two senses: either that in which 'accidental' means 'causeless', or that in which the accidental is equated (as it is in Hegel) with the contingent. If 'accidental' were to be understood in the first sense, the reign of determinism would indeed be broken, but this would also impugn the universal validity of the causal principle, which as we have seen, would be no more acceptable to dialectical materialism than it is to us. This meaning of 'accidental' is accordingly rejected.

The only remaining possibility, therefore, is to interpret the accidental as equivalent to the contingent. But then, however, the contingent acquires a certain hypothetical necessity: it can no longer fail to exist, once the efficient causes conditioning it are put into effect. It is non-necessary only in the sense that it is brought about either by a (rational) cause operating freely within the universe, or else, if it is governed by a cause which does not belong to the sphere

---

[1] T. I. Oyzerman: *Marxistsko–leninskoe reshenie problemy svobody i neobkhodimosti* (The Marxist-Leninist Solution of the Problem of Freedom and Necessity), *VF*, 1954, 3, pp. 16–33, *q.v.* p. 27.

of spiritual being, in the sense that it forms part of a universe that does not necessarily exist.

Hence it becomes clear that contingency only sets a limit to necessity insofar as the contingent gives expression to some kind of freedom: whether it be the freedom of a spiritual being within the world, or the free intervention of a supra-mundane cause which makes intelligible the actual existence of our whole contingent universe, existing as it does without any basis of inner necessity.[1]

The accidental may, however, be understood in yet a third sense, as that which has an efficient but not a final cause, *i.e.*, as something which results from the coincidence of two phenomena, each of which, taken by itself, is occasioned by efficient causes, but whose coincidence is determined neither on natural grounds, nor teleologically by an alien final cause. Plekhanov and the Deborinists conceived of the accidental in this fashion.

Certain consequences drawn by Soviet philosophy from this essentially correct notion of contingency are deserving of further and more detailed consideration.

Firstly it must be said that such a concept of contingency does not suffice, as the Soviet philosophers imagine, to limit the scope of determinism. For here the contingent is in fact causally conditioned, and hence in that sense necessary. And as we have previously observed, the power of necessity can only be broken by freedom.

---

[1] That contingency ultimately points to freedom of some kind can be seen even from the examples, ironically cited by Engels against determinism, of the five peas in a pod and the fleabite. That this pea-pod should contain five peas, and not four or six, is in fact the immediate outcome of various mechanical, chemical or biological processes actuated by natural necessity; but that I should have picked just this pea-pod and not some other one, that the gardener should have sown just this and not some other seedling in this and not some other less fertile bed, is no longer governed deterministically, since here already the free activity of rational beings intervenes. Of the example of the fleabite it may likewise be said, that this occurrence is immediately conditioned by a series of objectively working occasioning causes of which it is the unambiguous effect; here too, in the animal kingdom (as also in the already-mentioned example of the peas, drawn from the vegetable kingdom) a certain latitude is admitted, in that the causes which uniquely determine these effects are reckoned to include, not only the external stimuli, but also the specific state of the reacting organism itself; but in this example also the series of objectively working causes is further interrupted, as before, by a number of factors deriving from free human activity: that I went to bed that night at such-and-such an hour, and not an hour earlier or later; that on the previous day I took the tram-car, on which I caught the flea, instead of going on foot, and more to the same effect. It thereby becomes obvious that the 'contingency' in these examples is precisely due to the interpolation of intramundane free causes.

A further function assigned to contingency, so conceived, is that necessity is alleged to proceed from it. What Darwin maintained in the realm of biology, that modifications originally due to chance are retained in the morphological structure of the organism and transformed by way of the struggle for existence, natural selection and inheritance into necessary characteristics of the species—this law is adopted by dialectical materialism as a universal law of being, applicable to the whole of reality: necessary laws emerge as average regularities from a multitude of lawless individual deviations from the norm.

We touch here upon one of the most difficult problems in the modern philosophy of Nature, which has been posed to us, above all, by quantum mechanics and the 'statistical laws' laid down therein: how does 'chance' give rise to law? It is not possible in the present context to investigate this whole problem in detail, but we must at least offer a few critical remarks on the way this conception of law is employed in dialectical materialism:

(*a*) Dialectical materialism attributes to the whole of Nature, and ultimately to the whole of reality, a state of affairs established in the field of biology (and here indeed we must leave open the question whether the formation of new species by way of natural selection and inheritance is actually proved; the prevailing opinion is in fact against it); but as to this it must be observed that in Darwin's postulated transition from chance to law 'necessity' does not come about by a simple repetition of accidents, for contingency is transformed, rather, into necessity by natural selection and inheritance, and chance is supplemented in the process, not only by the element of frequency, but also by that of stability; but this is only possible in the realm of organic Nature and not in that of Nature as a whole.

(*b*) It is false in any case that all natural laws are of a statistical character. The essential impossibility of interpreting elementary processes within the individual atom in terms of strict dynamical causality is due, in effect, to an intrinsic uncertainty in the determination of two complementary quantities, the position and the velocity of the electron, owing to the dualism of wave and corpuscle. This uncertainty, however, is inversely proportional to the mass of the inert particles involved, and therefore disappears on the macrophysical scale. Hence not only the astronomical laws of motion, but also the minimum principles, the conservation theorems and many other laws may be regarded, not as statistical, but as strictly dynamical in character. The question whether all natural laws are essentially statistical is one of the most difficult problems in the contemporary philosophy of Nature. Many scientists, especially those positivistically-minded ones who deny the validity of the causal principle in the microphysical sphere, are inclined to regard all laws as statistical. Others, and Planck in particular, are firmly opposed to this view.

Here we shall merely confine ourselves to observing that the practice of Soviet philosophy in treating all laws as alike statistical is extremely difficult to reconcile with its simultaneous and determined adherence to the universal validity of the causal principle.[1]

A third function assigned in Soviet philosophy to the concept of 'contingency' and its dialectical unity with necessity, is that of accounting for finality in Nature. Here too we cannot undertake to expound the problem of finality in Nature at full length, and must be content with a few critical remarks on the manner of its solution in dialectical materialism. It will be expedient in this connection to separate the field of inanimate Nature from that of the animate. In animate Nature teleology is manifested chiefly in the adaptedness of organs to the performance of specific functions, notably in phenomena relating, *inter alia*, to the preservation of the individual or the species. The dialectical materialist account of finality ('chance' variations, initially of causal origin, which have proved themselves in life are transmitted to posterity and acquired by the species), is already untenable on this ground alone, that in order to transform the 'chance', the unique, into the 'necessary', *i.e.*, the permanent and law-abiding, it is obliged to invoke inheritance to explain the establishment of the acquired characteristic and its adoption by the species; but inheritance presupposes an organism already constituted as to its being, whereas finality must be taken to underlie the original constituting of such an organism; it is not a resultant phenomenon, but an original presupposition of the organic as such.

So far as concerns the field of inanimate Nature, however, the presence of teleology, of final as well as efficient causality, is contested.[2] It is generally agreed, however, that even though there may be no reason to credit inanimate Nature with finality in the properly Aristotelian sense, it does exhibit an 'order', evinced especially in the mathematical character of natural law, and one which, no less than finality, requires explanation in terms of a supernatural intelligence.[3]

---

[1] On this, *cf.* A. Gatterer, S.J.: *Das Problem des statistischen Naturgesetzes*, Innsbruck 1924, who comes to the conclusion that natural laws of a statistical type can only hold good (outside the field of biology) within the macrocosm, but that this, however, cannot be the case unless events within the microcosm are governed by dynamical natural law (p. 46). In his essay *Zufall und Gesetz im Naturgeschehen* (*Stimmen der Zeit*, Sept. 1930, p. 439), the same author summarizes his position as follows: 'Statistical laws of averages and probability in the macrocosm, yet, not in despite of this, but precisely because of it, exact dynamical laws of Nature in the microcosm; hence, not absolute, but only relative, chance.'

[2] *Cf.* J. Seiler: *Philosophie der unbelebten Natur*, Olten 1948, p. 276.

[3] *Cf.* J. Seiler: *Op. cit.*, pp. 279 f., who after having quoted a number of scientists (such as Eddington, for example: '... at that time it was the

Even from the standpoint of dialectical materialism it is difficult to think of this order as having arisen 'by chance', as a by-product of forces operating in a purely causal fashion, for the order in question includes the element of constancy, whose appearance in the process of transition from contingency to necessity is supposedly explained by dialectical materialism as due to such factors as 'natural selection', and 'inheritance', which obviously do not apply, however, in the field of inanimate Nature. To explain the 'cosmos', the inveterate constancy of the order prevailing throughout the world by virtue of the concurrence of innumerable causal sequences, as the chance by-product of a whole multitude of blindly operating efficient causes, would be much as if one were to maintain the fact that both hands of a clock point to 12 on the dial whenever the sun is at the zenith, to be wholly explicable on purely causal grounds, namely as the product of a chance coincidence of two effects, each of them determined purely by efficient causes, the one being due to the expansion of the clock-spring and the other to the rotation of the earth.

In general we may say that the dialectical materialist doctrine of necessity and contingency does nothing to restrict determinism and tips the balance unequivocally in favour of necessity. The same is true of the relationship of necessity to freedom, in which the bias in favour of necessity is still more strongly in evidence.

As regards the doctrine of freedom, we may begin by conceding to Plekhanov that a certain historical determinism, in the shape of a law and necessity governing the development of communities, does not necessarily rule out any sort of personal, individual freedom. Thus one may think of the laws inherent in the development of the community as being in the nature of statistical laws, which do not call for a rigid determinacy in every individual case. Social laws, with their historical necessity, would then bear a certain analogy to the statistical laws governing the microcosm. Even so, there would be this difference in the statistical character of the two types of law, that in quantum mechanics the irregular behaviour of the individual case must still, in the last resort, be causally determined in some way or other, even though this determinacy may be essentially beyond the

general assumption that the creation was the work of an engineer (not of a mathematician, as is the fashion nowadays)'), sets forth his own position in the following terms: 'Since these ideas, though formulable only in mathematical terms, are no less truly determinant of the occurrence and character of things than final causes are, they may be thought of either as *causae exemplares* in the Platonic sense, or, on the suggestion of F. Renoirte, as formal causes. At all events it seems that one cannot deny these mathematical norms a genuine causal meaning, even though they are accessible only to mathematical thought.'

physicist's comprehension, whereas in the case of statistical laws of historical development the individual case is not causally determined at all, since here we are dealing with individuals of a spiritual kind who are therefore equipped with free-will. It may indeed be granted as an element of truth in the Marxist conception of history, that the personal freedom of the individual agent is not necessarily bound to exclude a certain necessity or lawfulness, capable of formulation in historical laws, within the development of the community as a whole. It needs emphasizing here, however, that this historical necessity should not be construed in too absolute a sense. The fact is, rather, that despite its 'statistical' character, and unlike the statistical laws of physics, there still remains the fundamental possibility that it may be broken through from below, in virtue of the personal freedom of individuals (as for instance, by way of an intensification of the moral pressure exerted by the mass of private individuals).

But though we may accept, with reservations, Plekhanov's claim that individual freedom is not inconsistent with a certain determinism at the communal level, the philosophical reasons he gives for this, in common with Engels and Hegel, must nevertheless be rejected. Not that we wish to maintain by this that the concept of freedom so formulated is in itself untenable (*i.e.*, the notion of freedom as a 'conscious and free expression of necessity' presupposing a transcendence of that dualism of subject and object by which the subject is confined—as in the case of Hegel's 'Freedom is . . . the willing of nothing except itself'). But such a concept of freedom presupposes an infinite Being, in whom there is no room for such limitation by an external object standing over against Him, and for whom, therefore, the Hegelian 'willing of nothing except itself' could be wholly valid. Only in such a case would the situation be realized which Plekhanov assumes to be wholly self-evident: that actions directed to the realization (establishment) of necessity should at the same time be those most desirable to the subject who performs them. But all this has no application to our empirical world or to the actual freedom of man acting in history. It would need a powerful measure of optimism to maintain, say, that a revolutionary fighting to establish the dictatorship of the proletariat would find exile and imprisonment, or even, it may be, the loss of his own life, 'the most desirable of all possible actions'. If the attainment of such goals be really the most desirable as well as the most necessary of activities, why all the vast output of persuasion and revolutionary propaganda in order to induce people to lend their 'free' support to the realization of such 'necessary' goals? It is also a piece of wholly unwarranted optimism, and one which plainly discloses the actual contingency of particular historical events, to maintain that if one individual 'fails' in refusing to lend the support required of him to the realization of the necessary goal, another individual, roused by this very failure, will infallibly spring into the breach.

Thus we certainly do not wish to deny that Plekhanov's concept of freedom as necessary self-acquiescence is an inherently possible one. But it presupposes an infinite, absolute Being. It is the concept of freedom which we find realized in God, in whom the necessity of His own self-willing coincides with complete freedom, is 'transfigured into freedom'. But in our earthly, fallen condition, to speak of freedom as 'consciousness of necessity' ultimately means nothing else, in practice, than a denial of individual freedom and its deliverance into the power of what remains, despite all the professions of dialectical materialism with regard to 'contingency' and 'freedom', a still unbroken universal determinism.

4. POSSIBILITY AND ACTUALITY

As with Aristotle and the scholastics, becoming and development are interpreted by dialectical materialism as a transformation of the possible into the actual.[1] In spite of this, the Soviet authors applaud dialectical materialism as having

'for the first time in the history of philosophy provided a scientific solution to the problem of possibility and actuality'.[2]

In the development of the concept of actuality among the Soviet philosophers, it is possible, particularly in earlier years, but to some extent also in contemporary discussions of the problem, to trace the influence of the Hegelian concept of the 'rationality of the actual'. In the first edition of the *Great Soviet Encyclopaedia*, Shcheglov emphasized in defining the concept of the 'actual', that it means

'something deeper than the mere factual presence of individual things or their immediate external existence. The category of actuality already includes within its content an expression of the totality of all the internal and external moments, the reciprocal relationships of all these aspects, which go to make up objective reality. The category of actuality gives expression to the objective world, conceived as a necessary, internally-conditioned process governed by law.'[3]

In order to be actual, therefore, it is not enough that a thing should in fact exist. Just as, with Hegel, not everything that exists is therefore actual on that account, but only that which can be regarded as the

---

[1] Cf. Rozental'–Shtraks: *Op. cit.*, p. 252.

[2] I. A. Grudinin: *Dialektichesky materializm o vozmozhnosti i deystvitel'nosti* (Dialectical Materialism on Possibility and Actuality), Moscow 1955 p. 4.

[3] A. Shcheglov in *BSE* (1st edn.), XXII, col. 192.

actualization of an idea, so too in dialectical materialism, only that is actual which comes to pass out of inner necessity in the course of the world's process of development and is in accordance with the inner law of that development.

In the Preface to his *Philosophy of Right*, Hegel made the famous statement:

'What is rational is actual and what is actual is rational.' [1]

Many of his disciples have taken this remark—thanks, so it is believed in Soviet philosophy, to its 'idealist' mode of utterance—as an endorsement of all currently existing social arrangements. In Germany the Hegelian Right construed this maxim as a justification of the Prussian monarchy; in Russia, Belinsky employed the same argument for a time in defence of the rigid absolutism of Nicholas I. The Soviet philosophers, however, are ready on occasion to allow that Hegel himself, in his *Logic* and *Encyclopaedia* at least, interprets this principle in a revolutionary sense; although at a given moment an idea may appear to be in conflict with the established order, it may yet be actual if it gives expression to a still unrealized but inevitable tendency of historical development; and by contrast, an established order may nonetheless be unactual, *i.e.*, without a title to existence, if it lacks rationality and fails to correspond to an idea.

Dialectical materialism seeks to translate this principle from its idealist context into a materialistic one by substituting 'historically necessary' in place of 'rational':

'Everything rational, or in materialist terms, everything historically necessary, must become actual.' [2]

Here, for the first time, it becomes possible to see what is meant when the category of actuality is associated, in recent Soviet treatments of the subject, with those of necessity and law:

'The category of actuality is inseparably bound up with the categories of necessity and law. . . . Marxist philosophy maintains that any given actuality is brought about through the operation of definite objective laws.' [3]

This is not to imply that the rôle of contingent factors is thereby excluded; but their effect is limited to modifying the actual in matters of subordinate detail.[4]

But dialectical materialism was not content merely to reiterate the Hegelian thesis in a materialist terminology; the simple assertion that everything actual is historically necessary proved insufficient, for the

---

[1] G. W. F. Hegel: *Philosophy of Right* (trans. T. M. Knox), p. 10.
[2] M. B. Mitin: *Op. cit.*, p. 204.
[3] Rozental'–Shtraks: *Op. cit.*, p. 262.   [4] *Ibid.*, pp. 262 f.

emergence of such tendencies as economism and mechanism in Russian Marxism made it necessary to guard historical materialism against the danger of lapsing into fatalism. Otherwise Stammler would have been right in seeking to dispose of Marxism by the ironical argument, that if historical necessity guarantees the arrival of socialism there can be no need to exert oneself in bringing it about. For nobody would ever dream of founding a party in order to bring on a lunar eclipse.

The need to dissociate itself from a fatalist conception of historical determinism has given Soviet philosophy occasion to investigate the category of possibility as well as that of actuality, and also to inquire into the conditions under which the possible becomes actual.

The fatalism of the mechanists was due to the fact that they identified possibility with actuality: hence the realization of socialism, in their view, must necessarily come about by itself, by way of *samotek*, quite apart from human activity. As against this, Stalin makes it perfectly clear in his Report to the XVIth Party Congress, that possibility does not mean the same thing as actuality and that it requires a number of conditions for its realization, of which human activity is the most essential:

'The Soviet system provides colossal *possibilities* for the complete victory of socialism. But *possibility* is not *actuality*. To transform possibility into actuality a number of conditions are needed, among which the Party's line and the correct carrying out of this line play by no means the least rôle. . . . To convert possibility into actuality we must first of all cast aside the opportunist theory of things going of their own accord (*samotek*), we must . . . conduct a determined offensive against the capitalist elements in town and country.' [1]

But if dialectical materialism refuses on the one hand to identify the possible with the actual, it also guards itself on the other against the opposite extreme of cleaving an absolute gulf between possibility and actuality, as was done by Spinoza, Kant and others. The new actuality originates in the first place as a possibility in the womb of the old. Possibility is a necessary condition for the emergence of a new actuality. [2]

In order to steer a middle course between the mechanists' identification of possibility and actuality and the idealists' absolute separation between them, dialectical materialism again follows Hegel [3] in dis-

[1] J. V. Stalin: *Voprosy leninizma*, 9th ed., pp. 548 f. (*Works*, XII, p. 349).

[2] M. V. Taranchuk: *Marxistskaya dialektika o vozmozhnosti i deystvitel'-nosti* (The Marxist Dialectic on Possibility and Actuality), in *VF*, 1949, 1, pp. 109–27, *q.v.* p. 110; *cf.* also I. A. Grudinin: *Op. cit.*, p. 5.

[3] G. W. F. Hegel: *Science of Logic*, II, p. 174.

tinguishing between 'abstract' or 'formal' and 'real' possibility. The abstract, formal kind of possibility is that which:

'rests merely on abstract thought-constructions of formal logic, having no basis or precondition in objective reality and lacking determination by the given historical development'.[1]

The Soviet philosophers agree with Hegel that nothing much can be done with this kind of possibility; in this sense it is possible that the moon might fall to earth or an Indian rajah become pope.[2] Such abstract possibilities were also, in their day, considered to be exemplified in the 'equal opportunities' which the British delegates demanded for all countries at the Danube Conference, and which were opposed by the Rumanian representative, Anna Pauker, when she argued that despite such 'equal opportunities', Rumania, for example, had never established her commercial interests in Britain, France or the U.S.A., or imposed her will upon the Thames, the Seine or the Mississippi, whereas Englishmen and Frenchmen were claiming to themselves a major sphere of influence on the Danube and in Rumania.[3]

In contrast to this abstract possibility, real possibility

'has its ground in the given concrete historical circumstances, is evoked and determined by the existing actuality, and proceeds from the latter according to a necessary law'.[4]

Only such real possibilities can become actual. In his report *On the Draft Constitution of the U.S.S.R.*, Stalin maintained that, unlike the constitutions of bourgeois states, that of the U.S.S.R. did not confine itself to stating the formal rights of citizens, but stressed the guarantees of these rights and the means by which they could be exercised; the equality of the citizens, for example, was guaranteed by the abolition of exploitation, the right to work by the liquidation of crises, unemployment, etc.[5]

As to the relationships between these two types of possibility, it is held that 'abstract' possibility may, under certain conditions, become concrete (as with the dreams of earlier generations regarding flight), and contrariwise, that real possibility may again become abstract.

As for the transition from possibility to actuality, this is brought about in Nature on a basis of necessary law, through the operation of blind, elemental forces. But that is not the case in social life, where the transformation of the possible into the actual is assisted by the

[1] M. V. Taranchuk: *Op. cit.*, p. 110; so also *KFS*, p. 66.
[2] M. A. Leonov: *Ocherk* . . ., p. 199.
[3] M. V. Taranchuk: *Op. cit.*, pp. 110 ff.   [4] *Ibid.*, p. 112.
[5] J. V. Stalin: *Voprosy leninizma*, 11th edn., p. 518 (English, p. 551); *cf.* M. V. Taranchuk: *Op. cit.*, p. 113.

conscious activities of men. Consciousness therefore has a part here: men set themselves specific goals and struggle to achieve them. Nevertheless, in antagonistic societies the end-product of historical development is not what was aimed at by men in their conscious activity; it comes about unconsciously, through natural necessity, and regardless of the subjective aims of the individuals concerned, for the inhabitants of such a society neither have nor can have any common will. In the socialist classless society, however, the case is altered, for there, thanks to the moral and political unity of the people, and its common will, the end-product of historical development, the translation of the possible into the actual, is accomplished by means of a planned and conscious effort.[1]

The translation of possibility into actuality therefore calls for

'the union of objective possibility with purposeful and skilled human activity'.[2]

This statement is directed on the one hand against 'fatalism' (the Economists' theory of *stikhiynost'*, Bukharin's of *samotek* . . .), which has overlooked the subjective element, the importance of active, conscious intervention on the part of man; and on the other against subjectivism (the 'heroic' theory of the *Narodniks*, Trotsky's ultra-revolutionary adventurism . . .), which has underestimated the importance of the objective possibilities.[3]

What chiefly occasioned the development of this whole theory in its day, was the controversy as to whether it was possible to realize socialism in one country; Stalin, of course, decided that there was such a possibility. In his view, as we know already, the Soviet system offers enormous possibilities for the complete victory of socialism. But if these possibilities are to be translated into actuality, crucial importance attaches to the work of the Bolshevik Party and the Soviet State, the subjective factor in general, the will, determination, vigour and efficiency of organizations, and the like. The building of socialism in one country, a possibility which has been actualized in the U.S.S.R., creates in turn the necessary conditions for the actualization of communism in a single country also.[4]

It is an indication of continuity in the ideological field, despite the de-Stalinization campaign, that Khrushchev, in his Report to the XXth Party Congress, should have adopted almost word for word the Stalinist formula of the transformation of possibility into actuality. In speaking of the real possibility that the sixth Five-Year Plan might be not only fulfilled but over-fulfilled, he observed:

[1] M. V. Taranchuk: *Op. cit.*, pp. 114 f.; *cf.* Rozental'-Shtraks: *Op. cit.*, pp. 265, 273 ff.

[2] M. V. Taranchuk: *Op. cit.*, p. 116.   [3] *Ibid.*, pp. 116 f.
[4] *Ibid.*, pp. 118 f.

'However, as everyone knows, possibilities are not yet realities.'

To transform them into actuality would require hard work on the part of all Soviet organizations and strenuous endeavours from the entire Soviet people.[1]

The Soviet philosophical discussions of the categories of possibility and actuality deserve the closest attention. The basic idea involved, that motion and development represent a transition from the possible to the actual, is a perfectly sound one. It is also correct to emphasize that these two categories must certainly be distinguished. For if the possible and the actual were to coincide, this would not only make a non-fatalistic conception of development impossible, but would in general rule out all development, process or becoming in the world, leaving only pure actuality or necessary being.

There is much of value in the insight here attained by dialectical materialism, namely that possibility does not become actual of itself alone, requiring rather the intervention of a cause to enable it to do so. In the realm of conscious human activity, this necessity has been clearly worked out by dialectical materialism; it is less clear in its allusions to Nature, where the transition from the possible to the actual is said to be effected by the 'elemental power of natural forces'.[2] For if the possible and the actual are not to coalesce in a necessary *being*, but are to part company in a mutual tension, thereby leaving room for *becoming* (necessary or otherwise), what is needed, whether we are dealing with human affairs or with necessary occurrences in Nature, is the operation of something else, itself already actual, whereby possibility may be transformed into actuality.

A further notable vista opens up at this point: for since this additional third thing will doubtless itself be undergoing development of some sort and thus be in certain respects a 'possibility' in process of becoming 'actual', it too will in turn require a further thing; and since we cannot go on indefinitely in this fashion without leaving the entire motion of all these intermediaries hanging in the air, we must necessarily light somewhere upon a thing of this sort in which possibility and actuality coalesce in the form of necessary being, which is therefore responsible for setting in motion the whole of the world's process of development. Thus Stalin's 'possibility is not actuality' still ends by leading us back to that 'First Mover' which dialectical materialism is so assiduously anxious to avoid.

---

[1] *Pravda*, 15th Feb. 1956, p. 9 (English in *Soviet News* booklet, No. 4, p. 76).
[2] Rozental'–Shtraks: *Op. cit.*, p. 265.

5. FORM AND CONTENT

These two categories also form part of the stock-in-trade of dialectical materialism. In the days of Stalinism, when the theory of categories had no place of its own within the system of Soviet philosophy, these categories were generally dealt with in connection with the fourth principal feature of the dialectic, the law of the unity and struggle of opposites.

Content, in Soviet philosophy, is held to be

'the most important aspect of the object, that which characterizes its very essence, the basis which emerges in the properties and features of the object'.

Form, on the other hand, is

'the internal organizatión of the content, that which binds the elements of the content into unity, and in whose absence the content itself is impossible'.[1]

The definition given in the collective *Categories of the Materialist Dialectic* is even more obscure and less exact.[2]

Thus in the atom, for example, the elementary particles represent the content and their arrangement the form; in the organism it is the cells and organs, on the one hand, and their organization and specific structure on the other; in social production, content is provided by the productive forces, and form by the relations of production; in mental activity, the thought is the content and the word the form; in literary and artistic production, content consists in the social relations expressed (labour, the class-struggle), while form resides in the composition, the subject, the language, and so on.[3]

In contrast to 'metaphysics', which is accused of setting up form as something external and alien to its content, dialectical materialism proclaims a dialectical unity between the two categories: every object has its form and its content; there is no content absolutely without form, just as there is no form without content.[4] But within this unity, content has priority as the determining element. As against this, however, form in turn has an effect upon content, albeit in a secondary fashion, being itself dependent on content. Once it has arisen, it does not remain passive, but exercises an active influence on the development of content. Literature and art, provided they combine wealth of idea-content with power of artistic form, may come to be factors of enormous significance in the historical process.

---

[1] *KFS*, p. 520.
[3] *Ibid.*, pp. 215 f.
[2] *Cf.* Rozental'–Shtraks: *Op. cit.*, p. 215.
[4] *Ibid.*, p. 218.

The dialectical unity of form and content only emerges in its character of contradictoriness when form and content are regarded, not as static, but as dynamic features in the developmental process of the object. Up to a certain stage of development, content may go on developing unhindered within the framework of a given form. But then a point is reached beyond which the old form begins to fetter the further development of the content; the contradiction between the two thereupon makes itself felt and struggles to resolve itself, and this is finally effected by the old form being cast aside and giving place to a new:

'Conflict of content and form, and *vice versa*. Discarding of form, transformation of content'—

such is Lenin's formulation of the 15th element in dialectic.[1]

The classical example of this dialectic is the contradiction between the development of productive forces and that of the relations of production, of which Marx speaks in his 'classical' formulation of the materialist conception of history, in the Introduction to his *Critique of Political Economy*. In the development of productive forces, there comes a moment when the existing relations of production change from forms of development of the forces of production into fetters hampering their further progress. This ushers in a period of social revolution, in which the relations of production are transformed. Thereafter the new relations of production have a stimulating effect in turn on the development of the productive forces—this being taken by Soviet philosophy to confirm the thesis of the active rôle which form also plays in relation to content.

Another example of the dialectical relationship between form and content is invariably quoted from Lenin; though it is perhaps less interesting in this context of formal dialectics than in regard to another question which it raises. Lenin applies the categories of form and content to democracy also, and maintains at one point that Soviet democracy represents a new form of democracy, but again elsewhere that it also involves a new content. In the course of centuries, so he argues, the forms of democracy change. It would therefore be the height of foolishness to suppose that the greatest of all revolutions in the history of mankind could take place within the framework of the old, bourgeois conception of democracy, 'without creating new forms of democracy'.[2] On the other hand, however, Soviet democracy is novel, not only in form, but also in content, and

---

[1] *FT*, p. 193 (146); *cf.* p. 120 above.

[2] V. I. Lenin: *I Kongress kommunisticheskogo Internatsionala 2–6 marta 1919* (The First Congress of the Communist International, 2–6 March 1919), *Sochineniya*, XXVIII[4], pp. 431–51, *q.v.* p. 442.

the new content of this new form of democracy consists, in fact, in the destruction of classes:

'The proletariat needs the abolition of classes—such is the *real* content of proletarian democracy, of proletarian freedom . . . proletarian equality. . . . He who has failed to understand that *this* is the content of the dictatorship of the proletariat . . . takes the name of the dictatorship of the proletariat in vain.' [1]

This is a noteworthy admission. For if proletarian democracy differs alike in form and content from democracy as hitherto understood, one may legitimately ask what the two kinds of democracy continue to have in common, apart from the name itself.

The chief thing to be complained of about the dialectical materialist treatment of this pair of categories is again the lack of accuracy in the framing of definitions. There is no means of seeing from the definitions provided, how the category of 'content' differs in any way from that of 'essence'. And a definition certainly ought to be so formulated that it applies only to the definiendum.

Nor is there any justification for the accusation levelled against metaphysics, that it separates form from content; at the very least, it should be stated more clearly to whom this objection refers. Aristotle, indeed, from whom the framing of this pair of categories derives (though he used the term 'matter' instead of 'content'), envisaged the unity between these two principles of being in a manner which might well have served as an example to dialectical materialism. In his view, neither form nor matter could exist separately, but only in the unity of the material substance constituted by them. It is therefore incomprehensible that he should be accused of supposing that form could exist prior to matter.[2]

Here we may conclude our sketch of the theory of categories. In expounding it we have confined ourselves to those categories which already form part of the traditional stock of dialectical materialism. As we have seen from the lists of categories given at the outset, there are wide variations as between one author and another. The straightening-out of this portion of dialectical materialist theory has only just been resumed in Soviet circles, and hence is still too much in flux to yield, as yet, any generally accepted arrangement or detailed exposition of category-theory.

[1] V. I. Lenin: *O zadachakh III Internatsionala* (The Tasks of the Third International), *Sochineniya*, XXIX[4], pp. 456–73, *q.v.* p. 473 (English, *LSW*, X, pp. 52 f.).
[2] Rozental'–Shtraks: *Op. cit.*, p. 212.

CHAPTER V

Dialectical Materialism and Modern Science

W E have seen above,[1] that in Engels' view there is no room within the framework of Marxist philosophy for a true philosophy of Nature. For all that, it was he himself, in his *Dialectics of Nature*, who first provided an impetus towards the establishment of a philosophy of Nature on the basis of dialectical materialism. A further decisive impulse in this direction was also furnished by Lenin's campaign against 'physical idealism',[2] and by his distinction between the physical and philosophical concepts of matter. Just as, at that time, the first incursions of science into the field of sub-atomic structure had confronted Marxist materialism with serious philosophical problems, so now the later advances in the progress of physics and chemistry, more especially the establishment of quantum physics and relativity theory, have thrown up new philosophical quandaries. It is therefore not surprising that, despite the prohibition

[1] *Cf.* above, p. 254.

[2] Under the term 'physical idealism' Lenin refers to those physicists who had thought it possible, on the strength of the discovery of sub-atomic particles, to speak of a 'dematerialization of matter'; under this head he included not only Mach, Poincaré, Duhem and Karl Pearson, but 'the German immanentists, the disciples of Mach, the French neocriticists and idealists, the English spiritualists, the Russian Lopatin and, in addition, the one and only empirio-monist, A. Bogdanov' (*ME*, p. 290 (315, 356 f.)). More recently this term has been used to embrace a variety of tendencies: such, for example, as the Copenhagen School, on account of their idealistic proclivities in the interpretation of quantum physics, or those physicists who have interpreted Einstein's principle of the inertia of energy in terms of a mutual interchangeability of mass and energy (see below).

thus imposed by Engels, we should be able, as time goes on, to observe an increasing revival of nature-philosophy within dialectical materialism, albeit under the pseudonym of 'philosophy of science'. Particularly in the years after the Second World War, the problems of the philosophy of Nature represented a very definite centre of interest in Soviet philosophy.

In this the efforts of the Soviet philosophers have not been confined merely to providing an answer, from the standpoint of dialectical materialism, to the philosophical problems raised in particular by quantum physics and relativity theory. Their principal endeavours are directed, rather, at proving that modern science affords a 'dazzling confirmation' of dialectical materialism.

The task of the present chapter is therefore twofold: first we must show in what manner Soviet philosophy seeks the solution of the problems created by the modern natural sciences, from quantum physics and relativity theory to the Pavlovian physiology of higher nervous activity and to psychology. But in addition to this we must also pay particular critical attention to the question whether, and to what extent, the modern natural sciences actually confirm dialectical materialism.

In the lay-out of this chapter we shall follow, in broad outline, the ground-plan of the projected Soviet compilation 'Dialectical Materialism and Modern Science', which has already been referred to above, but which, so far as we know, has not yet appeared.[1] It is worth noting, incidentally, that psychology is still included here. This is no doubt connected with the fact that Soviet ideology continues to divide the whole of reality into the two great regions of Nature and Society. Hence those branches of science which do not consider man in the first place as a social being, come within the scope of the natural sciences.

1. QUANTUM PHYSICS

In the field of quantum physics, the main object of the Soviet philosophers is to counter positivistic and idealistic interpretations of the phenomena in question. From this point of view it is chiefly the so-called 'Copenhagen School' (Bohr, Heisenberg and others) that is attacked, mainly on account of their championship of the Complementarity Principle, their indeterminism, and the interpretation which they have given to quantum statistics.

In classical physics it is possible, by determining the position and momentum of a macrophysical body, to fix uniquely the further

[1] *Cf.* above, p. 245; *cf. Vestnik Akademii Nauk SSSR*, 1951, 11, pp. 82 f.

course of its motion. This predictability, and the predetermination of the behaviour of the body which follows from this, is indeed regarded as the essence of physical causality. But now it has turned out, in the realm of microphysics, that it is in principle impossible to measure or predict the position and momentum of a micro-particle with complete exactness at one and the same instant. According to Heisenberg's 'uncertainty-relation' the fact is, rather, that in simultaneous measurement or prediction of the position and momentum, both measurements or predictions are subject to an uncertainty, such that the product of both uncertainty-values is at least of the order of magnitude of Planck's quantum of action h:

$$\Delta_x . \Delta_{\neg \tau} \geqslant h$$

Thus the more exactly the position of a particle is measured, or can be predicted, the more impossible does it become, not only in fact, but in principle, to measure or predict the momentum exactly; and *vice versa*.

The uncertainty-relation is founded on a *dualism of waves and particles*, i.e., on the fact that, for purposes of physical description of the behaviour of a microphysical 'particle', we sometimes need to employ the picture of a corpuscular particle, and in other cases require that of a wave. Two pictures must therefore be employed which in one sense are mutually exclusive, but in another are so far complementary that only both pictures taken together make it possible to give a complete description of a microphysical object. This curious relationship of mutual exclusion and simultaneous supplementation is described by Bohr as '*Complementarity*'. It holds, not only for the wave-and-particle picture, but quite generally for the members of those pairs of properties such, for example, as position and momentum, or time and energy, simultaneous knowledge of which would be required for the complete description of a physical object as understood in classical physics. It would lead to internal contradictions if one were simultaneously to ascribe to a microphysical object *both* properties (*e.g.*, position *and* momentum); only one of its two 'sides' can ever be ascribed to microphysical reality, and the other 'side' is thus necessarily excluded (*Complementarity Principle*). But since two mutually exclusive states cannot be ascribed to an object existing independently of the knowing subject (as understood within a realistic epistemology), the Copenhagen school is inclined to restrict the concept of reality in general to 'physical reality', *i.e.*, to those properties which can actually be attributed to micro-objects by way of physical description. Questions concerning an objective reality existing 'in itself', and such as to underlie physical measurement and description, are dismissed, rather in the positivistic manner, as 'meaningless'.

This basic viewpoint involves a certain tendency towards idealism. Which properties of a microphysical object can be ascribed to it at any time, and which not, are dependent on the measuring-apparatus employed; in so far as the measuring-apparatus represents an 'extension' and refinement of the sense-organs of the physical observer, and thus of the knowing subject, 'physical reality' is dependent upon the cognitive orientation of the observing subject. Hence, in so far as 'physical reality' is forthwith identified, in the positivistic manner, with reality proper, the theory cannot well be acquitted of a somewhat idealistic approach.

Given such a positivistic approach, moreover, acceptance of the uncertainty-relation was bound to lead also to a denial of causality. For if reality is confined to the facts of observation, and the question as to the nature of the things underlying these phenomena regarded as meaningless, causality too can no longer be understood as a real relation between cause and effect, but implies merely a regular and predictable temporal succession of phenomena. But since, according to the uncertainty-relation, the field of microphysical phenomena no longer affords the presuppositions for this, namely, the simultaneous determination of the position and momentum of particles, the causal law, so understood, loses its validity in this sphere. Thus when physicists speak of 'laws' in the atomic field, these laws are of an essentially different kind from those which hold in the sphere of the macrophysical: whereas the latter are regarded as 'dynamic', in that they require a strict causal determinacy in the individual case, the former are 'statistical' in character, in that they merely refer to the probable or average situation in a large class of cases. Bohr, Jordan, Born and others have denied the validity of strict causality in the atomic field. De Broglie, Einstein, Schrödinger and Planck, on the other hand, have insisted that the observations relate to reality, continue to uphold the universal validity of the causal law, and hope that a later development of physics will make it possible to give a realistic and deterministic interpretation to microphysical facts.

Soviet philosophy is vehemently opposed to this philosophical interpretation of quantum physics on the part of the Copenhagen school. It does not, indeed, deny the physical facts underlying the complementarity principle, but objects to the Copenhagen school on the ground that they turn this principle into 'a philosophical conception of complementarity which characteristically denies the causality and objectivity of microphenomena'.[1] The basic error of the Copenhagen school is that they regard the wave-function which describes the state of the micro-particle, not as an objective characteristic of the micro-object itself, but merely as an expression of

[1] D. I. Blokhintsev: *Grundlagen der Quantenmechanik*, Berlin 1953, pp. 498 f.

'the knowledge of the observer';[1] the Copenhagen school consider the wave, not as a real property of the micro-object, but simply as a wave of probability, a mere expression of the probability of encountering a micro-object, one-sidedly regarded as a particle (such as an electron), at a particular place.[2]

Among Soviet interpretations of quantum physics, the greatest authority appears to attach to that put forward by D. I. Blokhintsev and various others (such as M. E. Omel'yanovsky and Y. P. Terletsky). Blokhintsev starts from the assumption that the wave-function does not characterize the behaviour of the individual micro-particle, but must be referred primarily to the behaviour of a 'totality' (*ensemble*),[3] meaning by the word 'totality' here, those particles which are subject to the same conditions within the macrophysical environment.[4] Thus in describing the particle as belonging to a particular macrophysical environment, the wave-function always presupposes a particular environment of this type. If the latter changes, the totality also changes. This is the true situation underlying what is commonly referred to as the 'influence of the measuring-apparatus' on the state of this system; but strictly speaking this influence is merely a special case of the macrophysical situation.[5] In this connection Blokhintsev denies the conclusion drawn by the Copenhagen school from this 'influence', namely that it is impossible to investigate microphenomena objectively. In order to inquire into the nature of the totality it is sufficient, merely, to investigate a small part of it. This part may well in fact be altered in the process of measurement, but the totality as a whole remains unchanged. In other words, the degree of isolation of the totality as a whole remains virtually unaltered by measurement. Blokhintsev concludes from this, that the wavefunction ψ, when applied to the totality, conforms to Schrödinger's equation

$$ih\frac{\partial\psi}{\partial t} = H\psi,$$ which makes it possible to determine this function for

any given instant, so long as it is known for the starting-point.

[1] *Ibid.*, p. 499.

[2] *Cf.* M. E. Omel'yanovsky: *Dialektichesky materializm i tak nazyvaemy printsip dopolnitel'nosti Bora* (Dialectical Materialism and Bohr's so-called Complementarity Principle) in the collection *Filosofskie voprosy sovremennoy fiziki* (Philosophical Problems of Modern Physics), Moscow 1952, pp. 396–431, *q.v.* pp. 401, 421.

[3] D. I. Blokhintsev: *Kritika filosofskikh vozzreny tak nazyvaemoy 'Kopenhagenskoy shkoly' v fizike* (Critique of the Philosophical Views of the So called 'Copenhagen School' in Physics), in *Filosofskie voprosy sovremennoy fiziki*, pp. 358–95, *q.v.* p. 377.

[4] D. I. Blokhintsev: *Otvet akademiku V. A. Foku* (Reply to Academician V. A. Fok), *VF*, 1952, 6, pp. 171–5, *q.v.* p. 173.

[5] D. I. Blokhintsev: *Kritika . . .*, p. 377.

Thus, by way of the totality, the physicist has access, in principle, to knowledge of the individual microphenomenon, and this consists in investigating the statistical laws of the collective:

'Quantum mechanics investigates the properties of the individual microphenomenon by investigating the statistical laws of the collectivity of such phenomena.' [1]

Omel'yanovsky sees the reason for this in the fact that the statistical average

'gives quantitative expression, not to the particularity which distinguishes one individual magnitude from another, but to that which is valid for the species to which these individual magnitudes belong, *i.e.*, to that which unites these magnitudes and makes them magnitudes of one and the same kind'.[2] According to the theory of totalities,

'the properties of micro-objects are reflected in the properties of totalities, which can be known to us by experiment'.[3]

On the strength of these considerations, Blokhintsev and his school think themselves in a position to make concrete assertions about the properties of micro-objects: and in particular this, that micro-particles must not be regarded as objects 'to which the concept of motion along a path can be applied',[4] and that the micro-object must be credited, not only with real particle-properties, but with equally real wave-properties as well.[5]

On the subject of indeterminism, the Soviet philosophers in general, and not merely the school of Blokhintsev, are strenuous defenders of a philosophical determinism, in face of the indeterminism of quantum physics. But in order to obviate misunderstandings, they emphasize that this determinism of theirs is not to be regarded as a strict determinism of the Laplacean sort,[6] which would exclude all contingency.

'According to Engels, necessity and contingency are not mutually

---

[1] D. I. Blokhintsev: *Kritika . . .*, p. 379.

[2] M. E. Omel'yanovsky: *Op. cit.*, pp. 424 f.   [3] *Ibid.*, p. 422.

[4] D. I. Blokhintsev: *Kritika . . .*, p. 389.

[5] M. E. Omel'yanovsky: *Op. cit.*, pp. 411 f.

[6] The most complete formulation of a consistently mechanistic worldview is probably that to be found in Laplace: 'Given for one instant an intelligence which could comprehend all the forces by which Nature is animated and the situation of the beings who compose it—an intelligence sufficiently vast to submit these data to analysis—it would embrace in the same formula the movements of the greatest bodies of the universe and those of the lightest atom; for it, nothing would be uncertain and the future, as the past, would be present to its eyes.' 'It is possible to imagine the attainment of a level of natural knowledge in which the entire world-

exclusive categories. The contingent has a ground, and the necessary emerges from within the contingent. There is no impassable barrier between the contingent and the necessary.' [1]

But unfortunately we get no further philosophical elaboration of this notion, as to how the necessary arises from out of the contingent.

So far as the problem of quantum statistics is concerned, Soviet philosophy is averse to the idea that the merely statistical character of quantum laws arises, as the positivists maintain, from the absence of lawful connections among the individual microphenomena. There is a similar aversion to Bohr's view, that these statistics are due to an uncontrollable influence of the measuring-apparatus on the micro-object.[2] Blokhintsev himself gives the following explanation of quantum statistics: Owing to the atomic character of action, there are no closed, isolated micro-systems; every quantum-'totality' involves, rather, an interconnection of micro- and macro-systems. This impossibility of isolating the micro-system from the macro-environment is also the reason why the Newtonian or Laplacean determinism no longer operates in the field of individual microphenomena, being here replaced by statistical laws:

'Thus quantum statistics has its basis in the mutual connection of micro- and macro-phenomena.' [3]

In view of their deterministic principles, the Soviet philosophers observe with satisfaction that even among Western physicists there are signs, at present, of a return to a deterministic interpretation of quantum physics, a tendency which was particularly noticeable in a series of essays contributed to the collective volume *Louis de Broglie, physicien et penseur*, which was published on the occasion of Louis de Broglie's sixtieth birthday.[4] In recent years the journal *Voprosy filosofii* has on two occasions actually published articles by de Broglie in Russian translation,[5] in which there was evidence of this return to

process would be represented in a single mathematical formula, an immeasurable system of simultaneous differential equations, from which the position, direction of motion and velocity of every atom in the universe could be calculated for any given instant.' (P. S. de Laplace: *Essai Philosophique sur les Probabilités*, Paris 1814; the English version, from the 6th edn. (New York–London 1902) includes only the first of these passages).

[1] D. I. Blokhintsev: *Kritika* . . ., p. 375.

[2] *Ibid.*, pp. 375, 379. [3] *Ibid.*, p. 377.

[4] G. Y. Myakishev: *V chem prichina statisticheskogo kharaktera kvantovoy mekhaniki?* (What is the Reason for the Statistical Character of Quantum Mechanics?), *VF*, 1954, 6, pp. 146–59, *q.v.* p. 146.

[5] Louis de Broglie: *Ostanetsya li kvantovaya mekhanika indeterministskoy?* (Is Quantum Mechanics still Indeterministic?), *VF*, 1954, 4, pp. 105–118; this article is a translation of a lecture given by de Broglie on

412   *Dialectical Materialism and Modern Science*

a deterministic position, together with an original article by Vigier, apparently written specially for *Voprosy filosofii*.[1]

Finally, we would also draw attention to an interesting epistemological premiss of Omel'yanovsky's, whereby the latter seeks to overcome the difficulties confronting an objective interpretation of the account of Nature in quantum physics. He thinks it possible to avoid the difficulties presented by the complementarity principle in this regard by referring to the merely *analogical* character of the concepts we form in respect of macrophysical objects:

'Quantum magnitudes (*i.e.*, quantum coordinates and moments) are differentiated from the *analogous* "classical" magnitudes (coordinates and moments) by new properties. . . . Quantum magnitudes are *not identical with the analogous* classical magnitudes.' [2]

And he believes that in the course of its further development physics will progress towards adequate concepts for the interpretation of micro-phenomena, and that the current difficulties in quantum physics will thereby be overcome. W. Büchel[3] and F. Selvaggi[4] have adopted a similar attitude from the critical realist point of view. Büchel, however, is of the opinion that it may never be possible to overcome the merely analogical character of our conceptual scheme, and hence the apparently contradictory character of the various assertions made in quantum physics.

In outlining the interpretation of quantum physics adopted in Soviet philosophy, we have so far chiefly relied on the accounts given by Blokhintsev and his supporters. But although this is evidently the dominant view, it is not the only one among the Soviet philosophers.

In its day a good deal of comment was occasioned by an article by

31st October 1952 at the Centre International de Synthèse and published in the *Revue d'Histoire des Sciences et de leurs Applications* (1952, No. 4). *Cf.* also, *Interpretatsiya volnovoy mekhaniki* (The Interpretation of Wavemechanics), *VF*, 1956, 6, pp. 80–90 (translated from the periodical *Atomes*, Jan. 1956).

[1] J. P. Vigier: *K voprosu o teorii povedeniya individualnykh mikroobyektov* (The Problem of a Theory of Behaviour for Individual Micro-objects), *VF*, 1956, 6, pp. 91–106.

[2] M. E. Omel'yanovsky: *O tak nazyvaemom sootnoshenii neopredelennostey v kvantovoy mekhanike* (On the So-called Uncertainty Relation in Quantum Mechanics), *VF*, 1954, 1, pp. 203–10, *q.v.* p. 209 (G. W.'s italics).

[3] W. Büchel: *Die Diskussion um die Interpretation der Quantenphysik* in *Scholastik* 29 (1954), pp. 235–44, *q.v.* pp. 241 f.; *cf.* also *Individualität und Wechselwirkung im Bereich des materiellen Seins*, in *Scholastik* 31 (1956), pp. 1–30, *q.v.* pp. 14–17.

[4] F. Selvaggi: *Le rôle de l'analogie dans les théories physiques*, in *Actes du XIᵉ Congrès Internationale de Philosophie*, Vol. VI, Amsterdam–Louvain 1953, pp. 138 ff.

M. A. Markov, *On the Nature of Physical Knowledge*, which appeared in the second number of the first volume (1947) of *Voprosy filosofii*.[1] Markov sets out from the concept of 'physical reality' adopted by the Copenhagen school. Owing to the difference between the microphysical and macrophysical worlds, micro-phenomena can only be grasped by means of a 'translation' into the macrophysical 'language' through the medium of the macrophysical apparatus. But in the course of this translation the microphysical phenomenon is necessarily altered, owing to its interaction with the apparatus. The outcome of this change, this 'translation', is 'physical reality'. According to Markov, this latter is indeed in a certain sense subjective and dependent on human activity, since it presupposes the presence of the measuring-apparatus. But in so saying Markov is by no means wishing to deny the existence of an objective reality, or even to describe it as in principle unknowable; yet this 'physical reality' serves the precise purpose of translating microphysical data into the macrophysical conceptual scheme; it is, as it were, 'a macrophysical mirror-image of the microphysical world'.[2]

This did not, however, prevent Markov from being violently attacked. He was accused of 'Kantianism', 'agnosticism' and even 'idealism'.[3] In the postscript with which the new editors of *Voprosy filosofii* hastily ended this whole discussion, Markov was subjected to what was indeed the much more valid reproach, that his theory was

[1] *Cf.* above, p. 188.

[2] M. A. Markov: *O prirode fizicheskogo znaniya* (On the Nature of Physical Knowledge), *VF*, 1947, 2, pp. 164 f.

[3] So, for example, A. A. Maximov in the Discussion, *VF*, 1948, 3, p. 225. It is interesting to note the course taken by this controversy. In the first number of the 1948 volume the Editors of *Voprosy filosofii* published a series of contributions to the discussion. A contribution from A. A. Maximov, already set up and passed for press by the author on April 10th, was nonetheless withdrawn from this issue by the Editors before finally going to press, since a similar intervention in virtually identical terms had been published by Maximov on this same 10th of April in the *Literaturnaya Gazeta*; though in this case, not as a contribution to the discussion, but as an unconcealed attack both on Markov and also on the Editors of *Voprosy filosofii*, which step had clearly been taken with the connivance of the Editors of the *Literaturnaya Gazeta*. In an editorial note on the incident the Editors of *Voprosy filosofii* registered an energetic protest against this manner of proceeding and attacked the Editors of the *Literaturnaya Gazeta* in a style which called for no little courage in the Stalinist era. The result was that Kedrov was removed from his post as Chief Editor of *Voprosy filosofii* and the new editors went on, in the third number of 1948, to publish the contributions of Maximov and Terletsky, and finally broke off the whole discussion with an editorial postscript, apparently written by Omel'yanovsky.

a new version of Plekhanov's 'hieroglyphic theory'. Even so, it is another question, whether the formal correspondence between perception and thing-in-itself, which is assumed by defenders of the Leninist copy-theory, can be rendered consistent with modern physics.

Serious objections were brought against Blokhintsev's theory of totalities by Academician V. A. Fok in an article in *Voprosy filosofii*, 'On So-called Totalities in Quantum Mechanics'.[1] Fok objects to 'totalities' on the ground that they represent 'speculative constructions'.[2] He himself takes the view that the wave-function reflects the real state of the individual micro-object.[3]

The theory of 'totalities' is also rejected by A. D. Alexandrov (not to be confused with G. F. Alexandrov the philosopher). His own view of the electron is an interesting one: a definite position and velocity are given, in the electron, merely 'as possibilities'; under given macroscopic conditions these possibilities are realized, whether it be as the position of the electron or as its velocity.[4]

It is no part of our business to pass judgement upon the Soviet interpretation of quantum physics from the point of view of the physicist. The chief question which interests us is, how much there is in Omel'yanovsky's claim that,

'Modern physics . . . confirms dialectical materialism and throughout its entire content confronts the scientist with the task of consciously applying dialectical materialism to the investigation of Nature.' [5]

How, in detail, do the Soviet philosophers see in quantum physics a confirmation of dialectical materialism?

To this we obtain the following answer: only the law of the unity and struggle of opposites can help us to explain such 'contradictory development' (an example of such 'contradiction' being the wave-and-corpuscle character of matter);[6] this wave-and-corpuscle char-

---

[1] V. A. Fok: *O tak nazyvaemykh ansamblyakh v kvantovoy mekhanike*, VF, 1952, 4, pp. 170–4.

[2] *Ibid.*, p. 170. [3] *Ibid.*, p. 172.

[4] A. D. Alexandrov in *Vestnik Leningradskogo Universiteta*, 1949, 4, p. 65, quoted by M. E. Omel'yanovsky: *Protiv idealistischeskogo istolkovaniya statisticheskikh ansambley v kvantovoy mekhanike* (Against an Idealistic Interpretation of Statistical Totalities in Quantum Mechanics), *VF*, 1953, 2, pp. 201–9, *q.v.* p. 207.

[5] M. E. Omel'yanovsky: *Filosofskie voprosy kvantovoy mekhaniki* (Philosophical Problems of Quantum Mechanics), Moscow 1956, p. 33.

[6] M. E. Omel'yanovsky: *Dialektichesky materializm i sovremennaya fizika* (Dialectical Materialism and Modern Physics), in *Kommunist*, 1956, 5, pp. 72–87, *q.v.* p. 75.

acter of the electron, and of light, is an indication of the fact that in reality these latter are neither corpuscles nor waves, but a 'dialectical structure', a 'unity of opposition';[1] the fact that quantum physics extends the boundaries of our knowledge is regarded as a confirmation of the Leninist thesis of the inexhaustibility of matter.[2] We have already referred above to the way in which the Soviet philosophers think they have found the answer to the problem of determinism in quantum physics in the shape of the dialectical materialist theory of the relation between necessity and contingency.

To all this it may be said, that if one takes for granted the philosophical foundations of dialectical materialism it is then possible—as the Soviet physicists have shown—to put forward a scientifico-philosophical interpretation of the data of quantum physics from this point of view. If one starts from a positivistic or idealist type of epistemology, it is equally possible to account for the facts from this point of view as well; so much has been shown by the Copenhagen school. Thus the scientifico-philosophical explanation of the physical facts is not uniquely determined on these grounds alone, but depends essentially on the philosophical starting-point adopted in the first place. Hence it cannot be said that modern physics confirms dialectical materialism; all that the Soviet physicists have shown is that the latter can be rendered consistent with quantum physics.

There is one further point of importance: the whole discussion has really nothing to do with the antithesis between idealism and materialism; the issue lies, rather, between an idealist or positivistic epistemology and a realistic one. Throughout we can discern the efforts of Soviet philosophy to counter certain idealistic and positivistic tendencies in the interpretation of quantum physics. We must merely be on guard against the misuse of the concept of 'materialism', customarily practised in this context, in that here too the concept of 'materialism' is confused with that of 'realism'. When it is argued that the micro-particle represents a reality existing independently of the process of observation and measurement, this is not a 'materialistic' interpretation, but a 'realistic' one. The acknowledgement of a reality independent of the knowing subject is not 'materialism', since this does nothing to settle the question as to the nature of this reality, *i.e.*, as to whether matter is the only and ultimate reality.[3]

[1] S. I. Vavilov: *Filosofskie problemy sovremennoy fiziki i zadachi sovetskikh fizikov v bor'be za peredovuyu nauku* (Philosophical Problems of Modern Physics and the Tasks of Soviet Physicists in the Struggle for a Progressive Science), in *Filosofskie voprosy sovremennoy fiziki*, pp. 5–30, *q.v.* p. 14.

[2] M. E. Omel'yanovsky: *Op. cit.*, p. 77; *cf. ME*, p. 249 (271, 318–19).

[3] It is a pity that W. Heisenberg (*The Development of the Interpretation of the Quantum Theory*, in *Niels Bohr and the Development of Physics*, ed.

2. RELATIVITY THEORY

In the field of quantum physics, Soviet criticism has been directed mainly against Western theories, and against Russian ones only insofar as they have been drawn into the wake of Western views. So far as relativity theory is concerned, it was again the philosophical interpretation frequently given to it in the West which initially formed the chief target of Soviet criticism. But the arguments brought against it were often of an extraordinarily elementary kind, and even the physical content of the theory of relativity was rejected, so that in recent years there has been a reaction, beginning even before Stalin's death. Reputable Soviet mathematicians have carried on a successful campaign against these simplifications on the part of certain Soviet theorists, so that their position has come to be generally rejected as representing a 'nihilistic attitude' towards relativity theory.

The rejection of relativity had originally gone so far, that not only were doubts entertained as to the facts discovered through relativity theory proper, such as the relativity (or dependence on the observer's standpoint) of lengths and intervals, but there was even opposition to the relativity-principle of Galileo. As is known, it was already realized before Einstein, that all *mechanical* processes occur in exactly the same manner, whether the system of reference be stationary or in uniform motion in a straight line (Galileo's relativity-principle). From the behaviour of an object falling to earth in a moving train, no conclusions can be drawn as to the state of motion of the train itself. This means that there is no preferred 'absolute' system of coordinates, but that all coordinate-systems in uniform rectilinear motion relative to one another are equivalent; more particularly it means that there is no 'absolute' path of fall, it being equally legitimate to say of a stone falling from a moving train that it describes a straight line (*i.e.*, in relation to the moving system of reference known as the 'train') or that it describes a parabola (*i.e.*, in re-

W. Pauli, London, 1955, pp. 12–29) should also adopt this fallacious use of the word 'materialism', when he says of the various opponents of quantum physics that they are united in wishing 'to return to the reality concept of classical physics or, more generally expressed, to the ontology of materialism; that is, to the idea of an objective real world, whose smallest parts exist objectively in the same way as stones and trees, independently of whether or not we observe them'. The 'ontology of materialism' claims, in the first instance, that there is nothing else in the world except matter, and that spiritual phenomena are in some way derivative from matter; the objective existence of things independent of the knowing subject or observer is upheld by materialism, not because it rests on the basis of a materialist ontology, but insofar as it adheres to realism in epistemology.

lation to the reference-system of a pointsman standing alongside the train).

In virtue of certain experiments, this principle of relativity, which originally had a purely mechanical application, was extended by Einstein to all processes (including those of an optical or electro-magnetic kind); he thereby arrived at the first principle of the ('special') theory of relativity: within systems in uniform rectilinear motion (= inertial systems) *all* natural processes take place in pre-cisely the same fashion. From this there emerged as a second basic premiss the principle of the 'constant velocity of light', namely, that the latter remains constant (at 300,000 km/sec.), whether the light-source represents a stationary inertial system or a moving one.

From these two principles there arose further consequences of a very radical kind, which it would take us too far afield to pursue here in detail: the relativity of lengths and times, *i.e.*, the fact that the physical length of a moving body and the physical duration of pro-cesses occurring in it have a different value for an observer moving with the body and for one at rest outside it; and the relativity of simultaneity, whereby two occurrences which are reckoned as simul-taneous in one system of reference are no longer so in another.

According to relativity theory the transition from one system of reference to another is governed by the formulae of the so-called Lorentz transformation. It was later found by Minkowski that the scope of these formulae is greatly increased if one introduces a four-dimensional system of coordinates, in which the 'time-axis' is added as a fourth dimension to the three spatial coordinates, and movement in the three-dimensional space is thereby regarded as a 'world-line' in a four-dimensional world (not to be confused with a four-dimensional space). This 'world-line' is now the same in all systems of reference, and therefore represents the true absolute, a description of Nature independent of the choice of a 'standpoint'.

It follows, moreover, from the formulae of the Lorentz transforma-tion, that the extension of a body moving with the speed of light would be equal to zero, since the speed of light, on this view, repre-sents the greatest possible velocity. And it also follows that with increasing velocity the mass also increases, and on reaching the speed of light would become infinitely large.

There is a further point connected with this. It was already known before Einstein that light-waves and electro-magnetic waves, on encountering a material object, produce a radiation-pressure, *i.e.*, the energy somehow manifests itself in the form of 'inert mass'. On the basis of the special theory of relativity, Einstein was now able to generalize this individual case to the 'principle of the inertia of energy': all energy possesses an inertial mass corresponding to the formula $E = mc^2$. This means that mass and energy are basically one and the same; the principle of the conservation of mass is thereby combined with that of the conservation of energy into a common principle.

According to the 'special theory of relativity' just described, which holds only for systems in uniform rectilinear motion, it was still possible to recognize an 'absolute' acceleration, or an 'absolute' motion of rotation, from the inertial forces thereby engendered. In introducing the 'general theory of relativity', Einstein subsequently set himself to remove this limitation and to treat acceleration as relative also, so that all systems of reference in the universe, including those in acceleration or in relative rotatory motion, would be given equal status; Ptolemy and Copernicus would thereby be shown to be equally correct.

Einstein now went on to realize this aim by equating inertia and gravitation. In working out his theory, he made use of Riemann's investigations into non-Euclidean geometries. But in general relativity, as also in the special theory, we are concerned, not merely with space, *i.e.*, not with geometry alone, but with motion in space, that is with kinematics, into which there enters also the component of time. Thus even in special relativity, time (in the Minkowski world) had already been added as a fourth dimension to the three dimensions of space. But whereas, in special relativity, the measuring-relations, *i.e.*, the 'metric' of this four-dimensional space-time, were still Euclidean, this is no longer the case in general relativity. The situation here, rather, is that the 'degree of curvature' [1] of space-time is governed by the presence of large masses, *i.e.*, by gravitational fields. At a great distance from such masses the Euclidean metric still holds (approximately), and so too does the kinematics of special relativity. But in the neighbourhood of such masses, these are replaced by another metric (and kinematics), namely those required by the gravitational field in the locality. In other words, the gravitational field is identical with the 'curvature of space' prevailing there.

From this Einstein then draws, among others, the conclusions that all clocks in the neighbourhood of large masses will go more slowly, and that the sum of the angles of a triangle having such masses within its boundaries, will be the more in excess of 180°, the larger the enclosed masses are.

Among those Soviet philosophers who adopted an emphatically dissenting attitude towards relativity theory, the chief spokesman was

[1] By 'degree of curvature' we are to understand the mathematical expression used to formulate the exact nature and extent of the differences between the figures of Euclidean, and the corresponding figures of non-Euclidean, geometry.

that same A. A. Maximov who, in the quarrel about quantum physics, had been responsible for the downfall of Markov, and with him also, the Chief Editor of *Voprosy filosofii*. Maximov's objections to relativity theory are very characteristic. In attempting to prove that a trajectory is something objective, independent of any system of reference (and so absolute), he relies on the fact that a meteorite falling to earth ploughs a channel into the earth's surface, whose form reproduces the trajectory of the meteorite.[1] In order to arrive at an absolute path, Maximov is prepared to recognize as the only true path of the body, that which the latter describes in relation to its environment. He goes on to defend the objectivity of lengths and time-intervals, and also of simultaneity, upon similar lines. In the latter case, Einstein's error consists in the fact that the only method of measurement of time and simultaneity that he accepts, involves the employment of systems of reference situated outside the body under consideration. But one can also determine time according to the stages of development in any such system of reference, from the incidence of decay-products, for example, in radio-active materials, or from the stage of development in plants, animals and so forth.[2] The essays on relativity theory by Kuznetov and Steinman, in the already oft-quoted collection *Philosophical Problems of Modern Physics* (1952), are in similar vein.[3]

But even within Stalin's lifetime, a reaction against such over-simplified rejections of relativity theory had already set in. It was urgently necessary, indeed, to adopt a different attitude towards relativity theory, inasmuch as the special theory at least had been brilliantly confirmed by experiment; the whole of modern atomic physics would be unthinkable without Einstein's formula, $E = mc^2$. Thus already in 1951, the Editors of *Voprosy filosofii* had opened a discussion on relativity theory, with an article by the young Esthonian physicist G. I. Naan.[4]

Maximov apart, there were other Soviet theoreticians who thought

[1] A. A. Maximov: *Marxistsky filosofsky materializm i sovremennaya fizika* (Marxist Philosophical Materialism and Modern Physics), *VF*, 1948, 3, pp. 105-24, *q.v.* pp. 114 f.
[2] A. A. Maximov: *Bor'ba za materializm v sovremennoy fizike* (The Struggle for Materialism in Modern Physics), *VF*, 1953, 1, pp. 175-94, *q.v.* p. 192.
[3] I. V. Kuznetsov: *Sovetskaya fizika i dialektichesky materializm* (Soviet Physics and Dialectical Materialism), in *Filosofskie voprosy sovremennoy fiziki*, pp. 31-86; P. Y. Steinman: *Za materialisticheskuyu teoriyu bystrykh dvizhenly* (Towards a Materialistic Theory of Rapid Motions), *ibid.*, pp. 234-98.
[4] G. I. Naan: *K voprosu o printsipe otnositel'nosti v fizike* (Problems of the Relativity Principle in Physics), *VF*, 1951, 2, pp. 57-77.

it their duty to dialectical materialism to cling somehow to the absolute nature of position and path; such, for example, were G. A. Kursanov[1] and V. Stern,[2] a German author from the Soviet occupation-zone, who frequently holds forth on problems of natural philosophy and who also took part in this discussion. D. I. Blokhintsev likewise considers the problem of absolute motion to be not without meaning, since inertial systems are only given approximately in reality. Absolute motion, for him, is motion in relation to 'the most inertial system of reference', and science is endeavouring to discover this.[3]

However, this naïve treatment of relativity theory on the part of Maximov, Kuznetsov and others, has been energetically repudiated by other Soviet philosophers, and above all by the mathematicians: such, for example, as I. P. Bazarov,[4] V. A. Fok[5] and the already-mentioned Leningrad mathematician, A. D. Alexandrov.[6] It would take us too far afield to enter further into the course of this discussion.[7] It reached its conclusion in the first number of the 1955 volume of *Voprosy filosofii*, in an editorial article which summarized the results of the discussion up to that point and gave decisive preference to the views of the authors last mentioned. Maximov was accused of having taken up a 'vulgarizing' and 'subjectivist' attitude, which had led him to 'nihilistic views about one of the most important theories in modern physics'.[8] This may well have been the reason why, in the fifth number of this volume, Maximov no longer appears as a member of the Editorial Board of the periodical in question, whereas A. D. Alexandrov and, it must be admitted, I. V. Kuznetsov also, make their appearance for the first time.

[1] G. A. Kursanov: *K kriticheskoy otsenke teorii otnositel'nosti* (Critical Examination of the Theory of Relativity), *VF*, 1952, 1, pp. 169–74.

[2] V. Stern: *K voprosu o filosofskoy storone teorii otnositel'nosti* (Concerning the Philosophical Aspect of Relativity Theory), *VF*, 1952, 1, pp. 175–81.

[3] D. I. Blokhintsev: *Za leninskoe uchenie o dvizhenii* (In Defence of a Leninist Theory of Motion), *VF*, 1952, 1, pp. 181–3.

[4] I. P. Bazarov: *Za dialektiko-materialisticheskoe ponimanie i razvitie teorii otnositel'nosti* (Towards a Dialectical Materialist Conception and Development of Relativity Theory), *VF*, 1952, 6, pp. 175–85.

[5] V. A. Fok: *Protiv nevezhestvennoy kritiki sovremennykh fizicheskikh teoriy* (Against Ignorant Criticism of Modern Physical Theories), *VF*, 1953, 1, pp. 168–74.

[6] A. D. Alexandrov: *Po povodu nekotorykh vzglyadov na teoriyu otnositel'nosti* (On Certain Conceptions of Relativity Theory), *VF*, 1953, 5, pp. 225–45.

[7] Further details will be found in A. Buchholz: *Ideologie und Forschung in der sowjetischen Naturwissenschaft*, Stuttgart 1953.

[8] *K itogam diskussii po teorii otnositel'nosti* (On the Outcome of the Discussion on Relativity Theory), *VF*, 1955, 1, pp. 134–8, *q.v.* p. 136.

The views of V. A. Fok and A. D. Alexandrov appear nowadays to enjoy the greatest esteem, since both these authors were also responsible for the article on 'Relativity Theory' in the new edition of the *Great Soviet Encyclopaedia*. Hence the account which follows of the philosophical interpretation of relativity theory on the part of Soviet philosophy is based primarily upon the writings of these two authors.

According to Alexandrov, relativity theory is not a purely geometrical theory, but a physical one; it is concerned with space and time, and these, according to dialectical materialism, are forms of existence of matter. The spatial and temporal connections between phenomena are therefore governed by the material connections between objects.[1]

The main point of relativity theory, as Alexandrov sees it, lies, not in its generalization of the principle of relativity, but in its discovery of the unity of space and time:

'The essence of relativity theory lies precisely in the fact that it demonstrates this connection between space and time. Space and time are united into a common form of existence of matter, spacetime.'[2]

Taken separately in themselves, space and time are merely relative, but still, for all that, objective aspects of absolute space-time. In the confusion between 'relative' and 'non-objective', Alexandrov, like Naan before him, sees the root of the trouble in the whole controversy about relativity theory. The division of the space-time unity into space and time is not fixed in itself, but merely in relation to this or that system of reference.[3]

Alexandrov has no desire to interpret the system of reference as a 'mode of representation', a fictitious network of coordinates, as Eddington, and after him Terletsky, have done; he sees it, rather, as an objectively real coordination of the objects and processes in the world, which all stand, in various ways, in real relationships one with another. Hence all bodies are in some way 'bodies in relation'. The conventional representation of an event by means of the three spatial coordinates x, y, and z, and the time-co-ordinate t, is merely an abstract representation of this objective coordination of events in space and time.[4]

The essence of general relativity is also seen, from the Soviet point

[1] A. D. Alexandrov: *Op. cit.*, pp. 226, 238. [2] *Ibid.*, p. 227.
[3] *Ibid.*, pp. 227, 238; *cf.* also *BSE*, XXXI, p. 411.
[4] A. D. Alexandrov: *Po povodu* ..., p 227; *cf.* Y. P. Terletsky: *O soderzhanii sovremennoy fizicheskoy teorii prostranstva i vremeni* (On the Content of the Modern Physical Theory of Space and Time), *VF*, 1952, 3, pp. 191-7, *q.v.* p. 193.

of view, not as a generalization of the relativity principle, but as a demonstration of the fact that the unity of space and time set forth in special relativity is not homogeneous, its metric being dependent, rather, on the distribution and motion of matter. General relativity asserts that this dependence is exhibited in gravitation, represents, as it were, the 'geometrical aspect' of the gravitational field, and thereby serves to explain the law of gravitation.[1] V. A. Fok accordingly rejects Einstein's progression from special to general relativity (the extension of the relativity principle from uniform rectilinear motion to accelerated and rotary motion) and attempts to derive the connection between the two theories from the equation for the expansion of the front of a light-wave.[2]

The significance for dialectical materialist philosophy which the Soviet theorists attribute to relativity theory, so conceived, can be summed up under the following heads:

Firstly it represents a 'splendid confirmation' of the fundamentals of dialectical materialism: above all of its doctrine of space and time as forms of existence of matter, this theory being yet further extended by the establishment of the unity of space and time, in that such a space-time must now be regarded as a *single* unitary form of the existence of matter; the discovery of the interconnections between space and time, mass and energy, etc., represents a confirmation of the dialectical materialist thesis as to the reciprocal interconnection and mutual conditioning among all phenomena; the establishment of the connection between mass and energy, and the dependence of the space-time metric upon the presence and motion of matter, confirms the doctrine of the inseparability of matter and motion, and so forth.

But when the Soviet philosophers drag in this connection between mass and energy as a confirmation of dialectical materialism, they take violent exception, in doing so, to that interpretation of the formula $E = mc^2$ which would treat it as indicating the possibility of transforming mass into energy, or even, as the 'physical idealists' and 'energeticists' maintain, of changing matter into energy, and thereby implying the disappearance of matter. But we shall be returning to this in more detail later on.

Soviet philosophers of all camps attach great philosophical importance to the problem of the equal validity of all systems of reference, whereby Copernicus and Ptolemy must be reckoned to be equally in the right. A. D. Alexandrov connects this 'error' of Einstein's with the fact that he falsely believed general relativity to be a generalization of the special theory.[3] The reason for the great significance attached to this question is an ideological one: the Soviet authors

[1] A. D. Alexandrov: *Op. cit.*, p. 229.
[2] V. A. Fok, in *BSE*, XXXI, p. 410.
[3] A. D. Alexandrov in *BSE*, XXXI, p. 412.

being still addicted to the belief that a religious world-outlook stands or falls by the acceptance of the geocentric system.[1]

The same ideological background explains why Soviet philosophers of all persuasions should be unanimous in rejecting the conclusion drawn by Einstein, admittedly with the help of an auxiliary hypothesis, from general relativity theory, with its doctrine of the 'curvature of space': namely, that the universe, though unbounded, is not infinite, resembling in this the surface of a sphere. A spatially finite universe seems to the Soviet philosophers to imply also a beginning in time, and hence to involve the necessity of a creation of the world, which would, however, run counter to dialectical materialism.

In conclusion, we may refer briefly to an interesting article by a Soviet philosopher, A. I. Uemov: *Can the Space-Time Continuum Interact with Matter?* [2] Uemov treats the relationship of space-time and matter in terms of the categories of form and content, and claims that they interact in the same way as form and content do. He thus arrives at a position very close to the Aristotelian hylomorphism, which regards all material things as having been produced from two essential principles, matter and form. But what Aristotle claims for individual things, Uemov here extends to the world as a whole, in which space-time plays the part of form and matter the part of content, or, in Aristotelian terminology, of 'matter', the result being that the world as a whole appears as a *single* substance.[3]

The chief intention of the foregoing account has been to point out the manner in which Soviet philosophy sets about giving a philosophical interpretation to relativity theory. There is, of course, no occasion for us here to enter into extensive discussion of the numerous problems thus created. As in the case of quantum physics, the chief thing which interests us here is to discover to what extent relativity theory does in fact constitute a confirmation of dialectical materialism.

In the first place, it is interesting to note that relativity theory originally met with very decided rejection in the name of dialectical

[1] A. I. Uemov: *Geliotsentricheskaya sistema Kopernika i teoriya otnositel'-nosti* (The Heliocentric System of Copernicus and the Theory of Relativity), in *Filosofskie voprosy sovremennoy fiziki*, pp. 299–331, *q.v.* p. 310.

[2] A. I. Uemov: *Mozhet li prostranstvenno-vremennoy kontinuum vzaimo-deystvovat' s materiey?*, in *VF*, 1954, 3, pp. 172–80.

[3] It may be mentioned in this connection that W. Büchel (*Individualität und Wechselwirkung im Bereich des materiellen Seins*, in *Scholastik*, 31, 1956, pp. 1–30) has recently attempted, from a scholastic standpoint, to represent the whole of the inorganic world as a single substance, in the philosophical sense of the term.

materialism itself, and that it took a considerable time before it was recognized to provide any confirmation of dialectical materialism; this raises an antecedent suspicion that such 'confirmation' is not entirely unambiguous. In actual fact it consists, at most, in the confirmation of a number of theses that dialectical materialism shares with many other philosophical systems—unless we are to reckon with such feeble platitudes as that enunciated by Stalin, to the effect that everything in the world is connected with everything else. It will be evident that this does nothing to support the basic axiom of dialectical materialism, namely that there is nothing in the world except matter. For this question cannot in principle be settled in terms of physics, since it is a purely philosophical question.

3. MASS AND ENERGY

We have seen in the previous section how Einstein, on the basis of special relativity and the already-discovered fact that electro-magnetic waves exert pressure, arrived at the principle of the 'inertia of energy', whereby all energy possesses an inert mass in accordance with the formula $E = mc^2$.[1] This law has become a fundamental principle in all atomic physics, and finds its chief application in the exploitation of atomic energy. Since this nuclear transformation exhibits a phenomenon referred to as 'mass-defect', it is customary to speak (in somewhat misleading fashion) of a transformation of mass into energy, or even of a transformation of matter into energy. From this it is often rather hastily inferred by philosophers that matter is dissolved into nothing, and hence that materialism has been shown to be false.

It is therefore not surprising to find the Soviet philosophers de-voting no little trouble to campaigning against this new form of 'energeticism' and 'physical idealism'. The positions they chiefly have in mind are those of writers like Jeans and Eddington, who con-sidered the radiation of energy by the sun and stars to be due to an 'annihilation of matter'; reference is made to expressions occasionally used by certain physicists, as, for example, when K. Darrow speaks of decay in uranium as a 'transformation of matter . . . into some-

---

[1] As regards the discovery of the principle of the inertia of energy, Soviet physicists lose no opportunity of attributing the decisive part to the Rus-sian physicist P. N. Lebedev, who established the fact of light-pressure in 1899, while they frequently make no mention at all of Einstein in this con-nection. Now it is certainly true that Lebedev showed that light exerts pressure; but to treat this as equivalent to discovering the principle of the inertia of energy is a gross exaggeration, since it was only Einstein, in the special theory of relativity, who first recognized radiation-pressure as a special case of the general concept of the inertia of energy.

thing that is not matter', or when C. Chase and L. Barnett refer to mass, or matter, as a 'form of energy', and derive the action of the atomic bomb from a 'transformation of matter into energy'.[1] Crown-witnesses for the 'idealist' conclusions drawn from these premisses are found, for example, in E. S. Brightman the American 'personalist', who designates 'God', or 'higher personality' as the bearer of energy, and sees it as 'divine will in action', or even in P. Jordan, who observes, in his *Physics in the Twentieth Century*, that the new physics has destroyed the scientific foundations of materialism.[2]

The Soviet philosophers are therefore much exercised, in the field of atomic physics, with giving a dialectical materialist interpretation to those facts which are generally brought forward on behalf of the apparent transformation of mass into energy. The most prominent of these are the 'mass-defect' which is to be observed both in the build-up of nuclei from protons and neutrons and also in the breakdown of heavier nuclei into lighter ones, and the transformation of an electron-positron pair into energy-quanta (gamma-photons).

In order to understand what follows, it must be premised that, as already mentioned, Soviet philosophy believes that matter occurs in two forms: as 'stuff' and as 'light' in a broad sense, *i.e.*, as an electro-magnetic field. The elementary particles of 'stuff' consist of electrons, protons, neutrons etc.; those of the electro-magnetic field of photons, which are regarded as differing 'qualitatively' from one another, according to the wave-length of radiation to which they are assigned (radio-waves have the longest wave-length; the scale then descending *via* heat- and light-waves to X-rays, and finally arriving at the shortest wave-length in gamma-radiation). Both forms, stuff and electro-magnetic field, possess both mass and energy. But Vislobokov sees the main difference between them in the fact that the elementary particles of 'stuff' exhibit both 'mass of motion' and rest-mass, whereas photons have no rest-mass. Hence the particles of stuff can have various velocities, though they never reach the speed of light, whereas photons, of whatever wave-length, travel only at this speed. Moreover, particles of stuff may carry a positive or negative electric charge, or be uncharged, whereas photons are invariably uncharged.[3]

Now as against 'energeticism' and 'physical idealism', Soviet philosophy maintains that both photo-radiation and the phenomena of mass-defect are not based on any transformation of 'mass' into

---

[1] *Cf.* N. F. Ovchinnikov: *Ponyatiya massy i energii v sovremennoy fizike i ikh filosofskoe znachenie* (The Concepts of Mass and Energy in Modern Physics and their Philosophical Significance), in *Filosofskie voprosy sovremennoy fiziki*, pp. 445-88, *q.v.* p. 481; A. Vislobokov: *O nerazryvnosti materii i dvizheniya* (On the Inseparability of Matter and Motion), Moscow 1955, p. 104.

[2] A. Vislobokov: *Op. cit.*, pp. 110 f.   [3] *Ibid.*, pp. 74 ff.

'energy', there being merely a change from 'stuff' into 'electro-magnetic field', in which the total sum both of mass and energy remains constant, and energy is nowhere created at the expense of mass.

So far as 'mass-defects' in nuclear reactions are concerned, Vislobokov maintains that in such reactions there is not only a mass-defect to be recorded, but also a corresponding loss of sub-atomic energy. The energy of an atom consists of two parts: the energy of the electronic shell, and that of the nucleus. Most of the energy of the atom is concentrated in the latter. It is the energy of the forces whereby the parts of the nucleus—protons and neutrons—adhere together, and is therefore called the 'binding-energy'. If the latter is divided by the number of protons and neutrons contained in the nucleus, the resultant 'binding-energy per nuclear particle' is greatest among the elements in the middle part of the Mendeleyev table; it becomes weaker among the lighter elements, and among the heavier ones smaller still. Hence it comes about, that nuclear energy can be released in two different ways: (a) by splitting the atomic nuclei of heavier elements, and (b) by the formation of heavier nuclei out of lighter ones. Thus all atomic nuclei, with the exception of those of the middle elements, can be used as 'fuel' for nuclear reactions.

Vislobokov now explains that the mass-defect in the fission-reaction involves no 'transformation' of the lost mass into energy, by taking as his example the reaction of a lithium atom under bombardment by a proton. The result of this encounter is the formation of two alpha-particles (helium nuclei), which fly off with great rapidity in opposite directions. This is expressed by the formula $Li_3^7 + H_1^1 \rightarrow 2He_2^4$. The binding-energy in the lithium nucleus amounts to 39 megaelectron-volts (MeV), that in each of the alpha-particles to 28 MeV, making 56 MeV in all. Now this means that the sub-atomic energy of the two alpha-particles is 17 MeV less,[1] as compared with that of the lithium nucleus. But that, however, is

[1] The reason why this quantity of 17 MeV must be regarded as a *loss* and not an increase of subatomic energy, is given as follows: The binding-energy here under discussion is defined as the energy which must be *applied* in order to *detach* the constituents of the atomic nucleus from one another, or which is *liberated* when these constituents *unite* under the influence of the attractive forces between them (just as energy is liberated when a stone falls from a great height, under the influence of gravity, towards the centre of the earth). The greater the binding-energy, the more firmly do the particles cling together. The fact that the binding-energy of the two alpha-particles taken together is greater than that of the lithium nucleus, means that the protons and neutrons in the alpha-particles are more firmly united than in the lithium nucleus, and that less energy is therefore required to separate the constituents of the latter than is gained when these constituents unite with the incoming proton to form two alpha-particles.

exactly the value of the kinetic energy of the flying alpha-particles. But to this loss of energy there corresponds a mass-defect exactly in accordance with the formula $E = mc^2$. The sum of the masses before the reaction amounted to 8·026294 mass-units; after it, to 8·007720; and the defect therefore amounts to 0·018574. However, this lost mass has not been transformed into kinetic energy, as the 'physical idealists' maintain, but has been changed from 'rest-mass' into 'mass of motion', *i.e.*, it now represents the mass of the energy of motion which must be added to the alpha-particles on the ground of their high velocity (about 1/20th of the speed of light).

The same holds for other decay-processes in which, as for example in the breakdown of uranium, as exploited in the atomic bomb, gamma-rays are often emitted as well. In such breakdown-processes we therefore have, in consequence, the following changes of mass and energy: the greater part of the mass of the initial nucleus is conserved as rest-mass of the 'fission-products' and of the particles (neutrons) that are emitted; a smaller part is changed into 'mass of motion' of the fission-products and neutrons, and a further portion appears as mass of the electro-magnetic energy contained in the photons of the gamma-radiation. There is also a corresponding distribution of energy of the shattered nucleus: the greater part of it goes over into the subatomic energy of the newly-created atomic nuclei, a smaller part into their kinetic energy, and the remainder into electro-magnetic energy.[1]

The opposite process, in which heavier atomic nuclei are formed out of lighter ones, also gives rise to the appearance of the mass-defect, which is interpreted as a transformation of mass into energy. Under natural conditions, such processes do not occur on earth, but they are exceedingly abundant in the sun and stars. In the development of stars, increasing age is marked by a decrease of mass. This lost mass is that of the energy which has been radiated in the form of heat and light.

In order to show that such processes no more involve the transformation of mass into energy than the previous ones, Vislobokov refers to the so-called Bethe-cycle, which takes place on the sun and which, after a series of intermediate reactions, eventually results in the formation of a helium-nucleus from four protons. Thus the lighter element hydrogen is transformed into the heavier element helium. But the mass of the isolated protons would be 4·03416 mass-units (MU), whereas the actual mass of the helium-nucleus amounts only to 4·00384 MU. We are therefore confronted with a mass-loss of 0·03032. But now in the case of this Bethe-cycle, it must be noted that in some of the intermediate reactions gamma-rays are also emitted,

[1] *Cf.* A. Vislobokov: *Op. cit.*, pp. 89–94; also N. F. Ovchinnikov: *Op. cit.*, p. 478.

which possess high energy and also mass. Here too, therefore, according to Vislobokov, there is a partial transformation of 'stuff' into electro-magnetic field. The above-mentioned mass-defect is therefore explicable, in that a part of the mass of the 'stuff', quantitatively equal to the mass-defect, is transformed into photons and carried off by them.[1]

Apart from the mass-defect observable in nuclear transformation-processes, the 'physical idealists' have also instanced the change of an electron-positron pair into gamma-photons. After the positron had actually been discovered, in 1932, it was soon established also that a collision of these two particles results in their both ceasing to exist and being transformed into two gamma-photons. Vislobokov now argues that in this case too there can be no talk of a transformation of mass into energy, since the photon also has mass. When the pair are thus transformed into photons, both mass and energy are quantitatively conserved, being equally distributed between the two photons.[2] The same holds for the reverse process of pair-formation, in which a gamma-photon passing close to the nucleus of a heavy element is transformed into an electron-positron pair. A similar transformation of electro-magnetic field into 'stuff' takes place, according to Vislobokov, when electrically-charged particles are accelerated in a magnetic field (as with an electron in a synchrotron): such a particle receives an acceleration, and its 'mass of motion' thereupon increases proportionately to its kinetic energy; but in both cases this is achieved at the expense of the corresponding factors in the electro-magnetic field.[3]

In reporting the standpoint of Soviet philosophy on this question of the possibility of transforming matter into energy, we have chiefly relied upon Vislobokov. But this position appears to be the prevailing one in the Soviet Union. Vislobokov cites a number of other names in support of his views, some of them very authoritative: S. I. Vavilov, President of the Academy of Sciences of the U.S.S.R., who died in 1951, together with D. I. Blokhintsev,[4] B. M. Kedrov, I. V. Kuznetsov, S. G. Suvorov and N. F. Ovchinnikov. As against this, he accuses certain Soviet physicists, such as A. F. Ioffe,[5] A. F. Kapustinsky[6] and T. P. Kravtsev,[7] of having spoken up in favour of the

---

[1] A. Vislobokov: *Op. cit.*, pp. 94 f.   [2] *Ibid.*, p. 97.   [3] *Ibid.*, pp. 96 f.

[4] *Cf.* D. I. Blokhintsev and S. I. Drabkina: *Teoriya otnositel'nosti A. Einsteina* (Einstein's Theory of Relativity), Gostekhizdat 1940.

[5] A. F. Ioffe: *Osnovnye predstavleniya sovremennoy fiziki* (Fundamental Ideas of Modern Physics), Gostekhizdat 1949.

[6] A. F. Kapustinsky: *Energiya atoma* (The Energy of the Atom), Goskul'tprosvetizdat 1947.

[7] T. P. Kravtsev: *Evolyutsiya ucheniya ob energii* (The Development of the Theory of Energy), in *Uspekhi fizicheskikh nauk*, Vol. 36/3 (1948).

identity of matter and energy, the transformation of matter into energy, the conception of energy as a substance, and so forth. A. A. Maximov, the philosopher, is reproached for having given countenance to 'energeticism' by extending the concept of energy more widely than that of matter, when he writes:

'The concept of energy includes not only that of motion, but also that of matter (which is physically defined in terms of mass, charge, etc.).'[1]

The philosophical viewpoint which Vislobokov extracts from his discussions of nuclear processes and the transformation of electron-positron pairs into photons is as follows: in all these processes we are concerned, not with an 'annihilation' of matter, but with a transformation of 'stuff' into 'light', the elementary particles of each being qualitatively different from the other and the transition from one to another being accomplished by way of a 'dialectical leap', whereby the mass and energy of the one are transformed into those of the other.

'The major achievements of modern physics . . . once again provide a complete refutation of the fantasies of the idealists as to the presence of an immaterial motion and confirm beyond all doubt the correctness of the theses of dialectical materialism as a whole (!) and thereby also the doctrine of the inseparable connection between motion and matter.'[2]

According to the Soviet philosophers, this inseparable connection between matter and motion is the true meaning of Einstein's formula $E = mc^2$. It does not represent a possibility of transforming mass into energy. Vislobokov also refuses to speak of the 'equivalence' of mass and energy; those forms of energy are equivalent which can also be transformed into one another; the use of this expression to designate the relationship between mass and energy would readily encourage the idea that they too could be mutually transformed into one another.[3] The true meaning of this formula is as follows, namely that

'any given material object having a mass of this or that nature necessarily also possesses the corresponding type of energy'.[4]

Hence the Soviet philosophers regard this physical principle as proof

[1] A. A. Maximov: *Vvedenie v sovremennoe uchenie o materii i dvizhenii* (Introduction to the Modern Theory of Matter and Motion), Sotsekgiz 1941, p. 154. *Cf.* on all this, A. Vislobokov: *Op. cit.*, pp. 116 ff.
[2] A. Vislobokov: *Op. cit.*, p. 100.   [3] *Ibid.*, p. 106.
[4] N. F. Ovchinnikov: *Material'nost mira i zakonomernosti ego razvitiya* (The Materiality of the World and the Laws of its Development), *VF*, 1951, 5, pp. 135–52, *q.v.* p. 145.

of the dialectical materialist thesis of *self-movement*, whereby there can no more be matter without motion than motion without matter, and from this they conclude that all motion, including that in inanimate nature, must be regarded as self-movement.[1]

The dialectical materialist thesis of the eternity of the world is also supposed to find confirmation in the physical theory of mass and energy. The laws of the conservation of mass and energy, which have been combined by means of the principle of the inertia of energy ($E = mc^2$) into a common law of conservation, have been regarded, ever since Engels' day, as a proof of the eternity of the world. Engels saw in the law of conservation of energy a proof of the fact that the universe is both indestructible and incapable of being created, and hence must have existed from all eternity.[2] Lenin likewise saw in this law 'the establishment of the basic principles of materialism'.[3] We shall only be able to go into this question in detail later on, when we come to deal with the problems of cosmology and cosmogony.[4]

Other dialectical materialist theses are also alleged to receive confirmation from modern atomic physics: the material unity of the world is evident in the possibilities of mutual transformation amongst elementary particles and the chemical elements.[5] Kedrov sees the Leninist thesis of the 'inexhaustibility' of the electron confirmed in the infinity and inexhaustibility of mutual interchange among the elementary particles, which implies the 'infinity and inexhaustibility of every individual particle, including also the electron'.[6] He likewise attempts to find an expression of this 'inexhaustibility' of the electron in the electronic mist (*i.e.*, in the fact that in its revolution around the atomic nucleus the electron does not always describe the same path), and also in the fact of spin.[7]

If we disregard these last-mentioned 'confirmations' of dialectical materialism, which are scarcely in need of discussion (since they have no bearing at all upon the decisive question, whether there are any non-material realities over and above matter), we shall find the really central claim of Soviet philosophy in the field of atomic physics to consist in its demonstration of the self-movement of matter. Even from our own non-materialistic standpoint, we have absolutely no difficulty in crediting inanimate matter with self-movement in the sense assigned to it above by the Soviet philosophers, *i.e.*, in acknow-

[1] N. F. Ovchinnikov: *Ponyatiya massy* . . ., pp. 480, 458.
[2] F. Engels: *Dialectics of Nature*, pp. 93–4.
[3] *ME*, p. 318 (346 n., 382 n.)   [4] *Cf.* below, p. 441.
[5] N. F. Ovchinnikov: *Material'nost* . . ., p. 137.
[6] B. M. Kedrov: *Leninsky vzglyad na elektron i sovremennaya fizika* (Lenin's Concept of the Electron and Modern Physics), in *Bol'shevik*, 1948, 3, pp. 44–61, *q.v.* p. 58.
[7] *Ibid.*, pp. 51 f.

ledging that every movement (every event) presupposes a substantial substratum, and that on the other hand substantial material being carries within itself those forces which continually actuate the process of becoming in physical Nature. (This does nothing, as yet, to settle the question whether matter, with these forces it possesses, exists from itself alone, *i e.*, whether it bears within itself its own ultimate cause, or whether it presupposes an act of creation on the part of a transcendent God.)

The Soviet philosophers imagine, however, that the admission of 'self-movement' in matter, in the sense that matter and motion are inseparable, necessarily also implies acceptance of materialism. Thus Vislobokov writes, in the Introduction to his oft-cited work:

'The idealists have thought and continue to think of motion as independent of matter. They have reckoned mere sensations, images and concepts, divorced from matter, to be capable of motion, and have never abandoned the attempt to refute the thesis of the materiality of motion. . . . Thus a defender of modern idealism, the Jesuit Gustav Wetter, declares, in his booklet [*sic*] *Dialectical Materialism. A Historical and Systematic Survey of Philosophy in the Soviet Union*, lately published in 1952 in Vienna, that the dialectical materialist thesis of the inseparability of matter and motion is merely postulated, *i.e.*, enunciated without proof, and that this thesis appears to be untenable either from a philosophical or from a scientific point of view.' [1]

The notion underlying these observations, and the whole of Vislobokov's book, is this: There can be no motion without a substantial substratum. But any such substantial substratum can consist only of mass, *i.e.*, matter. Hence all motion, all becoming, is necessarily bound up with matter. Hence there can be no other reality apart from matter, and philosophical materialism is proved.

We entirely accept the first premiss of this argument, but are decidedly opposed to the second, or at least assert our right to demand of it some show of proof. We admit, that is, that *material* motion must have a *material* substantial substratum. But precisely because we agree with dialectical materialism in accepting the first proposition, that there can be no motion or becoming without a substratum, we must insist that a process such as the mental movement of thought, which transcends material forces, (and which even dialectical materialism recognizes to be mental, *i.e.*, essentially different from physico-chemical processes), must also have a corresponding mental substratum.

[1] A. Vislobokov: *Op. cit.*, pp. 3 f.

To illustrate the reliability of Soviet authors in reporting on works of a contrary tendency, it may be pointed out that in the corresponding passage from the first German edition of the present book it was expressly stated:

'As regards the foregoing thesis of dialectical materialism, that motion is inseparable from matter and that hence absolute rest (in the sense of absolute lack of change) is nowhere to be found in the universe, we have nothing further to say against it.' [1]

The campaign which the Soviet philosophers are here conducting against 'philosophical idealism' is therefore directed, in this instance, against a view which also appears extremely dubious from the standpoint of a non-materialistic philosophy. Such a view has been encouraged by certain physicists, who, as we have already seen, have drawn very questionable philosophical conclusions from physical facts. If it be supposed that a transformation of mass, or matter, into energy represents a 'dematerialization', we are confronted here with a very odd way of speaking. The expression 'dematerialization' rests upon the fact that in the physical mode of speech particles possessing rest-mass are described forthwith as 'material' particles. But it does not follow from this that, philosophically speaking, light-quanta are not also to be assigned to the realm of the material. And if, on occasion, energy has been described as 'the divine will in action', such a view is based upon a highly materialistic concept of God. The passion with which the Soviet philosophers assail the interpretation of the formula $E = mc^2$, as implying the possibility of transforming matter into energy, appears, therefore, to be largely unwarranted, since this view must also be rejected by a non-materialistic philosophy.

4. CHEMISTRY

In the field of chemistry, it was structural chemistry which formed the subject of an altercation among Soviet scientists and philosophers in the years 1949–51. Here it was a matter of combating the resonance theory, put forward in 1932–4 by the American chemist L. Pauling, and further extended by J. W. Wehland, together with the theory of mesomerism developed by Ingold in Britain.

Structural chemistry attempts, on the basis of the various valencies exhibited by individual atoms, to sketch out a picture of their actual arrangement in the molecule, thereby producing a diagram of the latter's 'structure'. In most cases it turns out that one and the same

[1] G. A. Wetter: *Der dialektische Materialismus. Seine Geschichte und sein System in der Sowjetunion*, Vienna–Freiburg i. B. 1952, p. 330.

chemical bond between atoms allows of formally different, though equally valid, structural diagrams. Thus the benzene molecule, C_6H_6, for example, allows of five different structural diagrams:

Anthracene would admit of 429 schemas of this type.

The resonance theory goes on to apply quantum mechanics and Dirac's principle of superposition to the theoretical description of the molecule. In so doing, it resolves the wave-function ψ into a series φ_i and proceeds to coordinate each member of this series with one of the possible structural formulae. Now according to the resonance theory, the real structure of the molecule is to be found, not in any single one of these formulae, but is obtained by superposition of all the possible individual structures, or by their 'resonance'. The individual schemas and formulae serve merely as 'rough descriptions', being purely ideal constructions which are not to be construed as objective.[1]

The theory of mesomerism pursues a similar course in order to arrive at a result in complicated cases of this type, in which the real structure of the molecule cannot be determined by means of the normal valency formulae. In this case Ingold proposes to set up two limiting structural diagrams and to determine the actual structure of the real molecule as an intermediate value base upon these two fictitious structures.

In the Soviet Union the resonance theory has gained currency mainly through the work of Professor Y. K. Syrkin and his collaborator M. E. Dyatkina, who were joint-authors of a textbook published in 1946 and intended for chemistry faculties in universities, *The Chemical Bond and the Structure of Molecules*,[2] and who have translated various works by Pauling and Wehland into Russian. In the years 1949–51 these theories were subjected to heated discussions in various Institutes, and finally became the topic of an 'All-Union Conference on the Theory of the Chemical Structure of Organic Bonds', organized from 11th to 14th June 1951 by the Chemistry

[1] *Cf.* B. M. Kedrov: *Protiv 'fizicheskogo' idealizma v khimicheskoy nauke* (Against 'Physical' Idealism in Chemistry), in *Filosofskie voprosy sovremennoy fiziki*, pp. 539–75, *q.v.* especially pp. 546–51; and *Protiv idealizma i mekhanitsizma v organicheskoy khimii* (Against Idealism and Mechanicism in Organic Chemistry), in *Bol'shevik*, 1951, pp. 13–24, *q.v.* p. 14. *Cf.* also the article *Resonansa teorlya* (Resonance Theory) in *BSE*, XXXVI, pp 280 f.

[2] Y. K. Syrkin, M. E. Dyatkina: *Khimicheskaya svyaz' i stroenie molekul*, 1946.

section of the Academy of Sciences of the Soviet Union.[1] The Editors of *Voprosy filosofii* also carried on a discussion on this theory in their journal, introduced by an article by Tatevsky and Shakhparonov *On a Machist Theory in Chemistry and its Propagandists*,[2] and concluded by an editorial note in the second number of the 1950 volume.

It would take us too far to enter into the details of this discussion;[3] it ended in both these theories being decisively rejected. The resonance theory was accused of subjective idealism, agnosticism and mechanism: idealism, because it turned a fictitious diagram (the individual schemas and formulae, which were regarded as mere 'ideal constructions') into a real object, in that real active properties were ascribed to it (that of being overlaid one upon another in superposition, and that of 'resonating'!); agnosticism, because it denied the possibility of reproducing *one* object (the organic molecule) by means of *one* structural formula; and mechanism, insofar as the resonance theory attempts to 'reduce' the laws of organic chemistry to those of quantum mechanics. Of the theory of mesomerism it is said that it essentially comes to the same thing as the resonance theory, and that similar objections must therefore be held against it.[4]

A very weighty objection raised against Soviet supporters of the resonance theory, and wholly in the spirit of the patriotic line pursued in these years, was that they were overlooking the theory of the Russian chemist A. M. Butlerov. The latter enjoyed particular esteem among the Soviet philosophers in that, already in the second half of the previous century, he had fought against the 'mechanism' and 'agnosticism' to be found in Kekulé's theory of chemical structure. This 'mechanism' and 'agnosticism' was alleged of Kekulé in that he did not regard the chemical formula as a picture of the real structure of the molecule, and merely took account of the purely quantitative side of atomic valency, without attending to the qualitative aspect, which consists in the reciprocal influence of the atoms and the changes in their chemical properties which are engendered thereby. In contrast to such views, Butlerov had already published, in 1861, a truly 'materialistic' and at the same time 'dialectical' theory of the chemical structure of the molecule. The chief content of Butlerov's theory is held to lie in the following points: the chemical formula

---

[1] Proceedings of this Conference in: *Sostoyanie teorii khimicheskogo stroeniya, Vsesoyuznoe soveshchanie 11–14 iyunya 1951 g.* (The Theoretical Situation in Chemical Structure. All-Union Conference of 11–14 June 1951. Verbatim Report), Moscow 1952.

[2] V. M. Tatevsky and M. I. Shakhparonov: *Ob odnoy machistskoy teorii v khimii i ee propagandistakh*, VF, 1949, 3, pp. 176–92.

[3] These may be pursued in A. Buchholz: *Op. cit.*, pp. 38–43.

[4] *Cf.* B. M. Kedrov: *Protiv 'fizicheskogo' idealizma . . .*, pp. 574 f.

expresses the real bonding of atoms in the molecule, and thereby conveys to us a picture of the latter's structure ('agnosticism' vanquished); the atoms in the molecule are not merely linked externally with one another, but influence each other reciprocally and thereby undergo *qualitative* changes ('mechanism' vanquished). It must be the task of Soviet chemists to build further upon the theory founded by Butlerov and later extended by his pupil V. V. Markovnikov.[1]

It is certainly true that the diagrammatic formulae of molecular chemical bonding, which are established on the basis of the valency of the atoms, do more than express the merely quantitative relationship between the atoms of the individual elements, and that they also, at least approximately, convey a picture of the structure of the molecule and the arrangement of the atoms within it.

But when the resonance theory is accused of relapsing into 'idealism' or 'agnosticism', things are not so simple as Soviet criticism would have it appear. For the chemical formulae of structure based upon valencies have lately shown themselves to be merely an approximate picture of the molecule. In recent years, indeed, the whole theory of valency has had to be considerably revised, 'valencies' themselves having been replaced by Werner coordination-numbers. Since it is still not possible, in the present state of knowledge, to provide an exact structural picture of the molecule, the resonance theory seeks to be nothing more than a practical aid, which, in order to provide a more convenient grasp of physical states of affairs, deliberately makes allowance for a certain freedom in the selection of initial structures, a disadvantage which is compensated, however, by its enormous practical success in the solution of chemical problems. The founders of this theory have themselves given warning, indeed, against ascribing to these structures, which they would wish to see regarded as speculative magnitudes, a physical meaning they do not possess. There is no question here, therefore, either of 'idealism' or 'Machism',[2] but merely of pure working hypotheses.

But it may well be that the real meaning of this controversy is to be sought elsewhere; for it occurred during the heyday of the struggle against 'cosmopolitanism' and 'servility towards bourgeois culture', the struggle for 'Soviet patriotism'. One gets the impression that at this period virtually everything was seized upon and correspondingly inflated, which could in any way offer a handle for convicting

---

[1] *Cf.* B. M. Kedrov: *Op. cit.*, pp. 541 ff.; also *Ot redaktsii* (Editorial), *VF*, 1950, 2, pp. 194–6.

[2] V. M. Tatevsky and M. I. Shakhparonov: *Ob odnoy machistskoy teorii . . .*, pp. 176 f.

Western theories of 'idealism', 'Machism', etc.; just as the possibility of embracing Butlerov's theories offered a welcome opportunity for a display of 'Soviet patriotism'.

5. COSMOGONY

The ideological slant which we have been able to detect in all fields of Soviet natural philosophy so far examined, is to be met with in even greater degree in the territories of cosmology and cosmogony. Here the postulates of dialectical materialism are openly taken as a *starting-point* in the erection of hypotheses :

'The Marxist-Leninist doctrine of the infinitude of the universe is the *fundamental axiom* at the basis of Soviet cosmology. . . . The denial or abandonment of this thesis . . . leads inevitably to idealism and fideism, *i.e.*, in effect, to the negation of cosmology, and therefore has nothing in common with science.' [1]

Similar views have been expressed by other Soviet astronomers, including those of repute, such as V. A. Ambarzumyan.[2]

In the field of *Cosmology*, it is the first concern of Soviet scientists to refute the conclusion of an unavoidable 'heat-death', which is often drawn from the second law of thermodynamics. Since, according to this law, energy that has been transformed into heat cannot again be turned back entirely into higher forms of energy, our universe must be tending towards a state of affairs in which all higher forms of energy have been changed into heat and the latter in turn has been equally distributed throughout the entire universe, with the result that all macrophysical processes would have come to a standstill. From the necessity of such an end-state of thermodynamic equilibrium, it is also concluded that there must necessarily have been a beginning to this process in the past, and hence some sort of creation of the world, since if this process had been going on indefinitely the heat-death must already have supervened long ago.

In Soviet eyes, the basic error of Clausius, who initiated these arguments about the heat-death, lies in the fact that laws holding for finite systems cannot be transferred without further ado to a universe postulated to be infinite. Statistical physics and thermodynamics are concerned with systems of an admittedly very great

[1] M. S. Eigenson: *K voprosu o kosmogonii* (On the Problem of Cosmogony), in *Circular No. 30, Ministerstvo Vysshego Obrazovaniya SSSR, L'vovsky Gosudarstvenny Universitet, Astronomicheskaya Observatoriya,* 1955, pp. 1–12, *q.v.* p. 10 (our italics—G. W.).

[2] V. A. Ambarzumyan: *Kosmogoniya* (Cosmogony), in *BSE*, XXIII, pp. 103 f.

but nonetheless finite number of parts, whereas the universe, according to dialectical materialism, must be regarded as infinite.[1]

A further major concern of Soviet cosmology consists in discovering an interpretation of the red shift in the spectral lines of all distant nebulae, which shall be consistent with the eternity of the universe. As is known, the red shift is normally interpreted in terms of a 'Doppler effect',[2] and from this it is then concluded, somewhat as follows, that the universe must have had a beginning in time: interpreted as a Doppler effect the red shift implies that the nebulae are receding from us with enormous velocities, and it appears, moreover, that these velocities increase, the greater the distance of any given nebula from us. But, accepting the formula given by the Belgian, Canon Lemaître, who is Professor at the University of Louvain, it is possible to calculate from these measurements the point in time at which the universe must have been of zero volume. This originally led to a figure of about 2,700 million years (though it must now be corrected to 4,000 million). But in considering these speculations about the red shift, it must be observed, however, that they depend upon interpreting it as a Doppler effect, and this is a matter upon which even Western physicists are by no means unanimous.

Here too, the Soviet thinkers make use of the principle enunciated by Zhdanov in his speech at the Philosophical Discussion of 1947, and already referred to above, namely that the results of investigation in the portions of the galactic system in our immediate neighbourhood, should not be transferred to the whole universe and extrapolated at will into the past.[3] Barabashev thinks that the red shift can

[1] *Cf.* A. L. Zel'manov: *Kosmologiya* (Cosmology), in *BSE*, XXIII, p. 110.

[2] By 'Doppler effect' is meant, of course, the change of frequency in a wave-process when the wave-source is altering its position in relation to the observer. This is why the horn note of a car passing us at high speed seems distinctly higher on approaching than afterwards, when it is travelling away from us. In the case of light it is the spectral colour which corresponds to the frequency. If a light-source is moving sufficiently rapidly towards us, the spectral lines will be displaced towards the violet (the shorter the wave-length, the higher the frequency); in the opposite case, towards the red (the longer the wave-length, the lower the frequency). From the degree to which the lines are shifted it is possible to calculate the speed with which the object in question is moving towards or away from us. *Cf.*, for instance, F. Sherwood Taylor: *The World of Science*, London 1936, ch. 13.

[3] 'Contemporary bourgeois science supplies clericalism and fideism with new arguments which must be mercilessly exposed . . . Many followers of Einstein, in their failure to understand the dialectical process of knowledge, the relationship of absolute and relative truth, transpose the results of the study of the laws of motion of the finite, limited sphere of the universe

perhaps be explained by the fact that the light must pass through gravitational fields on its way towards us; or if there is in fact a motion of recession, this may perhaps be of the same character as the dispersive motion of stars or star-clusters within our own Milky Way.[1] But to this it could be replied that there should then be nebulae that are also moving towards us, which, so far as we know, is not the case.

However, it is not only an expanding universe that is rejected in Soviet cosmogony, but also an oscillating one, though one might indeed have expected that the assumption of an oscillation would have been a very convenient way of combining the recession of the galaxies with the eternity of the universe. Nevertheless, Barabashev describes all theories tending in this direction as 'false and absolutely untenable speculations, remote from all genuine science'. What is meant by 'genuine science', in this connection, emerges very clearly from the sentences which immediately follow: such theories

'are completely untenable and wholly at variance with dialectical materialism, since they either lead . . . to the assumption of an act of creation, or they presuppose the appearance of new material bodies and new space in the course of the expansion of the universe and their destruction and disappearance into nothing during the phase of contraction. It is evident that both these assumptions are unscientific, anti-dialectical and lead to open and undisguised popery'.[2]

In the field of Soviet *Cosmogony*, a special place is occupied by the theory put forward by Academician O. Y. Schmidt (d. September 1956) concerning the formation of the solar system. According to his theory the origin of the earth and planets is due to the fact that the sun, on its journey round the centre of the Milky Way, passed through a cloud consisting of gas, dust and larger particles, and dragged out a part of this cloud along with it. This swarm of material possessed a significant momentum which ultimately passed over into the orbital and rotational momentum of the planets. Since the angular momentum of the planets would have been governed by the speed of motion of the sun in relation to the gas and dust cloud,

to the whole infinite universe and arrive at the idea of the finite nature of the world, its limitedness in time and space. The astronomer Milne has even "calculated" that the world was created 2 billion years ago'. (A. A. Zhdanov; *Vystuplenie na diskussii . . .*, *VF*, 1947, 1, p. 271; English version: *On Literature . . .*, p. 110).

[1] N. P. Barabashev: *Bor'ba s idealizmom v oblasti kosmogonicheskikh i kosmologicheskikh gipotez* (The Struggle against Idealism in the Field of Cosmogonical and Cosmological Hypotheses), Kharkov 1952, p. 117.

[2] *Ibid.*, pp. 116 f.

this theory avoids the major difficulty confronting the Laplacean hypothesis, namely that 98 per cent of the angular momentum of the solar system as a whole is concentrated in the planets, whereas 99 per cent of the mass belongs to the sun. The earth, according to this theory, was cold in origin and is undergoing a continual process of heating, due to the breakdown of radio-active elements, since in radio-active breakdown the resultant gain of heat is many times greater than the loss due to radiation.[1]

Schmidt's theory appears to have the greatest authority in the Soviet Union today. It has been taken over as a basis by other neighbouring branches of Soviet science, such as geology for example, and geophysics,[2] and has also been accepted by Oparin as the basis of his theory about the origin of life on earth. With certain reservations, it was approved by the first 'Conference on Problems of the Cosmogony of the Solar System' convened in Moscow by the Academy of Sciences of the U.S.S.R. from 16th to 19th April 1951.[3] The most important objection, which was brought forward by Academician V. G. Fesenkov, pointed out that Schmidt had considered the problem of the origin of the planets in isolation from that of the origin and development of the sun and stars; since the age of the sun and planets appears to be about the same, it is reasonable to assume that both sun and planets must have come into being at about the same time.[4]

The chief Soviet workers in the field of stellar cosmogony (origin and development of stars and galaxies) are V. A. Ambarzumyan,[5] B. V. Kukarkin, V. A. Krat, P. P. Parenago and others. Ambarzumyan upholds the view that the process of star-formation in our galaxy

---

[1] O. Y. Schmidt: *Problema proiskhozhdeniya zemli i planet* (The Problem of the Origin of the Earth and Planets), *VF*, 1951, 4, pp. 120–33; *cf.* also the same author's *Chetyre lektsii o teorii proiskhozhdeniya zemli* (Four Lectures on the Theory of the Origin of the Earth), 2nd edn. 1950.

[2] *Voprosy geologii i geofiziki v kosmogonicheskoy teorii akademika O. Y. Schmidta: Soveshchanie v Leningrade* (Problems of Geology and Geophysics in the Cosmogonical Theory of Academician O. Y. Schmidt: A Conference in Leningrad), in *Vestnik AN SSSR*, 1953, 4, pp. 88–90.

[3] V. S. Safronov: *Problema proiskhozhdeniya zemli i planet: Soveshchanie po voprosam kosmogonii solnechnoy sistemy* (The Problem of the Origin of the Earth and Plants: A Conference on Problems of the Cosmogony of the Solar System), in *Vestnik Akademii Nauk SSSR*, 1951, 10, pp. 94–102.

[4] V. G. Fesenkov: *O kosmogonicheskoy gipoteze akademika O. Y. Schmidta i o sovremennom sostoyanii kosmogonicheskoy problemy* (On the Cosmogonical Hypothesis of Academician O. Y. Schmidt and the Present State of the Cosmogonical Problem), *VF*, 1951, 4, pp. 134–47, *q.v.* esp. p. 134.

[5] V. A. Ambarzumyan: *Evolyutsiya zvezd i astrofizika* (Stellar Evolution and Astrophysics), Erivan 1947.

is still going on. He bases his theory on the so-called 'star-associations' discovered and investigated by him in 1947–48, together with B. E. Markaryan. These, according to Ambarzumyan, are systems with 'positive total energy', in which the speed of motion of the individual members around the centre of the system is so great that the forces of mutual attraction are not sufficient to confer stability on the system. Hence he concludes that these associations must have a tendency to disperse, a conclusion which is said to have been confirmed in 1951 by the work of the Dutch astronomer Blaauw (whose results, however, are by no means assured). Ambarzumyan argues from this that the stars originate in groups. In the case of a group having positive energy, as with the associations, it must quickly fall apart. If the energy of the system is negative, then it is stable and maintains itself for a considerable period. The majority of star-groups (double stars, multiple stars, star-clusters) represent systems of negative energy. Since the age of these associations is relatively low, Ambarzumyan deduces that the process of star-formation must still be going on. But as to the nature of the 'proto-stars' from which these star-groups originate, he does not venture to supply any further details.[1]

From the above account of the basic themes of Soviet cosmology and cosmogony it will be seen that they have two main objects particularly in view: the first is to banish from modern astronomy all theories which in any way involve the assumption that the universe had a beginning in time or is spatially finite, and thereby encourage the idea of a creation of the world. In addition to this we find, in the field of cosmogony, the same fear of geocentricity which we were already able to note in dealing with relativity theory. If Jeans' theory of the origin of the solar system is so decidedly rejected,[2] the reason for this is that his theory leans much too strongly towards geocentricity.[3] Schmidt's theory, on the other hand, enjoys such high regard because in it the process of planetary formation appears, not as an exceedingly rare and exceptional case in the history of our

---

[1] V. A. Ambarzumyan: *Problema vozniknoveniya zvezd v svete novykh rabot sovetskikh astrofizikov* (The Problem of the Origin of the Stars in the Light of Recent Work in Soviet Astrophysics), in *Vestnik Akademii Nauk SSSR*, 1953, 12, pp. 49–60.

[2] Jeans attributed the origin of the planets to the passage into the sun's neighbourhood, many millions of years ago, of another extremely massive star, which drew out matter from the sun, this matter then coalescing to form the planets. Such an event would, however, be of the rarest occurrence in the universe.

[3] *Cf.* N. P. Barabashev: *Op. cit.*, p. 93.

universe, but as the normal one.[1] Our earth therefore occupies no special position in the universe.

One thing is particularly evident at this point: the guidance exercised by dialectical materialism over the sciences is much greater than the official version would have it appear.[2] Dialectical materialism manifests itself here, not merely as a 'generalization' of the results attained by the sciences; nor does it merely permeate the sciences as a 'methodology'. It also claims to give them guidance as an *account of reality*, whose theses are already laid down in cut-and-dried form before ever the sciences are at liberty to pursue their inquiries in this direction. Nor has the situation altered significantly since Stalin's death.

A peculiar vicious circle is thereby created: on the one hand the Soviet cosmologists maintain that dialectical materialism is the only scientific philosophy, since it is based on the findings of the sciences; but in those fields where science has been unable, as yet, to produce any final conclusions (as in the question whether the universe is spatially limited, or had a beginning in time), we find, on the other hand, that the only solutions accepted in advance as 'scientific' are those which conform to the purely *a priori* canons established by dialectical materialism. Indeed, as N. I. Guriev has pointedly remarked, the only 'scientific' evidence underlying Soviet championship of the spatio-temporal infinity of the universe, consists in the psychological impossibility of imagining a finite space or finite number-series; but in neither case does this have anything to do with science.[3]

Now as for the particular question of an opposition between 'science' and the religious belief in creation, it must be pointed out that on this subject there can, in principle, be no sort of conflict, since science is basically in no position to determine anything as to whether the world *in fact* had no beginning in time. All its assertions can at best lead only to the conclusion that the physical processes occurring in our world are so constituted that they either necessitate a beginning in time, or else do not require such a beginning, and *could* have been going on from all eternity. But whether they *in fact* had no beginning is something which neither atomic physics, nor astrophysics, nor astronomy, etc., can help us to decide. The controversy between dialectical materialism and the doctrine of creation cannot be resolved in this fashion. For supposing it were proved that the world might have existed from all eternity, adherents of the

---

[1] *Ibid.*, p. 101.　　　　　　　　　　　　　[2] *Cf.* above, p. 252.

[3] N. I. Guriev: *Sovetskaya kosmologiya na sluzhbe offitsial'nogo mirovozzreniya* (Soviet Cosmology in the Service of the Official Ideology), in *Vestnik instituta po izucheniyu istorii i kul'tury SSSR*, No. 1, Munich 1951, pp. 30-7, *q.v.* p. 33.

belief in creation would then appeal to the fact that, in virtue of its contingency, even an eternal world would require a creator.[1] For even on the assumption that the world does have a beginning in time, the act of creation must be thought of, not as a mere calling of the world into being for the first time, but also as an act which continues to maintain it in being. But once it has been shown on philosophical grounds that a creator is necessary in either case, it becomes possible in principle to accept a temporal creation of the world on grounds of revelation also, supposing the structure of the universe does not point back (as in the theory of the 'expanding universe', based on the red shift) to a temporal zero-point; for the creator himself must likewise be granted the possibility of creating the world either at the zero-point, or at any other desired juncture along its line of development. These considerations at least serve to show that the problem of the creation of the world cannot be decided on the scientific plane at all, but only along philosophical and, on occasion, theological lines.

6. THE ORIGIN OF LIFE

Not without justification does A. I. Oparin describe the problem of the origin of life as a

'subject of sharp ideological combat between the two irreconcilable philosophical camps—materialism and idealism'.[2]

And here our primary task must be to determine philosophically whether there is any justice in the dialectical materialist claim to be able to explain the spontaneous emergence of the higher from the lower.

On this problem as to the nature of life, dialectical materialism occupies a curious middle position between vitalism and mechanism. In common with the first, it is quite definite in rejecting the mechanist claim to deduce life without remainder from mechanical and chemical laws (the machine theory), and to interpret the origin of life as a product of chance, which has brought it about that, after an almost endless series of vain attempts, the atoms and molecules on one occasion entered 'by chance' into that extraordinarily rare combination which is required to provide the structure of a functional living form. Oparin himself gives a very striking indication of the hopelessness of any such claim:

[1] *Cf.* above, p. 353.
[2] A. I. Oparin: *Problema proiskhozhdeniya zhizni v svete dostizheniy sovremennogo estestvoznaniya* (The Problem of the Origin of Life in the Light of the Achievements of Modern Science), in *Vestnik Akademii Nauk SSSR*, 1953, 12, pp. 39-48, *q.v.* p. 39 (English in *The Origin of Life*, Moscow 1955, p. 5).

'This would be much as if we were to shake up a collection of printers' types, consisting of 28 different letters, in the hope that they would one day arrange themselves by chance into some poem or other with which we were familiar. Only if we know the order of letters and words in the poem can we derive the latter from them.' [1]

By the same token he also argues against the machine theory of mechanism that here it has forgotten

'that the internal purposiveness in the construction of the machine is governed by the creative will of its maker'.[2]

In strange contrast to this admission of the need for a creative principle to account for the origin of life ('knowledge' of the order of the letters, the 'creative will' of the maker of the machine), dialectical materialism allies itself on the other hand with mechanism, and against vitalism, in decisively rejecting the presence of any sort of ideal principle in the living creature ('entelechy', 'soul', 'life-force', or whatever it may be called) and *a fortiori* in rejecting the existence of a spiritual creative force on the supernatural plane. Vitalism is accused of conceiving matter as an 'inert' principle, which can only be animated by an immaterial one.

Dialectical materialism therefore advances the thesis that life represents something intrinsically different from, and higher than, inorganic matter, which interposes a 'qualitative' distinction between the two. The 'biological form of motion' in matter is a special form of motion and essentially higher than the 'physico-chemical form'.

Now what does the essence of this 'biological form of motion' in matter consist in? So far as Soviet philosophy is concerned, the definition given by Engels still retains its authority here:

'*Life is the mode of existence of albuminous substances*, and this mode of existence essentially consists in the constant self-renewal of the chemical constituents of these substances.' [3]

Oparin points out that Engels himself had already noted that this definition of his was inadequate, since it did not include all organic phenomena, but was confined to the simplest and commonest of these.[4] He himself sees the crucial feature of life in that 'purposiveness' whereby tens and hundreds of thousands of individual chemical

---

[1] A. I. Oparin: *Proiskhozhdenie zhizni* (The Origins of Life), Moscow 1954, p. 46 (*cf.* English version, p. 50).

[2] A. I. Oparin: *Zhizn'* (Life) in *BSE*, XVI, p. 141.

[3] F. Engels: *Anti-Dühring*, p. 93; *cf.* also *Dialectics of Nature*, p. 396.

[4] A. I. Oparin, in *BSE*, XVI, p. 139; *cf. Anti-Dühring*, p. 95.

reactions 'are strictly coordinated in point of time,' and in such a way that

'that order itself is directed towards . . . the self-renovation and self-preservation of the entire living system as a whole, in law-governed conformity with environmental conditions'.[1]

This ordering of the individual chemical reactions and the directional character of their sequence in time, their marvellous interplay, is something which cannot be deduced from physical and chemical laws at the sub-molecular level. Knowledge of the chemical properties of the individual components of organic matter exhibits, according to Oparin,

'merely the general, potentially possible transformations of organic matter, but can tell us nothing as to *how these possibilities are actually realized in the metabolism of living substances*'.[2]

It must be acknowledged that here the essential superiority of living to inorganic matter is very clearly brought out, and the problem of the origin of life stated with great distinctness. However, the solution given to it by dialectical materialism is a disappointing one: the origin of life is the result, not of chance, but of an extraordinarily lengthy development,

'which *necessarily* produces precisely that organization of the living substance which makes possible its continual metabolism and adjustment to the environment'.[3]

In what follows we shall present the course of this process of development in the form in which Oparin conceives it. Despite certain criticisms which have lately been directed by Soviet writers against individual points in his theory, the latter may still be regarded as having both the greatest authority and also the best claim to be taken seriously.

Oparin divides the process of the ascent of matter towards life into three stages: (*a*) origin of organic substances; (*b*) origin of large-molecule polymers from amino-acids, *i.e.*, origin of proteins; (*c*) origin of proteinous *substances*, having the power of metabolism, *i.e.*, origin of life. The formation of cells and multi-cellular organisms, the emergence of consciousness as the 'highest stage in the process of biological development', to be followed by the various 'social forms

[1] A. I. Oparin: *Problema* . . ., p. 45 (English, p. 76).
[2] A. I. Oparin, in *BSE*, XVI, p. 141 (our italics—G. W.).
[3] *Estestvoznanie i religiya* (Science and Religion), a collective work, edited by V. P. Dobrokhvalov, G. V. Platonov and E. V. Shorokhova for the Philosophical Institute of the Academy of Sciences of the U.S.S.R., Moscow 1956, p. 71.

of motion' in matter—all this already belongs to a later phase of development.[1]

In dealing with the *first stage*, Oparin sets out, in his more recent publications, from the cosmogonical theory of O. Y. Schmidt. Previously it was thought that organic substances could only be produced by living creatures. Recent discoveries have shown, however, that the simplest organic compounds—hydrocarbons and their derivatives—are also present in the stars, and that under conditions which completely exclude their biological origin; in particular the diffuse matter from which, on Schmidt's theory, the earth originated, will also have contained ammonia and water and possibly other more complex hydrocarbons.

'Consequently, in its earliest infancy the Earth absorbed elementary hydrocarbons, water, and ammonia from gas and dust matter, that is to say, everything required for the formation of primary organic substances.' [2]

With this, Oparin considers the first part of the problem of the origin of life to have been in principle solved.

In accounting for the *second stage* in the development of life, Oparin attaches decisive importance to two recently performed experiments. In 1953 the American biochemist Stanley L. Miller subjected a mixture of gases, which (as Oparin particularly emphasizes) must, in his opinion, have been present in the primeval atmosphere—a mixture, that is, of methane, ammonia, hydrogen and water-vapour—to constant increases of energy by means of electrical discharges, and produced amino-acids (glycocoll, alpha- and beta-alanin and small quantities of asparagin and alpha-amino-butyric acid); these are all substances which even today are still employed by organisms in the build-up of their proteins.

Now the protein molecule is a giant molecule in which large numbers of such amino-acids, often with thousands or tens of thousands of atoms, are linked together in a chain, the so-called peptide chain. And this in turn requires the application of considerable amounts of energy. In seeking an explanation as to how these polypeptide linkages could have come about, Oparin attaches a very crucial importance to the method of 'resynthesis' developed in 1947 by the Leningrad Professor, S. E. Bresler. Bresler took amino-acids, which he had obtained by breaking down existing proteins, and reconstituted them by the addition of enzymes under very high

[1] A. I. Oparin: *Problema . . .*, p. 40. For what follows, *cf.* also his book *Vozniknovenie zhizni na zemle* 2nd edn., Moscow 1941; 3rd, completely revised edn., Moscow 1957; English, *The Origin of Life* (tr. A. Synge), Edinburgh 1957. The latter versions appeared too late for discussion here.

[2] A. I. Oparin: *Problema . . .*, p. 41 (English, p. 35).

pressure (5,000–10,000 atmospheres). Since such pressures are to be found in Nature in the depths of the sea, Oparin believes that Bresler's experiments have opened up a promising road towards explaining the spontaneous formation of proteins 'in the Earth's primitive ocean'.

Oparin believes, therefore, that although in the present state of inquiry many gaps remain in our understanding of the second stage of the development of life, the lines of further investigation have already been laid down.[1]

In the *third stage*, on the other hand, as Oparin admits, even the problem itself has not yet been sufficiently clarified. Starting from the properties of colloids, in which protein solutions are included, he proposes the following hypothesis for further inquiry: if several protein-solutions are mixed, the individual macromolecules combine into droplet-formations, the so-called *coacervates*. These have the property of taking up various substances from the fluid surrounding them. Now if they enter into chemical combinations with the protein molecule, the latter grows and thereby changes its chemical structure. But in addition to these processes of synthesis, opposite processes of breakdown can also occur. Both can be accelerated by suitable catalysts, which may be contained in the substances taken up. Coacervates in which the processes of growth go on more rapidly than the opposite processes of breakdown, prove themselves dynamically stable, and are in a favourable position. At this point Oparin brings in the operation of 'natural selection'. The dynamically stable particles must have gone on growing. After reaching a certain limit, they were

'bound to break up into separate parts or pieces on the strength of purely mechanical reasons. The "filial" drops which thus came into being possessed roughly the same physico-chemical organization as the "parental" coacervate.'[2]

Parallel to this multiplication-process, natural selection must also have brought about a continual improvement in the direction of a completely controlled and ordered sequence in the process, which would provide for continual self-maintenance and self-renewal.

'Ultimately, at long last, this will have led to the development of proteinous substances equipped with an ordered cycle of chemical changes, to the development of systems whose very existence would be possible only in the presence of metabolism and continuous interaction with the environment, *i.e.*, to the development of life.'[3]

[1] A. I. Oparin: *Problema* . . ., pp. 41–3 (English, pp. 51–3).

[2] A. I. Oparin: *Proiskhozhdenie zhizni*, p. 76 (English, p. 81).

[3] A. I. Oparin: *Problema* . . ., pp. 46 f.; *cf.* also *Proiskhozhdenie zhizni*, pp. 75–81 (English, pp. 80–6).

As already indicated, there has lately been some criticism in the Soviet Union directed against this coacervate theory of Oparin's. Numerous authors have argued against him that life does not first make its appearance in supramolecular forms, but that even the individual protein-molecule must itself be regarded as alive. Their main argument, however, is drawn from a passage in Engels, who wrote, in his *Dialectics of Nature*:

'In the organic world . . . all chemical investigations lead back in the last resort to a body—protein—which, while being the result of ordinary chemical processes, is distinguished from all others by being a self-acting, permanent chemical process.' [1]

Thus it is maintained, for example, by Professors Konikova and Kritzman, that the properties of self-renewal, which they regard as crucial for life, are already present in the individual isolated protein-molecule. They point to experiments in which they have been able to show that isolated proteins, such as blood-plasma, casein, and also certain enzymes (trypsin, chemo-trypsin and papain), are capable of using amino-acids in their build-up, and this without the aid of biological structures.[2]   Stukov and Yakushev also maintain, against Oparin, that the qualitative leap from chemistry to life is already operative in the individual protein-molecule.[3] Skabichevsky criticizes Oparin on similar lines for his introduction of the category of 'natural selection' *prior* to arriving at the biological realm proper; he thereby carries over to the as yet inanimate coacervate-droplets a whole series of expressions appropriate only to life: they grow, they multiply, they leave descendants behind them, transmit their characteristics to the latter, and so forth.[4] Nudel'man likewise argues against Oparin that, even in the elementary protein-molecule, the qualitative leap from the inorganic to the organic has already occurred, and attempts to show that the 'metabolism' of the individual protein-molecule already exhibits a 'directedness' of the individual reactions in time, such as Oparin considers to be characteristic of the organic.[5] A whole series of other authors adopt the same

[1] F. Engels: *Dialectics of Nature*, p. 339.

[2] A. S. Konikova and M. G. Kritzman: *K voprosu o nachal'noy forme proyavleniya zhizni* (On the Problem of the Initial Form of the Emergence of Life), *VF*, 1954, 1, pp. 210–16, *q.v.* p. 211.

[3] A. P. Stukov and S. A. Yakushev: *O belke kak nositele zhizni* (On Protein as the Bearer of Life), *VF*, 1953, 2, pp. 139–49.

[4] A. P. Skabichevsky: *Problema vozniknoveniya zhizni na zemle i teoriya akad. A. I. Oparina* (The Problem of the Origin of Life on Earth and the Theory of Academician A. I. Oparin), *VF*, 1953, 2, pp. 150–5, *q.v.* p. 154.

[5] Z. N. Nudel'man: *O probleme belka* (On the Protein Problem), *VF*, 1954, 2, pp. 221–6, *q.v.* p. 224.

viewpoint, namely that life already begins with the protein-molecule: Sisakyan,[1] Sysoev,[2] Takach,[3] Emme,[4] etc.

In spite of these criticisms, however, Oparin still goes on expounding his coacervate theory even in his latest writings.[5] Other Soviet authorities also share this view that life only emerges in supramolecular protein-formations, Braunstein,[6] for example, Sukhov,[7] Bresler,[8] and others.

It may also be appropriate to say something at this juncture about the virus problem. It is interesting that the Soviet philosophy of Nature does not credit this problem with any very important rôle in its account of the origins of life. Viruses in general are regarded, indeed, as genuinely alive, this being the view, for example, of the leading Soviet authority on viruses, V. L. Ryzhkov,[9] K. S. Sukhov,[10] and others. But as to the question of their origin, the general opinion seems to be that nothing can as yet be said about it at the present time.[11] Oparin, roundly describes the viruses as 'a product of regression';[12] Sukhov is also inclined to attribute their origin to a

---

[1] N. M. Sisakyan: *Biologichesky obmen veshchestv—kachestvennaya osobennost' zhivogo* (Biological Metabolism as a Qualitative Property of the Living), *VF*, 1954, 3, pp. 89–105.

[2] A. F. Sysoev: *Samoobnovlenie belka i svoystvo razdrazhimosti- vazhneyshie zakonomernosti zhiznennykh yavleniy* (Protein Self-Renewal and the Property of Irritability as the Major Laws of Organic Phenomena), *VF*, 1956, 1, pp. 152–5.

[3] L. Takach: *K voprosu o vozniknovenii zhizni* (On the Problem of the Origin of Life), *VF*, 1955, 3, pp. 147–50.

[4] A. M. Emme: *Neskol'ko zamechaniy po voprosu o protsesse vozniknoveniya zhizni* (Remarks on the Problem of the Mode of Origin of Life), *VF* 1956, 1, pp. 155–8.

[5] A. I. Oparin: *Novoe o proiskhozhdenii zhizni na zemle* (New Light on the Origin of Life on Earth), Moscow 1956.

[6] Quoted by A. S. Konikova and M. G. Kritzman, in *VF*, 1953, 1, p. 144.

[7] K. S. Sukhov: *Problemy sovremennoy virusologii* (Problems of Modern Virology) in the collective work *Filosofskie voprosy sovremennoy biologii*, edited for the Philosophical Institute of the Academy of Sciences of the U.S.S.R. by I. I. Novinsky and G. V. Platonov, Moscow 1951, pp. 335–45, esp. p. 338.

[8] S. E. Bresler: *K probleme sinteza belka* (On the Problem of Protein- Synthesis), *VF*, 1951, 3, pp. 82–94.

[9] V. L. Ryzhkov: *Virusy* (Viruses), in *BSE*, VIII, p. 158; *cf.* also the same author's *O nekotorykh problemakh virusologii* (On Some Problems of Virology), in *Vestnik Akademii Nauk SSSR*, 1953, 1, pp. 42–6, *q.v.* p. 43.

[10] K. S. Sukhov: *Op. cit.*, p. 338.

[11] O. P. Peterson: *O prirode virusov i ikh znachenii v zhizni cheloveka* (On the Nature of Viruses and their Importance in Human Life), Moscow 1953, p. 27.

[12] A. I. Oparin: *Die Entstehung des Lebens auf der Erde*, Berlin–Leipzig 1949, p. 31.

degeneration from higher forms, such as the microbes.[1] Ryzhkov, in common with Western authors such as Friedrich-Freksa and A. Butenandt,[2] locates the importance of virus-investigation for the problem of the origin of life in the fact that the structure of the fluid crystals of viruses, such as that of the tobacco mosaic disease, has a considerable part to play as a *model*.[3]

The new conceptions which Soviet thinkers have imported into the controversy between vitalism and mechanism, can perhaps be reduced to the following two main points: (*a*) the essential 'qualitative' distinction between life and inorganic matter is to be explained, not by the appearance of an 'entelechy', or the like, in the course of the transition, but by, the *dialectic*, thanks to which the previous purely quantitative changes in the physico-chemical development of matter *necessarily* lead, at a certain point, and by way of a leap (breach of continuity), to the 'biological form of motion in matter'; (*b*) the extension of 'natural selection' to cover what is still a pre-biological process of evolution. The first of these ideas is common to all Soviet philosophers; the second is more characteristic of Oparin's theory. But are these two notions capable of providing a real solution to the problem? This, it seems, must certainly be denied.

As for the appeal to the 'dialectic', it must be said of this that here we are confronted either with a flight into irrationality, or else with a further relapse into the mechanistic position, according to which the emergence of life appears as a continuous prolongation of the chain of physico-chemical causes. For if this 'dialectical leap' is to be more than a stopgap, substituting a new word, merely, in place of an explanation, it would have somehow to account for the emergence of novelty from its causal antecedents, whether this be effected on the concrete scientific plane, by pointing out the immediate causes, or on a more abstract and philosophical level by at least drawing attention to the more deep-lying and general ontological connections. If the emergence of life is derived solely from the dialectical leap, how then are we to explain why, for example, in the case supposed, this leap is made upwards (*e.g.*, from the organic macromolecule to the living organism) and not downwards (as it might be to a piece of carbon, or to water)? Or how are we to account for the fact that the leap rises to this particular level and not higher still?[4] Confronted

---

[1] K. S. Sukhov: *Op. cit.*, p. 340.

[2] *Cf.* A. Butenandt: *Was bedeutet Leben unter dem Gesichtspunkt der biologischen Chemie?*, in *Schöpfungsglaube und Evolutionstheorie*, Stuttgart 1955, pp. 97–108, *q.v.* p. 107.

[3] V. L. Ryzhkov: *O nekotorykh problemakh . . .*, pp. 43 f.

[4] That the 'leap' represents an irrational transition from one form of being to another, and that this fails to explain why it should be an 'upward leap' and not a 'downward plunge', has been very aptly pointed out by

with these questions, dialectical materialism invariably seeks to extract an answer from the concrete physico-chemical processes occurring in the protein molecule, somewhat as we have already seen above with Oparin, albeit with certain modifications which other Soviet philosophers consider desirable. But this harking-back to the physico-chemical processes implies a tacit reversion to the standpoint of mechanism, representing as it does a further attempt to establish the continuity of the transitions from chemical reactions to life. The only meaning that can be attached to the leap in this context is that these reactions may perhaps occur with much greater violence at a certain juncture, but again this does not distinguish them 'qualitatively' or in principle, but merely quantitatively, from the processes preceding them.

Alternatively, dialectical materialism attempts to retain the discontinuity, and to seek an explanation for the leap, not on the scientific plane, but purely on the philosophical one. This explanation is contained, moreover, in the so-called fourth principal feature of the dialectic, which tells us

'that internal contradictions are inherent in all things and phenomena of nature . . . and that the struggle between these opposites . . . constitutes the internal content . . . of the transformation of quantitative changes into qualitative changes'.[1]

Philosophically speaking, therefore, the essence of the qualitative leap is supposed to lie in 'contradiction'. But this implies a flight into irrationality. For contradiction as such consists, not in the transition from a definite A (such as a protein-molecule) to a definite B (in this case the living organism), but in the transition from A to the quite infinitely broad indefiniteness of not-A (in this case anything whatsoever other than the protein-molecule). To derive the transition from one definite thing to another out of 'contradiction', or mere negation, is fundamentally to abandon all explanation of the second item and to relapse into irrationality. Thus the 'leap' is no more an explanation than 'chance'.

The reproach of relapsing into mechanistic positions, which dialectical materialism prides itself on having superseded, must also be levelled against Oparin's coacervate theory. And this not only because of the attempt it makes to restore continuity between the emergence of life and the physico-chemical processes antecedent to this, but especially also because life again figures here as a product of chance. We may recall the dialectical materialist doc-

B. Petrov, in his penetrating critique of dialectical materialism (*cf.* B. Petrov: *Filosofskaya nishcheta marxizma* (The Philosophical Poverty of Marxism), Frankfurt-a-M. 1952, pp. 20, 27).

[1] *DHM*, p. 539 (572–3, 109).

trine of contingency: the contingent is not causeless, but arises at the point where two causal series intersect to produce an effect which is not necessarily called for by either one of them.[1] That a coacervate drop should possess this particular structure and these particular properties is certainly the necessary result of the operation of physico-chemical processes. So too, the fact that this or that catalyst required by the coacervate drop was formed, and entered the drop's neighbourhood, is again the necessary result of a whole chain of causes, though a *different* chain from the first. The fact that the coacervate drop was able to take up from the environment this catalyst, necessary for its further development to a higher stage, is therefore no longer the necessary consequence of the whole of its development hitherto, but results from the fact that, at this particular juncture, its own chain of development intersected by chance with the second chain of causes referred to above. Thus we see that here too the origin of life appears once more as the result of chance.

But it is not only the *necessity* of the origin of life which remains unexplained on the coacervate theory; it is also questionable whether even the very *possibility* of such an origin can be explained in this way. For the crucial presupposition for this explanation is the possibility of a coacervate drop 'bequeathing' the properties it has acquired to its 'filial drops' after it has itself grown too large 'on the strength of purely mechanical reasons', and broken up into separate parts. But not all the molecules comprising the parental drop are exactly alike. Oparin himself underlines the rôle played by the individual *structure* of the coacervates, and which results from the fact that the individual molecules are ordered in a quite definite manner. Now if the coacervate breaks up, this structure is destroyed. But the dynamic stability of the parental drop was obviously not due to this or that protein-molecule, but was doubtless conditioned by the *total* organization of the drop as a whole. Now if the latter breaks up into separate parts, a completely new situation is created. The catalysts accelerating the process of growth are now distributed amongst the various droplets, and their interplay comes to an end. Hence it is not evident how, after the parental drop has divided in two, its acquired dynamic stability can be passed on to the filial drops and further improved upon by them. With the break-up of the coacervate drop the whole coacervate theory breaks up as well.

7. THE 'NEW CELL-THEORY' OF O. B. LEPESHINSKAYA

From the above account it will be clear that Soviet theorists in general accept the possibility of life in a pre-cellular state, and assume

[1] *Cf.* above, p. 384.

that in the course of its development it first emerged as non-cellular 'living matter'. The question now arises as to how cells came to be formed, Virchow's axiom *'Omnis cellula ex cellula'* having hitherto enjoyed universal acceptance. The endeavour to fill this gap was undertaken by O. B. Lepeshinskaya.[1] Since her theory has also been much discussed in the West, we may deal with it briefly here, the more so since it has lately fallen out of favour again, even in the Soviet Union.

Lepeshinskaya tells us how, in studying the changes due to ageing in the walls of the cell, she was led to the idea that the cell must have originated out of pre-cellular living matter. She investigated the blood of the tadpole and discovered in it yolk-globules in varying stages of development: one consisting only of yolk-granules, another having a nucleus, but lacking chromatin and with a few yolk-granules, a third with a fully shaped nucleus containing chromatin, and a fourth with a nucleus in process of karyokinetic division.

'I had before me a picture of the development of some kind of a cell from yolk-globules.' [2]

Encouraged by this, Lepeshinskaya went on to investigate yolk-globules in the eggs of hens, canaries, fish and simpler animals. She discovered in doing so,

'how the simplest, pre-cellular forms, without even a nucleus, are created from the yolk in the shape of yolk-globules. After going through a series of pre-cellular stages, a globule of this type forms a cell with a nucleus, which thereupon divides, just like other living cells. . . . The cells obtained from yolk-globules, have, as we have shown, nuclei with chromosomes, which do not differ in quantity or quality from the chromosomes in the normal cells from the organism of the fowl.' [3]

[1] Olga Borisovna Lepeshinskaya, b. 1871, member of the C.P.S.U. (or the Russian Social-Democratic Workers' Party, as it then was) from its foundation in 1898; banished to Siberia from 1897–1900, and then again, with her husband, in 1903. From 1903–6 she lived in exile in Geneva. Her academic career in the Soviet Union began in 1919. Since 1949 she has been head of the Section on the Development of Living Substance in the Institute of Experimental Biology of the Academy of Medical Sciences of the U.S.S.R.

[2] O. B. Lepeshinskaya: *Razvitie zhiznennykh protsessov v dokletochnom periode* (The Development of Living Processes in the Period before the Formation of Cells), in *Izvestiya AN SSSR. Seriya biologicheskaya*, 1950, 5, pp. 85–101 (English version in *The Origin of Cells from Living Substance*, Moscow 1954, pp. 49–50).

[3] O. B. Lepeshinskaya: *Tvorcheskoe znachenie trudov Marxa, Engelsa, Lenina, Stalina dlya razvitiya estestvoznaniya* (The Creative Significance of

Lepeshinskaya also claims to have obtained cells from living substance in other ways as well. She ground hydras in a mortar and centrifuged the resultant mass with a view to removing any cells remaining in it. After about an hour there formed, under the microscope, in the originally clear solution, glistening pin-point dots, coacervates, which continued to grow. After a nutrient medium had been added to the culture, in the form of an extract of cyclopes, the globules changed, so Lepeshinskaya believes, into cells which were capable of division. After a lapse of 24 hours in all, the original coacervate obtained from hydra-cells had formed a sizeable mass of some 30–35 'cells' of this kind.[1]

Lepeshinskaya's further investigations included the rôle of 'living substance' in the process of wound healing; she comes to the conclusion

'that in the process of wound healing new cells are formed not only by way of division of cells . . . but also from living substance in the form of tiniest grains which result from the destruction and disintegration of cells'.[2]

She also applied this theory of hers to the struggle against cancer and premature senility.[3]

The 'dialectical materialist nature of the new cell-theory' is seen by L. N. Plyushch in the fact that it considers cells in the course of their development, and that not only individually in ontogenesis, but also historically, in phylogenesis. The development of cells from precellular forms of living substance presents, in broad outline,

'an idea of the way in which cells have developed during the earth's history'.[4]

Moreover, the new cell-theory views the development of cells as a 'dialectical materialist unity of continuity and discontinuity': since, according to Lepeshinskaya, cell-division also represents a mode of formation of a new cell from living substance, the new cell-theory, in contrast to 'metaphysical, conventional evolutionism, with its notion of an endless, unbroken propagation of cells by means of division', also introduces the moment of 'discontinuity' into the development

the Works of Marx, Engels, Lenin and Stalin In the Development of Science), *VF*, 1953, 2, pp. 120–38, *q.v.* p. 129; (*cf. The Origin of Cells . . .*, pp. 49 ff.).

[1] O. B. Lepeshinskaya: *Razvitie . . .*, pp. 21 f. (*Origin of Cells*, pp. 65 ff.).

[2] *Ibid.*, pp. 25 f. (p. 72).

[3] O. B. Lepeshinskaya: *Tvorcheskoe znachenie . . .*, p. 133.

[4] L. N. Plyushch: *Ob osnovakh novoy kletochnoy teorii* (On the Foundations of the New Cell Theory), *VF*, 1953, 4, pp. 185–91, *q.v.* p. 187.

of organisms.[1] Here too is the point of contact with Michurin's doctrine of inheritance and Lysenko's theory of species-formation:

'When, in qualitative transitions, and especially in the formation of species, qualitatively new cells emerge, this implies that such cells have been newly formed and have not arisen by way of simple division from the old cells previously existing.' [2]

Lepeshinskaya had been working on this theory of hers from 1933 onwards. It was presented above all in her chief work, *The Origin of Cells from Living Substance*,[3] of which the first edition appeared in 1945. To begin with, she met with strong opposition even among Soviet theorists. But energetic support was forthcoming from well-known Soviet biologists, such as Lysenko and Oparin, and her theory was acknowledged at a Joint Conference, held on 22nd–24th May 1950, by the Biology Section of the Academy of Sciences and the Academy of Medical Sciences of the U.S.S.R., and also at two other conferences held in April 1952 and May 1953. At the request of the Academy of Sciences to the appropriate Ministries, Lepeshinskaya's theory was incorporated into the textbooks of biology, histology and cytology.

Shortly after Stalin's death, however, dissentient voices again made themselves heard. Lepeshinskaya's work was re-examined by a number of investigators and found to be not in accordance with the facts. The results of these inquiries are summed up in two articles by L. N. Zhinkin and V. P. Mikhailov.[4] The authors come to the conclusion,

'that the "new cell-theory" rests upon foundations which are not sufficiently convincing or well-established in respect of the facts'.

Thus, P. V. Makarov and V. Y. Kozlov, for example, have repeated

---

[1] L. N. Plyushch: *Op. cit.*, pp. 189 f.

[2] N. N. Zhukov-Verezhnikov, I. N. Maisky and L. A. Kalinichenko: *O nekletochnykh formakh zhizni i razvitii kletok* (On Non-Cellular Forms of Life and the Development of Cells), in *Filosofskie voprosy sovremennoy biologii*, Moscow 1951, pp. 318–34, *q.v.* p. 322.

[3] O. B. Lepeshinskaya: *Proiskhozhdenie kletok iz zhivogo veshchestva i rol' zhivogo veshchestva v organizme*, 2nd edn., Moscow 1950 (English version as above, n. 149).

[4] L. N. Zhinkin and V. P. Mikhailov: '*Novaya kletochnaya teoriya' i ee fakticheskoe obosnovanie* (The 'New Cell-Theory' and its Factual Basis), in *Uspekhi sovremennoy biologii*, 1955, vol. 39, pp. 228–44; and *O 'novoy kletochnoy teorii'* (On the 'New Cell-Theory'), in *Arkhiv anatomii, gistologii i embriologii* 1955, vol. 32, No. 2, pp. 66–71; both available in German in *Sowjetwissenschaft. Naturwissenschaftliche Abteilung* 1956, 2, pp. 155–82. (References are to the German version—Tr.)

Lepeshinskaya's experiment with hydras, but using material that had been killed off with formalin or osmium tetroxide, and was therefore certainly not 'living substance', but were still able to observe the same phenomena. From this they conclude,

'that it is not biological processes, but physico-chemical ones, which form the basis of the phenomena described by O. B. Lepeshinskaya in her experiments on hydras'.

The connection between species-formation and the origin of cells from living substance is also a pure invention and has no sort of factual justification.[1] To be sure, the two authors themselves share the view that as a matter of historical (*i.e.*, phylogenetic) development, cells have been formed from non-cellular living substance, but this is far from implying that such a process is still being repeated today in all plants and animals,

'and that in the course of its development every cell must still pass through the infinitely remote and primitive phase of non-cellular living matter'.[2]

As regards the generally accepted view among Soviet biologists that, at least in the course of its historical development on earth, life was at one time present in pre-cellular form and that present-day cells have arisen from this more elementary form of living substance, it must be said that up to now at least, Virchow's principle of *Omnis cellula ex cellula* has continued to prevail among Western biologists. All that modern microbiology has established is that there are cells, the nucleoids (Piekarski), of which it remains uncertain whether they contain nuclei or equivalent structures, although they incorporate the same substances as are present in higher-order nuclei.[3]

8. THE 'NEW THEORY OF INHERITANCE'.
I. V. MICHURIN, T. D. LYSENKO

The problem of inheritance may well be regarded as the most central feature of Soviet biology: here the pressure of ideology upon the sciences has certainly been felt most strongly; here the fiercest battles have been waged between supporters of the new, officially-approved doctrine and the representatives of classical genetics; here it is that the 'Soviet science' evolved by dialectical materialism has departed most widely from science in general (it need not be described as 'Western science', for it can also point to first-class

---

[1] L. N. Zhinkin and V. P. Mikhailov: *Op. cit.*, pp. 170–2.

[2] *Ibid.*, p. 180.

[3] *Cf.* O. Spülbeck: *Der Christ und das Weltbild der modernen Naturwissenschaft*[1], Berlin 1957, pp. 128 f.

exponents even in Russia itself). No other field has given rise to such a flood of literature as the new Soviet theory of inheritance, nor been so much reported on and discussed, even in the Western world.

The outward course of the struggle between supporters of the new and the classical theories of inheritance has already been described in Part One,[1] at least as regards its decisive phase at the 'historic August Session' of 1948. But the battle between the two schools has already been in progress for more than two decades by now. Apart from K. A. Timiryazev, who is regarded as a forerunner, it is I. V. Michurin and T. D. Lysenko who rank as the major authorities for the new doctrine.

Ivan Vladimirovich Michurin (1855–1935) was a highly successful plant-breeder, who is said to have reared up to 350 new varieties of berries and fruit. The chief methods he used consisted in the crossing of widely different species, sexual or vegetative hybridization (by grafting), and the so-called 'mentor-method'. Starting from the principle that, thanks to its exceptionally plastic character, the young vegetable organism is capable of 'training', Michurin thought that by guiding its development he could produce heritable changes therein.[2]

Trofim Denisovich Lysenko (b. 1898) is also a practical man, without any real scientific training. The son of a Ukrainian peasant, he graduated in 1921 from a horticultural college and in 1925 from the Kiev Agricultural Institute, having in the meantime taken a two-year course on selection and worked at the Belotserkov breeding-station. Lysenko has had great practical success, especially in the rearing of frost-resistant southern varieties for northern climates. Particularly well known is his method of 'yarovization' or 'vernalization', *i.e.*, the transformation of winter into summer crops by chilling the seed-corn, so that when sown in spring it produces ears in the summer of the same year. In 1929 Lysenko communicated results of his researches on this subject to a conference of geneticists at Leningrad. In the 'thirties his vernalization-technique was put into practice on the largest scale throughout the Soviet Union. The same period saw the beginnings of Lysenko's spectacular rise to positions of ever-increasing eminence: in 1934, Member of the Ukrainian Academy of Sciences; in 1938, President of the Lenin Academy of Agricultural Science of the U.S.S.R.; and three times a Stalin Prize winner (1941, 1943, 1949). Ashby, who has had the opportunity of personal acquaintance with Lysenko, gives the following account of his personality:

[1] *Cf.* above, pp. 189 f.
[2] S. I. Isaev: *I. V. Michurin—veliky estestvoispytatel', preobrazovatel' prirody* (I. V. Michurin—A Great Student and Transformer of Nature), Moscow 1955, pp. 13 ff.

'He is not a charlatan. He is not a showman. He is not personally ambitious. He is extremely nervous and conveys the impression of being unhappy, unsure of himself, shy, and forced into the rôle of leader by a fire within him. He believes passionately in his own theories, and he is not convinced by cold reasoning.' [1]

The central point in Lysenko's teaching is his theory of the inheritance of acquired characteristics, whose possibility he maintains in flat contradiction to the classical theory of heredity. According to the latter (originating from Mendel and Morgan), the bearers of inheritance are constituents of the cell-nucleus, the chromosomes, or the genes contained in them. The Mendelian laws of inheritance are governed by the mechanism of chromosome-division on fertilization, and the antecedent division of the mature germ-cells. Genuine changes of heredity, so-called 'mutations', are only possible, on the classical theory, when for any reason a change occurs in the constitution of the genes or chromosomes, which can in fact be achieved artificially, by the use of X-rays, mustard gas, etc.; though it is not yet possible, at present, to produce any given mutation at will.

Lysenko rejects this theory of the presence of specific carriers of inheritance in the organism. In elaborating his own theory he sets out from the thesis that organism and environment constitute a unity.

'According to the principles of Michurin's theory the organism and the conditions necessary to ensure its life must be considered as a unity.' [2]

Alteration of the environmental conditions therefore offers man the possibility of effecting a change in the organism which can be passed on by inheritance to its descendants. Changes of heredity occur, according to Lysenko, as

'the result of the realization of individual development, but deviating from the normal, usual course. Changes in heredity are, as a rule, the result of the organism's development under external conditions which, to one extent or other, do not correspond to the natural

---

[1] E. Ashby: *Scientist in Russia*, Pelican, 1947, p. 116. For the above biography of Lysenko, *cf. BSE*, XXV, pp. 498 f. and E. Sankewitsch. *Die Arbeitsmethoden der Mitschurinschen Pflanzenzüchtung*, Stuttgart/Ludwigsburg 1950, p. 28.

[2] T. D. Lysenko: *Agrobiologiya*, Moscow 1948; German version, *Agrobiologie*, Berlin 1951; English, *Agrobiology*, Moscow 1954, p. 484. (This version, from the fourth Russian edition, omits some material included in the German; occasional reference is therefore made to the latter for the extracts which follow—Tr.).

requirements, *i.e.*, its heredity. Changes in the conditions of life compel changes in the development of plant organisms. They are the root cause of changes in heredity.' [1]

Lysenko therefore defines heredity as

'the concentrate, as it were, of the environmental conditions assimilated by plant organisms in a series of preceding generations'. [2]

Lysenko distinguishes between conservative and 'destabilized' types of heredity:

'Usually the organism with a conservative heredity does not accept, does not assimilate conditions that are not native to it. That is why it is difficult for it to change, difficult for it to adapt itself to new conditions. Organisms with a destabilized heredity, however, act differently. They have not yet elaborated a fully developed stability, they lack conservatism with regard to electing conditions for assimilation. All that they have is a tendency, a preference for assimilating certain conditions. If these conditions are lacking in the given environment the organism having a destabilized heredity does not resist long, does not persist; it . . . assimilates the conditions which environ it with less discrimination, so to say, with greater appetite. A skilful experimenter can literally mould such organisms like clay and produce good, new and desirable races.' [3]

Lysenko lays down three ways of destabilizing heredity in this fashion:

'1. By grafting, *i.e.*, by uniting the tissues of plants of different breeds;
2. By bringing external conditions to bear upon it at definite moments when the organism undergoes this or that process of its development;
3. By cross-breeding, particularly of forms sharply differing in habitat or origin.' [4]

For the first way, Lysenko attaches special importance to the 'mentor method' developed by Michurin, which consists in choosing as root-stock a young hybrid seedling, which owing to its youth and hybrid character is reckoned to possess a 'destabilized heredity', and grafting on the latter as mentor or 'educator' a scion derived from a mature individual of a stable species, which therefore possesses a 'conservative heredity'. Now Michurin and Lysenko claim, by grafting as well as by crossing, to have obtained true hybrids which exhibit the specific and generic properties of both scion and root-

---

[1] T. D. Lysenko: *Op. cit.* (English), p. 487.
[2] *Ibid.*, p. 492.   [3] *Ibid.*, p. 347.   [4] *Ibid.*, p. 537.

stock. This 'vegetative hybridization' by means of grafting, which is completely ruled out from the standpoint of classical genetics, is brought in by Lysenko as an argument against the chromosome theory and in confirmation of his own teaching as to the possibility of transforming heredity:

'It follows that heredity may be shaped by the agency of nutrition, by the interchange of substances (in this case, between the scion and the stock). By changing the nature of the metabolic process we can achieve the directed alteration of the nature of the organism. . . . In the light of experiments with vegetative hybrids, nothing remains of the Morganist chromosome theory of heredity.' [1]

The second method given by Lysenko for destabilizing heredity is based on his theory of the 'phasic development' of plants. According to this theory the development of plants consists of individual, qualitatively distinct stages or phases. In order to pass through each of these stages, different external conditions (of light, temperature, etc.) are required.[2] Up to now Soviet biology has investigated only two of these stages: the 'vernalization phase' and the 'photo phase'. Lysenko now makes use of this fact in the vernalization of winter crops by exposing the seed-corn to low temperatures before sowing, and is thereby able to sow the seed in spring-time and to obtain a crop from it the same summer.

The third way of destabilizing heredity is represented by Michurin's method of 'distant crossing', which involves interbreeding species far removed from one another.

It may be noted specifically in connection with this third method that Lysenko also holds very strange views about the process of fertilization. In accordance with his notion of inheritance as a 'type of metabolism', he sees the essence of the fertilization-process, not as a new combination of hereditary factors, but as a reciprocal assimilation of the male and female germ-cells, whereby a new type of metabolism comes into being. He believes that in fertilization there is a selection-process at work: it is not just any one of the host of gametes which enters the egg-cell—what happens is a sort of 'marriage for love': the egg-cell is supposed to have an ability to select gametes of a particular physiological type; and it is also supposed to be evident in pollination that

'the stigma prefers the pollen that is biologically most akin to the maternal nature'.[3]

But the 'summit of fantasy' is reached, according to Hans Nachtsheim, in Lysenko's new theory of the transformation of one species

[1] *Ibid.*, p. 318.   [2] *Ibid.*, pp. 36 f.   [3] *Ibid.* (German only), p. 290.

into another.[1] In Darwin's opinion, the term 'species' is an arbitrary one; he explains the historical emergence of species as a result of natural selection and the elimination of intermediate forms, whereby, in the course of hundreds of thousands of years, species will have arisen from varieties, and genera, etc. from species.

Lysenko considers this a 'flat' form of evolution, since it recognizes only quantitative differences and not qualitative ones.[2] He himself gives the following definition of species:

'A species is a distinct, qualitatively definite state of living matter. Definite intraspecific interrelations between its members are an essential characteristic of each species of plant, animal and micro-organism. These intraspecific interrelations differ qualitatively from the interrelations between individuals of different species. Therefore, the qualitative difference between intraspecific and interspecific interrelations is one of the most important criteria for distinguishing between species and varieties.'[3]

Sub-species, on the other hand,

'are forms of existence of a given species and not steps in its transformation into another species'.[4]

In the above definition of species there is said to be a basic difference between intraspecific and interspecific interrelations. Lysenko means by this that there is no struggle for existence between individuals of the same species, but only mutual support with a view to preserving the species in competition with others. He finds confirmation of this thesis in the Russian rubber-plant, the kok-saghyz. It has been shown to thrive much better when it is not spaced out at a distance in rows, but is subjected to so-called hill-planting, whereby some 100–200 seeds are sown in a single hill.[5] Lysenko advocated the same method in his directive: *Experimental Hill Sowing of Forest Belts*,[6] for the purpose of creating protective strips of woodland in order to implement the general plan laid down in 1948 for the campaign against drought. However, his proposals turned out to be a failure and ran into criticism from the Deputy Minister of Forests, Koldanov, and more especially from the arboriculturist Sukachev. He therefore drew up a new instruction in 1950, which

[1] H. Nachtsheim: *Biologie und Totalitarismus* in: *Veritas, Justitia, Libertas* (A *Festschrift* for the Bicentenary Celebrations of Columbia University, New York, presented by the Free University of Berlin and the German School of Political Studies in Berlin), Berlin 1954, pp. 294–320, *q.v.* p. 315.

[2] T. D. Lysenko: *Op. cit.* (English), p. 571.   [3] *Ibid.*, p. 574.
[4] *Ibid.*, p. 575.   [5] *Ibid.*, pp. 458 ff.
[6] *Ibid.*, pp. 555–69.

concedes the value of other methods of cultivation in addition to hill sowing.[1] Lysenko claims to have proved the possibility of transforming one species into another by changing hard wheat (*Triticum durum*) with 28 chromosomes into soft wheat (*Triticum vulgare*) with 42 chromosomes.[2]

These, in broad outline, are the main ideas in Lysenko's teaching. He himself describes them as a 'creative Darwinism' which develops further the 'rational core' of Darwinian theory and overcomes its deficiencies. Now where, in general, do the supporters of Michurinist biology, locate the achievements and deficiencies of Darwin's view? His main achievement is held to lie in his theory of the ascending development of organisms and in his 'rational interpretation' of teleology, which he explains as the result of a causal process of selection. The main deficiencies in his theory are listed, above all, under two heads: (*a*) his carrying-over into the biological field of the Malthusian theory, which considered overpopulation to be the source of the struggle for existence (and therefore advocated birth-control); (*b*) his 'flat evolutionism' which only allows for gradual quantitative changes and denies the occurrence in Nature of qualitative leaps (*Natura non facit saltus!*).

Against this claim of the Michurinists to have made an advance upon Darwin's theory, it has often been pointed out, however, that the theories of Michurin and Lysenko owe a great deal more to Lamarck, since it is precisely Lamarck rather than Darwin whom they subscribe to on the vital point, namely the theory of the transmission of inherited and acquired characteristics.

With the exception of his last point about the formation of species, Lysenko's doctrine held undisputed sway from the 'historic August Session' of 1948 until the time of Stalin's death. His theory of species-formation alone met with prompt contradiction. Its main opponent was the already-mentioned V. N. Sukachev, who contends that the struggle for existence also goes on within the species, and takes this to be a presupposition of the evolutionary process. In this he was soon joined by N. V. Turbin, N. D. Ivanov and other Soviet biologists. Since 1953 especially, full-dress discussions on the problem of species-formation have been held in a number of scientific journals. Lysenko's opponents have chiefly congregated around the *Botanichesky Zhurnal* (Botanical Journal) edited by Sukachev. Towards the end of 1954, *Voprosy filosofii* also opened a discussion with an article by G. V. Platonov, *Some Philosophical Problems in the Discussion on Species and their Formation.*[3]

[1] *Ibid.* (German only), pp. 599-601.

[2] *Ibid.* (English), p. 543.

[3] G. V. Platonov: *Nekotorye filosofskie voprosy diskussii o vide i vidoobrazovanii*, VF, 1954, 6, pp. 116-32.

Platonov attacks Sukachev's belief in an intraspecific struggle for existence as a necessary presupposition of evolution. But he is not altogether in agreement with Lysenko either, who completely rules out this struggle and seeks to replace it by the factors of 'self-thinning' (*samoizrezhivanie*) and 'self-restraint' (*samougnetenie*). Platonov himself attempts to take up a middle position between Lysenko and Sukachev, holding that there is no justification for a complete denial or either self-thinning of mutual competition within the species. Nor is he prepared to support the charge of 'flat evolutionism' levelled against Darwin by Lysenko.[1]

Among other contributions to the discussion, the article by Prezent and Khalifman, and Kedrov's reply to it, are particularly interesting. Prezent and Khalifman devote themselves to proving that Lysenko was right in accusing Darwin of 'flat evolutionism',[2] while Kedrov strongly defends Darwin against this charge. It was not Darwin, but Spencer, who advocated 'flat evolutionism'. When Darwin discounts the possibility of 'leaps' in Nature, it is Cuvier's 'catastrophic' theory that he has in mind; a 'leap' in his sense is equivalent, therefore to the Stalinist term *vzryv* ('explosion').[3] Kedrov accuses Prezent and Khalifman of entertaining a false conception of the dialectical 'leap': a qualitative change, in their view, always takes place in this fashion, while gradual transitions are typical only of the preceding quantitative changes; but this is false, since qualitative transitions can also occur gradually. Flat evolutionism means, not gradualness, but a denial of qualitative differences in evolution. And since Darwin certainly did not deny such differences, this accusation cannot be levelled against him.[4] P. D. Puzikov also takes the same view in his contribution to the discussion, that the whole period of transition to a new quality cannot be described as a 'leap'; Lysenko's own theory of 'phasic development' is itself a good example of the

[1] G. V. Platonov: *Op. cit.*, pp. 122, 125, 126.

[2] I. I. Prezent, I. A. Khalifman: *Nekotorye voprosy teorii biologicheskogo vida i vidoobrazovaniya* (Some Problems in the Theory of Species and Species-Formation), *VF*, 1955, 5, pp. 157–68.

[3] For the meaning of this term *cf.* above, p. 325. Here it is sufficient to remark that in his earlier work, *Anarchism or Socialism?*, Stalin was by no means unwilling to accuse Darwinism of an undialectical conception of evolution: 'On the other hand, Darwinism repudiates not only Cuvier's cataclysms; but also dialectically understood development, which includes revolution; whereas, from the standpoint of the dialectical method, evolution and revolution, quantitative and qualitative changes, are two necessary forms of the same movement' (*Sochineniya*, I, p. 309; *Works*, I, p. 312).

[4] B. M. Kedrov: *Ob otnoshenii marxizma k darvinizmu v svyazi s problemoy vidoobrazovaniya* (On the Relation between Marxism and Darwinism in regard to the Problem of Species-Formation), *VF*, 1955, 6, pp. 149–166, esp. pp. 156 ff.

fact that the transition from an old to a new quality need not always occur suddenly.[1]

V. G. Nesterov, in his contribution to the discussion on species-formation, attempts a deeper approach to the dialectical materialist theory of contradiction. He believes that gradual or sudden transitions between species are both equally possible. This 'either—or' is also typical of his attitude to the problem of an intraspecific struggle for existence: the struggle certainly occurs, but it is not the only form of intraspecific relationship.[2]

The essay by P. N. Golinevich contains a very interesting and detailed analysis of the concepts of 'overpopulation' and 'struggle for existence', on the strength of which the author mounts a sharp attack against the supporters of Lysenko's theory that there is no intraspecific struggle for existence. In particular, he comes down heavily on Nesterov, who in earlier works (prior to the above-mentioned article) had unambiguously declared his support for this view. More interesting than this polemic, however, is his criticism of Lysenko's concept of 'self-thinning', which he describes as 'complete nonsense', since it is impossible to explain how it comes about. The explanations attempted by Lysenko and his colleague, Academician M. Olishansky, presuppose that the growing plant is determined by events in the future, but this would imply that it is conscious. Golinevich shows this by reference to a more recent utterance of Lysenko's:

'It must be emphasized that the self-thinning or elimination of individual saplings within the group occurs, not because they are already cramped, but so that they shall not be cramped in the immediate future'.[3]

Lysenko has arrived at these conclusions on the strength of wrongly-conducted experiments, which he has entered into with his mind already made up in advance.[4]

Nor have these attacks on Lysenko been confined merely to the realm of theory. In May 1956 the journal *Partiynaya zhizn'* denounced certain agricultural experts in western Siberia, who, by obstinately

[1] P. D. Puzikov: *Nekotorye filosofskie voprosy biologicheskoy evolyutsii* (Some Philosophical Problems of Biological Evolution), *VF*, 1956, 4, pp. 179–83, *q.v.* p. 182.

[2] V. G. Nesterov: *Filosofskie kontseptsii po voprosam protivorechiy v zhivoy prirode* (Philosophical Conceptions of the Problems of Contradiction in Organic Nature), *VF*, 1956, 1, pp. 143–9, *q.v.* pp. 145, 149.

[3] T. D. Lysenko, in *Lesnoe khozyaystvo*, 1955, 3, p. 49; quoted in P. N. Golinevich: *Perenaselenie i bor'ba za sushchestvevanie* (Overpopulation and the Struggle for Existence), *VF*, 1956, 4, pp. 183–92, *q.v.* p. 190.

[4] P. N. Golinevich: *Op. cit.*, pp. 189 ff.

clinging to Lysenko's advice to sow winter wheat, had done great harm to farming in the area, since for years on end, over tens of thousands of acres, they had thereby failed even to recover the seed-corn expended.[1] It may well be that this revival of opposition was the reason for Lysenko's resignation, in April 1956, from the presidency of the Lenin Academy of Agricultural Sciences of the U.S.S.R. But this incident should not be overrated; it must not be invested with the importance which it might have had in Stalin's day, as though Lysenko and his theories had now fallen completely out of favour again. It does seem to be the case, however, that the chromosome theory is now beginning to be spoken of again with greater respect; the fact that the headship of the Moscow Institute of Genetics has been given back to Dubinin, who fell from grace in 1948, and that of the Leningrad Institute to the Morganist Navashin,[2] also shows at least that the Michurin–Lysenko theory of inheritance no longer retains the monopoly-status that it enjoyed during the five years following the 'historic August Session' of 1948. As against this, however, Krushchev, in three speeches delivered in quick succession in April 1957, has lately spoken of Lysenko in the highest terms, defending him against the assaults of his colleagues and recommending his method of hill-sowing in the planting of maize.[3]

Shortly after the 'historic August Session', *Pravda* wrote that Michurinist biology

'represents one of the most important constituents in the scientific foundation of the Marxist–Leninist world-outlook'.[4]

Now where in detail is the dialectical materialist importance of this theory considered to lie?

Firstly, it is again regarded as 'a dazzling confirmation and further scientific proof of Marxist philosophical materialism', as formulated by Stalin.[5] Stalin had laid it down as the first 'principal feature' of Marxist philosophical materialism that the world is by nature *material*, that all the various appearances in the world are merely different forms of motion in matter, and that the world has no need

---

[1] *Partiynaya zhizn'*, 1956, 9, p. 30.

[2] *Cf.* G. L. Stebbins: *New Look in Soviet Genetics* in *Science*, 123 (1956), pp. 721 ff.

[3] *Pravda*, 1st, 5th and 10th April 1957.   [4] *Ibid.*, 12th Aug. 1948.

[5] A. A. Rubashevsky: *Filosofskoe znachenie teoreticheskogo nasledstva I. V. Michurina* (The Philosophical Significance of the Theoretical Legacy of I. V. Michurin), Moscow 1949, p. 204.

of any 'world spirit' or the like in order to explain it. Now Michurinism is regarded as an embodiment of materialism and a conquest of idealism in biology because it explains the origin of the various forms of organic life in terms of the reciprocal dependence of the organism and its environment, without relying upon

'any sort of ideas, entelechies, factors of purposive activity or other idealistic lumber'.[1]

It has often and rightly been held against Michurin–Lysenko biology that it is far less materialistic than the Morgan–Weismann theory of inheritance.[2] It is, in fact, impossible to see why the inheritance-mechanism of the chromosome theory should be any less 'materialistic', or more in need of an entelechy, than Lysenko's theory of heredity. The very opposite is the case: if we recall what we have learnt above from Lysenko about the egg-cell's 'ability to select' in the course of fertilization, or about the 'self-thinning', whereby a certain number of closely-planted saplings die off, not *because* they are too cramped, but *in order that* they shall not become so in the immediate future, it is impossible to comprehend how such occurrences are to be accounted for on purely causal lines, without an 'entelechy' or other principle of that kind.

Lysenko's own views as to what constitutes 'materialism' or 'idealism' in biology are in any case very peculiar. He describes Michurinism in biology as materialistic, 'because it does not separate heredity from the living body and the conditions of its life',[3] as though Weismann's contrary standpoint, which distinguishes between 'germ plasm' and 'soma' in the living organism, could not also be materialist, *i.e.*, regard matter as the only reality. His notion of 'idealism' is equally curious. Of the Morganist conception of mutations as essentially unpredictable, he says:

'We have here a peculiar conception of unknowability; its name is idealism in biology.'[4]

But Michurinist biology is supposed to be not only 'materialistic', but also 'dialectical', and thereby to confirm dialectical materialism. The dialectical character of the theory is held to consist firstly in the fact that it conceives of Nature as in a constant state of motion and change, this motion having its source in itself[5] and leading to the emergence of new qualities; Michurin was the first to succeed in

[1] *Ibid.*, p. 205.
[2] See, for example, E. Sankewitsch: *Op. cit.*, pp. 142 ff.
[3] T. D. Lysenko: *Agrobiology*, p. 545.
[4] *Ibid.*, p. 527.
[5] A. A. Rubashevsky: *Op. cit.*, pp. 228 ff.

grasping the process of development in organic Nature as a transition from quantitative processes into qualitative ones.[1]

The dialectical character of Michurinist biology is also and pre-eminently exhibited in its recognition of contradiction as the source of development in Nature. The most fundamental contradiction is to be found in the mutual relationship of organism and environment.[2] For since the environment, which provides the organism with its living-conditions, is continually changing, the organism must also keep changing too. This dialectical unity of organism and environment finds its concrete realization in metabolism; it is 'the foundation underlying all bonds in organic Nature'.[3] Metabolism itself again represents a dialectical unity of mutually exclusive and mutually conditioned opposites, namely the unity of assimilation and dissimilation in the processes of growth and decay.[4]

The nature of the metabolic process is shaped, however, by a lengthy historical process of interaction between organism and environment. But since the environmental conditions are continually altering, a new tension arises, a contradiction between consistency and variability, between heredity and adaptation. It is this contradiction which actually provides the incentive to evolution and the formation of species.[5] The Michurinist method of deranging the heredity is directly derived from this dialectical struggle between variability and hereditary tendencies.[6]

Lysenko, in his law of 'phasic development', provided an instance of the dialectical transition from quantitative to qualitative change, insofar, that is, as plant development represents, not a straight-forward quantitative growth, but a series of qualitative transitions.[7]

The dialectical materialist doctrine of the relation between necessity and contingency[8] is also alleged to find its confirmation in Michurinist biology. The necessary always mirrors the most general and constant relations within a group of phenomena, whereas the contingent reflects the non-repetitive features, which do not arise by necessity from a given process. In the case of living organisms, the necessary consists in the demands imposed on the environment by the

[1] D. M. Troshin: *Dialektika razvitiya v michurinskoy biologii* (The Dialectic of Development in Michurinist Biology), Moscow 1951, p. 143.

[2] *Ibid.*, p. 121.

[3] V. P. Dobrokhvalov: *Filosofskie i estestvennonauchnye predposylki ucheniya I. V. Michurina* (The Philosophical and Scientific Presuppositions of the Teaching of I. V. Michurin), Moscow 1954, pp. 78, 100.

[4] A. A. Rubashevsky: *Op. cit.*, pp. 260 ff.

[5] D. M. Troshin: *Op. cit.*, pp. 121 ff.; A. A. Rubashevsky: *Op. cit.*, pp. 263 ff.

[6] D. M. Troshin: *Op. cit.*, p. 129.

[7] A. A. Rubashevsky: *Op. cit.*, p. 248.   [8] *Cf.* above, pp. 381 ff.

organism in virtue of its heredity; it is the outcome of a long historical process of organic adaptation to the environment, leading to the formation of numerous varieties and species. But this necessity makes its appearance in the manifold shape of a mass of unique, individual, physiological and morphological peculiarities, *i.e.*, as a sum of contingencies. The inheritance has arisen as an outcome of individual development on the part of particular organisms; thus contingency passes over into necessity.[1] It is from this dialectic of contingency and necessity that Michurinist biology infers the possibility of conscious guidance of species-formation on the part of man. Lysenko's objection to Mendelism–Morganism, on the other hand, is that:

'All the so-called laws of Mendelism–Morganism are based entirely on the idea of chance.' [2]

But Lysenko's logic here is too 'dialectical' to admit of being understood. It is possible to see why he should describe the origin of species, on Morgan's account, which attributes them to 'mutations', as a work of chance. But the notion that Mendel's own laws of inheritance, with their wonderful constancy, are also based on chance, is certainly rather steep.

The above-mentioned dialectic of necessity and contingency in Michurinist biology is also responsible for another basic idea, to which Lysenko and the Michurinists attach the greatest importance: that of

'the mutual conditioning of ontogenetic and phylogenetic development'.[3]

The ontogenesis appears as a concentrate of the historical development of the organisms (phylogenesis), and the phylogenesis as the hereditary element governing their ontogenesis and formed in the course of development of previous generations.[4]

Michurinist biology also conforms to a nicety with another dialectical materialist ordinance: the unity of theory and practice. Having developed out of agricultural practice, it is held out as providing the practical man with clear perspectives and the certainty of achieving practical success:

'It is the best form of unity of theory and practice in agricultural science.' [5]

Whereas one of the main arguments repeatedly used against Mendelism–Morganism is that it shows itself to be sterile in practice.[6]

[1] A. A. Rubashevsky: *Op. cit.*, pp. 280–6.
[2] T. D. Lysenko: *Agrobiology*, p. 551.   [3] *Ibid.* (German only), p. 607.
[4] *Cf.* D. M. Troshin: *Op. cit.*, pp. 160 f.
[5] T. D. Lysenko: *Agrobiology*, p. 553.   [6] *Ibid.*, pp. 529 ff.

This all-embracing concord between the Michurin–Lysenko theory and dialectical materialism doubtless explains the high favour it has enjoyed among the ruling elements in the Soviet Union. But as Jean Rostand has very properly observed:

'It is no concern of ours, however, whether Michurinism is more promising, more encouraging or more stimulating than Mendelism–Morganism. Nor are we concerned to know whether it consorts better with this or that philosophy or ideology, or even whether the evolution of species is "unthinkable" without it. . . . What we want to know is on which side the truth actually lies, or rather, the preponderance of truth.' [1]

And the leading biologists are unanimous in declaring that it does not lie on the side of Michurinism. Even before the 'historic August Session' which brought it so much notice in the West, the theory had already been fully stated and disposed of by Hudson and Richens.[2] According to H. Nachtsheim, geneticists the world over are agreed 'that Lysenko has produced not a shadow of proof for the truth of his fantastic notions of inheritance'. [3]

Nachtsheim attributes the main source of error in Lysenko's experiments to a failure to take the necessary precautions for conducting such experiments only on pure lines of stock.[4] He tells us that Käthe Brix has repeated the tomato-grafting experiments, from which Lysenko seeks to demonstrate the possibility of vegetative hybridization, and has come to the conclusion,

'that the great variability found by the Soviet agrobiologists in the tomato-stocks employed is due to the selection-effects of genetically non-uniform strains and to technical faults in the grafting experiments; but that these experiments yield no sort of answer to the problem of the inheritance of acquired characteristics '.[5]

Any really scientific settlement of the issue between Michurinists and exponents of classical heredity is, indeed, made difficult by the fact that, on the strength of their own theory, the Michurinists start by taking the possibility of inheriting acquired characteristics for granted, and therefore consider the provision of pure lines of stock to work from as a superfluous and unnecessary complication.

Since the inheritance of acquired characteristics must therefore

---

[1] J. Rostand: *Les grands courants de la biologie*, Paris 1952.

[2] P. S. Hudson and R. H. Richens: *The New Genetics in the Soviet Union*, Cambridge 1946.

[3] H. Nachtsheim: *Der Fall Lysenko*, in *Der Tagesspiegel* 10th Oct., 1948, p. 2; quoted in A. Buchholz: *Op. cit.*, p. 85.

[4] H. Nachtsheim: *Biologie und Totalitarismus*, op. cit., p. 317.

[5] *Ibid.*

be regarded as not proven, there is no need for extended consideration of the conclusions drawn from it in support of the truth of
dialectical materialism.

9. ANTHROPOLOGY AND PSYCHOLOGY. I. P. PAVLOV

Just as dialectical materialism was confronted with a crucial test of
its powers in the problem of the origin of life, so also the field of
anthropology and psychology provides a similar touchstone for its
claim to possess, in the materialist dialectic, a means of explaining
the spontaneous emergence of the higher from the lower. The
difficulty here is greater still, insofar as the difference between mental
and material phenomena is much more radical than that between
organic and inorganic matter. For the functions of life continue to
be exercised in physico-chemical reactions, and can therefore be
expressed and described in concepts and laws appropriate to the
latter, even though their ordered interplay should add something new
and higher of its own. This is not the case with the mental processes
of human consciousness. Admittedly, they are still linked to physiological processes. But in comparison with the latter they represent
something so different that it is no longer possible to depict their
course in terms of physiological processes or to attempt to identify
what is peculiar to them merely in some very special kind of arrangement among these processes. On the contrary, they represent something completely new in themselves, which lies on a quite different
plane from that of physiological processes. Now it is interesting to
notice that here too, as in the case of the nature of life, Soviet philosophy is very well aware of this basic difference and expounds it with
great precision—the essential distinction, that is, between the mental
and the physiological. But just as, on the previous occasion, it
endeavoured, in spite of this crucial difference, to represent life as
having arisen of its own accord from inorganic matter, so here too it
makes an attempt, already foredoomed to failure, to elaborate the
mental from the physiological, as a property of highly-organized
matter. The means of effecting a connection between these two realms
are discovered by Soviet ideology in I. P. Pavlov's theory of the
physiology of higher nervous activity.

But before embarking on an exposition of Pavlov's doctrine we
must first touch briefly on the problem of the *origin of man*.

Although the evidence adduced by modern science for a purely
evolutionary account of human origins is sufficient, at most, to endow
this opinion with the security of a well-founded hypothesis, it is
treated by Soviet scientists as an established fact. Apart from the
structural resemblance between man and the higher mammals, their
main arguments rely heavily on Haeckel's biogenetic principle, on

the occurrence of so-called atavisms, and on the presence of rudimentary organs.[1]

Lenin, in *State and Revolution*, lists three original stages in human development:

'a tribe of monkeys grasping sticks', 'primitive man' and 'men united in a tribal form of society'.[2]

'These definitions', says Okladnikov, in Volume I of the 10-volume *History of the World* issued by the Academy of Sciences, 'have been taken over by Soviet science in order to designate the three successive stages in human development and the origin of society'.[3]

The australopithecoids give us an idea of the first stage. Okladnikov and Vlastovsky still reckon them as apes who, owing to the great climatic changes at the end of the Tertiary and beginning of the Quaternary, and the steppe-conditions resulting, from loss of moisture, in Central and West Africa, had left the trees and descended to the ground.[4] This was enough to produce major changes in physique: an upright posture, a prehensile hand with the thumb emerging from the plane of the remaining fingers, a more vertical position of the skull, leading to further development of the brain, and so forth. Other finds made in the neighbourhood of the fossil remains indicate that *Australopithecus* used animal bones to slaughter his prey and lived on the meat so obtained. But it is worth noting that the Soviet authorities have resisted the attempts made by Schepers, Dart and Broom to elevate *Australopithecus* as nearly as possible to the human level of intellectual development. These Western experts have mainly relied, in doing so, on an examination of the skull and brain structure, and consider the development of the brain to be a crucial factor for 'man in the making'; but the Soviet specialists reject such an approach to the problem as 'idealistic' and decline to regard *Australopithecus* as an immediate ancestor of man.[5]

Man's true 'making' took place, in their opinion, with the transition to the second stage spoken of by Lenin, *i.e.*, with the emergence of

---

[1] *Cf.* V. G. Vlastovsky: *Sovremennye predstavleniya o proiskhozhdenii cheloveka* (Modern Conceptions of the Descent of Man), in *Estestvoznanie i religiya*, a collective work issued by the Philosophical Institute of the Academy of Sciences of the U.S.S.R., Moscow 1956, pp. 111–36, *q.v.* pp. 117 ff.

[2] V. I. Lenin: *Sochineniya*, XXV, p. 361 (LSW, VII p. 11).

[3] A. P. Okladnikov: *Vozniknovenie chelovecheskogo obshchestva. Ranniy drevnekamenniy vek (nizhniy paleolit)* (The Origin of Human Society. The Early Old Stone Age (Lower Palaeolithic)), in *Vsemirnaya istoriya* (History of the World), Vol. I, Chap. I, pp. 17–49, *q.v.* p. 18.

[4] V. G. Vlastovsky: *Op. cit.*, p. 122.   [5] *Ibid.*, pp. 124 f.

Pithecanthropus in all his various forms. The australopithecoids merely took ready-made objects, such as sticks and stones, for their tools; they were not yet capable of fashioning implements for themselves. This was reserved for the *pithecanthropus* group alone, and that is why this second phase of human evolution is of such cardinal importance.[1]

The stages of *Pithecanthropus*, *Sinanthropus* and *Neanderthal* man are thus major landmarks in the process whereby a 'tribe of monkeys grasping sticks' developed into the primal human society. But whereas among Western anthropologists there is a growing conviction that *Homo sapiens* is earlier in time than, and ancestral to, Neanderthal man,[2] Soviet science takes it as a known fact that Neanderthal man is the ancestor of *Homo sapiens*:

'Progressive science has demonstrated with complete clarity that the *Neanderthalers* (in a broad sense) were the immediate ancestors and forebears of the present-day type of man.'[3]

With the arrival of *Homo sapiens*, society reached a level at which the law of biological selection ceased altogether to control the formation of species. Since the end of the Ice Age, the type of *Homo sapiens* has maintained itself virtually unaltered until our own day. His subsequent development has since occurred *en masse*, according to social laws, which were unknown in the animal kingdom.[4]

The major difference between Soviet and Western theories is doubtless to be found in the significance attributed by Soviet writers, like Engels before them, to *labour* as a factor in human progress. Labour, in Engels' view, 'created man himself'.[5] Vlastovsky underlines the importance of dialectical materialism in the making of this palaeontological discovery:

'By a brilliant application of the laws of the materialist dialectic to investigation of the problem of human origins, Marx and Engels came to the conclusion that labour-activity has had a decisive influence on the process of man's formation.'[6]

---

[1] A. P. Okladnikov: *Op. cit.*, p. 21.
[2] *Cf.*, tor example, W. E. LeGros Clark: *The Fossil Evidence for Human Evolution*, Chicago 1955, Ch. 2.
[3] A. P. Okladnikov: *Razvitie pervobytno-obshchinnogo stroya. Pozdniy drevnekamenniy vek (verkhniy paleolit)* (The Development of the Primeval Community. The Later Old Stone Age (Upper Palaeolithic)), *Op. cit.*, pp. 50–88, *q.v.* p. 51.
[4] *Ibid.*, p. 53.
[5] F. Engels: *Dialectics of Nature*, p. 228.
[6] V. G. Vlastovsky: *Op. cit.*, p. 130.

The 'dialectic governing the transition from *Australopithecus* to man' is seen by this author in the

'contradiction between the feeble natural defences of this ape and the brutal necessity of protecting itself against enemies and obtaining food under the new conditions of existence'.[1]

As already said, the Soviet belief is that *Australopithecus* was still confined to using improvised working-tools in the shape of sticks and stones, *Pithecanthropus* being the first to make tools for himself, which is why man's true beginning is located at this point. But as to how and why this crucial change came about, our authors are as silent as Engels himself.

The use of labour resulted, moreover, in ever closer and more organized interrelations among men, and so it came about that the primeval horde gave place to human society. Labour also brought with it an increasing development of the human hand 'and with it the brain'.[2] Both factors, the closer unity of men in the labour-process, calling for enduring co-operation between them, and the perfecting of the brain, accomplished in the course of the same process of labour, were responsible for the creation of human *language*. As Engels puts it, labour brought men in the making to the point

'where they had something to say to one another. The need led to the creation of its organ; by modulation the undeveloped larynx of the ape was slowly but surely transformed . . . and the organs of the mouth gradually learned to pronounce one articulate letter after another'.[3]

Okladnikov stresses at this point 'that even the earliest language was primarily vocal in character'; sign-language through gestures had a merely subordinate part to play.[4]

So it was, according to the exponents of dialectical materialism, that primaeval man developed increasingly in the direction of the primitive society. Already in the Mousterian epoch, towards the end of this 'preparatory period', primitive man in his Neanderthal phase had reached a level which exhibits the rudiments of the original tribal order. As can be seen from the 'kitchen-middens' found in his cave-dwellings, he was increasingly mastering his animal egoism, no longer caring only for himself and his own family, but also for the community as a whole: he no longer devoured his prey on the spot, but dragged it into the cave, where the women looked after the household. The Soviet anthropologists also believe that they can already discern in this period the beginnings of matriarchy, which

---

[1] V. G. Vlastovsky: *Op. cit.*, p. 131.
[2] A. P. Okladnikov: *Vozniknovenie . . .*, p. 21.
[3] F. Engels: *Op. cit.*, p. 232.   [4] A. P. Okladnikov: *Op. cit.*, p. 36.

subsequently, in the later Palaeolithic, is supposed to have character-ized the first stage of development of primitive society.[1] Just as, in the theory of heredity, Soviet scientists have not yet taken account of the many queries and amendments which later inquiries have set against what once seemed so secure in the theory, so here too, in the field of ethnology, they are compelled by their subservience to the authority of Engels to go on clinging to the theories of Lewis Morgan, which are nowadays out of date.

Along with this development of man from the ape there also took place a parallel enlargement of his mental capacities, *i.e.*, in the terminology derived from Pavlov and now universally employed in Soviet science, of his 'higher nervous activity': man's 'first signalling system', consisting of so-called 'conditioned reflexes' and shared in common with the brute creation, is supplemented by his so-called 'second signalling system', which is 'qualitatively' different from the first and marks the corresponding distinction between the human and the animal mind.

Ivan Petrovich Pavlov (1849–1936) was a pupil of the 'Father of Russian physiology', Ivan Mikhailovich Sechenov (1829–1905). Sechenov's chief work, *Reflexes of the Brain*,[2] attempts a material-istic interpretation of mental processes and was therefore enthusiasti-cally received by the revolutionary circles of the time in Russia, with whom Sechenov was closely associated. Pavlov made further advances along the lines indicated by Sechenov. His works became widely known outside Russia. He was also the first Russian scientist to receive the Nobel Prize (1904).

Pavlov sets out in his inquiries, like Michurin in biology, from the unity of the organism and its environment. This is probably one reason for the high favour accorded to his doctrines in the Soviet Union. A living organism constitutes, in his view, a system in more or less stable equilibrium with its environment. Thanks to his nervous system, man (like the animals) is conjoined with the environment, from which he extracts the substances necessary for life. At the lowest level of organic life such interchanges are effected by direct contact between food and organism, or *vice versa*. In the higher animals this contact is brought about by means of a whole system of highly differentiated 'conditioned reflexes' which function as 'signals' of the presence of food (or of other biologically useful or harmful stimuli). Now what does Pavlov understand by 'un-conditioned' or 'conditioned' reflexes?

[1] *Ibid.*, pp. 43 f.
[2] I. M. Sechenov: *Refleksy golovnogo mozga*, Moscow 1952.

If a young dog, that has tasted no other food except its mother's milk, is shown a piece of bread, it will not react in any way. But if a piece is put in its mouth then, supposing it is hungry, it will secrete saliva and swallow the bread. The secretion of saliva here is an 'unconditioned' reflex. It is a permanent, inborn reaction of the body to an external or internal stimulus. Such reflexes are situated in the deep-lying cells of the brain.

But if this experiment is frequently repeated, then in due course the dog will already begin to salivate on merely seeing the bread. The same reaction can also be produced by the sound of a bell if it is regularly rung for a time before feeding. This phenomenon, which it was Pavlov's special achievement to have discovered, represents a 'conditioned reflex'. Conditioned reflexes are transitory in character and extremely sensitive to changes in the environment. They are located in the cortex of the cerebral hemispheres.

Now if the environmental conditions were to remain exactly the same, then according to Pavlov, mere unconditioned reflexes would be sufficient. But since these conditions are continually altering, the organism needs not only the unchanging absolute reflexes, but the changeable, adaptable conditioned reflexes as well. They are signals to the organism, enabling it to seek out favourable conditions and avoid unfavourable ones.[1]

Pavlov considers the work of 'analysers' (the 'so-called' sense-organs) to be a very important element in higher nervous activity. He defines an analyser as

'a nervous mechanism consisting of the following parts: a certain peripheral ending—eye, ear, etc.—the corresponding nerve and the end of this nerve in the brain'.[2]

It is the function of the analyser to break up the phenomena of the external world into their elements and to select those which correspond to the analyser in question.

The whole of higher nervous activity (*i.e.*, mental activity) in the higher animals consists essentially, so Pavlov tells us, of a totality of conditioned reflexes of every description. A large part of human mental activity, including sensations, ideas and impressions, must also be attributed to this conditioned-reflex activity. Hence the 'first signalling system' consisting of the totality of conditioned reflexes, is common to both man and beast. Man's exclusive prerogative consists in his so-called 'second signalling system', in the form of spoken, heard and visible words. Speech, for Pavlov, is 'the signal of

---

[1] *Cf.* I. P. Pavlov: *Polnoe sobranie trudov* (Complete Works), III, 1949, p. 560 (English in *Selected Works*, Moscow 1955 [cited hereafter as *PSW*], p. 314).

[2] *Ibid.*, p. 144 (not in *PSW*).

the first signals'. It has arisen on the basis of the primary signal as a result of social co-operation, the need for more extensive intercourse among the individuals of the human group.

'The fundamental laws governing the activity of the first signalling system must also govern that of the second, because it, too, is activity of the same nervous tissue.'[1]

Nevertheless, the second signalling system has special features of its own in contrast to the first, and these make it possible for man to behave in a way that is absolutely unattainable to the ape. Y. V. Shorokhova points out that on Pavlov's theory the difference between speech, as a specific stimulus of the second signalling system, and the stimuli of the first signalling system, consists in the fact

'that speech operates, not only through its acoustical or graphical material aspect, but also through the content which is conjoined with this . . . In animals one can set up a conditioned reflex to speech, but this stimulus operates like any other influence impinging on the auditory analyser. . . . In man speech emerges as a stimulus, a signal of signals, a generalized reflection of reality, behind which there is concealed, for man, a system of immediate influences on the part of objects and phenomena in the outside world.'[2]

But as N. D. Levitov[3] emphasizes, the second signalling system is regarded by Pavlov, not only as the foundation of human thought, but also as a regulator, a conscious, voluntary control:

'In the normally developed human being, says Pavlov, the second signalling system is the highest regulator of human behaviour.'[4]

Pavlov is accordingly an outspoken champion of determinism in psychology. Here he is advancing along the trail already blazed by Sechenov, who himself held that all conscious activities, including those regarded as spontaneous, were nothing other than reflexes. So too Pavlov: the kinaesthetic cells of the cerebral cortex, whose excitation corresponds to some definite movement,

---

[1] I. P. Pavlov: *Polnoe sobranie sochineniy*[2], III /2, p. 336; (*PSW*, p. 262).

[2] Y. V. Shorokhova, in the collective work *Uchenie I. P. Pavlova i filosofskie voprosy psikhologii* (The Teaching of I. P. Pavlov and the Philosophical Problems of Psychology), issued by the Philosophical Institute of the Academy of Sciences of the U.S.S.R. under the editorship of S. A. Petrushevsky (*et al.*), Moscow 1952; German edition, Berlin 1955, pp. 272–300, *q.v.* p. 287.

[3] N. D. Levitov: *Voprosy psikhologii kharaktera* (Problems of Character-Psychology), Moscow 1952, p. 29.

[4] I. P. Pavlov: *Op. cit.*, pp. 346 f. (*PSW*, p. 484); quoted in N. D. Levitov, *Loc. cit.*

'can and do establish connections with all the cerebral cells which represent the external influences as well as various internal processes of the organism. It is this that constitutes the physiological basis of the so-called voluntariness of movements, *i.e.*, of their dependence on the aggregate activity of the cortex'.[1]

The theory of higher nervous activity just outlined is also fundamental to the Pavlovian account of character. He distinguishes between the 'type' of nervous system (a concept in some respects akin to that of 'temperament') and character proper. The 'type' is the inborn nature of the nervous activity; Pavlov classifies this in terms of the following features: (*a*) the strength of the basic nervous processes—excitatory and inhibitory; (*b*) the equilibrium of these processes; (*c*) their mobility. Character, on the other hand, results from the interaction between the type and the manifold environmental influences to which the organism is exposed from birth, and to which it must inevitably respond by definite actions, which thereby often become fixed for life. Pavlov stresses the extraordinary plasticity of the nervous system on which the formation of character depends:

'nothing is immobile, unyielding; everything can always be attained, changed for the better, if only the proper conditions are created'.[2]

Hence it comes about that Pavlov, though admittedly with great caution, accepts the possibility that acquired reflexes may be inherited:

'It can be accepted that at a later stage some of the newly formed conditioned reflexes are transformed into unconditioned reflexes by heredity.'[3]

A. von Kultschytsky points out, in this connection, how Pavlov's teaching seems to open up opportunities for 'psychagogic moulding-processes', *i.e.*, for an unlimited power of shaping men and guiding their thought and behaviour by appropriate manipulation of their two 'signalling systems'; he thinks that this prospect may well be the real reason why Pavlovism has been accorded the high favour it enjoys in party circles.[4]

It cannot be denied that Pavlov's teaching does hold out this prospect, especially in view of its acceptance of the possibility of

---

[1] I. P. Pavlov: *Polnoe sobranie trudov*, III, p. 554 (*PSW*, p. 308).

[2] I. P. Pavlov: *Polnoe sobranie sochineniy*[2], III/2, p. 188 (*PSW*, p. 447); quoted in N. D. Levitov: *Op. cit.*, p. 26.

[3] I. P. Pavlov: *Polnoe sobranie trudov*, III, p. 217 (quoted in *PSW* (Introduction), p. 34).

[4] A. von Kultschytsky: *Die marxistisch-sowjetische Konzeption des Menschen im Lichte der westlichen Psychologie*, Munich 1956, pp. 98 f.

inheriting acquired conditioned reflexes. And it may also be that this was why the Party viewed it with such favour. But in Soviet publications we scarcely encounter the express references to this prospect, going beyond the utilization of psychology in character-formation and education, such as may actually be met with elsewhere. Thus K. M. Bykov, for example, writes:

'The most important point in Pavlov's theory of the type (which in another terminology is also called the theory of character or temperament) is his demonstration that formation of the type is basically dependent on conditions in the environment. The features of a type vary in accordance with the conditions of life of the animal. Moreover, under given stable conditions in the environment the altered type of nervous system becomes hereditarily fixed.' [1]

But here the express reference is only to the control of animal behaviour, though it would also have been relevant to draw the corresponding conclusions as regards the control of human behaviour, since the second signalling system follows the same laws as the first. N. P. Antonov is rather more explicit:

'Psychology is faced with the task of investigating not only the physiological, material basis of the mental, but also the laws of development and formation in the human psyche, the changes in consciousness on the basis of changes in being. To gain access to the human mind, to be able to influence its formation in the course of education and upbringing in the widest sense of the word—this is a vital task for psychology.' [2]

But this injunction of Antonov's can still be read in the context of a mere recommendation to make use of psychological discoveries in education. We therefore tend to agree with Buchholz, who remarks on this point:

'But despite occasional references to the possibility of inheriting acquired psychological characteristics, this question is not intruded into the foreground of discussion.' [3]

I. P. Pavlov's theory of 'higher nervous activity' at present constitutes the official basis of Soviet physiology, psychology and medicine. At the 'Joint Session of the Academy of Sciences of the

---

[1] K. M Bykov, in *Uchenie I. P. Pavlova . . .*, German edn., pp. 7–28, *q.v.* pp. 15 f.

[2] N. P. Antonov: *Dialektichesky materializm—teoreticheskaya osnova psikhologii* (Dialectical Materialism as the Theoretical Foundation of Psychology), *VF*, 1953, 1, pp. 195–202, *q.v.* p. 201.

[3] A. Buchholz: *Op. cit.*, p. 99.

U.S.S.R. and the Academy of Medical Sciences on Physiological Problems in the Theory of Academician I. P. Pavlov', held from 28th June to 4th July 1950, it was endorsed with acclamation. To ensure that the sciences in question were properly imbued with his teaching, a 'Scientific Council on Problems of I. P. Pavlov's Physiological Theory' was set up under the chairmanship of K. M. Bykov. On this occasion too, Pavlov's long-standing and most intimate collaborator, Academician L. A. Orbeli, who had already had to put up with vehement criticism at the Biological Discussion in 1948, was again one of those most heavily attacked.

The question arises, however, whether Pavlov's theory is actually in such perfect harmony with dialectical materialism as the official version would maintain it to be. Even the account of the theory just given already inspires certain doubts. One often gets the impression that Pavlov was much more of a mechanist than a dialectical materialist. And we are fortified in this very suspicion by the noisy asseverations put forth by exponents of the official doctrine whenever they light on some point in Pavlov's theory which *lends itself* to interpretation in terms of some thesis or other in dialectical materialism.[1]

The official theorists themselves admit that Pavlov often expressed himself in a thoroughly mechanistic fashion, but seek to 'interpret' such utterances somehow in the sense of orthodoxy. Thus A. Popovsky reports, for example, a remark made by Pavlov after visiting a hospital patient:

'Machines . . . machines and nothing more. An apparatus, a damaged apparatus';

but Popovsky endeavours to tone down these statements, arguing that they were not so intended, and must be regarded merely as polemical exaggerations directed against idealism, vitalism and dualism.[2] E. A. Asratyan attempts, in a curious article, to prove that, in spite of occasional interjections of this sort, Pavlov's theory represents the scientific foundation of the Leninist copy-theory.[3] But it is not only in such passing observations that Pavlov's mechanistic tendency is evinced; it lies far more deeply rooted in his thought. This is particularly evident in his bitter hostility to psychology, in which he went so far as to be unwilling even to concede it the status of a genuine science, and either avoided such terms as 'voluntary', 'mental' and 'ideal' altogether, or only used them ironically. In his

[1] Cf., for example, *BSE*, IX, p. 505.
[2] A. Popovsky: *Zakony zhizni* (The Laws of Life), Moscow 1955, p. 118.
[3] E. A. Asratyan: *Marxistsko–leninskaya teoriya otrazheniya i uchenie I. P. Pavlova o vysshey nervnoy deyatel'nosti* (The Marxist–Leninist Copy-Theory and the Teaching of I. P. Pavlov on Higher Nervous Activity), *VF*, 1955, 5, pp. 31–42.

Reply of a Physiologist to Psychologists he openly declares as his programme that

'uniting, identifying the physiological with the psychological, the subjective with the objective . . . is the most important scientific task of our time'.[1]

Whatever supporters of the official interpretation of his teaching may say to such statements, the basic element in his own theory, the doctrine of the first and second signalling systems, obviously displays a mechanistic tendency. Since Pavlov regards the conditioned reflexes as of the same kind as the unconditioned, the same laws hold for the second signalling system as for the first; and he finds the reason for this in the fact that the operations of the second signalling system occur in the same nervous tissue as those of the conditioned reflexes. What we have also learnt above from Pavlov, concerning the explanation of voluntary activity, again has a very mechanistic air.

As N. P. Antonov tells us,[2] before the Pavlov Conference there were also a number of Soviet psychologists who considered his theory mechanistic. Since the said conference, however, this appears to be no longer the case. But now the inadequate philosophical training of these psychologists has been leading them, by a mistaken application of Pavlovian physiology to psychology, into identifying the mental with higher nervous activity[3] and into calling for a fusion of psychology with physiology. Antonov registers a strong protest in his article against views of this type, and thereby precipitated a discussion which was carried on for years with considerable vehemence in the pages of *Voprosy filosofii*. Here, unfortunately, we must be content to give a brief account of the main arguments employed by the spokesmen on either side, without being able to enter into the details brought out in the numerous contributions to the discussion.

Antonov recalls how, after a lecture by Professor Ivanov-Smolensky, a note was passed up to the lecturer asking what the true subject-matter of psychology was and what its aims might be. The letter bore the subscription: 'A Group of Psychologists in Search of the Subject-matter of their Science'.[4] Antonov regards this episode as

---

[1] *Polnoe sobranie sochineniy*, III/2, p. 153 (*PSW*, p. 409; originally published in *The Psychological Review*, 1932.

[2] N. P. Antonov: *Op. cit.*, p. 195.

[3] So, for example, B. M. Teplov: *Ob obyektivnom metode v psikhologii* (On the Objective Method in Psychology), 1952.

[4] N. P. Antonov: *Op. cit.*, p. 195.

highly significant: if the mental is to be identified with higher nervous activity, it follows inevitably that it will be reduced to physiology, and the true subject-matter of psychology will have evaporated.[1] It is therefore impossible to equate mental and higher nervous activity; the latter is simply the material, physiological basis of mental activity:

'Mental and higher nervous activities are assuredly one and inseparably interconnected, but they are not identical with each other.'[2]

Here Antonov appeals to the formula coined by Stalin:

'A single and indivisible nature expressed in two different forms—material and ideal.'[3]

When the mental factor of thought and consciousness is explained as a property of highly-organized matter, this does not entail, even for materialistic monism, a reduction of the ideal to the material. If it is maintained that mental processes consist entirely of reflexes, this is to go the way of vulgar materialism. A reflex is a material, physiological process, in which excitations of the peripheral endings in the analyser are conveyed along the nerve-fibres into the central nervous system; there the various groups of excitations are combined together, whereupon the excitation is returned to its executive organ and there produces a motor or secretory reaction to the original stimulus. A mental process, on the other hand, is an ideal process whereby the objective world is subjectively mirrored in the human brain in the form of sensations, perceptions, thought and consciousness.[4] Dialectical materialism in no way denies the subjective character of mental phenomena.

'The subjective character of mental processes is governed by the fact that they exist merely in our consciousness, in our "self". Sensation and perception, thought and consciousness, exist always as sensation and perception in the individual man—the subject—and that is why they are also described as subjective.'[5]

There are two orders of phenomena, the mental and the physical, the material and the ideal, which must be regarded, from the standpoint of materialistic monism, as two sides of a Nature one and indivisible.

Antonov draws from all this the following conclusions as to the subject-matter of psychology:

'The object of psychology must be to investigate the specific laws of

---

[1] N. P. Antonov: *Op. cit.*, p. 195.   [2] *Ibid.*, p. 196.
[3] J. V. Stalin: *Sochineniya*, I, p. 312 (*Works*, I, p. 315).
[4] N. P. Antonov: *Op. cit.*, p. 197.   [5] *Ibid.*, p. 198.

the subjective reflection of the objective world in the human brain and man's relation to this world. Psychology is the science of the laws of development and formation of the psyche, man's consciousness, as a property of highly-organized matter, as a product of social development, and as a subjective reflection of the objective world in the human brain.'[1]

Positions similar to Antonov's were also taken up by A. I. Rozov,[2] K. M. Dedov,[3] F. I. Georgiev,[4] and others. Rozov gives a very clear account of the essential difference between mental and physiological phenomena: even so simple an occurrence as pain cannot possibly be grasped in physiological terms:

'Undoubtedly this phenomenon involves both excitation and also inhibition, induction, etc., but its specific character (that which distinguishes it from other phenomena) cannot be described in physiological terms. But if even so elementary a phenomenon as this is incapable of translation into the language of physiology, what are we to say of more complicated cases, such as interest, understanding, thought, and the like? These are all phenomena of a particular order, namely mental phenomena.'[5]

Antonov and those who thought like him were fiercely attacked, however, by another group of Soviet psychologists; though the members of this group were also engaged, with Antonov and his supporters, in a common campaign against authors such as Teplov and others, already mentioned above.[6] Antonov's main error, according to Simonov, is that he considers higher nervous activity to be purely physiological in character. But this is not so, since it also includes the mental as an integral component. Simonov gives the following account of the whole psycho-physical process:

'When an object impinges on the peripheral part of the analyser, a process of excitation arises in this part. . . . As soon as the spreading

[1] *Ibid.*, p. 201.
[2] A. I. Rozov: *Soobrazheniya ryadovogo psikhologa* (Reflections of a Simple Psychologist), *VF*, 1953, 3, pp. 177–9.
[3] K. M. Dedov: *K voprosu ob otnosheniyakh mezhdu psikhologiey i fiziologiey vysshey nervnoy deyatel'nosti* (On the Problem of the Relation between Psychology and the Physiology of Higher Nervous Activity), *VF*, 1954, 1, pp. 216–18.
[4] F. I. Georgiev: *Problema chuvstvennogo i ratsional'nogo v poznanii* (The Problem of the Sensory and the Rational in Knowledge), *VF*, 1955, 1, pp. 28–41.
[5] A. I. Rozov: *Op. cit.*, p. 178.
[6] *Cf.* A. V. Petrovsky: *Ob obyectivnom kharaktere psikhologicheskikh zakonomernostey* (On the Objective Character of Psychological Laws), *VF*, 1953, 3, pp. 173–7.

excitation reaches the central nervous system, a state of excitation arises in certain of its neurodynamic structures; subjective experience, sensation, the mental, is one aspect of this.'[1]

N. A. Khromov also defends against Antonov the incorporation of the mental into higher nervous activity:

'The conditioned reflex is not a purely biological phenomenon, it does not consist in a mere linkage between two points within the cerebral hemispheres. It is at once both a picture of the external world (a mental affair) and an expression of the connection between the organism and its conditions of life.'[2]

He is strongly averse to Antonov's proposal to distinguish two separate processes, one mental and one physiological; the mental should be regarded, not as an independent process, but merely as a 'product' of the activity of the brain:

'Thinking (consciousness) as a process in the brain is a material process; the mental (thought, consciousness) as a "product" of brain-activity, a reflection, an image of the external world in the human head, is already a non-material phenomenon. Here the mental (ideas, consciousness) appears as a property of the physiological form of motion in matter, a property of the brain, which finds expression in the latter's capacity to mirror the external world in a reflexive manner.'[3]

Antonov's acceptance of mental activity (thinking, consciousness) as a separate process over and above the physiological process of brain-activity inevitably leads to the admission of a non-material motion; but this contradicts both natural science and also the 'scientific principles of dialectical materialism'; Lenin himself, in his struggle against Ostwald's energeticism and 'in conformity with the natural sciences', had already discounted the existence of a 'mental form of motion in matter'.[4] Antonov should have borne in mind that, if mental activity is not viewed as activity of the brain, one arrives at a standpoint akin to that of Gestalt psychology, which alleges that in addition to the transitory nerve-connections (associations) in the brain we must also postulate something higher, standing over them, namely the soul.[5] But according to Pavlovian theory, all mental

---

[1] P. V. Simonov: *O termine 'vysshaya nervnaya deyatel'nost cheloveka'* (On the Expression 'Higher Nervous Activity in Man'), *VF*, 1953, 4, pp. 213–15, *q.v.* p. 214.

[2] N. A. Khromov: *O nauchnom ponimanii psikhicheskoy, ili vysshey nervnoy, deyatel'nosti* (On a Scientific Understanding of Psychical or Higher Nervous Activity), *VF*, 1953, 4, pp. 216–18, *q.v.* p. 216.

[3] *Ibid.*   [4] *Ibid.*, p. 217.   [5] *Ibid.*

processes have their common foundation in the reflex activity of the brain. It must be the aim of psychology to investigate the reflex processes in the human cerebral cortex.[1]

In outlining the above positions we believe ourselves to have reproduced the salient features which the Soviet psychologists and philosophers have contributed to the debate about the proper subject-matter of psychology. It would take us too far afield to embark on more detailed discussion of the other points of view on this problem.

From all that we have gathered about Pavlov's theory of the physiology of higher nervous activity, and also in regard to the psychological discussion, the difficulties of Soviet psychology will be clearly evident; it is prohibited, on the one hand, from postulating a soul as the substratum of mental processes, but must equally guard itself, on the other, against falling into the outlook of 'vulgar materialism', which reduces psychology to physiology. Here, in more acute form, we get a repetition of the situation which confronted us above when dealing with the problem of the origin of life. We saw on that occasion, how a detailed working-out of the position adopted by Soviet philosophy leads back eventually either to vitalism or mechanism; and so too, in regard to our present topic, the views of the Soviet philosophers would be bound, logically, to lead either to acceptance of the soul, or to vulgar materialism, if the problems involved were to be rationally thought out to a conclusion.[2]

The basic difficulty confronting dialectical materialism at this point lies in the fact that, on its own principles, it should really be obliged to postulate a substantial spiritual substratum for what it acknowledges to be mental activity. For when Lenin very rightly remarks, in his polemic against Ostwald in the field of physics, that there can be no motion without something being moved, this contention also gives rise to the further conclusion, that it is absurd not to postulate also a spiritual substratum for mental processes that fundamentally transcend the material laws of physiology. That mental processes *do* in fact fundamentally transcend physiology, was indeed very

---

[1] *Ibid.*, p. 218.

[2] It is significant in this connection that the inability to pursue the problems arising to a conclusion has actually been charged against the essays of Petrushevsky and Khromov, in the collective work already referred to, during a discussion held on this book. *Cf.* T. A. Sakharova: *Obsuzhdenie sbornika 'Uchenie I. P. Pavlova i filosofskie voprosy psikhologii'* (Discussion on the Collective Volume 'The Teaching of I. P. Pavlov and the Philosophical Problems of Psychology'), in *Vestnik AN SSSR* 1953, 5, pp. 79–82, *q.v.* p. 80.

clearly brought out in the psychological discussion above described (*cf.*, for example, the article by Rozov). But it was also no less evident from the discussion to what an impasse we are led by denial of a spiritual support for these processes. For if the spiritual character of mental phenomena be seriously accepted, we are logically bound to postulate also an element of spirituality in the substance underlying them. If, in order to avoid this consequence, we seek to attribute spirituality, not to the processes themselves, but merely to their outcome, there is no way of seeing how we shall not again be landed in vulgar materialism. This comes out very clearly in the discussion between Antonov and his opponents.

Antonov had emphasized the spiritual character of mental activity. He laid stress on the way mental processes are related to the subject: sensations, thought, and consciousness exist always as activities of a subject, the individual man, 'they exist merely in our consciousness, in our "self" '.[1] But what is the nature of this subject? Khromov argues against Antonov, that if conscious processes are taken to be different from, and higher than, the physiological processes of nervous conjunction (associations) in the brain, one must also postulate a soul to contain them. And Khromov is perfectly right in this. What is this 'self', indeed, which Antonov sets up as the subject of mental processes? He himself gives two answers to this question. In one instance he equates the self with consciousness. But since the latter, like thought, is also taken by him to be only one among the various mental processes, in this case the substratum of all these processes would be only one amongst them, which is obviously absurd. But in another passage Antonov nominates the brain as substratum:

'Mental activity and higher nervous activity are two aspects of the activity of one and the same material organ, the brain.'[2]

But here we encounter the alternative difficulty, that there is no seeing how one and the same organ can have two such radically different functions as those evinced in physical (reflexive) and mental (spiritual) processes; this would be an even greater absurdity than if we were to try to see with our ears or sing with our eyes.

It would be otherwise if Antonov were prepared to regard the subject himself as a corporeal-spiritual entity, as is maintained by scholasticism, in which man in his substantial unity is held to comprise both a material and a spiritual principle.[3] In this way man as a

---

[1] N. P. Antonov: *Op. cit.*, p. 198.   [2] *Ibid.*

[3] It should be noted here that the spiritual soul is not regarded, on the scholastic view, as a principle by nature completely independent of the

corporeal entity, with his corporeal organs, can be the vehicle of physiological processes, and as a spiritual entity, with his spiritual capacities, can engage in spiritual activity. But there is no comprehending how a merely material entity can exercise spiritual activities, or how a bodily organ can give rise to both physiological processes and mental ones as well.

In order to escape these difficulties, Antonov's opponents deny that mental activity represents a separate process over and above the physiological processes of higher nervous activity, or that there could be any such thing as a 'mental form of motion in matter'.[1] But Antonov replies to this and again rightly, that the denial of such a mental form of motion logically entails a relapse into vulgar materialism. As we have seen above, in dealing with the problem of the origin of life, dialectical materialism distinguishes living matter from the inorganic precisely by the fact that at the organic level the biological form of motion supervenes upon the physico-chemical one; to reject this, as the Soviet philosophers see it, would imply mechanism. But even on Soviet accounts of the mental, the difference between mental and physical is far more radical than that between life and inorganic matter. Hence, if denial of the biological form of motion already betokens a relapse into vulgar materialism, this is even more palpably true of the denial of a 'psychological form of motion'.

Moreover, the Khromov school also find themselves in considerable trouble when attempting to give a more exact account of the subject of mental phenomena. Khromov supposes the mental (conception, consciousness) to be a 'product' of brain-activity, and an immaterial product at that. But this is open to the same objection as we have already urged against Antonov. Khromov goes on to define the mental (idea, consciousness) as a

'property of the physiological form of motion in matter, or property of the brain'.[2]

But in both cases we are faced with a contradiction in terms, insofar, that is, as the 'non-material' (idea, consciousness) is construed as a property of the 'material' (physiological processes, the brain).

It will be seen that the Soviet psychologists and philosophers are assigned a by no means easy task: the very conditions imposed upon their enterprise, namely the construction of a psychology devoid of a psyche—or 'soul', without at the same time reducing the mental to

body; though it may indeed be capable of continuing to exist in what is to it an unnatural state of separation from the body, it nevertheless constitutes, in conjunction with the body, a *single* entity.

[1] N. A. Khromov: *Op. cit.*, p. 217.   [2] *Ibid.*, p. 216.

the physiological, compel them to enter a blind alley from which there is no escape. Under these circumstances, it is to be feared that the above-mentioned group of Soviet psychologists will still be a long time in search of the subject-matter of their science.

In attempting now, at the end of this chapter, to sum up briefly what we have learnt of the relation between dialectical materialism and modern science, we reach the following conclusions:

So far as the *content* of the problem is concerned, we have seen how the much-vaunted 'dazzling confirmation' of dialectical materialism on the part of science crumbles, on closer examination, into nothing. In most cases it is a matter of some individual thesis, which dialectical materialism also shares with other philosophies, but which does nothing to substantiate the basic contention of materialism, viz., that there is nothing in the world except matter, and that there neither is nor can be any other world besides the material one. We have actually met with an example where this abuse is committed, and the confirmation of such an isolated thesis is expressly claimed as an endorsement of the 'correctness of dialectical materialism as a whole'.[1]

To this it must be added that the further claim repeatedly met with in Soviet literature, namely that only on the basis of dialectical materialism can a solution be found to the philosophical problems thrown up by modern science, is equally without foundation. In two instances at least it has become patently clear how their very adherence to a dialectical materialist foundation has led the Soviet philosophers into an inescapable blind alley: this has proved to be the case in the problems of the origin of life, and of the subject-matter of psychology. The middle position prescribed to the Soviet philosophers in these fields—between mechanism and 'vulgar materialism' on the one hand, and vitalism, or the postulate of a spiritual soul, on the other—is possible only at the expense of not thinking the problems out to their conclusion. In this respect we may agree with A. Filipov, who, in his article *Marxism and Materialism*, expresses the opinion that dialectical materialism is in no way superior to 19th-century German materialism, which the classics of Marxist–Leninism contemptuously refer to as 'vulgar materialism', and indeed that owing to its eclectic combination of materialism and dialectics it is inferior to the latter.[2] In its intention of restoring the mental to a greater importance than was allowed to it by the earlier

[1] *Cf.* above, p. 429.
[2] A. Filipov: *Marxizm i materializm* in *Vestnik instituta po izucheniyu istorii i kul'tury SSSR*, No. 1, Munich 1951, pp. 7–29.

materialists, dialectical materialism is certainly an improvement on so-called vulgar materialism and mechanism. But since the Soviet philosophers are forbidden, for certain non-philosophical reasons, to pursue this path to its appointed conclusion, the result is that in logical consecutiveness their dialectical materialism does not even reach the level of the 'vulgar materialism' which they view with such disdain.

So far as concerns the *formal* aspect of the relation between dialectical materialism and natural science, we have seen that although, in recent years, there has been some weakening of the party dictatorship in the field of science, the basic character of this relationship still continues to be the same as before. Even in more recent publications, the fundamental division of science into 'progressive' (*i.e.*, communist) and 'bourgeois' (*i.e.*, reactionary) is still to be met with, as is the tendency to attribute particular standpoints in 'bourgeois' science to the 'interests' of the 'exploiters' or 'imperialists'. It has indeed been acknowledged in recent years that even bourgeois science can be credited with certain achievements and that lessons may be learnt therefrom. And this has brought about some revision of unduly exposed and oversimplified approaches to the philosophical treatment of the findings of the sciences. This tendency has been of most effect hitherto in the field of physics (relativity theory), has percolated less strongly into that of biology, and is weakest of all in anthropology and psychology.

Now as before, the Party exercises its direction over the sciences by imposing dialectical materialism upon them as an alleged 'methodological foundation'. But, as we have had occasion to observe, the dialectical materialist claim to leadership goes far beyond the rôle of a mere methodology, a whole string of its more concrete assertions being regarded as indisputable foundations and axiomatic premises for the sciences. Such suppositions as that the world had a beginning in time, or is spatially finite, or that there is such a thing as the soul, for example, are never disposed of by factual argument, but are refuted merely by pointing out that they contradict dialectical materialism, or lead to 'mysticism', 'fideism', 'undisguised popery', or whatever else these expressions may be taken to imply.

CHAPTER VI

The Dialectical Materialist Theory of Knowledge

IF we recall the two aspects which Engels attributes to 'the great basic question of all . . . philosophy',[1] the problem of the relation between thought and being, it will be seen that all our discussions hitherto have been concerned with the first of these, the problem of priority, the question: which is primary (in the temporal sense), thought or being, Spirit or Nature? All the tenets of dialectical materialism so far dealt with have had no other object than to demonstrate the priority of being, or 'matter', and to do so within the framework of a general theory of being, a general ontology.

We must now address ourselves to the second aspect of the relation between thought and being, namely to the question whether our thinking is capable of apprehending the real world—or in other words to the dialectical materialist epistemology.

The problem of knowledge is the main problem of philosophy to this extent, that its solution is logically prerequisite for the further solution of the ontological problem: the question, that is, as to the nature of the world and of reality generally.[2] Mitin doubtless has this situation in mind when he urges against the radical opponents of philosophy that all positive science presupposes an answer to the question whether the world it investigates is independent of our thinking or itself a product of thought, and hence that all positive science is founded upon a theory of the potentialities of thought.[3]

In spite of this, the Soviet accounts of dialectical materialism choose the opposite path and deal with the ontological problem

[1] Cf. above, p. 281.
[2] Cf. Paolo Dezza, S.J.: Filosofia, Rome 1944, p. 14.
[3] Cf. above, p. 139.

488

before the epistemological one. This is no less true of the earlier accounts (Mitin, Ral'tsevich), than of the later (Leonov, Alexandrov). Nor is this merely a matter of purely external priority in spatial arrangement, but rather of a logical priority, in that the dialectical materialist treatment of the problem of knowledge already presupposes in principle the presence of an objective reality independent of consciousness. Several authors actually make express declaration to this effect; Obichkin, for instance, who opens his account of the dialectical materialist theory of knowledge with the formal announcement:

'The Marxist–Leninist epistemology is based on an acknowledgement of the existence of an external material world, independent of human consciousness.' [1]

A similar assumption also underlies the historicism on which Soviet authors lay great emphasis in dealing with epistemology, and which is exemplified in their fundamental insistence that epistemological problems must be approached from a historical point of view; it is the business of dialectical materialism to investigate the ways in which the knowledge of social man has come to maturity, to show how in the course of centuries his knowledge of the world has increasingly perfected itself, in keeping with the progressive development of the means of production.

As to the method of this dialectical materialist approach to epistemology, we may make the following brief remarks at this point: it is undoubtedly true that from a position of genuine universal doubt the epistemological inquiry cannot be set in motion at all, and that such an inquiry cannot be conducted in advance, 'before' any concrete knowledge has been obtained, but only in the context of the concrete act of knowing itself. There may also be something to be said for the placing of epistemology after ontology. But to set up an external world independent of the knowing subject as the starting-point to epistemological inquiry, is to take for granted the very point to be proved.

The first aspect of the question as to the relation of thought and being, namely as to the temporal and genetic priority of matter over consciousness, has already served as the topic of our whole previous

---

[1] G. Obichkin: *Osnovnye momenty dialekticheskogo protsessa poznaniya* (Primary Features of the Dialectical Process of Knowledge), Moscow–Leningrad 1933, p. 5. Similar remarks continue to occur in more recent publications, *e.g.*, that of I. Andreyev: 'Dialectical materialism starts from the assumption that the material world around us exists outside and independently of us and of our consciousness'. (I. Andreyev: *Dialekticheskyy materializm o protsesse poznaniya* (Dialectical Materialism on the Knowing-Process), Moscow 1954, p. 9; so also in *DM*, p. 380.

discussion. In particular, we have seen from the preceding chapter how dialectical materialism actually conceives of the emergence of consciousness from matter in the course of the evolutionary process. In spite of this, we must first of all return, in the opening pages of the present chapter, to some subsidiary philosophical problems which are bound up with this first aspect of Engels' 'great basic question of all philosophy'. The later sections deal with the second aspect of the relation between thought and being, namely the properly epistemological question, whether consciousness is or is not capable of reflecting being aright.

1. THE PRIORITY OF MATTER OVER CONSCIOUSNESS

The first aspect of the question at issue is settled by dialectical materialism to the effect that matter is primary in respect of its origins, and that consciousness only arises later from matter. As we have seen, the general philosophical justification for this claim is supposed to be provided by the laws of the materialist dialectic. In addition to this, the Soviet philosophers also proffer a number of more concrete explanations to account for the emergence of life, whose activities differ so markedly from the behaviour of inorganic matter, and more particularly for the appearance of sensation and consciousness.

Thus we are already familiar with the explanation given for the emergence of life from inorganic matter: the physico-chemical reactions of inanimate matter already harboured the *possibility* of serving as a basis for the occurrence of vital processes. In the course of an immensely long process of evolution these possibilities were *necessarily* actualized, one by one. There is no need for any further return to the subject here.

The same principle is enlisted to explain the origin of *sensation*:

'Inorganic matter contains the *possibility* of the emergence of sensitive, and hence of thinking beings. But this possibility only becomes *actual* at a definite stage in the historical development of matter.' [1]

Lenin sees the potential presence of sensation (and hence of consciousness) in inanimate matter in its capacity for 'reflection' (in the physical sense of mirroring), which in one form or another is characteristic of all matter. 'Sensation' in the psychological sense he regards as

'the transformation of the energy of external excitation into a state of consciousness'. [2]

In this form it is typical only of the higher organisms; but something

---

[1] F. I. Khaskhachikh: *Materiya i soznanie* (Matter and Consciousness), Moscow 1951, pp. 47 f.   [2] *ME*, p. 39 (44, 118).

of the kind is already to be found even in the lower forms of material existence, namely reflection in the physical sense:

'. . . in its well-defined form sensation is associated only with the higher forms of matter (organic matter), while "in the foundation of the structure of matter" one can only surmise the existence of a faculty akin to sensation'.

'. . . But it is logical to assert that all matter possesses a property which is essentially akin to sensation, the property of reflection'.[1]

Sensation and consciousness, therefore, are not yet formally inherent in matter of lower order, they are merely the outcome of certain rudiments present in it, which have still to undergo a series of 'qualitative' changes. The theory of a kind of universal animation of matter, such as was developed by Plekhanov, who claimed to discern a sort of consciousness, albeit in varying degrees, within all matter, and who said that 'even a stone thinks', is therefore rejected as 'hylozoism'.[2]

If we now inquire as to the specific peculiarity of *consciousness*, the highest form of 'reflection' (whether at the level of sensation or of thought), the explanations we receive are distinctly vague. It consists in the ability of such matter to 'perceive' (*vosprinimat'*), to 'mirror internally', to reflect (*vnutrenne otrazhat'*), to 'bring to consciousness' (*osoznavat'*) the processes occurring inside and outside itself. Objective physiological processes are accompanied in our nerve-centres by their inner, subjective expression, which takes the form of consciousness. That which in itself is an objective material process is at the same time, for a being equipped with a brain, a subjective mental act. This mental act may well be inseparably associated with the objective process occurring in the nervous system, but is not identical with it.[3] In adopting this view of the psychophysical relationship, dialectical materialism approximates in a certain sense to the 'double-aspect theory' of Fechner, who regarded mental and physical as having the same relation to one another as the concave and convex aspects of the circumference of a circle, which are one and the same, but differently perceived according to whether the observer is located inside or outside the circle. How nearly this theory approaches the position of Soviet dialectical materialism was plainly evident, in its day, in the work of the Deborinist Bykhovsky:

'Physical and mental are one and the same process, only seen from two different sides. . . . That which is seen from the outer, objective side as a physical process is equally perceived from within, by the

[1] *ME*, pp. 34 (38, 113), 81 (88, 157).

[2] M. B. Mitin: *Dialektichesky materializm*, p. 116.   [3] *Ibid.*, p. 115.

material being itself, as a phenomenon of will or sensation, as mental in character.'[1]

But the same viewpoint is also echoed in Stalin's formulation of material monism, to which Antonov appeals in the course of the controversy about the subject-matter of psychology:

'A single and indivisible nature expressed in two different forms—material and ideal.'[2]

Within the phenomenon of consciousness, dialectical materialism also sets up a further 'qualitative distinction' between animal and human consciousness. In the previous chapter we have made the acquaintance of Pavlov's theory, according to which human mental activity is to be distinguished from animal by the fact that in man the second signalling system is superimposed upon the first. This implies on the one hand a certain kinship between human and animal 'higher nervous activity', but on the other also an essential superiority of the human over the animal.

Initially, this argues some degree of continuity between the two. Engels believed himself to have found evidence in animals of every kind of intellectual activity: induction and deduction, and hence also abstraction (thus he fancied, for example, that his dog Dido must possess generic concepts, since she was certainly able to distinguish quadrupeds and bipeds), analysis of unknown objects (the cracking of nuts), synthesis (the methodical performance of 'artful tricks' by animals), and experiment (in new situations and difficult circumstances); in all these cases it seemed to him that the workings of the animal understanding were similar in type to the human and differed merely in degree of accomplishment; only the dialectical activity of reason, in Engels' opinion, is solely confined to man.[3] Soviet scientists consider that they have found the makings of intellect among the more highly-developed anthropoid apes. These are capable of reaching a food-target, not directly accessible, by alternative roundabout routes, and even of employing various objects as 'tools' in doing so;[4] Ladygina-Kots claims also to have detected 'primary

[1] *Ocherk filosofii dialekticheskogo materializma* (Outline of the Philosophy of Dialectical Materialism), pp. 83 f.; quoted from N. O. Lossky: *Dialekticheskyy materializm v SSSR* (Dialectical Materialism in the U.S.S.R.), Paris 1934, p. 44.

[2] J. V. Stalin: *Sochineniya*, I, p. 312 (*Works*, I, p. 315); *cf.* above, p. 480.

[3] F. Engels: *Dialectics of Nature*, pp. 295–6.

[4] A series of such experiments is described by N. Y. Voytonis in his book *Predistoriya intellekta* (Prehistory of the Intellect), Moscow–Leningrad 1949, pp. 157 ff. He comes, however, to the conclusion: 'What man performs as a perfectly elementary act at the very start of his development, lies, for the ape, at the utmost limit of attainability.' (*Op. cit.*, p. 190.)

abstraction' among chimpanzees in their ability to separate colour-properties from those of shape and size.[1]

Soviet philosophy is nevertheless adamant on the point that all these manifestations of the animal mind represent only the 'pre-history' of the human intellect; an 'essential' ('qualitative') difference continues always to lie between the two.

'When we see an ape going in search of the stick it requires and then using it a moment later to secure the bait, we are inclined to interpret this procedure as a *rudimentary stage* of that behaviour which later, *in a qualitatively new form*, is characteristic of man in the deliberate pursuit of a definite goal.' [2]

Soviet philosophy agrees in the first place with Engels in finding the most essential distinction between the human and animal intellect in the fact that only the human understanding is capable of dialectical thought, and this because the latter presupposes 'investigation of the nature of concepts themselves'.[3]

On this question of animal mentality dialectical materialism differs equally from the school of those who (like Thorndike and others), discount even the rudiments of consciousness in animals, and from those who (like Köhler), attempt to explain animal behaviour by postulating a consciousness akin to the human. The first, because it leads to a denial of the genetic connection between animal and human consciousness, and is compelled accordingly to regard the emergence of human consciousness as a real 'miracle'; the second, because it obliterates the qualitative boundaries between animal mind and human consciousness.[4]

If dialectical materialism is thus to be found defending the thought and consciousness of man against identification with the animal mind, it is a great deal sharper still in its opposition to the 'vulgar material-ist' identification of thought and matter (Büchner, Vogt, Moleschott, and already in the 18th century, the physician Cabanis). To Vogt's opinion, that thought stands in the same relation to the brain as bile to the liver, or to Büchner's attempt, in his book *Force and Matter*, to reduce thought to physico-chemical motions in the brain, Marxist philosophical materialism replies that though thought must certainly be derived from matter, it cannot be reduced or assimilated thereto in any such primitive fashion. Engels writes, in the *Dialectics of Nature*:

'One day we shall certainly "reduce" thought experimentally to

---

[1] *Cf.* M. A. Leonov: *Ocherk* . . ., p. 521.
[2] N. Y. Voytonis: *Op. cit.*, p. 189.
[3] F. Engels: *Dialectics of Nature*, p. 296.
[4] M. A. Leonov: *Ocherk* . . ., p. 520; *cf.* F. I. Khaskhachikh: *Op. cit.*, pp. 82 ff.

molecular and chemical motions in the brain; but does that exhaust the essence of thought?' [1]

Dialectical materialism undoubtedly believes thought to be a product of matter—not in the sense of a material secretion, however, but rather as a special property of highly organized matter, *viz.*, the brain. Thought is one of those properties of matter which cannot be dealt with by the ordinary methods of material measurement; the brain is admittedly extended in three-dimensional space; but thoughts and feelings 'have neither length nor breadth, neither thickness nor height '.[2] Yet dialectical materialism is in no way tempted by this into acceptance of spiritual substance as such:

'Even though thought and consciousness may exhibit an ideal, spiritual character, they are nevertheless phenomena of the one material world and have no existence as substances in their own right.' [3]

We have already referred in the previous chapter to the rôle of labour in the transition from ape to man. But in addition to labour, a decisive significance for the development of human consciousness is also attributed, in Soviet thinking, to *language*.

Language is as old as consciousness, and like the latter a product of social life; both arise simultaneously in the course of the labour-process. Language is an embodiment of thought. Thought and language form a unity, though they are not identical.

'Language and thought are as intimately bound up together as form and content, and it is just as impossible to sever them as it is to separate a form from its content.' [4]

This unity of thought and word is also referred to by Stalin in the course of his letters on linguistics; there he expressly rejects the possibility that thoughts could arise without words.

'It is said that thoughts arise in the mind of man prior to their being expressed in speech, that they arise without linguistic material, without linguistic integument, in, so to say, a naked form. But that is absolutely wrong. Whatever thoughts arise in the human mind and at whatever moment, they can arise and exist only on the basis of the linguistic material, on the basis of language terms and phrases. Bare thoughts, free of the linguistic material, free of the "natural matter" of language, do not exist. "Language is the immediate reality of thought" (Marx). The reality of thought is manifested in language.

[1] F. Engels: *Op. cit.*, p. 328.
[2] M. A. Leonov: *Ocherk* . . ., p. 517.   [3] *Ibid.*
[4] I. Andreyev: *Op. cit.*, p. 71.

Only idealists can speak of thinking not being connected with the "natural matter" of language, of thinking without language'.[1]

Directed against Marr, these words of Stalin's are to some extent at variance with the traditional Marxist theory of 'hand language' and give rise to certain difficulties in accounting for the thought of deaf-mutes. So far as hand language, the 'language of gesture', is concerned, Stalin does not directly deny the possibility of its existence, but he nonetheless sees in spoken language the sole language of human society capable 'of serving as an adequate means of intercourse between people'[2]; history does not know of a single human society without spoken language. Gesture and spoken language, according to Stalin, are just as incomparable as are the primitive wooden hoe and the modern caterpillar tractor with its five-furrow plough or tractor row drill. And he attempts to neutralize the counter-argument about the thought of deaf-mutes by maintaining that in cases of this type the linguistic basis is replaced by another basis of an equally concrete and sensory kind:

'The thoughts of deaf-mutes arise and can exist only on the basis of the images, sensations and conceptions they form in every-day life on the objects of the outside world and their relations among themselves, thanks to the senses of sight, of touch, taste and smell. Apart from these images, sensations and conceptions, thought is empty, is deprived of all content, that is, it does not exist.'[3]

In thus emphasizing the unity of thought and language dialectical materialism makes a particular stand against the views of Russell and the semantic school.[4]

In regard to this topic of language, it may also be noted that Stalin's essay *Marxism and Problems of Linguistics*, on which this theory is chiefly based, is still cited as a foremost authority, even in the most recent Soviet publications.[5]

The dialectical materialist theory of the origins of life and consciousness has many advantages over the ordinary materialist view on this subject. A particular point in its favour is that it acknowledges the essential difference between life and inorganic matter, as also that between human thinking and the animal mind. Despite this, however, dialectical materialism still retains the untenable conception of a

---

[1] I. V. Stalin: *Marxizm i voprosy yazykoznaniya*, pp. 80 f. (English, p. 51).
[2] *Ibid.*, p. 96 (59).   [3] *Ibid.*, p. 98 (61).
[4] *Cf.* I. Andreyev: *Op. cit.*, pp. 76 f.
[5] *Cf.*, for example, E. M. Galkina-Fedoruk: *Slovo i ponyatie* (Word and Concept), Moscow 1956.

genetic emergence of the higher spheres (life and consciousness) from the lower.

It must be particularly stressed in this connection, that Soviet philosophy itself admits that, for the moment at least, this hypothesis has not been scientifically proved; the vague 'confirmations' on the part of science that we have recounted from time to time are very far from constituting conclusive proofs, nor are they regarded as such either by Soviet philosophy or Soviet science. The Soviet philosophers are compelled to admit, of every single 'dialectical' transition to a higher order of some kind, that this transition has 'not yet' been scientifically demonstrated. Leonov concedes this, of the transition from inorganic to living matter, in the following terms:

'As the natural sciences develop, ideas as to the ways and means whereby life has originated from inorganic Nature are liable to change, and are in fact doing so. But the truth of the teaching of Marxist philosophical materialism remains beyond all doubt, that at some time or other in the remote past life must have arisen from non-living matter, from inanimate structures in Nature, on the basis of the natural laws of their development, without the intervention of any forces of an immaterial, spiritual or "divine" character.' [1]

As for the spontaneous emergence of matter equipped with sensation, it is Lenin himself who confesses this claim unproved, when he allows that further investigation is needed as to

'how matter, apparently entirely devoid of sensation, is related to matter which, though composed of the same atoms (or electrons), is yet endowed with a well-defined faculty of sensation. Materialism clearly formulates the as yet unsolved problem and thereby stimulates the attempt to solve it, to undertake further experimental investigation'. [2]

The same is true of the transition to consciousness:

'Inasmuch as the materialist dialectic assigns consciousness to the general category of reflection, it confronts natural science *eo ipso* with the still unsolved problem as to how the highest form of motion and reflection in matter, that of consciousness, has emerged concretely from the motion and reflection of its lower forms.' [3]

The sole basis of this thesis of the spontaneous ascent from the lower to the higher therefore resides in the philosophical theory of dialect-

---

[1] M. A. Leonov: *Ocherk* . . ., p. 494.   [2] *ME*, p. 34 (39, 113).
[3] V. Ral'tsevich, in *BSE* (1st edn.), XXII, col. 200.

ical materialism, especially the principle of the transition from quantitative into qualitative change; but we do not need to go any further into this here.

More particularly, so far as concerns the appeal to the 'double-aspect theory', which is supposed to bridge the gap between matter and consciousness, the analogy between the concave and convex sides of a mirror offers no solution, for there the difference in the images produced remains within the common field of optical reflection, and exhibits no such essential distinctions as those between wave-motion, say, and the abstract idea of justice.

We need not linger here on the question whether human thought is essentially different from mind in animals, for Soviet dialectical materialism denies this difference as little as we do. The point on which our criticism must fasten is again the claim that human thought and consciousness are genetically derived from animal cognition. It is easy to maintain that apes were transformed into men when they first began using tools for purposes of labour. But the real question is, how the ape could ever possibly have come to use tools *on his own account*, i.e., to employ means to an end which did not yet exist and could be grasped only in intention, through intellectual activity. For natural history shows us that when animals are left to themselves they make no progress. The first apes appear in the Oligocene; some 10 million years have passed since then, and the apes have displayed not the smallest symptoms of progress. Man, on the other hand, first appears in Quaternary times, and in the relatively short period that has since elapsed he has made the enormous cultural advance from extreme primitivism to the position he occupies today. If Voytonis, as we saw earlier, had such difficulty in introducing the ape to the most elementary use of tools, and if he soon encountered an impassable barrier in doing so, how then can our 'forebears' be supposed to have arrived, at once and unaided, not only at using tools, but at seeking them out for themselves or even manufacturing them? To this the Soviet philosophers will reply that the apes were compelled, by climatic changes and the resultant steppe-conditions in Central Africa, to descend from the trees and to seek their food on level ground; this being connected with the transition to an upright posture, and the subsequent changes in skull-structure and enlargement of the brain, which gradually led to the formation of intellectual capacities. But against this it must be urged that, once on the ground, *australopithecus* would have found himself, as the Soviet authors themselves admit, under very difficult living conditions; having lost the rich store of vegetable sustenance previously available in plenty among the tree-tops, he would have had to depend on roots, without possessing limbs equipped for digging them, and on resort to a meat diet, without having the speed to compete with the beasts of prey.[1] All this would have compelled him to employ implements of various kinds. But the formation of intellectual capacities, whereby alone he could become capable of making and using such tools, would be dependent on extremely gradual changes in his physique. This again could only have come about after a very long period of time. But by then the luckless *australopithecus* would long since have perished under the new and difficult circumstances of his environment.

It must therefore be insisted that it is not the use of tools that creates the intellect, but on the contrary, that it is the already existing intellect which is capable of devising means for the realizing of an ideal, not yet existent, but already anticipated goal.

2. THE 'COPY-THEORY'

The foregoing discussions have shown us how dialectical materialism thinks of the priority of matter over knowledge in concrete terms. But in order to be a materialist it is not enough to acknowledge this priority on the part of matter; one must also think it possible for matter *to be known*.[2] The knowability of matter constitutes the second aspect of the problem as to the relation of thought and being.

Stalin formulates this position in the following terms:

'Contrary to idealism, which denies the possibility of knowing the world and its laws, which does not believe in the authenticity of our knowledge, does not recognize objective truth, and holds that the world is full of "things-in-themselves" that can never be known to science, Marxist philosophical materialism holds that the world and its laws are fully knowable, that our knowledge of the laws of Nature, tested by experiment and practice, is authentic knowledge having the validity of objective truth, and that there are no things in the world which are unknowable, but only things which are still not known, but which will be disclosed and made known by the efforts of science and practice.'[3]

Critical support for these claims is held to be found, on the one hand, in the 'copy-theory' propounded by Engels and further extended by Lenin, and on the other, in an appeal to the confirmation of knowledge by practice.

We have already had frequent occasion to observe that dialectical materialism is firmly committed to a realist point of view. In con-

[1] *Cf.* V. G. Vlastovsky: *Op. cit.*, p. 122.
[2] M. B. Mitin: *Op. cit.*, p. 117.   [3] *DHM*, p. 543 (577, 113).

sequence of this it is energetic in campaigning, not only against scepticism (Protagoras, Gorgias, Pyrrho, and among modern philosophers above all Hume), but also against any form of agnosticism. Under the catchword of 'agnosticism', the attack of Soviet science is chiefly directed upon Kant, Spencer, Comte and Du Bois-Reymond, together with Helmholtz, as the originator of the 'hieroglyphic theory'; Heisenberg's uncertainty relation is likewise rejected as agnosticism. Besides scepticism and agnosticism, Soviet theory of knowledge is also particularly averse to the various forms of subjective and objective idealism. Though Hegel certainly admits that the world is knowable, he is still considered to have a mistaken conception of knowledge, in that he views the latter, not as a reflection of the outer world arising from interaction between man and Nature, but as the outcome of the self-development and self-knowledge of the Absolute Idea; the correctness of our knowledge of reality is guaranteed, for Hegel, by the identity of knowledge with its object. And lastly, dialectical materialism is also naturally opposed to any sort of irrationalism or intuitionism, as involving the denial of our knowledge of reality in its most extreme form.

Pre-Marxian materialism is given credit for having always held firmly to the view that the external world is knowable and reflected in human consciousness. But it conceived of knowledge as a passive contemplation of reality, a purely mechanical reflection of the latter in consciousness; it had not yet grasped the whole complicated process of knowledge, nor did it ever progress to the point of applying the dialectic to this process.

Against all such defective theories of knowledge dialectical materialism advances its own copy-theory. According to this, our representations and concepts arise through the operations of the external world upon our sense-organs; they depict or 'mirror' the world outside. The first assertion is directed against idealism: representations and concepts are not produced by the subject; the second has particular reference to the hieroglyphic theory: representations and concepts are not just signs or symbols, having no inner resemblance to the objects known thereby, but are 'pictures', 'mirror-images', 'copies' of the objects so known, and therefore resemble them.

This reflection of reality in consciousness is not to be thought of, however, as a momentary act, like the process which gives rise to the dead, immobile imagery of a photograph. Just as the world is a process of development, so knowledge too must be viewed as a process in which we move from a state of 'ignorance' to one of 'knowing', and in which there is a parallel transformation of 'things in-themselves' into 'things-for-us': yesterday we did not know that coal-tar contains alizarin; today we do know this; nevertheless, there can be no doubt that coal-tar also contained alizarin yesterday, when we were still unaware of the fact. Lenin concludes from this:

'(1) Things exist independently of our consciousness, independently of our perceptions, outside of us. . . .

(2) There is definitely no difference in principle between the phenomenon and the thing-in-itself. . . . The only difference is between what is known and what is not yet known. . . .

(3) In the theory of knowledge, as in every other branch of science, we must think dialectically, that is, we must not regard our knowledge as ready-made and unalterable, but must determine how *knowledge* emerges from *ignorance*, how incomplete, inexact knowledge becomes more complete and more exact.' [1]

But if knowledge is therefore to be regarded as a dialectical process, it also has to be seen as a conflict of opposites and as involving 'contradictions'. The 'contradictory' aspect of the knowing-process lies mainly in the inexhaustible and unlimited character of the world to be known and the limitations of human knowledge at every concrete historical stage of its development.

In his *Philosophical Notebooks* Lenin dwells repeatedly on this dialectical, 'contradictory' character of the knowing-process:

'The reflection of Nature in human thought must be envisaged, not as "dead", or "abstract", or static, or free from contradiction, but as an eternal process of movement, in which contradictions are forever emerging and being resolved'. [2]

Two dialectical transitions in particular are acknowledged by Soviet dialectical materialism within the process of knowledge: one leads from matter to consciousness, and occurs in sensation; the other takes place in the formation of abstract concepts from sensations and representations.

In thereby distinguishing two phases in the knowing-process, dialectical materialism endeavours to avoid the extremes of a one-sided sensationalism and an equally one-sided rationalism. The rationalists (Descartes, Spinoza, Leibniz) thought it possible to attain knowledge of the world by speculative methods alone, without regard for sense-experience; at the same time they also postulated certain innate ideas. The sensationalists, on the other hand (Hobbes, Locke, Condillac, Feuerbach), regarded sense-perception as the only source of knowledge: *Nihil est in intellectu, quod non prius fuerit in sensu* (Locke); they underestimated the part played by theoretical thinking and overlooked the fact that the transition from sense-

[1] *ME*, pp. 90 f. (98, 166 f.).   [2] *FT*, p. 168 (German, p. 155).

perception to thought represents a qualitative leap. Avoiding each of these one-sided views, Marxist philosophical materialism looks upon both types of knowledge as essential stages in the knowing-process:

'From living intuition to abstract thought, and from thence to practice—that is the dialectical road to knowledge of the truth, to knowledge of objective reality.' [1]

So far as the first stage is concerned, Lenin, as we have already seen, defines sensation as 'the transformation of the energy of external excitation into a state of consciousness.' [2] But how this transition from physical to mental occurs in the concrete, dialectical materialism never actually informs us; Khaskhachikh admits that: 'the mechanism of this change has not as yet been sufficiently investigated'.[3] But very thorough attention is given instead to another question, namely how the sensation is related to that which is represented through it, *i.e.*, whether or not the sensation resembles its object. This is the celebrated problem as to the objectivity of sense-qualities.

The dialectical materialist attitude to this problem is not particularly clear. But there is sufficient evidence of a general tendency to answer this question along the lines of a critical realism attributing to specific sensations an objectivity that is not formal, but merely causal in character; yet a number of formulations given by various authors often appear to go further than this, ascribing them a formal objectivity as well. In order to take stock of the Soviet philosophical position and the various ways in which it has been formulated, we need to be acquainted with the views attacked by dialectical materialism.

Whatever the esteem accorded to Democritus as a pioneer of materialism in antiquity, there is a clear divergence from his doctrine that sense-qualities (colour, smell, etc.) do not belong to material things and hence are not exact copies of them. Locke's distinction between the primary (size, shape, number, motion and rest) and secondary qualities of bodies (colour, sound, smell and taste) is rejected, because he regards the secondary qualities as subjective, as not characterizing material things as such, and thereby 'makes a palpable concession to idealism'.[4] The mechanists, too, are accused of holding that colour, smell, etc., only exist subjectively, for the sensing subject alone; that a rose is red, for example, only so long as someone is observing it; thus the mechanist Sarab'yanov developed the theory that that which exists in consciousness as a determinate quality (colour, sound, etc.) is present outside consciousness as a

---

[1] *FT*, pp. 146 f. (89).
[3] F. I. Khaskhachikh: *Op. cit.*, p. 141.
[2] *ME*, p. 39 (44, 118).
[4] *Ibid.*, p. 124.

merely quantitative determination; on this view, characteristics such as 'hard', 'red', 'bitter', etc., would be merely 'our sensations and nothing more'.[1]

But dialectical materialism is particularly averse to 'physiological idealism', the theory that sensations (colour, smell, sound, etc.) are wholly and solely dependent on the physiological organization of the perceiving subject.[2] Exponents of this doctrine include the German physiologist Johannes Muller (1801–58), who held that the qualities of our sensations are determined, not by the qualities of the material stimulus, but solely by the specific structure of our sensory nerves and sense-organs. The same is true of his pupil Hermann Helmholtz (1821–94), who likewise regarded the quality of colour- and sound-sensations as exclusively dependent on the specific energy of the optic or auditory nerves; in Helmholtz's view the qualities of our sensations bear no resemblance to the properties of external objects; the differences between the sensations conveyed by the various sense-organs are entirely governed by the nature of the nerves involved, not by the character of the external stimulus. On the strength of these considerations, Helmholtz worked out his theory of symbols, according to which our sensations are merely signs or symbols for external objects, and do not represent them; every individual has to master these symbols through experience and the use of language, just as he has learnt to understand his mother-tongue.[3]

This theory of Helmholtz's later provided Plekhanov with the basis of his 'hieroglyphic theory'. In a note to the first edition of his translation of Engels' *Ludwig Feuerbach* (1892), Plekhanov writes as follows—his authority being the Russian physiologist Sechenov:

'Our sensations are a sort of hieroglyphics, which render us conscious of what is going on in reality. The hieroglyphics bear no resemblance to the occurrences mediated by them.' [4]

From the hostility evinced by dialectical materialism towards all these theories it would appear that it is not content with a purely causal objectivity of sense-qualities (an objectivity, that is, in the sense merely that sense-qualities are evoked by certain properties in objects but do not in themselves resemble these properties); but nor, on the other hand, is there any willingness to ascribe a formal objectivity to these qualities (in the sense that the properties exist in

---

[1] M. V. Vol'fson–G. M. Gak: *Ocherki . . .*, p. 31.
[2] F. I. Khaskhachikh: *Op. cit.*, p. 125; M. A. Leonov: *Ocherk . . .*, p. 501.
[3] F. I. Khaskhachikh: *Op. cit.*, pp. 133 ff.; M. A. Leonov: *Ocherk . . .*, p. 501.
[4] G. V. Plekhanov: *Sochineniya* (Works), VIII, p. 408.

the sense-organs in the same manner as they do in the object). This can be seen from the critical attitude taken by dialectical materialism towards the 'naïve realists', who hold that colour, smell, sound, taste, etc., are objective properties of material things, in the sense that they exist there exactly as we perceive them;[1] it also emerges from the disavowal of 'vulgar materialism', which regarded sensation as a simple mechanical reproduction of the object in the brain and supposed the existence in Nature of 'colours-in-themselves', 'sounds-in-themselves', etc., which are reflected in the corresponding sensations we have of them.[2]

The positive doctrine of dialectical materialism is summed up in the following two points:

(1) Colour, sound, smell, etc., exist as objective properties of material things, independent of man's consciousness and his sense-organs;

(2) Our sense-impressions are truthful reflections of these objective properties in material things.[3]

Particular reliance is placed at this point on a passage from Lenin's *Materialism and Empirio-Criticism*:

'The sensation of red reflects ether vibrations of a frequency of approximately 450 trillions per second. The sensation of blue reflects ether vibrations of a frequency of approximately 620 trillions per second. The vibrations of the ether exist independently of our sensations of light. Our sensations of light depend on the action of the vibrations of the ether on the human organ of vision. Our sensations reflect objective reality, *i.e.*, something that exists independently of humanity and of human sensations. That is how science views it.'[4]

What corresponds in objective reality to the sensation of 'red', therefore, is ether vibrations of a certain frequency. But how there can be any resemblance between these two phenomena it is not easy to see.

Nor do the commentaries of the Soviet philosophers do anything to clarify matters. Reference is made, for example, to the fact that sensations are supposed to be subjective in form but objective in content:

'Human sensations are subjective as regards their form (their subjectivity consists in the fact that they exist only in our consciousness),

---

[1] F. I. Khaskhachikh: *Op. cit.*, p. 125.
[2] M. A. Leonov: *Ocherk . . .*, p. 504.
[3] F. I. Khaskhachikh: *Op. cit.*, pp. 125 f.
[4] *ME*, pp. 288 f. (313 f., 355).

but are objective in respect of their content, their origin, their source.' [1]

Leonov again appeals to the almighty contradiction to resolve the difficulty:

'The resemblance between reflection and object is not a simple mechanical similarity, but a complex, contradictory resemblance. The sensory material, the living organism, reflects the operation of external objects and processes in its own fashion, on the basis of its own peculiar properties (the inner laws of its nature).' [2]

Mitin speaks of a 'relative' resemblance:

'The objective quality of the light-wave is reflected here in subjective form, in the form of sensation. The colour resembles the objective process consisting in the action of light which produces it, but only in a relative fashion.' [3]

The point which is supposed to be brought out in all these groping attempts to define the relation between the sensation and the property of the object thereby reproduced is doubtless the notion that something more than a causal relationship obtains between the two, that sense-impressions somehow reproduce objective properties in bodies, even though there is no formal resemblance between them.

The transition from matter to sensation constitutes the first dialectical 'leap' in the knowing-process. The second consists in the transition from sensory knowledge (sensation, perception, representation) to the abstract, logical concept.

For knowledge must be regarded not as a passive, immediate reflection of reality, but as a process in which the knowing subject takes an active part, ascending by abstraction from sensations to higher products of knowledge—in other words, as a process occurring by stages:

'Knowledge'—says Lenin—'is the reflection of Nature on the part of man. This reflection, however, is by no means a simple, immediate, total affair, but rather a process involving a series of abstractions, formulations, the framing of concepts, laws, etc.' [4]

Sense-perception merely reflects *appearance*. Admittedly the general aspect of things, their interconnectedness, also finds expression in the process, but it is only an outer generality, an outer connectedness

---

[1] F. I. Khaskhachikh: *Op. cit.*, p. 128; *cf.* also M. A. Leonov: *Ocherk* . . . p. 502.
[2] M. A. Leonov: *Ocherk* . . ., p. 504.
[3] M. B. Mitin: *Op. cit.*, p. 120.
[4] *FT*, p. 156 (German, p. 101).

(the presence of a common colour, for example, or the sequence of sound following upon a blow, and so on); sense-perception fails, however, to grasp the relationships and laws involved, the element of causal connection. This is the work of *logical* knowledge, which penetrates into the *essence* of things, seeking out the inner unity behind the outward resemblance. For this reason it constitutes an indispensable element in the development of human knowledge.[1]

This transition to logical knowledge, from the reflection of appearance to the reflection of essence, also has a dialectical character. For logical thought would certainly seem to lead us to some extent away from concrete things. Sense-perception is much closer to things, for it expresses them in all their concreteness, and with all their individual features. But in place of this, logical knowledge goes deeper than sensation, for it probes the essence of the thing:

'The movement of knowledge *towards* its object must always take place in dialectical fashion, withdrawing in order to grasp it more securely—*reculer pour mieux sauter.* . . .'[2]

'In ascending from the concrete to the abstract, thought—provided it is *correct*—does not get farther away from truth, but comes closer to it . . . *all* scientific . . . abstractions present a deeper, more faithful, *more complete* reflection of Nature.'[3]

Only logical knowledge can grasp an occurrence in its entirety:

'Representation cannot grasp motion *in its entirety*, thus it cannot grasp, motion at a speed of 186,000 miles per second, but *thought* can grasp it, and is obliged to do so.'[4]

The ascent from concrete appearance to general essence takes place by way of abstraction or 'generalization'. Individual objects of the same kind are initially distinct from one another, no one of them being exactly like the others in every respect. But nor, on the other hand, is there any one which does not have much in common with the remainder.

'The general exists only in the singular and through the singular. Every singular is (in one way or another) a general.'[5]

Now the task of logical knowledge is precisely that of discovering this general in the singular, of extracting the essential from the mass of accidental particulars. Thus logical generalizations also provide subjective pictures of the objective world, just as sense-perceptions

---

[1] M. A. Leonov: *Ocherk* . . ., pp. 574 f.; *cf.* F. I. Khaskhachikh: *Op. cit.*, pp. 148 f.
[2] *FT*, p. 261 (216). [3] *FT*, p. 146 (89). [4] *FT*, p. 199 (152).
[5] *FT*, 329 (287; *cf.* also *On Dialectics. LSW*, XI, p. 83).

do; but unlike sense-perceptions they are mediated reflections of reality. They are *concepts*, giving expression to the general and essential features of things.[1]

Sensory and rational, or (as the Soviet philosophers call it) logical, knowledge form in this way a unity, a single knowing-process in two stages. The cleavage made by empiricism and rationalism, each in its own fashion, between sensation and concept, is thereby bridged: the dialectical materialist recognition of the dialectical unity of sensation and concept is held to overcome the one-sidedness of both these views.[2]

Mitin goes on from this to dispose of an objection raised against Lenin's copy-theory by L. Axel'rod, *viz.*, that to regard sensations as images, pictures or 'copies' of things must lead to a new separation of subject and object, which would make things as such superfluous and turn them once more into genuine 'things-in-themselves'.[3] Mitin rejects this argument of Axel'rod's on the ground that it overlooks the dialectical character of the copy-theory.[4] It is precisely in virtue of the dialectical connection thereby established within the knowing-process that sensations do not separate us off from things, as Kant thought, but bring us into union with them.[5]

But this does not suffice, on the copy-theory, to furnish all the essential ingredients of the knowing-process. For this latter, which begins with sensation and advances to dialectical thought, completes itself

'on the basis of the development of socio-historical practice, which emerges in the class-society as the practice of a particular class'.[6]

Material reality is perfectly reflected only in social consciousness. Hence the knowing subject—and this, according to dialectical materialism, constitutes the fundamental error of traditional epistemology—must be conceived, not in an abstract idealist fashion as 'consciousness', 'soul' or 'thought', as a logical or psychological 'subject'; nor yet in the abstract materialist manner as 'man as such' in his natural and immediate givenness; but rather as man· the socially active being, the representative of a particular social class.[7]

---

[1] M. A. Leonov: *Ocherk* . . ., pp. 576 ff.; *cf.* F. I. Khaskhachikh: *Op. cit.*, p. 154.

[2] *Cf.* I. Andreyev: *Op. cit.*, pp. 24 f.   [3] *Cf.* above, p. 152.

[4] M. B. Mitin: *Op. cit.*, p. 261.   [5] *Ibid.*, p. 117.

[6] F. I. Khaskhachikh: *Op. cit.*, p. 145.

[7] V. Ral'tsevich, in *BSE* (1st edn.), XXII, col. 198.

3. PRACTICE AS THE FOUNDATION OF KNOWLEDGE AND CRITERION OF TRUTH

M. N. Rutkevich sums up the rôle of practice in the knowing-process under the following heads: firstly it is the foundation of knowledge, and secondly it also serves as the criterion of truth.[1]

The first thing is to make clear what the Soviet philosophers mean by 'practice'. Rutkevich, in a polemic against other Soviet viewpoints, describes it as the 'material activity of man', a definition directed particularly against those who also wanted to include under it theoretical and intellectual activity.[2] By 'material activity of man' he means above all the production of material goods, but also the class-struggle, political life and even the physical or material procedures involved in scientific or artistic activity. Khaskhachikh gives a similar interpretation of the term.[3]

The Soviet philosophers commonly base their theory of the rôle of practice in the knowing-process on a passage from Lenin's *Philosophical Notebooks*:

'From living intuition to abstract thought, and from thence to practice—that is the dialectical road to knowledge of the truth, to knowledge of objective reality.'[4]

But Rutkevich emphasizes that this observation of Lenin's does not mean that practice merely comes in as the 'third stage' in the knowing-process, or that the first two stages referred to by Lenin are not bound up with practice.

'Practice is the *foundation of the entire knowing-process*, from beginning to end.'[5]

Rutkevich sees the basis of this thesis in the social character of human thought.

'Unlike metaphysical materialism, dialectical materialism views the individual act of thought in any one of the innumerable human heads as a particle of the historical process of knowledge embracing the world as a whole, in which this particle is organically incorporated.'

---

[1] M. N. Rutkevich: *Praktika—osnova poznaniya i kriteriy istiny*, Moscow 1952.

[2] M. N. Rutkevich: *K voprosu o roli praktika v protsesse poznaniya* (On the Problem of the Rôle of Practice in the Knowing-Process), *VF*, 1954, 3, pp. 34–45, *q.v.* pp. 38 f.

[3] F. I. Khaskhachikh: *Op. cit.*, p. 191.   [4] *FT*, pp. 146 f. (89).

[5] M. N. Rutkevich: *Praktika . . .*, p. 125; so also F. I. Khaskhachikh: *Op. cit.*, p. 191.

Our thinking is not, therefore, that of an isolated individual. And since our knowing is a socio-historical process, it is also conditioned by the development of social practice.[1]

In the first place, even our powers of sensory perception are dependent on this historical practice. Here Rutkevich appeals to Marx, as having maintained that the development of the five senses is a product of the whole of world-history.[2] The physiological delicacy of the sensations received by eye, ear, hand, etc., develops in accordance with the progress of production and culture.[3]

The same holds true of intellectual knowledge. Thanks to this theory of socio-historical practice as the foundation of knowledge, Marxism, according to Rutkevich, is in a position to resolve the eternal quarrel between rationalism and sensationalism about 'innate ideas': certain propositions (such as those of mathematics) owe their axiomatic character to the fact that, parallel with the development of socio-historical practice, the capacity for thought also progressed along with its content,

'which found expression in the hereditary fixation of the peculiar properties of the physiological structure of the brain and nervous system, and in the further modification of this heredity'.[4]

The 'invisible presence' of practice in the pursuit of theoretical thinking is also shown by the fact that at every step in the formation of a theory we test the results of our thought against the facts; even the laws of logic, indeed, by whose aid concepts are incorporated into a system, have developed alongside the development of man's practical activity.[5]

The second task allotted to practice in the knowing-process is that of functioning as the criterion of truth. Dialectical materialism starts by rejecting a number of 'idealist' criteria: Descartes' 'clear and distinct ideas'; Hegel's identity of knowledge with its object, premising as it does that this is really an identity of knowledge with itself, since object and knowledge are one and the same; Mach's principle of intellectual economy, and Bogdanov's thesis that the true is that which has 'universal significance'. Pre-Marxian materialism too, though correct in its conception of truth as the correspondence of thought with reality, failed, however, to carry this forward into regarding practice as the criterion of truth, because it was orientated exclusively upon contemplative apprehension of the world and not upon the struggle to change it.[6] Marx was the first to

---

[1] M. N. Rutkevich: *Op. cit.*, p. 121.
[2] *Ibid.*, p. 123; *cf.* K. Marx, F. Engels: *Works* (Russian edn.) III, p. 627.
[3] M. N. Rutkevich: *Op. cit.*, p. 123.   [4] *Ibid.*   [5] *Ibid.*, p. 131.
[6] M. A. Leonov: *Ocherk* . . ., pp. 608 ff.; *cf.* M. N. Rutkevich: *Op. cit.*, pp. 136 ff.

rectify this basic fallacy of approach in all previous philosophy, when he laid down in his theses on Feuerbach:

'The philosophers have only *interpreted* the world in various ways; the point, however, is to change it.' [1]

This statement also pointed the way, in a logical sense, to the discovery of practice as the criterion of truth. Starting from this basis, Marx then postulates as much in his second thesis:

'The question of whether objective truth can be attributed to human thinking is not a question of theory but is a *practical* question. In practice man must prove the truth, that is, the reality and power, the this-sidedness of his thinking. The dispute over the reality or non-reality of thinking which is isolated from practice is a purely *scholastic* question.' [2]

Engels, in his *Ludwig Feuerbach*, endeavours to reinforce this thesis by appealing to experiment and industry, in which human foresight finds its confirmation in practice, and thereby gives proof both of the power of human knowledge over reality and at the same time of the falsity of the Kantian belief in an essentially ungraspable 'thing-in-itself':

'The most telling refutation of this as of all other philosophical crotchets is practice, namely, experiment and industry. If we are able to prove the correctness of our conception of a natural process by making it ourselves, bringing it into being out of its conditions and making it serve our own purposes into the bargain, then there is an end to the Kantian ungraspable "thing-in-itself". The chemical substances produced in the bodies of plants and animals remained such "things-in-themselves" until organic chemistry began to produce them one after another, whereupon the "thing-in-itself" became a thing for us, as, for instance, alizarin, the colouring matter of the madder, which we no longer trouble to grow in the madder roots in the field, but produce much more cheaply and simply from coal tar. For three hundred years the Copernican solar system was a hypothesis with a hundred, a thousand or ten thousand chances to one in its favour, but still always a hypothesis. But when Leverrier, by means of the data provided by this system, not only deduced the necessity of the existence of an unknown planet, but also calculated the position in the heavens which this planet must necessarily occupy, and when Galle really found this planet, the Copernican system was proved.' [3]

This argument of Engels met with severe criticism, it being pointed

---

[1] *MESW*, II, p. 367.   [2] *Ibid.*, p. 365.
[3] F. Engels: *Ludwig Feuerbach . . .*; *MESW*, II, p. 336.

out that Engels had completely failed to understand Kant. Plekhanov attempts to shield him against this objection and defends the correctness of his reasoning. Since the appearance, for Kant, is merely an outcome of the impression made on me by the thing-in-itself, the fact is that in experiment and industry I am compelling the thing-in-itself to affect me in a given fashion intended by myself; and from this it follows that I have at least a certain knowledge of some of its properties.[1] A second argument adduced by Plekhanov is better than the first. In experimental and industrial activity I compel the thing to affect me in a particular fashion, that is, I take up an active attitude towards it, as a cause. But according to Kant the category of causality has no validity outside the phenomenal order, and has no application to the thing-in-itself.

'Experiment refutes him (Kant) even better than he refutes himself, when he says that the category of causality relates to appearances (not to things-in-themselves), and at the same time maintains that the "thing-in-itself" acts upon our "self", *i.e.*, is the cause of appearances.'[2]

These considerations of Plekhanov's represent at best a justification of Engels' argument against the Kantians; they fail, however, to provide any positive basis for the doctrine of practice as the criterion of true knowledge, nor do they show to what extent practice contains the solution to the problem of knowledge. As Lossky remarks in passing,[3] even if confirmation in practical activity does actually give us the assurance that we are capable of authentic knowledge of the world, this does nothing to solve the epistemological problem; we still lack a theory of knowledge proper, whose task is to demonstrate the critical and ontological possibility ('the conditions of the possibility' as Kant would say), as to *how* the subject may have true knowledge, not only of his own experiences and acts of cognition, but also of the outside world independent of his knowledge.

Rutkevich emphasizes, furthermore, that confirmation by practice should not be taken to suggest that only propositions confirmed by experiment can advance any claim to truth. Marxism does not reduce practice to experiment. There are also observations (in

---

[1] G. V. Plekhanov, in his notes to the second Russian edition of Engels' *Ludwig Feuerbach* (Geneva 1905), p. 109. This argument appears unconvincing, for Kant would never allow that in experiment and industry the subject compels the thing-in-itself to impress itself on him 'in a given fashion'. The impressions produced by the thing-in-itself are for Kant an amorphous mass; all determination arises through the application to this amorphous mass of the *a priori* forms of the knowing subject.

[2] *Ibid.*   [3] N. O. Lossky: *Op. cit.*, p. 56.

astronomy, for instance) where no sort of experimental verification is possible. Hence the significance of experiment should not be overrated:

'Practice includes both experiment and observation, but the decisive rôle in the process is played by labour and the political activity of the masses—production and the class-struggle.' [1]

Another author goes further still and credits revolutionary practice with an even more decisive significance in the process of cognition:

'The Marxist-Leninist epistemology has no other aim beyond the service of revolutionary practice.' [2]

In connection with this dialectical materialist doctrine of practice as the criterion of truth, and more especially in consequence of the aforementioned text from Lenin's *Philosophical Notebooks* ('From living intuition to abstract thought, and *from thence to practice* . . .') a discussion has lately arisen among the Soviet philosophers as to whether practice must be incorporated as a 'third stage' in the knowing-process. Rutkevich definitely rejects this view, in an article in *Voprosy filosofii*, on the ground that it involves a two-fold error: (*a*) practice is thereby shifted into the sphere of knowing, and (*b*) if practice figures merely as a 'third stage' in the knowing-process, it ceases to be the foundation of the other two.[3] This opinion was specifically contested, in another contribution to the discussion, by V. M. Podosetnik.[4] Further essays on the same theme were published, together with an editorial postscript, in the 1st number of the 1955 volume of *Voprosy filosofii*. The outcome of the discussion, as laid down by the Editors in their postscript, constituted a rejection of Rutkevich's thesis; he was chided for having incorrectly set practice in opposition to intellectual activity:

'Only if knowledge is regarded as a purely intellectual process, having no extension beyond the boundaries of pure consciousness, is it possible to speak of a false incorporation of practice into the sphere of knowledge. But the situation is entirely different from this. It is only because Marxism has thrown down the barriers erected between knowledge and practice by the older philosophers, and boldly

---

[1] M. N. Rutkevich: *Op. cit.*, p. 167.

[2] F. I. Georgiev: *Problema chuvstvennogo i ratsional'nogo v poznanii* (The Problem of the Sensory and the Rational in Knowledge), *VF*, 1955, 1, pp. 28–41, *q.v.*, p. 40.

[3] M. N. Rutkevich. *K voprosu . . .*, pp. 36 ff.

[4] V. M. Podosetnik: *K voprosu o stupenyakh protsessa poznaniya istiny* (On the Problem of Stages in the Process of Knowing Truth), *VF*, 1954, 5, pp. 77–81.

carried practice into the sphere of knowledge, that it has been able to effect a transformation in the field of epistemology itself, and to create a truly scientific theory of knowledge.' [1]

Practice is assuredly the foundation of the knowing-process as a whole, and of each individual stage therein, inasmuch as both living intuition and the abstractive activity of thought are carried out under its decisive influence; but neither the first nor the second stage are capable in themselves of yielding reliable knowledge, if it is not confirmed in practice. Rutkevich also shows signs of an excessive separation of knowledge and practice in that he only reckons art and science under practice insofar as they involve physical or material procedures. [2]

But in spite of this criticism, Rutkevich's book, *Practice as the Foundation of Knowledge and Criterion of Truth*, still largely retains its authority, as is shown by the fact that, in the summer of 1957, the Dietz Press in East Berlin brought out a German translation, praising it in its announcements as follows:

'This book has caused a sensation among philosophers. . . . The philosophically-minded German reader will be rewarded, on reading it . . . with important philosophic insights.' (*Dietz-Mitteilungen*, No. 56, series 3/1957, p. 14.)

4. OBJECTIVE, RELATIVE AND ABSOLUTE TRUTH

In conjunction with the copy-theory, Soviet philosophy normally goes on to deal with the question of objective truth. Lenin already regards these two problems as internally linked with one another:

'To regard our sensations as images of the external world, to recognize objective truth, to hold the materialist theory of knowledge—these are all one and the same thing.' [3]

Lenin's occasion for enlarging on this theme was provided by Bogdanov, who had maintained in his book on empirio-monism that:

'As I understand it, Marxism contains a denial of the unconditional objectivity of any truth whatsoever, the denial of all eternal truths.' [4]

As we have already seen in dealing with this author, the objectivity of a physical phenomenon consists, in his view, in nothing else except its universal validity.

[1] *VF*, 1955, 1, pp. 147 f.   [2] *Ibid.*
[3] *ME*, p. 117 (128, 193).
[4] A. Bogdanov: *Empiriomonizm*, Bk. III, pp. iv f.; *cf. ME*, p. 109 (119, 185).

Soviet dialectical materialism also found opponents in the ranks of the mechanists. Sarab'yanov, for example, held that 'objective truth has no sort of existence; all truth is subjective';[1] and he goes on to explain this as follows:

'Why do I call all truth subjective? For this reason, because truth is not objective being, because truth is our representation of the world, of things and of processes.' [2]

In company with Lenin, Rutkevich takes objective truth to be

'the content of human thought, as tested in practice, which is in conformity with objects, and is thus independent of the subject, man and humanity in general'.[3]

This objective truth is discovered in the course of the historical development undergone by the knowledge of social man. It is not a static, dead affair, but a process: 'Truth is a process', says Lenin, commenting on the Hegelian theory that in its own nature the Idea is itself a process:

'Man advances from subjective idea to objective truth *by way of* "practice" (and technology).' [4]

But if objective truth has the character of a process, and if our own knowledge therefore has a similar character, it follows from this that a distinction must also be drawn within objective truth itself, between absolute and relative truth. On the one hand, acknowledgement of objective truth also requires the admission of absolute truth:

'To acknowledge objective truth, *i.e.*, truth not dependent on man and mankind, is, in one way or another, to recognize absolute truth.' [5]

Absolute truth is nothing other than the full range and extent of objective truth. But man is incapable of grasping the full extent of this absolute truth in one and the same instant; he can only come increasingly close to it and arrive there by gradual stages.

'Man is unable to grasp—reflect—copy—Nature as a *whole*, a complete thing, in its "immediate totality", he can only approach *eternally* closer to it, by creating abstractions, concepts, laws, a scientific world-picture, and so on, and so forth.' [6]

This progressive conquest of absolute truth is relative truth.

[1] *Cf.* above, pp. 501 f.

[2] In *Pod znamenem marxizma*, 1926, No. 6, p. 66; quoted in M. B. Mitin: *Op. cit.*, p. 125.

[3] M. N. Rutkevich: *Praktika . . .*, p. 142.   [4] *FT*, p. 174 (121).

[5] *ME*, p. 120 (130, 195).   [6] *FT*, p. 157 (101).

'Human thought then by its nature is capable of giving, and does give, absolute truth, which is compounded of a sum-total of relative truths.' [1]

Absolute truth is the sum of relative truths.

'Absolute truth stands to relative as whole to part.' [2]

But since the world is infinite, and human knowledge likewise an endlessly advancing process, it follows that absolute truth will never be attained by mankind. This conclusion is in fact drawn, on many occasions, by Soviet authors:

'This process of approximation to absolute truth, *i.e.*, to an exhaustive knowledge about the world, is an unending process, which will never reach its full conclusion.' [3]

Engels had already spoken in this connection of an 'asymptotic progress'.[4]

In spite of this, however, the Deborinists were attacked, in their day, when they openly admitted as much and so declared absolute truth to be a thing unattainable. For Deborin

'every given truth represents a relative, not an absolute truth . . . absolute truth itself, on the other hand, is something we never possess. We merely approach it continuously in our consciousness and in our activity.' [5]

In opposition to this Deborinist formula, Leninist dialectical materialism puts forward another, namely that absolute truth is attained in the relative:

'For objective dialectics there is an absolute even *within* the relative. For subjectivism and sophistry the relative is only relative and excludes the absolute.' [6]

Thus it is that the Soviet philosophers interpret absolute truth to consist in

'an absolutely exact agreement of thought with its object, *i.e.*, a content of our knowledge such that neither now nor in the future, in consequence of the further development of knowledge, can it ever be proved false'.[7]

[1] *ME*, p. 122 (132, 197).   [2] F. I. Khaskhachikh: *Op. cit.*, p. 177.
[3] M. N. Rutkevich: *Op. cit.*, p. 184.
[4] F. Engels: *Dialectics of Nature*, p. 311.
[5] A. M. Deborin: *Lenin kak myslitel'* (Lenin the Thinker), 3rd edn., p. 27; cited here from M. B. Mitin: *Op. cit.*, p. 128.
[6] *FT*, p. 328 (286); (*cf. On Dialectics, LSW, XI*, p. 82).
[7] M. N. Rutkevich: *Op. cit.*, p. 179.

Relative truth is thereupon taken to represent 'a moment or stage in the knowledge of absolute truth'.[1] This relativity does not imply any mutability in the object of knowledge, such that it might be so today and otherwise a hundred years hence, and thereby involve a change in our knowledge of this object; it indicates, rather,

'that the given, concrete, historical state of a phenomenon is reflected in man's consciousness with approximate, relative accuracy, up to a certain degree of depth'.[2]

Rutkevich also provides some examples of such 'absolute truths':

'All the fundamental theses and an enormous number of lesser tenets of Marxist–Leninist philosophy, economic science, and the theory of socialism and the class-struggle are absolutely true. That matter is primary and consciousness derivative, that the collapse of capitalism is inevitable, that "the socialist system will follow capitalism as inevitably as day follows night",[3] that the socialist economic system offers unlimited scope for the development of productive forces, etc. —these are all *absolute* truths, so far confirmed by practice that nothing in the future can ever refute them.' [4]

As has frequently been stressed already, the positive value of the copy-theory lies precisely in the emphatic realism of its point of view. It is also a great point in favour of this theory, especially the Leninist version of it, that again in striking contrast to the sensationalist opinions of earlier materialists, it insists, throughout the working-out of the 'dialectical' transition from the sensory to the 'logical' stages of knowledge, on preserving an essential distinction between the two, and thereby acknowledges the basic impossibility of assimilating intellectual cognition to sensory activity.

To be sure, the copy-theory itself still offers no sort of critical vindication of the real authenticity of human knowledge, nor does it ever get beyond the assertion of a naïvely realistic point of view.[5] As

[1] F. I. Khaskhachikh: *Op. cit.*, p. 177.
[2] M. N. Rutkevich: *Loc. cit.*
[3] J. V. Stalin: *Sochineniya*, 1, p. 340 (*Works*, 1, p. 341).
[4] M. N. Rutkevich: *Op. cit.*, p. 183.
[5] It is possibly of interest in this connection to point out that in Soviet philosophical usage the expression 'naïve realism' has a very peculiar meaning; we have already seen earlier (p. 503) that Khaskhachikh applies the term 'naïve realism' to that conception of the objectivity of sense-qualities whereby the latter are held to be located formally in things in the same manner as they are perceived by the sense-organs; but Mitin describes Machism as 'naïve realism', because it identifies the objective world with our sensations.

we saw above, a critical vindication of this kind is supposedly effected by the appeal to practice, and by proclamation of the dialectical unity of theory (knowledge and thought) and practice (whose concrete embodiment is the economic process of production). But such a justification fails to stand up to detailed criticism. Granted that the epistemological inquiry cannot be initiated on a basis of universal doubt, the theory of knowledge of Soviet dialectical materialism still presupposes too many premisses that stand in need of prior justification or proof, for it to be able to rank as a genuine critique of knowledge. Thus from the very outset it not only takes for granted the presence of an external world independent of the knowing subject, but also makes use of other derivative theses which should themselves have been the product of extensive preliminary inquiry, such as the validity of historical knowledge, which is assumed as self-evident by the historicism implicit in the dialectical materialist epistemology. Indeed the much-contested thesis of the materialist conception of history, which already belongs to the philosophy of history, is itself a premiss of this epistemology; for the 'dialectical unity' of theory and practice is intelligible only on the basis of the materialist conception of history, whereby intellectual activity is construed as a function of economic practice.

As for the theory of practice as the criterion of truth, it commits the logical fallacy of tacitly assuming the point to be proved. For confirmation in practice (in the shape of an experimental proof, for example) is also supposed to warrant the validity of our sensory knowledge. But again, the positive (or negative) outcome of the experiment cannot be perceived except by sensory awareness.

It is in any case impossible to derive the validity of the major principles of thought from confirmation in practice, *i.e.*, from experience. As we have seen, dialectical materialism deduces the validity even of mathematical axioms and logical principles from their confirmation in the practice of earlier generations, and inheritance of the brain-structure thereby brought about. But inheritance can at best do no more than account for the presence of psychological necessities of thought, not for insight into the truth and logical necessity of the propositions in question. Experience gives rise to necessary general propositions, not through a mere piling-up of experience itself, but by way of induction; this, however, already presupposes the validity of the primary laws of thought, notably the principle of sufficient reason.

Finally, we must ask, and more particularly in regard to the absolute validity of the various social laws allegedly 'proved' by social practice, how long a social doctrine has to maintain itself before it can claim the rank of an 'absolute truth'. For we have seen in our own day how particular social theories and movements may succeed for a time, and accomplish themselves, and eventually lead to catastrophe; take national socialism, for example, which certainly met with very great success, to begin with, in both internal and external affairs, but ultimately led to a fearful disaster. One may equally suppose, indeed, that communism will pursue a similar course, save only that it displays a somewhat greater historical 'wave length', and will therefore take longer before it falls into the trough.

CHAPTER VII

Logic

THE field of logic has lately been the scene of an extremely violent controversy among the Soviet philosophers. This has chiefly raged about the question whether the classical formal logic is the only one, or whether, in addition, a 'dialectical' logic is also possible and necessary. But before entering into the details of this dispute, we must first consider a thesis of Lenin's, on which the proponents of dialectical logic chiefly rest their case. This is the Leninist doctrine that the materialist dialectic itself comprises both a logic and a theory of knowledge.

1. THE MATERIALIST DIALECTIC AS LOGIC AND AS THEORY OF KNOWLEDGE

In the fragment *On Dialectics* Lenin refers to the materialist dialectic as also playing the part of a theory of knowledge:

'Dialectics *is* the theory of knowledge of (Hegel and) Marxism. This is the "side" of the matter . . . to which Plekhanov, not to speak of other Marxists, paid no attention'.[1]

And in a footnote to the *Philosophical Notebooks* it is said that the

'logic, dialectics and theory of knowledge of materialism (there is no need of three words: they are all one and the same)' are to be 'converted into a single discipline'.[2]

How, then, are we to construe this unity of dialectic, logic and epistemology to which Lenin here refers? We already know what is

[1] *FT*, p. 329 (*On Dialectics, LSW*, XI, pp. 83 f.)
[2] *FT*, p. 215 (German, p. 249).

518

meant by dialectic: it is the theory of the general laws of motion in reality, and therefore falls, in the first place, under what would otherwise be described as ontology. But how can this dialectic be at the same time both logic and theory of knowledge?

The situation becomes rather clearer if we refer back to Hegel. Before Hegel—in the opinion of the Soviet philosophers—there was basically nothing except formal logic, which was exclusively concerned with the correctness of thinking and not with the question of its truth—the question, that is, as to whether the content of thought was also in accordance with reality; it was precisely because of this disregard of the material aspect of the thought-content that it was described as 'formal logic'. Kant had already recognized this abstraction from the content of thought as a weakness in formal logic for which he sought to compensate by his own transcendental logic. But it was only Hegel—so it is held—who first actually created a logic which was not content with the purely formal side of thinking, but also took account of the content of concepts. Since Hegel conceives the Absolute as the Idea, in which thought and being are identical, the science of the Absolute is at once both logic and ontology. The dialectical unfolding of the categories in Hegel's *Science of Logic* is also at the same time an expression of the process of self-development in the Absolute itself.

Now if, like Soviet philosophy, we speak of 'dialectic' instead of 'ontology', it will be evident that in Hegel logic and dialectic immediately coincide. But a further consequence, on Hegel's view, is that epistemology also coincides with this 'dialectic' or 'logic', for he regards the process whereby the Absolute Idea unfolds itself in the categories as being also the process of its own self-knowledge. Thus when Hegel explains in his *Logic* how the Absolute Idea attains to knowledge of itself, he is simultaneously providing both a solution to the epistemological problem and a justification of the authenticity of this knowledge in relation to reality; 'dialectic', for Hegel, is therefore at the same time epistemology as well.

Now dialectical materialism seeks to emulate this performance, and attempts, as usual, to improve still further on Hegel in doing so, for in his case the assimilation of dialectic, logic and epistemology is effected by recourse to the 'idealistic principle of the identity of thought and being', an error that Marx was the first to correct.[1] In essence this had already been done by the founders of Marxism in putting the Hegelian dialectic on a materialist basis. A similar identification of dialectic and epistemology therefore holds good, in

[1] V. P. Rozhin: *O materialisticheskoy dialektike kak logike i teorii poznaniya* (On the Materialist Dialectic as Logic and as Theory of Knowledge), in *Vestnik Leningradskogo Universiteta*, 1956, 5, pp. 29–37, *q.v.* p. 30.

Lenin's opinion, for dialectical materialism also; in his essay on *Karl Marx* he observes that

'dialectics, as understood by Marx, and in conformity with Hegel, includes what is now called the theory of knowledge, or epistemology'.[1]

In the light of this dictum, Rozhin attempts a concrete demonstration of how dialectic, logic and epistemology coincide in Marxist materialism:

'The materialism of Marxist logic lies primarily in the fact that thinking is regarded as a product of a physical organ of the body, namely the human brain; thought is a function of the brain. Whereas idealism separates thinking from matter. . . . Marxist philosophical materialism considers thought and the laws and forms thereof, as a reflection of the objective, material world. . . . In opposition to the idealists . . . dialectical materialism teaches that the objective foundations of logical laws and forms of thought lie in the forms of being itself, in the forms of the external world and of human practice . . . The laws and forms of being determine the laws and thought-forms of logic. . . . Since thought is not something alien to Nature, but a product thereof, subjective thought and objective Nature are governed by one and the same set of laws and their eventual findings cannot contradict one another.' [2]

Since, therefore, thought is a product of Nature, the logical laws of thought are copies of natural laws, and thinking can do no more than truthfully reflect what Nature is like.

In all this, Leninist dialectical materialism is blindly reiterating the Hegelian principle of the coincidence of dialectic, logic and epistemology without asking itself whether such an equation is still feasible, now that Hegel has been subjected to the materialist 'inversion' and 'matter' has replaced the Idea. And in fact this possibility is no longer open to it. In the first place, so far as the assimilation of logic and dialectic is concerned, the impossibility of reconciling this with the dialectical materialist position emerges all too clearly from the very disputes about the relation of formal logic to dialectic which are currently going on among the Soviet philosophers, and which we shall shortly be investigating in greater detail. As for the other equivalence, that of dialectic and epistemology, this was possible for Hegel inasmuch as he regarded being—all being, that is—as consisting in its inmost essence of 'Idea'; the self-unfolding of the Idea in its being is therefore at the same time the process whereby it comes to self-knowledge, a knowledge which, thanks to

---

[1] V. I. Lenin: *Karl Marx* (1914), *Sochineniya*, XXI[4], p. 38 (English, *LSW*, XI, p. 17).

[2] V. P. Rozhin: *Op. cit.*, p. 33.

the identity of thought and being, must necessarily remain true to reality. But if 'matter' is now substituted in place of the Idea, the argument is no longer applicable. For either consciousness is regarded thereafter as a property of only a part of matter, namely 'highly-organized' matter—in which case being and consciousness are no longer identical, the developmental process in matter in respect of its being is thus no longer immediately coincident with its development in respect of its consciousness, the accordance of consciousness with reality is no longer given *eo ipso* by its very occurrence, and the problem of the bridge between knowledge and reality is raised once more in its most acute form. Alternatively, despite the 'inversion' of Hegel, being and thought are again equated, the only difference being that it is now called 'matter' instead of 'Idea'; and in fact an identification of this sort is not infrequently met with in the epistemological disquisitions of Soviet dialectical materialism, especially where it is said that the 'brain' is a part of 'Nature', and hence that in this its organ Nature comes to consciousness of itself, just as the Hegelian 'Idea' does in the case of 'Spirit'. But this would presuppose that 'matter' so conceived is already by origin in some way *essentially* 'consciousness', and does not merely become so in the case of its highest product; in that case, however, we should again have fetched up in Hegel's idealism, and the whole difference between Hegel and dialectical materialism would be simply a matter of terminology, in that 'matter' or 'Nature' is used instead of the word 'Idea'.

The same assimilation of dialectics and epistemology, and this on the ground of a fundamental identity between subjective and objective, is also to be found in Engels' doctrine of the coincidence of objective and subjective dialectics, according to which subjective dialectics so-called, *i.e.*, dialectical thought, is only a reflection of objective dialectics, *i.e.*, the motion through opposites which asserts itself everywhere in objective reality.[1] Engels thereby seeks to combine dialectics with the copy-theory. Marck, in criticism of this proposal, points to the unbalance and discordancy between the static character of the copy-theory, which presupposes a fixed object of knowledge and hence a similar fixity in knowledge itself, and the dynamism of the dialectical concept of knowledge.[2] Be that as it may, the invocation of the copy-theory in order to establish the necessary correspondence between subjective and objective dialectics has no warrant in any case. For this would necessarily presuppose that the dialectical process of knowledge runs absolutely parallel in time to the dialectical process of unfolding in objective reality; 'reflection'

[1] F. Engels: *Dialectics of Nature*, p. 280.
[2] S. Marck: *Die Dialektik in der Philosophie der Gegenwart*, I. Tübingen 1929, pp. 121 f.

implies simultaneity. If, however, the knowing-process is contracted, on occasion, into a relatively short space of time, we again encounter the full force of the critical problem of knowledge, namely what guarantee do we have that it truthfully reflects the process in reality, spread out as this is over an incomparably greater span of time? But that the two processes by no means coincide is already evident from the consideration that the knowing-process in many cases ascends from knowledge of effects to knowledge of causes, whereas the process in reality occurs in precisely the reverse order. It follows from this that the appeal to a correspondence of subjective and objective dialectics is again nothing more than a purely external imitation of Hegel, and in no way constitutes a solution of the critical problem of knowledge.

In justification of this thesis of the coincidence of dialectic with logic and epistemology, another method is also frequently employed, namely to start off from the principle of the unity of the logical and the historical. According to this, the historical development of human thought proceeds by the formation of various 'nodal points', which find their embodiment in philosophical concepts. The logical sequence within the system of philosophy is thereupon alleged to correspond to the genetic sequence of the said nodal points in the history of human practice and human knowledge.

'If, therefore, dialectic, logic and epistemology are viewed against the background of the history of human knowledge, each of them separately and all of them together turn out to be a schematic representation of the history of human knowledge, considered in terms of its nodal points. . . . Herein lies the identity of dialectic, logic and epistemology in dialectical materialism'.[1]

From this Lenin also draws in particular the conclusion that epistemology too must proceed on historical lines:

'Dialectics, as understood by Marx, and in conformity with Hegel, includes what is now called the theory of knowledge, or epistemology, which, too, must regard its subject matter historically, studying and generalizing the origin and development of knowledge, the transition from *non*-knowledge to knowledge,'[2]

This historical treatment of the epistemological problem is justified on the ground that it is impossible to embark on an appraisal of man's capacity for knowledge prior to any concrete act of knowing

---

[1] E. P. Sitkovsky: *Lenin o sovpadenii v dialekticheskom materializme dialektiki, logiki i teorii poznaniya* (Lenin on the Identity of Dialectic, Logic and Epistemology in Dialectical Materialism), *VF*, 1956, 2, pp. 77–90, *q.v.* p. 83; *cf.* also pp. 80 f.
[2] V. I. Lenin: *Op. cit.*, p. 38 (*LSW*, XI, p. 17).

on his part. Sitkovsky endorses Hegel's criticism of Kant, that he sought to determine the forms and limits of knowledge *prior to* and *apart from* the historical process of knowing:

'One cannot learn to swim without jumping into the water, one cannot define the limits of knowledge without overstepping those limits, and one cannot determine the forms of knowledge by isolating oneself from the history and practice of knowledge. The best theory of knowledge, said Hegel, . . . is the history of knowledge.' [1]

The intrinsically sound conception that it is basically impossible to justify the capacity of knowledge *in advance* of any concrete act of knowing, and that knowledge can therefore be justified only in its concrete exercise, leads dialectical materialism to the unwarranted conclusion that it is only the *historical* course of human knowledge that can furnish proof of its legitimacy. For we must distinguish two kinds of experience: the individual experience of the particular knowing subject, and the large-scale experience which mankind acquires in the course of the history of human thought, and which we may describe, in contrast to the former, as macro-experience. There is however, an internal connection between the two. The second is in a certain sense mirrored and reproduced in the first, insofar, that is, as the individual recapitulates to some extent in his own development the experience which mankind as a whole has already acquired in the course of its history. Macro-experience thereby takes on a significance which should not be underrated, in helping to substantiate individual experience as well—in a certain sense it corroborates the experience of the individual. Despite this, however, it has no meaning apart from individual experience. On the contrary, macro-experience presupposes the self-subsistency and primacy of individual experience, and in the absence of the latter it would hang to some extent in the air. And the reason for this is that historical knowledge, which underlies it, is only mediate knowledge. But in solving the epistemological problem we have to set out from a cognitive act in which an immediate unity obtains between the known object and the knowing subject, and this is only the case in an (individual) act of consciousness.

2. THE CONTROVERSY OVER FORMAL LOGIC

According to Lenin's pronouncement, already referred to, dialectics is supposed to be identical not only with epistemology, but also with logic. Now this confronts Soviet philosophy with the question, to what sort of logic is dialectics to be assimilated, to the

[1] E. P. Sitkovsky: *Op. cit.*, p. 84.

customary traditional 'formal' logic of Aristotle, or to a new 'dialectical' logic? And supposing it is the latter, what is then to become of the traditional formal logic?

In the 'thirties, this question was settled out of hand in favour of 'dialectical' logic. Formal logic was dismissed as 'metaphysical', being viewed as the logical foundation of the metaphysical habit of thought which recognizes only complete unchanging objects and knows nothing of becoming in things or their transformation one into another; for formal logic, as for the metaphysical mode of thought generally, its communication is simply 'Yea, yea; Nay, nay; for whatsoever is more than these cometh of evil.' In place of this it was proposed to institute a new 'dialectical' logic, which should not confine itself, like the traditional logic, to the formal aspect of thought, but was required to take account of the content of knowledge as well. A further and very important difference was also supposed to separate the new logic from its formal predecessor: the traditional logic rests fairly and squarely upon three basic principles: the law of identity, the law of contradiction and the law of excluded middle; the third law in particular lies at the heart of formal logic: a thing is either A or not A; there can be no third possibility. In radical contrast to this, dialectical logic sets out from the unity of opposites. This was not, however, intended to constitute an immediate rejection of formal logic; still less did the demand for a dialectical logic imply —even at that time—a denial of the law of contradiction.[1] But it was thought of as something barren, a 'sterile flower' (*pustotsvet*), to use an expression of Lenin's. In the Introduction to his translation of Engels' *Ludwig Feuerbach* Plekhanov was still prepared to grant formal logic a place as a 'moment' in dialectical logic:

'Just as rest is a special case of motion, so thought according to the rules of formal logic (the "laws" of thought) is a special case of dialectical thinking.'[2]

---

[1] At this time too the Soviet philosophers were insistent upon clear definition of concepts and campaigned against 'conceptual amorphism' (M. B. Mitin: *Op. cit.*, pp. 222 f.). According to Obichkin it is dialectical logic, indeed, which makes for clear and definite conclusions. This demand for clarity was founded on an appeal to Lenin: 'One may quarrel about tactics, but it is necessary, in doing so, to proceed with perfect clarity . . . In all these discussions the party of the militant class must never lose sight of the necessity for perfectly clear answers to the concrete questions of our political approach, answers which *do not admit of two different interpretations*: yes or no, ought we to do this now, at this moment, or not?' (V. I. Lenin: *Sochineniya*, IX⁴, p. 237).

[2] In F. Engels: *Lyudvig Feyerbach*, 2nd Russian edn., Geneva 1905, pp xxii f.; *cf.* also G. V. Plekhanov: *Fundamental Problems of Marxism* (tr E. and C. Paul), London 1929.

Mitin repudiates this, however: formal logic cannot be accommodated in dialectical, any more than alchemy can be regarded as a subordinate moment in chemistry, or astrology as a subordinate moment in astronomy.

Here too, as so often in the realm of Soviet ideology, a radical reversal has lately set in. In November 1946, by a decree of the Central Committee of the Bolshevik Party, logic was again introduced into the schools. The publication of new textbooks of formal logic was hastily put in hand, indeed, for lack of such, permission was actually given in 1946 for the provisional use, in revised form, of a pre-revolutionary textbook by Chelpanov. In 1947 there appeared a textbook by Asmus, but it ran into devastating criticism 'on account of its formalism, its acknowledgement of the idealist "logic of relations" as a sort of last word on the science of logic'.[1] Other attempts, the textbooks of Strogovich and Vinogradov for example, did not fare much better; a collection of essays on logic was actually confiscated by the Ministry of Higher Education.[2] It can be seen from this that no sort of clarity existed amongst the Soviet philosophers on the most fundamental issues relating to formal logic. In order to elucidate matters in this field a series of full-dress discussions was held, in 1948, 1949, and in 1950 on no less than two occasions, in March and December. At the last of these the plan of a book by N. I. Kondakov, *The Principles of Logic*, was dissected in detail,[3] from which it emerged that the Soviet philosophers were more divided on this topic than ever.

In the hope of reaching a final conclusion the Editors of *Voprosy filosofii* opened a discussion in the second number of the 1950 volume, which went on for over a year and attracted more than sixty contributions.

Whereas it was the reintroduction of formal logic as a teaching subject in secondary schools and colleges, and the consequent need to produce textbooks, which provoked the discussion on the theoretical foundations of logic, Stalin's letters on linguistics provided, on the other hand, a number of fixed points which made it easier to furnish a theoretical warrant for formal logic and to demonstrate its title to existence even from the dialectical materialist point of view. Stalin regards grammar as a science yielding abstract general rules for the formation of words and sentences independently of the content which these words and sentences express. Now this could also be applied without difficulty to the problem of formal

---

[1] V. I. Cherkesov: *O logike i marxistskoy dialektike* (On Logic and the Marxist Dialectic), in *VF*, 1950, 2, pp. 209–22, *q.v.* p. 210.

[2] *Ibid.*

[3] Report on the discussions of 1948, 1949 and March 1950 in *VF*, 1950, 3, p. 330; on that of December 1950 in *VF*, 1951, 1, pp. 218–22.

logic, just as could Stalin's remarks about the universal human character of language, which does not have a class-character and must be thought of as serving, not one class only, but the whole of society, of which it is the unifying tie.

But this was by no means sufficient to dispose of all the difficulties in the way of establishing formal logic on a philosophical footing from the dialectical materialist point of view. The main obstacle arose from the vacillating approach to formal logic displayed by the classical authorities. On the one hand it was possible to argue in favour of formal logic and its title to existence by appealing to Engels, in whose *Anti-Dühring* nothing is left standing of all previous philosophy except 'formal logic and dialectics'.[1] In the *Dialectics of Nature* Engels describes formal logic as the 'lower mathematics of logic', a notion which he develops more fully in *Anti-Dühring*:

'Even formal logic is primarily a method of arriving at new results, of advancing from the known to the unknown—and dialectics is the same, only in a much more important sense, because in forcing its way beyond the narrow horizon of formal logic it contains the germ of a more comprehensive view of the world. It is the same with mathematics. Elementary mathematics, the mathematics of constant magnitudes, moves within the confines of formal logic, at any rate taken as a whole; the mathematics of variable magnitudes, whose most important part is the infinitesimal calculus, is in essence nothing other than the application of dialectics to mathematical relations.'[2]

Lenin, too, in his article *Once Again on the Trade Unions*, had come out clearly in favour of formal logic:

'Formal logic, which schools confine themselves to (and which, with modifications, the lower forms should confine themselves to), takes formal definitions, and is guided exclusively by what is most customary, or most often noted. . . . Dialectical logic demands that we go further. . . .'[3]

In justification of the existence of formal logic, weight is also attached to the fact that the works of the Marxist classics are themselves permeated by an unanswerable logic:

'But what captivated me'—says Stalin—'in Lenin's speeches . . . was that irresistible force of logic in them which, although somewhat terse, gained a firm hold on his audience, gradually electrified it, and then, as one might say, completely overpowered it. . . .'[4]

[1] *Anti-Dühring*, p. 31.   [2] *Ibid.*, p. 151.
[3] V. I. Lenin: *Eshche raz o profsoyuzakh* (1921). *Sochineniya*, XXXII[4], p. 72; (*LSW*, IX, p. 66).
[4] J. V. Stalin: *O Lenine* (On Lenin), 1924. *Sochineniya*, VI, p. 55 (*Works*, VI, p. 57).

But as against this there are other utterances of the classics, notably Engels, in which formal logic comes off rather badly, and which are accordingly pressed into service by the opponents of formal logic. Thus Engels declares in the *Dialectics of Nature*:

'The science of thought is . . . like every other, a historical science, the science of the historical development of human thought' and hence 'the theory of the laws of thought is by no means an "eternal truth" established once and for all, as philistine reasoning imagines to be the case with the word logic . . . But it is precisely dialectics that constitutes the most important form of thinking for present-day natural science, for it alone offers the analogue for, and thereby the method of explaining, the evolutionary processes occurring in Nature, inter-connections in general, and transitions from one field of investigation to another.' [1]

'Fixed categories', according to Engels, retain their validity only for 'everyday use',[2] *i.e.*, in those fields

'where small dimensions or brief periods of time are in question; the limits within which [they] are usable differ in almost every case and are determined by the nature of the object'.[3]

For all that, Engels concedes that formal logic is not to be regarded simply as 'nonsense'.[4]

In the course of the logical discussion, three tendencies emerged among the Soviet philosophers: the first school supported the possibility of two logics, one formal and the other dialectical, coexisting alongside one another (M. S. Strogovich,[5] V. I. Cherkesov[6] the Professor of Logic at Moscow University, the Leningrad mathematician A. D. Alexandrov,[7] V. P. Rozhin[8] and others). The second group took the view that there could only be one logic, namely the formal variety (the chief exponent of this outlook being the Professor of Logic at the University of Tiflis, K. S. Bakradze[9]). Other authors

[1] F. Engels: *Dialectics of Nature*, pp. 58 f.
[2] *Ibid.*, p. 282.   [3] *Ibid.*, p. 286.
[4] *Ibid.*, p. 319.
[5] M. S. Strogovich: *O predmete formal'noy logiki* (On the Subject-Matter of Formal Logic) in *VF*, 1950, 3, pp. 309–17.
[6] *Cf.* above, p. 525, n. 1.
[7] A. D. Alexandrov: *O logike* (On Logic), *VF*, 1951, 3, pp. 152–63.
[8] V. P. Rozhin: *Neskol'ko zamechaniy po spornym voprosam logiki* (Some Remarks on Disputed Questions in Logic) *VF*, 1951, 4, pp. 238–41.
[9] K. S. Bakradze: *K voprosu o sootnoshenii logiki i dialektiki* (On the Problem of the Reciprocal Relation between Logic and Dialectics), *VF*, 1950, 2, pp. 198–209.

attempted in one way or another to adopt an intermediate position (I. I. Os'makov,[1] P. S. Popov,[2] B. M. Kedrov[3] and others).

The attitude of the first group may be typified in the views expressed by M. S. Strogovich, both in the essay already cited and also in his textbook *Logic*.[4] In Strogovich's opinion the above-mentioned passage from Lenin's article on the trade unions clearly indicates that the classics explicitly distinguished between a formal and a dialectical logic, and consider both to be valid. Hence the earlier standpoint of Soviet philosophy, such as is still to be found in the *Short Philosophical Dictionary*, can no longer be maintained; the position, that is, that 'the laws of formal logic are opposed to those of dialectical logic' and that formal logic is 'empty, impoverished and abstract' because the laws and categories it establishes fail to conform to objective reality.[5] The anti-Marxist views of Marr, who describes formal logic as an obsolete stage in the development of human thought, are brilliantly refuted in Stalin's letters on linguistics.[6] Both types of logic, formal and dialectical, are therefore justified, according to Strogovich, and their mutual relationship is so defined that formal logic, as compared with dialectical, represents the lower plane of knowledge.[7] Formal logic, with its four basic laws (Identity, Contradiction, Excluded Middle and Sufficient Reason), conceives of things statically, in a state of rest, and isolates them one from another. Dialectical logic, on the other hand, reflects motion and development, the unity and conflict of opposites; it is the 'subjective dialectics' which Engels contrasts with 'objective dialectics', the dialectical thought reflecting the motion through opposites which asserts itself everywhere in Nature.[8]

'Dialectic views the phenomena of reality in their development and motion, their connection and reciprocity; but this does not exclude the necessity of taking into consideration their more elementary relationships as well, of regarding them as phenomena possessing, at a specific period in time and under specific conditions, a stable, persistent and independent character.' [9]

[1] I. I. Os'makov: *O logike myshleniya i o nauke logike* (On the Logic of Thought and the Science of Logic), *VF*, 1950, 3, pp. 317–30.
[2] P. S. Popov: *Predmet formal'noy logiki i dialektika* (The Subject-matter of Formal Logic and Dialectics), in *VF*, 1951, 1, pp. 210–18.
[3] B. M. Kedrov: *Ob otnoshenii logiki k marxizmu* (On the Relation between Logic and Marxism), *VF*, 1951, 4, pp. 212–27.
[4] M. S. Strogovich: *Logika*, Moscow 1949.
[5] *Kratky filosofsky slovar'*, 1940, pp. 296 f.; *cf.* M. S. Strogovich: *O predmete* . . ., p. 309.   [6] M. S. Strogovich: *O predmete* . . ., p. 309.
[7] M. S. Strogovich: *Logika*, p. 63.
[8] F. Engels: *Dialectics of Nature*, p. 280.
[9] M. S. Strogovich: *Logika*, p. 66.

Dialectical logic is related to formal as higher mathematics is to lower. But dialectical logic in no wise upsets the validity of the laws of formal logic; even dialectical thought is strictly logical in the sense that it allows of no deviation from the laws of formal logic.[1] Though formal logic may be somewhat more imperfect than dialectical, that certainly does not mean that it is 'metaphysical' in character, as its opponents maintain. And though the classics may also have treated formal logic rather contemptuously at times, in limiting it to 'everyday use' or the instruction of lower forms in schools, that again does not mean that they regarded it as metaphysics. Engels and Lenin rejected metaphysics, but undoubtedly accepted the validity of formal logic; if they had equated formal logic with metaphysics, this would have meant that they also considered 'metaphysics' itself to be appropriate for 'everyday use', or for lower forms in Schools![2]

Cherkesov takes up an essentially similar position, save only that he restricts the domain of formal logic to the lower reaches of reality, the sphere of 'everyday use', and so differs on this point from Strogovich, who, as we have seen, upholds the validity of the laws of formal logic even in the field of dialectical thought.[3]

The position advocated by Bakradze is the diametrical opposite of this: there cannot be two logics alongside one another, one formal and one dialectical, both investigating the same subject-matter, namely the forms of thought and inference, and both setting up laws distinct from, and in part actually contradictory of, one another. Nor can it be the case, as Strogovich maintains, that formal logic deals with 'the simple relationships of things'; for in fact there can be no line drawn between simple and complex relationships among things. Bakradze formulates his own position in the following terms: there is only one logic, properly speaking, having as its object correct thinking, *i.e.*, thinking which is subject to the laws of identity, contradiction, etc. Dialectical logic is not a theory of the laws and forms of correct thinking; the classics identify dialectical logic with dialectics as such; this is what Lenin means when he speaks of the fact that logic, dialectics and epistemology coincide. Hence it is not formal logic that must be contrasted with dialectical logic, but only logic proper (as the theory of correct thinking) with dialectics (which, as the theory of the higher laws of development in Nature, society and human thought, also functions as an epistemology, and decides such questions as the following: is knowledge in general possible, what is knowledge, what is truth, what is the criterion thereof, etc.). Logic is thus a moment in dialectics conceived as epistemology. For according to Lenin the process of knowledge is the transition

[1] M. S. Strogovich: *O predmete . . .*, p. 315. [2] *Ibid.*, p. 313.
[3] V. I. Cherkesov: *Op. cit.*, p. 213.

'from living intuition to abstract thought and from thence to practice';[1]

though correct thinking plays an essential part in this. On the other hand logic is also dependent on dialectics: thus the view we take of the relation of universal to particular is of decisive importance for the rules of deductive inference: for if anyone denies the reality of the universal he has no right to assume the validity of deductive inference. For Bakradze too, logic is not class-conditioned, but holds good for all men. So far as Engels' contemptuous remarks about formal logic are concerned, and his restriction of the latter to the field of 'everyday use', these observations refer only to formal logic as corrupted by metaphysics. But it is essentially wrong to suppose that formal logic depicts the laws of metaphysical thought.[2]

Among those who adopt a middle position, P. S. Popov takes the view that there can only be one logic. Formal and dialectical logic merely represent two different stages of one and the same logic. Even in the dialectical sphere the laws of formal logic still retain their validity, while conversely, dialectical logic is already applicable even to the most elementary phenomena in reality; hence neither can be wrenched apart from the other.[3]

Os'makov makes a distinction between the logic of thought and the science of logic. The logic of thought is a copy of the logic of things in human consciousness. Hence its universal human character, its validity for all men and all orders of society; it cannot possess a class-character. Like language, it is a medium of understanding between men. But whereas language is ordinarily a bond of union only for a single people, logic constitutes a unifying tie for the whole of human society throughout all nations. Thus there cannot be a number of different kinds of logic, formal, dialectical, inductive, etc., but only the one logic of thought reflecting the logic of things. Lenin's assertion as to the unity of logic and dialectics applies only to this logic of thought; logic and dialectics are here inseparable. Logical thought characterizes the activity of the understanding, whereas dialectical relates to that of reason, signifying a penetration of consciousness into the inwardness of objects and phenomena in Nature and social life, a pursuit of the latter in their change and development.

With the science of logic the situation is different. In Os'makov's opinion it certainly has a class-character. Here too, there is recourse to the distinction between formal and dialectical logic. Formal logic represents a stage in the development of the science of logic, namely the stage of bourgeois science. Soviet logic cannot be metaphysical,

---

[1] *FT*, p. 146 (German, p. 89).   [2] K. S. Bakradze: *Op. cit.*, pp. 198–209.
[3] P. S. Popov: *Op. cit.*, pp. 210–18.

as formal logic is—it must be dialectical. All the same there is no need to call it 'dialectical'; that is superfluous, because all genuine science has a dialectical character, and it could easily lead to confusion with dialectical materialism: it is best described as logic *tout court*. Moreover, in decreeing the reintroduction of logic into the schools, the Central Committee did not call for instruction in formal logic, but for instruction in logic as such, which must be dialectical in character.[1]

This discussion was concluded by an editorial postscript in the sixth number of the 1951 volume of *Voprosy filosofii*. The official and generally prescribed standpoint was summed up under the following heads: Logic does not belong to the superstructure, and therefore has no class-character, but is common to all classes and nations;

'the forms and laws of thought are a reflection of one and the same objective reality, resulting from the numberless repetitions in man's practical activity'.[2]

The logical structure of thought and the laws thereof are continually changing, but gradually, as language does, without 'explosions'. Formal and dialectical logic both have a title to acceptance. The former is the science of the elementary laws and forms of correct thinking and as such needful, not only for the student, but for everybody. Dialectical logic is a qualitatively new and higher stage in the development of thought, the logic of which Lenin was speaking when he declared it to be identical with dialectic and epistemology. It sets out the organic connection between the laws and forms of thought and the laws of the objective world.[3]

But this did not by any means provide a final solution to the problem of logic in Soviet philosophy. Until Stalin's death, to be sure, the situation remained quiet. It would appear, however, that the subsequent change in the ideological 'atmosphere' put new heart into the champions of formal logic, so that they felt emboldened to renew their attempt to gain recognition for their point of view. This emerges from the fact that whenever the official organs have had occasion to review recent work in Soviet philosophy, the neglect of dialectical logic has repeatedly been referred to as a major defect.[4]

---

[1] I. I. Os'makov: *Op. cit.,* pp. 317–30.

[2] *K itogam obsuzhdeniya voprosov logiki* (On the Outcome of the Discussion on Problems of Logic), *VF*, 1951, 6, pp. 143–9, *q.v.* p. 145.

[3] *Ibid.*, pp. 146 f. Further details of the whole discussion, and its conclusion, may be found in A. Winkelmann: *Die Stellung der formalen Logik im Sowjetsystem*, in *Scholastik*, 31 (1956), I, pp. 85–9.

[4] *Cf.*, for example, *VF*, 1954, 5, pp. 16 f.; *Kommunist*, 1954, 14, p. 6; *Vestnik AN SSSR*, 1955, 9, p. 88; *Kommunist*, 1955, 5, p. 1, where Bakradze is accused, in practice, of denying dialectical logic and reducing it to formal.

For fear lest the revival of this group, who regarded formal logic as the only logic, should lead to a complete swamping of dialectical logic by formal, the Editors of *Voprosy filosofii*, in a leading article in the third number of the 1955 volume, delivered a violent attack on the two ringleaders of the opposing faction, K. S. Bakradze and N. I. Kondakov. The excuse for this was the appearance of the latter's book, *Logic*, which was published in 1954 under the imprint of the Academy of Sciences of the U.S.S.R. They also seized the occasion to pass further judgement on Bakradze's *Logic*, published in 1951, despite the fact that it had already been reviewed in *Voprosy filosofii* in 1952.

Bakradze's book again denies the existence of two logics; there is only one, namely formal logic. The author endeavours to show that the most important propositions in Marxist dialectics are basically applications of the rules of formal logic. Thus the principle of excluded middle, for example, is in no way contradictory of the dialectic, which proceeds from the very fact that the classics of Marxism always made use of this principle.[1] Bakradze also points out, very properly, the basis of the whole misunderstanding: the Soviet philosophers erroneously suppose that the explanation of motion and development in the world calls for a special 'dialectical' logic:

'The logical law of identity implies no denial of either change or development.'[2]

Kondakov's book on logic also takes the view that there can be only one logic, namely formal; when the classics of Marxism speak of a 'dialectical logic', they are thinking of Marxism as a whole and not of any one part of dialectical materialism. He attempts to prove that the passages cited from the classics as examples of the application of a dialectical logic are wholly in accordance with the laws of formal logic. In pursuit of this he offers a very clear-cut statement of the law of contradiction:

'Two opposed judgements cannot both be true of one and the same object, considered at one and the same time and in one and the same respect.'[3]

Obviously, to avoid the reproach of indulging in metaphysics and banishing contradiction from the real world, Kondakov formulates the law of contradiction, not in its Aristotelian form ('The same

[1] *Cf. Protiv putanitsy i vul'garizatsii v voprosakh logiki* (Against Confusion and Vulgarization in Problems of Logic), *VF*, 1955, 3, pp. 158–71, *q.v.* p. 161.

[2] K. S. Bakradze: *Logika*, Tiflis 1951, p. 417.

[3] N. I. Kondakov: *Logika*, p. 68.

attribute cannot at the same time belong and not belong to the same subject and in the same respect'), but as a mere law of thought.

In spite of this he was heavily attacked, in the article referred to, by the Editors of *Voprosy filosofii*. The very fact of his having framed the law of contradiction as a law of thought led to an accusation of separating the laws of thought from the laws of being. But the main reproach directed against him, as against Bakradze, was that of denying the existence of dialectical logic and recognizing the validity of formal logic alone.

The violence of the reaction among the defenders of dialectical logic was doubtless due to the fact that in the meantime the position taken by Bakradze and Kondakov had attracted quite a number of supporters among the Soviet logicians. At the time of the logic discussion in 1950–51, Bakradze had stood almost alone. But now, as the editorial in *Voprosy filosofii* complains, his views are no longer 'the private vagaries of an aberrant logician', but a

'pernicious tendency, obstinately defended by a number of our logicians'.[1]

The collective *Problems of Logic*[2] produced by the Philosophical Institute in 1955, also shares the outlook of Bakradze and Kondakov and so too, say the aggrieved Editors, does the collective *Logic*,[3] issued under the same auspices. Not only so, but formal logic has played a far more conspicuous part in philosophical literature, and not in articles only, but also in special monographs,[4] whereas dialectical logic can point only to a few contributions, mainly in article form.[5]

[1] *Protiv putanitsy . . .*, p. 158.
[2] *Voprosy logiki*, ed. P. V. Tavanets, Moscow 1955.
[3] *Logika*, ed. D. P. Gorsky and P. V. Tavanets, Moscow 1956; *cf. VF*, 1955, 3, p. 171; it can be seen that it is this work that the Editors have in mind, since they speak (in July 1955) of a 'manuscript lately prepared by the Philosophical Institute of the Academy of Sciences of the U.S.S.R.'; it actually went to press in September of the same year.
[4] Chief among them, V. F. Asmus: *Uchenie logiki o dokazatel'stve i oproverzhenii* (Logical Theory of Proof and Disproof), Moscow 1954; N. P. Popov: *Opredelenie ponyatiy* (The Definition of Concepts), Leningrad 1954; P. V. Tavanets: *Suzhdenie i ego vidy* (The Judgement and its Forms), Moscow 1953; also *Voprosy teorii suzhdeniya* (Problems of a Theory of Judgement), Moscow 1955; D. P. Gorsky: *Logika* (Logic), Moscow 1955. An extremely useful bibliographical handbook, covering Russian publications on logic from the 18th century to 1955 inclusive, has been compiled in A. P. Primakovsky's *Bibliografiya po logike* (Bibliography of Logic), Moscow 1955.
[5] *Cf.*, for example, B. M. Kedrov: *O soderzhanii i obyeme izmenyayushchegosya ponyatiya* (On the Content and Scope of a Changing Concept),

It is typical, however, of the present ideological situation in the Soviet Union, that these violent attacks by the 'dialecticians' should have had not the smallest effect in persuading the supporters of formal logic, and least of all Professor Bakradze, to lower their colours. On the contrary, Bakradze and Kondakov published open letters in *Voprosy filosofii*, protesting against the aspersions cast upon them.[1] And, doubtless at the former's instigation, the professors and lecturers in dialectical and historical materialism at the University of Tiflis also demurred against the claim, put forward in several articles in *Voprosy filosofii*, that the problem of the interrelations of logic and dialectics had ceased to be worth discussing, since it had already received a clear-cut solution in the teachings of Marxism; to this they replied, not only that they had no intention of breaking off the discussion at this point, but that, on the contrary, they were proposing to extend it on to a still broader front.[2] At present the controversy is still in full spate.[3]

The fundamental misconception which has induced a number of Soviet philosophers to excogitate their own dialectical logic is clearly brought out by Bakradze, when he insists that the law of identity involves no denial of change or development. The supporters of dialectical logic were afraid lest motion and change should fail to be comprehended under the static concepts and laws of formal logic, and they therefore sought to assimilate logic with dialectic, so that the laws and categories of thought might also participate in the

in *Filosofskie Zapiski*, Vol. 6 (1953), pp. 188–254; M. N. Alexeyev: *O dialekticheskoy prirode suzhdeniya* (On the Dialectical Nature of Judgement), *VF*, 1956, 2, pp. 49–61; V. I. Cherkesov: *Nekotorye voprosy teorii ponyatiya v dialekticheskoy logike* (Some Problems of the Theory of the Concept in Dialectical Logic), *VF*, 1956, 2, pp. 62–76.

[1] *Cf.* K. S. Bakradze: *Protiv nenauchnoy i nedobrozhelatel'noy kritiki* (Against an Unscientific and Malevolent Criticism), *VF*, 1956, 2, pp. 218–224; N. I. Kondakov: *O logike* (On Logic), *ibid.*, pp. 224–8; and the Editorial rejoinder, *Ne nastaivat' na oshibkakh i ne uglublyat', a preodolet' ikh* (*Ot redaktsii*) (One should not Persist in Errors and Deepen Them, but should Overcome Them [Editorial]), *ibid.*, pp. 229–36.

[2] A. A. Gelashvili, in *VF*, 1956, 3, p. 232.

[3] Space forbids us to pursue the matter further. A very exhaustive account, both of the problems involved and of the literary warfare between the two parties, is given by H. Dahm: *Renaissance der formalen Logik*, in *Ost-Probleme*, IX, No. 8 (22nd Feb. 1957), pp. 254–67. On the whole question of formal logic and dialectical logic, *cf.* also A. Philipov: *Logic and Dialectic in the Soviet Union*, New York 1952; George L. Kline: *Recent Soviet Philosophy*, in *Annals of the American Academy of Political and Social Science*, Jan. 1956, pp. 126–38.

dynamism which animates the objective world. But in order to accommodate a changing and developing object, it is by no means necessary for logical concepts and laws of thought to be themselves subject to change and development. An example will make this clear: in order to reflect a moving body, it is not necessary for the mirror itself to move. On the contrary, if it is also moved, along with the moving body, and if in addition they both share the same velocity, the mirror-image will certainly reproduce the body, but *not* its motion, indeed the body will remain stationary in the mirror. Similarly, it is unnecessary for categories of thought and the whole logical structure of human thinking to move and change in order for them to be able to grasp the motion and change in objective reality.

3. INDIVIDUAL LOGICAL OPERATIONS

As just seen, the official line in Soviet philosophy seeks to supplement the traditional formal logic by a new and dialectical one. It would therefore be interesting to learn how this dialectical logic appears in detail. But here, unfortunately, everything is still too much at the stage of preliminary studies to make it possible to attempt an outline of a dialectical logic of this kind. The logic textbooks mainly confine themselves, as we have already noted, to reproducing the doctrines of formal logic in regard to concepts, judgement, inference and so forth. To be sure, as early as 1944, Tavanets had demanded the replacement of formal logic by a logic 'imbued with content', in which the categories of formal logic (which abstracts from content) should be subjected to revision in the light of dialectic;[1] but he confines his reformation of 'traditional' logic to what are essentially matters of detail, such as a rearrangement in the classification of judgements, the recasting of the modalities of inference, etc.[2]

Yet certain beginnings towards a 'dialectical logic' are discernible nonetheless. One has to go back here, in the first place, to Engels' *Dialectics of Nature*; but a number of such attempts can be found among more recent authors as well. In what follows we shall be giving a brief account of these rudiments, and in doing this we shall follow the example of the Soviet philosophers, who decline to separate the 'logical stage' of knowledge' from the 'sensory', by refusing to confine ourselves merely to thought-contents proper (concepts, judgements and inferences) and making some preliminary observations about sensation, perception and representation as well.

[1] *Cf.* P. V. Tavanets: *K voprosu o razlichnom ponimanii predmeta logiki* (On the Problem of Differing Conceptions of the Subject-Matter of Logic), in *IAN*, I (1944), 6.

[2] P. V. Tavanets: *O vidakh suzhdeniya* (On the Types of Judgement), *Ibid.*, VII (1950), pp. 69–84, *q.v.* pp. 74, 78.

Sensation, according to Soviet dialectical materialism, is

'the result of the operation of external objects upon our sense-organs, a product of a particular mode of organization in matter'.[1]

For Lenin, as we already know, it is the

'transformation of the energy of external excitation into a state of consciousness'.[2]

Soviet philosophy considers it the sole starting-point of all knowledge:

'Marxist philosophical materialism teaches that the source of all our knowledge lies in sensation; the sense-organs are the only channels whereby the external world makes entry into our consciousness. A man deprived of all his sense-organs cannot be in any way acquainted with the world. A person having no sensation of anything knows nothing and understands nothing'.[3]

Stalin too, in his letters on linguistics, stressed the impossibility of thought without a basis of sensation.[4] Dialectical materialism is therefore entirely at one on this point with the Lockean *Nihil est in intellectu, quod non prius fuerit in sensu*, though it objects to the sensationalist interpretation of this statement, which Locke meant to be understood as implying the denial of any essential difference between sensory and logical knowledge.[5]

Dialectical materialism considers the difference between its own standpoint and that of pre-Marxian materialism to consist primarily in its employment, in this field also, of the principle of historicism. Sensation also develops, like everything else in the world. Better developed sense-organs also yield better knowledge. But the progress of sensation is bound up in a special degree with the development of technology and the means of production. Technical aids enable us to make our sensations sharper and more exact (the naked eye perceives about 5,500 stars, whereas the telescope can take in upwards of 100 million) or to extend them into regions which would otherwise remain completely inaccessible to perception (the inner world of the atom).[6] Rutkevich even considers the progress of culture and productive techniques to be responsible for a physiological sharpening of our sensations (the delicacy of the capacity of discriminating colours is supposed to increase with the development of the dyeing industry).[7]

---

[1] F. I. Khaskhachikh: *Op. cit.*, p. 140.   [2] *ME*, p. 39 (44, 118).

[3] F. I. Khaskhachikh: *Op. cit.*, p. 116; *cf. ME*, p. 288 (313, 355).

[4] *Cf.* above, p. 494.   [5] M. A. Leonov: *Ocherk* . . ., p. 565.

[6] *Ibid.*, pp. 570 ff.; *cf.* also V. Ral'tsevich in *BSE* (1st edn.) XXII, cols. 201 f.

[7] M. N. Rutkevich: *Praktika* . . ., p. 123.

The various qualities of sensation—sight, hearing, touch, etc.—
are conditioned on the one hand by differences in the objective
structure of the world, and on the other by differences in the organization of the sense-organs. This diversity among our sense-impressions
should not, however, be taken in too absolute a fashion. For each
of our various senses gives expression to reality in its own peculiar
manner; moreover there is also a certain inner connection between
them, in that hey can often replace and even rectify one another.
Thus the sensory illusion to which the eye is subject when it sees a
stick dipped in water as broken, can be corrected by feeling with the
hands.[1]

But sensation, as Soviet philosophy sees it, must not be interpreted
as a purely passive affair. It is not just a passive reflex, but also implies
at the same time an active attitude on the part of the knower. Besides
this active attitude of the knower in sensation, it also possesses
another essential feature which dialectical materialism upholds
against the mechanistic viewpoint, namely its social character, to
which reference has already been made above.

'Sensations . . . are always the sensations of man the social being.
The sensations of social man are always mediated by his social being,
by his social consciousness as a whole. . . . The sense-perceptions of
social man are mediated by his previous experience, by his practice,
by the practice of his class as a whole.'[2]

In the emphasis thus placed upon the social character of sensation,
and in the historical mode of approach already referred to, one may
discern what is perhaps the characteristic difference in treatment of
this question between 'dialectical logic' and the traditional view.

The next highest stage after sensation is *Perception*. In Nature
there are in fact no 'pure' properties, but only complete objects; so
too, in our sensory knowledge, we are also concerned, not with 'pure'
sensations isolated one from another, but with sensations organically
dovetailed as components into the perception of a total object.
Perception is the result of the analytico-synthetic activity of the
cerebral cortex and

'gives man awareness of a thing as a total object with its particu-
larities, properties and relations'.[3]

In adopting this view of the perceptual process, dialectical materialism aims to do away with atomistic sensualism.[4] On the other
hand the Soviet psychologists are continually inveighing, in this

---

[1] I. I. Khaskhachikh: *Op. cit.*, p. 116; V. Ral'tsevich: *Op. cit.*, col. 204.
[2] G. Obichkin: *Op. cit.*, pp. 13 f.; *cf.* also M. N. Rutkevich: *Praktika . . .*,
pp. 122 f.
[3] F. I. Georgiev: *Op. cit.*, p. 32.   [4] *Ibid.*

connection, against *Gestalt* psychology,[1] and especially against
Köhler and Koffka, who are accused of having 'made a mystery'
of the totalistic character of perception.[2]

It is interesting to find Soviet dialectical materialism of the opinion
that the occurrence of perception involves recourse to previous
sensory and intellectual knowledge:

'Sense-perceptions in man are interspersed with intellectual activity.
I look at a given object and perceive it as a clock; I take it for a clock
on this occasion because the idea of a clock has already arisen in me
on the basis of previous experience. This means that in perceiving
objects and phenomena man already has a certain stock of knowledge
in the shape of representations and concepts which operate as
premises in the knowing-process, though they are really a result of
the history of knowledge and practice.'[3]

The next stage above perception in the knowing-process is
Representation. It is the link between sense-perception and concept,
the elementary form of generalization. Like sensation, it is a subjective picture of the objective world, but differs from sensation in
that it is no longer so immediately dependent on the object sensed,
since in this case the presence of the object is no longer necessary. It
still adheres to the sensory form of the object but already omits
certain details and is confined to whatever happens to strike the eye
for any reason, even though it may not be by any means the most
important thing; in this respect it differs from the concept, which
singles out the essential features of the object.[4]

With the *Concept*, the knowing-process ascends to a new and
higher level, namely the 'logical', which differs qualitatively, *i.e.*,
essentially, from that of the senses. The concept too is a subjective
picture of objective reality, but unlike sensation and representation
it is no longer sensory in character but 'logical' or 'thought-created'.
The concept is no longer tied to the material order.

'Hence it can neither be contemplated nor represented. Value, for
instance, cannot be apprehended by the sense-organs. Any individual

---

[1] *Gestalt* psychology emphasizes the total character of our sensory perception. The whole, for it, is more than the part, inasmuch as *Gestalt*
perception is not exhausted by the mere sum of partial perceptions. The
Berlin school (Köhler, Koffka, *et al.*) saw in this *Gestalt* experience a mere
reflection of the physical *Gestalt* in the stimuli and brain-processes, whereas
others have sought to explain it by the intervention of various intellectual
functions. *Cf.* A. Willwoll, S.J.: *Seele und Geist*[2], Freiburg-i-B. 1953, p. 52.

[2] F. I. Georgiev: *Op. cit.*, p. 32.

[3] F. I. Khaskhachikh: *Op. cit.*, p. 142; *cf.* F. I. Georgiev: *Op. cit.*, p. 33.

[4] F. I. Khashachikh: *Op. cit.*, pp. 143 f.; *cf.* F. I. Georgiev: *Op. cit.*,
pp. 34 f.

commodity can be touched and seen, but value can neither be seen with the eyes, nor heard with the ears, nor felt with the hands, for as Lenin says, it is a category that is not bound to the matter of sensory experience.' [1]

Hence too the scope of the concept is incomparably greater than that of sensation or perception. What Lenin declared of the concept of velocity, namely that it can and must embrace speeds beyond the limits of imagination,[2] is equally true of many concepts of modern physics (think, for example, of the micro-particles of quantum physics, or even of the so-called radio stars, which cannot be observed at all by optical methods, but of which modern astronomy is capable of framing a still admittedly incomplete concept).[3] As regards the formation of general concepts, we have already indicated above that dialectical materialism adheres to a perfectly acceptable theory of abstraction.[4]

The dialectical character of the theory of concepts is supposed to be guaranteed in particular by two special features in the view taken of them: the rejection of 'fixed', unalterable concepts, and the doctrine of the 'concrete concept'.

Whereas 'metaphysics' regards concepts as absolute, fixed and unchanging, dialectics considers them to be essentially mutable in character; they possess a flexibility extending even to the identity of opposites. If this were not so they could not reflect a world itself conceived as in a state of perpetual flux.[5]

'Assuming that everything develops, does this also extend to the most general *concepts* and *categories* of thought? If not, that means that thought has no connection with being. If it is so, then this means that there is a dialectic of concepts and a dialectic of knowledge, having objective significance.' [6]

V. I. Cherkesov points, as an example of such mutable, dialectical concepts, to the notion of a 'revolutionary mass'. According to Lenin, it is sufficient, at the outset of a revolutionary struggle, that some thousands of workers should begin to engage in revolutionary activity, in order to be able to speak of a 'mass'. Later, when the revolutionary movement has spread sufficiently to turn it into a true revolution, this is no longer enough. The concept of 'mass' has changed; it now signifies the majority, and that not only the majority of the workers, but of all the dispossessed.[7] Mutable concepts of this

---

[1] F. I. Khaskhachikh: *Op. cit.*, p. 152.

[2] *FT*, p. 199 (German, p. 152); *cf.* above, p. 505.

[3] *Cf.* F. I. Georgiev: *Op. cit.*, p. 37.   [4] *Cf.* above, p. 505.

[5] F. I. Khaskhachikh: *Op. cit.*, p. 157.   [6] *FT*, p. 239; (German, p. 190).

[7] V. I. Cherkesov: *Nekotorye voprosy . . .*, p. 71; *cf.* V. I. Lenin: *Sochineniya*, XXXII[4], pp. 451 f.

sort, according to Cherkesov, also include such concepts as 'dictatorship of the proletariat', 'biological species' and 'the boiling of water at 100° C.' He describes them as 'concepts of changing relations'; they are not confined to the enumeration of essential features, isolated from the inessential; for the essence of things cannot be reduced to a sum of unalterable features, since it is always developing and changing; it incorporates, rather, a contradiction within itself, which can only be reproduced in our consciousness by a dialectically contradictory concept; a really profound, scientific concept must therefore include in its content the general, the necessary and the lawful, unseparated and unisolated from the opposed categories of the individual, the contingent, the particular, etc. In the concept of 'biological species', for example, the individual variants included under the species in question are not set aside and forgotten, but incorporated into it as 'its other'. Thanks to its dialectical interconnection of general and particular, this concept leads the biologist to reckon in advance with the possibility, and even the necessity, that new species may emerge from the old, and that under given conditions the essential may be transformed into the inessential, and *vice versa*.

The formation of such a concept does not occur by way of an enumeration of all the individual features and instances. So far as that goes, it would merely prove that the general is sometimes realized in a specific norm, that events do indeed repeat themselves, albeit with certain variations. It is precisely on this account that the dialectical concept enables man to grasp the concreteness of truth and of the actual situation, which has its special importance from the point of view of revolutionary tactics.[1]

Cherkesov's examples show very clearly, however, the misconception underlying this doctrine of the dialectical concept. When new species arise from an earlier one (leaving aside the question whether such processes actually occur), it is obviously not a matter of the species-concept having altered, but of certain organisms having so far altered in the course of evolution that they no longer belong to this particular species. Again, if a few thousand workers can form a 'revolutionary mass' in one particular historical situation, but not in another, this does not mean that the concept has altered, but that it also includes, as one of its features, a relation to the environment. If this relation is altered, on another occasion, by a shift in the balance of power, say, it may come about that the concept of 'revolutionary mass' is no longer applicable to a few thousand workers.

The same applies to the dialectical materialist doctrine of the 'concrete concept', by which is meant not merely the concreteness of the

---

[1] V. I. Cherkesov: *Op. cit.*, pp. 68 ff.

individual concept, but a concreteness in the concept of the universal, and even of the type.

The Hegelian legacy is again in evidence here. For in his *Science of Logic* Hegel had set himself this very goal of overcoming the abstract universality of the concept in formal logic, which becomes ever more impoverished in content the more its scope increases, and replacing it by the concrete concept as the expression of a concrete universality including within itself all the wealth of its subordinate concepts.

'It is only through a profounder acquaintance with other sciences'— says Hegel in his introduction to the *Logic*—'that logic discovers itself to subjective thought as not a mere abstract Universal, but as a Universal which comprises in itself the full wealth of Particulars.' [1]

Like the passages from Hegel's *Logic* on 'self-movement' which we referred to earlier, this idea also put Lenin into a state of high enthusiasm. Of the quotation cited above he remarks, in his *Philosophical Notebooks*:

'A splendid formula: "not a mere abstract Universal", but a Universal containing in itself the wealth of the particular, the individual, the singular . . .!! *Très bien!*' [2]

This idea, when fully worked-out, should indeed have led to the replacement of traditional formal logic by a new dialectical logic, as Hegel himself intended it should. But how does dialectical materialism set about solving this problem on a materialist basis? How is this unity of universal, particular and singular to be realized? In the fragment *On Dialectics* Lenin gives the following 'dialectical' account of the unity of universal and particular:

'Consequently, opposites (the singular as opposed to the general) are identical: the singular exists only in the connection that leads to the general. The general exists only in the singular and through the singular. Every singular is (in one way or another), a general. Every general is (a fragment, or a side, or the essence of) a singular. Every general only approximately comprises all the singular objects. . . . Every singular is connected by thousands of transitions with other *kinds* of singulars (things, phenomena, processes), etc.' [3]

In this formulation, which is not distinguished by undue precision, Lenin appears to regard the identity of general and singular in the concrete concept in such a way that a real connection only obtains between individual concrete things.

[1] G. W. F. Hegel: *Science of Logic*, I, p. 69.
[2] *FT*, p. 73 (German, p. 17).
[3] *FT*, p. 329 (*LSW*, XI, p. 83).

No more happy are the attempted solutions put forward by the Soviet philosophers. In most cases the concreteness of the general concept is derived from the unity of general, particular and singular, which is not only attributed to things in objective reality, but also required of concepts. Khaskhachikh thinks that *every* definition of a concept involves three moments:

'the general (the species), the particular (determinacy of the species) and the singular (the defined object);'

but this does not prevent him, a few lines later, from explaining that

'the concept "animal" is formed by leaving aside what distinguishes animals from one another and retaining only what is common to all of them'.[1]

Further on still, he gives a quite different account of the 'concreteness' of a concept:

'A concept which reflects the really existing world is a *concrete concept*';

by 'concrete' here he means, following Marx, 'the union of many determinations, a unity in multiplicity', and gives as an example the Stalinist definition of the concept of 'nation':

'A nation is a historically constituted, stable community of people, formed on the basis of a common language, territory, economic life and psychological make-up manifested in a common culture.' [2]

This 'concrete concept' too is supposed, like every other, to represent a 'unity of general, particular and singular'. But when Khaskhachikh attempts to illustrate this claim by an example, the singular tacitly drops out of sight once more:

'The concept "apple-tree", for example, simultaneously designates the common element characteristic of all trees and the particular features peculiar to fruit trees.' [3]

For Sitkovsky the concrete concept is imbued with content because it incorporates its negation, 'its other', a dialectical contradiction within itself. Here he is thinking primarily of the 'categories' of dialectical materialism, which are mostly listed in pairs, because each of them contains in its content and definition the category contradictorily opposed to it. Since the concrete concept therefore has a highly complicated, dialectical content, it also includes the judge-

---

[1] F. I. Khaskhachikh: *Op. cit.*, pp. 153 f.
[2] J. V. Stalin: *Marxizm i natsional'ny vopros* (Marxism and the National Question), *Sochineniya*, II, p. 296 (English, *Works*, II, p. 307); *cf.* F. I. Khaskhachikh: *Op. cit.*, p. 154.
[3] F. I. Khaskhachikh: *Op. cit.*, p. 155.

ment which gives expression to this content; it is to some extent a compendium or condensate of the many judgements which have gone to make it up.[1]

Keburiya has lately attempted to found the concreteness of the concept on a variety of other grounds as well. The concept, for him, is concrete insofar as it represents a 'nodal point' in the historical development of knowledge. The latter gives rise to a continuously increasing enrichment of the concept, *i.e.*, a continual growth in concreteness. The concept of the atom in contemporary physics differs, for example, from that of the ancient Greeks, by its greater content, depth and definiteness, '*i.e.*, by its greater concreteness'.[2] This concrete character of the concept is further governed by the fact that it reflects the *essence* of the object. For the essence is concrete because it represents the unity of a multiplicity, namely the 'wholeness of the essential features'. And finally he considers this concreteness to be still further conditioned by the fact that it represents the result of a 'scientific generalization'. Unlike the 'metaphysical' theory, however, the Marxist theory of the concept regards generalization as a process in which thought moves from the simple to the complex, and from the abstract to the concrete. The concept of 'capitalism', for example, is characterized by a whole series of determinations: goods, money, capital, surplus value, profit, etc. But in defining capitalism, all these individual determinations must not be mechanically listed together in a row, but developed one from another, as Marx does in *Capital*.[3]

From all the above-mentioned examples of 'concrete concepts' it will be clearly evident that they are in no need of any new 'dialectical' logic. The concepts of formal logic also reflect the real existing world; they also represent the unity of a multiplicity of features; and they are also often the result of a series of judgements and gain in depth of content through the progress of science. The speculations of those who champion concrete concepts are often founded on a confusion between the various types of general concept. Thus when formal logicians lay it down as a law of the general concept that the more its scope is enlarged the poorer it grows in content, it is the generic concept that they have in mind. Now though modern logic may still be far from possessing any universally acknowledged scheme for classifying general concepts,[4] there is agreement on this much at

[1] E. P. Sitkovsky: *Op. cit.*, p. 87.

[2] D. M. Keburiya: *K voprosu o konkretnosti ponyatiya* (On the Problem of the Concreteness of the Concept), *VF*, 1957, 2, pp. 22–38, *q.v.* p. 32.

[3] *Ibid.*, pp. 32–5; *cf.* also S. F. Efimov: *Konkretnoe ponyatie i chuvstvennoe znanie* (The Concrete Concept and Sensory Knowledge), *VF*, 1956, 3, pp. 59–73.

[4] *Cf.* Hans Wetter: *Zur Systematik der Allgemeinbegriffe* in *Blätter für Deutsche Philosophie*, XI (1937), pp. 24 ff.

least, that in addition to the generic concept proper there is also a whole series of other types of general concept, such as collective concepts, inclusive concepts (*e.g.*, 'the Renaissance', 'capitalism'), serial concepts (which designate a series, such as 'the spectrum'), and so on. When the Soviet philosophers offer as examples of the 'concrete universal' such concepts as 'nation', 'working-class', etc., what we are dealing with here are not generic concepts but collective or inclusive concepts, which even according to the laws of formal logic are by no means attenuated in content the wider their scope is extended (thus the concept of 'fleet', for example, is not diminished in content the more ships the fleet contains).

In its account of *Judgement* Soviet philosophy insists, with Engels, that dialectical logic, unlike formal, must not be content with enumerating the individual forms of motion of thought (judgement and inference), and placing them side by side without any connection; dialectical logic, on the contrary, must derive these forms out of one another and establish a relation of subordination between them, instead of putting them on an equal level.

Hegel's four groups of judgements (judgements of Inherence, judgements of Subsumption, judgements of Necessity and judgements of the Notion) are reduced by Engels to three: individual judgements (Hegel's judgements of Inherence), special judgements (Hegel's judgements of Subsumption and Necessity) and general judgements (Hegel's judgements of the Notion). In Engels' opinion, this subordination of judgements, their progression from individual to particular and from particular to universal, reflects the historical development of human knowledge. He shows this by way of the following example:

'That friction produces heat was already known practically to prehistoric man, who discovered the making of fire by friction perhaps more than 100,000 years ago. . . . But from that to the discovery that friction is in general a source of heat, who knows how many thousands of years elapsed? Enough that the time came when the human brain was sufficiently developed to be able to formulate the judgement: *friction is a source of heat.* . . . Still further thousands of years passed until, in 1842, Mayer, Joule and Colding . . . formulated the judgement: *all mechanical motion is capable of being converted into heat by means of friction.* . . . But from now on things went quickly. Only three years later, Mayer was able . . . to raise the judgement of subsumption to the level at which it now stands: *any form of motion, under conditions fixed for each case, is both able and compelled to undergo transformation, directly or indirectly, into any other form of motion.*' [1]

[1] F. Engels: *Dielectics of Nature*, pp. 297 f.

According to Kopnin, the most elementary form of thought is not the concept, but the judgement. The concept he considers to be a judgement

'whose predicate represents the thought of the general within phenomena'.[1]

He also believes that, unlike formal, dialectical logic is not confined to the question of the validity of the judgement, but also provides a method for determining whether a given judgement is true.[2]

Alexeyev distinguishes between elementary judgements (such as 'Ivan is a man'), whose formulation requires no acquaintance with dialectical logic, even though a dialectic is present within them, and dialectical judgements, which can only be formulated by the use of the dialectical method. As an example of such a judgement, he quotes a remark from Marx's *Capital*:

'Capital, therefore, cannot originate out of circulation; and yet it is no less impossible that it should originate apart from circulation. Consequently, capital must arise both in circulation and not in circulation';

in circulation, because only therein is there purchase of that specific commodity (namely labour-power) which creates surplus value; not in circulation, but in production, because labour-power only creates surplus value in the labour-process.[3] But in this sense we should equally have to call 'The Danube flows through Austria and does not flow through Austria' a dialectical judgement, since besides flowing through Austria it also flows through various other countries. It is not difficult to see, however, that formal logic can also make short work of 'dialectical' judgements of this sort.

It is not in judgement only, but also in *Inference*, that Soviet philosophy sees a copy of the processes, interconnections and reciprocal relations prevailing among objects in reality. According to Khaskhachikh, the various forms of syllogism reproduce the relations obtaining among things:

'The logical figures with which logic normally operates give expression to real relations and connections among things. Just as the connections and relations among things are numerous and manifold, so too are the forms of inference.' [4]

[1] P. V. Kopnin: *Formy myshleniya i ikh vzaimosvyaz'* (The Forms of Thought and their Reciprocal Connection), *VF*, 1956, 3, pp. 44–58, q.v. p. 45.

[2] *Ibid.*, p. 47.

[3] M. N. Alexeyev: *Op. cit.*, pp. 53 f.; cf. K. Marx: *Capital* (Everyman), I, pp. 152 f.

[4] F. I. Khaskhachikh: *Op. cit.*, p. 165.

Lenin goes further still and even maintains that the logical validity of
inference is derived from experience:

'When Hegel tries . . . to subsume the purposeful activity of man
under the categories of logic by saying that this activity is "inference",
that the subject (man) plays the part of a "term" in the logical
"figure" of the argument, etc.—this is not just a forced conclusion,
not just a game. On the contrary, it has a very deep, purely materialistic meaning. One must put the matter the other way round: man's
consciousness must have been led by his practical activity to recap-
itulate the various logical figures millions and millions of times, *in
order for* these figures to have acquired the significance of *axioms*
. . . It is precisely (and solely) on the strength of these millions of
repetitions that the figures themselves possess the fixity of preconceived notions and an axiomatic character.'[1]

Since dialectical materialism conceives of inference as the reproduction of a process and connection occurring in things themselves
—the 'conclusion from ideas' being simply a copy of the 'conclusion
from things',[2] it regards the procedure of inference as a means of
acquiring *new* knowledge; the conclusion gives us knowledge that we
should not have had from the premisses alone. Moreover, the conclusion can either reproduce what is past (from the fact that large
quantities of shells were found in the Alps it could be inferred that at
some earlier time the alpine rocks were once at the bottom of the sea),
or else be a means of foreseeing events still impending in the future.[3]

But this latter claim is scarcely in keeping with Lenin's thesis, that
the logical validity of inference reposes on the millionfold repetition
of the experience which accords with it. For if logical validity does
not depend on the knowledge of an unchanging essence contained in
the premisses (which does not first require a millionfold repetition of
experience for its discovery), and such that the connection expressed
in the conclusion necessarily follows from it, one may legitimately ask
on what other basis foreknowledge of the future can be supposed to
be possible.

According to the direction in which inference proceeds, a distinction must be made between *Induction* and *Deduction*. In inductive
inference thought proceeds from the particular to the general; in
deductive, on the other hand, from the general to the particular; both
forms have their own justification and meaning. Whereas 'metaphysical' thinking separates the two from one another, dialectical
materialism regards them, not as mutually exclusive methods, but as

---

[1] *FT*, pp. 164 (German, p. 110), 188 (139).
[2] V. Ral'tsevich in *BSE* (1st edn.), XXII, col. 218.
[3] F. I. Khaskhachikh: *Op. cit.*, pp. 163 f.

forms of thought which supplement and condition one another. Deduction is said to have particular importance in the field of mathematics and geometry; by the use of this method the whereabouts of the planet Neptune were calculated by Leverrier in 1846, some years before its discovery by Galle. Even so, the importance of deduction should not be exaggerated. For awareness of generality (concepts, laws . . .) is not the starting-point, but the outcome of the history of knowledge. Deduction therefore presupposes induction, whose task is precisely that of ascending from the singular to the general.[1] Kopnin, on the other hand, rightly emphasizes that induction without deduction is impossible, and this because

'induction alone is incapable of explaining the process of inductive inference. Every inference, including induction, proceeds on the basis of knowledge of generality.'[2]

Like induction and deduction, the methods of *Analysis and Synthesis* must also complement one another, according to dialectical materialism, and form a unity, in order not to lapse into the errors of 'metaphysical' thinking. Argument by *Analogy* is likewise reckoned to be justified under certain conditions, assuming, that is, that the qualitative peculiarities of the phenomena under comparison are taken into account.[3]

These are some of the indications pointing in the direction of a consciously-designed 'dialectical logic'. No complete and rounded treatment of the subject has yet been vouchsafed to us. The dialectical method of dealing with individual thought-contents emerges most clearly in the sections on concepts and on judgement. But we feel compelled to endorse the opinions of those Soviet philosophers who maintain that the matters brought into issue by the champions of 'dialectical logic' can all be equally well dealt with by means of the traditional logic.[4]

[1] *Ibid.*, p. 166.   [2] P. V. Kopnin: *Op. cit.*, p. 55.
[3] F. I. Khaskhachikh: *Op. cit.*, pp. 169 f.   [4] *Cf.* above, p. 532.

Conclusion

WE hope, in the foregoing pages, to have given a tolerably adequate account of the Soviet version of the system of dialectical materialism. The critical remarks occasionally added at the end of individual sections may in general have been enough to indicate the more salient philosophical weaknesses of this system and to stimulate further critical thought. By way of summing up we shall now, however, attempt to give an estimate, from various angles, of the significance of dialectical materialism as a rounded whole, in the officially prescribed formulation it has received through the teachings of the 'classics' of Marxist-Leninism.

If we begin by considering this significance in a quite general way, it seems to us to extend far beyond the fact on which chief emphasis is commonly placed, namely that the philosophy of dialectical materialism has come to be adopted as the official world-view of the Soviet state, and indeed of the world communist movement as a whole. This fact is certainly important, but it by no means exhausts the problem. For there is every reason to think that the outlook of which this system is the most thoroughgoing expression is not merely representative of the world-view of the various communist parties, but also reflects the often unconscious or unspoken attitude of the average citizen of today, so far as he is not positively religious and Christian in his beliefs; and does so regardless of his political affiliations and social status, which may often be such as to make this same average citizen an embittered opponent of communism. The doctrines underlying the entire system of dialectical materialism, that nothing exists apart from matter, and that the whole world as at present constituted has somehow come about 'of its own accord', are in accordance with the views held by what is doubtless the great majority of people nowadays, and not merely by those who are numbered in the ranks of the Communist Party. The penetrative power of the

548

communist ideology at the present time may well be largely due to this fact.

As regards the more strictly philosophical assessment of dialectical materialism, we may declare ourselves very largely in agreement with the judgement of Bocheński.[1] In the course of our survey we have found repeated confirmation of many of Bocheński's observations, more particularly, for instance, as to the technical and scientific primitiveness of Soviet philosophy, its lack of acquaintance with other systems of philosophy and its inability to examine these latter in a factual and unprejudiced way. As Bocheński also brings out in most revealing fashion,[2] dialectical materialism as a total system represents an eclectic medley of extremely diverse elements, often borrowed from philosophical positions totally at variance with one another; in part they consist simply of obvious truisms, in part also of perfectly sound philosophical truths, but most of them represent assertions which do not stand up to serious philosophical examination. It may not infrequently escape the philosophical tyro, however, that the positions taken up by dialectical materialism in the various branches of philosophy are in many cases mutually incompatible, and that views upheld in one field are irreconcilably opposed to those defended in another.

So far as individual philosophical doctrines are concerned, it cannot be denied that dialectical materialism contains a whole set of positive features which distinguish it, in particular, from popular mechanistic materialism. Above all we may applaud its efforts to justify the existence of philosophy in the face of repeated attempts to dismiss the latter as superfluous; another point in its favour is the gradual return to a number of philosophical disciplines—the philosophy of Nature, psychology, etc., which Engels' original version of dialectical materialism had banished from the realm of philosophy. We must also pay tribute to the emphatic realism of the dialectical materialist approach, which is carried to such lengths that the term 'materialism' often means nothing else than 'epistemological realism'.[3]

[1] I. M. Bocheński: *Der sowjetrussische dialektische Materialismus*, pp. 147 ff.

[2] *Ibid.*, pp. 152 ff.

[3] This view has lately been contested by Prof. J. Hommes (*Der technische Eros. Das Wesen der materialistischen Geschichtsauffassung*, Freiburg-i-B. 1955). In his opinion, the realism of Soviet philosophy again breaks down, in that we are dealing with a *dialectical* philosophy; but dialectic means that subject and object, man and Nature, are seized in an embracing unity, whereby the independence and self-subsistency of the object again come to naught. To us, however, it seems that in present-day Soviet dialectical

But the most considerable merit which dialectical materialism has over crude mechanistic materialism is to be found in its conception of motion, which is thought of not merely as change of position in space, but in the Aristotelian sense as 'change' in general; connected with this there is also the basic thesis concerning the emergence of qualitative distinctions in the course of the evolutionary process— these being viewed, however, as originally due to the occurrence of changes in quantity. Dialectical materialism is thereby able to admit of qualitative, *i.e.*, essential, distinctions between the different spheres of reality: life is not immediately reducible to physico-chemical laws, any more than human knowledge and consciousness can be derived from physiology. In conjunction with this, a further merit of dialectical materialism also comes to light, this time in the field of epistemology: its rejection of sensationalism and acknowledgement of a qualitative difference between the sensory and 'logical' levels of cognition, together with an essentially correct view of the nature of concepts and their formation by way of abstraction. All these positive elements in the ideal content of dialectical materialism can be related in one way or another to one of its two major constituents, namely the dialectic. It is this which supposedly helps to explain the essential distinction between the higher and the lower.

In irreconcilable contrast to all this there stands, however, the second main component of the system: its basic dogma of materialism. In accordance with this the reality just described, which elevates itself into ever higher, and ultimately even into spiritual forms of existence, is regarded, for reasons which are not rationally intelligible and may well be explicable only on psychological grounds, as essenti-

materialism there is no longer any trace of dialectic in this sense of the term. It may still be present, indeed, in the thought of the early Marx, and its influence may even be detectable in Lenin, albeit to a very much slighter degree. But present-day Soviet philosophy consciously dissociates itself from the early philosophy of Marx, since during this period of his development he had not yet sufficiently detached himself from Hegelian idealism. In the course of the development from early Marx to contemporary Soviet dialectical materialism, a breach occurred somewhere—and in our opinion it was definitely made by Engels. Hence it has come about that in Soviet philosophy nowadays dialectic simply betokens an evolutionism progressing *via* the emergence and dissolution of opposites. It may be that a truly philosophical working-out of certain of the positions entertained in modern Soviet philosophy would inevitably lead to a true dialectic, as Marx and Hegel conceived it. But the Soviet philosophers never pursue this in any systematic way. On the contrary, so strong is the emphasis on the objective, 'independent-of-man's-will' character of the laws of development in Nature and society, that students are bound to be brought up in a realistic frame of mind, rather than a truly dialectical one (in the sense envisaged by Hegel and the youthful Marx).

ally 'material' in character. As N. Berdyaev very properly emphasizes,[1] this either means giving a completely new sense to the word 'matter' and using it to designate attributes which are not only spiritual but actually divine, or else admitting a contradiction which runs through the entire system.

'Dialectic, which stands for complexity, and materialism, which results in a narrow one-sidedness of view, are as mutually repellent as water and oil.'[2]

And this contradiction does indeed poison the entire system and deprives the positive features just referred to of a large part of their value. The external world, whose independence of the knowing subject is so emphatically defended in the realism of Engels and Lenin, is quite unjustifiably restricted to the outer world which acts upon the senses; in this way realism is eventually converted into materialism. The acknowledgement of qualitative differences and changes in the process of development loses its value, in that the again quite unwarranted denial of a being outside and above the world compels dialectical materialism to think of the higher orders as having emerged from the lower by a natural process of evolution; but this, as we have repeatedly had occasion to note at key points in the system, can only be done at the cost of violating the causal principle, which in other connections is strenuously defended.

Hence it comes about that dialectical materialism not only proclaims in its teaching that contradiction is the most essential element of reality, but also exemplifies a single vast contradiction on its own account. And though we have repudiated the Soviet philosophers' theory of 'real contradictions' as the springs of development in material reality, we may yet be of the opinion that this fundamental contradiction in the system of dialectical materialism will prove to be the driving-force in the realm of thought, eventually demanding a solution, and thereby necessarily leading to the collapse of the whole intellectual edifice of dialectical materialism in general.

For all that, one may still, perhaps, find something of value in the very existence of this fundamental contradiction. For on the basis of popular mechanistic materialism, with its seemingly clear answers, its simplified, cut-and-dried solutions, stifling all impulse to inquiry in the minds of men, any further development of philosophy was rendered impossible. Popular materialism repudiates philosophy not only by what it says, but still more so by its whole nature. It is of much importance, therefore, that dialectical materialism has again served to make the world-picture somewhat less clear and simple, and

[1] N. Berdyaev: *Wahrheit und Lüge des Kommunismus*, Lucerne 1934, p. 84.
[2] N. O. Lossky: *Dialektichesky materializm v SSSR.*, p. 60.

—in theory and principle, at least, though not in actual fact—has reopened an approach to the deeper aspects of things. Despite its campaign against any sort of 'mysticism', dialectical materialism, with its doctrine of the 'contradictions' in the world, has restored to its adherents a feeling for the paradox and mystery of the world and has thereby prepared the ground for the revival of a truly philosophical 'sense of wonder'. By virtue of its dialectical character, it is a philosophy which again leads on to thought, inquiry and research. And this cannot but lead to a genuine renaissance of philosophy in Russia, so soon as the external conditions for this are again realized —above all, real freedom of thought and philosophical research.

We have just been referring to a point which was brought out in greater detail earlier on, in our treatment of the materialist dialectic, namely that dialectical materialism, despite its verbal hostility to all forms of 'mysticism', is nevertheless endued at bottom with a certain 'mystical' vein. This point deserves fuller consideration, for it directs our attention to the Russian environment which has set its stamp on Marxist dialectical materialism as it is today, and in which even positivism and materialism themselves take on a 'mystical' air.

We have seen in Part One, how the personality of Lenin has imposed on Russian Marxism in general a quite specific flavour which marks it off very distinctly from social-democratic doctrines of the Western European type: the difference ultimately rests, no doubt, upon a revival of the old Russian revolutionary tradition. And in our judgement, something of the same kind can also be discerned, in particular, within the field of Marxist philosophy and theory. At those very points where Lenin has exercised a decisive influence on Soviet philosophy, there are striking points of contact to be found between dialectical materialism and non-Marxist tendencies in Russian philosophy. In saying this, we must not be misunderstood as implying that Bolshevism is a purely Russian product, and that we would wish to relieve the West of responsibility for its emergence. In speaking here of points of contact between Soviet philosophy and certain intuitions dear to many non-Marxian Russian philosophers, we are thinking of the fact that even in the Soviet ideology, for all its materialist and levelling tendencies, there are certain aspirations still surviving, which animated the minds of many other Russian thinkers of the 19th and early 20th centuries. These contacts are also and above all concerned with that movement which is so radically opposed to Marxism and materialism generally, and in which, perhaps, a certain peculiar quality of Russian philosophy is most clearly exhibited: with the Slavophile movement in its religious and theological phase (Ivan Kireyevsky, Alexey Khomyakov), and with the powerful school of Russian religious thought which grew out of it, and which leads, through V. Soloviev, to such modern Russian philosophers of religion as S. Bulgakov, N. Berdyaev, S. Frank, P. Florensky, L. Karsavin and others.

This affinity can be apprehended most clearly, perhaps, in respect of a feature already dwelt upon, the adoption of the Hegelian dialectic, which despite its 'materialist inversion' continues to lend a certain touch of 'mysticism' to the dialectical materialist view. It is true, of course, that the union of materialism and dialectic had already been effected, in essentials, by Marx and Engels. But as regards profundity of conception, there is a great deal of difference between Engels and Lenin, as the latter's *Philosophical Notebooks* make particularly clear. Truly Russian, at least, is the excitement with which Lenin seizes upon the notion of a dialectical explanation of the universe; it is wholly in the spirit of that enthusiasm for Hegel so characteristic of Russia in the 'thirties and 'forties of the 19th century. It is probably no exaggeration to say that Hegel has found his most ardent votaries upon Russian soil. Many, even, of those Russian thinkers who later became violently hostile to Hegel's philosophy, had nevertheless begun their philosophical development as confessed devotees of Hegelianism (as was the case, for example, not only with Bakunin, Belinsky and Herzen, but also with their rivals in the Slavophile camp), nor were they ever able to shake off his influence for the rest of their lives. In virtue of this connection one may perhaps venture to assert that the element of 'mysticism' deriving from the dialectic is the very feature in Marxism which has enabled it to attain such sweeping success in Russia.

A further point of contact between Leninist dialectical materialism and Slavophile views has already been indicated at the appropriate place. For although the postulate of the unity of theory and practice connects Marxism in general with the various anti-idealist and anti-intellectualist reactions against Hegel's abstract idealism[1] (*Lebensphilosophie*, existentialism, etc.), it also exhibits, especially when taken in conjunction with the specifically Leninist postulate of the 'partisanship' (*partiynost'*) of theory, a surprising resemblance to the basic idea of Slavophile thought, the doctrine of 'total knowledge' (*tsel'noe znanie*). For Kireyevsky and Khomyakov likewise, cognition is not simply a theoretical affair, for it has an existential significance; indeed, as an existential encounter between the knowing subject and a substantial, personal truth, it involves a positively religious responsibility, and finds its consummation, not in the particular cognitive act of the solitary individual, but in the knowing process of a total organism embracing the whole of mankind, namely the

[1] On Hegel's 'abstract idealism', *cf.* p. 10, n. 2.

church, in which the individual knowing subject is merely a part and a moment.

And finally there is yet a third feature which brings out the striking affinity between Leninist philosophy and Russian religious thought: this is the typically romantic vision, again ultimately inherited from Hegel, of a reciprocal inner connection and unity pervading the infinite multiplicity of essences in the world. We may remember what it was in Hegel that so delighted Lenin: the idea, splendid in spite of its 'mysticism', of a 'living' (!) interconnection of everything with everything else.[1] And like the idea of the unity of opposites, this intuition also goes back to the conceptions prevailing in Platonic, and still more in neo-Platonic, mysticism. In the 5th *Ennead*, Plotinus declaims in inspired words of the splendour of *Nous*, in which the many things existing separately alongside one another in the world are mutually interfused in the most intimate unity:

Every being . . . contains all within itself, and at the same time sees all in every other, so that everywhere there is all, and all is all and each all, and infinite the glory. Each of them is great; the small is great; the sun, There, is all the stars; and every star, again, is all the stars and sun. . . . There each being is an eternal product of a whole and is at once a whole and an individual manifesting as part but, to the keen vision There, known for the whole it is. The myth of Lynceus seeing into the very deeps of the earth tells us of those eyes in the divine.'[2]

The idea of such a πάντα ἕν, in which all things are one, is similarly to be found in the patristic writers (Clement of Alexandria, Origen and others), and more recently has also become a recurrent theme in Russian religious philosophy. The entire philosophical development of V. Soloviev, perhaps its greatest representative, is dominated by this intuition of universal unity. The whole of the world-process is seen by him as nothing less than the breakdown of the originally perfect unity of the creation in God, brought about by its 'apostasy' from God, and the subsequent reascent of creation, which is now returning, by way of the cosmogonical and historical process, back to its initial unity. Various philosophical elaborations of the same ideas also underlie the systems of other leading representatives of Russian religious thought.

In reviewing the first version of the present book,[3] *L'Umanita*, the organ of Saragat's Italian Social-Democratic Party, laid particular stress on the fact that this work on Soviet dialectical materialism

---

[1] *Cf.* above, pp. 6 f., 119 f.

[2] Plotinus: *Enneads* (trans. McKenna), V, 8, 4.

[3] G. A. Wetter: *Il materialismo dialettico sovietico*, Turin 1948.

'should have had to come from a Jesuit father;—certainly a sign of the times we live in—times in which even the traditional religious "culture" accommodates itself to reality and has so far perfected its technique that it is even able to survey the historical phenomenon in abstraction from the stale and all-too-often interested standpoint of Catholic apologetics. Objectively speaking, it should be added at once, however, that the *forma mentis* of Father Gustav A. Wetter . . . is perhaps better equipped than any to appreciate the nuances of a philosophy, a whole world-view, indeed, which is essentially derived from the classical utterances of religious mysticism. This may well go far towards explaining the detachment and objectivity of this book. When Father Wetter writes, in his exposition of Lenin's doctrine, that for the Russian statesman "partisanship consists in the requirement that the proletarian philosopher should not be content to have an objective, purely theoretical knowledge of reality, but rather that in all evaluation of events he should openly and directly identify himself with the standpoint of a particular social group, namely that of the proletariat", we immediately feel from this that here the Jesuit is speaking from a first-hand experience of similar states of the soul, however obvious the differences may be between the standpoint of the militant Catholic and that of the bolshevik agitator.' [1]

These remarks raise problems of a very interesting kind. We have ourselves already formulated conclusions which go some way towards justifying the reviewer when, on the strength of a special capacity, he credits us Catholics with a deeper understanding of bolshevik philo-sophy, in so far as the latter is ultimately connected in some way with the 'classical utterances of religious mysticism', even if this connec-tion be not to be understood to mean that the philosophy of Bol-shevism itself represents a genuine form of 'mysticism'.

More notable still, however, are the further observations of the socialist reviewer, in which he credits the Catholic philosopher, and more especially the Jesuit, as a 'militant Catholic', with a *'forma mentis'* such that he can find a certain congeniality, a certain inner affinity, in the *'forma mentis'* of the bolshevik philosopher, and is thereby exceptionally well equipped for an adequate understanding of Soviet philosophy. Such a kinship has also frequently been imputed to the other side. Berdyaev has this in mind when he describes the Soviet philosophers as 'warriors of *philosophia militans*, having much in common with Catholic theologians'.[2] This sugges-tion of a resemblance between Soviet philosophers and Catholic theologians shows us the direction in which to look for a solution of the problem. The affinity between the *'forma mentis'* on either side

---

[1] *L'Umanita*, 30th March 1948.   [2] N. Berdyaev: *Op. cit.*, p. 62.

arises, in effect, from this, that the Soviet philosophers—as we have already had occasion to notice—base their inquiries, not on a philosophical method, but on an explicitly theological one; a method which asks, not whether a proposition is true or false in itself, but whether it figures in the corpus of revealed truth issuing from a demonstrably infallible source of dogmatic authority. This property of the theological method, which as such is common to all Christian theology, is reinforced in Catholic theology by the fact that here the authority of Holy Writ and tradition is supplemented by the infallible teaching of the Church itself.

But it must be insisted, in this connection, that this method is employed in Christian thought in *theology* only, and not in *philosophy*. In the latter field, even the Christian thinker recognizes an authority, in the last resort, only to the extent that his arguments carry proof. But the Soviet ideologue also employs this method in philosophy, when he treats certain propositions of Marxist–Leninism as admitting of no discussion.

And even in the field of theology, there is still a very important difference between the procedures of a Catholic theologian and a Soviet ideologue. For before the Catholic goes on to argue from the authority of divine revelation, he has already assured himself on purely philosophical grounds of God's existence, and has ascertained by purely scientific and historical methods of inquiry that this God has spoken to the world through positive revelation in Jesus Christ. For the Soviet philosophers, on the other hand, the authority of the 'classics' of Marxism admits of no argument, and has to be blindly taken on trust.

But the problem of the formal resemblance between Soviet philosophy and Catholic thought by no means ends at this point. For in actual fact it extends, not only to the parallel in 'theological' method already described, but also to a fairly comprehensive agreement in their conceptual scheme and manner of stating problems, more especially as between present-day Soviet philosophy and Scholasticism, however diametrically opposed the answers that each of them gives. One of the most surprising things that our exposition of the Soviet philosophical system has revealed to us is the existence of a very wide-ranging correspondence between certain fundamental categories of thought and lines of inquiry in Soviet philosophy on the one hand, and those of Scholasticism, or even Thomism, on the other. We think it no exaggeration to maintain that dialectical materialism, in its present-day official Soviet form, bears a far greater resemblance to the '*forma mentis*' of Scholasticism than to that of Hegelian dialectics, notwithstanding the presence of certain Hegelian concepts and expressions which are still adhered to, though robbed by the 'materialist inversion' of their idealistic meaning, and accorded an interpretation which is simply that appropriate to ordinary common sense. Indeed, the curse put upon the dialectic by its transference to the realm of Nature, like the special meanings attached to the Stalinist categories of 'possibility and actuality', are directly responsible for the fact that in contemporary Soviet dialectical materialism we find ourselves dealing with a mode of thought that is internally far more akin to the Aristotelian and Scholastic doctrines of act and potency than to the true Hegelian dialectic. The criticisms appended in Chapter III of Part Two to our account of the two most fundamental theses of dialectical materialism (the law of the transition from quantity to quality, and the law of the unity and struggle of opposites), have shown us clearly how easy it is to fit the 'materialist dialectic' into the categories of the theory of act and potency. In discussing the theory of the transition from quantitative to qualitative change we have had occasion to note its affinity with the scholastic doctrine of *mutatio substantialis*. In the theory of categories, the account of the concept of contingency corresponds in some respects to the scholastic notion thereof. When the Soviet philosophers dispute whether the space-time continuum of relativity theory can be regarded as form, and matter as its content, the Thomist immediately feels tempted to enter the fray from the standpoint of Aristotelian hylomorphism. When the Soviet psychologists argue whether mental activity can be a special process distinct from physiological processes, and yet still have its substratum in the material organ of the human brain, the scholastic again finds it easy to intervene in the controversy and to point out to the Soviet thinkers that, on the strength of certain principles they accept (motion is impossible without a substantial substratum), they are effectively obliged to push on and postulate a spiritual substance to support this process. In the field of epistemology, dialectical materialism goes so far, that in treating of the concept and its formation by abstraction, it even claims to have originated this very definitely Thomistic view.

This thoroughgoing parallelism often makes it seem as though somewhere at the root of matter, in some major thesis of dialectical materialism, it would be sufficient to rectify an obvious fallacy or an unfounded presupposition in order, not merely to convert the atheism of the theory into theism in general, but to carry it straightway into Thomism.

And yet it would be an illusion to regard such 'points of contact' as 'points of departure' for a reconciliation between dialectical materialism, or its vehicle, communism, on the one hand, and Christianity or Catholicism on the other. For it would at once emerge that the atheistic outlook of communism is not derived from theoretical considerations, but is in some sense the outcome of a prepossession whose roots lie in a region deeper than that of the

558 *Conclusion*

understanding. It is for this very reason that demonstration of the superfluity of God's existence is regarded by Soviet philosophy as its most essential aim, its authentic *raison d'être*, and that, precisely by virtue of the most basic law of the materialist dialectic, the law of the unity and struggle of opposites as the origin of motion, a First Mover or Creator-God is held to be excluded. Despite all the parallels which can perhaps be established in the formal sphere, the opposition of Soviet philosophy to Catholic thought, as to Christianity and theism generally, is irreconcilable, precisely on account of this basic subjective attitude, originating somehow in the sphere of the will. At this point it becomes palpably evident that dialectical materialism is not just one philosophical system among others, but a world-view, the credal embodiment of a temporal force at work in history.

This unbridgeable opposition in depth, despite certain 'points of contact' on the surface, which we have already been able to establish in the field of philosophy, enables us, however, to go a step farther and to interpret the situation thus disclosed as a partial aspect within a wider context. The 'religious' character of communism has often been noted. Jules Monnerot speaks of a '20th-century Islam'.[1] It may seem paradoxical to attempt to apply religious categories to a movement expressly dedicated to materialism and atheism. But in fact the atheism of dialectical materialism is concerned with very much more than a mere denial of God. The latter is the standpoint of that vulgar materialism which dialectical materialism attacks, and for which there is no hierarchy of higher and lower in the world, everything being reduced to the lowest level, that of inanimate matter. But the situation in dialectical materialism is entirely different. Here the higher is not, as such, denied; the world is interpreted as a process of continual ascent, which fundamentally extends into infinity. But it is supposed to be matter itself which continually attains to higher perfection under its own power, thanks to its indwelling dialectic. As Nikolay Berdyaev very rightly remarks, the dialectical materialist attribution of 'dialectic' to matter confers on it, not mental attributes only, but even divine ones.[2] And we find in fact that on such a view matter is eternal, infinite in space and time and internal potency of being, that at a certain stage of development it also acquires mental properties, and that it even has a genuine power of creation, so far as it is capable of bringing forth the higher from the lower, the more perfect from the less perfect, a task which would certainly call for genuine creative power.

Matter here appears as a new absolute, a new divinity replacing the transcendent Creator-God, and as such unable to tolerate any

[1] Jules Monnerot: *Sociology of Communism*, London 1953.
[2] N. Berdyaev: *Op. cit.*, p. 84.

other sort of deity by its side. The communist warfare against religion is not a casual historical misunderstanding, but proceeds from its innermost nature.

But we must go yet further still, and point out that communism—precisely because of its world-outlook, as represented by dialectical and historical materialism—is not merely a new sort of religion, or rather pseudo-religion, but in actual fact a sort of pseudo-Christianity, a perversion, in effect, of true religion, namely Christianity, and a sort of anti-church.

It has often been remarked that communism incorporates a whole series of particular Christian doctrines in secular form: like the Christian, the communist sets out in his attitude from the fact that he is confronted with a world which is not as it should be, which 'lieth in wickedness'. As with the Christian, so also for communism, this corruption of the world is the outcome of a sort of 'fall', occurring in the earliest days of man's history; for Marxism, it was the introduction of private property through the transition from primitive communism to a slave-owing society. This initial error works itself out throughout history as a sort of 'original sin'. This wickedness of our world is not due, initially, to the individual shortcomings of this or that exploiter; it is more in the nature of a supra-individual guilt, in which the individual (exploiter) necessarily participates by virtue of his existence, his membership of a particular social class. Redemption from this primary and original sin has come about—and here Marx was consciously taking over a Christian heritage—through the atonement of a sinless sacrificial lamb: the proletariat, by its undeserved suffering, must pay the price for the emancipation, not of its own class alone, but of the whole of human society. And as in Christianity, this redemption is bound up with a sort of revelation: Marx's discovery of the laws of social development was not the achievement of a thinker of genius, such as might equally well have been effected by any other thinker at any other time; on the contrary, it was a discovery that could only have been made at this particular juncture, at this crucial point in the Marxist pseudo-history of salvation, once 'the fullness of time' had in some sense come to pass. As in Christianity too, this 'revelation' has been primarily vouchsafed in a sort of 'Holy Writ': we find an essential distinction in Marxism between writings having a certain absolute authority, the works of the 'classics', and the productions of second- or third-ranking authors, to which one may assent more or less. And as in the Roman church, this deposit of faith is entrusted to an 'infallible authority': the Central Committee of the Communist Party claims to be regarded, not merely as a focus of organization, but also as a focus of theory; its decrees must be accepted by theorists as 'inexhaustible springs of Marxist–Leninist wisdom' and made fundamental to their work. In

general, the Communist Party figures as a sort of new 'church'; this
comes out most clearly in the requirement of 'partisanship', to which
all Marxist theoreticians are obliged to adhere: according to communist doctrine, that is, a theoretician is only capable, in general, of
recognizing truth when he openly and consciously adopts in his work
the standpoint of the proletariat and its *avant-garde*, the Party. The
latter thereby represents a medium of life for the individual, who is
capable of participating in truth only when he stands in vital and
organic communion with this mighty organism, in which the spirit
of truth resides. We might pursue these parallels still further, but it
would take us too far afield to do so. And from what has been said
the drift of our intention will already be sufficiently clear.

However, the nature of communism, as a perversion of Christianity
and a counter-church, is still more plainly revealed as we pass from
such external matters to the innermost essence of these two spiritual
powers. For what is Christianity, in its inmost essence? It may perhaps be summed up as follows: it is the religion of a world redeemed,
transfigured and made holy, but all this accomplished by the saving
power of the incarnate Son of God. And how does the essence of
communism stand revealed, in the light of our analysis of its world-
outlook? As a similar aspiration towards the salvation and transfiguration of our world, a blasphemous pretension, indeed, of rendering it holy, but all this, not only to the exclusion of any prior descent
of God into the world, but in positive rejection of a transcendent
Creator, and in forthright declaration of war upon Him. Here indeed
it becomes evident how communism, for all its manifold formal
resemblances, is essentially a perversion of Christianity, precisely in
so far as the latter is the religion of incarnation, and itself an incarnation continued throughout the ages in the Church.

Hence, despite all superficial 'points of contact', which merely confirm the old saying that extremes meet, communism appears in its
inmost nature as the true antagonist of Christianity; an antagonist
appearing not only in the guise of a social doctrine and a political
power, but more and more in the shape of a pseudo-religious
spiritual movement. This cardinal feature of Bolshevism had already
been prophetically anticipated by Dostoyevsky:

'Our people are not only becoming atheists, but believe in atheism as
if it were a religion.'

And that of all the historical forms of Christianity it should prove to
be Catholicism which exhibits the largest number of formal similari-
ties with Bolshevism, albeit with the signs reversed, is perhaps an
indication that, on the other side, the opposition between Bolshevism and the Catholic church is also the most radical of all.
This essential incompatibility of Christianity and communism was

recognized by Pope Pius XI, when in his Encyclical *Divini Redemptoris* he urged the Catholic episcopate:

'Venerable Brethren, see that the faithful are put on guard against these deceitful methods. Communism is intrinsically evil, and therefore no one who desires to save Christian civilization from extinction should render it assistance in any enterprise whatever.' [1]

These words remain valid so long as communism itself treats the ideological sphere as an exception to the principle of coexistence. Khrushchev, as we have seen, regards it as a 'harmful' error to extend the principle into ideological matters, or to suppose that it implies any relaxation of the struggle against bourgeois opinions or the survivals of capitalism in the minds of men.[2] It is no secret that communism also ranks religion as one of these survivals. Coexistence between Christianity and communism would only become possible if the latter were prepared, not merely to permit freedom of worship within its dominions, but to allow full opportunity for religious expansion, and in particular the same liberty to proclaim the Christian message, not forgetting the press and the schools, as it claims for the propagation of Marxist materialism. But it is very much to be doubted if communism will ever concede this. For in so doing it would trespass against one of its most fundamental postulates, the demand for unity of theory and practice, and would thereby cease to be communism.

[1] Encyclical *Divini Redem toris*, in *Acta Apostolicae Sedis*, 31st March 1937, p. 96 (English version in *Church and State through the Centuries* (ed. Ehler and Morrall), London 1954, p. 570).

[2] *Cf.* above, p. 267.

Bibliography

THE following list of books and articles on the subject makes no
pretence at completeness; it is confined for the most part to works
which are either cited in the text or whose subject-matter is closely
related thereto. Thus the very extensive literature on the subject of
'historical materialism', *i.e.*, the philosophy of history and political
theory of the Soviet ideology, has been left out of account. Publications having only a marginal bearing on dialectical materialism, but
which it seemed advisable to mention for the reader's benefit, are
occasionally referred to in the footnotes alone. The principle followed is that on first mention of any work in a footnote full bibliographical details are given; for subsequent references the opening
words of the title are generally employed by way of abbreviation, but
these can readily be identified by turning to the alphabetical bibliography.* In addition, for the more important periodicals and a few
works quoted with especial frequency, the following abbreviations
are used:

Anti-Dühring = F. Engels: *Herr Eugen Dühring's Revolution in
Science.*

BSE = *Bol'shaya Sovetskaya Entsiklopediya* (Great Soviet
Encyclopaedia); 2nd edn., unless otherwise
indicated.

DHM = J. V. Stalin: *O dialekticheskom i istoricheskom
materializme*, in *Voprosy leninizma*, 11th edn., pp.
535–63; English Version: *On Dialectical and Historical Materialism*, in *Problems of Leninism*, pp.

* *Translator's Note*. Quotations in the text have been drawn, so far as
possible, from existing translations. For Russian works, page references
are given to the original, as well as to the English version. For German
works (and secondary sources generally) it has not normally been thought
necessary to retain the original pagings, more especially since the number
and variety of editions involved makes it difficult, in some cases, to specify
them without risk of confusion.

569–95; originally published in *Istoriya Vseso-yuznoy Kommunisticheskoy Partii* (*bol'shevikov*). *Kratky kurs*, pp. 99–127; English Version: *History of the Communist Party of the Soviet Union* (*Bolsheviks*), pp. 105–31; often published separately. Page references are to *Voprosy leninizma* and (in brackets) to both English versions.

DM   = G. F. Alexandrov: *Dialektichesky materializm* (Dialectical Materialism).

FT   = V. I. Lenin: *Filosofskie tetradi* (Philosophical Notebooks). Page references are to the Russian and German versions, or, on occasion, to the fragment included in *LSW*, XI.

FZ   = *Filosofskie Zapiski* (Philosophical Studies), issued by the Philosophical Institute of the Academy of Sciences of the U.S.S.R., I (1946), II (1948), III, IV (1950).

IAN = *Izvestiya Akademii Nauk SSSR. Seriya istorii i filosofii* (Bulletin of the Academy of Sciences of the U.S.S.R. History and Philosophy Series), I (1944)–VIII (1951).

KFS = *Kratky filosofsky slovar'* (Short Philosophical Dictionary).

KMSW = K. Marx: *Selected Works*, I–II.

LSW = V. I. Lenin: *Selected Works*, I–XII.

ME   = V. I. Lenin: *Materialism and Empirio-Criticism*; also in *LSW*, XI. Page references are to the Russian and both English versions.

MEGA = K. Marx–F. Engels: *Historisch-kritische Gesamtausgabe*.

MESW = K. Marx–F. Engels: *Selected Works*, I–II.

PSW = I. P. Pavlov: *Selected Works*.

VF   = *Voprosy filosofii* (Problems of Philosophy), issued by the Philosophical Institute of the Academy of Sciences of the U.S.S.R., 1947–57 (2 numbers per year in 1947, 3 from 1948 to 1950, and 6 annually from 1951 on).

ADLER, MAX: *Marx als Denker, Zum 25. Todesjahre von Karl Marx*, Berlin 1908.
Lehrbuch der materialistischen Geschichtsauffassung (*Soziologie des Marxismus*), I, Berlin 1930.
ALEXANDROV, A. D.: *O logike* (On Logic), *VF* 1951, 3, pp. 152–63.
Po povodu nekotorykh vzglyadov na teoriyu otnositel'nosti (On Certain Conceptions of Relativity Theory), *VF* 1953, 5, pp. 225–45.

564 Bibliography

ALEXANDROV, G. F.: *Istoriya zapadnoevropeyskoy filosofii* (History of Western European Philosophy), Moscow 1946.

Kosmopolitizm—ideologiya imperialisticheskoy burzhuazii (Cosmopolitanism—the Ideology of the Imperialist Bourgeoisie), *VF* 1948, 3, pp. 174–92.

Trudy J. V. Stalina o yazykoznanii i voprosy istoricheskogo materializma (J. V. Stalin's Writings on Linguistics and the Problems of Historical Materialism), Moscow 1952.

Dialekticheskymaterializm (Dialectical Materialism), issued by the Philosophical Institute of the Academy of Sciences of the U.S.S.R., under the editorship of G. F. Alexandrov, Moscow 1954; *cf.* the discussion on this book in *VF* 1954, 3, pp. 181–6; 4, pp. 202–9; 5, pp. 190–204.

ALEXEYEV, M. N.: *O dialekticheskoy prirode suzhdeniya* (On the Dialectical Nature of Judgement), *VF* 1956, 2, pp. 49–61.

AMBARZUMYAN, V. A.: *Evolyutsiya zvezd i astrofizika* (Stellar Evolution and Astrophysics), Erivan 1947.

Problema vozniknoveniya zvezd v svete novykh rabot sovetskikh astrofizikov (The Problem of the Origin of the Stars in the Light of Recent Work in Soviet Astrophysics), in *Vestnik Akademii Nauk SSSR*, 1953, 12, pp. 49–60.

ANDREYEV, I.: *Dialektichesky materializm o protsesse poznaniya* (Dialectical Materialism on the Knowing-Process), Moscow 1954.

ANTONOV, N. P.: *Dialektichesky materializm—teoreticheskaya osnova psikhologii* (Dialectical Materialism as the Theoretical Foundation of Psychology), *VF* 1953, 1, pp. 195–202.

ARKHIPTSEV, F. T.: *Leninskoe uchenie o materii—obrazets tvorcheskogo marxizma* (The Leninist Theory of Matter as an Example of Creative Marxism). *VF* 1951, 6, pp. 41–59.

ASHBY, E.: *Scientist in Russia*, London 1947.

ASMUS, V. F.: *Logika* (Logic), Moscow 1947.

Uchenie logiki o dokazatel'stve i oproverzhenii (The Logical Theory of Proof and Disproof), Moscow 1954.

ASRATYAN, E. A.: *Marxistsko–leninskaya teoriya otrazheniya i uchenie I. P. Pavlova o vysshey nervnoy deyatel'nosti* (The Marxist–Leninist Copy-Theory and the Teaching of I. P. Pavlov on Higher Nervous Activity), *VF* 1955, 5, pp. 31–42.

AXEL'ROD (ORTODOX) L.: *Filosofskie ocherki* (Philosophical Studies), St. Petersburg 1906.

Idealisticheskaya dialektika Hegelya i materialisticheskaya dialektika Marxa (The Idealist Dialectic of Hegel and the Materialist Dialectic of Marx), Moscow–Leningrad 1934.

BAAS, E.: *L'humanisme marxiste, Essai d'analyse critique*, Colmar-Paris n.d.

BAKRADZE, K. S.: *K voprosu o sootnoshenii logiki i dialektiki* (On the Problem of the Reciprocal Relation between Logic and Dialectics), *VF* 1950, 2, pp. 198–209.

Logika (Logic), Tiflis 1951.

Protiv nenauchnoy i nedobrozhelatel'noy kritiki (Against an Unscientific and Malevolent Criticism), *VF* 1956, 2, pp. 218–24.

BARABASHEV, N. P.: *Bor'ba s idealizmom v oblasti kosmogonicheskikh i kosmologicheskikh gipotez* (The Struggle against Idealism in the Field of Cosmogonical and Cosmological Hypotheses), Kharkov 1952.

BAUER, R. A.: *The New Man in Soviet Psychology*, Cambridge 1952.

BAZAROV, I. P.: *Za dialektiko-materialisticheskoe ponimanie i razvitie teorii otnositel'nosti* (Towards a Dialectical Materialist Conception and Development of Relativity Theory), *VF* 1952, 6, pp. 175–85.

BELOV, P. T.: *I. V. Michurin kak dialektichesky materialist* (I. V. Michurin as a Dialectical Materialist), *VF* 1948, 3, pp. 125–42.

BEL'TOV, N.: See Plekhanov.

BERDYAEV, N.: *Sub specie aeternitatis. Opyty filosofskie sotsial'nye i literaturnye* (Sub Specie Aeternitatis. Philosophical, Social and Literary Essays), St. Petersburg 1907.

Wahrheit und Lüge des Kommunismus, Lucerne 1934.

The Origin of Russian Communism, London 1937 (Reprinted 1948).

BLOKHINTSEV, D. I.: *Za leninskoe uchenie o dvizhenii* (In Defence of a Leninist Theory of Motion), *VF* 1952, 1, pp. 181–3.

Otvet akademiku V. A. Foku (Reply to Academician V. A. Fok), *VF* 1952, 6, pp. 171–5.

Kritika filosofskikh vozzreny tak nazyvaemoy 'Kopenhagenskoy shkoly' v fizike (Critique of the Philosophical Views of the So-Called 'Copenhagen School' in Physics), in *Filosofskie voprosy sovremennoy fiziki*, pp. 358–95.

Grundlagen der Quantenmechanik, Berlin 1953.

BLOKHINTSEV, D. I.–DRABKINA, S. I.: *Teoriya otnositel'nosti A. Einsteina* (Einstein's Theory of Relativity), Gostekhizdat 1940.

BOCHEŃSKI, I. M.: *Der bolschewistische Katechismus*, in *Schweizer Rundschau*, XLVIII (1948/9), 2, pp. 237–44.

Der sowjetrussische dialektische Materialismus (Diamat), Berne–Munich 1950.

BOGDANOV, A.: *Empiriomonizm. Stat'i po filosofii* (Empiriomonism. Essays in Philosophy), 3rd edn., Moscow 1908.

Tektologiya (Tectology), Berlin–Petrograd–Moscow 1922.

BOGRACHEV, Y. L.: *Voprosy kommunisticheskoy etiki v nauchnom nasledstve A. S. Makarenko* (Problems of Communist Ethics in the Scientific Remains of A. S. Makarenko), *VF* 1949, 1, pp. 244–64.

BOLDYREV, N. I.: *O moral'nom oblike sovetskoy molodezhi* (The Moral Face of Soviet Youth), Moscow 1954.

Bols'haya Sovetskaya Entsiklopediya (BSE) (Great Soviet Encyclopaedia), I–LXV, Moscow 1926 ff.; Supplementary Vol.: *Soyuz Sovetskikh Sotsialisticheskikh Respublik* (The Union of Socialist Soviet Republics), Moscow 1948; 2nd edn. (so far published) I–XLVI Moscow 1949 ff.

BRESLER, S. E.: *K probleme sinteza belka* (On the Problem of Protein-Synthesis), *VF* 1951, 3, pp. 82–94.

BRIEM, E.: *Kommunismus und Religion in der Sowjetunion. Ein Ideenkampf*, Basle 1948.

BUCHHOLZ, A.: *Ideologie und Forschung in der sowjetischen Naturwissenschaft*, Stuttgart 1953.

BUKHARIN, N.: *Teoriya istoricheskogo materializma*, Moscow 1921; translated as *Historical Materialism. A System of Sociology*, London 1926.

BUKHARIN, N.–PREOBRAZHENSKY, E.: *Das ABC des Kommunismus. Populäre Erläuterung des Programmes der Kommunistischen Partei Russlands (Bolshewiki)*, Moscow 1921.

BULGAKOV, S.: *Religiya chelovekobozhestva u L. Feuerbacha* (The Religion of Man-God in L. Feuerbach), Moscow 1906.

BYKHOVSKY, B.: *Ocherk filosofii dialekticheskogo materializma* (Outlines of the Philosophy of Dialectical Materialism), Moscow–Leningrad 1930.

CALVEZ, J.-Y.: *La pensée de Karl Marx*, Paris 1956.

CATHREIN, V.: *Der Sozialismus*, 16th edn., Freiburg-i-B. 1923.

CHAMBRE, H.: *Le Marxisme en Union Soviétique*, Paris 1955.

CHERKESOV, V. I.: *O logike i marxistskoy dialektike* (On Logic and Marxist Dialectic), *VF* 1950, 2, pp. 209–22.
Nekotorye voprosy teorii ponyatiya v dialekticheskoy logike (Some Problems of the Theory of the Concept in Dialectical Logic), *VF* 1956, 2, pp. 62–76.

CHERNOV, F.: *Burzhuazny kosmopolitizm i ego reaktsionnaya rol'* (Bourgeois Cosmopolitanism and its Reactionary Rôle), *Bol'-shevik* 1949, 5, pp. 30–41.

CHERNYSHEVSKY, N. G.: *Izbrannye filosofskie sochineniya* (Selected Philosophical Essays), Moscow 1951; English version, Moscow–London 1953.

CHESNOKOV, D.: *Voprosy marxistskoy filosofii v trude J. V. Stalina 'Ekonomicheskie problemy sotsializma v SSSR'* (Problems of Marxist Philosophy in J. V. Stalin's *Economic Problems of Socialism in the U.S.S.R.*), *Kommunist* 1952, No. 21, pp. 24–48.

CHIZHEVSKY, D.: *Filosofskiya iskaniya v Sovetskoy Rossii* (Philosophical Research in Soviet Russia), in *Sovremennyya Zapiski* XXXVII (1928), pp. 501–24.

Hegel v Rossii (Hegel in Russia), Paris 1929.

Hegel bei den Slaven, Reichenberg 1934.

Continuity and Change in Russian and Soviet Thought, ed. with Introduction by Ernest J. Simmons, Cambridge (Mass.) 1955.

CONZE, E.: *Der Satz vom Widerspruch. Zur Theorie des dialektischen Materialismus*, Hamburg 1931.

CORETH, E.: *Hegel und der dialektische Materialismus*, in *Scholastik*, 1952, pp. 55–67.

CORNU, A.: *Karl Marx. L'homme et l'œuvre. De l'hégélianisme au matérialisme historique (1818–1845)*, Paris 1934.

Karl Marx und Friedrich Engels. Leben und Werk (Vol. I, 1818–44), Berlin 1954.

DAHM, H.: *Renaissance der formalen Logik*, in *Ost-Probleme*, 9, No. 8 (22nd Feb. 1957), pp. 254–67.

DAL, J.: *De Marx à Stalin. Les conceptions philosophiques des soviets*, 1937.

DALLIN, D. J.–NICOLAEVSKY, B. I.: *Forced Labour in Soviet Russia*, London 1948.

DANZAS, J.: *Sous le drapeau du marxisme*, in *La Vie Intellectuelle* 1936, pp. 422–45.

DEBORIN, A. M.: *Vvedenie v filosofiyu dialekticheskogo materializma* (Introduction to the Philosophy of Dialectical Materialism), Petrograd 1916.

Lenin kak myslitel' (Lenin the Thinker), Moscow 1924.

Dialektika i estestvoznanie (Dialectics and Natural Science), Moscow–Leningrad 1930.

DEDOV, K. M.: *K voprosu ob otnosheniyakh mezhdu psikhologiey i fiziologiey vysshey nervnoy deyatel'nosti* (On the Problem of the Relation between Psychology and the Physiology of Higher Nervous Activity), *VF* 1954, 1, pp. 216–18.

DEUTSCHER, I.: *Stalin. A Political Biography*, London–New York–Toronto 1949.

Dialektichesky materializm. Marx, Engels, Lenin, Stalin (Dialectical Materialism. Marx, Engels, Lenin, Stalin), Moscow 1933.

Dialektichesky materializm (Dialectical Materialism), in *BSE* XXII (1935), cols. 45–235; compiled, under the editorship of M. Mitin and V. Ral'tsevich, by G. Adamyan, M. Konstantinov, S. Lapshin, M. Mitin, I. Razumovsky, V. Ral'tsevich, A. Saradzhev, A. Shcheglov.

Diskussionsreden auf dem XX Parteitag der KPdSU (14–25 Feb. 1956), Berlin 1956.

DOBROKHVALOV, V. P.: *Filosofskie i estestvennonauchnye predposylki ucheniya I. V. Michurina* (The Philosophical and Scientific Presuppositions of the Teaching of I. V. Michurin), Moscow 1954.

Documents sur l'organisation de la recherche scientifique en URSS, in *La documentation française*. *Notes et études documentaires*, Paris 1952.

DOSEV, P. (T. PAVLOV): *Teoriya otrazheniya. Ocherki po teorii poznaniya dialekticheskogo materializma* (The Copy Theory. Studies in the Epistemology of Dialectical Materialism), Moscow–Leningrad 1936.

DREWS, W.: *Materialismus militans*, in *Theologische Blätter* 1932, pp. 269 ff.

DVORYANKIN, F.: *Pobeda michurinskoy biologicheskoy nauki* (The Triumph of Michurinist Biological Science), *Bol'shevik* 1948, 16, pp. 30–9.

DZHANDIL'DIN, N.: *Ob osobennostyakh postupatel'nogo razvitiya sotsialisticheskogo obshchestva* (On the Distinguishing Features of the Upward Development of Socialist Society), *VF* 1950, I, pp. 58–76.

EASTMAN, M.: *The Last Stand of Dialectical Materialism*, New York 1934.

Edinstvo teorii i praktiki (Unity of Theory and Practice), *VF* 1954, 2, pp. 3–14.

EFIMOV, S. F.: *Konkretnoe ponyatie i chuvstvennoe znanie* (The Concrete Concept and Sensory Knowledge), *VF* 1956, 3, pp. 59–73.

EIGENSON, M. S.: *K voprosu o kosmogonii* (On the Problem of Cosmonogy), In *Circular No. 30, Ministerstvo Vysshego Obrazovaniya SSSR, L'vovsky Gosudarstvenny Universitet Astronomicheskaya Observatoriya*, 1955, pp. 1–12.

EL'MEYEV, V. Y.–KAZAKOV, A. P.: *Zakon otritsaniya otritsaniya i preemstvennost' v razvitii* (The Law of the Negation of the Negation and the Continuity of Development), *Vestnik Leningradskogo Universiteta*, 1956, 23, pp. 77–84.

EMME, A. M.: *Neskol'ko zamechaniy po voprosu o protsesse vozniknoveniya zhizni* (Remarks on the Problem of the Mode of Origin of Life), *VF* 1956, I, pp. 155–8.

ENGELS, F.: *Ludwig Feuerbach and the End of Classical German Philosophy* (Stuttgart 1888), in *MESW*, II, Moscow–London 1950/51.

Socialism: Utopian and Scientific (London 1892), in *MESW*, II, Moscow–London 1950/51.

Herr Eugen Dühring's Revolution in Science (*Anti-Dühring*) (3rd edn., Stuttgart 1894), London 1934, Moscow–London 1955.

Dialectics of Nature (Moscow 1925), London 1940 (based on 1935 edn.); New Revised edn. Moscow–London 1954/55.

EPSTEIN, P. S.: *The Diamat and Modern Science*, in *Bulletin of the Atomic Scientists*, vol. 8, 1952, 6, pp. 190–4.

ERMILOV, A. P.–BELOV, M. V.: *K itogam koordinatsionnogo sove-*

shchaniya po filosofskim problemam (On the Results of the Co-ordinating Session on Philosophical Problems), *VF* 1955, 2, pp. 228-34.

Estestvoznanie i religiya: (Science and Religion), collective volume issued by the Philosophical Institute of the Academy of Sciences of the U.S.S.R. under the editorship of V. P. Dobrokhvalov, G. V. Platonov and E. V. Shorokhova, Moscow 1956.

ETCHEVERY, A.: *La philosophie du communisme* (Archives de Philosophie 15), Paris 1939.

FEDOROV, G.: *Bor'ba mezhdu novym i starym v usloviyakh sovetskogo obshchestva* (The Struggle between New and Old under the Conditions of Life in Soviet Society), *Bol'shevik* 1947, 19, pp. 36-49.

FEDOSEYEV, P.: *O svyazi filosofii i politiki* (On the Connection between Philosophy and Politics), *Kommunist* 1956, 3, pp. 33-48.

FESENKOV, V. G.: *O kosmogonicheskoy gipoteze akademika O. Y. Schmidta i o sovremennom sostoyanii kosmogonicheskoy problemy* (On the Cosmogonical Hypothesis of 'Academician O. Y. Schmidt and the Present State of the Cosmogonical Problem), *VF* 1951, 4, pp. 134-47.

FETSCHER, I.: *Stalin. Über dialektischen und historischen Materialismus.* Complete text and critical commentary by I. F., Frankfurt-a-M.-Berlin-Bonn 1956.

Von Marx zur Sowjetideologie, Frankfurt-a-M.-Berlin-Bonn 1957.

FEUERBACH, L.: *Sämtliche Werke,* ed. W. Boli and F. Jodl, I-X, Stuttgart 1903-11. See also *The Essence of Christianity* (Tr. M. Evans), London 1881.

FILIPOV, A.: *Marxizm i materializm* (Marxism and Materialism), in *Vestnik instituta po izucheniyu istorii i kul'tury SSSR*, Munich 1951, 1, pp. 7-29. (See Philipov.)

Filosofskie voprosy sovremennoy biologii (Philosophical Problems of Modern Biology), issued by the Philosophical Institute of the Academy of Sciences of the U.S.S.R., under the editorship of I. I. Novinsky and G. V. Platonov, Moscow 1951.

Filosofskie voprosy sovremennoy fiziki (Philosophical Problems of Modern Physics), issued as above, under the editorship of A. A. Maximov, I. V. Kuznetsov, Y. P. Terletsky and N. F. Ovchinnikov, Moscow 1952.

Filosofskiya techeniya russkago marxizma (Philosophical Tendencies in Russian Marxism), in *Vestnik Evropy* XLIV (1909), 3, pp. 355-63.

FISCHER, L.: *The Life and Death of Stalin*, London 1953.

FOK, V. A.: *O tak nazyvaemykh ansamblyakh v kvantovoy mekhanike* (On so-called 'Totalities' in Quantum Mechanics), *VF* 1952, 4, pp. 170-4.

Protiv nevezhestvennoy kritiki sovremennykh fizicheskikh teoriy (Against Ignorant Criticism of Modern Physical Theories), *VF* 1953, 1, pp. 168–74.

FOMINA, V. A.: *Rol' G. V. Plekhanova v rasprostranenii marxistskoy filosofii v Rossii* (The Rôle of G. V. Plekhanov in the Diffusion of Marxist Philosophy in Russia), in the collective *Iz istorii russkoy filosofii*, ed. I. Y. Shchipanov, Moscow 1951.

Filosofskie vzglyady G. V. Plekhanova (The Philosophical Opinions of G. V. Plekhanov), Moscow 1955.

FRENKEL', Y. I.: *Statisticheskaya fizika* (Statistical Physics), Moscow–Leningrad 1948.

GAK, G. M.: *Voprosy etiki v marxistsko–leninskom mirovozzrenii* (Problems of Ethics in the Marxist–Leninist World-view), *Bol'-shevik* 1948, 9, pp. 25–40.

GAK, G. M.–MAKAROVSKY, A.: *Zhurnal 'Voprosy filosofii'* (The Journal *Problems of Philosophy*), *Bol'shevik* 1947, 15, pp. 50–8.

GAK, G. M.: See Vol'fson-Gak.

GALKINA–FEDORUK, E. M.: *Slovo i ponyatie* (Word and Concept), Moscow 1956.

GARAUDY, R.: *La liberté*, Paris 1955.

GARDEIL, H. D.: *Le matérialisme dialectique*, in *La Vie Intellectuelle*, LV (1938), pp. 406–20.

GEORGIEV, F. I.: *Problema chuvstvennogo i ratsional'nogo v poznanii* (The Problem of the Sensory and the Rational in Knowledge), *VF* 1955, 1, pp. 28–41.

GERMAN, L. I.: *Filosofiya voinstvuyushchego katolitsizma* (The Philosophy of Militant Catholicism), *VF* 1948, 1, pp. 261–77.

GIUSTI, W.: *Due secoli di pensiero politico russo. Le correnti 'progressiste'*, Florence 1943.

Il pensiero di Trotzky, Florence 1949.

GLEZERMAN, G. E.: *Klass i natsiya* (Class and Nation), *VF* 1950, 1, pp. 259–75.

Marxizm-leninizm o bazise i nadstroyke (Marxist-Leninism on Basis and Superstructure), *Bol'shevik* 1950, 18, pp. 41–56; German version in *Ost-Probleme* II (1950), 51/52, pp. 1615–25.

GOLINEVICH, P. N.: *Perenaselenie i bor'ba za sushchestvovanie* (Overpopulation and the Struggle for Existence), *VF* 1956, 4, pp. 183–92.

GORSKY, D. P.: *O kategoriyakh materialisticheskoy dialektiki* (On the Categories of the Materialist Dialectic), *VF* 1955, 3, pp. 17–31.

Logika (Logic), Moscow 1955.

GORSKY, D. P.–TAVANETS, P. V.: *Logika* (Logic), Moscow 1956.

GRADOBOYEV, N.: *Stalin dopolnyaet marxizm* (Stalin Augments Marxism), in *Vestnik instituta po izucheniyu istorii i kul'tury SSSR*, 1951, No. 1, pp. 38–50.

G. F. Alexandrovs dialektische Laufbahn, in *Ost-Probleme* III (1951), 28, pp. 855–8.

Stalins gesammelte Werke, ibid., 32, pp. 982–4.

GRÉGOIRE, F.: *Aux sources de la pensée de Marx. Hegel, Feuerbach*, Louvain–Paris 1947.

GRUDININ, I. A.: *Dialektichesky materializm o vozmozhnosti i deystvitel'nosti* (Dialectical Materialism on Possibility and Actuality), Moscow 1955.

GURIEV, N. I.: *Sovetskaya kosmologiya na sluzhbe offitsial' nogo mirovozzreniya* (Soviet Cosmology in the Service of the Official Ideology), in *Vestnik instituta po izucheniyu istorii i kul'tury SSSR*, No. 1, Munich 1951, pp. 30–7.

HAAS, A.: *Gelenkte Naturforschung*, in *Stimmen der Zeit* LXXIV (1949), pp. 383–8.

HARPER, J.: *Lenin als Philosoph* (Bibliothek der Rätekorrespondenz I), 1936.

HARTMAN, N.: *Die Philosophie des deutschen Idealismus, II. Hegel*, Berlin–Leipzig 1929.

HARTWIG, T.: *Zur Frage des dialektischen Materialismus*, in *Dialectica* 1948.

HEGEL, G. W. F.: *Science of Logic* (Tr. Johnston and Struthers), London 1929.

The Logic of Hegel (Tr. Wallace) = Part I of the *Encyclopaedia of the Philosophical Sciences*, 2nd edn., Oxford 1892.

Philosophy of Right (Tr. Knox), Oxford 1945.

HOMMES, J.: *Der technische Eros. Das Wesen der materialistischen Geschichtsauffassung*, Freiburg-i-B. 1955.

HUBATKA, C.: *Die materialistische Geschichtsauffassung im Lichte der Scholastik*. Diss. Pont. Univ. Gregorianae, Rome 1940.

HUDSON, P. S.–RICHENS, R. H.: *The New Genetics in the Soviet Union*, Cambridge 1946.

HUNT, R. N. C.: *Theory and Practice of Communism*, 5th edn., London 1957.

Informatsionnoe soveshchanie predstaviteley nekotorykh kompartiy v Polshe v kontse sentyabrya 1947 g. (Briefing Conference for Delegates from a Number of Communist Parties, held in Poland, End of September 1947), Moscow 1948.

IOFFE, A. F.: *Osnovnye predstavleniya sovremennoy fiziki* (Fundamental Ideas of Modern Physics), Gostekhizdat 1949.

IOVCHUK, M T.: *Leninizm i peredovaya russkaya kul'tura XIX veka* (Leninism and the Progressive Russian Culture of the 19th Century), Moscow 1946.

O nekotorykh problemakh nauchnogo issledovaniya istorii russkoy materialisticheskoy filosofii (On some Problems of Scientific Research into the History of Russian Materialist Philosophy), *IAN*, IV (1947), 4, pp. 305–23.

O samostoyatel'nosti russkoy materialisticheskoy filosofii, ee tradit-siyakh i ikh preemstvennosti (On the Independence of Russian Materialist Philosophy, its Traditions and their Continuity), *VF* 1948, 3, pp. 193–221.

Rol' sotsialisticheskoy ideologii v bor'be s perezhitkami kapitalizma (The Rôle of Socialist Ideology in the Struggle with the Survivals of Capitalism), *VF* 1955, 1, pp. 3–16.

ISAEV, S. I.: *I. V. Michurin—veliky estestvoispytatel', preobrazovatel' prirody* (I. V. Michurin—A Great Student and Transformer of Nature), Moscow 1955.

Istoriya Vsesoyuznoy Kommunisticheskoy Partii (bol'shevikov). Kratky kurs. Pod redaktsiey komissii TsK VKP(b). Odobren TsK VKP(b) 1938 god., Moscow 1945. English version: *History of the Communist Party of the Soviet Union (Bolsheviks). Short Course. Edited by a Commission of the Central Committee of the C.P.S.U.(B)*, London 1939. The Italian version assigns authorship to: Stalin, Kalinin, Molotov, Voroshilov, Kaganovich, Mikoyan, Zhdanov and Beria, 'under the Editorship of Stalin'.

ISVOLSKY, H.: *La vie de Bakounine*, Paris 1930.

IVANENKO, D. D.: *Elementarnye chastitsy i ikh vzaimodeystviya* (Elementary Particles and their Interactions), in *Uspekhi khimii*, XVII, 5, 1948.

IVANOV-RAZUMNIK: *Istoriya russkoy obshchestvennoy mysli* (History of Russian Social Thought), 2 vols., St. Petersburg 1911.

Iz istorii filosofii XIX veka. Sbornik statey pod redaktsiey i s predis-loviem I. K. Luppola (From the History of Philosophy in the 19th Century. A Collection of Essays, Edited with a Preface by I. K. Luppol), Moscow 1933.

JAKOVENKO, B.: *Filosofiya bol'shevizma* (The Philosophy of Bolshevism), Berlin 1921.

Dějiny ruské filosofie (History of Russian Philosophy), Prague 1939.

Josif Vissarionovich Stalin. Kratkaya biografiya, Moscow 1945; English Version: *Stalin; A Short Biography*, London 1943.

KAFTANOV, S. V.: *Vsemerno uluchshat' prepodavanie osnov marxizma-leninizma v vysshey shkole* (An All-out Drive to Improve the Basic Teaching of Marxist-Leninism in Higher Education), *Bol'shevik* 1949, 12, pp. 22–33.

KAGANOV, V. M.: *O svyazi i vzaimnoy obuslovlennosti yavleniy v prirode* (On the Interconnection and Interdetermination of Phenomena in Nature), *VF* 1949, 1, pp. 128–46.

KALININ, M. I.: *On Communist Education*, Moscow–London 1951.

KAMENSKY, Z. A.: *K voprosu o traditsii v russkoy materialisticheskoy filosofii XVIII–XIX vekov* (On the Problem of Tradition in Russian Philosophy of the 18th and 19th Centuries), *VF* 1947, 1; discussion thereon in *VF* 1948, 1, pp. 184–202.

KAMMARI, M. D.: *Printsip bol'shevistskoy partiynosti v otsenke isto-richeskikh deyateley* (The Principle of Bolshevist Partisanship in the Judgement of Historical Personages), *VF* 1947, 2.

Stalin o marxizme v yazykoznanii (Stalin on Marxism in Linguistics), *VF* 1950, 2, pp. 9–30.

O novom vydayushchemsya vklade J. V. Stalina v marxistsko-leninskuyu filosofiyu (On J. V. Stalin's Latest Outstanding Contribution to Marxist–Leninist Philosophy), *VF* 1952, 6, pp. 18–40.

KAPUSTINSKY, A. F.: *Energiya atoma* (The Energy of the Atom), Goskul'tprosvetizdat 1947.

KARISCH, R.: *Der Christ und der dialektische Materialismus*, 2nd edn., Berlin 1956.

KARPUSHIN, V. A.: *Razrabotka K. Marxom materialisticheskoy dialektiki v 'Ekonomichesko-filosofskikh rukopis'yakh' 1844 goda* (Karl Marx's Working-Out of the Materialist Dialectic in the *Economico-Philosophical Manuscripts* of the Year 1844), *VF* 1955, 3, pp. 104–14.

Kategorii dialekticheskogo materializma (The Categories of Dialectical Materialism), Uchenye Zapiski Yaroslavskogo gosudarstvennogo pedagogicheskogo instituta im. K. D. Ushinskogo, vyp. XVI (XXVL), edited by G. M. Shtraks, N. V. Pilipenko and N. V. Medvedev, Yaroslavl' 1954.

KAZAKEVICH, T. A.–ABOLENTSEVA, A. G.: *Nekotorye voprosy zakona otritsaniya otritsaniya* (Some Problems concerning the Law of the Negation of the Negation), *Vestnik Leningradskogo Universiteta*, 1956, 23, pp. 67–76.

KDYRNIYAZOV, G. N.: *O khimicheskikh i biologicheskikh protsessakh organizma* (On Chemical and Biological Processes in the Organism), *VF* 1951, 1, pp. 83–97.

KEBURIYA, D. M.: *K voprosu o konkretnosti ponyatiya* (On the Problem of the Concreteness of the Concept), *VF* 1957, 2, pp. 28–38.

KEDROV, B. M.: *O kolichestvennykh i kachestvennykh izmeneniyakh v prirode* (On Quantitative and Qualitative Changes in Nature), Moscow 1946.

Engels i estestvoznanie (Engels and Natural Science), Moscow n.d.

Ponyatie 'khimichesky element' i ego logichesky analiz (The Concept of 'Chemical Element' and its Logical Analysis), *FZ* 1 (1946), pp. 118–78.

O znachenii leninskikh 'Filosofskikh tetradey' dlya estestvoznaniya (On the Significance of Lenin's *Philosophical Notebooks* for Natural Science), in *Vestnik Akademii Nauk SSSR* 1947, 1, pp. 5–22.

Leninsky vzglyad na elektron i sovremennaya fizika (Lenin's View of the Electron and Modern Physics), *Bol'shevik* 1948, 2, pp. 44–61.

Ob otnoshenii logiki k marxizmu (On the Relation of Logic to Marxism), *VF* 1951, 4, pp. 212–27.

Protiv idealizma i mekhanitsizma v organicheskoy khimii (Against Idealism and Mechanicism in Organic Chemistry), *Bol'shevik* 1951, 19, pp. 13–24.

Protiv 'fizicheskogo' idealizma v khimicheskoy nauke (Against 'Physical' Idealism in Chemistry), in *Filosofskie voprosy sovremennoy fiziki*, pp. 539–75.

O soderzhanii i obyeme izmenyayushchegosya ponyatiya (On the Content and Scope of a Changing Concept), *FZ* 6 (1953), pp. 188–254.

Postepennost' kak odna iz form perekhoda ot starogo kachestva k novomu kachestvu (Gradualness as a Form of Transition from an Old Quality to a New), *VF* 1954, 2, pp. 50–70.

Ob otnoshenii marxizma k darvinizmu v svyazi s problemoy vidoobrazovaniya (On the Relation between Marxism and Darwinism in regard to the Problem of Species-Formation), *VF* 1955, 6, pp. 149–66.

O klassifikatsii nauk (On the Classification of the Sciences), *VF* 1955, 2, pp. 49–68.

KEDROV, B. M.–GURGENIDZE, G.: *Za glubokuyu razrabotku leninskogo filosofskogo nasledstva* (For a Thorough Study of Lenin's Philosophical Remains), *Kommunist* 1955, 14, pp. 45–56.

KHASKHACHIKH, F. I.: *O poznavaemosti mira* (On the Knowability of the World), 2nd edn., Moscow 1950.

Materiya i soznanie (Matter and Consciousness), Moscow, 1951.

KHROMOV, N. A.: *O nauchnom ponimanii psikhicheskoy, ili vysshey nervnoy deyatel'nosti* (On a Scientific Understanding of Psychical or Higher Nervous Activity), *VF* 1953, 4, pp. 216–18.

KHRUSHCHEV, N. S.: *Report of the Central Committee to the XXth Party Congress*, in *Pravda*, 15th Feb. 1956; English version in *Soviet News* booklet No. 4.

K itogam diskussii po teorii otnositel'nosti (On the Outcome of the Discussion on Relativity Theory), *VF* 1955, 1, pp. 134–8.

K itogam obsuzhdeniya voprosov logiki (On the Outcome of the Discussion on Problems of Logic), *VF* 1951, 6, pp. 143–9.

KLINE, G. L.: *Recent Soviet Philosophy*, in *Annals of the American Academy of Political and Social Science*, Jan. 1956, pp. 126–38.

A Philosophical Critique of Soviet Marxism, in *The Review of Metaphysics*, IX, 1, Sept. 1955.

KOLBANOVSKY, V. N.: *Za marxistskoe osveshchenie voprosov psikhologii* (Towards a Marxist Solution of the Problems of Psychology), *Bol'shevik* 1947, 17, pp. 50–6.

Ukreplenie sem'i v sotsialisticheskom obshchestve (The Establishment of the Family in Socialist Society), *Bol'shevik* 1949, 15, pp. 53–63.

Kommunisticheskaya moral' i byt (The Communist Morality and Way of Life), Moscow 1955.

KOLLONTAI, A.: *Novaya moral' i rabochy klass* (The New Morality and the Working Class), Moscow 1919.

KOLOGRIWOF, I.: *Die Metaphysik des Bolschewismus*, Salzburg 1934.

KONDAKOV, N. I.: *Logika* (Logic), Moscow 1954.

KONIKOVA, A. S.–KRITZMAN, M. G.: *Zhivoy belok v svete sovremennykh issledovaniy biokhimii* (Living Protein in the Light of Modern Research in Biochemistry), *VF* 1953, 1, pp. 143–50.

K voprosu o nachal'noy forme proyavleniya zhizni (On the Problem of the Initial Form of the Emergence of Life), *VF* 1954, 1, pp. 210–16.

KONSTANTINOV, F. V.: *Istorichesky materializm* (Historical Materialism), issued by the Philosophical Institute of the Academy of Sciences of the U.S.S.R., under the editorship of F. V. K., Moscow 1951; 2nd edn., Moscow 1954; *cf.* the discussion on this 2nd edn. in *VF* 1955, 2, pp. 213–28.

KOPNIN, P. V.: *Formy myshleniya i ikh vzaimosvyaz'* (The Forms of Thought and their Reciprocal Interconnection), *VF* 1956, 3, pp. 44–58.

KORSCH, K.: *Marxismus and Philosophie*, 2nd edn. 1930.

KRAVKOV, S. V.: *Ocherk obshchey psikhofiziologii organov chuvstv* (Outline of a General Psychophysiology of the Sense Organs), issued by the Academy of Sciences of the U.S.S.R., 1946.

KRAVTSEV, T. P.: *Evolyutsiya ucheniya ob energii* (The Development of the Theory of Energy), in *Uspekhi fizicheskikh nauk*, Vol. 36/3 (1948).

(*P. A.*) *Kropotkin i ego uchenie. Pod redaktsiey i s primechaniyami G. P. Maximova* (P. A. Kropotkin and his Teaching. Edited and annotated by G. P. Maximov), Chicago 1931.

KUCHARZEWSKI, J.: *The Origins of Modern Russia*, New York 1948.

KULTSCHYTSKY, A. VON: *Die marxistisch-sowjetische Konzeption des Menschen im Lichte der westlichen Psychologie*, Munich, Institut zur Erforschung der UdSSR, 1956.

KURSANOV, G. A.: *Dialektichesky materializm o prostranstve i vremeni* (Dialectical Materialism on Space and Time), *VF* 1950, 3, pp. 173–91.

K kriticheskoy otsenke teorii otnositel'nosti (Critical Examination of the Theory of Relativity), *VF* 1952, 1, pp 169–74.

KUZNETSOV, I. V.: *Protiv putanitsy v voprose o ponyatii materii* (Against Confusion over the Concept of Matter), *IAN* IX (1952), 3, pp. 251–72.

Sovetskaya fizika i dialektichesky materializm (Soviet Physics and Dialectical Materialism), in *Filosofskie voprosy sovremennoy fiziki*, pp. 31–86.

LABRIOLA, A.: *La concezione materialistica della storia* (1895), 2nd edn., Rome 1945; English version, Chicago 1908.
La filosofia del comunismo (= *Doctor Communis, Acta et Commentationes Pontificiae Academiae Romanae S. Thomas Aquinatis*, II/III, Maii–Decembris 1949), Turin.

LANGE, M. G.: *Marxismus, Leninismus, Stalinismus. Zur Kritik des dialektischen Materialismus*, Stuttgart 1955.

LAURENTIUS: *Kropotkins Morallehre und deren Beziehungen zu Nietzsche*, Dresden–Leipzig 1896.

LAUTH, R.: *Einflüsse slawischer Denker auf die Genese der Marx'schen Weltanschauung*, in *Orientalia Christiana Periodica*, XXI, Nos. 3–4, Rome 1955, pp. 399–450.

LAVAUD, B.: *La philosophie du bolchévisme*, 2nd edn., Liège 1935.

LAZITCH, B.: *Lénine et la III Internationale*, Neuchâtel 1951.

LEFEBVRE, H.: *A la lumière du matérialisme dialectique. I. Logique formelle, logique dialectique*, Paris 1947.
Le matérialisme dialectique, Paris 1949.
Le marxisme, Paris 1956.

LEGAULT, H.: *Le marxisme et la critique de la religion*, Dissertation, Quebec 1944.

LENIN, V. I.: *Sochineniya* (Complete Works), 4th edn., I–XXXV, Moscow 1941/51; vols. IV, XIII, XVIII, XIX, XX, XXI, XXIII available in English. See also: *Selected Works* (12 vols.), Moscow–London 1936–9; *The Essentials of Lenin* (2 vols.), Moscow–London 1947; *Selections from Lenin* (2 vols.), London 1928; and pamphlets in the 'Little Lenin Library'.
Filosofskie tetradi (Philosophical Notebooks), Moscow 1947; German Version: *Aus dem philosophischen Nachlass. Exzerpte und Randglossen*, Berlin 1949.
Materialism and Empirio-Criticism. Critical Comments on a Reactionary Philosophy (= vol. XIV of the *Collected Works* and vol. XI of *LSW*), Moscow–London 1952.
Lenin, Vladimir Ilyich. A Short Biography, Moscow 1956.

LEONOV, M. A.: *Marxistsko-leninskaya nauka—osnova nauchnogo predvideniya* (Marxist–Leninist Science—the Foundation of Scientific Prediction), *Bol'shevik* 1946, 1, pp. 26 ff.
Marxistsky dialekticheskymetod (The Marxist Dialectical Method), Moscow 1947.
Ocherk dialekticheskogo materializma (Outline of Dialectical Materialism), Moscow 1948.
Kritika i samokritika—zakonomernost' razvitiya sovetskogo obsh-

chestva (Criticism and Self-Criticism—a Law of the Development of Soviet Society), *Bol'shevik* 1948, 5, pp. 24–36.

Stalinsky etap v razvitii dialekticheskogo materializma (The Stalinist Stage in the Development of Dialectical Materialism), *IAN*, VI (1949), 6, pp. 501–20.

Klassiki marxizma-leninizma o predmete dialekticheskogo materializma (The Classics of Marxist-Leninism on the Content of Dialectical Materialism), *IAN*, VI (1949), 4, pp. 297–312.

LEONTIEV, A. N.: *Ocherk razvitiya psikhiki* (Outline of the Development of the Psyche), MS copy, Moscow 1947.

LEPESHINSKAYA, O. B.: *Razvitie zhiznennykh protsessov v dokletochnom periode* (The Development of Living Processes in the Period before the Formation of Cells), *IAN SSSR. Seriya biologicheskaya*, 1950, 5, pp. 85–101.

Proiskhozhdenie kletok iz zhivogo veshchestva i rol' zhivogo veshchestva v organizme (The Origin of Cells from Living Substance . . .), 2nd edn., Moscow 1950.

Tvorcheskoe znachenie trudov Marxa, Engelsa, Lenina, Stalina dlya razvitiya estestvoznaniya (The Creative Significance of the Works of Marx, Engels, Lenin and Stalin in the Development of Science), *VF* 1953, 2, pp. 120–38; (English versions of the above in *The Origin of Cells from Living Substance*, Moscow 1954.

Le '*Testament de Lénine*' in *Est et Ouest* (B.E.I.P.I.), vol. 8, No. 151 (1–15 May 1956), pp. 14–16.

LEVITOV, N. D.: *Voprosy psikhologii kharaktera* (Problems of Character-Psychology), Moscow 1952.

LIEBER, H. J.: *Die Philosophie des Bolschewismus in den Grundzügen ihrer Entwicklung*, Frankfurt-a-M.–Berlin–Bonn 1957.

LOMBARDI, R.: *La dottrina marxista*, Rome 1947.

LOSSKY, N. O.: *Dialektichesky materializm v SSSR* (Dialectical Materialism in the U.S.S.R.), Paris 1934.

Filosofiya i psikhologiya v SSSR (Philosophy and Psychology in the U.S.S.R.), in *Sovremennyya Zapiski* LXIX (1939), pp. 364–73.

LÖWITH, K.: *Von Hegel bis Nietzsche*, Zürich–New York 1941, 2nd edn., Stuttgart 1950.

LUPPOL, I.: *Lenin und die Philosophie. Zur Frage des Verhältnisses der Philosophie zur Revolution*, translated from the Russian, Berlin 1929.

LYSENKO, T. D.: *O polozhenii v biologicheskoy nauke* (The Situation in Biological Science), in *Pravda*, 4th and 5th Aug. 1948; see also under *O polozhenii* . . .

Agrobiologiya, Moscow 1948; English version; *Agrobiology*, Moscow 1954.

Malaya Sovetskaya Entsiklopediya (Little Soviet Encyclopaedia), I–X, Moscow 1928–32.

578   *Bibliography*

MALININ, V.–TARAKANOV, N.–SHCHIPANOV, I.: *Protiv sovremennykh burzhuaznykh fal'sifikatorov istorii russkoy filosofii* (Against the Modern Bourgeois Falsifiers of the History of Russian Philosophy), *Kommunist* 1955, 10, pp. 62–76.

MARCK, S.: *Die Dialektik in der Philosophie der Gegenwart*, I–II, Tübingen 1929–31.

Lenin als Erkenntnistheoretiker, in *Der Kampf* 1928, 10, Vienna.

MARKOV, M. A.: *O prirode fizicheskogo znaniya* (On the Nature of Physical Knowledge), *VF* 1947, 2; Discussion thereon in *VF* 1948, 1, pp. 203–32; 3, pp. 222–35.

MARX, K.: *Das Kapital. Kritik der politischen Ökonomie*, I–III, Hamburg 1890–4; English version of Vol. I: *Capital* (Tr. E. and C. Paul), I–II, London 1930.

Zur Kritik der politischen Ökonomie, Stuttgart 1897; English (Preface only) in *MESW* I.

Die Frühschriften (ed. S. Landshut), Stuttgart 1953; English (in part) in *Selected Essays* (by K. M.—Tr. H. J. Stenning), London 1926.

MARX, K.–ENGELS, F.: *Selected Works*, I–II, Moscow–London 1950/ 1951; largely supersedes the earlier Karl Marx: *Selected Works*, I–II, London 1942.

Historisch-kritische Gesamtausgabe, issued by the Marx–Engels–Lenin Institute in Moscow, Frankfurt–Berlin 1927–33 (still incomplete).

Marxismusstudien. Schriften der Studiengemeinschaft der Evangelischen Akademien, 3; ed. Hans Frhr. von Campenhausen *et al.*, Tübingen 1954; 2nd Series, ed. I. Fetscher, Tübingen 1957.

MASARYK, T.: *Die philosophischen und sociologischen Grundlagen des Marxismus*, Vienna 1898.

The Spirit of Russia, I–II, London 1919; New edn., 1955.

'MATERIALIST': *Otets iezuit v roli kritika dialekticheskogo materializma* (A Jesuit Father as Critic of Dialectical Materialism), *VF* 1952, 6, pp. 127–37.

MAXIMOV, A. A.: *Lenin i estestvoznanie* (Lenin and Natural Science), Moscow–Leningrad 1933.

Vvedenie v sovremennoe uchenie o materii i dvizhenii. Filosofskie ocherki po voprosam teoreticheskoy fiziki (Introduction to the Modern Theory of Matter and Motion. Philosophical Studies in Problems of Theoretical Physics), Moscow 1941.

Marxistsky filosofsky materializm i sovremennaya fizika (Marxist Philosophical Materialism and Modern Physics), *VF* 1948, 3, pp. 105–24.

Bor'ba Lenina s 'fizicheskim' idealismom (Lenin's Fight against 'Physical' Idealism), *Bol'shevik* 1949, 2, pp. 21–33.

Bor'ba za materializm v sovremennoy fizike (The Struggle for Materialism in Modern Physics), *VF* 1953, 1, pp. 175–94.

MAYER, G.: *Friedrich Engels. Eine Biographie*, 2 vols. and Supplement, Berlin 1920; English version, London 1935.

MEHNERT, K.: *Stalin versus Marx. The Stalinist Historical Doctrine*, London 1952.

MERLEAU-PONTY, M.: *Les aventures de la dialectique*, Paris 1955.

MEYER, A. G.: *Marxism. The Unity of Theory and Practice. A Critical Essay*, Cambridge 1954.

MICHE, I. V.: *Manuale di filosofia bolscevica*, Rome n.d.

MICHURIN, I. V.: *Sochineniya* (Works); English versions in *Selected Works*, Moscow–London 1954.

MITIN, M. B.: *O filosofskom nasledstve V. I. Lenina* (On the Philosophical Heritage of V. I. Lenin), in *Pod znamenem marxizma* 1932, 3/4.

Boevye voprosy materialisticheskoy dialektiki (Burning Questions of Materialist Dialectics), Moscow 1936.

Filosofskaya nauka v SSSR za 25 let (25 Years of Philosophical Science in the U.S.S.R.), Moscow 1943.

Pobeda michurinskoy biologii (The Triumph of Michurinist Biology), *IAN*, V (1948), 5, pp. 411–21.

Rol' i znachenie raboty tovarishcha Stalina 'O dialekticheskom i istoricheskom materializme' v razvitii marxistsko–leninskoy filosofskoy mysli (The Rôle and Significance of Comrade Stalin's *Dialectical and Historical Materialism* in the Development of Marxist–Leninist Philosophical Thought), *Bol'shevik* 1949, 1, pp. 19–38.

J. V. Stalin, korifey marxistsko–leninskoy nauki (J. V. Stalin, a Coryphaeus of Marxist–Leninist Science), *VF* 1949, 2, pp. 17–39.

MITIN, M. B.–RAZUMOVSKY, I.: *Dialektichesky i istorichesky materializm* (Dialectical and Historical Materialism), issued by the Philosophical Institute of the Communist Academy under the Editorship of M. Mitin and I. Razumovsky.

    Part I: *Dialektichesky materializm*, ed. Mitin, Moscow 1933.

    Part II: *Istorichesky materializm*, ed. Mitin and Razumovsky, Moscow 1932.

MOLODTSOV, V. S.: *J. V. Stalin o raskrytii i preodolenii protivorechiy* (J. V. Stalin on the Discovery and Overcoming of Contradictions), *VF* 1949, 2, pp. 205–26.

Voprosy dialekticheskogo materializma v trude J. V. Stalina 'Marxizm i voprosy yazykoznaniya' (Problems of Dialectical Materialism in J. V. Stalin's *Marxism and Problems of Linguistics*), *VF* 1951, 5, pp. 3–17.

MOLOTOV, V. M.: *Tridtsatiletie Velikoy Oktyabr'skoy revolyutsii* (Thirtieth Anniversary Celebration of the Great October Revolution), Moscow 1947.

MONNEROT, J.: *Sociology of Communism*, London 1953.

MYAKISHEV, G. Y.: *V chem prichina statisticheskogo kharaktera kvantovoy mekhaniki?* (What is the Reason for the Statistical Character of Quantum Mechanics?), *VF* 1954, 6, pp. 146–59.

NAAN, G. I.: *Sovremennyi 'fizichesky idealizm' v SSA i Anglii na sluzhbe popovshchiny i reaktsii* (Modern 'Physical Idealism' in the U.S.A. and England in the Service of Clericalism and Reaction), *VF* 1948, 2, pp. 287–308.

K voprosu o printsipe otnositel'nosti v fizike (Problems of the Relativity Principle in Physics), *VF* 1951, 2, pp. 57–77.

NACHTSHEIM, H.: *Biologie und Totalitarismus* in: *Veritas, Justitia, Libertas* (A *Festschrift* for the Bicentenary Celebrations of Columbia University, New York, presented by the Free University of Berlin and the German School of Political Studies in Berlin), Berlin 1954, pp. 294–320.

NARSKY, I.: *Filosofiya neopozitivizma i nauka* (The Philosophy of Neo-Positivism and Science), *Kommunist* 1955, 13, pp. 70–85.

Nauchnaya sessiya posvyashchennaya problemam fiziologicheskogo ucheniya Akademika I. P. Pavlova 28 iyunya–4 iyulya 1950 g. (Scientific Session on Problems of the Physiological Theory of I. P. Pavlov, 28th June–4th July 1950), Verbatim Report, Moscow 1950; English version: *Scientific Session on the Teachings of Pavlov*, Moscow 1951.

NAVILLE, P.: *Psychologie, Marxisme, Matérialisme. Essais critiques*, 2nd edn., Paris 1949.

NESTEROV, V. G.: *Filosofskie kontseptsii po voprosam protivorechiy v zhivoy prirode* (Philosophical Conceptions of the Problems of Contradiction in Organic Nature), *VF* 1956, 1, pp. 143–9.

NIKOL'SKY, V. K.–YAKOVLEV, N. F.: *Osnovnye polozheniya materialisticheskogo ucheniya N. Y. Marra o yazyke* (Basic Principles of N. Y. Marr's Materialist Theory of Language), *VF* 1949, 1, pp. 265–85.

NOVIK, I. B.: *O sootnoshenii prostranstva, vremeni i materii* (On the Reciprocal Relations of Space, Time and Matter), *VF* 1955, 3, pp. 140–6.

NUDEL'MAN, Z. N.: *O probleme belka* (On the Protein-Problem), *VF* 1954, 2, pp. 221–6.

O bazise i nadstroyke (On Basis and Superstructure), in *Pravda* 5th Oct. 1950; German version in *Ost-Probleme* II (1950), 44, pp. 1389–90.

OBICHKIN, G.: *Osnovnye momenty dialekticheskogo protsessa poznaniya* (Primary Features of the Dialectical Process of Knowledge), Moscow–Leningrad 1933.

OYZERMAN, T. I.: *Marxistsko–leninskoe reshenie problemy svobody i neobkhodimosti* (The Marxist–Leninist Solution of the Problem of Freedom and Necessity), *VF* 1954, 3, pp. 16–33.

Bibliography 581

OMEL'YANOVSKY, M. E.: *V. I. Lenin i fizika XX veka* (V. I. Lenin and Twentieth-Century Physics), Moscow 1947.

Fal'sifikatory nauki (Falsifiers of Science), *VF* 1948, 3, pp. 143–62.

Dialektichesky materializm i tak nazyvaemy printsip dopolnitel'nosti Bora (Dialectical Materialism and Bohr's so-called Complementarity Principle), in *Filosofskie voprosy sovremennoy fiziki*, Moscow 1952, pp. 396–431.

Protiv idealisticheskogo istolkovaniya statisticheskikh ansambley v kvantovoy mekhanike. (Against an Idealistic Interpretation of Statistical Totalities in Quantum Mechanics), *VF* 1953, 2, pp. 201–9.

O tak nazyvaemom sootnoshenii neopredelennostey v kvantovoy mekhanike (On the So-called Uncertainty Relation in Quantum Mechanics), *VF* 1954, 1, pp. 203–10.

Dialektichesky materializm i sovremennaya fizika (Dialectical Materialism and Modern Physics), *Kommunist*, 1956, 5, pp. 72–87.

Filosofskie voprosy kvantovoy mekhaniki (Philosophical Problems of Quantum Mechanics), Moscow 1956.

O nauchnoy rabote Instituta filosofii AN SSSR. (On the Scientific Work of the Philosophical Institute . . .), *VF* 1955, 5, pp. 191–9.

OPARIN, A. I.: *O nekletochnykh formakh zhizni i proiskhozhdenii kletok* (On Non-Cellular Forms of Life and the Origin of Cells; Conference Report), in *Vestnik AN SSSR* 1950, 7, pp. 119–22; German version in *Sowjetwissenschaft, Naturwissenschaftliche Abteilung*, vol. 3, 1950, 2, pp. 111–13.

Zhizn' (Life), in *BSE XVI* (1952), p. 141.

Problema proiskhozhdeniya zhizni v svete dostizheniy sovremennogo estestvoznaniya (The Problem of the Origin of Life in the Light of the Achievements of Modern Science), in *Vestnik AN SSSR* 1953, 12, pp. 39–48.

Proiskhozhdenie zhizni (The Origin of Life), Moscow 1954.

Novoe o proiskhozhdenii zhizni na zemle (New Light on the Origin of Life on Earth), Moscow 1956.

Vozniknovenie zhizni na zemle, 2nd edn., Moscow 1941; English version: *The Origin of Life*, New York (Macmillan) 1938; another: Moscow 1955; 3rd., completely revised edn., Moscow 1957; English version, Edinburgh 1957.

O polozhenii v biologicheskoy nauke. Stenograficheskyy otchet sessii Vsesoyuznoy Akademii sel'skokhozyaystvennykh nauk imeni V. I. Lenina. 31 iyulya–7 avgusta 1948 g., Moscow 1948; English Version: *The Situation in Biological Science. Proceedings of the Lenin Academy of Agricultural Sciences of the U.S.S.R. (July 31–August 7, 1948). Verbatim Report*, Moscow 1949.

OS'MAKOV, I. I.: *Vsesoyuznoe soveshchanie po logike* (The All-Union Conference on Logic), *VF* 1948, 2, pp. 376 f.

582   *Bibliography*

O logike myshleniya i o nauke logiki (On the Logic of Thought and
the Science of Logic), *VF* 1950, 3, pp. 317–30.

O sovetskom patriotizme. Sbornik statey (On Soviet Patriotism. A
Collection of Essays), issued by the Philosophical Institute of the
Academy of Sciences of the U.S.S.R., Moscow 1950.

OSTER, G.: *Scientific Research in the U.S.S.R. Organization and
Planning*, in the collective *The Soviet Union since World War II*,
1949, pp. 134–40.

OURALOV, A.: *Staline au pouvoir*, Paris 1951.

OVANDER, N. E.: *Ob objektivnom kharaktere zakonov razvitiya
sovetskogo sotsialisticheskogo obshchestva* (On the Objective
Character of the Laws of Development in the Soviet Socialist
Society), *VF* 1953, 4, pp. 40–9.

OVCHINNIKOV, N. F.: *Material'nost mira i zakonomernosti ego
razvitiya* (The Materiality of the World and the Laws of its
Development), *VF* 1951, 5, pp. 135–52.

*Ponyatiya massy i energii v sovremennoy fizike i ikh filosofskoe
znachenie* (The Concepts of Mass and Energy in Modern Physics
and their Philosophical Significance), in *Filosofskie voprosy
sovremennoy fiziki*, pp. 445–88.

PALÉOLOGUE, M.: *Les précurseurs de Lénine*, Paris 1938.

PASTORE, A.: *La filosofia di Lenin*, Milan 1946.

PAVLOV, I. P.: *Polnoe sobranie sochineniy* (Complete Works), Vols.
I–VI, 2nd edn., Moscow 1951/52; English versions in I. P.
Pavlov: *Selected Works (PSW)*, Moscow 1955.

PERLOV, I. S.: *Neobkhodim konkretny podkhod k voprosu o protivorechiyakh* (The Problem of Contradictions must be Approached Concretely), *VF* 1956, 4, pp. 164–9.

PERUCATTI, A.: *Saggio di critica scientifica sul materialismo dialettico*, Naples n.d.

PETERSON, O. P.: *O prirode virusov i ikh znachenii v zhizni cheloveka*
(On the Nature of Viruses and their Importance in Human
Life), Moscow 1953.

PETROV, B.: *Filosofskaya nishcheta marxizma* (The Philosophical
Poverty of Marxism), Frankfurt-a-M. 1952.

PETROVSKY, A. V.: *Ob obyektivnom kharaktere psikhologicheskikh
zakonomernostey* (On the Objective Character of Psychological
Laws), *VF* 1953, 3, pp. 173–7.

PHILIPOV, A.: *Logic and Dialectic in the Soviet Union*, New York
1952.

PLATONOV, G. V.: *Nekotorye filosofskie voprosy diskussii o vide i
vidoobrazovanii* (Some Philosophical Problems in the Discussion
on Species and their Formation), *VF* 1954, 6, pp. 116–32.

PLEKHANOV, G. V.: *Osnovnye problemy marxizma*, 1910; English
version: *Fundamental Problems of Marxism*, London 1929.

Istoriya russkoy obshchestvennoy mysli (History of Russian Social Thought), I–III, Moscow 1914–17.

Sochineniya (Works), ed. D. Ryazanov, I–XXVI, Moscow 1922–7.

Materialismus militans, Moscow–Leningrad 1931.

Protiv filosofskogo revizionizma. Sbornik statey so vstupitel'noy statey V. Vandeka i B. Timosko (Against Philosophical Revisionism. Essays, Collected, with an Introduction, by V. Vandek and B. Timosko), Moscow 1935.

K voprosu o roli lichnosti v istorii, Moscow 1948; English version: *The Rôle of the Individual in History*, London 1940.

('BEL'TOV, N.): *K voprosu o razvitii monisticheskogo vzglyada na istoriyu* (On the Question of the Development of the Monist View of History), 4th edn., St. Petersburg 1906; English version: *In Defence of Materialism*, London 1947; another: Moscow 1956.

PLYUSHCH, L. N.: *Ob osnovakh novoy kletochnoy teorii* (On the Foundations of the New Cell Theory), *VF* 1953, 4, pp. 185–91.

PODOSETNIK, V. M.: *K voprosu o stupenyakh protsessa poznaniya istiny* (On the Problem of Stages in the Process of Knowing Truth), *VF* 1954, 5, pp. 77–81.

POLITZER, G.: *Principes fondamentaux de philosophie*, Paris 1954.

POPOV, N. P.: *Opredelenie ponyatiy* (The Definition of Concepts), Leningrad 1954.

POPOV, P. S.: *Predmet formal'noy logiki i dialektika* (The Subject-Matter of Formal Logic and Dialectics), *VF* 1951, 1, pp. 210–18.

POPOVSKY, A.: *Zakony zhizni* (The Laws of Life), Moscow 1955.

PREZENT, I. I.–KHALIFMAN, I. A.: *Nekotorye voprosy teorii biologicheskogo vida i vidoobrazovaniya* (Some Problems of the Theory of Species and Species-Formation), *VF* 1955, 5, pp. 157–168.

PRIMAKOVSKY, A. P.: *Bibliografiya po logike* (Bibliography of Logic), Moscow 1955.

PROKOFIEV, P.: *Sovetskaya filosofiya* (Soviet Philosophy), in *Sovremennyya Zapiski* XXXIII (1927), pp. 481–501.

Krizis sovetskoy filosofii (The Crisis in Soviet Philosophy), in *Sovremennyya Zapiski* XLIII (1930), pp. 471–88.

Protiv burzhuaznoy ideologii kosmopolitizma (Against the Bourgeois Ideology of Cosmopolitanism), *VF* 1948, 2, pp. 14–29.

Protiv putanitsy i vul'garizatsii v voprosakh logiki (Against Confusion and Vulgarization in Questions of Logic), *VF* 1955, 3, pp. 158–171.

PUZIKOV, P. D.: *Nekotorye filosofskie voprosy biologicheskoy evolyutsii* (Some Philosophical Problems of Biological Evolution), *VF* 1956, 4, pp. 179–83.

RAL'TSEVICH, V.: *Na dva fronta* (On Two Fronts), Moscow–Leningrad 1931.

See *Dialektichesky materializm*.

RAUCH, G. VON: *Die Hochschulen der Sowjetunion*, in *Osteuropa* II/1 (Feb. 1952), pp. 1–9.

Geschichte des bolschewistischen Russlands, Wiesbaden 1955.

ROZENTAL', M. M.: *Marxistsky dialektichesky metod* (The Marxist Dialectical Method), Moscow 1947.

Zadachi sovetskoy estetiki (The Tasks of Soviet Aesthetics), Report on Rozental's lecture on this subject and the ensuing discussion, *VF* 1948, 1, pp. 278–92.

Razvitie V. I. Leninym marxistskoy teorii poznaniya (V. I. Lenin's Contribution to the Development of the Marxist Epistemology), Moscow 1950.

Voprosy dialektiki v 'Kapitale' Marxa (Problems of Dialectic in Marx's *Capital*), Moscow 1955.

ROZENTAL', M. M.–SHTRAKS, G. M.: *Kategorii materialisticheskoy dialektiki* (The Categories of the Materialist Dialectic), Moscow 1956.

ROZENTAL', M. M.–YUDIN, P.: *Kratky filosofsky slovar'* (Short Philosophical Dictionary), 4th edn., Moscow 1955; English version, Moscow 1958 (?).

ROZHIN, V. P.: *Neskol'ko zamechaniy po spornym voprosam logiki* (Some Remarks on Disputed Questions in Logic), *VF* 1951, 4, pp. 238–41.

O materialisticheskoy dialektike kak logika i teorii poznaniya (On the Materialist Dialectic as Logic and as Theory of Knowledge), *Vestnik Leningradskogo Universiteta* 1956, 5, pp. 29–37.

ROZOV, A. I.: *Soobrazheniya ryadovogo psikhologa* (Reflections of a Simple Psychologist), *VF* 1953, 3, pp. 177–9.

RUBASHEVSKY, A. A.: *Filosofskoe znachenie teoreticheskogo nasledstva I. V. Michurina* (The Philosophical Significance of the Theoretical Legacy of I. V. Michurin), Moscow 1949.

RUBINSTEIN, S. L.: *Osnovy obshchey psikhologii* (Foundations of General Psychology), 2nd edn., Moscow 1946. *Cf.* on this, E. T. Chernakov in *VF* 1948, 3, pp. 301–15.

RUTKEVICH, M. N.: *Praktika—osnova poznaniya i kriteriy istiny* (Practice as the Foundation of Knowledge and Criterion of Truth), Moscow 1952.

K voprosu o roli praktika v protsesse poznaniya (On the Problem of the Rôle of Practice in the Knowing-Process), *VF* 1954, 3, pp. 34–45.

RYZHKOV, V. L.: *O nekotorykh problemakh virusologii* (On Some Problems of Virology), *Vestnik A N SSSR* 1953, 1, pp. 42–6.

SAFRONOV, V. S.: *Problema proiskhozhdeniya zemli i planet: Soveshchanie po voprosam kosmogonii solnechnoy sistemy* (The Problem of the Origin of the Earth and Planets: A Conference on

Problems of the Cosmogony of the Solar System), *Vestnik A N SSSR*, 1951, 10, pp. 94–102.

SAGER, P.: *Die theoretischen Grundlagen des Stalinismus und ihre Auswirkungen auf die Wirtschaftspolitik der Sowjetunion*, Berlin 1953.

SAKHAROVA, T. A.: *Obsuzhdenie sbornika 'Uchenie I. P. Pavlova i filosofskie voprosy psikhologii'* (Discussion on the Collective Volume *The Teaching of I. P. Pavlov and the Philosophical Problems of Psychology*), *Vestnik A N SSSR* 1953, 5, pp. 79–82.

SANDER, P.: *Histoire de la dialectique*, Paris 1947.

SANKEWITSCH, E.: *Die Arbeitsmethoden der Michurinschen Pflanzenzüchtung*, Stuttgart–Ludwigsburg 1950.

SCHEIBERT, P.: *Von Bakunin zu Lenin. Geschichte der russischen revolutionären Ideologien 1840–1895* (Vol. I only, so far), Leyden 1956.

SCHMIDT, O. Y.: *Chetyre lektsii o teorii proiskhozhdeniya zemli* (Four Lectures on the Theory of the Origin of the Earth), 2nd edn., 1950.

Problema proiskhozhdeniya zemli i planet (The Problem of the Origin of the Earth and Planets), *VF* 1951, 4, pp. 120–33.

SECHENOV, I. M.: *Refleksy golovnogo mozga* (Reflexes of the Brain), Moscow 1952.

SEILER, J.: *Philosophie der unbelebten Natur*, Olten 1948.

SELEKTOR, M. Z.: *Dialektichesky materializm i teoriya ravnovesiya* (Dialectical Materialism and the Equilibrium Theory), Moscow–Leningrad 1934.

SESEMANN, W.: *Die bolschewistische Philosophie in Sowjet-Russland*, in *Der Russische Gedanke* 1931, 2, pp. 176–83.

SHARIKOV, I. S.: *Kritika i samokritika—dvizhushchaya sila razvitiya sovetskogo obshchestva* (Criticism and Self-Criticism—a Driving-Force in the Development of Soviet Society), *VF* 1950, 1, pp. 35–57.

SHARIYA, P. A.: *O nekotorykh voprosakh kommunisticheskoy morali* (On Some Problems of Communist Ethics), Moscow 1951.

SHCHEGLOV, A. V.: *Kratky ocherk istorii filosofii* (Short Outline of the History of Philosophy), Moscow 1940.

See *Dialektichesky materializm*.

SHCHIPANOV, I. Y.: *Protiv burzhuaznogo obyektivizma i kosmospolitizma* (Against Bourgeois Objectivism and Cosmopolitanism), *VF* 1948, 2, pp. 213–27.

SHEINMAN, M. M.: *Vatikan mezhdu dvumya mirovymi voynami* (The Vatican between the World Wars), Moscow–Leningrad 1948.

Reaktsionnaya sotsiologiya sovremennogo Vatikana (The Reactionary Sociology of the Vatican Today), *FZ* II (1948), pp. 158–86.

Ideologiya i politika Vatikana na sluzhbe imperializme (The Ideology and Politics of the Vatican in the Service of Imperialism), Moscow 1950.

Deklaratsiya voinstvuyushchego mrakobesiya (A Declaration of Militant Obscurantism), *VF* 1951, 1, pp. 169–73 (against the Encyclical *Humani generis*).

Sovremenny Vatikan (The Modern Vatican), Moscow 1955.

SHIROKOV, M.: *A Textbook of Marxist Philosophy*, prepared by the Leningrad Institute of Philosophy . . ., tr. A. C. Moseley, ed. J. Lewis, London 1937.

SHISHKIN, A. F.: *Burzhuaznaya moral'—oruzhie imperialisticheskoy reaktsii* (Bourgeois Ethics—a weapon of Imperialist Reaction), Moscow 1951.

Osnovy kommunisticheskoy morali (Foundations of Communist Ethics), Moscow 1955.

SHUB, D.: *Lenin. A Biography*, New York, 1949.

SIDOROV, M. I.: *Ob itogakh obsuzhdeniya knigi M. A. Leonova 'Ocherk dialekticheskogo materializma'* (On the Findings of the Examining Committee on M. A. Leonov's *Outline of Dialectical Materialism*), *VF* 1948, 3, pp. 315–23.

O filosofskom nasledii G. V. Plekhanova (On the Philosophical Legacy of G. V. Plekhanov), *Kommunist* 1956, 6, pp. 120–8.

SIMONOV, P. V.: *O termine 'vysshaya nervnaya deyatel 'nost cheloveka'* (On the Expression 'Higher Nervous Activity in Man'), *VF* 1953, 4, pp. 213–15.

SISAKYAN, N. M.: *Biologichesky obmen veshchestv—kachestvennaya osobennost' zhivogo* (Biological Metabolism as a Qualitative Property of the Living), *VF* 1954, 3, pp. 89–105.

SITKOVSKY, E. P.: *Lenin o sovpadenii v dialekticheskom materializme dialektiki, logiki i teorii poznaniya* (Lenin on the Identity of Dialectic, Logic and Epistemology in Dialectical Materialism), *VF* 1956, 2, pp. 77–90.

SKABICHEVSKY, A. P.: *Problema vozniknoveniya zhizni na zemle i teoriya akad. A. I. Oparina* (The Problem of the Origin of Life on Earth and the Theory of Academician A. I. Oparin), *VF* 1953, 2, pp. 150–5.

SMITH, I.: *Soviet Philosophy*, in *New Scholasticism*, 1947.

SOMERVILLE, J. M.: *Dialectical Materialism*, in D. D. Runes: *Twentieth Century Philosophy*, New York 1943.

Soviet Philosophy. A Study of Theory and Practice, New York 1946.

Sostoyanie teorii khimicheskogo stroeniya, Vsesoyuznoe soveshchanie 11–14 iyunya 1951 g. (The Theoretical Situation in Chemical Structure. All-Union Conference of 11–14 June 1951. Verbatim Report), Moscow 1952.

SOUVARINE, B.: *Stalin. A Critical Survey of Bolshevism*. London 1939.

SPIRITO, U.: *La filosofia del comunismo*, Florence 1948.

SPÜLBECK, O.: *Der Christ und das Weltbild der modernen Naturwissenschaft*, 4th edn., Berlin 1957.

STÄHLIN, K.: *Geschichte Russlands von den Anfängen bis zur Gegenwart*, I, Stuttgart–Berlin–Leipzig 1923, II–IV (1, 2), Königsberg–Berlin 1930–9.

STALIN, J. V.: *Sochineniya* (Works), Moscow 1946 on, I–XIII; English version: *Works*, Moscow–London 1952/3 on, I–XIII (still uncompleted).

Voprosy leninizma, 9th edn., Moscow 1933; 11th edn. (somewhat altered), Moscow 1947; English version (from the 11th edn.): *Problems of Leninism*, Moscow–London 1947.

O Velikoy Otechestvennoy voyne Sovetskogo Soyuza (On the Great Patriotic War), 5th edn., Moscow 1947; English version: *War Speeches*, London 1946.

Rech' na predvybornom sobranii izbirateley Stalinskogo izbiratel'nogo okruga g. Moskvy 9. fevralya 1946, Moscow 1946; English version in: *Speeches Delivered at Meetings of Voters of the Stalin Electoral District, Moscow*, Moscow–London 1950.

Marxizm i voprosy yazykoznaniya, Moscow 1950; English version: *Marxism and Problems of Linguistics*, Moscow–London 1954/5.

Ekonomicheskie problemy sotsializma v SSSR, Moscow 1952; English version: *Economic Problems of Socialism in the U.S.S.R.*, Moscow 1952.

Stat'i tovarishcha Stalina po voprosam yazykoznaniya i zadachi v oblasti istoricheskikh i filosofskikh nauk (Comrade Stalin's Articles on Problems of Linguistics and the Tasks in the Fields of Historical and Philosophical Science), *IAN*, VII (1950), 4, pp. 322–59.

STEBBINS, G. L.: *New Look in Soviet Genetics*, in *Science*, 123 (1956), pp. 721 ff.

STEINBERG, H.: *Marxismus, Leninismus, Stalinismus. Der geistige Angriff des Ostens*, Hamburg 1955.

STEINMAN, P. Y.: *O reaktsionnoy roli idealizma v fizike* (On the Reactionary Rôle of Idealism in Physics), *VF* 1948, 3, pp. 163–173.

STEPANOV, I. I.: *Istorichesky materializm i sovremennoe estestvoznanie* (Historical Materialism and Modern Science), 1924.

STEPANYAN, TS. A.: *Protivorechiya v razvitii sotsialisticheskogo obshchestva i puti ikh preodoleniya* (Contradictions in the Development of Socialist Society and the Means of Resolving Them), *VF* 1955, 2, pp. 69–86.

STERN, V.: *Stalin als Philosoph*, Berlin 1949.

K voprosu o filosofskoy storone teorii otnositel'nosti (Concerning the Philosophical Aspect of Relativity Theory) *VF* 1952, 1, pp. 175–181.

STOLETOV, V. N.: *Printsipy ucheniya I. V. Michurina* (Principles of the Teaching of I. V. Michurin), *VF* 1948, 2, pp. 148–70.

Rabota V. I. Lenina 'Materializm i empiriokrititsizm' i voprosy biologii (V. I. Lenin's *Materialism and Empirio-Criticism* and the Problems of Biology), *VF* 1949, 1, pp. 85–108.

Dialektichesky materializm i michurinskaya biologiya (Dialectical Materialism and Michurinist Biology), *VF* 1949, 3, pp. 126–46.

STOLYAROV, A.: *Dialektichesky materializm i mekhanisty. Nashi filosofskie raznoglasiya* (Dialectical Materialism and the Mechanists. Our Philosophical Differences), Leningrad 1930.

STROGOVICH, M. S.: *Logika* (Logic), Moscow 1949.

O predmete formal'noy logiki (On the Subject-Matter of Formal Logic), *VF* 1950, 3, pp. 309–17.

Studien über Materialismus: in *Osteuropa* I/1 (Oct. 1951), pp. 31–8; I/2 (Dec. 1951), pp. 107–15; II/1 (Feb. 1952), pp. 29–34; II/2 (Apr. 1952), pp. 102–7.

STUKOV, A. P.–YAKUSHEV, S. A.: *O belke kak nositele zhizni* (On Protein as the Bearer of Life), *VF* 1953, 2, pp. 139–49.

SUKHOV, K. S.: *Problemy sovremennoy virusologii* (Problems of Modern Virology) in *Filosofskie voprosy sovremennoy biologii*, Moscow, 1951, pp. 335–45.

SVETLOV, V.–OYZERMAN, T.: *Vozniknovenie marxizma—revolyutsionny perevorot v filosofii* (The Rise of Marxism—a Revolutionary Upheaval in Philosophy), *Bol'shevik* 1948, 7, pp. 28–41.

SVIDERSKY, V. I.: *O filosofskom i estestvenno-nauchnom ponyatiyakh prostranstva i vremeni* (On the Philosophical and Scientific Concepts of Space and Time), in *Uchenye Zapiski Leningradskogo Gosudarstvennogo Universiteta, seriya filosofskikh nauk*, 2, No. 109, 1948.

Filosofskoe znachenie prostranstvenno-vremennykh predstavleniy v fizike (The Philosophical Significance of Spatio-Temporal Conceptions in Physics), Leningrad 1956.

SYRKIN, Y. K.–DYATKINA, M. E.: *Khimicheskaya svyaz' i stroenie molekul* (The Chemical Bond and the Structure of Molecules), 1946.

SYSOEV, A. F.: *Samoobnovlenie belka i svoystvo razdrazhimosti vazhneyshie zakonomernosti zhiznennykh yavleniy* (Protein Self-Renewal and the Property of Irritability as the Major Laws of Organic Phenomena), *VF* 1956, 1, pp. 152–5.

TAKACH, L.: *K voprosu o vozniknovenii zhizni* (On the Problem of the Origin of Life), *VF* 1955, 3, pp. 147–50.

TARAKANOV, N. G.: *Fal'sifikatory istorii russkoy filosofskoy mysli* (Falsifiers of the History of Russian Philosophical Thought) *VF* 1955, 3, pp. 73–85.

TARANCHUK, M. V.: *Marxistskaya dialektika o vozmozhnosti i deystvitel'nosti* (The Marxist Dialectic on Possibility and Actuality), *VF* 1949, 1, pp. 109–27.

TATEVSKY, V. M.–SHAKHPARONOV, M. I.: *Ob odnoy machistskoy teorii v khimii i ee propagandistakh* (On a Machist Theory in Chemistry and its Propagandists), *VF* 1949, 3, pp. 176–92.

TAVENETS, P. V.: *K voprosu o razlichnom ponimanii predmeta logiki* (On the Problem of Differing Conceptions of the Subject-Matter of Logic), *IAN*, I (1944), 6.

Klassifikatsiya umozaklyucheniy (Classification of Inferences), *FZ*, I (1946), pp. 84–117.

O vidakh suzhdeniya (On the Types of Judgement), *IAN*, VII (1950), 1, pp. 69–84.

Kritika istolkovaniya prirody suzhdeniy logikoy otnosheniy (A Criticism of the Exposition of the Nature of Judgements in terms of the Logic of Relations), *IAN*, VII (1950), 4, pp. 360–72.

Suzhdenie i ego vidy (The Judgement and its Forms), Moscow 1953.

Voprosy teorii suzhdeniya (Problems of a Theory of Judgement), Moscow 1955.

TEPLOV, B. M.: *Ob obyektivnom metode v psikhologii* (On the Objective Method in Psychology), 1952.

TERLETSKY, Y. P.: *O soderzhanii sovremennoy fizicheskoy teorii prostranstva i vremeni* (On the Content of the Modern Physical Theory of Space and Time), *VF* 1952, 3, pp. 191–7.

THALHEIMER, A.: *Einführung in den dialektischen Materialismus*, Berlin 1928.

THEIMER, W.: *Der Marxismus*, Berne 1950.

TROSHIN, D. M.: *O korennoy protivopolozhnosti dvukh kontseptsiy razvitiya* (On the Radical Opposition of the Two Conceptions of Development), *VF* 1950, 1, pp. 139–56.

Dialektika razvitiya v michurinskoy biologii (The Dialectic of Development in Michurinist Biology), Moscow 1951.

TROTSKY, L.: *Istoriya russkoy revolyutsii*, I–III, Berlin 1931; English Version: *History of the Russian Revolution*, I–III, London 1932.

TSCHAGIN, B. A.: *Die Entwicklung der marxistischen Philosophie nach der Pariser Kommune (1871–1895)*, Berlin 1951.

TUGARINOV, V. P.: *Sootnoshenie kategoriy dialekticheskogo materializma* (The Correlation of the Categories of Dialectical Materialism), *VF* 1956, 3, pp. 151–60.

Sootnoshenie kategoriy dialekticheskogo materializma (The Correlation of the Categories of Dialectical Materialism), Leningrad 1956.

TUGARINOV, V. P.–MAYSTROV, L. E.: *Protiv idealizma v matematicheskoy logike* (Against Idealism in Mathematical Logic), *VF* 1950, 3, pp. 331–9.

TYMYANSKY, G. S.: *Vvedenie v teoriyu dialekticheskogo materializma* (Introduction to the Theory of Dialectical Materialism), 2nd edn., Moscow–Leningrad 1931.

Über die Kategorien des dialektischen Materialismus. Special pamphlet issued by the monthly *Sowjetwissenschaft, Gesellschaftswissenschaftliche Beiträge*, 2nd edn., Berlin 1956.

Uchenie I. P. Pavlova i filosofskie voprosy psikhologii (The Teaching of I. P. Pavlov and the Philosophical Problems of Psychology), issued by the Philosophical Institute of the Academy of Sciences of the U.S.S.R. under the editorship of S. A. Petrushevsky (*et al.*), Moscow 1952; German edition, Berlin 1955.

UEMOV, A. I.: *Geliotsentricheskaya sistema Kopernika i teoriya otnositel'nosti* (The Heliocentric System of Copernicus and the Theory of Relativity), in *Filosofskie voprosy sovremennoy fiziki*, Moscow 1952, pp. 299–331.

Mozhet li prostranstvenno-vremennoy kontinuum vzaimodeystvovat' s materiey? (Can the Space-Time Continuum Interact with Matter?) *VF* 1954, 3, pp. 172–80.

VALENTINOV, N. (= VOL'SKY): *Vstrechi s Leninym* (Encounters with Lenin), New York 1953.

VAVILOV, S. I.: *Lenin i sovremennaya fizika* (Lenin and Modern Physics), Moscow 1944.

Filosofskie problemy sovremennoy fiziki i zadachi sovetskikh fizikov v bor'be za peredovuyu nauku (Philosophical Problems of Modern Physics and the Tasks of Soviet Physicists in the Struggle for a Progressive Science), in *Filosofskie voprosy sovremennoy fiziki*, Moscow 1952, pp. 5–30.

Velikoe leninskoe filosofskoe nasledstvo (The Great Philosophical Heritage of Lenin), *VF* 1955, 2, pp. 3–15.

VENTURI, F.: *Il populismo russo*, 2 vols., Turin 1952.

VIGNEAUX, P.: *Le ressort de la dialectique marxiste: l'aliénation*, in *La Vie Intellectuelle* 1936.

VINOGRADOV, S. N.–KUZ'MIN, A. F.: *Logika. Uchebnik dlya sredney shkoly* (Logic. A Textbook for Middle Schools), Moscow 1949.

VINOGRADOV, V.: *O lingvisticheskoy diskussii i rabotakh J. V. Stalina po voprosam yazykoznaniya* (On the Linguistic Discussion and the Works of J. V. Stalin on Problems of Linguistics), *Bol'shevik* 1950, 15, pp. 7–23.

VISLOBOKOV, A.: *O nerazryvnosti materii i dvizheniya* (On the Inseparability of Matter and Motion), Moscow 1955.

VLASTOVSKY, V. G.: *Sovremennye predstavleniya o proiskhozhdenii cheloveka* (Modern Conceptions of the Descent of Man), in *Estestvoznanie i religiya*, Moscow 1956, pp. 111–36.

VOL'FSON, M. V.–GAK, G. M.: *Ocherki istoricheskogo materializma* (Outline of Historical Materialism), Moscow 1931.

Voprosy dialekticheskogo i istoricheskogo materializma v trude J. V. Stalina 'Marxism i voprosy yazykoznaniya' (Problems of Dialectical and Historical Materialism in J. V. Stalin's *Marxism and Problems of Linguistics*), 2 vols., Moscow 1951/52.

Voprosy dialekticheskogo materializma (Problems of Dialectical Materialism), a collective work, issued by the Philosophical Institute of the Academy of Sciences, Moscow 1951.

Voprosy geologii i geofiziki v kosmogonicheskoy teorii akademika O. Y. Schmidta: Soveshchanie v Leningrade (Problems of Geology and Geophysics in the Cosmogonical Theory of Academician O. Y. Schmidt: A Conference in Leningrad), *Vestnik A N SSSR*, 1953, 4, pp. 88–90.

Voprosy logiki (Problems of Logic) issued by the Philosophical Insitute of the Academy of Sciences, under the editorship of P. V. Tavanets, Moscow 1955.

Voprosy marxistsko–leninskoy filosofii. Sbornik statey (Problems of Marxist–Leninist Philosophy. A Collection of Essays), issued by the Academy of Sciences, Moscow 1950.

VORLÄNDER, K.: *Von Macchiavelli bis Lenin*, Leipzig 1926.

VOROBIEV, M. F.: *O soderzhanii i formakh zakona otritsaniya otritsaniya* (On the Content and Forms of the Law of the Negation of the Negation), in *Vestnik Leningradskogo Universiteta* 1956, 23, pp. 57–66.

VOSTOKOV, P.: *La philosophie russe durant la période post-révolutionnaire*, in *Le Monde Slave* IX (1932), 11/12, pp. 286–305, 432–57.

VOSTRIKOV, A. V.: *Voprosy teorii poznaniya v trudakh J. V. Stalina* (Problems of Epistemology in the Works of J. V. Stalin), *VF* 1949, 2, pp. 184–204.

VOYSHVILLO, E. K.: *O knige 'Logika' prof. V. F. Asmusa* (On Prof. V. F. Asmus' *Logic*), *VF* 1947, 2.

VOYTONIS, N. Y.: *Predistoriya intellekta* (The Prehistory of the Intellect), Moscow–Leningrad 1949.

Vsesoyuznoe soveshchanie zaveduyushchikh kafedrami marxizma–leninizma i filosofii vysshikh uchebnykh zavedeniy (All-Union Conference of Holders of Chairs of Marxist–Leninism and Philosophy in Institutions of Higher Education), *VF* 1949, 1, pp. 366–379.

VUL, B. M.: *K voprosu ob izuchenii mekhanicheskogo dvizheniya v klassicheskoy i kvantovoy fizike* (On the Problem of Investigating Mechanical Motion in Classical and Quantum Physics), *VF* 1949, 3, pp. 165–75.

WALTER, G.: *Lénine*, Paris 1950.

WETTER, G. A.: *Der dialektische Materialismus. Seine Entwicklung in der Sowjetunion*, in *Wort und Wahrheit* II (1947), 8, pp. 463–74.

Der dialektische Materialismus II. Das System der Sowjetphilosophie, in *Wort und Wahrheit* II (1947), 9, pp. 544–58.
Sowjetwissenschaft, in *Wort und Wahrheit* IV (1949), 8, pp. 570–86.
Der dialektische Materialismus und das Problem der Entstehung des Lebens. Zur Theorie von A. I. Oparin, Munich–Salzburg–Cologne 1958.

WINKELMANN, A.: *Die Stellung der formalen Logik im Sowjetsystem*, in *Scholastik* 31 (1956), I, pp. 85–9.

WOLFE, B. D.: *The New Gospel of Stalinism*, in *Problems of Communism*, Washington, Jan. 1953.

YAKOVLEV, B. A.: *Academic Freedom under the Soviet Régime. A Symposium*, New York 1954.

Za boevoy filosofsky zhurnal (For a Militant Philosophical Journal), in *Pravda*, 7th Sept. 1949; also in *VF* 1949, 1, pp. 7–10.

Za bol'shevistskuyu partiynost' v filosofii (For a Bolshevik Partisanship in Philosophy), *VF* 1948, 3, pp. 3–15.

Zadachi sovetskoy estetiki (Tasks of Soviet Aesthetics), *VF* 1948, 1, pp. 278–92.

Za leninsky printsip partiynosti v ideologicheskoy rabote (For the Leninist Principle of Partisanship in Ideological Work), *VF* 1956, 6, pp. 3–10.

Za tvorcheskoe izuchenie marxistsko–leninskoy teorii (For a Creative Study of Marxist–Leninist Theory), *Kommunist* 1954, 14, pp. 3–12.

Za tvorcheskuyu razrabotku voprosov dialekticheskogo materializma (For a Creative Working-Out of the Problems of Dialectical Materialism), *VF* 1954, 5, pp. 3–19.

ZAVADSKAYA, N. V.: *Filosofiya obrechennykh—khristiansky ekzistentsializm* (The Philosophy of the Doomed—Christian Existentialism), *VF* 1948, 2, pp. 278–86.

ZELENOV, T.: *Izdanie i rasprostranenie proizvedeniy J. V. Stalina* (Editions and Circulation-Figures of the Works of J. V. Stalin), *Bol'shevik* 1949, 23, pp. 85–96.

ZEN'KOVSKY, V. V.: *O mnimom materializme russkoy nauki i filosofii* (On the Alleged Materialism of Russian Science and Philosophy), Munich 1956.

ZHDANOV, A. A.: *Vystuplenie na diskussii po knige G. F. Alexandrova 'Istoriya zapadnoevropeyskoy filosofii'* (Speech in the Discussion on G. F. Alexandrov's *History of Western European Philosophy*), Moscow 1951; also in *Bol'shevik* 1947, 16, pp. 7–23, *VF* 1947, 1, and as a separate pamphlet; English version in A. A. Zhdanov: *On Literature, Music and Philosophy*, London 1950, pp. 76–112.

ZHEBRAK, A. R.: *Soviet Biology*, in *Science* CII, No. 2649 (5th Oct. 1945), pp. 357 ff.

ZHINKIN, L. N.–MIKHAILOV, V. P.: *O 'novoy kletochnoy teorii'* (On the 'New Cell-Theory') in *Arkhiv anatomii, gistologii i embriologii* 1955, vol. 32, No. 2, pp. 66–71.

'*Novaya kletochnaya teoriya*' *i ee fakticheskoe obosnovanie* (The 'New Cell-Theory' and its Factual Basis), in *Uspekhi sovremennoy biologii* 1955, vol. 39, pp. 228–44. Both in German versions in *Sowjetwissenschaft. Naturwissenschaftliche Abteilung* 1956, 2, pp. 175–82 and 155–74.

ZHUKOV-VEREZHNIKOV, N. N.–MAISKY, I. N.–KALINICHENKO, L. A.: *O nekletochnykh formakh zhizni i razvitii kletok* (On Non-Cellular Forms of Life and the Development of Cells), in *Filosofskie voprosy sovremennoy biologii*, Moscow 1951, pp. 318–34.

ZVONOV, L.: *Partiynost' filosofii* (The Partisanship of Philosophy), Moscow–Leningrad 1932.

XIX syezd Kommunisticheskoy partii i voprosy ideologicheskoy raboty (The XIXth Congress of the Communist Party and Questions of Ideological Work), *VF* 1952, 6, pp. 3–17.

XX syezd KPSS i voprosy ideologicheskoy raboty (The XXth Party Congress of the C.P.S.U. and Questions of Ideological Work), *VF* 1956, 2, pp. 3–18.

Index of Names

Main references are given in bold type.

Index of Subjects